China 2030

China 2030

Building a Modern, Harmonious, and Creative Society

The World Bank

Development Research Center of the
State Council, the People's Republic of China

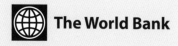 The World Bank

Contents

Part I Overview

China 2030: Building a Modern, Harmonious, and Creative Society 3

Part II   Supporting Reports

Boxes

Figures

Tables

Foreword

China's economic performance over the past 30 years has been remarkable. It is a unique development success story, providing valuable lessons for other countries seeking to emulate this success—lessons about the importance of adapting to local initiative and interregional competition; integrating with the world; adjusting to new technologies; building world-class infrastructure; and investing heavily in its people.

In the next 15 to 20 years, China is well-positioned to join the ranks of the world's high-income countries. China's policy makers are already focused on how to change the country's growth strategy to respond to the new challenges that will come, and avoid the "middle-income trap." That is clearly reflected in both the 11th and 12th Five Year Plans, with their focus on quality of growth, structural reforms to harness innovation and economic efficiency, and social inclusion to overcome the rural-urban divide and the income equality gap.

The idea behind this study was developed in 2010, at the celebrations for the 30th anniversary of the China–World Bank partnership. To commemorate that milestone, former World Bank Group President Robert Zoellick proposed to Chinese leaders to work jointly on identifying and analyzing China's medium-term development challenges looking forward to 2030. Together, China and the World Bank would conduct research drawing on lessons from international experience as well as China's own successful development record, and prepare a strategic framework for reforms that could assist China's policy making as well as guide future China–World Bank relations. China's state leaders welcomed and supported the proposal.

This report, *China 2030: Building a Modern, Harmonious, and Creative Society*, represents the results of that work. The research was organized jointly by China's Ministry of Finance (MOF), the Development Research Center of the State Council (DRC), and the World Bank. The report was written and produced by a joint team from DRC and the World Bank who worked together as equal partners. The team held numerous workshops, prepared several studies and background papers, and forged common ideas as well as bonds of friendship and mutual respect. A preliminary report was discussed at a high-level international conference held on September 3, 2011, at which many Chinese and international experts provided helpful comments and guidance. Building on these comments and additional work commissioned by the team, a conference edition of *China 2030* was launched at a meeting in Beijing on February 27, 2012. Since that launch, there has been considerable interest in this joint study both within China and around the world. This final version of *China 2030* could further enrich discussions in China and elsewhere, especially in middle-income countries that face similar issues.

The report is based on the strong conviction that China has the potential to become a modern, harmonious, and creative society by 2030.

In order to reach that objective, however, China must change its policy and institutional framework. China's next phase of development will need to build on its considerable strengths—high savings, plentiful and increasingly skilled labor, and the potential for further urbanization—and capitalize on external opportunities that include continued globalization, the rapid growth of other emerging economies, and promising new technologies. At the same time, China will need to address a number of significant challenges and risks, such as an aging society, rising inequality, a large and growing environmental deficit, and stubborn external imbalances.

The report proposes six strategic directions for China's new development strategy.

First, rethinking the role of the state and the private sector to encourage increased competition in the economy. Second, encouraging innovation and adopting an open innovation system with links to global research and development networks. Third, looking to green development as a significant new growth opportunity. Fourth, promoting equality of opportunity and social protection for all. Fifth, strengthening the fiscal system and improving fiscal sustainability. Sixth, ensuring that China, as an international stakeholder, continues its integration with global markets.

Using the 12th Five Year Plan as a starting point, and the six strategic directions as a policy framework, this report lays out a time frame for and sequencing of reforms that can take China toward its vision for 2030. We hope that it can provide a practical guide to help China's policy makers successfully navigate this next phase of China's development journey. We also hope that it will mark the beginning of another period of fruitful partnership between China and the World Bank.

Robert B. Zoellick
President, 2007–2012
The World Bank Group

LI Wei
President
Development Research Center
of the State Council, P.R.C.

Jim Yong Kim
President
The World Bank Group

Acknowledgments

This research was organized jointly by China's Ministry of Finance (MOF), the Development Research Center of the State Council (DRC), and the World Bank. The report was prepared by a World Bank and DRC joint team, led by DRC Vice Minister Shijin Liu, World Bank Country Director for China and Mongolia Klaus Rohland, and World Bank Chief Economist for East Asia and the Pacific Region Vikram Nehru.

President Robert B. Zoellick of the World Bank, Minister Xuren Xie of MOF, and Minsters Wei Li and He Liu of DRC provided valuable guidance and strong support throughout. A Chinese internal steering committee comprising former Minister of DRC Yutai Zhang, Vice Minister of the Ministry of Finance (MOF) Yong Li, Vice Minister of DRC Shijin Liu, Director-General of DRC's General Office Junkuo Zhang, Director-General of the International Department of MOF Xiaosong Zheng, and Deputy Director-General of the International Department of MOF Shixin Chen, and a World Bank internal steering committee comprising Sri Mulyani Indrawati, Lars Thunell, Justin Yifu Lin, Otaviano Canuto, Joachim von Amsberg, James Adams, and Klaus Rohland, guided this research.

The overview report was prepared by a joint team led by Shijin Liu, Klaus Rohland, and Vikram Nehru, and comprising Junkuo Zhang, Yongzhi Hou, Guoqiang Long, Shiji Gao, Yongsheng Zhang, Sen Gong, Wenkui Zhang, Pei-Lin Liu, and Changsheng Chen from DRC, and Ardo Hansson, Shahid Yusuf, Carter Brandon, Philip O'Keefe, and Hans Timmer from the World Bank. The joint team is grateful to David Bulman, Aart Kraay, and Antonio Ollero for analytical support and background papers. Yukon Huang, advisor to the World Bank team, as well as members of the Chinese Advisory Board comprising Jinglian Wu, Bin Xia, Fei Feng, Wei Lv, and Yanfeng Ge provided helpful advice and suggestions. The team benefited greatly from comments by peer reviewers Pieter Bottelier, Bert Hofman, and Barry Naughton. The team is also grateful for comments from Fang Cai, Yuanzheng Cao, Yoon Je Cho, Evan Feigenbaum, Shuqing Guo, Motoshige Ito, David Lampton, Lawrence Lau, Jiange Li, Peilin Li, Dwight Perkins, Il SaKong, Pingping Wang, Yiming Wang, Fuzhan Xie, Shanda Xu, Lan Xue, Weimin Yang, Linda Yueh, and Yuyan Zhang. Most of those comments were received at an international conference organized by MOF, DRC, and the World Bank in Beijing on September 3, 2011.

The five supporting reports were prepared under the overall guidance of Shijin Liu, Klaus Rohland, and Vikram Nehru.

Supporting report 1 on structural reforms was prepared by a joint team led by Wenkui Zhang (DRC) and Ardo Hansson (World Bank) and included Jianwu He, Louis Kuijs, Ulrich Schmitt, Jun Wang, Anbo Xiang, and Min Zhao. Critical guidance, inputs, and advice were provided by Daofu Chen, Jianwu He, Shouying Liu, Hongri Ni, Jianing Wei, and Chenghui Zhang (all DRC), and by Robert Cull, Asli Demirguc-Kunt, Juan Feng, Yukon Huang, Guo Li, Haocong Ren, Tunc Uyanik, Xiaoli Wan, Ying Wang, and Luan Zhao (all World Bank). The report builds on new background papers or notes prepared by Ehtisham Ahmad (consultant, fiscal policy), David Bulman (consultant) and Aart Kraay (World Bank, economic growth), Yoon Je Cho (consultant, financial sector), Andrew Hilton and Paul Munro-Faure (Food and Agriculture Organization, land), Hironori Kawauchi (World Bank, Japan), Chul Ju Kim (World Bank, Korea), Ping Li (Landesa, land), and Wenkui Zhang and Anbo Xiang (DRC, enterprise sector). The team benefited from useful discussions and comments from (in alphabetical order by surname) Carter Brandon, Loren Brandt, Nigel Chalk (IMF), Shixin Chen (MOF), Klaus Deininger, Peiyong Gao (CASS), Sudarshan Gooptu, James Hanson (consultant), Ede Ijjasz-Vasquez, Kang Jia (Institute for Fiscal Sciences), Il Houng Lee, Lili Liu, Shangxi Liu, Xiaofan Liu, Millard Long, Philip O'Keefe, Thomas Rawski, Elaine Sun, Eric Thun, Rogier van den Brink, Dimitri Vittas, Yan Wang, Li Xu, Shanda Xu, Chunlin Zhang, and Zhuoyuan Zhang. In preparing the report, the team was ably supported by Jianqing Chen, Yan Wang, and Shanshan Ye.

Supporting report 2 on innovation was prepared by a joint team led by Shiji Gao of DRC, and Shahid Yusuf of the World Bank and comprising Zhiyan Sun, Jietang Tian, Xiaowei Xuan and Yongwei Zhang from DRC, and Luan Zhao, Lopamudra Chakraborti, and Rory Birmingham from the World Bank. We thank Hamid Alavi, Cong Cao, Mark Dutz, Xin Fang, Zhijian Hu, Gary Jefferson, Yuan Ma, Jamil Salmi, Changlin Wang, Chunfa Wang, Jun Wang, Lan Xue, and Chunlin Zhang for their most helpful comments and suggestions. In addition, Jingyue Huang and Bo Lv prepared some of the background company case studies.

Supporting report 3 on green development was prepared by a joint team led by Yongsheng Zhang of DRC and Carter Brandon of the World Bank and comprising Ede Ijjasz, Kirk Hamilton, and Chris Sall (World Bank) and Shouying Liu, Xiaowei Xuan, Yongwei Zhang, Xiaoming Wang, Jianwu He, and Jianjun Dai (DRC). This report also benefited from background papers by Xiaodong Wang, Noureddine Berrah (clean energy); Victor Vergara, Zhi Liu, Wanli Fang, Holly Krambeck, Axel Baeumler, Meskerem Brhane, and Andrew Saltzberg (urban development); Lee Travers, Sudipto Sarkar, and Paul Kriss (water); Sina Johannes (pollution and waste); Luc Christiaensen (agriculture); Katrina Brandon (natural resource management); Urvashi Narain and Gordon Hughes (adapting to a changing climate); Kirk Hamilton and Maryla Maliszewska (simulating a carbon price for China); and Chris Sall (China's future green export markets, and using urban quality of life indices to evaluate government performance). Additional comments and guidance from World Bank colleagues were provided by Andrew Steer, Ken Chomitz, and Michael Toman (peer reviewers), and Gailius Draugelis, Marianne Fay, Kathryn Funk, Marea Hatziolos, Dan Hoornweg, Vijay Jagannathan, Abed Khalil, Paul Kriss, Xiaokai Li, Magda Lovei, Gayane Minasyan, John Roome, Stefanie Sieber, Xuemen Wang, and Yanning Wang. Comments from DRC and other reviewers were provided by Zhigang Chen, Fei Feng, Ross Garnaut, Stephen Howes, Carlo Jarger, Kejun Jiang, Nick Johnstone, Frank Jotze, Hongri Ni, Jiahua Pan, Ye Qi, Heling Shi, Fangfang Tang, Simon Upton, Jinzhao Wang, Yi Wang, Yiming Wei, Ming Xu, Qian Ye, and Xinye Zheng. Zijing Niu and Hua Zhu (World Bank), Jianpeng Chen and Haiqin Wang (DRC) provided excellent support throughout.

Supporting report 4 on social development was prepared by a joint team led by

Sen Gong (DRC) and Philip O'Keefe (World Bank) and comprising Dewen Wang (World Bank) and Liejun Wang (DRC). The team also included Jin Song (World Bank), and Changsheng Chen, Yang Su, and Dong Yu (DRC). The Director-General of DRC's social development research department, Yanfeng Ge, provided constructive comments for the report. It benefited from background papers by Carl Mason and Quilin Chen (social spending modelling); Toomas Palu (primary health care); Sen Gong and Dong Yu (citizen participation); Liejun Wang and Sen Gong (doctor and teacher pay), Scott Rozelle (human capital); Kin Bing Wu, Christine Boscardin, and Peter Goldschmidt (education); Fang Cai, Yang Du, and Meiyan Wang (labor market overview, and labor market institutions); John Giles, Dewen Wang, and Wei Cai (labor supply and retirement); Dewen Wang and Philip O'Keefe (hukou); Sen Gong and Liejun Wang (hukou) John Giles and Dewen Wang (social security); and Laurie Joshua (aged care). The team also benefited from comments from Tamar Manuelyan-Atinc, Arup Banerji, Eduardo Velez Bustillo, Fang Cai, Gong Chen, Ariel Fiszbein, Gerard La Forgia, Emmanuel Jimenez, John Langenbrunner, Peilin Li, Xiaoyan Liang, Albert Park, Hainan Su, Adam Wagstaff, Liping Xiao, Xiaoqing Yu, Li Zhang, and Bingwen Zheng. The team is grateful to the Korea Development Institute and Japan-China Economic Association for making arrangements for DRC study tours in Korea and Japan, respectively, and to local Development Research Centers of Chengdu and Nanjing, and the Hangzhou Government for joint field visits and meetings. Finally, the team is grateful for assistance in preparing the document from Limei Sun and Tao Su.

Supporting report 5 on China and the global economy was prepared by a joint team led by Guoqiang Long of DRC and Hans Timmer of the World Bank and comprising Dilek Aykut (service sector FDI), Charles Blitzer (renminbi), Deborah Brautigam (official finance), Allen Dennis (voluntary export restraints), Jin Fang (cross-border investment), Jianwu He (growth prospects), Gang Lv (foreign trade), Maryla Maliszewska (forecasts for the global economy and the scenarios for the impact of climate change), Aaditya Mattoo (trade), Francis Ng (trade), William Shaw (main author), Dominique van der Mensbrugghe (forecasts for the global economy and the scenarios for the impact of climate change), Lucio Vinhas de Souza (international banking regulation), Hongqing Xu (foreign aid), and Liping Zhang (opening of the financial sector and internationalization of RMB). Jin Fang helped coordinate the revision for this supporting report. Yongsheng Zhang provided important suggestions on climate change issues. We thank Jiyao Bi, Qisheng Lai, Hong Song, Youfu Xia, Xiangchen Zhang, and Xiaoji Zhang for their helpful comments and suggestions. Excellent data work and other inputs were provided by Yueqing Jia, Sergio Andres Kurlat, Jose Alejandro Quijada, and Sachin Shahria. The team also benefited from excellent support provided by Maria Hazel Macadangdang and Rosalie Marie Lourdes Singson.

Pei-Lin Liu, Changsheng Chen, Wei Xu, Xian Zhuo, and Ting Shao thoroughly reviewed and proofread the Chinese version of the overview report and all supporting reports under the guidance of and with personal involvement of Shijin Liu.

Coordination teams led by Yongzhi Hou, Shixin Chen, Elaine Sun, and Shiji Gao and comprising Chunquan Yin, Wei Wang, Licheng Yao, Weijie Liu, Jiangnan Qian, Yanning Wang, Yunzhong Liu, Zhiyan Sun, Xian Zhuo, Guangqin Luo, and Li Li provided strong support for the successful completion of the study. Chunquan Yin helped organize a series of important meetings, while Yi Li, Lihui Liu, Hao Dong, Hui Han, and Li Zhu helped in communications, coordination, and other ad hoc tasks. Tianshu Chen of the World Bank served as interpreter at innumerable meetings, participated in the translation of the report, and organized and coordinated the translation work. The World Bank's Elaine Sun,

Kathryn Funk, and Li Li managed coordination and production of the English edition. The team is grateful to Patricia Katayama and Susan Graham of the World Bank's Office of the Publisher for the editing and layout of the English edition. The International Department of MOF, the General Office and International Department of DRC, and the World Bank provided support in organizing numerous conferences, discussion meetings, small seminars, and international field study trips throughout this research.

This research also benefited enormously from comments and suggestions from Chinese ministries and local governments, including Ministry of Foreign Affairs, National Development and Reform Commission, Ministry of Education, Ministry of Science and Technology, Ministry of Industry and Information Technology, Ministry of Public Security, Ministry of Civil Affairs, Ministry of Human Resources and Social Security, Ministry of Land and Resources, Ministry of Environmental Protection, Ministry of Housing and Urban-Rural Development, Ministry of Agriculture, Ministry of Commerce, Ministry of Health, National Population and Family Planning Commission, The People's Bank of China, State-owned Assets Supervision and Administration Commission, State Administration of Taxation, National Bureau of Statistics, State Intellectual Property Office, China Banking Regulatory Commission, National Council for Social Security Fund, National Energy Administration, State Administration of Foreign Experts Affairs, as well as governments of Beijing, Jilin, Heilongjiang, Shanghai, Jiangsu, Anhui, Henan, Guangdong, Chongqing, Shaanxi, Gansu, and Xinjiang Uygur Autonomous Region. The joint research team is grateful for all their comments and suggestions.

Background to This Research

This research was conducted by a joint research team with experts from the World Bank and China, the first time such research has been conducted in the history of cooperation between the two. The research was organized by China's Ministry of Finance, the Development Research Center of the State Council (DRC), and the World Bank. The research work and report writing was undertaken by a joint team from the World Bank and the DRC.

The joint team formally launched the research at its first working-level seminar held at Fragrant Hills in Beijing on November 23–26, 2010. The seminar set the vision of the research as building a modern, harmonious, and creative high-income society in China by 2030. Five research groups were established to study the subjects of *structural reforms, innovation, green growth, social development, as well as China and the world*. Over the following year, Chinese and foreign experts wrote background reports and jointly held a dozen seminars. The experts from the World Bank and the DRC also held working-level seminars, conducted interviews and field research in relevant government agencies, cities, rural areas, and enterprises in China, and visited countries like Indonesia, Republic of Korea, and the Philippines. After finishing the first draft of the research report, the team solicited opinions from many experts. At a high-level international seminar held at the Diaoyutai State Guesthouse, both renowned domestic and international experts as well as leaders of China's government departments and high ranking executives of China's enterprises commented on the draft and raised many critical and constructive ideas. The team also asked for opinions and suggestions of relevant central government departments and local governments during different phases of the project. The team revised the report in line with these comments and suggestions and held a series of special seminars to address some prominent issues. The final report managed to reflect many of these diverse views, but without losing its focus and realism.

Needless to say, the research was challenging. This was the first time that joint research was conducted by experts from the World Bank and China, who approached issues from different vantage points, held beliefs shaped by different experiences, and used different ways of organization and coordination. Moreover, China's challenge over the next two decades will be nothing short of historic—taking 1.3 billion people from middle- to high-income status with the backdrop of an ongoing global financial crisis. While the research was more difficult than expected, it was always stimulating and occasionally fun. It was a good opportunity for sharing knowledge and experience, conducting joint analysis, and learning from Chinese and international experts of different persuasions. The research was a relentless process of identifying and discussing problems, deepening understanding, and attempting to bring forward creative ideas. Second, all members of the team approached the work with an open mind, and solicited opinions and suggestions from experts inside and outside China to push the discussions forward. Hours of debate helped in converging viewpoints and developing a common understanding. Finally, shared objectives and mutual respect between the Chinese and World Bank experts, their professionalism, and their effective collaboration ensured that the research work went smoothly. Hopefully, experience from this research will pave the way for more cooperative undertakings between China and the World Bank in the future.

Executive Summary

By any standard, China's economic performance over the last three decades has been impressive. GDP growth averaged 10 percent a year, and over 500 million people were lifted out of poverty. China is now the world's largest exporter and manufacturer, and its second largest economy.

Even if growth moderates, China is likely to become a high-income economy and the world's largest economy before 2030, notwithstanding the fact that its per capita income would still be a fraction of the average in advanced economies.

But two questions arise. Can China's growth rate still be among the highest in the world even if it slows from its current pace? And can it maintain this rapid growth with little disruption to the world, the environment, and the fabric of its own society?

This report answers both questions in the affirmative, without downplaying the risks. By 2030, China has the potential to be a modern, harmonious, and creative high-income society. But achieving this objective will not be easy. To seize its opportunities, meet its many challenges, and realize its development vision for 2030, China needs to implement a new development strategy in its next phase of development. The reforms that launched China on its current growth trajectory were inspired by Deng Xiaoping, who played an important role in building consensus for a fundamental shift in the country's strategy. After more than 30 years of rapid growth, China has reached another turning point in its development path when a second strategic, and no less fundamental, shift is called for. The 12th Five Year Plan provides an excellent start. This report combines its key elements to design a longer-term strategy that extends to 2030. More important, it focuses on the "how," not just the "what." Six important messages emerge from the analysis:

First, implement structural reforms to strengthen the foundations for a market-based economy by redefining the role of government; reforming and restructuring state enterprises and banks; developing the private sector; promoting competition; and deepening reforms in the land, labor, and financial markets. As an economy approaches the technology frontier and exhausts the potential for acquiring and applying technology from abroad, the role of the government and its relationship to markets and the private sector needs to change fundamentally. While providing relatively fewer "tangible" public goods and services directly, the government will need to provide more intangible public goods and services like systems, rules, and policies, which increase production efficiency, promote competition, facilitate specialization, enhance the efficiency of resource allocation, protect the environment, and reduce risks and uncertainties.

In the enterprise sector, the focus will need to be further reforms of state enterprises (including measures to recalibrate the role of public resources, introduce modern corporate governance practices, such as separating ownership from management, and implement gradual ownership diversification where necessary), private sector development and fewer barriers to entry and exit, and increased competition in all sectors, including in strategic and pillar industries. In the financial sector, it would require commercializing the banking system, gradually allowing interest rates to be set by market forces, deepening the capital market, and developing the legal and supervisory infrastructure to ensure financial stability and build the credible foundations for the internationalization of China's financial sector. In the labor market, China needs to accelerate phased reforms of the *hukou* system to ensure that by 2030, Chinese workers can move in response to market signals. It also needs to introduce measures to increase labor force participation rates, rethink wage policy, and use social security instruments (pensions, health, and unemployment insurance) that are portable nationwide. Finally, rural land markets need to be overhauled to protect farmer rights and increase efficiency of land use, and policies for acquisition of rural land for urban use must be thoroughly overhauled to prevent urban sprawl, reduce local government dependency on land-related revenues, and address a frequent cause of complaint from farmers.

Second, accelerate the pace of innovation and create an open innovation system in which competitive pressures encourage Chinese firms to engage in product and process innovation not only through their own research and development but also by participating in global research and development networks. China has already introduced a range of initiatives in establishing a research and development infrastructure and is far ahead of most other developing countries. Its priority going forward is to increase the quality of research and development, rather than just quantity. To achieve this, policy makers will need to focus on increasing the technical and cognitive skills of university graduates and building a few world-class research universities with strong links to industry; fostering "innovative cities" that bring together high-quality talent, knowledge networks, dynamic firms, and learning institutions, and allow them to interact without restriction; and increasing the availability of patient risk capital for private startup firms.

Third, seize the opportunity to "go green" through a mix of market incentives, regulations, public investments, industrial policy, and institutional development. Encouraging green development and increased efficiency of resource use is expected to not only improve the level of well-being and sustain rapid growth, but also address China's manifold environmental challenges. The intention is to encourage new investments in a range of low-pollution, energy- and resource-efficient industries that would lead to greener development, spur investments in related upstream and downstream manufacturing and services, and build international competitive advantage in a global sunrise industry. These policies have the potential to succeed, given China many advantages—its large market size that will allow rapid scaling up of successful technologies to achieve economies of scale and reduced unit costs; a high investment rate that will permit rapid replacement of old, inefficient, and environmentally damaging capital stock; its growing and dynamic private sector that will respond to new signals from government, provided it gets access to adequate levels of finance; and a relatively well-developed research and development infrastructure that can be harnessed to reach and then expand the "green" technology frontier.

Fourth, expand opportunities and promote social security for all by facilitating equal access to jobs, finance, quality social services, and portable social security. These policies will be critical in reversing rising inequality, helping households manage employment-, health-, and age-related risks, and increasing labor mobility. China's relatively high social and economic inequality (some dimensions of which have been increasing) stems in large part from large rural-urban differences in access to jobs, key public services, and social protection. Reversing this trend requires three coordinated actions: delivering more and better quality public services to underserved rural areas and migrant populations from early childhood to tertiary education institutions and from primary health care to care for the aged; restructuring social security systems to ensure secure social safety nets; and mobilizing all segments of society—public and private, government and social organizations—to share responsibilities in financing, delivering, and monitoring the delivery of social services.

Fifth, strengthen the fiscal system by mobilizing additional revenues and ensuring local governments have adequate financing to meet heavy and rising expenditure responsibilities. Many of the reforms proposed in this development strategy—enterprise and financial sector reforms, green development, equality of opportunity for all—have implications for the level and allocation of public expenditures. Over the next two decades, the agenda for strengthening the fiscal system will involve three key dimensions: mobilizing additional fiscal resources to meet rising budgetary demands; reallocating spending toward social and environmental objectives; and ensuring that budgetary resources available at different levels of government (central, provincial, prefectural, county, township, village) are commensurate with expenditure responsibilities. Without appropriate fiscal reforms, many of the other reform elements of the new development strategy would be difficult to move forward.

Sixth, seek mutually beneficial relations with the world by becoming a proactive stakeholder in the global economy, actively using multilateral institutions and frameworks, and shaping the global governance agenda. China's integration with the global economy served it well over the past three decades. By continuing to intensify its trade, investment, and financial links with the global economy over the next two decades, China

will be able to benefit from further specialization, increased investment opportunities and higher returns to capital, and a mutually beneficial flow of ideas and knowledge. As a key stakeholder in the global economy, China must remain proactive in resuscitating the stalled Doha multilateral trade negotiations, advocate "open regionalism" as a feature of regional trading arrangements, and support a multilateral agreement on investment flows. Integrating the Chinese financial sector with the global financial system, which will involve opening the capital account (among other things), will need to be undertaken steadily and with considerable care, but it will be a key step toward internationalizing the renminbi as a global reserve currency. Finally, China must play a central role in engaging with its partners in multilateral settings to shape the global governance agenda and address pressing global economic issues such as climate change, global financial stability, and a more effective international aid architecture that serves the cause of development in poor nations less fortunate than China.

* * *

These six priority reform areas lay out objectives for the short, medium, and long term, and policy makers need to sequence the reforms within and across these areas appropriately to ensure smooth implementation and to reach desired outcomes. A successful outcome will require strong leadership and commitment, steady implementation with a determined will, coordination across ministries and agencies, and sensitive yet effective management of a consultation process that will ensure public support and participation in the design, implementation, and oversight of the reform process. And since the global economy is entering a dangerous phase and China itself will be transitioning from middle-income to high-income status, the government will need to respond to a variety of risks, shocks, and vulnerabilities as they arise; in doing so, it must hold fast to the principle that policy responses to short-term problems should uphold, not undermine, long-term reform priorities.

Abbreviations

5YP	Five Year Plan
ALTC	Aged and long-term care
APEC	Asia Pacific Economic Corporation
BITs	Bilateral investment treaties
BRICS	Brazil, the Russian Federation, India, China, and South Africa
CBRC	China Bank Regulatory Commission
CCS	Carbon capture and sequestration
CCT	Conditional cash transfer
CO_2	Carbon dioxide
CPC	Communist Party of China
CPCC	Communist Party Central Committee
CPI	Consumer Price Index
CSRC	China Securities Regulatory Commission
DRC	Development Research Center of the State Council, P. R. China
ECDE	Early childhood development and education
EFTA	European Free Trade Association
EU	European Union
FDI	Foreign direct investment
GATT	General Agreement on Tariffs and Trade
GDP	Gross domestic product
GEM	Growth enterprises market
GNI	Gross national income
GPT	General purpose technologies
HRS	Household responsibility system
ICOR	Incremental capital-output ratios
ICT	Information and communication technology
IMF	International Monetary Fund

IT	Information technology
KBA	Key biodiversity areas
KWh	Kilowatt hour
LED	Light-emitting diode
LFPR	Labor force participation rate
M&A	Mergers and acquisitions
MFN	Most-favored nation
MIIT	Ministry of Industry and Information Technology
MSME	Micro, small, and medium enterprises
NBSC	National Bureau of Statistics of China
NBFI	Nonbank financial institutions
NDRC	National Development and Reform Commission
NO_2	Nitrous oxide
NPL	Nonperforming loan
OECD	Organisation of Economic Co-operation and Development
OPEC	Organization of Petroleum Exporting Countries
PBC	People's Bank of China
PISA	Programme for International Student Assessment
PM_{10}	Small particulate matter
PPP	Purchasing power parity
PSU	Public service unit
R&D	Research and development
ROE	Return on equity
RMB	Renminbi
SAMC	State asset management company
SASAC	State Owned Assets Supervision and Administration Commission
S&T	Science and technology
SFI	State financial institutions
SME	Small and medium enterprise
SO_2	Sulphur dioxide
SOE	State-owned enterprise
TCE	Tons of coal equivalent
tCO_2	Tons of CO_2
TFP	Total factor productivity
TVET	Technical and vocational education and training
UDIC	Urban Development Investment Corporations
UN	United Nations
UNEP	United Nations Environment Programme
VAT	Value added tax
WIPO	World Intellectual Property Organization
WTO	World Trade Organization

Part I

Overview

China 2030:
Building a Modern, Harmonious,
and Creative Society

China 2030:
Building a Modern, Harmonious, and Creative Society

Introduction

From the early 1500s until the early 1800s, China's economy was the world's largest. By 1820, it was one-fifth again as big as Europe's and accounted for a third of world gross domestic product (GDP). But the next two centuries were tumultuous for China. The country experienced catastrophic decline between 1820 and 1950 and then, starting in 1978, meteoric rise (Maddison 2001). Today, China is once again among the largest economies of the world, having overtaken Japan in 2010. Its economy is now second only to that of the United States (third, if the European Union [EU] is counted as one economy), and it is the world's largest manufacturer and exporter. The East Asian miracle may have lost some of its luster after the financial crisis of 1997–98, but China's performance continues to impress. Even if China grows a third as slowly in the future compared with its past (6.6 percent a year on average compared with 9.9 percent over the past 30 years), it will become a high-income country sometime before 2030 and outstrip the United States in economic size (its per capita income, however, will still be a fraction of that in advanced countries). If China achieves this milestone, it will have avoided the "middle-income trap" by traversing the seemingly impossible chasm between low-income and high-income status within a generation and a half—a remarkable achievement for any country, let alone one the size of China.

But two questions arise. Can China's growth rate still be among the highest in the world even if it slows from its current pace? And can it maintain this rapid growth with little disruption to the world, the environment, and the fabric of its own society? We answer "yes" to both, but only if China transitions from policies that served it so well in the past to ones that address the very different challenges of a very different future.

This overview, followed by five supporting reports, identifies these challenges of tomorrow, points to key choices ahead, and recommends not just "what" needs to be reformed, but "how" to undertake the reforms. The overview is divided into nine chapters. The first chapter examines the characteristics of China's development since 1978; considers future opportunities, challenges, and risks; and describes a vision of China in the year 2030. The second chapter maps a new strategy that will realize this vision, focusing on the key choices ahead for China to sustain rapid economic and social development and become a modern, harmonious, and creative high-income society before 2030. Chapters 3–8 elaborate on each of the six pillars of the new strategy: consolidating China's market foundations; enhancing innovation; promoting green development; ensuring equality of opportunity and social protection for all; strengthening public finances; and achieving mutually beneficial win-win relations between China and the rest of the world. The ninth and final chapter addresses implementation challenges, including the sequencing of proposed reforms and overcoming obstacles that are likely to emerge.

Chapter 1   China's Path: 1978 to 2030

Unique Factors behind China's Economic Success

Over the past three decades, China's two historic transformations, from a rural, agricultural society to an urban, industrial one, and from a command economy to a market-based one, have combined to yield spectacular results. Not only did economic growth soar, but the poverty rate fell from more than 65 percent to less than 10 percent as some 500 million people were lifted out of poverty, and all the Millennium Development Goals have been reached or are within reach. Although growth rates differed across China, growth was rapid everywhere. Indeed, if mainland China's 31 provinces were regarded as independent economies,[1] they would be among the 32 fastest-growing economies in the world (figure O.1). Such rapid growth has been accompanied by many other achievements: for example, 2 of the world's top 10 banks are now Chinese;[2] 61 Chinese companies are on the Global Fortune 500 list;[3] and China is home to the world's second-largest highway network, the world's 3 longest sea bridges, and 6 of the world's 10 largest container ports.[4] The country has also made large strides in health, education, science, and technology, and is quickly closing the gap on all these fronts with global leaders.

Many unique factors lie behind China's impressive growth record, including the initial conditions of the economy in 1978 that made it particularly ripe for change. The spark came in the form of agricultural reforms, including the household responsibility system that foreshadowed sustained reforms in this and other areas over the next 30 years. To summarize, key features of the reforms included:

Pragmatic and effective market-oriented reforms. China's uniqueness among developing countries is not what it did to achieve success, but how it did it. China adapted a strategy known as "crossing the river by feeling stones," which encouraged local governments to undertake bold pilot experiments within the broader context of reform priorities. By introducing market-oriented reforms in a gradual, experimental way and by providing incentives for local governments, the country was able to discover workable transitional institutions at each stage of development. One key feature of these reforms was their "dual-track" nature—supporting state-owned firms in old priority sectors while liberalizing and encouraging the development of private enterprises (Lin 2012). The economy was allowed to "grow out of the plan" until the administered material planning system gradually withered. As a result of continuous and decentralized trial-by-error exploration, institutional arrangements evolved as new and different challenges needed resolution. Indeed, different localities often adopted their own unique institutions tailored to their specific situations.

Balancing growth with social and macroeconomic stability. The difficult economic situation at the start of reforms in 1978 made economic growth an urgent priority. Early reform successes quickly transformed this priority into a national objective that was effectively used to mobilize all quarters of society—individuals and firms as well as local governments—to focus their collective efforts on economic development. The government employed a mix of fiscal, administrative, and employment policies to maintain social stability during a period of rapid economic and structural change. This was no mean achievement, given the need to employ an additional 9 million new entrants into the labor force each year while also absorbing workers affected by policy shifts (such as the 1998 reforms of state-owned enterprises, or SOEs), frictional unemployment, and occasional external economic shocks.

Rapid growth and structural change also presented macroeconomic challenges. The economy experienced occasional bouts of serious inflation, such as in the late 1980s and early 1990s. But macroeconomic stability was effectively restored through a combination of traditional monetary and fiscal policies, as

FIGURE O.1   China's impressive economic performance

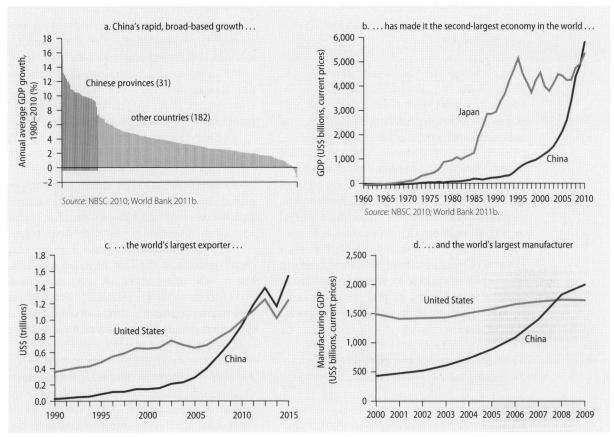

a. China's rapid, broad-based growth . . .

Source: NBSC 2010; World Bank 2011b.

b. . . . has made it the second-largest economy in the world . . .

Source: NBSC 2010; World Bank 2011b.

c. . . . the world's largest exporter . . .

Source: NBSC 2010; World Bank 2011b.

d. . . . and the world's largest manufacturer

Source: UNSD 2010.

well as administrative means when necessary. As a result, the authorities were broadly successful in keeping inflation low throughout the period and protecting the rural and urban poor from relative price increases in key necessities.

Interregional competition. China built on its strong local governments at various levels by allowing them to compete in attracting investment, developing infrastructure, and improving the local business environment. Decentralization policies, including fiscal reforms in 1994 (which significantly increased resource transfers from the central government), gave subnational governments the incentives and the resources to aggressively pursue local development objectives. Increased factor mobility meant that resources flowed to jurisdictions most supportive of growth. Finally, China's vast size

and regional differences meant that local governments could experiment with and champion specific reforms suited to their circumstances, while operating within the parameters established by central authorities. Officials were rewarded for delivering key reform goals: growth, foreign direct investment (FDI), employment, and social stability. The resulting competition between local governments and regions was fierce—and became a strong driver of growth—far beyond the expectations of the authorities.

Domestic market integration. A key element of the reforms was the dismantling of regional barriers to the movement of goods, labor, and capital and the establishment of a single national market. Major infrastructure investments connecting regions and the interior to the coast helped. A large and integrated domestic market allowed firms to achieve scale economies, and the large variation in income levels and consumption patterns across the country gave their products a longer life cycle.

Steady integration with the global economy. With the establishment of special economic zones, Deng Xiaoping's remarks during his famous South China tour, and accession into the World Trade Organization (WTO) as milestones, China expanded and deepened its economic integration with the global economy. This policy reaped large dividends for China, bringing investments, advanced technologies, and managerial expertise; opening the international market for China's goods and services; and giving a boost to China's internal economic reforms. The proximity of Hong Kong SAR, China, and Taiwan, China, helped, as did a large Chinese diaspora dispersed across the globe.

Trends and Characteristics at Home and Abroad in the Next Two Decades

China's reforms, still ongoing, have facilitated regional concentration of activities and captured agglomeration economies in coastal provinces, encouraged mobility of factors and goods across provinces and with the rest of the world, and established a high savings- and investment-led growth process disciplined by the competitive pressures of globalization. Most important, China has avoided economic setbacks: not only did economic growth average nearly 10 percent over more than three decades, it fell measurably below 8 percent only twice. During the recent global financial crisis, China's continued rapid growth was a significant stabilizing force that partly counterbalanced the impact on global economic activity of the downturn and subsequent tepid recovery in the advanced economies.

Will China be able to sustain this performance over the next two decades? Much depends on how the global environment evolves and on the structural forces that are already at work within China. But this much is certain: trends at home and abroad will be very different over the next 20 years compared with the past 30, not only because China and other emerging markets have fundamentally reshaped the global economy— a trend that was accelerated by the recent global financial crisis—but also because new global challenges and opportunities are emerging that will significantly affect the future trajectory of the world's economies.

Global Megatrends

The last three decades saw a supportive global environment that undoubtedly assisted and accommodated China's rapid growth. Key elements included relatively open trade, rising flows of foreign direct investment, steady growth in the world's major markets, sharply declining transport costs, increased intraindustry trade, and the introduction and spread of information and communications technology. While extrapolating linearly from the past may be dangerous, some of these trends are indeed likely to persist.[5] There is widespread consensus, for example, that in addition to China, other developing countries, especially middle-income emerging markets, will continue to outperform the advanced economies as they have for the past decade. One reason is their continued potential for technological catch-up. The other is continued slow growth in advanced economies owing to deleveraging and the impact of high sovereign debt burdens. By 2030, developing countries are expected to contribute two-thirds of global growth (40 percent, excluding China) and half of global output (30 percent, excluding China), and will be the main destinations of world trade. The larger emerging markets—China more so than others—will act as additional growth poles in a multipolar world economy.

Perhaps the most important global megatrend is the rise of China itself. No other country is poised to have as much impact on the global economy over the next two decades. Even if China's growth rate slows as projected, it would still replace the United States as the world's largest economy by 2030, its share in world trade could be twice as high, it is likely to remain the world's biggest emitter of carbon dioxide, and, notwithstanding shrinkage in its trade surplus, it is expected to remain the world's largest creditor. Some have argued that by 2030, China's influence in the global economy could approach that of the United Kingdom in 1870 or the United States in 1945 (Subramanian 2011).

Continued rapid growth in emerging markets will give rise to an unprecedented expansion of the global middle class (by one estimate, from less than 1.8 billion people in 2009 to about 5 billion in 2030, of whom nearly two-thirds will be in Asia).[6] That expansion will trigger an explosion in demand for housing and consumer durables, including automobiles. The pressure on global supplies of energy, natural resources, food, water, and the environment will ratchet up rapidly. Climate change effects could exacerbate food and water shortages in some areas. The price of raw materials will remain elevated and volatile. Higher prices for scarce natural resources highlight the need to introduce "green growth" strategies that could potentially become a new source of growth.

Notwithstanding the potential for rapid growth in emerging markets, there are also reasons to believe that growth in developing countries, including China, will slow. First, as populations age, the growth rate of the labor force will slow, and in some countries (such as China and the Russian Federation) will even decline, leading to higher dependency ratios and lower savings and investment. Second, although emerging market economies will retain a comparative advantage in manufacturing, rising unit labor costs will further increase their relative share of services; overall growth would thus slow because productivity growth in services is usually lower than in manufacturing.

While protectionism may occasionally rear its head, especially in advanced countries where the impact of the recent financial crisis has been particularly severe, the forces of globalization will remain irresistible, and further cross-border movements of goods, services, finance, people, and knowledge will endure and deepen. Production chains across borders will continue to flourish, and intraindustry and intrafirm trade will intensify.

As global trade continues to grow at a more rapid rate than GDP, the new frontier will be trade in services, now the fastest-growing component of global trade. Thanks to new informational technologies, services previously considered nontradable (such as health and education) will be routinely provided across national borders just as manufactures are now. In addition, the world is continuing to see further global relocation of industries (and, increasingly, tasks within industries) in the incessant search for global competitiveness.

The number of free trade arrangements in the world has multiplied manifold over the past two decades; over the next two, trade integration will intensify and production networks will expand further. Intra–East Asian trade could rival that of intra-European trade (as a share of GDP). Emerging markets will develop an increasing stake in an open global trading system. The resolution of climate change, international financial stability, international migration, health pandemics, water management, and other global challenges will require new approaches to transnational and global governance arrangements.

The U.S. dollar will likely remain the world's major international reserve currency, especially given weaknesses in the Euro Area and Japan. But expansionary monetary policies in the advanced countries, including the United States, will cause instability in the international monetary system, and uncertainty in key exchange rates will add to costs of international monetary and trade transactions. China's growing weight in world trade, the size of its economy, and its role as the world's largest creditor will make the internationalization of China's renminbi inevitable, but its acceptance as a major global reserve currency will depend on the pace and success of financial sector reforms and the opening of its external capital account (see chapter 8).

Technological breakthroughs, unpredictable as they may be, are more likely in some areas, such as clean water, energy storage, and biotechnologies, than in others. A breakthrough in clean coal technologies would give China an obvious advantage, given its huge coal reserves. Renewable energy technologies could also become more economically viable. The recent pattern has been for such technological breakthroughs to occur in advanced countries, with their application in commercial and mass production usually transferred to developing countries. This pattern is likely to continue; adoption, adaptation, and mastery of existing technologies will remain an important growth driver in developing countries. At the same time, however, as emerging markets develop their own technological capability, new and disruptive technologies will appear in the developing world and raise the chance of "leapfrogging" over advanced countries in a few areas.

Major Trends within China

Just as growth is expected to slow in some emerging markets over the coming two decades, many signs point to a growth slowdown in China as well (Liu et al. 2011). Indeed, we expect GDP growth to decline gradually from an average near 8.5 percent in 2011–15 to around 5 percent in 2026–30 (see table O.1). One reason for the slowdown is that much of the growth contribution from shifting resources from agriculture to industry has already occurred. And going forward, the continued accumulation of capital, although sizable, will inevitably contribute less to growth as the capital-labor ratio rises (even though capital stock per worker, now an estimated 8.7 percent of the U.S. level, underscores the need for further capital accumulation). Moreover, China is poised to go through wrenching demographic change: the old age dependency ratio will double in the next two decades, reaching the current level in Norway and the Netherlands by 2030 (between 22 and 23 percent);[7] and the size of China's labor force is projected to start shrinking as soon as 2015. Yet workers will become more productive as physical and human capital stock per worker continues to rise. Finally, total factor productivity (TFP) growth—a measure of improvements in economic efficiency and technological progress—has also declined, in part because the economy has exhausted gains from first-generation policy reforms and the absorption of imported technologies. As a result, the distance to the technological frontier has shrunk, and second-generation policy reforms are likely to have a smaller impact on growth.[8]

These factors, together with "rebalancing" policies to emphasize domestic growth sources, will contribute to a higher share of services and consumption in the economy and a lower share of exports, savings, and investment. The challenge will be to support these growth and structural transitions while avoiding sudden slowdowns and possible crises.

China's external accounts are expected to show a decline in the trade surplus—export growth will slow as China's global market share rises and markets in advanced countries grow more slowly, while import growth will be driven by continued expansion in domestic demand. At the same time, however, the external capital account will show a rising deficit as Chinese savings flow abroad in search of better returns and to counter protectionist pressures abroad. This trend will serve not only to keep in check further accumulation of external reserves but also to facilitate the transformation of Chinese enterprises into global players.

China's current pattern of development has also placed considerable stress on the environment—land, air, and water—and has imposed increased pressure on the availability of natural resources. The challenge going forward will be to convert these pressures into new sources of growth by adopting a green growth model that taps into new global markets in green technologies while at the same time solving many of China's own pressing environmental concerns. If successful, the energy and commodity intensity of production is expected to decline significantly by 2030 for three reasons: a smaller share of industry in GDP; a smaller share of resource- and pollution-intensive firms in the industrial sector; and better pricing of energy, commodities, and environmental services (see chapter 5).

Income inequality in China, which climbed continuously over the past two decades, is showing some tentative signs of beginning to flatten and possibly even decline. In the coming decades, three underlying structural factors could serve to confirm this inflexion point. First, acceleration of growth in the middle and western regions will continue, so the income gap between

TABLE O.1   China: Projected growth pattern assuming steady reforms and no major shock

Indicator	1995–2010	2011–15	2016–20	2021–25	2026–30
GDP growth (percent per year)	9.9	8.6	7.0	5.9	5.0
Labor growth	0.9	0.3	−0.2	−0.2	−0.4
Labor productivity growth	8.9	8.3	7.1	6.2	5.5
Structure of economy (end of period, %)					
Investment/GDP ratio	49	42	38	36	34
Consumption/GDP ratio	47	56	60	63	66
Industry/GDP ratio	46.7	43.8	41.0	38.0	34.6
Services/GDP ratio	43.1	47.6	51.6	56.1	61.1
Share of employment in agriculture	36.7	30.0	23.7	18.2	12.5
Share of employment in services	34.6	42.0	47.6	52.9	59.0

Sources: NBSC and DRC.

the coast and the interior will narrow. Second, migrant wages will continue to rise rapidly, reducing the income gap with urban residents. The role of policy will be to support these structural forces by increasing the equality of opportunity (see chapter 6). Third, even though the urbanization rate is expected to continue its rise, rural-urban migration will gradually slow over the period as the structural shift from agriculture to manufacturing eases, and the rural-urban wage gap narrows (the urban-rural income ratio is expected to fall from 3.2 : 1 in 2010 to 2.4 : 1 in 2030).

At the same time, rising educational standards and brisk growth in tertiary education is rapidly increasing the numbers of skilled workers and helping China move up the value chain, and this process is likely to accelerate in coming decades. The growing skill base will facilitate a further shift in production from labor-intensive to skill-intensive activities and an increase in the pace of innovation. Indeed, just as in the 1980s and 1990s when hundreds of millions of unskilled Chinese workers joined the global labor force as part of China's "opening up" strategy, so too will tens of millions of tertiary-educated Chinese workers join the global workforce to significantly expand the global supply of skill-intensive products. Indeed, the number of college graduates could swell by 200 million over the next two decades—more than the entire labor force of the United States.[9]

At the same time, China's existing comparative advantage in low unit labor costs will shrink gradually. Rapidly rising real wages for unskilled workers in coastal provinces are encouraging firms to relocate to neighboring interior provinces where labor and land are more plentiful and relatively cheap. Thanks to continuous improvements in connective infrastructure between the interior and major cities and ports, the incremental transport costs from interior locations will be outweighed by the benefits of lower input costs.

The rise in wages associated with increased productivity will continue to spur rapid expansion in the ranks of the middle class, which, in turn, will increase consumption of consumer durables and raise the share of consumption in GDP. And, as international experience shows, a growing middle class will also act as a catalyst for improved governance, better delivery of public services, and the empowerment of civil society.

And finally, China's urbanization—a driver of much of China's increased global competitiveness—is poised to grow rapidly. Over the coming two decades, the increase in the urban population will be the equivalent of more than one Tokyo or Buenos Aires each year as the share of urban residents in the total population climbs from about one-half to near two-thirds in 2030.[10] This will act as another powerful driver of growth, although much will depend on how well urban development policies are designed and implemented.

Opportunities and Risks Going Forward

These global and internal trends offer China many opportunities that could support rapid growth in the next two decades—and give rise to many risks that could threaten that growth. Any development strategy going forward would need to build on the opportunities and manage the risks.

First consider the *opportunities*. Continued rapid economic development and decreases in inequality will swell the ranks of the middle class and accelerate domestic demand for income-elastic products, such as consumer durables, leisure activities, and housing, as well as better health and education services. This, together with the rapid growth of other emerging markets where similar transformations are taking place (albeit at a slower pace) will afford new opportunities to Chinese enterprises, enable economies of scale in production and marketing, and provide fresh incentives to increase international competitiveness through innovation and technological development.

Increased specialization, intraindustry trade, and the two-way flow of investment will allow China to continue to exploit opportunities to narrow the gap between its capabilities and the technological frontier through adoption, adaptation, and mastery of existing technologies. The country's high savings rates will allow it to replenish its capital stock relatively quickly, and that will continue to facilitate rapid technological catch-up (figure O.2). And with improvements in its own research and development capabilities, China itself could become a global source of product and process innovation as well as occasional technological breakthroughs.

China's growing technological prowess will lead to rapid change in its industrial structure, which will create new areas of dynamic comparative advantage. Just as its construction industry has become a global leader in construction projects internationally, so too will other industries become a

competitive force in global markets in their own right. This transition would present an opportunity to improve quality, safety, and environmental standards that would provide a competitive edge abroad and improve consumer experience at home.

Growing recognition within China that the current pattern of production and growth is unsustainable is giving rise to new approaches toward realigning government priorities. A fresh emphasis on the quality—not just the pace—of growth provides a promising opportunity to encourage competition between local governments on the basis of a broad development index incorporating a mix of social and environmental measures that can be added to existing indicators of economic growth. Realignment of priorities would also be consistent with the expected increase in demand from the rising number of middle-class Chinese seeking improvements in their quality of life.

At the same time, global and domestic trends are also likely to give rise to many *risks* that could slow economic growth and disrupt China's progress to become a high-income, harmonious, and creative society. Managing the transition from a middle-income to a high-income society will itself prove challenging, and a global environment that will likely remain uncertain and volatile for the foreseeable future makes the task doubly daunting. The next five years will be particularly risky as the global economy enters a new and dangerous phase and works its way through the aftereffects of the global financial crisis and adjusts to the "new normal."

There is broad consensus that China's growth is likely to slow; annual average growth over the next 20 years is expected to be one-third less than annual average growth for the past 30 years (6.6 percent versus 9.9 percent). While this will be enough to propel China into high-income status by 2030, there is no saying whether this slowdown will be smooth or not. Any sudden slowdown could unmask inefficiencies and contingent liabilities in banks, enterprises, and different levels of government—heretofore hidden under the veil of rapid growth—and could precipitate a fiscal and financial crisis. The implications

FIGURE O.2   Savings in China compared to other economies

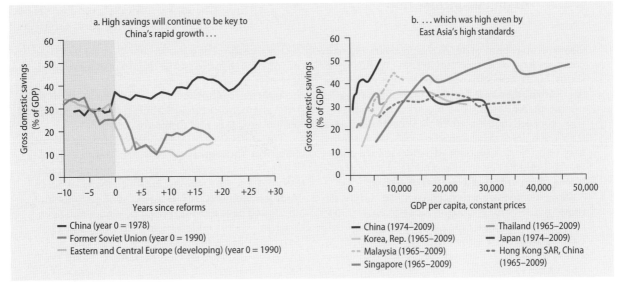

Source: World Bank 2011b.

for social stability would be hard to predict in such a scenario.

How government responds to a rapid slowdown will depend on its causes. One cause could be a macroeconomic shock, say, a sudden decline in real estate prices and a sharp contraction in construction and investment, or a rapid growth slowdown in the advanced economies leading to sharply lower global trade and growth. Such risks could be significant in the short term, and there is a likelihood that China could face just such challenges over the course of the next two decades. Fortunately, unlike many other countries, China's fiscal and debt position allows it the space to respond with countercyclical measures. But these short-term policy responses should also be supportive of long-term structural reforms (such as those recommended in this report).

Another cause of a growth slowdown—arguably one of greater concern—could be structural in nature, the so-called middle-income trap (box O.1). If, instead of responding with policy reforms to address structural problems, the government applies macroeconomic measures to stimulate the economy, then inflation and instability could result, possibly undermining investor confidence and ultimately leading to slower growth and

even stagnation. Over the past half century, many countries have entered middle-income status, but very few have made the additional leap to become high-income economies. Rather, several faced sudden, sharp decelerations in growth and have been unsuccessful in addressing the root structural cause of the slowdown. China does not have to endure this fate. Successful implementation of the reform policies, contained in this report, aimed at finding new growth drivers—increased efficiency in input use, higher human capital investments, increased innovation, and a shift to high-value services—will help China avoid the middle-income trap and maintain an expected average growth rate of between 6 and 7 percent a year in the coming two decades, compared with an average of nearly 10 percent a year in the past three decades.

The risk of sharply lower growth rates is exacerbated by China's relatively high income and asset inequality, low consumption, and unequal access to quality public services (figure O.3). Notwithstanding massive internal migration from farms to cities, barriers to labor mobility (the household registration, or *hukou*, system, the lack of portability of pension plans, weak labor market institutions, and inadequate job market information) have

BOX O.1   The middle-income trap

Growing up is hard to do. In the postwar era, many countries have developed rapidly into middle-income status, but far fewer have gone on to high-income status. Rather, they have become stuck in the so-called middle-income trap.[a] The factors and advantages that propelled high growth in these countries during their rapid development phases—low-cost labor and easy technology adoption—disappeared when they reached middle- and upper-middle-income levels, forcing them to find new sources of growth.

Low-income countries can compete in international markets by producing labor-intensive, low-cost products using technologies developed abroad. Large productivity gains occur through a reallocation of labor and capital from low-productivity agriculture to high-productivity manufacturing. As countries reach middle-income levels, the underemployed rural labor force dwindles and wages rise, eroding competitiveness. Productivity growth from

sectoral reallocation and technology catch-up are eventually exhausted, while rising wages make labor-intensive exports less competitive internationally. If countries cannot increase productivity through innovation (rather than continuing to rely on foreign technology), they find themselves trapped.[b]

The concept of a middle-income trap has some empirical backing. Latin America and the Middle East provide compelling support for the trap hypothesis: in these two regions, most economies reached middle-income status as early as the 1960s and 1970s and have remained there ever since (see figure BO.1.1a). Of 101 middle-income economies in 1960, only 13 became high income by 2008 (see figure BO.1.1b)—Equatorial Guinea; Greece; Hong Kong SAR, China; Ireland; Israel; Japan; Mauritius; Portugal; Puerto Rico; Republic of Korea; Singapore; Spain; and Taiwan, China.

Figure BO.1.1   Few economies escape the middle-income trap

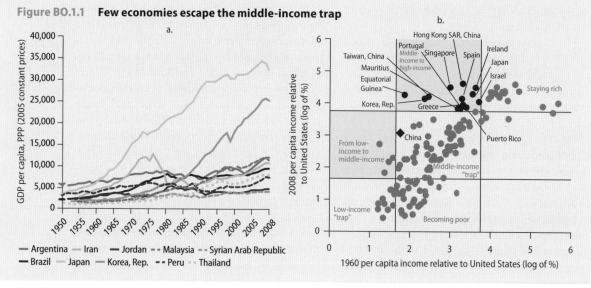

Source: Heston, Summers, and Aten 2011.
Note: PPP = purchasing power parity.

Source: Maddison database.

a. The term "middle-income trap" was first defined in Gill, Kharas, and others (2007). "Middle-income economies" are defined in accordance with classifications by income group as given in: http://data.worldbank.org/about/country-classifications.
b. In today's increasingly globalized world, escaping the middle-income trap may be even more difficult (Eeckhout and Jovanovic 2007).

trapped tens of millions of farm families in low-paying, low-productivity work. These barriers, combined with factor and resource price policies that favor enterprise profits and implicitly tax household incomes, have contributed to the declining share of wages and

rising share of capital in national income. Furthermore, the quality gap in public services available to rural and urban households has widened, and the "opportunity gap" between urban and rural areas has grown. Social tensions have ratcheted up in some

FIGURE O.3 China's economic challenges

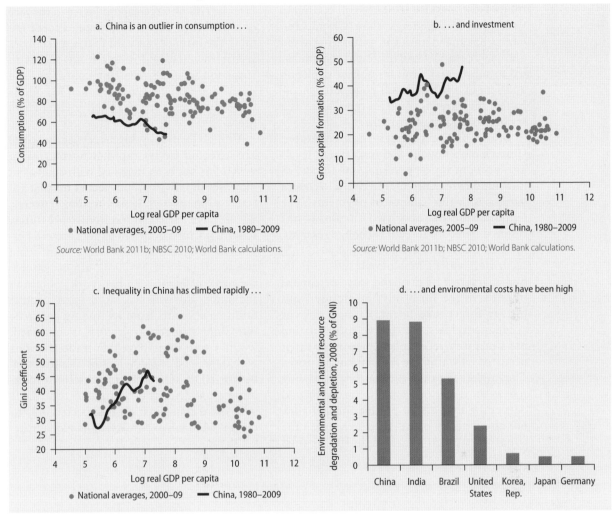

Source: World Bank 2011b; NBSC 2010; World Bank calculations.

Source: World Bank 2011b; NBSC 2010; World Bank calculations.

Source: Milanovic 2005; World Bank calculations.

Source: World Bank 2011b.

areas, resulting in a growing number of public protests. Unresolved, these tensions could pose a threat to growth and stability in coming decades.

Social risks are also expected to arise from another direction. If the experiences of other countries is any guide, the rising ranks of the middle class and higher education levels will inevitably increase the demand for better social governance and greater opportunities for participation in public policy debate and implementation. Unmet, these demands could raise social tensions; but if the government finds ways to improve consultation and tap the knowledge and social capital of

individuals and nongovernment agencies, these demands can be transformed into a positive force supportive of improved governance and public policy formulation.

Another risk relates to China's growth pattern, which has been particularly intensive in energy and natural resource use, contributing to a widening environmental deficit and exposing the economy to commodity price shocks. While the energy intensity in most individual industries has been declining steadily, rapid growth, growing urbanization, and structural change within manufacturing have combined to make China the world's largest energy user, outstripping the

United States in 2010 (although, on a per capita basis, the United States still consumes five times more energy than China, and China has raced ahead in generating wind and solar energy). Similarly, rapid growth has led to substantial natural resource depletion and serious environmental pollution. Uncorrected, these trends could, in time, serve as a serious constraint on growth.

Many of the policies that generated China's high savings and investment levels also account for its external imbalance, as measured by its current and capital account surpluses in the balance of payments. The combination of these two surpluses has resulted in record foreign exchange reserves, most of which are invested in low-yield U.S. securities, while China pays a substantially higher interest or dividend rate for capital imports in the form of "hot money" and foreign direct investment. China's current account surpluses and reserve accumulation are a relatively recent phenomenon, one that occurred only after the Asian financial crisis. They reflect not only the country's growing role as the center of a rapidly expanding and deepening East Asian production network but also a policy objective to strengthen the country's foreign exchange buffer against external shocks. Ironically, these reserves face the risk of large capital losses in the face of a weakened dollar. Efforts to export capital in the form of outward FDI, especially to secure raw material supplies, has met with suspicion in some receiving countries, and unless appropriate steps are taken to address these problems, such risks and friction could grow.

China's relations with the rest of the world are affected by its rapid export growth, which has not been matched with equivalent increases in import volumes, and by bilateral trade surpluses with its key trading partners, which have fueled protectionist pressures. Indeed, if China's current export growth persists, its projected global market share could rise to 20 percent by 2030, almost double the peak of Japan's global market share in the mid-1980s when it faced fierce protectionist sentiments from its trading partners. But China's current trajectory, if continued, would cause unmanageable trade frictions with developed and developing countries well before 2030. The anemic growth of high-income countries as they continue to struggle with fiscal consolidation is expected only to magnify China's expansion of its global market share.

Chapter 2   A New Development Strategy for 2030

China' successful development strategy over the past three decades has made it an upper-middle-income economy today. But the opportunities and challenges in the next two decades will be unlike those it encountered in the past and will demand a new development strategy. This strategy will need to build on China's opportunities, meet its challenges, manage its risks, and realize the country's long-term objectives. But what are those objectives—and what kind of strategy does China need to achieve them? This chapter begins with a discussion of China's vision of itself in 2030, identifies the core elements of a strategy that would help it realize that vision, and examines the characteristics that such a strategy should have.

The 2030 Vision: To Build a Modern, Harmonious, and Creative Society

In a recent landmark study, the Commission on Growth and Development (2008) identified five common features in countries that sustained rapid growth and development for extended periods: They exploited opportunities in the world economy by maintaining open trade and investment policies; they maintained macroeconomic stability; they enjoyed high savings and investment rates; they allowed markets to allocate resources; and they were led by committed and credible governments. China belongs to this select group and has demonstrated all five of these features. The architect of China's reforms was Deng Xiaoping, who played an important role in building consensus for a fundamental shift in the country's strategy. After more than 30 years of rapid growth, China has reached another turning point in its development path, one that calls for a second strategic, and no less fundamental, shift. If managed well, China could become a modern, harmonious, creative, and high-income society by 2030. Each element of the phrase "modern, harmonious, creative, and high income" has specific significance

in China that guides the analysis and recommendations in this report.

A *modern society* is industrialized and urbanized and enjoys a quality of life that is on par with developed countries. This society would have modern values, a modern economic and social structure, with access to contemporary, state-of-the-art product and process technologies, and would engage and contribute as an equal with other nations in the discourse of the modern world on all subjects.

As a *harmonious society*, China sees three interrelated goals. First, its own policies need to be inclusive and just, aimed at eliminating most social and economic boundaries and at building a society in which everyone has a common stake in the country's economic, social, legal, and political institutions. China would like to see a society where people show mutual respect, disputes are resolved justly and peacefully through accepted norms, laws, regulations, and practices—and the institutional structure is quick to adapt to society's changing needs and aspirations. Second, China sees itself living in balance with nature, in which its ecological footprint—the use of resources and creation of waste—are consistent with the biological capacity of its (and the world's) land, water, and air resources given existing technology. And third, China would like to see itself as an equal, constructive, and accepted partner in the community of nations, working peacefully and cooperatively toward common goals, and engaging constructively on global issues and in global institutions.

As a *creative society*, China sees itself building its future prosperity on innovation in which everyone's creative potential is tapped. Its success will lie in its ability to produce more value, not more products, enabling it to move up the value chain and compete globally in the same product space as advanced countries. Creativity will manifest itself not just in product and process technology, but also in cultural and artistic pursuits. If successful, China's experience could potentially be a beacon for other middle-income developing countries to follow.

As a *high-income society,* China's aspiration is to enjoy a per capita income on par with advanced economies; have a large middle class that acts as a force for stability, good governance, and economic progress; eliminate poverty as it is known today; and promote social harmony by increasing equality of opportunity and lowering inequality in all its economic and social dimensions.

If China achieves its goal of becoming a high-income society by 2030, it will be the world's largest economy using market prices (indeed, if GDP is measured by purchasing power parity, it could well outstrip the United States later this decade). China's incremental size in the coming two decades will be equivalent to 15 of today's Republic of Korea's. Even so, its annual per capita income will still be around $16,000, more than three times today's level, close to today's Slovak Republic or Korea, and slightly more than a third of today's United States.

Another reality in 2030 that can be foretold with some accuracy will be China's demographic transition. Simply put, China will grow old before it grows rich. Its low fertility rate and consequent low population growth rate will mean a rising share of old people in the economy. The old-age dependency ratio—defined as the ratio of those aged 65 and over to those between the ages of 15 and 64—will double over the next 20 years (UN 2010; UN 2009). By 2030, China's dependency ratio will reach the level of Norway and the Netherlands today. Just as important, China's working-age population will decline after 2015. The urban share of the population is expected to rise from around 50 percent today to near two-thirds by 2030, an average growth of 13 million people each year (NBSC 2011; UN 2010).

Compared with today, China's economy in 2030 will be more complex, market driven, knowledge centered, and oriented toward services. Its trade and financial integration with the global economy will make it more interdependent with other economies and at the same time more vulnerable to external shocks. It will have deeper and more stable financial markets, which can lay the foundation for an open capital account and broad acceptance of the renminbi as an international reserve currency. The government's economic priority will shift to maintaining macroeconomic stability, creating an investment and regulatory environment conducive for enterprise development, and financing public goods and services. China will be competing internationally in the same product space as the advanced economies; its university graduates will have tripled in number; and its environment will be significantly cleaner. Moreover, with a larger urban population and more efficient transportation and movement of labor between cities and the countryside, inequality between urban and rural areas will continue to decline.

The Case for a New Strategy

Realizing China's vision for 2030 will demand a new development strategy. The development strategy it pursued over the past three decades was directed at meeting the challenges of a different era. Not only have the challenges changed, so have China's capabilities. No strategy lasts forever. Successful strategies must be flexible and adjust in accordance with changing conditions. Middle-income countries unable to make such adjustments have stumbled into the middle-income trap. China's top decision makers recognize this and have made transforming the economic development pattern the country's most important economic policy priority.

Changing the development model is urgent because, as an economy approaches the technology frontier and exhausts the potential for acquiring and applying technology from abroad, the role of the government needs to change fundamentally. Initiating this change early helps smooth the transition from importing new technologies to innovating and creating new technologies.

Developing countries tend to benefit from the latecomer's advantage by following a development path adopted by others. This path makes the role of government relatively straightforward—providing roads, railways, energy, and other infrastructure to complement private investment, allowing open trade and investment policies that encourage technological catch-up, and implementing industrial policies when market and coordination failures inhibit the development of internationally competitive industries consistent with the country's comparative advantage. The development strategies of East Asia's successful economies—Japan; Korea; Hong Kong SAR, China; Singapore; and Taiwan, China—have all broadly reflected these features.

But when a developing country reaches the technology frontier, the correct development strategy ceases to be so straightforward. Direct government intervention may actually retard growth, not help it. Instead, the policy emphasis needs to shift even more toward private sector development, ensuring that markets are mature enough to allocate resources efficiently and that firms are strong and innovative enough to compete internationally in technologically advanced sectors.

The role of the private sector is critical because innovation at the technology frontier is quite different in nature from simply catching up technologically. The process becomes essentially one of trial and error, with the chances of success highly uncertain. Innovation is not something that can be achieved through government planning. Indeed, the more enterprises are involved in the trial-and-error process of innovation, the greater are the chances for technological breakthroughs, and the more likely that new discoveries will be translated into commercially viable products. As enterprises take a leading role, the government needs to adopt a more supportive and facilitating role.

One of the key supportive roles the government can play is enhancing the quality of human capital. China's rapid growth has been accompanied by a gradual decline in its agricultural surplus labor and a steady rise in real wages in manufacturing, a trend that appears to have accelerated recently. Without concomitant increases in labor productivity, real wage increases could lead to a steady decline in international competitiveness. Increasing the quality of human capital will not only increase labor productivity and maintain China's competitiveness; it will also allow Chinese manufacturing and services to move up the value chain. Improvement in

the quality of human capital will require better education, health care, and social security. And it will demand a marked increase in equal employment opportunities and self-employment, as well as greater lateral mobility of labor from rural to urban areas and across towns, cities, provinces, and occupations, and vertical mobility through the social, economic, and political hierarchies.

Another supportive role the government can play is encouraging greater participation in the development process. The expanding middle class is increasingly vocal in its demand to participate in the discussion of public policy. This demand points to a broader need to empower people to contribute to the country's development efforts, be creative, and improve standards of living through their own efforts. The government should respond proactively to these needs and grant rights to individuals, households, enterprises, communities, academia, and other nongovernmental organizations through clear rules that encourage broad participation. By doing so, the government can gradually transfer some of its previous functions to society at large, allow nongovernmental players to form networks in new and interesting ways, and create space for innovation and creativity. Moreover, empowering society, especially those who are disadvantaged, will help unleash new ideas and approaches toward increasing equality of opportunity, ensuring inclusive growth, and achieving a balance between a caring and a competitive society.

Last, while the government reduces its role in markets, resource allocation, production, and distribution, it should step up its role in financing public goods and services, protecting the environment, increasing equality of opportunity, and ensuring an environment conducive for private sector development. Playing such an indirect and supportive role is complicated but will have a wide impact, with greater leverage through the private sector and social organizations. While providing fewer "tangible" goods and services directly, the government will need to provide more intangible public goods and services, like systems, rules, and policies, that increase production efficiency, promote competition, facilitate specialization, enhance the efficiency of resource allocation, and reduce risks and uncertainties. It requires designing and implementing incentive structures that lead to desired and sustainable outcomes.

One key area, for example, is the financing of basic public services such as pensions, medical care, education, and housing, where the government can invest more, drawing on resources it had previously devoted to infrastructure and manufacturing. Equally important, the government should be less concerned with whether the private or the public sector provides these public goods and services—but instead focus on ensuring they are delivered efficiently and to the requisite quality. Encouraging the private provision of public goods and services and forming public-private partnerships where appropriate will not only inject new skills and ideas into public service delivery but also empower the private sector and encourage greater participation in the development process. Another example is the environment, an area requiring strong action by the government. Not only will green development improve the quality of life in China, it will contribute to global efforts at mitigating climate change. As the second-largest economy with the largest population in the world, China is bound to shoulder increasing global responsibilities and play an important role in delivering global public goods. To do this, it will need to align its national interests to global concerns and build its capacity to participate actively in global affairs and to design global rules instead of merely accepting them.

In sum, it is imperative that China adjusts its development strategy as it embarks on its next phase of economic growth. At its core, this adjustment requires changing the role of government and its relations with the market, the private sector, and society at large. While the government needs to withdraw from direct involvement in production, distribution, and resource allocation, it will need to focus greater attention on designing and implementing the policy and regulatory framework that empowers others to participate in economic decision making so that the desired outcome of rapid, inclusive, and sustainable growth is achieved. To play

this role, the government will need to transform itself into a lean, clean, transparent, and highly efficient modern government that operates under the rule of law. In redefining its role, the government will need to accelerate reforms in the state-owned sector and combine it with further development of the private sector. It will also need to advance reforms in factor markets (capital, land, and labor) to help strengthen the foundations of a market economy and promote greater competition and innovation. At the same time, society's role will need to change significantly, with the middle class becoming a major force in promoting harmonious development through greater participation of the people in the development process.

Key Characteristics of the New Strategy

Before describing a proposed development strategy, it is worth highlighting five characteristics that should lie at its core.

The first is improvement in the quality of growth while continuing to increase incomes. Not only does China aspire to become a high-income society that enjoys sustained growth, it would like to see growth measured in qualitative as well as quantitative terms. Rising incomes need to be accompanied by increased leisure, a better physical environment, expanding arts and cultural activities, and a greater sense of economic and social security. Correspondingly, the incentive structure that drives central and local government performance will also need to reflect this changed emphasis. China needs to develop a new metric to measure progress over the coming decades that balances growth and income objectives with broader welfare and sustainability goals.

The second is to achieve balanced and sustainable growth, consistent with market forces. There is broad recognition in China—as reflected in the 11th and 12th Five Year Plans—that the country's pattern of investment and growth has become largely unsustainable. Spurred by high savings, cheap finance, and export-oriented policies, China's impressive growth rate has been capital intensive, industry led, and export dependent for several years. Compared with rapidly growing manufacturing, the development of services has lagged (though the statistics may exaggerate the degree of lag). The shares of wages and consumption in national income have fallen steadily; the shares of capital and investment have climbed. Rural-urban inequality has expanded since the 1990s. China is home to more than a million millionaires,[11] while more than 170 million live on less than $2 a day.[12]

Returning to balanced and sustainable growth will require a rise in the shares spent on services and consumption as per capita income increases. This will be achieved, in part, by correcting factor price distortions that implicitly tax labor and subsidize capital. Correcting such distortions and allowing market-driven structural change will not only help achieve greater balance between manufacturing and services but also in the distribution of income between capital and labor and between rural and urban households.

The third is to strengthen innovation and creativity. While development of services will need to be a priority in the coming decades, manufacturing growth will continue to be an important growth driver. After all, notwithstanding recent rapid increases in real wages, China's low-cost labor, especially in interior, less-developed provinces, will remain an advantage for many years to come. But rather than focus purely on growth, policies will need to encourage manufacturers to move up the value chain and advance rapidly to the global technology frontier (and, in some areas, push that technology frontier forward). Services like research and development (R&D), finance, logistics, training, information services, and after-sale services will help. Achieving this will require further integration with the global economy and increased specialization, as well as participation in global R&D networks and marketing arrangements.

But it would be a mistake to believe that innovation will be restricted to manufacturing. If China is successful in nurturing a culture of open innovation, then the services sector could also be an important beneficiary, and there is no reason why China should not become an important exporter of high-end

services. Most services have become tradable internationally, and China can benefit from agglomeration economies and international specialization in services just as it has in manufacturing. For example, if China succeeds in becoming a leading innovator in the field of green development, then its expertise and knowledge on this subject will likely be sought worldwide. Similarly, if China's financial sector is strengthened to the point that the capital account can be liberalized and the renminbi become a key international reserve currency, then China could become a key exporter of financial services.

The fourth is unleashing China's full human potential. Equality of opportunity will not only help unleash China's full human potential, it will also support inclusive growth and improve income distribution. Increasing equality of opportunity should not be restricted only to public services, such as health or education; it should also include economic opportunities such as access to jobs, finance, or official permits to start a business. One way to increase equality of opportunity in the enterprise and financial sectors will be to allow more competition in factor markets (labor, land, and capital) as well as product markets. More competition, of course, can come from abroad through boosting exports and lowering import barriers, but it can also be encouraged by easing the entry and exit of firms in the domestic market, giving small and medium enterprises (SMEs) greater access to finance and market opportunities, opening up public procurement by making procedures transparent, and creating new opportunities for the private provision of public services by separating financing from delivery. Smarter and more effective regulation can do more than just help level the playing field between big enterprises and small ones. It can also help protect consumers, workers, and the environment; safeguard private and intellectual property rights; ensure greater financial sector stability; and provide a solid foundation for corporate governance to guide enterprises.

Equality of opportunity also means higher public participation in public policy formulation, implementation, and oversight. As economies grow in size and complexity, the task of economic management becomes more complicated, and governments usually find that they alone do not, indeed should not, have all the answers. Governments, therefore, tend to tap the knowledge and social capital of individuals and nongovernment agencies, including universities, communities, and think tanks. One of the hallmarks of advanced economies is their public discussion of public policies. Indeed, such discussions are already beginning in China, but there is a long way to go. Public consultations and policy debate ensure that all points of view are considered before government reforms are introduced. These discussions not only shrink the distance between the government and the citizens and communities it serves, but they also encourages stakeholders' ownership of new policies, help render reform proposals intelligible to citizens and firms, and enhance the chances of success.

The fifth (and last) values the role of the market, rule of law, social values, and high moral standards. As the government transitions away from direct intervention in enterprise and market activities and toward creating a policy and regulatory environment supportive of free and fair competition, it must also safeguard the rule of law. In a similar vein, as the Chinese economy grows in complexity, not only must rules and regulations evolve to reflect changing reality and emerging priorities, but they should be fairly and effectively enforced. If the enforcement of standards varies from sector to sector, region to region, entity to entity, and sometimes even person to person, then it will not only discourage innovation and lead to inefficient economic outcomes, it will also contribute to feelings of injustice. Where contract disputes arise, whether between private parties or between private entities and the State, the disputants should have access not only to legal recourse but also to a transparent and effective judicial system that imparts justice without fear or favor.

Similarly, social values and high moral standards will be important. There is widespread concern in China over many recent instances of "moral failures" that were reported widely in the media. As China becomes a high-income society, its social values and moral standards should be reexamined and reinforced. From a social perspective, not only will this contribute to improving the quality of life, it will also provide a greater sense of community and enhance social cohesion. From an economic perspective, it will reduce transaction costs and improve the quality of economic governance. Promoting social values and high moral standards is not only the job of government; it is also the duty of social organizations and, indeed, every citizen. Moral awareness, not legal compulsion, should be the hallmark of a high-income, harmonious society.

Six Key Directions of the New Strategy

Over the next two decades, China will face many challenges in its quest to become a modern, harmonious, and creative high-income society. These include transitioning government from being an active participant in the economy to developing the legal, regulatory, and institutional framework supportive of a competitive market environment; implementing a "smart" urbanization strategy; encouraging innovation and industrial upgrading; reducing income inequality and ensuring equal opportunity for all; modifying its approach toward handling economic relations with other countries; and playing a more constructive role in a rapidly changing system of global governance. In reality, the list of challenges is much longer. While some consensus has emerged with respect to a few of those issues, controversies remain and an intense debate is ongoing over key aspects. This report evaluates the major challenges China needs to tackle in the next two decades and identifies six new strategic directions that will form the core components of the new strategy.

The first new strategic direction is the appropriate role of the government, the state, and the private sector. The recent global financial crisis in the advanced economies and, in stark contrast, China's continued rapid growth despite the global slowdown, have led some in China to conclude that China's state dominance in key industrial and service sectors should continue (especially in the financial sector).[13] Others, however, counter that China's vision of itself in 2030 as an innovative, high-income society will require markets and the private sector to play a bigger role in resource allocation decisions. They consider the dominance of the state in the economy as potentially inhibiting China's efforts to move up the value chain. This report makes two points: first, that government should encourage increased competition in the economy, including by increasing the ease of entry and exit of firms as soon as possible; and second, that public resources should be used to finance a wider range of public goods and services to support an increasingly complex and sophisticated economy. Reforms of state enterprises and banks would help align their corporate governance arrangements with the requirements of a modern market economy and permit competition with the private sector on a level playing field. This would create the appropriate incentives and conditions for increased vigor and creativity in the economy in support of China's successful transformation into a high-income society.

The second new strategic direction is encouraging systemwide innovation and adopting an "open" innovation system with links to global R&D networks. Although China's R&D investment as a share of GDP is high by international standards for a country at its per capita income level, much needs to be done to ensure that this investment yields commercially viable innovations that will help Chinese firms move up the value chain and compete effectively in the same product space as advanced economies. Ensuring free and fair competition for all enterprises would be the single most important policy to encourage innovation, which is likely to be driven by large private firms. Without competition, the effects of other policies aimed at encouraging innovation will unlikely have much effect. At the same time, technology development worldwide has become a collaborative exercise in which countries benefit from specialization, just as they do in manufacturing or services. China would therefore benefit from participation in global R&D networks just as it benefited from participation in global production networks. A "closed" technology

strategy may yield short-term gains but will be ultimately self-defeating, while an open innovation strategy promises more sustained long-term rewards.

The third new strategic direction is that China should "grow green." Instead of considering environmental protection and climate change mitigation as burdens that hurt competitiveness and slow growth, this report stresses that green development could potentially become a significant new growth opportunity. Much will depend on how effectively government policies make firms internalize negative externalities and motivate firms to innovate and seek technological breakthroughs. China does not want to replicate the experience of advanced countries that became rich first and cleaned up later. Instead, China intends to grow green by following a pattern of economic growth that boosts environmental protection and technological progress, a strategy that could become an example to other developing countries and perhaps even advanced economies.

The fourth new strategic direction is to promote equality of opportunity and social protection for all. China's high inequality in incomes and assets can, in part, be attributed to unequal access to quality public services, particularly those that help accumulate human capital and increase public participation in the development process. Policies should promote the equality of opportunity to help all members of society, especially the disadvantaged, who have the same rights as everyone else to access social and economic services as well as employment opportunities. Promoting equality of opportunity will largely entail increasing the quality of public services available to rural residents, migrants in urban areas, and those in poor, interior provinces. While increasing the efficiency of public service delivery can save public resources that can then be used to increase the quality of public services, there will still be a need to increase the allocation of public resources toward this objective. Given China's sound fiscal situation, the temptation will be to design a public service and welfare system that is comparable to advanced economies. But China needs to ensure that spending on public services is increased prudently and in line with available fiscal space. China does not intend to fall victim to the "high-income trap" whereby publicly financed social entitlements become fiscally unsustainable.

The fifth new strategic direction is to build a sustainable fiscal system that will meet expected public finance challenges over the next two decades. Over the coming two decades, China's fiscal system will face three major challenges. The first will be to make the fiscal system resilient to macroeconomic shocks and a protracted growth slowdown; the second will be to accommodate new public expenditure demands linked to the adoption of the new development strategy; and the third will be to make the fiscal system transparent and responsive to policy adjustments. Given the likelihood of a protracted growth slowdown at some point in the next two decades, it is important that China's fiscal system is able to adjust public expenditures in line with an expected rapid deceleration in revenue growth. It is also important for China to maintain adequate fiscal space to deal with macroeconomic shocks, some of which may originate abroad, given the continued uncertainties in the global economy.

Moreover, the budget will need to accommodate expected increases in public expenditures linked to expansions in public service delivery and the proposed green development program, while at the same time ensuring that fiscal sustainability is not impaired. Finally, compared with other countries, China's fiscal system remains opaque, intergovernmental fiscal relations have not been fully reformed and codified, and fiscal risks and large contingent liabilities remain significant. Tackling these challenges will require a fiscal system that is flexible, transparent, prudently managed, and responsive to emerging priorities. The efforts to strengthen and reform the fiscal system will also need to be aligned with the broader objective of reorienting the role of government vis-à-vis the private sector and with the longer-term needs of a changing economy.

The sixth new strategic direction is to develop mutually beneficial relations for the rest of the world. Notwithstanding tepid growth in advanced countries likely for the foreseeable future, China must continue its integration with global markets even as it reorients the economy toward domestic sources of growth. While further integration may bring its own risks, the benefits of openness will be central to increasing efficiency, stimulating innovation, and promoting international competitiveness. Opening up served China well in the past, especially after its entry to the World Trade Organization (WTO), and further integration will serve it well in the future, particularly for the development of the services sector. China also needs to engage with global governance institutions proactively as an international stakeholder to help shape the global policy environment in a manner that is mutually beneficial for China and the world.

The six new strategic directions provide an internally coherent policy framework and form the key pillars of the proposed development strategy for the next two decades. Some may argue that they may not include some important policy areas, but the pillars can be applied to explain virtually every significant development issue facing China. Box O.2, which describes China's urbanization challenge, provides a good example.

China's senior leaders have recognized for some time the urgent need to adjust the country's development strategy and transform the growth pattern. To some extent, China is already beginning to do this. A new policy direction for the next five years has been elaborated in China's 12th Five Year Plan and other policy documents and includes macroeconomic, social, and environmental targets as well as pilot applications of the "happiness" index to evaluate local government performance. The plan is the first step in a longer-term shift in China's development strategy and is consistent with the reform program described in this report.

Chapters 3–8 discuss the six new strategic directions in greater detail.

BOX 0.2   Smart urbanization

Meeting China's urban challenge presents an interesting example of how the policy priorities highlighted in this report—economic policies, innovation, green development, social policies, fiscal strengthening, and global integration—need to interact with one another to bring about desired change.

Over the long term, the health and vitality of China's rapidly growing urban areas will not only be central to continued rapid growth but will also hold the key to greater equality and less resource-intensive growth. In 1978, less than a fifth of China's population resided in cities; by 2009, urban residents made up close to half the population; and by 2030, the share is expected to swell to near two-thirds. That means about 13 million more urbanites each year, or the equivalent of the total population of Tokyo or Buenos Aires. Rapid as this may seem, China's urbanization level by 2030 will be broadly in line with other countries with a similar per capita income. Interestingly, China's 20 fastest-growing cities are located inland with per capita incomes that are rapidly catching up with coastal cities. These cities can access the main metropolitan centers thanks to low-cost transport links and communications facilities, while at the same time derive advantages from the ease of face-to-face communication and social capital accumulation facilitated by spatial compactness.

Most urban growth in the future will result from the expansion of existing cities through migration from rural areas. As recent research shows, cities are strong engines of growth. They permit economies of scale and scope in production and distribution and facilitate technology spillovers. Thanks to higher population densities in cities, private and public investments are more cost-effective and yield higher returns. And by bringing a critical mass of talent together in compact space, cities often become crucibles for innovation.

But for urbanization to be supportive of rapid and efficient growth, it should be "smart" as well as rapid. Smart urbanization involves delivering

adequate levels of public services—especially health, education, transport, water, and energy—in ways and at prices that encourage efficient use. Finally, cities that invest in effective risk reduction and disaster response capabilities often find these will be among the best public investments they make.

Perhaps the most important recommendation for smart urbanization is the critical need to improve the fiscal strength of municipalities (along with other local governments) and reduce the large disparities in resource availability between cities. Strengthening the resource base of cities will require improved arrangements for tax sharing and transfer payments with the central government as well as new tax instruments, such as land and property taxes, that permit an elastic tax base. There are two reasons why this is a priority. The first obvious one is that city governments need adequate resources to meet the needs of recurrent expenditure and investment, taking into account the future growth of population and economic activities. Second, in the absence of such tax instruments, local governments will continue to use land sales as a key source of revenues. Besides increasing the pressure on arable land, this practice also tends to continuously expand city size, contributes to urban sprawl, reduces population densities, and raises costs of transport and infrastructure.

The second complementary policy would be to restrain the geographic expansion of cities and increase the population density of cities. Several Chinese cities are already quite densely populated by international standards, but for those that aren't, further increases in density will lower the cost of public and infrastructural services, improve energy and transport efficiency, and reduce the loss of arable land. There remain large tracts in the core of major cities that are underused owing to ownership still vested in state enterprises or local interest groups that prevent efficient urban development. Increased population density can be consistent with growth in value added only if urban land and property markets

(box continues next page)

BOX O.2   (continued)

function smoothly. Of course, increased density has its limits, but expanding city areas should be undertaken carefully and only when other alternatives to combat congestion are exhausted. Adequate density needs to be accompanied by increased intra- and intercity connectivity. Intracity connectivity, critical to reducing the carbon footprint of cities and boosting city efficiency, requires providing viable options to private automobiles. Increasing connectivity between cities reduces economic distances, encourages growth of satellite cities, advances specialization, supports greater scale economies, and increases international competitiveness.

The third is the importance of strengthening urban land use planning. Planning is important to ensure an appropriate balance between green areas, residential areas, factories, businesses, shopping areas, and recreational facilities such as parks and playing fields. Urban areas that mix residential, recreational, shopping, and business facilities tend to develop more vibrant communities, have a smaller ecological footprint, enjoy lower crime rates, and generally improve the quality of life. At the same time, planning has its limits and planners cannot anticipate the future perfectly. City designs therefore need to evolve continuously to respond to the needs of citizens as lifestyles change. This requires constant public and private investments, reinforcing the need for sound fiscal systems. It also demands a new role for government and emphasizes the importance of good governance.

The fourth is effective and good urban governance, which goes beyond efficiency, integrity, and transparency, although these are very important. It includes responsiveness to citizen needs, and the ability to use the energy and capabilities of private enterprises and civil society organizations. One way is to invite citizen participation in land use planning and zoning, which not only harnesses public creativity but also reminds officials to look beyond the interests of individual sectors. Another way is through designing citizen report cards and other similar methods of surveying that regularly assess public satisfaction with the level and quality of public services and seek

suggestions on how they can be improved. A third way is to support the participation of social and voluntary organizations in delivering services (including health and education). Experimentation is already ongoing along these lines in many cities but needs to be encouraged and expanded, and substantial changes need to be made in government practice and attitude. The government can then focus on being a regulator and coordinator. Identifying the services that can be provided in this way should be the outcome of discussions and decisions at the local level, with guidance from the central government.

The fifth recommendation is to advance the government's efforts to make cities knowledge centers and incubators for innovation. The government has already identified 20 pilot cities for those efforts. But what more can it do? One approach is to ensure that as many cities as possible provide the essentials for becoming knowledge centers—sound infrastructure, modern transport and telecommunication facilities, local universities and research centers, and a critical mass of skilled labor. Those that do not make the leap to becoming knowledge centers will still be better positioned to attract manufacturing or service industries. Those fortunate enough to attract world-class firms or world-leading technology R&D centers beyond a particular threshold could receive local and central government support in the form of additional ancillary services, including research institutes, universities, and related and sponsored links to other research organizations. Some urban centers have already made this leap and are becoming recognized knowledge and innovation centers—opto-electronics for Wuhan, aviation for Chengdu, financial and engineering services for Shanghai, logistics and business services for Shenzhen, information technology (IT) and software for Beijing—and should be supported in becoming centers of excellence. In others, such as Chongqing, efforts are ongoing. In identifying what to support, governments need to remind themselves that innovation does not always mean high tech. Experience has shown that firms in mature industries can also be transformed through innovation and become globally competitive.

Chapter 3   Structural Reforms for a Market-Based Economy with Sound Foundations

Since 1978, China has made full use of its late-comer advantages in a globalized economy, experiencing rapid structural change, becoming the world's largest manufacturer and exporter, and rapidly moving toward the technology frontier in many industries. The introduction of the market mechanism and openness to trade provided strong incentives for efficient resource allocation and boosted productivity growth.

But the forces supporting China's continued rapid progress are gradually fading. The productivity benefits from structural change are expected to decline. As China approaches the technology frontier, total factor productivity growth from technology adoption, adaptation, and dissemination will also almost certainly decline. At the same time, the government's continued dominance in key sectors of the economy, while earlier an advantage, is in the future likely to act as a constraint on productivity improvements, innovation, and creativity.

At the same time, China's transition to a market economy is incomplete in many areas. A mix of market and nonmarket measures shapes incentives for producers and consumers, and there remains a lack of clarity in distinguishing the individual roles of government, state enterprises, and the private sector. It is imperative, therefore, that China resolve these issues, accelerate structural reforms, and develop a market-based system with sound foundations in which public resources finance the delivery of key public goods and services—while a vigorous private sector plays the more important role of driving growth. This challenge is bigger than it may appear because many other constraints to growth, including an anemic global economy and a shrinking and aging labor force, also need to be overcome.

Private Sector Development and State Enterprise Reforms

Going forward, a vibrant corporate sector will be critical for sustaining relatively fast growth. China's rapid growth, particularly since 2003, benefited from SOE restructuring and expansion of the private sector. Many small and medium-sized SOEs became privately owned. In line with these developments, the new policy direction has been to diversify the ownership of state enterprises. Indeed, many large state enterprises have been "corporatized" and some of the biggest (including those directly monitored by the central government) are now not only listed on stock exchanges but have also improved their governance structure, managerial professionalism, and profitability.

Key Issues

Relative to the private sector, SOEs consume a large proportion of capital, raw materials, and intermediate inputs to produce relatively small shares of gross output and value added. A large share of state enterprise profits comes from a few state enterprises where profitability is often related to limits on competition and access to cheaper capital, land, and natural resources.[14] Meanwhile, the financial performance of some state enterprises has been weak, in part because they have been responsible for delivering public services or have been constrained by regulated prices. In fact, more than one in every four state enterprises makes a loss. A recent study also shows that between 1978 and 2007, total factor productivity growth (a measure of efficiency improvements) in the state sector was a third that of the private sector,[15] which has proved to be the more powerful engine of growth and innovation.

State enterprises have close connections with the Chinese government. State enterprises are more likely to enjoy preferential access to bank finance and other important inputs, privileged access to business opportunities, and even protection against competition (Li and others 2008). This discourages new private sector entrants and reduces competition and innovation. Some state enterprises operate outside their mandated area (many invest in real estate and the shadow banking system), because they can keep their earnings and invest them with limited external control or oversight. A new issue needing attention is the recent rapid expansion of some state enterprises owned by subnational governments; their growth will likely further crowd out private sector activity, dampen competition, and conflict with efforts to build sound foundations for a market-based economy.

The cost of reforming and restructuring state enterprises will not be trivial. Reforms in the late 1990s, in which many small state enterprises were closed, incurred a cost exceeding RMB 2 trillion—more than 20 percent of GDP at the time—a measure of how difficult and costly such reforms can be. Potential costs of reforming and restructuring state enterprises may have climbed significantly because opaque accounting practices and lack of transparency mean that some SOEs have accumulated large contingent liabilities that will need to be revealed and reduced over time.

Finally, the Chinese authorities have implemented a complex set of industrial policies that are the responsibility of different agencies at different levels of government. In some instances, these policies may have helped by overcoming coordination failures and promoting infant industries effectively, but in others, they did not yield the intended results. Some government departments are keen to adopt industrial policies and view such policies as a close substitute for planning; they consequently often prefer large-scale investments by SOEs instead of achieving the same ends through incentives, market forces, and private sector initiatives. Industrial policy initiatives by different departments can sometimes conflict and interact with one another, making the overall policy framework complicated and opaque and the results ambiguous and unpredictable.

Many studies suggest the potential for significant growth dividends from giving the private sector a greater role in competing with state enterprises in key sectors. The greatest benefit is likely to accrue in so-called "strategic" sectors where competition has been curtailed. In 2006, China identified seven strategic sectors where the state would keep "absolute control"—defense, electricity generation and distribution, petroleum and petrochemicals, telecommunications, coal, civil aviation, and waterway transport.[16] In these sectors, a handful of state firms might compete with one another, but they are protected by barriers that discourage new entrants. The Chinese authorities have also designated "basic" or "pillar" industries—machinery, automobiles, electronics and information technology, construction, steel, base metals, and chemicals—where the state is expected to retain a "somewhat strong influence" (Owen and Zheng 2007). Although formal barriers to entry may be low in these industries, informal entry barriers convey the clear policy message—competition from private firms is not welcome. These barriers, together with less favorable regulatory treatment tend to inhibit private sector growth and development, dampen innovation and creativity, and slow productivity growth.

Key Reform Recommendations

Reforms in the enterprise sector must begin with the recognition that government ownership is widespread and varied, covering most sectors and ranging from outright ownership to controlling interest to minority shareholder. The challenge, therefore, is twofold: How can public resources best be used; and how can China best transition from its current approach to managing its portfolio of state enterprises to an approach that is best suited for its long-term development objectives?

The response to the first challenge is straightforward. Public resources should be used solely or mainly for the provision of public goods and services, the production or consumption of which result in unremunerated positive externalities.[17] These goods and services range from defense at one end to infrastructure, social protection, and basic R&D at the other, and their scope could evolve as conditions change. The recent emphasis on public housing for the poor is a good example of how government resources can be used to address a pressing social need. Indeed, the scope of public goods and services can be quite broad, and can even include reliable energy supplies and the widespread availability of communications and postal facilities. The share of public resources applied in a particular area will depend on the nature of the public good or service being supplied. In areas considered to be of high national priority, like defense, government resources would be expected to provide the full or dominant share of finance. But in most areas, a smaller share is usually sufficient to achieve the government's objectives. Most important, in many cases, private sector firms will be fully capable of delivering public goods and services, even though the government may provide the bulk or some part of the finance. The private delivery of public goods and services (with public financing) introduces the added dimension of competition and helps lower production and distribution costs.

The response to the second question is less straightforward. First, the government could securitize its implicit equity in state enterprises as soon as possible (in listed state enterprises, the value of the equity is already known). This would pave the way for state enterprise reform by separating ownership from management and introducing modern corporate governance practices, such as appointment of senior management, public disclosure of accounts in accordance with international practice, and external auditing. Second, the government could consider establishing several state asset management companies (SAMCs) that would represent the government as shareholder and would professionally manage and trade these assets in financial markets where feasible. Each SAMC could specialize in certain sectors. They could then, on behalf of government, gradually diversify the portfolio over time. The dividends of state enterprises would need to be paid to the SAMCs who, in turn, would transfer them to the budget. Finally, a portion of state assets could be transferred to the national pension fund with the flow of returns being used to help meet future pension obligations.

While the operational details of the proposed SAMCs can be elaborated later, it is important that key principles are established early. It is critical, for example, that the State-Owned Assets Supervision and Administration Commission (SASAC) confine itself to policy making and oversight, leaving asset management to the SAMCs. The SAMCs should have clear mandates, be independently and professionally managed, and be subject to publicly announced performance benchmarks (depending on the nature of the enterprises in their portfolio). In addition, they will need to adhere to international standards for transparency, including on operations and results, value creation, profitability, and dividend payments.

More competition—domestic and international—will be key to improving the efficiency and innovation capability of Chinese enterprises. To increase competition in domestic markets, further reforms will be needed to support private sector firms, such as lowering barriers to firm entry and exit, breaking up state monopolies or oligopolies in key industries (petroleum, chemicals, electricity distribution, and telecommunications), promoting the growth of dynamic SMEs and increasing their access to finance, stimulating much needed regional and local specialization, and encouraging spontaneous state enterprise reforms through competition. China's own past experience, together with that of other countries, shows that increased domestic competition can result in significant improvements in productivity. With these reforms, state enterprises can, over time, withdraw gradually from contestable markets. Starting in the late 1990s, for example, ownership diversification and market reforms stimulated entry and competition in most manufacturing subsectors. Even in some strategic or pillar industries, such as telecommunications, the breaking up and corporatization of incumbent enterprises created new competitive forces.[18] Easing the entry of private firms into these areas and giving them access to adequate levels of finance from state-owned banks will further promote efficiency and competitiveness.

And with an eye to redefining further the role of government, policies should encourage the private provision of public services, and public procurement should be further opened to competition by private firms. Where natural monopolies exist (for example, in rail services), the monopolist enterprise should be subject to independent and strict oversight to ensure that the lack of competition does not lead to monopoly pricing and the abuse of market power that could harm downstream industries. Further efforts are also needed to level the playing field, especially between smaller and larger firms, and between state and nonstate firms—with a special focus on laws and regulations, and access to credit from state-owned banks. This will also require review and modernization of China's "industrial policies" to support the growth of firms in dynamic new sectors, improve resource allocation, and stimulate innovation.

In addition, competitiveness and innovation will be encouraged by measures to enhance *international competition* through further integration with the global economy (see chapter 8), and a reduction in behind-the-border barriers to trade. China's accession to the World Trade Organization in 2001 triggered economy-wide improvements in efficiency and spurred technology acquisition and adaptation. More recently, the phasing out of incentives that had favored foreign investors stimulated competition by leveling the playing field with domestically owned firms.

Factor Market Reforms

To complete the transition to a market economy and further strengthen its foundations, China needs to also focus attention on factor markets—capital, land, and labor—where market reforms have tended to lag, and consequently, the remaining distortions are particularly large. Price, regulatory, and institutional changes are essential to ensure that resources flow to economic activities that yield the highest returns.

Capital

Despite impressive progress in reforming and deepening the financial sector in the past three decades, China's financial system remains repressed and suffers from key structural imbalances. The current system, characterized by dominance of state-owned banks, strong state intervention, and remaining controls on interest rates, has been remarkably successful in mobilizing savings and allocating capital to strategic sectors during China's economic take-off. Going forward, however, such benefits are increasingly likely to be outweighed by many costs. The first cost is the disintermediation of the non-state sector, especially micro, small, and medium enterprises that have significantly less access to formal financial institutions than state enterprises and large firms. Second, low lending rates have contributed to excessive investment and high capital intensity. Third, the government's important role in credit allocation at the central and provincial levels is leading to the accumulation of contingent liabilities not easily quantified owing to limitations on monitoring, data collection, and interagency data exchange. And fourth, the financial system is growing more complex—markets and institutions are increasingly intertwined across borders, and informal credit markets, conglomerate structures, and off-balance-sheet activities are on the rise.

Not only do the above characteristics of, and trends in, the financial system pose significant systemic risks, they will eventually prevent China's financial system from serving an increasingly dynamic, sophisticated, internationally integrated economy, driven, in large part, by private sector firms. Banks, capital markets, and other financial intermediaries will need to raise and allocate capital efficiently; adopt modern corporate governance arrangements; provide access to micro, small, and medium borrowers; assess and manage risks using best-practice techniques; and provide a broader variety of financial services to an increasingly diversified clientele. At the same time, an increasing number of Chinese enterprises will go global, placing pressure on China's domestic financial system to adopt global standards to ensure seamless integration with foreign financial institutions and global capital markets. Rising income and accumulation of wealth within China will increase the demand for new financial products and investment opportunities. And finally, in the event of financial crises emanating from inside or outside China, adequate systems (including adequate capital buffers and clear accountabilities) will need to be in place for an orderly and systematic resolution of bad debts and either the recapitalization or the closing of insolvent financial institutions. Instead of persisting in pushing problems into the future, financial sector reforms in the next two decades should be decisive, comprehensive, and well coordinated.

The aim of financial sector reforms should be to build a competitive, balanced, efficient, safe, and sound financial system that meets the demands of the corporate, household, and government sectors. A well-functioning financial system capable of sound risk management is essential to mobilize savings; allocate capital efficiently to an increasingly complex and sophisticated economy; and ensure access to finance for all sections of the economy including individuals, households, the poor, and businesses of all sizes.

To reach these objectives, financial sector reform should follow an implementation road map that is properly sequenced, and, because the financial sector will remain vulnerable to crises, be sustained as a priority through the next two decades. Much has been learned from China's own experience as well as the successes and failures of other countries that have sought to reform their financial sectors.

The first priority should be to make interest rates more flexible, and endeavor to move to a point where interest rates, not quantity controls, clear the credit market. In addition, greater exchange rate flexibility is needed to help cool inflation and take pressure off reserve requirements, together with the deployment of a combination of monetary and macroprudential measures to pursue growth, inflation, and financial stability objectives.

In parallel, direct and indirect controls of financial institutions must give way to arm's-length market-based arrangements. This would mean an autonomous central bank adopting open market operations and using interest rates, rather than credit ceilings, to manage liquidity. Commercial banks would use commercial principles and creditworthiness analysis, rather than follow government signals, to guide lending (an exception could be made for one or more policy banks that would continue to finance government priority programs). Such reforms may require a thorough overhaul of governance structures in state-owned financial institutions, in which existing state ownership functions, agencies, and practices are reviewed, using lessons from examples of international best practice and failures. In addition, efforts should be made to further diversify the ownership structure in state-owned banks and further reduce the shares held by the state.

Second, although its huge foreign reserves give China a strong safety net against the possibility of a financial or currency crisis, it nevertheless must be prepared in case a crisis occurs. To achieve this, the government needs to strengthen the independence, effectiveness, staffing, and funding of regulatory bodies, including supervisory agencies (at the central and provincial levels), and to give them greater enforcement and resolution powers. A high-level financial committee on the basis of the existing framework could also be established, with the main objective of monitoring and managing systemic risk and maintaining financial stability. Limits need to be placed on emergency liquidity support to solvent banks facing short-term liquidity problems. Standing facilities should operate automatically to provide liquidity support to all domestically incorporated institutions, and clear guidelines should govern and limit the use of fiscal resources. Stress testing should be continued and improved to take account of emerging risks, and "financial war games" should be conducted regularly to fine-tune the institutional arrangements for dealing with a financial crisis if and when one occurs. The government should establish an efficient legal framework; insist on higher standards of disclosure, auditing, and accounting; and streamline the court system to deal with troubled banks and firms in a timely fashion. A functioning deposit insurance scheme to underwrite risks faced by small depositors should be established. Such arrangements will not only help ensure financial stability but also provide the credible foundations for the eventual integration of China's financial sector with the global financial system.

Third, the capital market will need to be deepened and reformed to make available more equity and securitized financing, an important ingredient for more dynamic and innovative industries. To achieve this, China could shift the way it handles initial pubic offerings from the current merit-based approval system to a disclosure-based system and focus on improving the capital market's legal framework, enforcing laws and regulations, upgrading the financial infrastructure, and imposing stringent rules on information disclosure. Adequate and accurate disclosure and transparency supported by credible accounting and auditing practices can go a long way in supporting financial development by minimizing informational friction. China could also promote the corporate bond market, which would not only open up new channels of financing and further diversify financial markets but also create conditions conducive for further liberalization of interest rates, the opening of the external capital account, and internationalization of the renminbi. Financial infrastructure needs to be further upgraded to facilitate transactions in the financial market in general and the capital market in particular.

Fourth, after the above institutional and governance structures are in place, the Chinese authorities can also prepare and implement a plan that phases out the ceiling on deposit rates and the floor supporting lending rates; this step will facilitate the commercialization of banks and ensure stability in the financial sector. And as is actually well recognized and understood in China, this final stage of interest rate liberalization will have to be properly sequenced—long-term market instruments first, and short-term deposit rates last. Careful monitoring of the progress of liberalization will be crucial to ensure that banks do not indulge in destabilizing competition that erodes margins or in reckless lending that harms the quality of the loan portfolio, and that any emerging risk of distress is dealt with swiftly.

Land

Over the next 20 years, land will be increasingly scarce, and its efficient use will become critical for a range of China's long-term objectives—food security, efficient and innovative cities, equality of opportunity, and social stability. Better land policies will help secure farmers' rights over land use and promote agricultural investments and productivity; ensure that land is used for the highest productive purposes, whether in urban or rural areas; help reduce rural-urban inequality; and promote more efficient and sustainable urban development.

Policies affecting land face three key challenges. The first challenge is insufficient security of rural land tenure. Despite a relatively clear legal and policy framework, rural households continue to possess weak land rights and often face expropriation risks. In addition, serious difficulties remain in the implementation of policies and laws, governance and accountability at the local level, documentation of land rights, and increasing citizens' awareness of existing rights.

The second challenge lies in the process of converting rural land for urban use. During 2003–08, the government requisitioned 1.4 million hectares of agricultural land for urban use, and another 450,000 hectares were reported to have been requisitioned illegally.[19] In China, the government has unusually wide powers by international standards to requisition agricultural land for urban use. The exercise of this power has led to four consequences: the government has reserved for itself the sole right to requisition agricultural land for urban purposes; the acquisition price of the land is its net present *agricultural* value, not the (usually much higher) market price of land, which is its opportunity cost; local governments, which acquire land at the acquisition price and then sell at the market price, have come to rely on land acquisition as a revenue earner to finance the delivery of public services, especially infrastructure; and the consequent rapid growth of urban boundaries has resulted in urban sprawl (figure O.4). The lack of transparency in land acquisition and the large difference between the price paid to affected farmers (after a portion is held back by the collective) and the price received when the land is auctioned has led to a sense of injustice and been a factor in increasing rural unrest.

The third challenge is the use of land as a source of revenue for some local governments and collateral for borrowing by special purpose vehicles established to circumvent restrictions on local government borrowing. Revenues from land acquisition now constitute a significant share of total government revenues and have become an indispensable funding source that local governments use to finance heavy expenditure requirements. In addition, thousands of special purpose vehicles have been established (by one measure more than 5,000) that use local government land as collateral to raise funds from the banking system. The National Audit Office estimates that local-government-related debts exceeded RMB 10 trillion by the end of 2010, of which a significant share were deemed to be nonperforming.[20]

Meeting these three challenges will require a mix of policy reforms and institutional development that will take time to design and implement but that is essential for the success of the reform program as a whole. Without these reforms, agricultural investment could suffer, rural-urban inequality could continue to rise, urban sprawl could stymie environmental and economic goals, and the efficiency of land use could decline.

The first priority is implementation of measures that ensure the security of agricultural land tenure, including rolling out the recent policy decision to grant indefinite land use rights to farmers, expanding land registration and strengthening rural land markets, and reforming and modernizing the governance structure of rural collectives and dispute resolution mechanisms. A second priority involves reforming land acquisition and compensation practices, including strategic land use planning at the municipal, regional, and national levels. A third priority involves substituting property and other local taxes for land requisition as a revenue source as well as allowing local governments to borrow from domestic capital markets subject to strict controls and regulations.

In rural areas, the government could begin by legally granting farmers indefinite user rights to land they cultivate. It is important

FIGURE O.4 **Urban land has expanded faster than urban population**

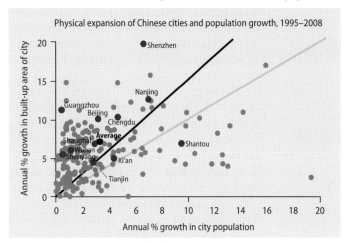

Source: NBSC, various years; World Bank staff estimates.
Note: The green line is the line of equality. The black line is the linear regression between the two variables. The blue circles are China's 11 largest cities.

that the Communist Party's 2008 Policy Decision regarding this issue be enshrined in law soon. The law will need to clarify who will be eligible for such rights; what the residual role of the collective will be; the actual terms of the document that grants land user rights (a common title document used nationwide would be ideal); and the rights and responsibilities of land users as well as sanctions in case of violations.

Effective implementation of land user rights will require some degree of clarity about the land's location and delineation. Over the coming years, various land registration pilots need to be scaled up. Lessons from other countries indicate that placing land registration and administration of the land registry under a single agency is the most efficient, because such an arrangement avoids overlapping and competing jurisdictions.

Developing rural land markets will greatly assist in improving the efficiency of land use. The transition to transparent and efficient rental markets for user rights can potentially raise productivity by 60 percent (Jin and Deininger 2009) and facilitate labor mobility and land consolidation. Such markets have developed rapidly since the 1990s, (they now cover about 20 percent of cultivated land), but the absence of enforceable contracts continues to inhibit growth, and most transactions remain informal. Expanding such markets will require improvements in land registration and documentation (and the latest land-mapping technologies make this cost-effective) as well as the establishment of credible and trusted dispute resolution mechanisms.

Governance standards in rural collectives need improvement. One of the key causes of land insecurity in rural areas is the abuse of power by some village cadres at the expense of the members of the collective. Land readjustment or sales are often undertaken in collusion with commercial developers with little transparency or accountability. Although the frequency of such events may have declined, one survey showed that every village experienced at least one reallocation during the period 1998–2008 (Wang, Tao, and Man 2010). Going forward, and especially in light of the policy supporting indefinite land use rights, the role of the collective will need to be reexamined, with a view to improving governance standards.

Policies governing acquisition of rural land for urban use need to be overhauled. Because the state has used its untrammeled acquisition authority to raise revenues, the urban land area in China has grown much more rapidly than the urban population. Two reforms are needed: First, local governments should be allowed to acquire rural land for urban areas only if the urban development plans have been vetted and approved by a higher level of government, and the approval process should take into consideration regional land area priorities and urban land use efficiency. Second, the current practice of compensation—a frequent cause of complaints—needs to be reviewed. One approach would be to pay the going market price to the collective (with total pass-through to the farmer) but then impose a transparent capital gains tax. The current practice of expropriating the entire difference between the agricultural value of the land and its urban market value is equivalent to a 100 percent capital gains tax; a lower figure would be a reasonable compromise between the need for more local government revenue and some benefits for the farmer whose land is acquired and way of life changed forever. Part of the capital gains tax revenue could be used for rural development within the county where the land is located.[21]

In addition to revenues from land acquisition, some local governments have also become increasingly reliant on resources raised by land banks that use land as collateral, and, as recent events have shown, this practice may lead to significant financial losses and transmit these risks to the broader banking system. The challenge lies in replacing these socially and financially costly forms of raising revenues with a more efficient and sustainable revenue base. Over time, other revenue sources, including a property tax, may help make up the difference (see chapter 7). A few countries, such as the United States and Canada, raise 3–4 percent of their GDP from property taxes, while the average among members of the Organisation for Economic Co-operation and Development (OECD) is near 2 percent.[22] China is already piloting property taxes in two cities but is finding that its introduction is usually difficult for technical, institutional, and social reasons. This argues for its gradual introduction and for modest expectations about its contribution to revenues.

Labor

Just as land and capital need to be used where they provide the highest returns, so too should labor be allowed to move to where the most productive and best-paying jobs are. But China's hukou, or household registration, system and its locally administered insurance and pension systems make mobility difficult. In addition, the labor force is expected to start shrinking in a few years, and a declining labor force participation rate among older workers is likely to make this downtrend worse. Together, these two constraints threaten to undermine China's efforts at becoming an innovative and internationally competitive economy. To compete against advanced economies in global markets, China will need a more flexible and dynamic workforce that can adjust quickly to changing market conditions. In the Republic of Korea, some 45 percent of the population migrated across provincial boundaries, contributing to extraordinarily rapid urbanization, concentration of economic activity, and flexible reallocation of labor;[23] in China's case, 19.5 percent of the population migrated in 2010; nearly 85 percent of the migrants moved from rural to urban areas.[24]

Over the coming decades, notwithstanding a decline in China's overall labor force, hundreds of millions will move in search of better jobs,[25] and their absorption will require labor markets that are flexible and institutions that protect workers by providing some employment predictability, social security, and portable rights to affordable health care and financial security in their old age. Government leadership will be crucial in helping people obtain equal opportunities to access jobs, education, and health care services, and to manage rising risks stemming from further structural change, difficult global conditions, and increased competition. Developing a flexible and dynamic labor market will be central to China's future success as a high-income, open economy; whether that can be done will depend critically on whether production and employment patterns adjust quickly to changing demand conditions globally and domestically. Phased reforms of the hukou system to ensure that, by 2030, Chinese workers can move to where the jobs are; measures to increase labor force participation rates; and reforms in labor taxation, hiring policy, and wage policy will all be essential to success.

Hukou reform will be a top priority in the coming decades and needs to be completed by 2030, but progress will likely be slow because it will depend on fiscal reforms. The hukou system no longer restricts movement of labor from rural to urban areas.[26] But rural migrants without urban hukous are still denied access to social entitlements—health care, education, and housing—that urban residents receive. One of the key constraints to hukou reform is that local governments have neither the resources nor the incentives to extend public services to migrants and their families. So the speed of hukou reform will depend on the rapidity with which local governments strengthen their fiscal systems (see chapter 7) and how financing responsibilities are shared between central and local governments. The inability to provide migrants social entitlements on par with urban residents not only increases inequality but also discourages mobility. Local hukou reforms have been ongoing but, owing to fiscal constraints, have progressed least in large cities where rural migrants are most concentrated. In contrast, migrants to small and medium cities receive a modicum of social services and social protection. Taking these factors into account, a systematic approach to propel hukou reform forward would include: (1) delinking the hukou from access to public services and using a residential permit instead to determine eligibility to receive services; (2) encouraging pilot reform programs at the local level; and (3) redefining financing responsibilities between central and local governments as an incentive for reform.

To increase the labor force participation rate, especially among older workers, the government could increase the retirement age of men and women, which has the additional benefit of reducing the burden on pension systems (see chapter 6). Many OECD and transition countries have tried this in recent years, with the annual increase in the retirement age ranging from six months a year in transition countries to one to three months a year in OECD countries. The government could also promote flexible working arrangements and strengthen mid-career training and life-long learning opportunities.

China should also reduce the level of social insurance contributions required for employed workers. This implicit employment tax imposed on employers, amounting to about 45 percent of the wage rate on average, is high by international standards. Because minimum contributions are set at a rate applied to 60 percent of the *average* wage, the implicit tax rate is much higher for workers earning low wages. Employers therefore avoid formalizing employment. Many employers and employees also "opt out" of social insurance schemes. The total number of contributing urban workers in 2010 ranged from 237 million for health insurance and 236 million for pensions, compared with only 134 million for unemployment insurance and only 80 million for housing funds.[27]

Finally, China's public sector entities should be "equal opportunity employers," that is, their recruitment practices should be transparent, based on merit, and impose no restrictions on place of birth or possession of an appropriate hukou.

Chapter 4   Increasing the Pace of Innovation

Notwithstanding reforms in factor markets and development of the private sector, sustaining high growth poses a considerable challenge. With population growth slowing sharply and investment rates also set to decline, growth will be more dependent on gains in total factor productivity. During the past decade, TFP growth averaged 3 percent a year, which is high by international standards and attributable in large part to rapid structural change; product and process technology spillovers from high levels of foreign direct investment; the speed of technological catch-up made possible by the buildup of physical, human, and financial capital; the progressive easing of infrastructure constraints; and the creation of a more competitive and open economy.

The potential productivity benefits from catching up in industry and services, from measures to enhance competition in the domestic market, and from the accumulation of human and knowledge capital, are far from exhausted. But there can be little doubt that many segments of Chinese industry are approaching the technology frontier, that intersectoral transfers of labor will diminish, and that the contribution of capital as a growth driver will decline. Recognizing these facts, China is turning to innovation as a means of achieving rapid and sustainable growth while coping with looming challenges associated with resource scarcities, climate change, and environmental degradation.

Is innovation the answer? Over the long term, high levels of investment will remain a major driver of growth in China through embodied technological change, but its importance is likely to decline while TFP growth from innovation is expected to become increasingly significant. Were investment to fall to European levels of around 25 percent of GDP or less, growth would trend toward 4–5 percent a year. But a more innovative China that continues to invest at least a third or more of its GDP has a high probability of meeting its growth targets buoyed by above-average advances in TFP.

Even so, much will depend on complementary domestic reforms and the global environment—merely investing another 1 percent of GDP in research and development will be insufficient. Many complementary ingredients in China's innovation policy, including private sector development and increased competition, reforms in factor markets, adoption of a green growth strategy, human capital deepening, and the effective harnessing of urban agglomeration economies to advance ideas and technologies, are discussed in other chapters of this report. This chapter focuses on policy reforms needed to develop a system of incentives and institutions that could specifically support broad-based, economy-wide innovation.

Innovation Advantages

As it begins its journey toward an innovative economy, China possesses several advantages. First, China's spending on research and development is on a steep upward trend. Second, China's manufacturing sector is large and possesses wide-ranging capabilities. Third, having expanded its education system, China's efforts to innovate are being supported by a rising supply of science and engineering skills of improving quality. Fourth, an elastic supply of patient capital is being mobilized to support innovative firms and scale up the production capacity of new entrants with good ideas. Fifth, China's large and expanding market of urban middle-class consumers—expected to double in the next decade—is attracting leading innovative multinationals, encouraging local innovators, allowing domestic producers to attain scale economies, and permitting formation of clusters and agglomerations. Sixth, a pro-business, entrepreneurial culture in several of China's provinces, including Guangdong's Pearl River Delta, Zhejiang, and Fujian, is supportive of small firms and start-ups. Seventh, considerable potential is inherent in China's relatively underdeveloped services sector. Eighth, and finally, not only is China urbanizing, some Chinese cities are realizing that the productivity and growth of urban economies will rest upon the quality of life and how effectively these cities can attract and retain global talent.

Innovation Weaknesses

China's rising supply of skills and its large and advanced industrial base notwithstanding, the reality is that government and state enterprises conduct the bulk of research and development—and part of this effort still seems divorced from the real needs of the economy. True, China has seen a sharp rise in scientific patents and published papers, but few have commercial relevance and even fewer have translated into new products or exports (the honorable exception being telecommunications and consumer electronics). Part of the problem may lie in weak incentives for indigenous, government-backed research institutes to work with commercial users of new technologies. In addition, research institutes may not be capturing opportunities to leverage their capabilities by networking within the country and connecting with global R&D networks. China has the potential to improve the institutional arrangements needed to encourage broad-based innovation—such as ease of firm entry and exit, increased competition, enforcement of laws protecting intellectual property rights, quality tertiary education, the availability of risk capital for small and medium enterprises, evaluation of government R&D expenditures, and standard setting in government procurement. In the long run, the objective should be to develop a system that stimulates broad-based creativity and innovation.

Key Reform Recommendations

A better innovation policy in China will begin with a redefinition of government's role in the national innovation system, shifting away from targeted attempts at developing specific new technologies and moving toward institutional development and an enabling environment that supports economy-wide innovation efforts within a competitive market system.

The central government will need to take greater initiative in building countrywide *research networks* that mobilize national talent and reduce the isolation of firms in some cities by including them in research consortia that also involve advanced firms (including multinationals) from coastal cities. The governments of Japan and the United States have successfully sponsored such consortia in their countries; similar efforts in China could potentially develop more "global challengers." These domestic networks can also link to global R&D networks in ways that leverage Chinese efforts with research activities in other parts of the world. The natural inclination may be to protect domestic research efforts and innovative companies, but that would prevent Chinese researchers from interacting with external research efforts, cut them off from new ideas, and lower opportunities to adopt foreign technologies. Links with global networks would also help address constraints in domestic research capacity and overcome perceptions in foreign countries about China's research and development program. Moreover, the trend in global R&D is rather similar to other kinds of economic activity, such as increased specialization, more intense exchange of ideas and know-how, and frequent exchange of research personnel. In such a model, China will be a participatory member in a global research effort in which it is a consumer as well as a producer of new ideas, new inventions, and new ways of doing business.

Many *high-tech multinational corporations* have invested in R&D facilities in China (including in inland cities such as Xian and Chengdu). Such investment should be further encouraged because of its significant spillover effects, the reputational gains for those Chinese cities that are fast becoming science hubs, and the contribution this research can make to industrial upgrading. Closer collaboration and partnerships with multinationals on the basis of mutual trust and recognition will contribute to the creation of a dynamic and open innovation system. In this context, an efficient patenting system that reflects the experience of the U.S. and European systems (both of which are in the throes of reform) and effective protection of intellectual property, especially in fields such as biotechnology, nanotechnology, software, and multimedia, will expedite the growth of China's innovation capabilities.

China's innovation policy needs to reflect the lesson borne from international experience that most applied research and innovation is done within *large private sector firms*. Large private firms tend to make innovation a central plank of their competition strategies, respond to market demand and government incentives, and provide researchers with the freedom to pursue interesting ideas and interact with other researchers both at home or abroad. A range of incentives—through fiscal, financial, and regulatory instruments—needs to be applied to encourage such firms to emphasize research, development, and innovation, and to give them a large enough market to ramp up production of new products and achieve economies of scale. In addition to tax deductions for R&D spending, these incentives could include temporary consumer subsidies for the purchase of new products that have proven positive externalities (such as electric automobiles, for which China is already providing consumer subsidies).

At the other end of the size spectrum, SMEs should also be seen as an important source of innovation, especially in sunrise industries.[28] SMEs, after all, are the big firms of the future, and every effort should be made to ensure they are not disadvantaged by regulations and are encouraged through tax incentives. Innovative new entrants, especially SMEs, face a perennial shortage of *risk capital*. True, local governments and state-owned enterprises are increasingly becoming sources of venture capital and private equity funds. Nevertheless, venture capital is scarce for smaller private firms and SMEs trying to scale up. One partial solution is to increase lending by banks to small, hi-tech, private firms. The resulting creation of bank-led relational networks seems to work in other countries, such as the United Kingdom and the United States, and complements other sources of financing. Another approach is to ensure that capital markets both allow SMEs access to funding, even though they may be located in interior provinces, and permit venture capital owners an exit option. Finally, governments could help innovative SMEs by establishing public technology platforms that provide SMEs access to laboratory, metrology, testing, and certification facilities.

Then there is the direct role of government in R&D. Central and provincial governments are seeking to enlarge spending on R&D and also raise the share of *basic research* supported by universities and research institutes. Support of basic research is more likely to succeed through well-targeted incentives, by committing a sufficient volume of funding to a few high-caliber institutions, and by sustaining that funding. One example is the National Institutes of Health in the United States, which plays a central role in boosting innovations in life sciences because it enjoys large and stable funding. Another is the Defense Advanced Research Project Agency, also in the United States. To maximize spillovers from government-sponsored research, findings would need to be made widely available. Beyond that, it is up to firms to transform the research findings into profitable products and services.

But increasing R&D spending to the government's target of 2.2 percent of GDP, expanding basic research, and emphasizing publishing and patenting is likely to have only a small impact on productivity growth, unless the quality of this research and its commercial relevance and uptake are substantially increased. Good research must be complemented by a stringent and disciplined process of *refereeing and evaluating* research findings. The research community needs to take the initiative here, although the government could provide the parameters.

China's innovation objectives, increased effectiveness of its basic research, and development of high-technology industries envisaged in the 12th Five Year Plan all depend on the availability of a vast range of *technical skills* for research, design, fabrication, production, information and communication technology (ICT) support, and eventually marketing. By 2030, China is expected to have up to 200 million college graduates, more than the entire workforce of the United States. Moreover, the quality of university training is improving rapidly:

FIGURE O.5　**The quality of China's tertiary education system is improving rapidly**

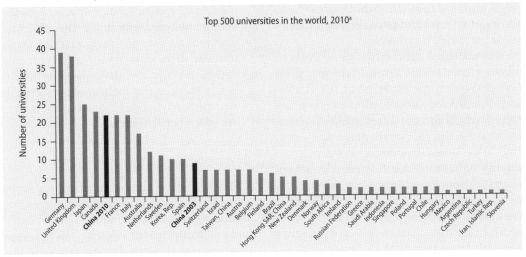

Top 500 universities in the world, 2010[a]

Source: Shanghai Jiao Tong University 2010.
a. The United States, which has 154 top universities, is not shown.

in 2010, only five countries had more universities than China in the top-ranked 500 universities of the world. China had 22 universities in this list in 2010, compared with 9 in 2003 (figure O.5).

Even so, the quality of tertiary education more broadly is a matter of concern, and employers are experiencing a serious shortage of skills. To address this shortfall, China needs to further accelerate governance reform in universities, giving them greater autonomy while, at the same time, tightening ethical standards in research. The best universities must be allowed to mobilize funding and appoint faculty that ensure high-quality, cross-disciplinary, postgraduate, and postdoctoral programs. They also need to develop innovative approaches to imparting knowledge and analytical skills and set up well-staffed specialized research institutes. In this regard, China should encourage leading foreign universities to set up campuses in China jointly with domestic universities and impart modern governance standards, teaching methods, and research management.

In addition, both the private sector and the government need to invest more in improving the *quality of human resources*. Public-private initiatives can secure and replenish the base of technical skills essential for innovative industries. The education system should emphasize competencies, not

qualifications, and do away with the rigid boundaries that separate academic streams from technical and vocational education and training. To achieve the desired increase in the volume and quality of skills and maximize the returns from the limited supply of quality instruction and teaching facilities, China will also have to rely more on innovations in ICT and pedagogical techniques involving the greater use of multimedia and flexible online training customized to the varying needs of students. The traditional education approach of lecturing to large classes may need to be rethought, with institutions being encouraged to experiment and given the autonomy to do so. Universities can also take the lead in promoting public lectures and exhibitions and in contributing to the teaching of science in local schools. In this context, opening the tertiary education sector to foreign investment and increasing the participation of leading foreign universities in China may help stimulate domestic university reforms.

There is also scope for encouraging innovation through demand-side instruments such as *government procurement* and standard setting. The key to success will lie in genuine open competition. One way to begin would be to take EU or U.S. standards as a technical starting point while looking for ways to advance product performance;

another would be to involve industry leaders when setting standards. A third would be to get industry associations to develop industry standards based on consensus.

Technological capability is more likely to advance in *innovative cities*. In the past three decades, coastal cities served as the incubators of technology development by attracting large levels of foreign direct investment. But industrial cities are not the same as innovative cities. Innovative cities have depth and quality of human capital (especially a high share of science and technology workers) as well as mechanisms that support the generation, debate, testing, and perfecting of new ideas. Innovative cities have local knowledge networks, institutions that support innovation, an industrial base that employs scientific and technological talent, a few major dynamic firms that invest heavily in R&D, and digital networks and online services. Such cities thrive on the heterogeneity of knowledge workers drawn from all over the country and the world. Moreover such cities are closely integrated with other global centers of research and technology development. Finally, innovative cities are "sticky" because their leading edge in design, assets, attributes, and governance attracts global talent and does not let it go. Industrial cities can become innovative cities—such as Tokyo, Stuttgart, Munich, Seoul, Seattle, and Toulouse. But innovative cities do not have to be industrial, as Cambridge (U.K.), Helsinki, San Francisco, and Kyoto all show.

International experience suggests that innovative cities usually include one or more *leading research universities* that compete and collaborate with each other. These universities must interact with employers to mix technical and soft skills as well as impart the latest industry know-how. Possible areas of research include challenges associated with:

- Rapid urbanization—the development of energy-saving building materials, efficient large-scale public transportation systems with low carbon emissions, and the infrastructure needs of intelligent cities;
- Health care—including basic research in science and medicine, biomedicine, application of ICT in health care management, and institutional arrangements for health care management and financing; and
- Green development—including the development of more-economical renewable energy sources and new green technologies, as well as the application of incentive structures to change behaviors and encourage green consumption.

Sequencing

The chapter on economic restructuring highlighted the urgent importance of increasing competition and lowering barriers to entry and exit for increased efficiency and international competitiveness. These reforms are also central in providing incentives for research and innovation activities. With more investment in R&D, perhaps an equally important priority is to introduce an unbiased and independent evaluation system for R&D spending and current industrial policies supportive of targeted technology development. Such a system would give the government rigorous analysis to show what works and what doesn't, and where government financial support needs to be reallocated.

Policies that will take longer to implement include the institutional arrangements for innovation—university development, establishment of venture capital financial institutions, and creation of nationally integrated R&D networks linked with global R&D networks. Many of the reforms will depend on other areas of the economy, notably fiscal and financial sector reforms, but work on these can nevertheless begin soon, recognizing they will take time to bear fruit.

As far as outcomes are concerned, once a sound institutional framework is in place and as firms near the international technology frontier, a concerted effort will be needed to strengthen basic research. The success of China's innovation policy will depend on how effectively all branches of the research and innovation network (research institutes, universities, central and local governments, state and private enterprises) function together and how these efforts are leveraged internationally through global networks.

Chapter 5   Seizing the Opportunity of Green Development

Concerned that past and current economic growth patterns are environmentally unsustainable and that the environmental base needed to sustain economic prosperity may be irreversibly altered, the Chinese authorities proposed a new approach toward green development in the 12th Five Year Plan. The plan emphasizes continued rapid growth together with ambitious targets for energy efficiency, natural resource management, and environmental sustainability. This approach is consistent with the concept of green development used in this study, namely, a pattern of development that decouples growth from heavy dependence on resource use, carbon emissions, and environmental damage, and that promotes growth through the creation of new green product markets, technologies, investments, and changes in consumption and conservation behavior.[29]

Why a Green Development Strategy?

China should give high priority to green development for many good reasons, both domestic and international.

First, new technological opportunities make green development not just a realistic possibility but a potential driver of economic growth. If successful, green development will create new business opportunities, stimulate innovations in technology, and potentially make China globally competitive in sunrise industries.

Second, quite apart from stimulating growth, green development would significantly improve the quality of China's economic growth. For example, less production and use of fossil fuels would greatly reduce health losses from air and water pollution, water scarcity, and land subsidence. The costs of environmental degradation and resource depletion in China are estimated to approach 10 percent of GDP, of which air pollution accounts for 6.5 percent, water pollution 2.1 percent, and soil degradation 1.1

percent.[30] And although air pollution levels may be on a consistent downward trend, the cost of illnesses from pollution has climbed as the population ages and urban populations and urban incomes grow.

Third, green development will help address a wide range of sector-specific issues, such as energy security, urban livability, agricultural output, and infrastructure constraints. The rapid growth of energy consumption has strained domestic supplies of electricity, raised coal prices, and made China increasingly dependent on imported energy. With unchanged policies, China may have to import 75 percent of its oil (making it the world's largest oil importer) and 50 percent of its natural gas by 2030. The efficient use and better governance of land will help reduce urban congestion and sprawl. Improving the quality of land and water will help raise agricultural output. Better energy efficiency will ease infrastructure constraints, particularly for handling coal.

Fourth, given rising and volatile commodity prices, lowering the resource intensity of production will improve international competitiveness and partially insulate domestic prices from fluctuations in international prices.

Fifth, while China's green development strategy is driven almost entirely by domestic considerations, it will make a significant contribution to tackling global climate change. China is now the largest energy user in the world and the largest emitter of carbon dioxide emissions, although its cumulative emissions remain significantly below that of the United States (Baumert, Herzog, and Pershing 2005). Its annual per capita emissions have already exceeded the world average and are still rising rapidly. Furthermore, China is one of many countries that are likely to be most seriously affected by climate change. Vigorous implementation of a green development strategy will not only benefit China but also contribute toward global efforts to reduce emissions and mitigate climate change.

Green Development as a Source of Growth

There are also many reasons why green development can be a potential driver of growth.

The first is *the greening of traditional sectors*. A large number of existing conventional techniques and management models can both reduce energy use and emissions and improve the level of corporate profitability. Although the greening of traditional sectors may seem less dramatic and revolutionary than the development of cutting-edge new technologies, it is clear that with information and financing, many energy-efficient investments are also cost-effective and yield high economic returns.

Second, going green can drive growth through the *expansion of emerging green industries*, including solar and wind energy, together with upstream and downstream industries such as relevant equipment manufacturing and electric vehicle industries. More broadly, however, new markets and incentives, supported by innovation and research, will likely stimulate new low-carbon, reduced-resource, and environmentally friendly technologies, goods, and exports. In addition, increased public awareness will help shift consumer demand toward green products.

Third, *services will also expand as a complement to new green product markets and changes in consumer preferences*. Not only will the rising share of services in GDP help reduce the economy's carbon intensity, specialized services are likely to develop that specifically support green development. Examples are ecosystem services, carbon asset management services, carbon trading, and contract energy management.

Fourth, by anticipating climate impacts on agriculture, low-lying coastal areas, and areas vulnerable to extreme weather events, green development *will promote sustainable growth and development, reduce climate-related risks, and improve investor and consumer confidence*. International experience shows that preventive measures are usually far more cost-effective than ex-post reconstruction and rehabilitation.

China's Many Advantages in Moving toward Green Development

By some measures, China's quality of growth has shown improvement in the past two decades, although it has a long way to go. For example, although its energy efficiency improved faster than that of any other country, it is still one of the least efficient energy users in the world. The share of fossil fuels in China's energy mix has fallen since 1990 but is still much higher than that of advanced countries. China's expenditures on energy research have been the highest in the world as a share of GDP, however, and these expenditures appear to be having an impact. The efficiency of coal-fired plants has shown impressive progress, and China possesses the world's largest capacity for renewable energy generation. It is a world leader in small hydroelectricity generation, has doubled its wind-driven turbine capacity every year since 2005, and has become the world's largest manufacturer of solar panels.

Going forward, China can build on this progress and on its many strengths and advantages. First, the Chinese leadership has reached consensus on green development, and the government's strong implementation capability will play an important role in facilitating change. Second, China's relatively low urbanization rate and high level of investment as a share of GDP allows for a rapid turnover of the capital stock, permitting old technology to be replaced with new relatively quickly, thus avoiding the lock-in costs associated with old buildings and aging infrastructure. Third, it can potentially use its newcomer status in green industries and technologies to leapfrog current capabilities in the advanced countries. Fourth, the size of its domestic market can support rapid achievement of scale economies. Fifth, its increasingly educated workforce will provide abundant skilled manpower; this, together with foreign partnerships and appropriate policies and institutions, is likely to accelerate the pace of innovation. And finally, its abundant wind, solar, biogas, and shale gas resources give it many options to reduce its dependence on fossil fuels and improve its energy security.

Obstacles to Green Development

While China has many advantages that would help it implement a green development strategy, many obstacles and difficulties also need to be overcome. Most important among these is the price of energy, water, raw materials, and natural resources, which remain distorted to different degrees and do not reflect either the negative externalities associated with their use or their true scarcity value. The result is high resource intensity in production and associated wastage and pollution. A second and related obstacle is excessive dependence on administrative mechanisms to deal with environmental and natural resource management issues. In the absence of market-based mechanisms, the government is forced to make decisions that appear arbitrary and occasionally even heavy-handed. At the same time, other fiscal and regulatory incentives for environmental protection are either weak or weakly enforced; as a result, pollution and greenhouse gas emissions remain high.

A green development strategy will also face implementation and incentive constraints within government, and may face opposition from workers and enterprises that benefit from the current pattern of growth, exports, and investment. The strategy will require coordination across many government ministries and agencies, many of whom may oppose it because it reduces their discretionary power to make decisions. In addition, while a green development strategy will be of considerable long-run benefit, it will in the short run conflict with other economic objectives (for example, meeting employment and industrial targets for the five-year plan). Resolving these conflicting objectives will require job retraining, skill development, and similar policies to smooth the adjustment toward the new pattern of green development, and will need clear and strong leadership from the highest levels.

Recommended Reforms

Economic activities are replete with externalities and market failures that require government intervention through market and nonmarket policy instruments. To promote green development and control environmental degradation and carbon emissions, governments must intervene to allow economically and environmentally efficient markets to fully play their role.

Applying this principle, the promotion of green development in China will involve five distinct but coordinated policy levers: long-term market incentives to encourage enterprises and households to "go green"; better designed and enforced regulations requiring changes in behavior in situations where market incentives do not work; public investments that deliver key environmental goods and services with high positive externalities and that explicitly incorporate climate risk management; measures to strengthen local government institutions; and safety net schemes to mitigate any short-term negative employment effects of green development reforms.

Long-term market incentives. A key goal of using market incentives is to harness the creativity and entrepreneurial energy of China's private sector and state enterprises to protect the environment and turn China's green industries into an important source of growth by making them world-class innovators and competitors. Market incentives are also the best way to foster efficiency, which, in the case of green development, goes beyond financial efficiency to include resource use efficiency and the reduction of environmental externalities.

So far, China has mainly employed regulations and edicts to enforce its environmental and emissions targets. Old power plants have been retired and polluting factories closed, with measurable benefits in improved environmental quality. But as the scale and complexity of the Chinese economy and the environmental challenge grow, the disadvantages of this approach will (indeed, already have) become more apparent. Instead, the government should consider market mechanisms such as taxes, fees, tradable permits, tradable quotas, and eco-labeling. In degraded ecosystems, rehabilitation is warranted, especially through expanded payments for ecological services in poor and ecologically important rural areas (for example, upriver watersheds or downriver floodplains).

There is no better place to begin than by ensuring that market prices of goods and services reflect the true cost of production and consumption to society. For example, the price of oil, water, coal, and other natural resources should include a tax to reflect the social and environmental costs incurred with their use. Complementary actions would involve removing direct and indirect subsidies, raising pollution taxes, and canceling export tax rebates for high-pollution, high-emissions, and resource-intensive industries. (Indeed, export targets for these industries should also be curtailed, if not abolished altogether.) Mining companies, state and nonstate, should pay royalties for the state-owned mining resources they use. These measures, together with enforcement of the "polluter pays" principle, will help internalize the pollution costs of enterprises and reflect the true scarcity of the resources they use, as well as reflect their real competitiveness in domestic and world markets.

Such "no-regrets" policies not only improve efficiency, they also support sustainable growth. But China's green development strategy has a loftier objective, which is to make green industries a source of growth. To achieve this goal, industries that use green technologies should be open to private and foreign enterprises that compete on a level playing field. Public investment should focus on public goods and services such as basic research, appropriate infrastructure (for example, smart grids), and a supportive environment for private and foreign investment such as streamlined investment and copyright approval and rapid endorsement of new technologies and products.

Because innovation is fundamental to green growth, the government should foster the conditions for creativity by permitting new entrants as well as the import of high-level talent for innovative firms. New entrants will stimulate competition and innovation; the production of electric vehicles, for example, should not rely solely on traditional automobile manufacturers. Once such public policies spur private sector development in a green sector, the focus could shift to the next vanguard sector. In this way, state investment can play a key role in spurring private sector–driven technological innovation. State enterprises, on the other hand—especially if they enjoy monopoly power, are subsidized implicitly or explicitly, or are favored in any way by discretionary government actions—are more likely to hinder, rather than encourage, green innovation.

In the early stages of developing green industries, the government could "grow bigger fish by adding more water." During the formative period of green firms, the authorities could offer temporary tax relief, fiscal subsidies, preferential land allocation, and below-market financing. Once these firms are established, however, such preferential policies should be withdrawn. Any initial loss in tax revenues will be more than made up by later increases. At the same time, if it becomes clear that international competitiveness is unlikely to be achieved, this financial support should be withdrawn.

Given the global push on climate mitigation, the most effective way for China to establish itself as a global green technology leader is by implementing stringent and effective policies to reduce greenhouse gas emissions and to internalize the cost of carbon emissions in the operating costs of enterprises. Stringent emissions reduction policies, achieved through such diverse market mechanisms as carbon trading, a carbon tax on fuels, technology standards, and regional carbon partnerships, can act as a powerful mobilizing force for innovation in green technologies. This, in turn, will help lower economic costs associated with improving the quality of the environment and help drive overall growth.

The 12th Five Year Plan commits China to experiment with a carbon cap-and-trade scheme to be rolled out gradually and on a voluntary basis. As China embarks on its own pilot emissions-trading schemes, it needs to evaluate policy choices between price and quantitative instruments under the guiding principles of efficiency and effectiveness. Beyond the more conceptual differences between these two approaches, China can find valuable lessons in the experiences of many OECD countries, including existing and proposed carbon-trading schemes in Australia, Canada (Alberta), the European Union, New Zealand, Switzerland, Tokyo, and the United States (both national and state-level schemes).

Better designed and enforced regulations. Regulations are an important complement to market-based incentives to promote green development, provided the authorities are able to monitor and enforce compliance effectively. One important step will be the establishment of strong environmental and emissions technical standards that will shape behavior and create market incentives for green technologies. A key example is in the automobile industry, where standards can be set for fuel consumption. Another is in the appliance and lighting industry, where new standards for energy efficiency can have a direct and widespread impact, especially given the scale of urban construction. A third involves setting national standards for climate-robust green buildings, urban design, and transportation to avoid locking in existing carbon footprints. Compliance with these standards can be increased through tougher inspections and buttressed by market-based incentives (such as insurance policies that require flood proofing or compliance with energy efficiency standards). A fourth is the establishment of labels and standards for green products, services, and technologies so they are easily recognizable and understood by consumers. And a fifth is the implementation of recycling guidelines to reduce the need for new urban landfills or incinerators by reducing the volume of waste at the source. The government could also signal its seriousness about environmental goals by changing the way it conducts its own business. The most important and pervasive approach would be to introduce green standards for the roughly RMB 1 trillion in government procurement each year;

these standards could open up a huge market for green products and usher in a period of robust growth in relevant industries.

Public investment. While the bulk of new investment in green industries and technologies will be through enterprises, a sound green development strategy will also require incremental public investments over and above the huge amount the government is already doing. While China's annual investment in the treatment of industrial pollution is roughly comparable to Europe's, its total expenditure on environmental protection activities is less than Europe's by 0.3–1.1 percent of GDP.[31]

To improve environmental quality over the longer term, China's government expenditures related to the environment should be at least half a percentage point of GDP higher than current levels. Incremental expenditures should be focused not only on reducing pollution and solid waste but also on protecting and restoring the health of China's ecosystems, water, and soil, and reducing potential damage from flooding. Evidence from other countries indicates that such expenditures have extremely high economic rates of return. Therefore, a relatively modest incremental increase in environment-related expenditures would go a long way toward reducing the annual costs of environmental degradation and depletion (as noted, these costs are approaching 10 percent of GDP).

One of the most important areas for increased public investment will also be adaptation to climate change and, more broadly, the development of a climate risk management framework. Four of the ten Asian cities most vulnerable to rising sea levels are in China. Careful planning and large public investments will be required to protect ports, infrastructure, and housing in these cities from extreme climate events. The government could invest more in public institutions to analyze and disseminate weather-related and emergency response information, and it could also update and develop new climate-robust technical standards for infrastructure. Follow-on actions could include relocating transmission lines and distribution systems for power grids in coastal areas exposed to natural hazards, and redesigning storm water drainage systems in cities so they can handle extreme weather events projected for the next several decades.

The government also needs to prepare for climate-induced effects on agriculture and to invest early in flood control, water management, drought-resistant plant varieties and agricultural methods, and research on climate-induced effects on the economy. These investments would earn higher economic rates of return if they were complemented by measures to improve water use efficiency (for example, through consumption-based allocation and trading of water rights) and expanded pollution regulation that includes coverage of nonpoint sources of pollution. Finally, expanding current programs that restore forest cover and watersheds to meet the objective of restoring ecosystem health will have even broader benefits. When investing in environmental improvements, it is important to use instruments that give value to environmental quality and then reflect these values in measures used to monitor and rank the performance of local governments.

To mobilize collective action on environmental protection and climate change, the government needs to launch mass education campaigns to increase public awareness of these issues and the actions that individuals and households can take to contribute toward the national effort. China can make emissions reduction and environmental protection a desirable lifestyle, thereby increasing market demand for green products. To do so, it could mobilize nongovernmental organizations, industry associations, and the media. It can also change consumer behavior by providing better information, through energy efficiency labeling, for example.

Local institutional strengthening and reform. In the past, some of China's most successful reforms, such as the household responsibility system, originated as local experiments that were later scaled up. The same could be said for green development. In a few cities such as Baoding and Rizhao,

bold efforts are under way to deploy clean technologies, improve energy efficiency, and reduce greenhouse gas emissions. But green successes in some areas are not being scaled up because most local officials remain under more traditional pressure to grow their economies and protect jobs.

One way to align national and local objectives is to introduce explicit performance indicators for local governments that support green growth. China could consider using some of the measurable indicators suggested by the OECD (2010), along with other indicators that have been developed by local governments themselves. For example, some subnational governments—typically more affluent ones—have introduced quality-of-life indexes into performance appraisals for public officials. Meaningful ratings depend on publicly disclosed information, such as on the levels of air and water pollution and on the levels of environmental compliance across industries. Fujian Province has included ratings for environmental quality, energy consumption, R&D, public safety, education, and rule of law in its performance evaluations. Guangdong Province recently started using a "happiness index" as a supplementary measure of performance. A national poll in 2011 found an overwhelming 89 percent of respondents in favor of including a happiness index as part of local government performance evaluations (Feng 2011).

Two other important ways to strengthen local institutions include, first, adjusting the local tax structure away from land sales and in favor of property and value-added taxes (see chapter 7). Among other benefits, greater use of property taxes would provide additional incentives for local governments to increase land values by improving the local environment. Another step is to strengthen interregional coordination to better manage regional transportation, natural resources, and pollution control facilities. Urban, transport, ecosystem, and environmental problems are not confined to local boundaries. Incentives are needed to encourage smart urban planning and risk management by local and regional governments across an entire region. Transjurisdictional bodies, such as river basin commissions and regional planning boards need to be given more authority.

Reduce negative impacts on specific sectors or groups. The introduction of reforms, whether fiscal and financial incentives or nonmarket policy instruments (such as new standards and regulations), will inevitably alter relative prices and change the profitability of different sectors. Pollution-intensive sectors will see profitability reduced while green sectors will see profitability enhanced.

To handle objections of those likely to be affected negatively, the government will need to be ready with a range of policy measures. First, compensation for carbon pricing (whether through taxation or tradable permits) could be made through fiscal transfers. If done in a fiscally neutral manner, carbon revenues could replace other taxes that may be more regressive. In addition, progressive "social" tariffs could be introduced where price increases in water, electricity, oil, and gas specifically do not affect low-income groups.

Second, if carbon trading is introduced, the original allocation of permits, both by sector and across regions, can be done equitably with the cost of low carbon transition in mind. Less developed areas may not use their full allocation and could potentially earn revenues from the sale of the excess. High-emission enterprises that may be affected by carbon emission limits (especially industries that are still subject to price controls or that cannot pass on the cost of carbon emissions to consumers) could receive free allocations at the beginning, moving to a partial and then full auction over time.

Third, job retraining will be needed for displaced workers, as will labor market policies that permit workers to move jobs and locations at relatively low cost. Managing this transition, and ensuring that the pace of change is well within the capacity of the economy to absorb, will require careful policy planning and proactive implementation of social safeguards.

Conclusion

Green development can drive growth and address past environmental deficits, but its success will take active government policies—applying market and nonmarket policy instruments—together with competitive and well-functioning markets for goods and services. Valuing natural assets and applying a price to pollution will lie at the heart of China's green growth strategy. Therefore, a key priority would be to price electricity, oil, gas, water, and other key natural resources not only to reflect scarcity value but also to incorporate the environmental costs associated with their use. Enterprises and households will need to respond to price signals and regulatory standards and restrictions. A cap on greenhouse gas emissions together with an emissions trading scheme—combined, perhaps, with a fuel tax to encourage emissions reduction in transport (which is not amenable to inclusion in carbon trading systems)—will be essential to ensure an optimal allocation of emissions rights.

As a result of these policies, returns to investments in green products and services will increase, and "brown" industries will be discouraged. More important, the expansion of green industries will contribute to economies of scale in production and to R&D. Competitiveness honed in the domestic market could accelerate the competitiveness of Chinese green firms in a rapidly growing international market. Net job creation is likely to be positive. In the long run, green development will derive from new product and process opportunities afforded by innovation aimed at addressing environmental concerns, more efficient use of resources through the removal of price distortions that lead to environmentally harmful practices, more rigorous appraisal of the costs and benefits of alternative government policies and public investments, and lower economic costs associated with growing green now rather than growing now and greening later.

Chapter 6 Equal Opportunity and Basic Security for All

China's social development over the past three decades has been impressive. The country has universalized compulsory primary education, expanded participation in higher levels of education, sharply reduced the burden from infectious diseases, and dramatically increased health insurance coverage. Labor has become more mobile, and a growing number of rural migrants have moved to cities in search of employment. The "iron rice bowl" social protection system based on state enterprises has been transformed into a set of social protection programs that are being expanded and consolidated.

Going forward, social policy will need to focus on establishing a welfare system appropriate for China in 2030—one that promotes human capital development, provides basic social welfare but avoids welfare dependency, and creates social conditions supportive of growth and development. Its foundation should be a basic level of security provided to all, with a particular focus on the poor. Just as important, policies should promote equality of opportunity in education, health, employment, and entrepreneurship to realize everyone's full potential and substantially narrow disparities in income, living conditions, and wealth that will allow people to enjoy a higher standard of living and share the fruits of development.

Key Problems and Risks

China's social policy faces four broad problems and risks. The first is *relatively high inequality,* some dimensions of which may have even worsened in recent years. Inequality remains high in incomes, consumption, and asset ownership, as well as in access to quality education, health, jobs, and social protection programs across and within regions and especially between rural and urban areas. Although regional inequality appears to have narrowed to some extent, other dimensions of inequality, such as housing wealth (accounting for some 60 percent of total household wealth), have increased. Rising inequalities increase the risk of reduced vertical mobility

in China and gradual ossification of social structures. In addition, many who escape poverty remain near poor, and a shock, such as an illness, injury, or layoff, could easily thrust them back into poverty (box O.3).

Part of China's income and consumption inequality is the result of the "Kuznets effect"—which comes from structural change as labor moves from low-productivity agriculture to higher-productivity manufacturing. But there are three other drivers of inequality, all related primarily to the inequality of opportunity in accessing social services and social entitlements:

- China's decentralized fiscal system and the mismatch at the local government level between resource availability and social spending responsibilities have led to large differences in government expenditures per capita on social services—between rural and urban areas within provinces, and between coastal and interior provinces. The inadequacy of fiscal resources at subprovincial levels also makes many public service units (PSUs) behave like private sector profit-maximizing units and distorts incentives for service provision. Spending differentials have resulted in disparities in access. For example, progression rates of rural students to senior secondary school remain far below those of their urban counterparts, and relatively few of them are entering universities. Another example is public subsidies on health care, which differ by several multiples between urban and rural residents. Just as important, spending differentials have resulted in "inequality of quality" in education and health services and in the degree of financial protection offered by pension and health insurance programs. Such disparities in turn lead to inequality in job opportunities, productivity, and eventually incomes, as well as in risk management capacities.
- Institutional arrangements and policies reinforce and, in some cases, accentuate inequalities; examples include the different rural and urban social entitlements

BOX O.3   Reducing poverty

Over the past three decades, more than 500 million Chinese have moved out of the ranks of the poor—an achievement of historical significance. At the same time, China still has a large number of poor people—204 million in 2005 when applying a $1.25 a day poverty line (purchasing power parity) and household consumption as the measure (Ravallion and Chen 2008). Reaching those that still remain below this international poverty line will prove difficult. Many are in remote western provinces, and the rest are dispersed throughout the country. Many more are "near poor"—just above the poverty line and only one crisis away from falling back into poverty. The challenge facing the country will therefore increasingly be to reduce risks faced by the near-poor and tackle transient poverty. The recommendations below are designed to meet this challenge.

First and foremost is the need for continued rapid growth. Throughout the world, higher growth has meant greater likelihood that incomes and consumption rise above the poverty line for increasing numbers of people. But poverty is not just about income—it is also about access to affordable quality health care and education and the ability to deal with risks. Indeed, China's rising inequality is largely the result of inequality of opportunity; one's connections, place of birth, employer, and parental circumstances still play a large role in gaining access to critical social services.

Second, it follows that identifying the poor and vulnerable through a metric broader than just income—one that includes access to public services and ability to deal with uninsured risks—will help targeted poverty reduction programs and keep poverty reduction at the top of the government's development agenda. China has developed a household-based targeting system for providing direct assistance to the poor, but there seems to be scope to improve this program through a more explicit proxy-means targeting system based on easily observed household characteristics that are correlated with income.

Third, universal access to quality health care, secondary and higher education services, and finance for agricultural investments can improve the conditions of poor rural residents and migrants, while also improving opportunities in agriculture through additional investments in rural infrastructure (notably water, renewable energy, and roads).

Fourth, returns to labor can be raised by relaxing disincentives to rural-urban migration and providing migrants affordable access to urban services through the phased reform of the *hukou* system. These steps would not only raise household incomes of the poor and reduce poverty and inequality, they would also boost household consumption, and at the same time allow firms more time to make the adjustment from labor-intensive to skill-intensive production. Complementary efforts could include improving the education and skill base of potential migrants before they migrate, providing assistance to migrants to reduce job search and information costs, increasing connectivity between rural and urban areas, and improving the investment climate in the poorest western provinces where the bulk of poor potential migrants reside.

Fifth, notwithstanding significant improvement in recent years, social protection instruments—health, unemployment, and pension insurance—need to be strengthened to meet two objectives: insuring the poor against a variety of risks with adequate but sustainable financial protection; and making full portability of entitlements a reality to promote occupational and geographical flexibility for workers, giving them the freedom to seek better and more productive jobs wherever they may be.

Finally, because local governments shoulder the bulk of the responsibility for implementing and financing these programs, they cannot be expanded without fiscal reforms (identified in chapter 7). Bridging the gap between expenditure responsibilities and revenue sources is one priority, and reducing regional disparities in fiscal performance is another. This in turn warrants strengthening the fiscal system so it can shoulder these additional responsibilities.

created by the hukou system, and the fragmented institutional arrangements and delivery systems that limit portability of entitlements and impede labor mobility. Thus, notwithstanding recent local hukou reforms, there remain obstacles to migration from rural areas to cities, from interior to coastal provinces, or even from city to city, because most migrants are denied access to affordable health, education, housing, and pension coverage to which urban residents have access by right.

- Other factors also contribute. For example, high taxes on labor—to pay for social insurance—limit formal sector employment opportunities, lower remuneration for workers, and bias investment toward capital-intensive technologies. In addition, weak labor market institutions, in particular the wage determination system, do not provide an effective platform for balancing the interests of workers, employers, and sustained competitiveness to ensure the growth of labor earnings in line with increasing profits. The labor market is segmented between and within localities, often according to the hukou, income, and social status of workers. As a result, workers without family or social connections are disadvantaged in accessing government or public enterprise jobs. The lack of portability of social entitlements and differences in worker wage and entitlement terms between the formal and informal sectors, and between the private and public sectors (state enterprises, PSUs, and government departments) exacerbate the segmentation.

A second challenge is inefficiencies in social service delivery stemming from *distorted incentives and market structures*. Public organizations and agencies exercise a monopoly or quasi-monopoly in delivering social services and face little competitive pressure to improve efficiency or quality. Pressure from users of services is also limited because government incentive structures are not based on downward accountability. As noted, the revenue and incentive structure in health and, to some extent, education services encourages public providers to maximize revenues and to act as profit-maximizing private sector entities. This results in some undesirable outcomes: for example, between a third and a half of admissions to hospitals in China are estimated to be unnecessary; the average number of days in hospital is double the OECD average (World Bank 2010); and school selection fees in urban areas drive a further funding wedge between "key" schools and regular schools, excluding many deserving students.

The third challenge is *rapid aging of the population*. China's demographic transition will be among the most rapid ever seen and poses future challenges for social policy formulation and the economy more broadly. With rising life expectancy and with total fertility at only around 1.5, the country is "growing old before growing rich." As the country ages, the labor force will peak around 2015 and then start to shrink (albeit gradually at first), and health and pension costs will escalate. A smaller workforce, combined with higher dependency rates, puts a premium on deepening human capital to enhance labor productivity, places additional demands on education and training systems to increase relevant skills, and heightens the importance of ensuring that labor is allocated efficiently. Moreover, the aging of the population means that the disease profile has changed sharply toward noncommunicable diseases—a trend that will only accelerate—requiring a shift in health care strategy from curative to preventive care and better health education for children and adults. The fiscal costs of health and pension programs will need to be contained through greater emphasis on primary care rather than hospitals, structural reforms in pension systems, efficiency improvements in service delivery driven by information and communications technology (ICT), and better incentives for health care providers.

And the fourth challenge is *rising expectations*, especially among second-generation migrants and a rapidly growing middle class, for higher wages, greater income security, better social services and greater equality in access, and a voice in the design and delivery of those social services. There is growing dissatisfaction with service providers and increasing expectations for more accountable, affordable, and equitable social programs. The expectations and interests of different groups may not be aligned, however, and may even conflict with one another, raising concerns that unless these deep inequalities are reduced, social unrest could grow.

Proposed Reforms

Based on these problems and challenges, social policy reform has three objectives. The first is to reverse rising inequalities in income, consumption, and access to public services and ultimately to ensure that equal opportunities are available to all, irrespective of whether someone is migrant or local, old or young, in the city or countryside, or from the coast or interior. The second is to help households better manage employment, health, and age-related risks, and ensure a basic level of security. The third is to promote greater accountability of service providers, public and private, to ensure that services are made available in the right amount, at the right place, and of the right quality.

To achieve equality of opportunity for all by 2030, the policy focus will require expanding opportunities to include all citizens so they can access quality, affordable health and education services and share in, as well as contribute to, the country's prosperity through equal participation in the labor market. To become a competitive high-income economy, China must deepen and broaden its human capital base and put it to the most productive use.

A more complex and dynamic economy also brings greater risks for workers during and after their working lives, and reducing these risks requires measures that enhance security in old age and help workers better manage risks inherent in a more flexible labor market. The provision of such "flexicurity" requires making structural reforms in pension and unemployment insurance systems so that workers have reasonable and portable support in old age or when unemployed, while avoiding an ever-increasing burden on the working population; ensuring comprehensive coverage of pension insurance, in particular for rural citizens, migrants, and informal sector workers in urban areas; preparing for and gradually expanding long-term care for the aged and terminally ill; and strengthening labor market institutions to enable wage bargaining and dispute settlement mechanisms that balance the interests of workers and employers.

Underpinning these reforms is the crosscutting need to promote greater accountability for results in social services and social protection programs. Accountability would need to come through three channels: administrative systems that monitor performance and encourage quality and equity in service delivery; market-based mechanisms that encourage the private delivery of public services and rely on competition with appropriate regulation; and accountability to citizens for quality services by increasing the role of civil society organizations in monitoring and in some cases giving them co-responsibility for managing social services. Emerging local experience in China with citizen participation in oversight and management of service delivery (for example, through school councils, election of school principals, and medical dispute mediation councils), and in providing feedback on service quality (for example, through web-based public feedback and citizen score cards) suggests that China can benefit from more active citizen participation in service delivery as many other countries have.

To achieve these objectives, China needs to *develop a vision*, core values, and guiding principles for social policy reforms. Policy makers need to ask two questions: What level of social services and protection should the state aim to finance, and how much of the burden should be shouldered by individuals and households? And what should be the roles in service provision of government, the private sector, and communities? In China, the answer to the first question will depend on the amount of fiscal resources the government intends to devote for this purpose. Extending the current level of urban services and social protection to rural residents and migrants—well over half the population—will itself impose a significant burden on fiscal resources. Therefore, additional government-financed social services should be undertaken with considerable caution and only if they do not strain the fiscal system (see chapter 7). At the same time, international experience suggests that social spending accounts for the bulk of incremental public expenditure as countries get wealthier. China will want to strike the appropriate balance and avoid the current predicament that many advanced countries face—a fiscal crisis that has arisen, in part, from financially unsustainable entitlement programs.

Achieving Equality of Opportunity

Providing equal access to quality, affordable education and health care for all by 2030 requires action in several areas. In the first place, the challenge will be to continue fiscal and structural reforms that ensure the wider framework for equitable and sustainable service delivery. But these will need to be accompanied by sectoral reforms that promote opportunities to build human capital and allow people to be healthy and productive across the life cycle.

Based on a vision of China's future social policy, the government will need to put in place the *appropriate fiscal measures*—increased aggregate social public spending commensurate with the level of development, lower payroll taxes to increase labor intensity in production and encourage formal sector employment, and stronger fiscal equalization across local governments at the subprovincial level (see chapter 7).

In addition to fiscal measures, several *structural reforms* in the social sectors can improve the efficiency of service delivery and help achieve equality of quality. First, human resource management should be reformed for service providers, through effective monitoring of performance on key outcomes, strengthening the link between provider performance and career progression, providing incentives that discourage rent-seeking, and ensuring that the best health providers and teachers also provide services to underprivileged urban and rural areas (for example, through rotation policies for teachers and outreach programs for hospital doctors to periodically provide services to poor patients).

Second, nonstate provision of social services should be increased, and different stakeholders (communities, commercial and nonprofit providers, and even households themselves) given greater co-responsibility. The state cannot and probably should not "do it all" as it seeks to provide a wider and deeper range of social services and social protection programs. Involving the nonstate sector will open up new possibilities, from private hospitals and clinics, to private preschools and universities, to involvement of private insurers and third-party administrators. In some fields, such diversification may also benefit from enhanced partnerships with international firms. New approaches to financing will also be required. Greater plurality of service provision also offers a greater role for communities and the nongovernmental sector, often with financial support from the state. The experience of OECD countries suggests a range of innovations in unbundling financing, provision, and regulation of social services that China could consider. At the same time, achieving plurality of social service provision while ensuring quality will require the state to assume a greater role in licensing, accreditation, oversight, and regulation of providers.

Third, integration of ICT in social service and social protection delivery systems should be increased. This integration could include electronic medical records, telemedicine, distance learning, and high-functionality smart cards that allow individuals easy access to their key medical data from anywhere. A good ICT system will permit exchange of data and financial information across the country, dramatically reducing administrative costs and costs to the population. But realizing such gains requires harmonization of data standards and systems to end the current situation of major investments by local authorities in IT systems that are incompatible with one another.

Fourth, intra- and intersectoral coordination is needed for policy development and delivery of social services. As economies age and grow richer, effective social services increasingly require better cross-sectoral coordination. For example, within health services, coordination of care across levels of service is critical for managing noncommunicable diseases, and for education, the boundary between technical and vocational education and training and academic streams becomes more porous. Across sectors, new needs such as long-term care require inputs from social welfare, health, and other agencies, while labor policy for older workers requires coordination of social security and training initiatives. Developing an administrative system of cross-sectoral coordination requires the transformation of government functions and responsibilities.

These structural reforms need to be complemented by a range of sector-specific policies to promote equality of quality from young children to the elderly.

Education. A key priority in improving equality of quality will need to be an equal start in life for all children, especially in the areas of early childhood nutrition and education for rural and poor children. These are some of the highest return social investments in the next generation. The government should prioritize nutritional supplements for children ages zero to three and for pregnant or lactating women in all poor rural counties, especially in the central and western provinces, and for migrant children in urban areas. The cost of such a program is not prohibitive—this intervention is in fact very cost-effective in light of the high returns to health, cognitive development, and productivity. Over time, the focus of child nutrition efforts would increasingly need to shift to stemming the incidence of childhood obesity, which is already approaching Western levels in a number of China's coastal cities.

Similarly, *early childhood education* for three- to six-year-olds is another relatively low-cost, high-return public investment. In the coming five to ten years, the program should focus on children in poor rural counties, gradually expanding to rural areas in central and western provinces, and migrant children in urban areas (figure O.6). The financing can come through supply-side subsidies to providers and fee exemptions for targeted households. Another option could be the use of conditional cash transfers (CCTs) targeted to poor households. CCTs have proven to be effective in other developing countries, and pilots in China indicate that they have significant potential.

Another priority will be extending affordable access to *secondary education.* High fees are a key reason why a significant portion of rural children fails to enter senior secondary schools (fees are high because schools are encouraged to use them to make up for inadequate financing through local government budgets). Yet, given the needs of the Chinese economy over the next two decades, and given the experience of countries that have moved from middle to higher income, providing free senior secondary level education will be essential. China has set itself a 90 percent senior secondary enrollment target

FIGURE O.6   Unequal spending on early childhood development across Chinese provinces

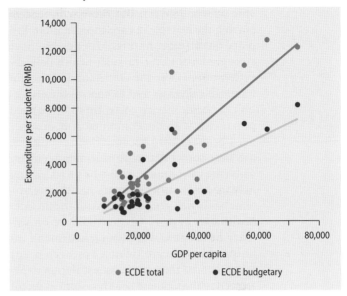

Source: World Bank staff estimates based on data from Chinese authorities.
Note: ECDE = early childhood development and education.

by 2020—comparable to Korea's senior high enrollment rate in 2000. Following the example of the abolition of fees for compulsory (primary and junior secondary) education, a similar policy is needed for senior secondary schools in rural areas, together with a parallel initiative for poor and migrant children in urban areas. This could be financed in part by the incremental public funding that China has already committed in its Education Law (4 percent of GDP, around half a percentage point above current levels).

Health. Just as in education, much needs to be done in health. Deepening health reform is one of China's biggest social challenges in the coming years. At the same time, Chinese and international experience demonstrates that health sector reform is one of the most complex and politically challenging reforms that governments confront, a challenge exacerbated in China by the rapid pace of population aging and the explosion of noncommunicable diseases, which, in 2009, accounted for more than 80 percent of all deaths in China and 82 percent of the total disease burden.

A critical challenge is reorienting China's three-tier health delivery system away from the current hospital-centric model to one that manages care across levels of the system with a revitalized *primary health care system* playing the key role in care coordination. Primary health care, in turn, will need to have stronger links to the broader health delivery system to manage the epidemic of noncommunicable diseases and to control the escalation of health service costs. Up to 85 percent of patients with noncommunicable diseases need primary care because their conditions are best controlled with self-management. This care can—and should—be provided and managed by a strong primary health care system that is well-coordinated with the broader health care system. Greater reliance on primary health care will mean less demand for hospital-based care, which has been a key factor behind the major cost escalation experienced in the Chinese health system in recent years. Unnecessary admissions and overtreatment have made hospital costs in China a significant outlier compared to a range of OECD countries.

The necessary reorientation to primary and preventive care in China will be difficult to achieve without further progress on hospital reform. Fundamentally, it will be necessary to change the current incentives for public hospitals and doctors to behave like private providers. The key reform will be setting firm budget constraints on public hospitals through a more active purchasing role for health insurance agencies and the use of information to monitor and provide better incentives for improved provider performance. Evaluating the experience in improving hospital governance and management will also be important. Given the diversity in hospital organizational reforms across China, it is necessary in the short run to have more rigorous evaluation of different models and the lessons from them.

Reforms of the health delivery system will be effective, however, only with a broader reform of the incentive structure for health care providers, including *health financing and provider payment* arrangements in particular. An initial step will be to raise the pooling level of the health insurance system to harmonize benefits across different schemes, promote administrative efficiency, and facilitate portability of entitlements. Greater pooling would also pave the way for greater integration of schemes across rural and urban areas. In this process, health insurance agencies could gradually ensure value and quality of health services, including through contracts with public and private providers. More broadly, the experience with the New Cooperative Medical Scheme and urban residents' health insurance schemes points to the need to consider over time an appropriate balance between financing from health insurance contributions and from the budget. Developments in the rest of Asia point to an increasing role for general revenues in financing health care, especially for the poor.

In parallel, provider payment reform must be accelerated to increase the incentives for all health providers to produce efficiency and quality. A number of efforts have been made to control costs in the health system, including drug lists, zero markup policies, and controls on the use of costly medical equipment and procedures. But without a more fundamental shift away from the current provider payment systems, the basic provider incentive structure will continue to drive inefficiencies and inappropriate care. Changes in incentives will need to be complemented with a stronger emphasis on professional ethics among providers and tools for greater accountability of providers to patients.

Going beyond the health system, China's aging population will increasingly require *aged and long-term care (ALTC)*, as the 4-2-1 extended family structure places greater care burdens on adult children. To date, the policy framework for ALTC is limited, and its multisectoral nature has posed institutional challenges to developing a coherent approach. Nor are there enough appropriately trained personnel to provide required services. Given the early stage of development of ALTC in China, a first need is deciding on the appropriate mixture of public and private financing and provision and the role of the public sector for different population groups. These decisions would benefit from extensive piloting and local experimentation. Another key issue will be the institutional and coordination arrangements for the ALTC sector, given the number of public and private actors involved. Once these questions are decided, a framework for ALTC can be developed that involves mixed models of providers (state, nonstate, communities, and households) and ensures that basic standards of care are met.

Achieving Flexicurity

An increasingly open economy with greater labor market flexibility brings greater risks for workers during and after their working lives. To help them manage these risks requires flexicurity—labor market and social security institutions that promote flexible and efficient allocation of workers and also ensure they have decent working conditions and adequate social protection during and after their working lives.

A first element of flexicurity is a set of *labor market policies and institutions* that promote an internationally competitive workforce in which workers share in the benefits of growth and also enjoy some social protection. This would first require eliminating the remaining barriers to labor mobility—the most critical measure being phased reform of the hukou system (see chapter 3). To improve labor mobility, segmentation among social protection programs needs to be reduced to promote an integrated and seamless social security system. Social security entitlements should be portable within and across provinces, and with central government involvement reducing interprovincial disparities in social insurance protection. In parallel, labor market institutions will be needed to support wage determination that is driven less by administrative direction and more by collective bargaining where the interests of workers and employers are balanced. Finally, by 2030, as people live longer and healthier lives, the retirement age will need to rise gradually. Flexible work arrangements could make continued work more attractive, and life-long learning opportunities for workers would help reduce the depletion of human capital with age.

The second element of flexicurity is a *robust but sustainable social protection system*. Since the 1990s, China has put in place a comprehensive package of social protection programs at a speed that is unprecedented internationally. These include pension programs for urban and rural residents; pension, unemployment, sickness, workplace injury, and maternity insurance for urban sector workers; and a national social assistance scheme that now covers more than 70 million people, among others. But there remains a big unfinished agenda to deepen the reforms already introduced.

The first item on this agenda is the need *to expand coverage of the pension system* among rural residents, migrants, and other urban informal sector workers. Until very recently, China had pension coverage well below that expected of a country with its per capita income (figure O.7). Low coverage has been driven by the absence (until very recently) of a national rural pension program, the very low participation rates of migrant workers in urban schemes, and the absence until mid-2011 of a pension scheme for urban informal sector workers (30–40 percent of the urban labor force). Current policies commit to comprehensive coverage of the pension system by 2020, and new schemes for rural workers and urban residents represent a major step in this direction. To achieve comprehensive coverage, the authorities could consider a system with three pillars: a basic benefit pillar that provides minimum poverty protection to the elderly through noncontributory social pension benefits (this would build on the general approach being taken in the new rural and urban residents' pension schemes); a contributory pillar with a mandatory notional defined contribution scheme for workers with wage incomes (modifying the current urban pension system) and a voluntary defined contribution pension savings scheme for urban and rural residents with nonwage incomes; and a supplementary savings pillar for the urban and rural population providing voluntary occupational and personal pensions that may supplement other pension benefits.

The second priority is the need to ensure the *fiscal and financial sustainability* of existing urban pension systems in order to ensure

FIGURE O.7   Pension coverage rate of the active labor force, various countries, mid-2000s

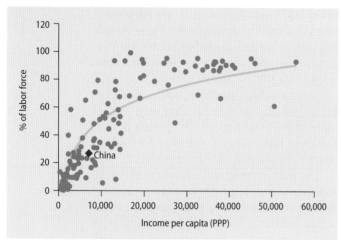

Source: Holzmann, Robalino, and Takayama 2009.
Note: PPP = purchasing power parity.

a credible commitment to basic security in old age. Pension reform will need a robust financing strategy that ensures basic benefits consistent with fiscal constraints. A key step is phased increases in the retirement age in line with higher life expectancy, and gradually harmonized retirement ages for men and women. In addition, there is a need to address the issue of inadequate returns on contributions in the current urban system, while controlling investment risks (for example, through a notional defined contribution approach). Pension reform will also require a strategy for financing the legacy costs of the urban system. Pension liabilities for those under the previous pension regime—so-called legacy costs—are estimated to range from 82 to 130 percent of 2008 GDP, depending on assumptions. An appealing option for financing this obligation would be to gradually pay it down through incremental fiscal resources, while all the time ensuring that assets accumulating in pension funds are properly managed and yield rates of return adequate to meet future liabilities. This approach in turn would create space for future reduction in

pension contribution rates to enhance the competitiveness of Chinese workers. Finally, voluntary supplementary saving arrangements will need to be expanded for those workers wanting pension replacement rates above the basic level.

The third priority is the *reduction of fragmentation* across different subsystems of the pension system. The integration agenda has both a spatial dimension and a cross-program dimension. Across space, greater portability in the short run would be complemented by pooling funds at higher levels over time, first at the provincial level and ultimately at the national level. Across programs, within the urban schemes, PSU and civil servant schemes should be gradually merged with the urban workers' scheme in line with emerging global practice. In addition, national policy can build on the growing provincial practice of merging rural and urban residents' schemes so that mobile workers have a more harmonized and ultimately integrated system as they follow productive work opportunities.

Finally, there is a broader need to build a more coherent social protection system, where the individual elements are aligned and the system is more than the sum of its parts. The Chinese government has committed to guaranteeing the poor a decent living with access to public services, including education, health, and housing by 2020, and the social protection system will play an important role in this process by assuring a minimum standard of welfare for the poor (State Council 2011). In addition, the medium- to long-term agenda in social protection will require greater coherence across insurance, social assistance, and other welfare and antipoverty programs to ensure not only that the poor are protected but also that the near-poor are not subject to "poverty traps," where low-wage earners are worse off than those receiving social assistance.

Chapter 7 Strengthening the Fiscal System and Aligning It with the Evolving Role of Government

Over the past two decades, China has reformed its fiscal system significantly. A major overhaul in 1994 focused on enhancing revenue mobilization and revamping national-provincial fiscal relations. A new tax system with a value added tax at its core laid the foundations for a significant increase in the ratio of revenue to GDP. The reforms also launched important changes in China's system of intergovernmental fiscal relations. Changes in tax assignments increased central government revenues, laying the foundation for larger and more rules-based transfers to subnational governments to help tackle fiscal disparities. The combination of these reforms put public finances on a solid footing, allowed China's government spending to grow to levels comparable with other economies with similar incomes, and paved the way for increased social and environmental expenditures.

Key Fiscal Challenges

Now a key challenge is to further strengthen China's fiscal system, improve fiscal sustainability, and align it with the evolving role of government to support the delivery of a large economic, social, and environmental agenda by 2030. For example, in the economic sphere, improvements in the efficiency and independence of the financial system will mean that some of its quasi-fiscal functions will need to be transferred gradually to the fiscal system. Additionally, as state enterprises are subjected to hard resource constraints and better credit evaluation criteria, their restructuring, closure, or ownership diversification may require budgetary support. A strong fiscal system will also be central to China's objectives to meet domestic and external economic shocks as and when they arise—the 2009–10 fiscal stimulus package being an example of what can be achieved when an economy has adequate

fiscal space. Finally, although the share of public expenditures on social and environmental services has climbed in recent years, the large social and environmental agenda over the next two decades will entail further increases in public spending.

At the same time, it is important that China preserve fiscal stability to protect against future macroeconomic shocks. The demand for additional budgetary resources to address social and environmental needs will arise at a time when China's total public spending is already high relative to GDP, and the emergence of structural budget deficits could potentially erode available fiscal space and pose a risk for future fiscal stability. So the challenge China faces is to contain the level of government expenditures as a share of GDP while at the same time changing the composition of those expenditures to address evolving strategic priorities. This will require fiscal discipline as well as budgetary procedures that allow reallocation of resources over time from lower- to higher-priority government programs. How China deals with two key factors—its decentralized fiscal system, and its public finance management system—will be central to achieving these objectives. Consider each in turn.

China is among the most decentralized countries in the world when it comes to government expenditures, but government revenues are highly centralized. Its subnational governments account for around 80 percent of total budgetary expenditures and bear responsibility for the provision of vital public services including basic health and education, pensions, unemployment insurance, disability, housing, infrastructure maintenance, and minimum income support. But local government revenues—available through the tax revenue-sharing mechanism and intergovernmental fiscal transfers—are not commensurate with local government expenditure responsibilities. On average, these "revenues" from the center finance 40–50 percent of the expenditure burden of local governments. Moreover, provincial governments have considerable discretion in transferring resources to subprovincial governments, and it is at the local level in poorer jurisdictions that the imbalance is most acute between available resources and responsibility for public service delivery.

While intergovernmental transfers are common in most large countries, China is unusual in the discretionary power wielded by provincial governments and the fiscal stress experienced at the lowest level of local government responsible for service delivery. In pursuit of rapid growth and motivated to "collect resources to do big projects," subnational governments have identified innovative ways to raise resources locally. China's subnational governments derive substantial revenues from fees of various kinds, the sale of land use rights, and taxes on real estate transactions. Distorted incentives to develop land can lead to corruption, forced land acquisition, inefficient use of land, and abuse of government power. Because local governments are prohibited from borrowing directly from banks, they have established special purpose vehicles that are free to borrow for infrastructure and urban construction, financed principally by local land sales and bank loans, often with land as collateral. Such activities have contributed to systemic risks in the financial sector (see chapter 3).

Arguably, the availability of revenue and borrowing outside the general budget has fostered some degree of local government independence (especially because most transfers from higher levels of government are for earmarked expenditures). But not only have locally generated revenues led to distortions in land and financial markets, they may also have exacerbated inequalities. Some poor provinces, townships, and villages may not be able to raise enough resources locally to provide quality services, and poor households cannot afford their high cost (see chapter 6).

Finally, *government financial management, fiscal transparency, and accountability* are key issues. China currently runs four budgets—the general budget (comprising the bulk of government expenditures, including center-provincial revenue sharing and resource transfers), the government-funded budget (comprising off-budget revenues and expenditures), the state capital budget (financed by dividend payments from state enterprises), and the social security fund budget. The absence of a comprehensive budget makes it difficult to assess or alter the aggregate allocation of government resources across priority sectors and programs. Ministries have substantial latitude in allocating earmarked transfers to the provinces. Few budget details are made available, and there is little oversight by higher authorities or discussion about implicit intra- or cross-sectoral priorities. Moreover, little information is available on whether governments spend money according to budgetary allocations (except at the broadest levels), whether government expenditures and programs lead to the desired outputs, and whether the outputs lead to the expected outcomes. Internal audits focus on detecting malfeasance, not program performance. Additionally, the budget cycle and the expenditure cycle are not synchronized. Thus, even though the fiscal year starts at the beginning of the calendar year, the budget is not finalized until the end of the first quarter of the calendar year. This delay forces government departments to start program implementation before budgetary authorization. While that may seem a small procedural matter, it tends to reinforce the view that the budget itself is a formality with little operational significance for local governments and central ministries.

Proposed Reforms

Over the next two decades, then, China's challenge is to reform its fiscal system in the following four ways: first, to contain government expenditures as a share of GDP but change their composition in line with China's new challenges, with higher allocations for social and environmental public investment and recurrent expenditures; second, to improve the efficiency of revenue mobilization, including through changes in the structure of revenues; third, to reform intergovernmental fiscal relations, including through better alignment between resource availability and expenditure responsibility at different levels of government; and, fourth, to strengthen the management of government finances and improve the efficiency of public expenditures.

Containing Growth of Government Expenditures While Altering Their Composition

The composition of government spending will need to evolve to reflect China's changing development challenges. Most notably, the next 20 years will see a pressing need to further increase spending on health, social protection, and environmental protection. These increases will be important to provide social security and a basic set of public services and to build human capital and expand opportunity (see chapters 5 and 6).

The amount of public spending relative to GDP for social and environmental protection will depend on choices the authorities make in the current and upcoming five year plans. While China's reported spending on environmental protection appears to be in line with OECD and upper-middle-income country standards, the significant backlog and new challenges in this area could well require a further scaling up of such expenditures over the next two decades. In health, however, the scaling up of China's public expenditures will need to be significant. If high-income countries are used as benchmarks, the share of public spending on health in GDP can range from 4 percent (in Switzerland) to near 8 percent (in Iceland). China's current spending is about 2.5 percent of GDP.

Using these and other international benchmarks as reference, China could potentially aim to increase public expenditures by 1–1.5 percentage points of GDP for education, 2–3 percentage points for health care, and another 3–4 percentage points to fully finance the basic pension pillar and to gradually meet the legacy costs of existing pension obligations. These add up to an incremental fiscal outlay of around 7–8 percent of GDP, a reasonable estimate to bring China's aggregate "social expenditures" by 2030 to near the lower end of the range of high-income countries. Part of

these incremental expenditures could be met through efficiency improvements in current expenditure programs and the rest through reallocation away from lower-priority investment budgets (such as infrastructure).

Managing such a fundamental shift in government expenditure composition by 2030 while containing its total share in GDP will prove to be a major challenge. China's total government budget and off-budget expenditures as a share of GDP are about the same as some other upper-middle- and high-income countries. It would be inappropriate to push it higher. At no point should China fall into the "high-income trap" by expanding entitlements to the point that they become fiscally unsustainable in the long run. To prevent such an occurrence, a debt and fiscal sustainability analysis that accounts for contingent liabilities and considers alternative stress tests should be required as a condition for the approval of each annual budget.

Improving the Efficiency of Revenue Mobilization

Since the 1994 fiscal reforms and subsequent improvements, China has been very successful in mobilizing revenues. But it has significant untapped potential to increase the efficiency of its tax structure. These are concentrated in six areas.

First, higher taxes on energy (carbon), water, natural resources, and pollution will encourage resource conservation while improving environmental outcomes and generating revenues (see chapter 5).[32] Second, raising SOE dividend payments to the general budget (perhaps through the intermediary structure of state asset management companies; see chapter 3) will spur more efficient investment planning in SOEs while also generating significant budgetary resources.[33] Third, additional revenues can potentially be mobilized from personal income taxes. These taxes make up only 1 percent of China's GDP, compared with an average of 5.85 percent in high-income countries.[34]

Fourth, enhanced taxation of motor vehicles and parking (as a near-term option) and congestion pricing (as a longer-term option) would lead to more efficient and livable cities and better environmental outcomes. Fifth, property taxes will encourage more efficient use of land while also reducing urban sprawl and lowering local government dependence on funds from land acquisition. While promising, property taxes are unlikely to become a major source of overall revenues for some time; very few developing countries raise more than 1 percent of GDP from this source (Bahl 2009). Sixth and finally, the government could capture important economic rents by auctioning public resources such as bandwidth user rights, franchises for public utilities, and exploitation rights for natural resources. Not only will such measures raise government revenues, they would prevent politically powerful interests from capturing these economic rents for free.

Make Resource Availability Commensurate with Expenditure Responsibility at All Levels of Government

Local governments are responsible for 80 percent of government expenditure responsibilities but receive only slightly more than 40 percent of tax revenues (in the form of transfers from the central government) (figure O.8). The recentralization of revenues in 1994 strengthened the central government's capacity to redistribute in favor of poorer provinces. The most serious disparities in resource availability, however, occur at the subprovincial level, which was not included in tax-sharing arrangements in 1994 and which is responsible for more than 50 percent of total public spending. Fiscal transfers to subprovincial levels remain largely at the discretion of powerful provincial governments and are subject to negotiation, leading to high disparities across subprovincial local governments.

One way to deal with the disparity in government resource availability across and within provinces would be to introduce rules governing resource transfers from the provincial to the township and municipality level. Increasing the autonomy and capabilities of local governments is a common trend in other countries, even in unitary states. But in China, such increases will have

FIGURE O.8   Local governments: Large expenditure responsibilities, inadequate revenues

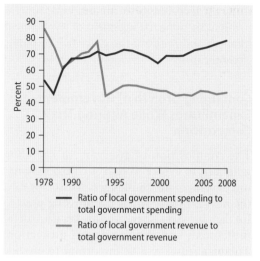

Source: NBSC, various years.

to be implemented in a manner consistent with ongoing discussions regarding reforms in the number, structure, and hierarchy of subnational governments. In addition, it may be appropriate to selectively raise some expenditure responsibilities to higher levels of government or to pool their financing at these higher levels. Scope for such reforms lies largely, but not exclusively, in health and pension spending (see chapter 6). Ultimately, any such solutions will need to be guided by a clear understanding of the functions and responsibilities of subnational governments in China.

Subnational governments will be able to increase their fiscal autonomy if they are given increased scope to raise their own revenues. The high disparity in development across different countries, townships, and villages warrants some flexibility in revenue assignment. China could consider first granting new sources of "own" revenues—such as property taxes and capital gains taxes on agricultural land acquired for urban development (see chapter 3)—to subnational governments in relatively developed cities to replace revenues from land acquisition. This step would free up fiscal resources at the center for additional transfers to poorer regions and help bring a larger share of subnational financing on budget. In addition, citizens are likely to hold officials more accountable if local public services are financed to a significant extent from locally imposed taxes.

Increasing the fiscal autonomy of local governments can be supplemented by allowing them to prudently expand on-budget borrowing. In the past, local governments have circumvented the rule against borrowing by establishing Urban Development Investment Corporations and other special purpose vehicles that can borrow using land as collateral. Total local government debt in 2010 reached as high as 26 percent of GDP, according to the National Audit Office.[35] Such indirect borrowing played a significant role in financing infrastructure investment and thus supported rapid industrialization and urbanization. But lack of transparency and regulation has created potential risks to fiscal sustainability,[36] and such quasi-fiscal financing also obscures the true size and composition of public spending and revenues. China has recently introduced a pilot program that allows selected local governments to issue bonds. There is a pressing need to revise the Budget Law and establish the institutions for bond issuance by local governments. Over time, subnational governments should be allowed to borrow from the domestic capital market on the strength of their own creditworthiness but subject to a prudential regulatory and institutional framework for subnational debt.

Improve Government Financial Management

China could introduce a number of public finance management reforms to improve the efficiency and effectiveness of public finances, but here we just mention nine possibilities.

- First, it could bring all off-budget government revenues and expenditures on budget and prepare a comprehensive budget that combines the general budget, the government-funded budget, and the state capital operating budget, and includes current and capital expenditures together with transfers.
- Second, China could complete the ongoing move from five to three (budgetary) levels of government in a manner consistent with reforms, also under way, to the structure of subnational governments. This step is a key toward streamlining the size of government, improving the efficiency of government services, and empowering county governments.
- Third, to discipline the budgetary process, the budget and expenditure cycles need to be synchronized by either finalizing the budget two months before the start of the fiscal year or moving the start of the fiscal year to April 1.
- Fourth, independent agencies should be used to conduct rigorous performance evaluations of government programs on a random basis. These evaluations will help provide feedback on the allocation of resources and identify programs that are delivering the right outcomes and those that are not.
- Fifth, treasury management and budget accounts, together with cash management, could be strengthened to streamline disbursements, introduce fiduciary controls, and prevent fraud and corruption.
- Sixth, a strict tally could be kept of contingent liabilities accumulating in the banking sector, state enterprises, and local governments and conduct regular fiscal sustainability analyses, accounting for these liabilities under different stress scenarios.
- Seventh, all levels of government should complete the process of bringing all public revenues and expenditures on budget in accordance with the latest Ministry of Finance regulations.
- Eighth, the central government should change the criteria for performance evaluation of local officials from an emphasis on growth to a focus on a "harmonious society."
- Ninth, and perhaps most important, all levels of government should publish and make transparent all budgetary revenues and expenditures from aggregate sectoral allocations and outturns to project level allocations and outturns. In the experience of other countries, this disclosure has been one of the most powerful ways to improve expenditure efficiency and ensure that budgetary resources are used in accordance with budgetary priorities.

Chapter 8 Achieving Mutually Beneficial Relations with the Rest of the World

China has benefited enormously from globalization and by opening to the global economy. Open trade policies worldwide helped sustain global demand for Chinese products just as opening its market has sustained Chinese demand for global products. China's openness to foreign capital helped improve domestic economic efficiency by encouraging competition within China and providing access to cutting-edge technology. China imported foreign practices in a host of areas ranging from banking regulation to product standards. And substantial inflows of foreign direct investment helped drive productivity in domestic firms through competition, workforce training, and demonstration of new technologies.

Other countries have similarly benefited from China's rise. The rapid growth of China's exports has been largely driven by its participation in the global production value chain; nearly half of its exports are processing trade—imports that are further processed and then exported—and multinational companies that have invested in China produce more than half of its exports. Therefore, China is part of a broader success story in which enterprises from many countries and territories have benefited, directly or indirectly. Furthermore, China is now not only the world's second-largest import market, it is also its fastest growing. Its strong demand for raw materials, advanced machinery, and consumer products has benefited developed and developing countries alike.

At the same time, China's relations with the world have changed over the past decade. It is now the world's second-largest economy and its largest exporter. Its foreign exchange reserves are the highest in the world, and they provide a large amount of sovereign debt financing for the United States and European countries. China's economy is now so large that its domestic policies have an impact on the global economy. If China had not implemented such a strong fiscal stimulus package in 2009 and grown as robustly as it did during the recent global financial crisis, the

global effects of the Great Recession might have been even worse than they were. In addition, China's outward foreign investment is playing an increasingly important development role in developing countries.

Going forward, this mutual dependence between China and the world economy will only increase. China's large and growing middle class will become an even more important source of global demand, the country's industrial upgrading and expanding trade will lead to further specialization and increased efficiency in world markets, and its increasingly educated labor force will become a force for global innovation. It is now in the world's interest to see a growing and thriving China that will contribute a positive force in support of global economic recovery and sustainable global growth. The world outside China will change dramatically too. In 2030 the contribution of other developing countries to global growth will exceed 40 percent, far more than the contribution of all (current) high-income economies together, which will contribute roughly one-third. This shift will dramatically change China's relations with its trading partners and its comparative advantage relative to other countries.

With this backdrop of mutual dependence, China's strategy toward the world will need to be governed by a few key principles: open markets, fairness and equity, mutually beneficial cooperation, global inclusiveness, and sustainable development. And China should help shape global governance structures that will accommodate its own evolution while promoting global growth and providing opportunities for the development of other countries. As with other large economies, China's long-term interest lies in global free trade and a stable and efficient international financial and monetary system. China benefited enormously from entering the WTO and is now an important stakeholder in the existing global trading system. Similarly, it will want to see stable international financial markets and a well-regulated international monetary system supported by stable currencies and underpinned by sound monetary policies. And finally, to ensure sustainable global growth, it is in China's interest to work toward a global climate change agreement that is fair and effective.

Key Issues in China's External Economic Relations

Notwithstanding slower growth in the advanced economies for the foreseeable future, greater integration with the global economy will further increase China's international competitiveness in a number of ways: through the specialization of Chinese manufacturing firms in the international value chain and greater economies of scale; increased specialization and productivity in services, where China would benefit from more international competition; continued access to international technologies and greater participation in the global R&D network; and increased inward and outward foreign direct investment that would build on the comparative advantage between China and its trading partners.

The hard fact is that unless China moves up the value chain, the future *contribution of exports to economic growth* will decline for three reasons. First, China's penetration in key markets is already large, and further expansion of China's market share is limited within the current export structure. Second, rising costs for unskilled labor are changing China's international comparative advantage within the export sector and will require China to move up the value chain to remain internationally competitive. And, third, reforms in input markets and natural resource pricing designed to correct distortions will help increase the efficiency of resource allocation, but, if labor productivity does not increase to compensate for higher production costs, international competitiveness will erode in traditional energy- and resource-intensive industries.

As China moves up the value chain, it will inevitably have to manage rising trade and investment tensions (in part, because of China's sheer size). Increasingly, China will compete internationally in the same product space as advanced countries and other emerging markets. Reflecting these trends, the number of disputes in the WTO involving China has accelerated in recent years and currently stands at 107 (78 as third party, 21 as respondent, and 8 as complainant). These are expected to rise in the short term. The share of developing-country antidumping actions against China (as a share of their total actions) increased from 19 percent in 2002 to 34 percent in 2009.[37]

With services rising as a share of GDP, productivity growth in services will become increasingly important in maintaining overall rapid growth, and this growth can be boosted by further opening the services sector to global competition. Moreover, a more efficient services sector will also advance the competitiveness of manufacturing as China moves up the value chain. In stark contrast to the important position China holds in global trade is its virtual lack of *presence in international financial markets*. In the next two decades, Chinese firms are likely to become regional and global companies, and they will need to invest and raise funds abroad. The international presence of Chinese commercial banks and other financial institutions that have close relations with Chinese firms can help in this process.

Moreover, China's emerging multinationals will face new challenges as they seek to become global players. China's *outward flows of foreign direct investment* have climbed rapidly over the past decade. Even as the stock of China's foreign investment remains a minuscule share of the global stock, efforts by Chinese companies to invest in other countries have already faced market access restrictions in several countries, and these tensions are likely to rise. Such restrictions are misguided, because Chinese multinationals can play an important role in a host country's development, by transferring technology and by integrating business practices and organizational approaches.

China faces other challenges in its external accounts. The combination of its current and capital account surpluses has resulted in record foreign exchange reserves, exposing China to notably increasing risks from any depreciation of the U.S. dollar or the euro and to limits on its macroeconomic policy space to contain inflation and domestic overheating.

As its interactions with the global economy continue to intensify, China will need to continue to protect its economic security and respond properly to risks that arise in other countries. The opening of the capital account as part of a possible initiative to internationalize the renminbi will, however, increase international capital movements and sudden changes in asset prices. China will also be more reliant on imported energy and raw materials, placing it at greater risk of supply disruptions arising from sharp price movements in global commodity markets. And the wide and increasingly deep application of the Internet and other information technologies will increase risks regarding information and financial security.

Finally, China is becoming an important source of development assistance to other developing countries, but its conditions, procedures, and approaches differ noticeably from those of some international donors. These differences did not matter when China's official development assistance was still small, but it is beginning to matter now and will be of increasing importance in coming years. China's processes—on tying aid, transparency of terms and conditions, and application of environmental and other safeguards—will come under increasing scrutiny as its development aid program grows in size.

Recommendations for Achieving Mutually Beneficial Trade and Investment Relations

Improving the external economic and trading environment. Given its high trade-to-GDP ratio relative to other large economies, the environment for international trade is crucial for China's future development, so promoting an open global trading system should remain an important policy objective. In the absence of a successful Doha Round, a multitude of bilateral and multilateral free trade agreements have emerged around the world (most notably in East Asia), and the number of preferential agreements has increased from about 70 in 1990 to almost 300 today; this poses a major challenge for China's future trade because Chinese exporters are increasingly excluded from the same preferential access as other exporters to key international markets.[38] China should adopt a strategy of emphasizing both multilateral and regional arrangements—abiding by and protecting existing multilateral agreements as well as pushing for further opening of global markets using multilateral channels. It should also proactively push ahead with the negotiations for accession to the WTO government procurement agreement as part of its effort to improve procurement procedures, enhance transparency, reduce costs, and enhance quality in government purchases. At the same time, China needs to proactively participate in regional trade agreements that lower trade barriers at and behind borders and introduce trade facilitation arrangements. Where possible, China should advocate "open regionalism," which requires that tariff levels agreed among regional partners be offered to other nonmember countries on a most-favored-nation basis.[39]

Further opening of the services sector to international trade and investment. Notwithstanding rapid opening up of China's services sector since its entry into the WTO, its policies on services trade remain more restrictive than policies in many developing countries and much more so than in high-income countries.[40] Further opening up the services market will help introduce advanced technology and managerial expertise, promote reforms, increase competition, and ultimately enhance the efficiency and competitiveness of China's services sector while, at the same time, providing China leverage in international trade negotiations to further open the services markets of trading partners.

Promoting outward FDI. By becoming global players, Chinese companies can capture higher value-added segments of the global production chain and exploit economies of scale. It can also be an effective strategy in anticipation of increased scarcity of low-skilled labor within China. Moreover, increased outward FDI can limit the continued expansion of foreign exchange reserves (in part to temper international protectionist sentiment). To facilitate the globalization of Chinese firms, the government should further promote outward FDI and perhaps even liberalize outward flows of portfolio capital. Bilateral investment protection agreements could help create a better investment environment for Chinese enterprises investing abroad. Given doubts about foreign investments made by Chinese state-owned enterprises, the focus should be on promoting outward FDI by private enterprises, thus enhancing their ability to operate internationally and, over time, to become global companies.

China should also consider supporting a multilateral investment agreement that liberalizes FDI flows, provides basic guarantees, and includes binding dispute resolution mechanisms. China's contribution toward the shaping of such a multilateral agreement would be to ensure that the terms would be appropriate for developing-country circumstances. Achieving stronger protection and easier access for all investors, including Chinese investors, would require granting reciprocal concessions to foreign investors in China, implying a dismantling of most restrictions on FDI inflows—something that would also be in China's long-term interest.

Steadily pushing ahead with the internationalization of the renminbi. Internationalizing China's currency will bring important long-term benefits for China. The renminbi is already being used increasingly as the currency for cross-border settlement (figure O.9). If a substantial portion of China's assets and trade were denominated in renminbi, then fluctuations in the dollar-renminbi exchange rate would have few implications for domestic stability. But internationalizing the renminbi requires opening the capital account, and that can be done only after China has in place a stable financial sector with improved corporate governance in banks and other financial institutions; well-functioning legal, supervisory, regulatory, and crisis management frameworks; deep financial markets with credible indirect monetary controls to manage liquidity; and an exchange rate that

FIGURE O.9   The renminbi is increasingly being used as the currency for cross-border trade settlement

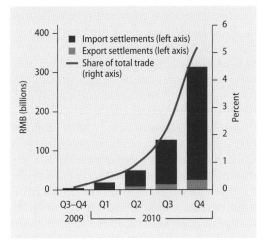

Source: People's Bank of China.
Note: China's total exports 2010: $1.75 trillion; China's total imports 2010: $1.52 trillion. Q = quarter; RMB = renminbi.

is made flexible over time. The many prerequisites for an open capital account was the main reason why many European countries took nearly 20 years after the collapse of the Bretton Woods system to achieve full capital account liberalization.[41] In the case of China, therefore, a relatively prudent approach, stretching over many years, is recommended in transitioning safely to a more open and efficient financial and exchange rate system.

A Stakeholder That Plays a Positive Role in Global Governance

With its growing share in the world economy and its rising per capita income, China has become an essential partner in the provision of global public goods. A growing number of global problems cannot be solved without China's active participation. China's future prosperity depends to a large extent on the capability of global collective action to make available key global public goods. It is in the common interests of the international community (and China) for China to become a key proactive stakeholder in these global governance arrangements. The fact that China is the second-largest economy in the world and yet ninety-third in terms of per capita income has created a huge gulf between the world's expectations about China's ability to shoulder important roles and responsibilities in global governance and China's perceptions of its own capabilities to do so. The process of China's participation in global governance will inevitably be gradual as the international community and China make constant adjustments to accommodate each other.

As China's strength in the global economy rises, the international community will expect China to play a more proactive role as a key stakeholder in *international governance rules for trade and capital flows*. In multilateral negotiations, China could capitalize on its unique position of straddling the interests of virtually the entire range of economies from low to high income. Its responsibilities will correspondingly increase. China can also wield enormous influence in shaping these rules to ensure that they are supportive of Chinese development. In particular, China's considerable impact on the global economy means that it can take, and would benefit from taking, a proactive stakeholder role in the design of such multilateral agreements.

China should continue to proactively *push forward global climate change negotiations*. China's 12th Five Year Plan already includes declining intensity of carbon dioxide emissions as a binding target. A fair and balanced global climate agreement could leverage these planned domestic actions by China, and make them more effective, without placing China at a competitive disadvantage. China's earnest efforts to reach this target and establish a market-based emissions reduction mechanism within the country will provide a solid basis to help shape a global agreement and create crucial win-win solutions. Failure on the part of major countries to reach agreement on climate change and contain the climate crisis will lead to serious consequences for the world economy and, in particular, developing countries, including China, that are likely to be the most severely affected by climate change. Such an agreement is also needed to create a level playing field and to avoid carbon tariffs, which can easily turn into protectionist measures. China's proactive role in the climate change negotiations is important

to put policies in place—such as international carbon trading—that are fair for developing countries and create win-win solutions for the world. Once carbon mitigation policies are implemented globally, incentives increase to invent and implement new green technologies. The resulting technological progress and economic growth can potentially turn the reduction of emissions into an opportunity instead of a burden.

China should proactively push for the reform of the international financial system. China's role in discussions on reforming the *international financial architecture* should be to ensure that the final outcome not only is consistent with China's own plans to liberalize its foreign exchange system, financial sector, and capital account, but is also appropriate for developing country conditions and suitable for strengthening the financial systems and the reduction of financial risks in developing countries. For example, it is necessary to assess the appropriateness of international prudential norms for China's financial system and their implications for China's interactions with global financial markets. Another example is the need to consider the proposal of establishing a derivatives clearinghouse and the capital needs for such institutions to ensure that they can reduce systemic risks facing China's financial system.

China also needs to be an active stakeholder in shaping the *international aid architecture*. As China has become a more significant source of concessional assistance, it can better improve aid effectiveness, by further enhancing the transparency of its foreign aid program, strengthening communication with OECD donors, and enhancing aid project management techniques.

Finally, China should increase its participation, contribution, and predictability in global governance in the international community and play a role commensurate with its capabilities. Over time it can better play its role as an international stakeholder if it strives to learn from the experience of other major powers in global governance, train its representatives in international governance institutions to be world class, and enhance the mechanism for and efficiency of internal coordination in international affairs.

Chapter 9   Overcoming Obstacles to Implementing Reforms

So far, this report has described a proposed medium-term reform program composed of six new strategic directions to make China a modern, harmonious, creative, and high-income society. Reaching this goal is important for China and for the world, but much will depend on the design and direction of the reforms as well as on their implementation.

International experience shows that the presence of a crisis may help a country reach internal consensus for action on reforms, but it also tends to make reform costs high and outcomes uncertain. Crises narrow policy options, dictate the pace of reform implementation, and prevent adequate preparation. The advantage of appropriately timing and sequencing policy reforms is lost. In some cases, crises also set in motion events that spin out of control and irreversibly shift economies to a lower growth path. Conversely, initiating reforms proactively allows adequate time for good policy design, appropriate sequencing, steady implementation, and corrective actions when necessary. Yet proactive reforms tend to be opposed by vested interests, and reaching consensus is difficult, requiring governments to be clear about objectives, communicating them well, consulting widely, and working to overcome obstacles.

In China's current situation, the case for reform is urgent. The world economy is entering a dangerous phase in its recovery from the global financial crisis, and the next five years could prove to be particularly difficult. At the same time, China's economic, social, and environmental challenges are increasing. China could postpone reforms and risk the possibility of an economic crisis in the future—or it could implement reforms proactively. Clearly, the latter approach is preferable. Over the past three decades, proactive policy change has been key to China's economic success, and the calls for reforms within the country have never been louder. In pushing for reforms proactively, China possesses the considerable advantage of good

economic conditions, robust growth, and the largest stock of foreign exchange reserves in the world. Moreover, it has able and effective central and local governments that have demonstrated strong capabilities for mobilization, organization, management, and implementation and, as in the past, can make the important collective action decisions needed to ensure successful outcomes.

Sequencing Reforms

The six priority reform areas lay out objectives for the short, medium, and long term, and policy makers need to sequence the reforms within and across these areas appropriately to ensure smooth implementation and to reach desired outcomes.

Highest priority should be given to actions that enjoy broad support, are likely to encounter little resistance, and are relatively easy to implement. Examples include increasing investment in human capital, encouraging public participation in the reform and development process, introducing a broad set of indicators to assess economic, social, and environmental progress and to measure the performance of local governments.

High priority should also be accorded to actions that deliver "quick wins" and address short-term risks. These actions include increasing the flexibility of bank deposit and lending rates and lowering high interest rate spreads; increasing SOE dividend payments to the national budget; stopping forced conversion of rural land for urban use, with any conversions based on vetted urban plans, payment of market prices for acquired land, and the introduction of a reasonable capital gains tax; raising the retirement age for men and women (which can be started soon but implemented gradually); removing fees for secondary education in rural areas; changing local government growth targets from indexes based on GDP to those based on "quality of growth"; raising energy, water, and carbon prices to reduce bottlenecks and shortages, encourage efficiency, and lower carbon emissions; and aggressively expanding public transport options.

The next priority is for actions that will form the basis of future reforms, offer incentives for innovation, and lay the foundations for future sustainable growth. These include introducing fiscal transparency as well as independent and rigorous evaluation of public expenditures; mobilizing additional fiscal revenues, including by rapidly ramping up implementation of property taxation in urban areas; recentralizing expenditure responsibility for key social security programs, such as the basic pension system and unemployment insurance, which will encourage labor mobility and integrate the labor market; phasing out the *hukou* system; lowering entry and exit barriers for firms; and imposing a carbon emissions quota, adopting tougher ecological and environmental standards, and introducing new building codes to meet energy efficiency and safety standards.

It is also important that the government make breakthroughs in core reforms to cement the foundations of a market economy and form the foundations for the rest of the reform program. The core of the program comprises the fiscal, financial, and enterprise reform components—key here are enterprise reforms (especially measures promoting competition) and pricing reforms for natural resources, including energy and raw materials. Not only are these very closely tied to one another, they are building blocks upon which the innovation, environmental, and social components rest. These core reforms are key to China's efforts to consolidate the foundations of a market economy. Their success will determine the success of the other elements needed to achieve sustainable and innovation-driven development.

In the medium term, efforts should focus on promoting innovation, green development, and participation in the reform and support for global governance.

Overcoming Opposition to Reform

Finally, as China knows only too well, and as is also the experience of other countries,

reforms and change always meet opposition. In China, this opposition is likely to take many forms, and the policy response should be accordingly varied and flexible. In summary, we identify three kinds of possible opposition.

The most resistant group is likely to be vested interests—such as those enterprises that enjoy partial or full monopoly (or monopsony) in key markets as well as firms, groups, institutions, and individuals who obtain special privileges and benefits or enjoy preferential treatment from the current power structure and institutional setting. These groups gain from a special relationship with decision makers or reap economic rents from distortions implicit in the current price, institutional, and administrative structures. Not only are these vested interests unlikely to surrender their privileged position easily, they are likely to be very influential, powerful, resourceful, and resolute in protecting their interests. Overcoming such opposition will require political courage, determination, clarity of purpose, and adroit leadership qualities at the highest level of the government.

A second group that may oppose the reform agenda are those who are likely to be hurt from reforms in the short term, even though they will gain in the long term. An example would be those affected by the proposal to reform the *hukou* system. In the long run, this reform would clearly be beneficial to China by helping to develop a more integrated and efficient labor market and also by lowering inequality in incomes and access to social services, which would reduce social tensions. But urban *hukou* holders, driven by concerns that their privileged access to public services and social security may be threatened, may not be supportive of these reforms. Similarly, workers in loss-making enterprises, energy- and pollution-intensive industries, and unregulated financial institutions may think the reforms will hurt their economic interests. If this were to happen, the government could not only provide appropriate information and guidance but also allocate such groups transitional assistance in the form of temporary income support and training in new skills. The government could also take steps to ensure that local governments do not thwart or undermine the reforms by placing local interests above national interests.

A third group is opinion makers who equate today's problems as outcomes of earlier reforms rather than of the distortions that remain. Some, for example, attribute the deterioration in the natural environment (air, water, land) to the market mechanisms rather than to ineffective implementation of existing laws, rules, and regulations, or inappropriate price and incentive structures. Their impact on public opinion is usually significant and out of proportion to their small numbers. It is important that such influential voices have access to the thinking, analysis, and rationale underlying the reform program. Government departments, think tanks, research institutions, and universities should be encouraged to analyze reform issues and disseminate their results. Indeed, involving the participation of civil society organizations not only will rally support for reforms but could improve the design of the reform program itself.

Winning over opposition to reforms will need to be a key part of the strategy and will require a calibrated response depending upon the reasons for the opposition. Strong leadership and commitment to the reforms will provide important signals, facilitate coordination across ministries and agencies, and ensure that opposition to reforms is dealt with sensitively and effectively.

As a practical matter, a high-powered reform commission needs to be established by—and with the full support of—the highest level of government. This commission should be made responsible for the design and implementation of the reform program. Only with such high-level support can reforms be implemented steadily and with a determined will. Commission members will need to undertake extensive and genuine consultations and discussions with all stakeholders so that everyone respects and understands the objectives of the reforms and the underlying rationale for policy changes and so that a proper balance is struck between the interests of various stakeholders. At the same time, reforms should be designed so that they do not create new interest groups supportive of distortive policies. Thus, fiscal or financial

incentives introduced to assist those who may be hurt by structural reforms should be temporary, and the conditions for their termination clearly established at the time of their initiation.

Finally, local governments and line ministries should be allowed to experiment with certain reforms within the framework of national policy objectives, and successful examples scaled up. China's success in previous reforms has built on the strength, flexibility, and adaptability of its institutions. Its future institutional evolution should continue to be firmly rooted within China's own reality and experience. Interest groups that oppose change usually find it difficult to argue against success—and successful reforms at the local level tend to grow their own champions who see benefits from the new policies. Moreover, it is only through learning-by-doing that implementation problems in reforms can be ironed out, so that when scaled up, the potential for opposition is minimized.

Managing Macroeconomic Risks and Vulnerabilities

Macroeconomic and social stability is not only key for innovation, investor confidence, and sustainable growth, it is also a fertile environment in which reforms—short and long term—can achieve desired outcomes. Over the next 20 years, it is important that China's record of stability be maintained given the possibility of greater risks. These risks include greater susceptibility to external economic shocks resulting from China's tighter economic integration with the world; weaknesses in government finances or in the financial and enterprise sectors, which might be revealed in a slowdown in China's economic growth as it is transitioning from middle-income to high-income status; possible social unrest, which could erupt in the face of perceived injustices; and greater danger from natural disasters (rise in sea levels, earthquakes, floods, droughts, tsunamis, pandemics), which are likely to be magnified by increasing urbanization.

Usually, risks are idiosyncratic, that is, they occur randomly. But occasionally, they can be covariant or systemic, when they occur together or have economy-wide effects. Economies can usually cope with idiosyncratic risk, but covariant or systemic risks are more difficult to manage. China is well prepared to deal with idiosyncratic risks, but it must anticipate the possibility of systemic risks and prepare appropriate responses.

Thanks to its impressive capacity for collective action, China has shown itself to be particularly effective at dealing with macroeconomic shocks (including those from abroad). The challenge to China is not whether it can respond well to crises but whether it can further lower the risk of future crises. Indeed, all risks—natural, economic, or social—are essentially contingent liabilities that can translate into actual liabilities for either government or households. Most important, measures to reduce risk are not only possible, they are usually cost-effective. For example, adequate prudential safeguards that prevent reckless behavior in the financial and enterprise sectors can help governments avoid costly expenses in the wake of a macroeconomic crisis; such safeguards can reduce the probability and the costs of a financial crisis. The benefits of such measures are often orders of magnitude higher than their costs.

Notwithstanding government efforts to ensure stability, the risk of macroeconomic shocks and instability cannot be completely eliminated and will need to be dealt with in a way that promotes medium-term reforms rather than sacrificing them. When shocks occur, the policy response should depend on the cause. If growth slows because of a temporary slowdown in demand, then countercyclical policies may be appropriate. But if the potential growth rate decreases, then countercyclical policies would be inappropriate, and instead, additional emphasis would need to be given to structural reforms.

The government should also take preventive action to reduce the size of "shock amplifiers"—which tend to be high debt (including high contingent debt) ratios in key parts of the economy such as banks, firms, households, and governments. Careful supervision of banks will need to ensure

that capital ratios are adequate, nonperforming loans accounted for properly and kept within prudential limits, and currency and asset-liability mismatches kept to a minimum. Balance sheets of banks, systemically important state enterprises, and local governments should be able to pass a variety of periodic stress tests (such as interest rate variability, exchange rate fluctuations, growth slowdowns, and capital flight).

International experience has shown how quickly a small spark can ignite widespread social unrest. According to surveys in China, the public's trust in the judicial system and public services is very low, and social frustration has been building. This situation points to the critical importance of building an impartial and effective legal and justice system and improving equality of opportunity and accessibility to high-quality social services. An essential element of reforms in these areas will be greater consultations and participation of the public in decision making and oversight of service delivery (including by the justice system), increased transparency in the operations of these branches of government, and greater accountability to stakeholders and citizens.

If one thing has been learned from systemic crises, it is the importance of avoiding overconfidence and remaining vigilant against potential problems from social, economic, and natural causes. Countries need to ensure that such vigilance is incorporated into the national risk management system. That can be done in five ways:

First, risk management requirements should be embedded firmly in national regulations, policies, and public investments. In addition, weaknesses in economic and financial systems should be probed constantly to identify where a crisis may arise and appropriate preventive action taken. Regular risk audits for critical parts of the financial infrastructure and systemically important enterprises can reveal where structural or other flaws may expose the broader economy to unnecessary risk.

Second, because risk management tends to cut across institutional jurisdictions, not only is coordination needed across different agencies and levels of government, so too is clarity on who is responsible and accountable for what.

Third, the government can and should make information more easily accessible to help individuals, households, and firms take risk mitigation measures or preventive action.

Fourth, risk management institutions need to be capable of quick and decisive action when crises occur, be receptive to all ideas from all sources, and be able to build partnerships for collective action, especially with communities that hold a stake in the outcome.

Fifth, neither prevention nor mitigation can completely eliminate risk, so insurance is needed to soften the blow when macroeconomic disasters unfold. One insurance policy is China's already large external reserves. Another would be to keep adequate fiscal space by maintaining a prudent public debt burden. A third would be strong supervision of the financial system. And a fourth would be a deposit insurance program that discourages reckless lending and encourages prudent financial management, such as observance of capital requirements.

In managing social and macroeconomic risks, three principles need to be kept in mind: the first is to guard against a retreat from the market mechanism and a return to administrative measures; the second is to press ahead with long-term reforms, because structural factors usually lie at the root of many of China's periodic episodes of macroeconomic overheating; and the third is to ensure that risk mitigation strategies are consistent with, and reinforce, the long-term strategy.

China's road toward a modern, harmonious, creative, and high-income society will be filled with challenges; but the goal has never been closer. The world's economic landscape will change when China becomes a high-income country. China's rapid growth and poverty reduction over the past three decades—achieved through domestic reforms and opening up to the global economy—was nothing short of a miracle. The next two decades could witness another miracle in which China's economic, social, and cultural contributions will not only benefit China's own people but also contribute to global economic prosperity and stability. Much will depend on the wisdom, strength, and determination of the Chinese leadership in pressing ahead with reforms in the six key areas highlighted in this report.

Notes

1. The term "provinces" here includes municipalities and autonomous regions that have the same status as provinces.
2. http://www.bankersalmanac.com/addcon /infobank/bank-rankings.aspx).
3. http://money.cnn.com/magazines/fortune /global500/2011/.
4. http://aapa.files.cms-plus.com/PDFs /WORLD%20PORT%20RANKINGS%20 2009.pdf.
5. Although the reputation of forecasting is rightly in disrepute, even for the short term, let alone the medium or long term, national development strategies do need to consider future trends in the global environment, difficult as that may be. The authors recognize that discontinuities and shocks, by their very nature, are difficult to anticipate. Ideas, technologies, events, and individual actions can sometimes snowball into powerful forces of change—the so-called "butterfly effect" that occurs when initial conditions are such that a small change triggers large consequences.
6. Estimates of the scope of the middle class vary depending on the definition. The estimate quoted here is from Kharas and Geertz (2010), who define the middle class as falling within the threshold levels of $10 a day to $100 a day per capita (measured in 2005 PPP terms).
7. The old age dependency ratio is defined as the ratio of the number of people aged 65 years and older to those aged between 15 and 64 years.
8. During 1994–2009, particularly high TFP growth continued in part because of SOE restructuring, WTO accession, and very successful integration in the world economy of China's manufacturing industry and associated economies of scale. With a lower contribution expected from such forces, TFP growth (excluding the contribution of human capital formation), is expected to fall by half a percentage point to 2.5 percent a year in 2010–15 and ease thereafter to around 2 percent in 2026–30. By way of comparison, in 1966–90, annual TFP growth in Hong Kong SAR, China; the Republic of Korea; Singapore; and Taiwan, China, averaged between 1.7 and 2.3 percent. This average includes the

contribution of human capital accumulation, which is separated out in our analysis.

9. The U.S. labor force numbers about 155 million. The calculation assumes that over the next decade, China's tertiary education completion rate rises to the advanced country average, where the advanced country average is determined based on data from Barro and Lee (2010).

10. The population of Hong Kong SAR, China is around 7 million.

11. Based on the global wealth study prepared by the Boston Consulting Group (2011).

12. Estimate for 2010 using 2005 purchasing power parity prices based on staff calculations in Povcalnet (http://web.worldbank .org/wbsite/external/extdec/extresearch /extprograms/extpovres/extpovcalnet/).

13. The term "state dominance" goes beyond just state ownership and includes active state involvement in investment and other management decisions.

14. Unfortunately, the average profitability of the rest of the SOEs cannot be calculated for lack of data.

15. TFP growth in the state sector was 1.5 percent a year, whereas the nonstate sector's TFP grew at a rate of 4.6 percent a year; see Brandt and Zhu (2010).

16. For example, in 2006, state enterprises accounted for the production of all petroleum, natural gas, and ethylene; all basic telecoms services; about 55 percent of electricity generation; and 82 percent of airline and air cargo traffic (see Owen and Zheng 2007).

17. A pure "public good or service" is one whose consumption by one individual does not reduce its availability for consumption by others, and when no one can be effectively excluded from using the good. The term, as used in this report, applies to those goods and services that, when produced or consumed, result in positive externalities that are not remunerated, and hence tend to be underproduced.

18. However, in some sectors such as telecoms, the splitting up was along geographic lines, still leaving a single dominant provider in any given area.

19. Land Resources Statistical Yearbooks 2002–09, published by the Ministry of Land Resources.

20. The National Audit Office report is available at http://www.audit.gov.cn/n1992130 /n1992150/n1992500/2752208.html.

21. An alternative approach could be the one adopted by Korea, which provides affected farmers with a plot located within a developed urban area equivalent to 40 percent of the acquired land area. Such a program, however, may incur administrative delays and lead to very different outcomes for farmers affected by the same land acquisition transaction.

22. OECD Stat Extracts: http://stats.oecd.org /index.aspx?DataSetCode=REV.

23. Based on data from Sam Ock Park (2009).

24. Sixth National Population Census, National Bureau of Statistics of China (NBSC), People's Republic of China.

25. The amount of "surplus labor" in rural areas, and therefore the number of potential rural-urban migrants, is the subject of much study and controversy; see Knight, Quheng, and Shi (2010).

26. There remain cases in very large cities where this process remains incomplete, such as in Beijing where applicants for government jobs and for many enterprises require a Beijing *hukou* to be considered.

27. MOHRSS (Ministry of Human Resources and Social Security) data from end-2010.

28. Sunrise industries are the opposite of sunset industries—relatively "young" industries with future growth prospects, unlike sunset industries that are mature and likely to decline in relative size.

29. The three key underlying concepts are that growth and resource use can be "decoupled," that the process of "going green" can itself be a source of growth, and that green development and economic growth could potentially reinforce one another.

30. World Bank estimates using 2008 data. In addition, more than half of China's water is polluted, over 300 million people use contaminated water supplies, a third of China's waterways are below the government's own safety standards, and about a fifth of China's farmland has been contaminated with heavy metals (Ministry of Environmental Protection 2011).

31. For 2008, the last year for which data is available.

32. Several such taxes address negative externalities. Unlike many other taxes, such taxes present few if any trade-offs when viewed in a more holistic way than through GDP alone, because they make prices better reflect the true marginal cost of a particular activity, including the damage to environment.

33. Zhang (2010) provides a detailed discussion on SOE dividend policy and international practices.

34. Furthermore, the "revenue productivity" of personal income taxes (PIT), measured as the revenue collected as a share of GDP divided by the weighted average PIT rate, is only 15 percent of global averages and 11 percent of high-income country averages.

35. http://www.audit.gov.cn/n1992130 /n1992150/n1992500/2752208.html.

36. Liu (2010) and Liu and Pradelli (forthcoming) give a detailed discussion on the regulatory framework of subnational government debt management.

37. Antidumping is not the only mechanism used to discriminate against China's exports. Others include the Transitional Product-Specific Safeguard Mechanism (a unique feature of China's WTO accession that allows importers to invoke safeguards against China through 2014, with less evidentiary requirements than under the normal safeguards regime), the traditional safeguards regime, voluntary export restraints (particularly as a result of U.S. and EU investigations of China's textile and apparel exports, and despite the banning of voluntary export restraints under the WTO Agreement on Safeguards), and countervailing measures under antisubsidy policies (Bown 2007). Recourse to such instruments will become more difficult when China attains market economy status in 2016.

38. Only 6 percent of China's exports enjoy preferential access, well below the world average.

39. "Open regionalism" ensures that "regional agreements will in practice be building blocks for further global liberalization rather than stumbling blocks that deter such progress" (Bergsten 1997).

40. Insurance remains closed in many respects, majority foreign ownership is prohibited in some sectors (such as telecommunications and air transport), and provision of domestic legal services is restricted.

41. The end of the Bretton Woods system between 1968 and 1973 was meant to eliminate the need for capital controls, but European countries did not achieve full capital account liberalization until the late 1980s and early 1990s, and then only because liberalization was seen as a step toward monetary integration.

References

Bahl, Roy. 2009. "Fixing the Property and Land Tax Regime in Developing Countries." Draft, February 25, 2009.

Barro, R. J., and J. W. Lee. 2010. "A New Data Set of Educational Attainment in the World, 1950–2010." Working Paper 15902, National Bureau of Economic Research, Cambridge, MA.

Baumert, Kevin A., Timothy Herzog, and Jonathan Pershing. 2005. *Navigating the Numbers: Greenhouse Gas Data and International Climate Policy*, chapter 6. Washington, DC: World Resources Institute.

Bergsten, C. Fred. 1997. "Open Regionalism." Working Paper 97-3, Petersen Institute for International Economics, Washington, DC. http://www.iie.com/publications/wp /wp.cfm?ResearchID=152.

Boston Consulting Group. 2011. "Shaping a New Tomorrow: How to Capitalize on the Momentum of Change." Boston (June 21) http:// www.bcg.com/media/PressReleaseDetails .aspx?id=tcm:12-77753.

Bown, C. P. 2007. "China's WTO Entry: Antidumping, Safeguards, and Dispute Settlement." Working Paper 13349, National Bureau of Economic Research, Cambridge, MA.

Brandt, L., and Xiaodong Zhu. 2010. "Accounting for China's Growth." Working Paper 395, Department of Economics, University of Toronto, Toronto (February).

Commission on Growth and Development. 2008. *The Growth Report Strategies for Sustained Growth and Inclusive Development*. Washington, DC: World Bank.

Eeckhout, Jan, and Boyan Jovanovic. 2007. "Occupational Choice and Development." Working Paper 13686, National Bureau of Economic Research, Cambridge, MA.

Feng, Shao. 2011. "Introducing a Public 'Happiness Index' into Government Performance Appraisals" (in Chinese). *Decision Making and Information* 314: 58.

Gill, Indermit, Homi Kharas, and others. 2007. *An East Asian Renaissance: Ideas for Economic Growth*. Washington, DC: World Bank.

Heston, Alan, Robert Summers, and Bettina Aten. 2011. Penn World Table Version 7.0. Center for International Comparisons of Production, Income and Prices at the University of Pennsylvania, Philadelphia (May).

Holzmann, Robert, David Robalino, Noriyuki Takayama, eds. 2009. *Closing the Coverage Gap: The Role of Social Pensions and Other Retirement Income Transfers*. Washington DC: World Bank.

Jin, Songqing, and Klaus Deininger. 2009. "Land Rental Markets in the Process of Rural Structural Transformation: Productivity and Equity

Impacts from China." *Journal of Comparative Economics* 37: 629–46.

Kharas, H., and G. Geertz. 2010. "The New Global Middle Class: A Cross-Over from West to East." In *China's Emerging Middle Class: Beyond Economic Transformation,* edited by C. Li (chapter 2). Washington, DC: Brookings Institution Press.

Knight, John, Deng Quheng, and Li Shi. 2010. "The Puzzle of Migrant Labor Shortage and Rural Labor Surplus in China." Discussion Paper Series 494, Department of Economics, University of Oxford, Oxford, U.K. (July).

Li, H., L. Meng, Q. Wang, and L. Zhou. 2008. "Political Connections, Financing and Firm Performance: Evidence from Chinese Private Firms." *Journal of Development Economics* 87 (2008): 283–99.

Lin, Justin Yifu. 2012. *Demystifying the Chinese Economy.* Cambridge, U.K.: Cambridge University Press.

Liu, Lili, 2010. "Strengthening Subnational Debt Financing and Managing Risks." In *Review of Economic Research.* Ministry of Finance, China; August 16, 2010, 46 F-9. Beijing.

Liu, Lili and Juan Pradelli. Forthcoming. "China Financing Infrastructure and Monitoring Fiscal Risks at Subnational Level: Strategic Considerations and Policy Options." Policy Note, World Bank, Beijing.

Liu, Shijin, et al. 2011. *The Trap or the Wall: The Real Challenges to China's Economy and Its Strategic Choices.* Beijing: CITIC Press.

Maddison, Angus. 2001. *The World Economy: A Millennial Perspective.* Paris: OECD Publishing.

———. 2010. Statistics on World Population, GDP and Per Capita GDP, 1-2008 AD. http://www.ggdc.net/MADDISON/oriindex.htm.

Milanovic, B. 2005. Worlds Apart: *Measuring International and Global Inequality.* Princeton NJ: Princeton University Press.

Ministry of Environmental Protection and Chinese Academy of Engineering. 2011. *Macro-Strategy for China's Environment: Strategy for Protection of China's Environmental Factors* (in Chinese). 2 vols. Beijing: China Environmental Sciences Press.

Ministry of Land and Resources PRC. 2002–09. *China Land and Resources Statistical Yearbook.* Beijing: Geological Publishing House (GPH) of China.

NBSC (National Bureau of Statistics of China). Various years. *China Statistical Yearbook.* Beijing: China Statistics Press.

OECD (Organisation for Economic Co-operation and Development). 2010. "Green Growth Strategy: Implementing Our Commitment for a Sustainable Future." Statement of a meeting of the OECD Council at Ministerial Level, Paris. May 27–28.

Owen, Bruce, and Wentong Zheng. 2007. "China's Competition Policy Reforms: The Antimonopoly Law and Beyond." Discussion Paper 06-32, Stanford Institute for Economic Policy Research, Stanford, California.

Park, Sam Ock. 2009. "An History of the Republic of Korea's Structural Transformation and Spatial Development." In *Reshaping Economic Geography in East Asia,* edited by Y. Huang and A. Magnoli Bocchi, 320–37. Washington, DC: World Bank.

The People's Bank of China. "China Monetary Policy Report." Various issues, 2009q1–2011q2. Available at http://www.pbc.gov.cn.

Ravallion, Martin, and Shaohua Chen. 2008. "The Developing World Is Poorer than We Thought, But No Less Successful in the Fight against Poverty." Policy Research Working Paper 4703, World Bank, Washington, DC.

Shanghai Jiao Tong University. 2010. "Academic Ranking of World Universities." Institute of Higher Education, Shanghai Jiao Tong University. http://www.arwu.org.

State Council. 2011. "Outline for Poverty Reduction and Development of China's Rural Areas (2011–2020)." Information Office of the State Council, Beijing.

Subramanian, Arvind. 2011. *Eclipse: Living in the Shadow of China's Economic Dominance.* Washington, DC: Peterson Institute of International Economics.

UN (United Nations). 2009. "World Urbanization Prospects: The 2009 Revision." UN Department of Economic and Social Affairs, Population Division, Geneva.

———. 2010. "World Population Prospects: The 2010 Revision." UN Department of Economic and Social Affairs, Population Division, New York.

UNSD (U.N. Statistics Division). 2010. "National Accounts: Estimates of Main Aggregates." New York.

Wang, Hui, Tan Tao, and Joyce Yanyun Man. 2010. "To Reallocate or Not? Reconsidering the Dilemma for China's Agricultural Land Tenure Policy." Peking-University–Lincoln Institute Working Paper Series 040. Beijing (October) http://www.plc.pku.edu.cn/en _publications.aspx.

World Bank. 2010. "Fixing the Public Hospital System in China." China Health Policy Notes, World Bank, Washington, DC.

World Bank. 2011a. Global Development Horizons 2011. Washington, DC: World Bank.

———. 2011b. *World Development Indicators.* Washington, DC: World Bank (September).

Yao, Yang. 2010. "Is the Era of Cheap Chinese Labor Over?" *Economist,* July 16 .http://www.economist.com/economics/by -invitation/guest-contributions/no_lewisian _turning_point_has_not_yet_arrived.

Zhang, Wenkui. 2010. "The Direction and Task for China's SOEs Reform in the 12th five-Year Plan Period." (in Chinese). Research Report 203, Development Research Center, Beijing.

Part II

Supporting Reports

China: Structural Reforms for a Modern, Harmonious, Creative Society

China's remarkable economic growth over the past three decades has brought many positive results and set the country on a path to become a high-income economy. But the pattern of growth has introduced new economic, social, environmental, and external challenges that could ultimately slow growth and work against the stated goal of building a "harmonious society."

To become a high-income economy by 2030, China will need to sustain relatively rapid economic growth. However, three factors look set to contain growth going forward. First, the contribution from labor will decrease in line with lower and eventually negative expansion of the working-age population. Second, the need to achieve more "intensive" and more balanced growth may require a gradual decline in the ratio of investment to gross domestic product (GDP), albeit the ratio will remain at very high levels. Third, the scope for gains in total factor productivity (TFP) from rapid factor reallocation and the simple copying or transfer of technology will taper off as China approaches the later stages of industrialization.

In this setting, the key to sustaining relatively fast growth will be keeping the rate of increase in TFP growth near its past high rates, through policies and reforms to further improve economic efficiency. Within-firm improvements in *technical efficiency* can be generated by technological innovation, better management, exploitation of scale economies, agglomeration economies linked to successful urbanization, and productivity improvements spurred by enhanced competition. Improvements in *allocative efficiency* would come through the movement of factors of production from lower to higher productivity uses (firms, sectors, locations). Better resource allocation would sustain the pace, alter the pattern, and boost the quality of growth. Such efficiency gains have been an important part of China's growth story to date and are far from exhausted. To unleash such efficiency gains, China needs to move from a growth model appropriate for a period of "catch up" to one driven by efficiency and innovation. Building on modeling results, the report argues that sustained reforms could deliver growth rates that, while lower than those of the past three decades, will still allow China to join the group of high-income countries by 2030.

However, as long recognized by China's leaders, growth is no longer enough. Simultaneously achieving a "harmonious society" will also require progress in making growth more equitable, environmentally sustainable, and balanced. Specific challenges include creating conditions for more employment generation and for improvements in "the distribution of primary income," in the quality of and access to public services, in expanded social security and other reductions in vulnerability, and in efforts to create a less resource-intensive form of growth.

Indeed, the report shows how concerted reforms to address key remaining distortions can put China on a development path that delivers both relatively fast growth and improvements in key social, environmental, and external indicators. In contrast, such an outcome is inconceivable under broadly unchanged policies. In fact, an attempt to sustain the past growth model for an extended period could lead to a forced change in course as China finally reaches some of the limits of economic, social, environmental, or external sustainability. Whether through a controlled change in policy or through a crisis, such a hasty shift would lead to sharply lower savings and investment rates, putting China on a slower growth path. This reality further strengthens the case for proactive reforms.

Such fundamental policy reforms will need to go hand in hand with increases in some categories of public spending. These needed increases have two implications. First, the fiscal system needs to be strengthened to help deliver the level and quality of public social, environmental, and infrastructural services deemed central to the vision of China 2030. Second, public resources will need to be raised efficiently and allocated in a way that rapid growth is maintained even as China approaches the technology frontier in a number of sectors. This is a bigger challenge than it may appear at first blush since many other constraints to growth—including an anemic global economy and a shrinking and aging labor force—also need to be overcome. This report argues they can be overcome through reforms in China's enterprise sector as well as in its input markets—land, labor, and capital.

The fiscal system. The large social and environmental agenda over the next two decades will entail significant expansion of social protection, health care, environmental public investment, and recurrent expenditures, mostly by subnational governments. However, such increases will need to be achieved while maintaining fiscal sustainability, avoiding levels of taxation that could harm growth, easing the fiscal pressures on subnational governments, and strengthening fiscal institutions. Over the next two decades, then, the challenge will be sixfold: changing the composition and improving the efficiency of public expenditures in line with China's evolving development objectives; improving the efficiency of revenue mobilization; realigning revenues with expenditure responsibilities by raising selected functions to higher levels of government and allowing some governments to charge local taxes; bringing on budget all subnational government borrowing and the associated spending, and putting them under strict controls; equalizing subprovincial transfers across lower levels of government; and improving the accountability and transparency of governments.

The enterprise sector. A vibrant corporate sector will be critical for sustaining relatively fast growth. The central elements will be further increases in competition, especially (but not only) between the state and nonstate (including private) enterprises in the "strategic" and "pillar" industries where competition has been curtailed, and redefinition of the function of state capital. To promote the securitization and trading of state capital, state capital should be used solely for the provision of public goods and services. This reform requires restructuring the state-owned enterprise (SOE) sector, dismantling monopolies and oligopolies in sectors where competition would yield superior results, introducing oversight arrangements where monopolies are considered necessary to ensure that market power is not abused and does not act as a drag on the economy, and lowering entry and exit barriers for all enterprises. Improved allocative efficiency will also require further efforts to level the playing field, especially between smaller and larger firms, and between state-owned and nonstate firms, not only in a legal sense, but also in the access to key inputs. The portfolio of SOEs should be diversified, some state shares should be sold in the market over time, and modern corporate governance practices should be exercised in SOEs. Finally, this restructuring will require a review and modernization of the extensive "industrial policies" that the authorities have used to influence the structure within and across sectors.

The allocation of factors of production. If anything, improving the efficiency in the use of factors of production—land, labor, capital—will be more challenging than reforming the enterprise sector. However, this sphere is also the one in which many significant distortions remain, suggesting much potential from reforms to improve resource allocation.

In land, the principal challenges are to enhance security of rural land tenure and to ensure the equal treatment of rural and urban land tenure and property rights for social stability, particularly in rural areas; to modernize the institution of the rural collective so that it remains relevant in the face of evolving shifts in law and policy; to address the strict separation of rural and urban land tenure systems, which currently drives the inefficiencies and inequities generated by the process of converting rural land into urban use, by reducing the role of state in the land conversion process and by allowing for more market-based allocation of land; to ensure the protection of priority farmland for food security through comprehensive land use planning; and to introduce taxation of land and property to help ease the distortions and social pressures created by subnational governments' reliance on revenues from land transfer fees.

The financial sector faces a few key reform challenges. First, there is a need to commercialize and rationalize financial institutions and markets to meet the diverse demands of households, enterprises, and government sectors for financial services and products. To this end, financial institutions should be better governed and operate in a conducive policy environment under competitive pressure

and effective regulation and supervision. In addition, there is a need to further liberalize interest rates; deepen the capital market; upgrade financial infrastructure and the legal framework; strengthen the regulation and supervision framework; build a financial safety net and develop crisis management and insolvency schemes; and recast the rights and responsibilities of government.

These reforms are united by one common theme—"reforming government." For much of the past three decades, and unlike in countries that belong to the Organisation for Economic Co-operation and Development (OECD), government has maintained a direct role in allocating resources, with instruments such as industrial policy and state ownership leading to tight interconnections between governments and enterprises. In contrast, in health, education, social security, and other areas typically considered to require state involvement because of market failures, China's government had initially retreated. Traditional arrangements were abandoned, and government spending lagged behind. The report identifies specific ways in which the role of the government can be recalibrated, generally toward a more limited direct role in resource allocation, a more arm's-length relationship between government and business, and an enhanced role in delivering public goods and services and ensuring equality of opportunity. Reviewing the interrelationships between various tiers of government will play a key role in this recalibration.

Setting the Stage: China's Past Economic Performance, Key Challenges, and Future Growth Potential

Rapid Past Growth and its Sources

China's remarkable economic development over the past three decades has brought many positive results. Growth averaged 10 percent a year, far faster than in nearly any other country. This growth drove a parallel reduction of the poverty rate from 65 percent to well below 10 percent (World Bank 2009a).

As a result, China has become the world's second largest economy (accounting for 9.5 percent of global GDP in 2010), its largest exporter (with a global market share of over 10 percent and rising) and manufacturer, and an increasingly important engine of global growth.

As elaborated in annex 1A, China's fast growth can be explained from various perspectives. It was a type of growth characteristic of a catch-up phase, where the combination of government-driven resource mobilization and pragmatic and effective market-oriented reforms allowed the country to exploit the "advantages of backwardness." Additional factors such as China's large market size, a "demographic dividend," the successful harnessing of globalization, and a large and disciplined workforce contributed to China's boom in manufacturing. Market-oriented reforms unlocked a vast pool of entrepreneurial talent, which further contributed to vigorous growth.

While the market mechanism was continuously expanded and now plays the lead role in resource allocation, the government has played a strong role during China's economic take-off. In general, the government has used its regulations and powers in ways that favor the extensive input of capital and other factors to foster fast industrialization and urbanization. The government's focus on expanding industrial investments has helped to promote reallocation of factors from low-productivity agriculture to higher-productivity manufacturing. Over time, however, the government's strong role, especially its influence on factor allocation, has contributed to ever more serious economic imbalances and social disharmonies. Going forward, this strong role can also be detrimental to improvements in technical efficiency, creative power, and entrepreneurship at a time when China's growth will depend more on innovation.

The Emergence of Imbalances

This rapid growth and the accompanying structural change, while serving China well in many respects, also introduced new economic, social, environmental, and external challenges that work against the government's stated goal of building a "harmonious society."[1] Spurred by high savings, cheap finance and other inputs, and export-oriented policies, China's growth has been investment- and industry-led. The priority accorded to industry stunted the development of services, while the emphasis on physical investment led to lower investment in human capital. In turn, highly capital-intensive growth meant that China's economy created few jobs per unit of urban GDP growth.[2] With wages lagging behind productivity growth, the share of wage income in GDP declined to 48 percent by 2008, driving the share of consumption in GDP to unprecedentedly low levels for a major economy. These trends contributed to high and widening income disparities. Social imbalances were exacerbated by pronounced unevenness in access to public services and by tensions surrounding land acquisition. On the environmental front, rapid growth, a shift in production toward more energy-intensive industries, and urbanization have combined to make China the world's largest energy user. Fast growth has also led to substantial depletion of natural resources and serious environmental pollution. Finally, many of the policies that generated China's internal imbalances also contributed to its twin current and capital account surpluses. Together with China's expanding global market share, they fueled protectionist pressures in key foreign markets.

Avoiding the "Middle-Income Trap" while Addressing Key Imbalances

To become a modern, harmonious, and creative high-income society by 2030, China will need to sustain relatively rapid growth while addressing the noted economic, social, environmental, and global imbalances. In countries near China's level of per capita GDP, the first challenge is often termed that of avoiding the "middle-income trap" (Gill and Kharas 2007).

Two factors are set to contain China's growth rate going forward. The contribution from labor will decrease in line with lower, and eventually (from around 2015) negative, expansion of the working-age population. Similarly, if some income will be transferred from enterprises to households either because of a need to achieve social objectives or because of a tightening labor market, and if growth must become more "intensive" to meet environmental goals, the ratio of investment to GDP could gradually decline, albeit still remaining at very high levels.[3] In addition, somewhat lower investment rates will reduce the scope for the transfer of technologies embedded in new equipment. In any case, as China moves from a technological "catch-up phase" toward the frontier, a smaller share of productivity improvements will take such embedded form.

In this setting, the key to avoiding the middle-income trap is keeping TFP growth near its past high rates, through policies and reforms to further improve the efficiency of China's economy. Without new impulses to raise TFP, growth could slow rapidly, exposing China's economy to heightened risks. Within-firm improvements in *technical efficiency* can be generated by technological innovation, better organization and management, exploitation of scale economies (including from consolidation of supply chains), agglomeration economies linked to successful urbanization, and productivity improvements spurred by enhanced competition. Parallel improvements in *allocative efficiency* would come through the movement of factors of production from lower- to higher-productivity uses (firms, sectors, locations). Better resource allocation would sustain the pace, alter the pattern, and boost the quality of growth. As elaborated in box 1.1, such efficiency gains have been an important part

BOX 1.1   Significant potential remains for further productivity gains through factor reallocation

Several detailed studies of China's past performance support the conclusion that factor reallocation has been a major contributor to its productivity growth. Hsieh and Klenow (2009) seek to measure the degree to which resource misallocation has lowered aggregate total factor productivity (TFP) in China and India. They model how distortions that drive wedges between the marginal products of capital and labor across firms will lower aggregate TFP. Using microdata, they find large gaps in marginal products of capital and labor across plants within narrowly defined industries in China compared with the United States. By hypothetically reallocating capital and labor to equalize marginal products to the extent observed in the United States, they calculate potential manufacturing TFP gains of 50.5 percent in China in 1998. By 2005, these potential gains had been reduced to 30.5 percent, indicating progress in improving resource allocation in the intervening period as well as large remaining scope for further improvements.

Brandt and Zhu (2010) seek to quantify the sources of China's past growth. The authors consider three sectors: agriculture, the state part of non-agriculture, and the nonstate part of nonagriculture. They find the increase in TFP in the latter sector to be the key driver of growth. They also find significant misallocation of capital, with the less efficient state sector absorbing over half of all fixed investment, while representing only 13 percent of employment. The authors calculate that if capital had been allocated efficiently across the state and nonstate sectors, with more going to the latter, China could have achieved the same growth without the observed increase in the rate of aggregate investment from 21 percent of GDP in 1978 to 40 percent in 2007. Looking forward, reducing distortions in capital markets could help China maintain relatively rapid growth while simultaneously reducing the imbalances between consumption and investment.

Bai, Hsieh, and Qian (2006) also look at the dispersion of returns to capital across sectors, regions, and types of ownership. They find clear evidence of misallocation but also some evidence that it may have lessened over time, thus contributing to China's growth performance. Bulman and Kraay (2011) find that factor reallocation has accounted for about 2.2 percentage points of growth over the period 1979–2008, or more than one-half of the total growth in TFP. This contribution appears to have been on a declining trend.

BOX 1.2   **How fast will China need to grow to achieve high-income status by 2030?**

Between 1989 and 2009, the World Bank threshold between upper-middle-income and high-income countries grew by an average of 3.5 percent a year (nominal U.S. dollars). Assuming that this threshold continues to grow at the same rate, the high-income threshold in 2030 would be $24,079 per capita. To reach this level by 2030, China's GDP per capita in dollars would have to grow at an average of 8.9 percent a year. Based on a projected population growth of 0.4 percent a year, this would require average GDP growth of 9.3 percent a year, in dollar terms. Assuming 2.3 percent U.S. inflation, average annual real GDP would have to grow 6.2 percent if real

exchange rate appreciation is 0.8 percent a year, and 4 percent average real GDP growth if real exchange rate appreciation is 3 percent a year.

Alternative assumptions about each indicator are easy to apply in this simple framework. For example, if the threshold were assumed to grow by around 4.5 percent a year instead of 3.5 percent, the required GDP growth rate would rise to 5–7.2 percent. Similarly, targeting a 2030 GDP per capita 10 percent above the formal high-income threshold would require a 0.5 percentage point higher average growth rate.

of China's growth story to date. They are far from exhaustion, however, and can be unlocked through further reforms.

China could formally reach high-income status with average GDP growth rates quite a bit below those it achieved over the past three decades. The threshold beyond which an economy is deemed to be high, middle, or low income is naturally arbitrary. Nonetheless, the World Bank employs such thresholds for classifying its client members. Box 1.2 provides illustrative calculations of the growth rates needed to carry China to the Bank's high-income threshold by 2030. Because global growth is moving this marker, while the relevant Chinese growth rate is the product of domestic GDP growth and the evolution of the yuan-dollar exchange rate, these calculations produce a range of estimates from 4 percent to 6.2 percent. Reaching a higher level above this very minimal threshold would require faster average growth; the average per capita income of high-income countries is more than three times this threshold level.

Prominent projections of China's future potential growth bracket this range of growth rates, suggesting that high-income status by 2030 is achievable. For example, Lin (2011) argues that China could still grow at around 8 percent a year over the next 20 years, based on a comparison with the performance of

Japan, Republic of Korea, and Taiwan, China, over periods when their per capita GDP relative to that of the United States was similar to that of China today. In a recent multicountry review of growth performance, Eichengreen, Park, and Shin (2011) project China to grow by 6.1 to 7.0 percent a year in the 2011–20 decade and by 5.0 to 6.2 percent a year over 2021–30. Finally, Lee and Hong (2010) forecast average growth over the period 2011–30 of 5.5 percent under a "baseline" scenario and 6.6 percent under a "reform" scenario. Our own projections (given later) imply average growth of 6.6 percent over the next 20 years under a reform scenario, also suggesting that such a target is within reach.

However, growth is no longer enough. Simultaneously achieving a "harmonious society" along with high-income status will also require progress in making growth more equitable, environmentally sustainable, and balanced. Specific challenges include creating conditions for more employment generation and for improvements in the distribution of "primary income," in the quality of and access to public services, in expanded social security and other means of reducing vulnerability, and in efforts to create a less resource-intensive form of growth.

China's top leaders have long recognized this need. As a result, the need for a new growth model has been the paramount objective of all key government policy statements since the annual Central Economic Work Conference of December 2004.[4] The following year, changing the growth pattern became an overarching thrust of the 11th Five Year Plan (5YP) 2006–10. In a major shift from previous plans, where growth was the dominant objective, the 11th 5YP also emphasized environmental and social objectives. While some progress has been made, the agenda is far from complete (World Bank 2009c). These aims have now been maintained and reinforced as central pillars of the 12th 5YP.[5] The need for more fundamental structural change to achieve such objectives has also long been stressed by many analysts of China's economy.[6]

Possible Scenarios to 2030

This understanding is also supported by the results of economic modeling, which deliver two strong messages. The first is a positive one. Concerted reforms to address key remaining distortions can lead China to a development path that delivers both relatively rapid growth and improvements in key structural, social, environmental, and external indicators. Second, and in contrast, such an outcome is inconceivable under broadly unchanged policies. Under such a scenario, while growth could still remain relatively high, key social, environmental, and external indicators would worsen significantly.

How might China's economy evolve over the next 20 years under a scenario of substantial additional reform? Given the fundamentals, how high could trend growth be? How would the structure of the economy evolve? To examine the impact of different long-run strategies on the speed and quality of China's future growth (including on resource use, income inequality, and the external balance), the Development Research Center (DRC) of the State Council has updated its computable general equilibrium model, which incorporates the detailed structure of production, demand, income distribution, and resource use in China to conduct illustrative alternative long-term scenarios.[7]

A reform scenario that assumes substantial policy reform along the lines sketched out in the report is first developed and quantified. We then consider alternative, more qualitative scenarios where such reform is not forthcoming or is of lower quality.[8]

Under the modeled reform scenario, overall GDP growth would slow over time, but to rates that still could ensure high-income status by 2030. All the main drivers of growth evolve gradually. Although more employment-friendly labor market policies and more labor-intensive production allow employment to grow slightly faster than the working-age population, demographic factors still cause employment to begin shrinking around 2015. With the beneficial impact of opening up the economy and integration into the world economy expected to phase down, with China moving closer to the technological frontier, and with declining potential to remove distortions, TFP growth edges down over time, although to a still high level by regional standards. Finally, the contribution of capital accumulation to growth also declines but remains sizable. Restructuring the economy takes time, while the need remains for high levels of manufacturing activity and for further investment, notably in infrastructure but also for industrial upgrading. The capital stock per worker is now an estimated 8.7 percent of the U.S. level, underscoring the need for further capital accumulation. GDP growth would gradually decline from an average of 8.6 percent in 2011–15 to an average 5 percent in 2026–30.

Such a growth slowdown would be independent of policies to transform the economic development pattern. Relative to an alternative "on past trends" scenario described below, this scenario features significantly lower investment, hence a smaller contribution from capital accumulation. However, this effect would be broadly offset by still high TFP growth, driven by factors such as more reallocation of labor (both across firms and from rural to urban areas), more financial sector reforms, better corporate governance, fewer distortions and barriers to services sector activities, more research and

TABLE 1.1   China: Projected growth pattern assuming steady reforms and no major shock
Percent

Indicator	1995–2010	2011–15	2016–20	2021–25	2026–30
GDP growth (annual)	9.9	8.6	7.0	5.9	5.0
Labor growth	0.9	0.3	–0.2	–0.2	–0.4
Labor productivity growth	8.9	8.3	7.1	6.2	5.5
Structure of economy (end of period)					
Investment/GDP ratio	49	42	38	36	34
Consumption/GDP ratio	47	56	60	63	66
Share of industry in GDP	46.7	43.8	41.0	38.0	34.6
Share of services in GDP	43.1	47.6	51.6	56.1	61.1
Share of employment in agriculture	36.7	30.0	23.7	18.2	12.5
Share of employment in services	34.6	42.0	47.6	52.9	59.0

Sources: NBSC and DRC.

development (R&D), and more development of human capital.

Over a 20-year horizon, this scenario also sees significant changes in the structure of the economy, supporting a reduction of economic, social, environmental, and external imbalances (table 1.1). Key specific trends include:

- The importance of industry declines and that of the service sector rises. The share of industry in GDP gradually declines by 12 percentage points, from 47 percent in 2010 to 35 percent in 2030, while that of the tertiary sector rises by a significant 18 percentage points from 43 percent in 2010 to 61 percent in 2030.
- The share of consumption in GDP rises from 47 percent in 2010 to 66 percent in 2030, reversing the past steady decline. Reforms that encourage urban job creation and greater upward pressure on wages boost the share of wages and household income in GDP, increasing the role of household consumption. Government consumption rises on the back of increasing social spending and spending on operations and maintenance.
- Investment as a share of GDP declines over time. This ratio trends down by 15 percentage points to a more sustainable 34 percent in 2030, well below both current levels and levels under any alternative "on past trends" scenario. Despite lower

investment, the current account surplus gradually declines over time, as a share of GDP, easing external imbalances.
- The economy creates more urban jobs and, as a result, more rural-urban migration, higher rural productivity and income, and less urban-rural inequality. More urbanization stimulates the service industry, including through spending patterns of urban residents. The share of employment in agriculture falls to 12.5 percent in 2030.[9] This decline works to support the growth of labor productivity in agriculture, hence income growth in that sector. The decrease in the productivity gap between agriculture and the other sectors underlies lower urban-rural income inequality.
- The economy will be less commodity and energy intensive. That is because it has less industry and, within industry, less heavy and dirty industry, in large part because of better pricing of energy, commodities, and environmental degradation.

Alternative scenarios are possible. Differences in global developments would naturally affect China's prospects. Because the resulting possible range of domestic exogenous and policy scenarios is vast, we discuss the key features of these alternatives in more qualitative terms.

One alternative domestic scenario would see much less progress with economic restructuring. Under this "on past trends" scenario, policy settings and trends would remain broadly unchanged. As a result, factors and resources would continue to be channeled toward industry, with the share of industry in GDP edging down only slightly between 2010 and 2030. The share of services would still increase, but to a low level compared with countries at a similar stage of development. Already very high investment and savings would increase further and already very low consumption would decline further. Overall, the current account surplus would remain high despite increasing levels of investment. Labor migration out of agriculture and urbanization would continue, but at a slower pace. More modest urban job creation would limit the increase in the household income share, while the labor productivity gap between agriculture and the rest of the economy would remain high. Both factors would further accentuate urban-rural income disparity and overall inequality. Finally, in this industry-led scenario, energy and resource intensity would remain high, and pollution and emissions would continue to rise.

In fact, continuing with the past pattern would become increasingly difficult, if not impossible. While this scenario can be modeled, a more likely outcome would be a future forced change in course as China finally reaches some of the limits of economic, social, environmental, or external sustainability.[10] Whether through a controlled change in policy or a crisis, such a hasty shift would lead to sharply lower savings and investment rates, putting China on a slower growth path than under the reform scenario. This possibility further strengthens the case for up-front reforms to get China on a new growth path.

Promoting Efficiency and Equity through Structural Reform

Changing the Role of the State

To achieve its vision for 2030, China needs to shift from factor input-driven to efficiency-driven growth, from direct state intervention to more reliance on markets and entrepreneurship, and from technology absorption to technology innovation, while simultaneously correcting economic imbalances and social disharmonies. Doing so will require a sense of the policy areas that offer particular promise for promoting rapid and harmonious development and of the specific reforms that would be required. This report now turns to examining such issues. It argues that these reforms will need to focus on three broad areas that promise particularly significant gains in efficiency or reductions in imbalances. First, the enterprise sector needs to be further reformed to facilitate more efficient resource use and motivate innovation and entrepreneurship. Second, reforms of input markets—land, labor, and capital—need to be advanced to rectify distortions in factor allocation.[11] Third, the fiscal system needs to be improved to help sustainably deliver the level and quality of public social and environmental services central to the vision of China 2030. The remaining resources available for investment will need to be raised and allocated so that rapid growth is maintained even as China approaches the technology frontier in a number of sectors.

These reforms are united by one common theme—"reforming government." For much of the past three decades, while the market mechanism has been demonstrating its effective function in allocating resources and spurring economic growth, the government has maintained a direct role in allocating resources and deciding business affairs. It does so by maintaining significant ownership stakes in some important enterprises in "strategic" sectors and by deploying a range of industrial interventions to influence resource allocation. It also exercises complicated regulations and oversight to channel factors at low cost into industrialization and urbanization. In contrast, in health, education, social security, and other areas typically considered to require government involvement because of market failures, China's government had initially retreated. Traditional arrangements were abandoned, and government spending lagged behind. Also many public entities such as hospitals and schools had to "fend for themselves," becoming responsible for their own revenue generation.

China's strong track record under the existing policies, especially its relatively good performance during the recent global crisis, is no reason to avoid reforming government. China's past success was the combined result of market and government forces and actions. A strong government used direct interventions to push forward industrialization and urbanization, to overcome market failures, and to facilitate factor accumulation while the market unleashed the power of the enterprise sector. As described by economists like Gerschenkron (1962) and Rosenstein-Rodan (1961), such policies to reap the "advantages of backwardness" are not unusual. However, as China approaches the general technological frontier and finds it harder to sustain an extensive form of growth, this previous advantage can become the disadvantage. Over time, specific incumbent enterprises can solidify their privileged access to resources and government support. In China, many such firms are larger state-owned enterprises, because SOEs are naturally connected to the government and often seen as strategically important. This biased business environment can jeopardize fair competition, efficiency improvement, and innovation and thus be an obstacle for an economy trying to complete its industrialization and join the club of high-income countries. The economic imbalances and social disharmonies will also become more and more difficult to handle.

The report identifies specific ways in which the role of the government and its relationship with enterprises can be recalibrated to achieve rapid sustained growth driven by efficiency and innovation. It calls generally for moving toward a more limited direct (more arm's-length) role in resource allocation and an enhanced role in delivering public goods and services and ensuring equality of opportunity. As economic development progresses, markets function increasingly well, and the economy becomes increasingly sophisticated, the benefit of direct government involvement in allocating resources weakens. In this connection, it is useful for China to review the role of government in input markets, in state ownership of companies, and in industrial and competition policies. At the same time, in line with the aim to become a harmonious society, there is scope for more government involvement in health, education, and social security. Reviewing the interrelationships between various tiers of government will play a key role in this recalibration.

From Catch-Up Growth to Endogenous Growth

Government reform will be crucial for helping China move from its previous catch-up growth approach to a more endogenous development approach. So far, this shift has proven very challenging. While a 2003 plenum of the Communist Party of China (CPC) vowed to transform the government's function in economic management (especially through reform of the administrative approval and investment systems), limited progress has been made. Going forward, such progress in government reform will be promoted by reform of the fiscal system, the enterprise sector, and factor allocation.

The fiscal system. The large social and environmental agenda over the next two decades will entail significant expansion of social protection, health care, public investment in the environment, and recurrent expenditures, mostly by subnational governments. However, such increases will need to be achieved while maintaining fiscal sustainability, avoiding levels of taxation that could harm growth, easing the fiscal pressures on subnational governments, and strengthening fiscal institutions. Over the next two decades, then, the challenge will be sixfold: changing the composition and improving the efficiency of public expenditures in line with China's evolving development objectives; improving the efficiency of revenue mobilization; realigning revenues with expenditure responsibilities by recentralizing some selected functions and allowing some subnational governments to charge local taxes; bringing all subnational government borrowing and associated spending on budget, subject to strict controls; making subprovincial transfers more equalizing across lower levels of government; and improving the accountability and transparency of governments.

The enterprise sector. A vibrant corporate sector will be critical for sustaining relatively fast growth. A central element will be further increases in competition, especially (but not only) between the state and nonstate (including private) enterprises in the "strategic" and "pillar" industries where such competition has been curtailed. The role of state capital, after being securitized and made tradable, should be calibrated to provide public goods. That requires dismantling monopolies and oligopolies in sectors where competition would yield superior results, introducing oversight arrangements where monopolies are considered necessary to ensure that market power is not abused and does not serve as a drag on the economy, and lowering entry and exit barriers for all enterprises. Improved allocative

efficiency will also require further efforts to level the playing field, especially between smaller and larger firms, and between state-owned and nonstate firms, not only in a legal sense but also in the access to key inputs. Finally, this will require a review and modernization of the extensive "industrial policies" that the authorities have used to influence the structure within and across sectors.

The allocation of factors of production. If anything, improving the efficiency in the use of factors of production—land, labor, capital—will be more challenging than reforming the enterprise sector. However, as shown in box 1.3, this is also the sphere in which many significant distortions remain, suggesting much potential from reforms to improve resource allocation.

In land, the principal challenges are to enhance rural land tenure security and ensure the equal treatment of rural and urban land tenure and property rights for social stability, particularly in rural areas; modernize the

---

BOX 1.3   Where are the largest remaining distortions in product and factor markets?

In a series of recent papers, Yiping Huang and collaborators (Huang 2010; Huang and Tao 2010; Huang and Wang 2010) show that China's specific reform approach has led to extensive liberalization of product markets, with prices of more than 95 percent of products being market determined, but with continued distortions in factor markets. The authors focus on labor, capital, land, resources, and the environment. They present crude estimates of the cost of remaining distortions in each area, with particularly high measures for capital and labor. Such distortions acted like implicit subsidies and artificially raised the profits of production, increased returns to investment, and increased China's external competitiveness. While such asymmetric liberalization was a fundamental cause of China's extraordinary growth performance, it also contributed to the observed growing structural (including global) imbalances and risks. Future efforts should focus on comprehensive market-oriented reform of factor markets.

Similarly, Chen, Jefferson, and Zhang (2011) investigate the impact of structural reform during

the period 1980–2008 using the input-output panel of 38 two-digit industrial sectors in China. They find that, on average, factor allocative efficiency plays a substantial role in industrial growth by increasing productivity. Based on their analysis, the most urgent reforms are to continue the development of factor markets (including by providing nonstate enterprises equal access to resources and developing nonstate financial institutions) and to deepen the restructuring of state industry.

Zhang and Tan (2007) examine and estimate the changing patterns of distortions during the reform process. They find that China's product markets have become more integrated after an initial period of fragmentation in the early reform period. The large shift from farm to nonfarm employment and relaxed constraints on migration also indicate increased labor market integration. However, intersectoral differences in marginal product of capital have grown during the reform period, suggesting remaining distortions concentrated in financial and land markets.

institution of the rural collective to remain relevant in the face of evolving shifts in law and policy; address the strict separation of rural and urban land tenure systems—which currently drives the inefficiencies and inequities generated by the process of converting rural land into urban use—by reducing the role of state in the land conversion process and by allowing for more market-based allocation of land; ensure the protection of priority farmland for food security through comprehensive land use planning; and introduce taxation of land and property to help ease the distortions and social pressures created by subnational governments' reliance on revenues from land transfer fees.

The financial sector faces several reform challenges too. First, there is a need to commercialize and rationalize the financial institutions and markets to meet the diverse demands of households, enterprises, and government sectors for financial services and products. To this end, financial institutions should be better governed and operate in a conducive policy environment and under competitive pressure and effective regulation and supervision. In addition, there is a need to further liberalize interest rates, deepen the capital market, upgrade financial infrastructure and the legal framework, strengthen the regulation and supervision framework, build a financial safety net and develop crisis management and insolvency schemes, and recast the rights and responsibilities of government.

Supporting Report 4 on social development addresses the issues of improving the flexibility and efficiency of labor markets in China, as many of the constraints and issues are interrelated with social protection and insurance.

While discussed individually here, reforms of the fiscal system, the enterprise sector, and factor allocation are highly interrelated. For example, incentives created by the fiscal system influence the form of industrial policy, particularly the actions of local authorities. The differential access to finance of various enterprises influences China's industrial structure. The ability of governments to capture the rents created by China's dual system of

rural and urban land influences the structure of government revenues and expenditures. Especially during crises, limits of the fiscal system have encouraged governments (including subnational governments more recently) to employ the financial sector as a quasi-fiscal tool to support state enterprises and public and social infrastructure. As a result, the banking system has needed to be periodically recapitalized, with fiscal repercussions. Thus, making the fiscal system stronger is a critical element of making the financial sector more competitive and commercial.

Such reforms must also be carefully sequenced. While the following sections provide specific suggestions on the sequencing of reforms within a given area, there also are some general lessons for sequencing across broad areas of policy. First, in the most general terms, enterprise reforms should precede financial sector reforms. Otherwise, a liberalized financial sector channeling resources to a still distorted enterprise sector could in fact exacerbate distortions in resource allocation and raise risk levels. In contrast, once major price and other distortions have been removed, once enterprises have begun to face a truly hardened budget constraint, and once important sources of moral hazard have been addressed, the financial sector will be much better placed to allocate capital in line with its social rate of return. Of course, that does not mean that all financial sector reforms should be delayed. In fact, it places a premium on early action to strengthen regulation and supervision, enhance commercialization, and gradually lower floors on lending rates and raise ceilings on deposit rates within a still controlled setting.

In broad terms, fiscal reform should move in tandem with or even slightly in advance of enterprise sector reforms. Remaining tax distortions and incentives created by the system of intergovernmental finance are combining with other policies to distort China's industrial structure. Remaining weaknesses in the fiscal system have forced local governments to rely on off-budget borrowing, further distorting resource allocation and raising risk levels. Thus, a front-loading of fiscal reforms, particularly in the spheres of revenues (especially the channeling of SOE dividends to the budget) and local borrowing could create conditions for more effective enterprise and financial reform.

The rest of this chapter examines four specific areas where policy reform will be crucial for achieving China's 2030 vision. In each of these areas, what is the vision for 2030? What progress has already been made, and what are the key current challenges in getting on a critical path for achieving the vision? What more specific steps should be taken in the near-, medium- and longer term? The chapter highlights key points.

Strengthening the Fiscal System

Fiscal System Reform in Line with the Evolving Role of the State

Fiscal policy is a key determinant of efficiency and equity and thus of China's ability to achieve its 2030 vision. By efficiently mobilizing and spending around 30 percent of GDP, government can increase the availability of crucial public goods and services, address key externalities, and support increases in overall efficiency. Tax policies have indirect incentive effects on the savings, investment, and consumption decisions of firms and households. Government also has a central role in reducing inequalities in opportunity and maintaining macroeconomic and financial stability. Well-designed fiscal reform can help sustain rapid growth, address important social gaps, and make the development path more environmentally friendly.

Over the past two decades, China has greatly reformed its fiscal system. A major overhaul in 1994 focused on enhancing revenue mobilization and revamping national-provincial fiscal relations. A new tax system with the value added tax (VAT) as its core laid the foundations for a significant growth in the revenue-to-GDP ratio. This increased revenue allowed China's public spending to grow to levels comparable with other economies with similar incomes, bringing significant improvements in public goods and

services. The reform also launched important changes in China's system of intergovernmental fiscal relations. Changes in tax assignments significantly strengthened the central government's revenue base, laying the foundation for greater and more rules-based transfers to begin tackling fiscal disparities. Further incremental reforms followed in a range of areas. Fiscal policies also played an active role in China's industrialization. For instance, China successfully attracted foreign investment through preferential tax treatment and other incentives provided by subnational governments.

By 2030, China will need a financially strong and effective fiscal system capable of meeting the economic, social, and environmental needs of a complex and sophisticated economy. In particular, as outlined below, the government will have to meet increasing demands for public goods and services, an expanded social safety net, and improvements in human capital. Despite China's substantial existing fiscal space and major untapped sources of fiscal revenues, the scale of looming expenditure pressures combined with the lessons provided by the ongoing sovereign debt problems of several developed regions attest to the importance and difficulty of maintaining fiscal sustainability. Fiscal costs need to be honestly estimated when initiating new social programs, and containment of some expenditures should be considered. In addition, fiscal system reform will be a key instrument for recalibrating the role of the state and strengthening governance and self-regulation to meet China's emerging challenges. Such reforms would focus on provision of public goods and services, including regulatory institutions, and on providing appropriate incentives for subnational governments to carry out their functions in a financially sustainable and operationally self-disciplined manner. Over the next two decades, successful reform and institutional strengthening would fundamentally transform China's fiscal system in five important dimensions:

1. The *composition of spending* would be different from what it is today, reflecting

changes in the function of government as China attains higher income levels, places greater emphasis on social and environmental outcomes, and faces the need to operate and maintain its rapidly growing stock of infrastructure.

2. Most remaining distortions in *the revenue system* would have been addressed with a view to improving efficiency and equity, and with several currently minor or nonexistent revenue sources (such as carbon taxes, personal income taxes, and SOE dividends) playing significant roles in both mobilizing on-budget revenues and addressing key distortions.

3. While public spending may or may not play a larger role in the economy than it does today, the relative *levels of spending and revenue* would be in line with macroeconomic stability, balancing the tensions arising from pursuing the dual objectives of rapid growth and greater social and environmental sustainability.

4. *Intergovernmental fiscal arrangements* would be better balanced, both vertically (between levels of government) and horizontally (across jurisdictions), especially at the subprovincial level. This would promote the adequate provision of local infrastructure, social protection, and basic public services.

5. A significant strengthening of budget system institutions (including full consolidation of spending and revenues) would have greatly enhanced *accountability and transparency*, improved budget planning and execution at all levels of government, and thus improved the effectiveness of government.

This report argues that such a transformation can be achieved through a continuation and deepening of the fiscal reforms that China has pursued over the past decades. Past and present policies have been broadly appropriate given the challenges of the time, and much has already been accomplished. However, more remains to be done to complete the reform agenda, to align with evolving challenges, and to benefit from past improvements in institutional capacity. Within each of the five priority areas, the report explores policy options and tools that could be useful for China to manage its new challenges and contain emerging risks.

China's Fiscal System: Key Developments to 2010

Government spending has supported the country's development strategy and has evolved in response to changing development objectives. Expenditures heavily tilted toward physical investments supported rapid growth in a "catch-up" phase during which the removal of physical bottlenecks offered high rates of return. While off-budget investment by local governments obscures the size and composition of such investments, total public spending on infrastructure is estimated to have reached over 10 percent of GDP (Liu 2010), compared with 3–4 percent in many other developing countries. More recently, spending has begun to be shifted toward promoting equity and more balanced growth, in line with China's development strategy outlined in the 11th 5YP. To this end, the government has expanded its network of social protection, such as urban and rural minimum income support, rural medical cooperative schemes, medical assistance for the poor, and central transfers to expand rural education. It has also increased expenditures on rural areas and agriculture, abolished agricultural taxes, significantly narrowed the fiscal disparities across provinces through transfers, and improved provision of public services.

A large share of government spending has been devoted to "economic activities," while gaps in core public services such as health and social protection remain significant. According to the International Monetary Fund (IMF), total general government spending reached 25.7 percent of GDP by 2008.[12] As table 1.2 shows, China's public spending on social protection and health as a share of GDP is well below that in OECD and upper-middle-income country averages. If such spending is excluded, the remaining nonredistributive government spending is

TABLE 1.2   Size and composition of public expenditures, cross-country comparisons as a share of GDP
Percent of GDP

Expenditure	High income	Middle income		China
	OECD	Upper middle	Lower middle	
Total outlays	41.6	33.1	36.1	25.7
General public services	5.6	5.6	5.5	2.9
Defense	1.6	1.5	2.2	1.3
Public order and safety	1.6	2.0	2.6	1.3
Economic affairs	4.2	5.3	6.1	7.9
Environment protection	0.7	0.5	0.3	0.5
Housing and community amenities	0.8	1.2	3.0	1.9
Health	6.3	3.3	3.1	1.0
Recreation, culture, and religion	1.2	0.8	1.0	0.5
Education	5.4	3.9	5.4	3.7
Social protection	15.2	9.0	6.9	4.7
Memo: total outlays excluding health and social protection	20.1	20.8	26.2	20.0

Sources: Government Finance Statistics (IMF), World Development Indicators, and World Bank staff estimations.
Note: Data are for 2007, except for China, where they are for 2008. China's social protection includes outlays for both the pension fund and health insurance. The total public expenditure on health financed from the general budget was about 2.5 percent of GDP in 2008.

comparable with that in OECD countries. This imbalance reflects the active role of China's government in economic activities, including subsidies to firms and infrastructure spending. Part of infrastructure spending is financed by revenues from the sale of land use rights that are (correctly) excluded from the aggregates noted above but now subject to budgetary oversight. However, a more significant amount of investment is funded through borrowing by local Urban Development Investment Corporations (UDICs), whose activities are off budget by definition. Adding their expenditures would raise the total public spending in 2008 to around 30 percent of GDP.[13] While an active government role in resource allocation is appropriate in the catch-up phase of development, this role should shift toward the core business of government—provision of public goods and services—as China enters a more advanced stage of development.

On the revenue side, a series of reforms have addressed many past distortions. These reforms include unifying the corporate income tax (between domestic and foreign-funded enterprises), shifting from a production-based to a consumption-based VAT, lowering import tariffs, raising the threshold for personal income taxes, and introducing a fuel tax.

Improved revenue collection allowed spending to grow without compromising macroeconomic stability. Headline budgetary revenues have increased from less than 10 percent of GDP in the mid-1990s to around 20 percent of GDP today. The government also raises some 2 percent of GDP through "government funds" other than land revenue and about 4 percent of GDP through social protection contributions. In addition, subnational governments raise significant revenues from land assets and borrowing through UDICs, which have mainly been used to support land development and infrastructure investment.[14] The resulting modest fiscal deficits and reported government debts also allowed the government to effectively cushion the negative shock from the recent global financial crisis.

The recentralization of revenues in 1994 strengthened the central government's capacity to redistribute in favor of poorer provinces. Net transfers from the center make up an increasing share of subnational government resources (table 1.3). Among transfers, both general equalization grants and earmarked transfers (targeted at specific

TABLE 1.3   Subnational government finance

Item	1996 yuan (billions)	1996 %	2001 yuan (billions)	2001 %	2008 yuan (billions)	2008 %	2009 yuan (billions)	2009 %
Budgetary expenditures	578.6	100	1,313.5	100	4,924.8	100	6,104.4	100
Budetary revenues	374.7	64.8	780.3	59.4	2,865.0	58.2	3,260.3	53.4
Net transfer from center	211.9	36.6	541.1	41.2	2,204.4	44.8	2,856.4	46.8
Of which:								
General transfer	15.9	2.7	121.5	9.3	874.6	17.8	1,131.7	18.5
Earmarked transfer	48.9	8.5	223.7	17.0	996.7	20.2	1,236.0	20.2

Sources: Ministry of Finance and staff calculations.

development priorities) have been growing in recent years, allowing a welcome phased reduction of the "transitional systems transfer." Viewed at the provincial level, such transfers have vastly reduced, if not removed, the correlation between government expenditure per capita and the level of local economic development. The difference in expenditure per capita across provinces can be largely explained by factors that affect the delivery cost, including average wage and population density.

Finally, the efficiency of public expenditures has been improved through a range of measures to strengthen public financial management. Most extrabudgetary charges have been abolished or brought on budget, and plans are in place to bring the remainder on budget. As in many countries, although social security contributions and revenues from sale of land use rights and other government assets flow to separate funds, they have all been subject to budget-type management, and a more comprehensive view of public finances is emerging.[15] Dividends from SOEs have begun to grow, have been brought into a separate capital operating budget, and are gradually becoming available to finance the general budget. Single treasury accounts have been broadly established at the central and provincial levels and are being rolled out at lower government levels, laying the basis for enhanced monitoring and control of budget execution. Government accounting reform with improved classification of government activities made a strong foundation for improving transparency. Performance evaluation has been piloted in selected programs.

Challenges and Policy Options for Strengthening China's Fiscal System

The long-term vision and current starting point elaborated above imply a clear direction for fiscal reforms over the next two decades. In most aspects, the broad direction is understood by policy makers, and related programs have been included in the 12th 5YP. Within each of the five noted dimensions, this section highlights more specific areas that offer the greatest challenges as China seeks to get on a path to achieving its vision. Drawing on international benchmarking and experiences, it also suggests policy options and tools that could be applied in China.

Restructuring government expenditures. The composition of government spending needs to evolve to reflect China's changing development challenges as it transitions to high-income status. Most notably, providing social security and a basic set of public services, and building human capital and expanding opportunity will require additional spending on health, social protection, and environmental protection. As shown in table 1.2, China's public spending on social protection and health as a share of GDP is significantly below average levels in OECD and upper-middle-income countries. The gap in education spending is quite a bit smaller. While China's reported spending on environmental protection appears in line with OECD and upper-middle-income country norms, the significant backlog and new challenges in this area could well require a further scaling up of such expenditures.

FIGURE 1.1   Cross-country comparison of government expenditures as a share of GDP

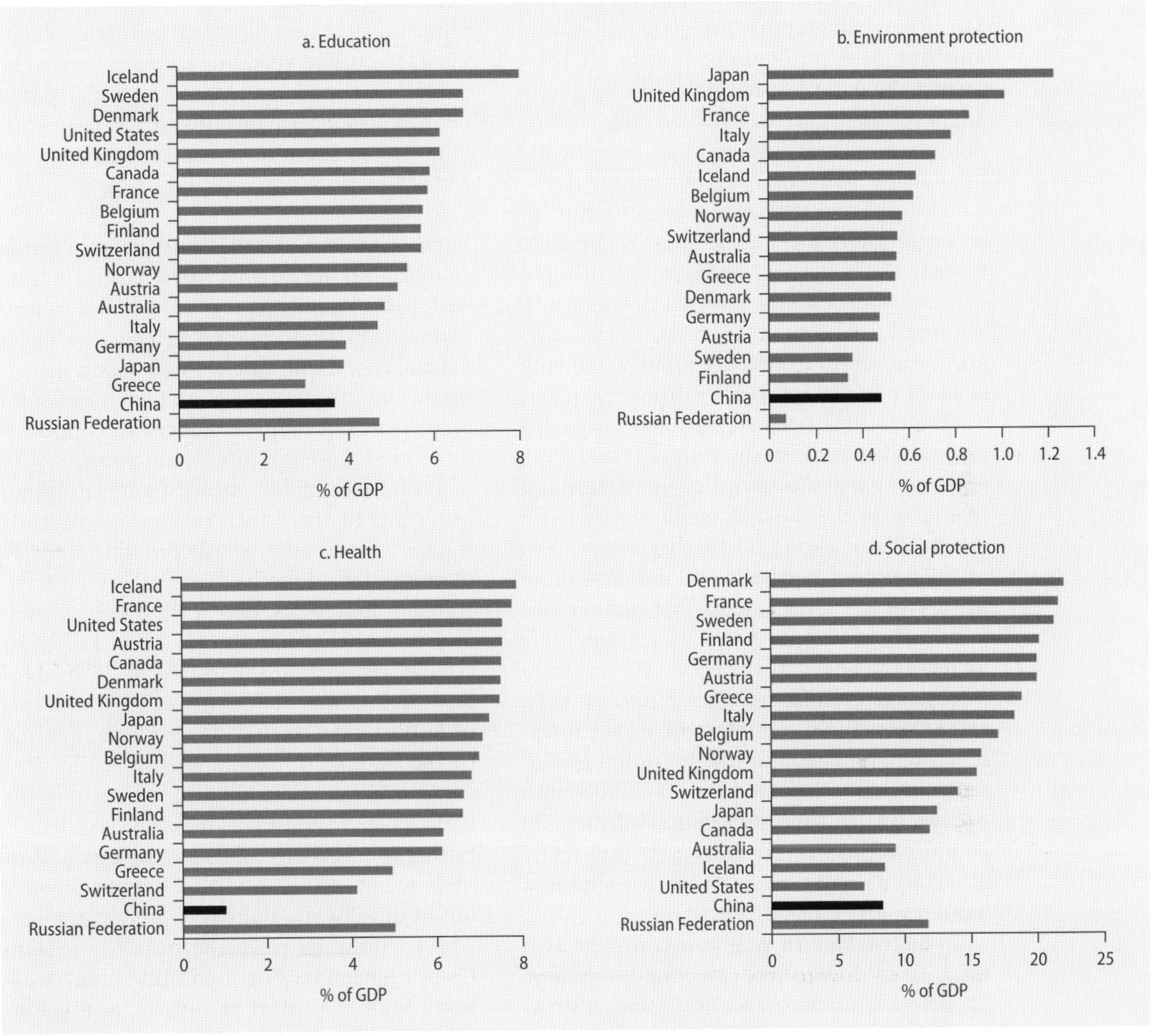

Source: *Government Finance Statistics* IMF 2007, 2009, and staff estimation.

There is no uniform high-income-country model for the size of such expenditures relative to GDP, especially for social and environmental protection. High-income countries tend to spend more on these items than middle-income countries, but with much variability. Figure 1.1 benchmarks China's spending on these four items against a range of high-income countries and the Russian Federation. For example, the share of public spending on health in GDP ranges from 4.1 percent in Switzerland to 7.9 percent in Iceland, and the share of social protection ranges from 7 percent in the United States to over 20 percent in Denmark and France. The overall cost depends greatly on the level of protection and the scheme design, which is ultimately a political decision of the country. Also, given the fiscal problems currently faced by many advanced economies, their current spending levels should not be compared very mechanistically.

Using these and other international benchmarks as reference, China could potentially aim to increase public expenditures by 2–3 percentage points of GDP for health care, 1–1.5 percentage points for education, and another 3–4 percentage points to fully finance the basic pension pillar and to gradually meet the legacy costs of existing pension obligations. These add up to an incremental fiscal outlay of around 7–8 percent of GDP—which is a reasonable estimate to bring China's aggregate "social expenditures" by 2030 to near the lower end of the range of high-income countries. Going forward, China will also need to allocate more resources to operating and maintaining its rapidly growing stock of physical infrastructure assets.

While infrastructure investment may need to be scaled back in the longer term, these and other expenditure reallocations need not be linear. In the short to medium term, still rapid urbanization and further integration of the national market could demand more infrastructure investment. The further rise in household income would correspondingly increase the financial and economic return to infrastructure, justifying such investments. Over the medium to long term, as the infrastructure stock is built, the marginal rate of return to infrastructure assets could begin to decline. By that time, public investment could be more rapidly phased down toward levels observed in higher-income countries, leaving more resources for other activities.

The structure of public investment also needs to evolve to meet emerging needs. The challenge is to choose projects that address current bottlenecks. As China develops, the bottlenecks are also changing. From a spatial perspective, no economy will develop equally, and cities are more likely to be the poles of growth (World Bank 2009d). For China, Luo (2005) finds that infrastructure investments in some inland regions such as Hubei and Sichuan could reduce the regional development gap without sacrificing much growth. Therefore, from the perspective of enhancing growth, more public investment could be spatially targeted to cities and selected regions.

In any case, the government needs to redefine its role and restructure its expenditures in line with its development goals. In China,

this role has evolved significantly over the past 30 years and should continue to do so. Once this has been decided, practical adjustments to current spending patterns need to be agreed and implemented, taking into account China's specific organizational arrangements. One way to begin this process is through the use of functional reviews (box 1.4).

Further reform of taxes and other revenue sources. To achieve its 2030 vision, China will need to adjust its revenue policies to generate adequate on-budget revenues to cover expenditures, cut efficiency-reducing distortions, and promote social and environmental objectives. The main challenges and opportunities are focused in three main areas.

First, China has significant untapped potential to introduce or expand revenue sources that simultaneously promote all three of the noted objectives. These are concentrated in four areas, two at the national level, and two at the subnational level. The most significant near-term source of additional revenues is the collection of higher levels of SOE dividends and their full channeling to the budget. This adjustment could spur more efficient investment planning in SOEs while also generating significant resources.[16] For example, were SOEs to pay out half of their profits to the budget—a ratio prevailing in developed countries—budgetary revenues would grow. In the near to medium term, higher taxes or prices on energy (carbon), water, natural resources, and pollution would encourage their more efficient use while improving environmental outcomes and generating major revenues.[17] For example, Stern (2011) estimates that a tax on coal at fairly modest carbon prices (for example, $20 a metric ton of carbon dioxide) could yield revenues equivalent to 2–3 percent of GDP. In addition, enhanced taxation of motor vehicle use and charges on parking (as a near-term option) and congestion (as a longer-term option) would lead to more efficient and livable cities and better environmental outcomes. Experience with motor vehicle taxes, piloted in Shanghai, and with congestion charges, such as in Singapore and

---

BOX 1.4   Functional reviews: A tool for designing reforms for a more efficient government

Functional reviews offer a flexible, problem-driven, and evidence-based framework that can help public sector organizations at various levels to identify key performance constraints, analyze the functions they perform, assess their relevance, and draw recommendations for organizational and process changes to enable more effective delivery. These reviews typically evaluate existing expenditure programs along two dimensions: efficiency and effectiveness. Each review varies by objectives and scope. In some cases, the focus is at the policy and program level on effectiveness concerns; in other cases, the focus is at the organizational level on efficiency concerns or a combination thereof.

Functional reviews have been applied in many countries. In Canada, a 1994 program review established a high-level special committee under the prime minister. The committee set performance-based guidelines and managed the review process that helped to generate substantial cuts (averaging 21.5 percent across departmental budgets). In New Zealand, an expert-based, top-down review of the state sector was undertaken without the participation of line agencies. Restructuring in many sectors

resulted in a 50 percent downsizing of the public sector. In Latvia, a 1999 functional review of the Ministry of Agriculture identified 161 separate functions, of which 9 were identified for privatization, 40 for rationalization, and 12 for transfer to other sectors. Implementation closely followed the proposed review.

The literature on functional reviews points to key success factors. First, such exercises involve setting general targets, but without specifying where they will be found. Second, aligning functional reviews with the budget process is essential to ensure that recommendations are provided at the appropriate point in the budget cycle. Third, one reason for successful reviews in high-income countries was that the legal mandates of the agencies and programs were flexible enough to allow relevant ministries to amend their own structure and services. Fourth, it is often difficult for such exercises to succeed in the absence of strong political leadership or of ownership and buy-in on the part of line ministries and departments. Finally, a compelling need for such reviews, such as a looming fiscal crisis, can help gain the consent of the public.

Source: World Bank 2009b.

London, could offer useful guidance. Finally, as elaborated in greater detail in the subsequent discussion of land policy, expansion of property taxes to residences would encourage more efficient use of land and also reduce urban sprawl. While promising, it will take time before property taxes become a major source of overall revenues—very few developing countries raise more than 1 percent of GDP from this source (Bahl 2009).

Second, reform of labor taxes can promote both greater efficiency and reduced imbalances. Figure 1.2 gives a comparative picture of the main tax rates on goods and services, corporate income, and labor income. The figure shows that while China's taxes on goods and corporate income are not out of line with Western European and Latin American averages, its marginal rates of labor taxation

FIGURE 1.2   Cross-country comparison of tax rates

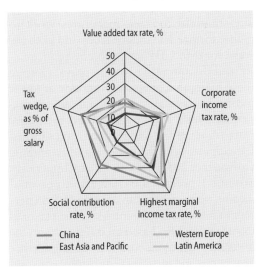

Source: Fiscal Reform and Economic Governance 2011.

FIGURE 1.3   Cross-country comparison of government revenue

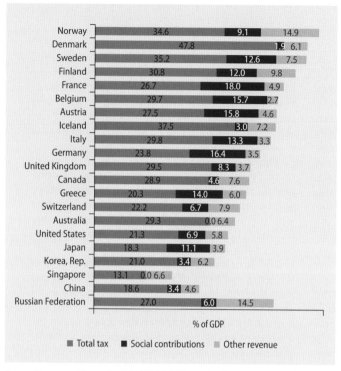

% of GDP

■ Total tax   ■ Social contributions   ▨ Other revenue

Sources: Government Finance Statistics IMF 2007, 2009, and staff estimations.

are far above global norms. Its top marginal rate for personal income tax (45 percent), total pension contribution rate (28 percent of average salary of formal employment), and the overall labor tax wedge are high by any standard.[18] These high rates work to reduce formal demand for labor and keep the wage share in GDP low, promoting inequality and discouraging consumption. Despite these high rates, major exemptions at lower income levels mean that China mobilizes surprisingly little from personal income taxes. Data from the U.S. Agency for International Development (Fiscal Reform and Economic Governance 2011) indicates that China raises around 1 percent of GDP from personal income taxes, against an average of 5.85 percent in high-income countries.[19] The personal income tax is also based on different rates for different types of income, introducing further distortions and inequities. At incomes beyond the basic exemption, the tax becomes highly

progressive (discouraging the formation of human capital), while the various social contributions are high and regressive, adding further distortions and encouraging evasion at both ends of the income spectrum. As a combined effect of still low levels of coverage, a narrow base, and high levels of in-kind compensation and informal employment, China also collects relatively little from social security contributions despite their high rates (figure 1.3).

A phased approach is advisable to reform the labor taxation. In the near term, the contribution rate for unemployment insurance could safely be reduced by around 1 percentage point. In the medium term, the personal income tax could be consolidated to cover incomes from all sources (including capital gains), its base expanded by scaling back currently significant exemptions, and simplified with a lower marginal tax rate. If the first two effects were to dominate, and to be supported by an enhanced collection effort, such a reform could possibly raise personal income tax revenues by around 1 percent of GDP in the medium term and 2 percent of GDP or more in the more distant future. In the longer term, China's social protection contributions could be reformed through reductions in average rates combined with efforts to address the regressivity introduced through high minimum contributions, complemented by other reforms to mitigate unintended effects on the finances of the respective social funds. The latter could include separating out the "legacy costs" of the pension system and funding these from general revenues.

Third, the taxation of land will need to shift away from transaction-related revenues toward a modern property tax. As elaborated in more detail later in this chapter, China's subnational governments derive substantial revenues from the sale of land use rights and taxes on real estate transactions. Because prices and trading volumes in the property market can be highly volatile, such revenues may not be reliable for financing essential public services and may put fiscal sustainability at risk. In addition, distorted incentives for officials in land development lead to inefficient use of land, corruption, and abuse of government power in land acquisition. Since changes in land compensation practices will in any case lower the net resources that subnational governments can derive from such sources, these governments will need to find new revenues to fund their operations. As detailed below, expanding property tax to cover residences offers such potential in the longer term.

Other important reforms on the revenue side would include further changes in the VAT, enterprise income tax, and consumption tax. These reforms could help rebalancing—making growth more domestically driven and services driven. Changing the excise tax on services to a value added tax would not only lower the tax burden but also improve services' competitiveness and promote specialization. China's current residence-based enterprise taxes deprive poor provinces of significant revenues because company headquarters are usually located in richer provinces. These taxes also have encouraged wasteful tax competition and beggar-thy-neighbor policies among subnational governments. In the medium term, while the collection of the VAT, enterprise income tax, and consumption tax could remain residence based, the income could be attributed to various locations, based on the headcount of registered household, consumption, or value added (Xu 2006).

Maintaining fiscal sustainability. Past fiscal reforms and prudent macroeconomic policies have left China with significant fiscal space. Over the past decade, fiscal balances have ranged from small surpluses to small deficits (a 1.6 percent deficit of GDP in 2010). While off-budget borrowing by subnational authorities complicates the measurement of overall public debt, a conservative estimate of the debt of subnational governments based on a recent report by the National Audit Office would put overall public debt at around 44 percent of GDP by the end of 2010.[20]

Several factors will work to preserve or even enhance this fiscal space. China's large growth potential creates the foundation for further growth of real revenues and favorable debt dynamics. China's government commands a large portion of assets including SOE shares and land, which represent a source of potential revenues going forward. Large national savings coupled with investment-grade sovereign risk ratings imply a relatively low cost of borrowing. Given these factors, China could in principle sustain somewhat higher annual fiscal deficits in the range of 3–4 percent of GDP.

At the same time, significant new pressures will challenge China in maintaining fiscal stability. Citizens' growing emphasis on social and environmental outcomes, rapid population aging, and further urbanization will put upward pressure on public spending. As noted, the combined effect of raising social expenditures toward levels observed at the lower end of the high-income spectrum could alone add around 7–8 percent of GDP to total spending. In the absence of reductions in the share of other spending items in GDP, China's total fiscal expenditure would reach around 40 percent of GDP. As shown by the current sovereign debt crises in some high-income countries, the revenue collection efforts required to finance such a level of spending could either be inconsistent with rapid growth or (if patently infeasible) with macroeconomic stability. The conversion of currently quasi-fiscal liabilities (of UDICs, for example) into explicit public debt could add further fiscal pressure. At the same time, slowing economic growth will cut the potential growth rate of total fiscal revenues below past levels, while the government faces pressure to cut taxes to boost household disposable income and facilitate restructuring.

Meeting the triple challenge of maintaining fiscal stability, sustaining rapid growth, and addressing social and environmental imbalances will require choices in the face of difficult trade-offs. Even among high-income countries, different countries handle such pressures in different ways, in line with their specific circumstances and preferences. If China does not want to grow its size of government to average levels in high-income countries, part of the adjustment will need to come from containment of some expenditures. In the near term, that could include cuts to capital transfers and other enterprise subsidies, streamlining government institutions and employment, and regulating "on-the-job consumption" (*san gong xiao fei* in Chinese). Over time, as China's front-loaded public investment program achieves its initial aims, such investment could begin to be scaled back. Given China's fiscal space and the existence of major untapped revenue sources, a large part can come from the scaling up of several taxes (noted above). Such trade-offs will be eased by reforms to enhance the efficiency of government, including through the functional reviews described above.

China could construct a macrofiscal framework (usually comprising medium-term budget plans and dynamic debt sustainability analysis), linked to the five-year development plan, as a specific tool for promoting fiscal sustainability. Such a tool, employed at both national and local levels, would help ensure the consistency of public spending with the country's development strategy and resource envelope. First, it would reveal the implications of current decisions on taxation and spending on future budgetary and financing needs. Second, it can expose the fiscal risks emanating from various sources such as contingent liabilities being called and global shocks hitting output growth. Third, it can help evaluate the government's capacity to meet current and future financial obligations. Were such analysis to show that debt limits are likely to be breached over the projection horizon, the government's plans would need to be revised accordingly.

Fiscal sustainability would also be promoted by bringing subnational government borrowing on budget. Currently, while such governments can formally borrow only with State Council approval, they circumvent this limit by borrowing through UDICs and other vehicles. Total subnational government debt has reached 26 percent of GDP according to the National Audit Office. Such indirect borrowing played a key role in financing important infrastructure investments and

thus supporting industrialization and urbanization. Debt financing will remain important for China's urbanization drive, which demands continuing large investments in urban transit including subways, power, water, sewage, and the like. However, limited transparency and regulation has created potential risks to fiscal sustainability and the quality of bank assets. Formally, borrowing through UDICs should be for revenue-generating purposes that can pay back the loan. In reality, a part of such borrowing appears to be for other purposes. Such quasi-fiscal financing also obscures the true size and composition of public spending and revenues. The lack of a unified planning, execution, and monitoring of public spending can also lead to inefficient and suboptimal allocation of public funds.

Allowing subnational governments to access the financial market could have important benefits. Matching the economic life of assets that the debt is financing with the maturity of debt is sound public policy because these infrastructure services can and should be paid for by the beneficiaries of the financed services. Market access and the operation of an active secondary market expose subnational governments to market disciplines and reporting requirements, helping to strengthen fiscal transparency, budget and financial management, and governance. A competitive subnational credit market with numerous buyers, sellers, and financial options, such as bonds that compete with loans, can help diversify financial markets and lower borrowing cost.

Moving forward, the central government needs to establish an institutional and regulatory framework to reap the benefits while mitigating the risks of subnational borrowing. As demonstrated by over 200 years of subnational infrastructure financing in the United States, subnational debt financing is viable under sound regulatory frameworks. The government's recent inventory of all subnational government borrowings is an important first step toward transparency in quantifying the liabilities of subnational governments and their entities and lays a good foundation for further steps. Box 1.5, based on Liu (2010) and Liu and Pradelli (2011), provides indicative elements of a regulatory framework for subnational debt management.

Direct borrowing by subnational governments could be phased in, beginning with authorities with the greatest revenue capacity and most reformed fiscal systems. Financially weaker localities could initially rely more heavily on transfers, with the central government establishing clear rules about when a subnational government can graduate from one status to another. Preconditions for UDIC borrowing would include corporate governance reform and clarity in its financial relationship with the subnational government. Credit ratings and disclosure of

---

BOX 1.5   Indicative regulatory framework for subnational government debt

Core components of a subnational government debt regulatory framework are ex ante regulation and an ex post insolvency system. In China, a complete regulatory framework would also include strict regulation on borrowing by Urban Development Investment Corporations (UDICs).

Ex ante regulation. The framework would spell out ex ante rules governing the purposes of subnational government borrowing (such as long-term borrowing for public capital investments only), types of debt allowed and disallowed (prohibiting exotic financial products, for example), and procedures for issuing debt. Fiscal targets can be established quickly by focusing on the debt service ratio, balanced operating budget, and guarantee limits, while developing thresholds for fiscal sustainability assessment would take more time and effort. Fiscal transparency would be a precondition for subnational governments and UDICs to access capital markets. Credit assessment by reputable rating agencies can be required of all subnational government and UDICS wishing to access the capital markets. Only those governments that have adopted fiscal transparency and budgetary reforms would be allowed access the markets.

Ex post insolvency system. International experiences have demonstrated that unconditional bailouts of subnational governments and their entities lead to moral hazard, encouraging irresponsible fiscal behavior and reckless lending by creditors. In the *near term*, China can develop two sets of monitoring indicators: one measuring fiscal deterioration and another one for fiscal insolvency. The key is to monitor, and intervene early, to prevent subnational governments from deteriorating into insolvency. Over the *longer term*, a more systematic insolvency system can be developed to include debt restructuring rules and a priority structure for settling claims.

Regulating UDICs. As part of ex ante regulations, UDIC long-term borrowing must be restricted to public capital investments, ratios of operating revenues to debt service must be established, and pledges of assets as collateral must be regulated. Subnational government guarantees of UDIC borrowing can play a useful role but would follow prescribed rules; for example, total guarantees provided must be below a percentage of the subnational's revenues, and no single UDIC borrower could have guarantees exceeding a certain percentage of total guarantees by a subnational government. The U.S. regulation for subnational special purpose vehicles can provide a useful reference.

To "ringfence" and reduce fiscal risks, China could develop regulatory frameworks for UDICs to issue revenue bonds. In contrast to general obligation bonds, revenue bonds are secured by the revenue stream generated by the project that the debt is to finance. Revenue bonds reinforce self-sustaining finance and allow the market to play a central role in enforcing debt limitation, pricing risks, and matching the maturities of liabilities with the economic life of assets. In the United States, revenue bonds account for about two-thirds of the US$3 trillion subnational debt outstanding.

Developing revenue bonds can be supported by complementary reforms, including corporate governance reform, regulatory frameworks for setting tariffs, and standardized reporting, audit, and market disclosure requirements. Financial strength is assessed through a credit rating system that assesses a borrower's ability to pay debt. Hard budget constraints on special purpose vehicles are a must.

audited financial accounts (for UDICs) and fiscal accounts (for subnational governments) are prerequisites for borrowing from the financial market. Those subnational governments and UDICs that are allowed to borrow should be subject to hard budget constraints, without recourse to central government support. It is important for the central government to send a credible "no-bailout" message to the market, one documented in legislation and demonstrated in action.

Further reforming the intergovernmental relationship. Achieving a harmonious high-income society by 2030 will require further complex reforms of China's system of local finance and intergovernmental fiscal relations. The key challenges for China's fiscal system in supporting this agenda remain high fiscal inequality and a decentralization of many functions that are usually financed or provided by higher levels of government in most high-income countries. Reforms in four areas stand out: completing the move from five to three levels of government; selectively raising some functions to higher levels of government; introducing some more formal central government involvement in subprovincial distribution; and introducing new sources of subnational own revenues.

First, the ongoing move from five to three (budgetary) levels of government should be completed. This is a key step toward streamlining the size of government, improving the efficiency of government services, and empowering county governments. Such reforms in the fiscal management system are already being introduced in 27 provinces, covering more than 900 counties (Ministry of Finance 2010). Most county governments

where reforms have already been introduced have witnessed improved revenue capacity with increased transfer directly from the province (circumventing the municipal level—a tier between province and county) and enhanced monitoring of county finances by provincial governments. Moving forward, a natural step would be to gradually expand this reform to the whole nation. While international experience provides limited clues, China's own pilot programs suggest it has strengthened the fiscal capacity of county governments, reduced the overall cost of government, and improved the delivery of public goods and services. Implementation of such reforms should pay due attention to avoiding gaps in, or shocks to, service delivery in the transition period.

Second, to enhance efficiency and equity and to strengthen the national market integration, some expenditure responsibilities or their financing could be raised to higher levels of government. The economic literature prescribes that a function should be assigned to the level of government that best matches benefits and costs of that function, whereas the "subsidiarity principle" would lead to assignment of a function to the lowest possible level (Dollar and Hofman 2006). These considerations still leave much scope for interpretation. In practice, there is considerable variety among countries in the assignment of functions. As table 1.4 shows, China is much more decentralized than high- and middle-income countries on the spending side. In several cases, China's assignment of functions is out of line with theory and global good practice. In most countries, income-maintenance responsibility (pensions, disability, and unemployment insurance) is the task

TABLE 1.4   **Share of subprovincial governments in total government revenues and spending**
Percent

Share provided by subprovincial governments	Developing countries	High-income countries	Transition countries	China
Tax revenues	9.3	19.1	16.6	34.2
Government expenditure	13.8	32.4	26.1	59.3

Sources: Dollar and Hofman 2006; staff calculations.

of the central government, for the good reason that centralization can help pool the risks across regions and encourage labor mobility and participation. In China, this also has an equalization effect, because some coastal provinces have relatively high employment-to-retiree ratios thanks to many migrant workers.

Third, China could consider introducing more formal direct central government involvement in subprovincial fiscal relations. Because the tax-sharing arrangements introduced in 1994 were not extended to the subprovincial level, the most serious fiscal disparities remain at that level, which accounts for nearly 60 percent of total public spending. In 2007, provincial governments on average took about 25 percent of total subnational revenue, municipal governments a further one-third, and county governments, which provide most services, took the remaining 41 percent. Subprovincial fiscal arrangements remain at the discretion of provincial governments, leading to high variation across provinces. For example, the share of provincial governments in subnational revenues ranged from 37 percent in Gansu to only 9 percent in Henan, while the county governments' share ranged from 30 percent in Helongjiang to over 68 percent in Zhejiang.[21] In general, the higher-level government grabbed a higher fraction of fiscal revenue than its share of expenditure responsibilities. As a result, the most serious vertical and horizontal imbalances are at the lower levels of government (counties and below).

One option for addressing subprovincial disparities would be to set some limits on the expenditure autonomy of subnational governments. Any such solutions would be guided by (and possibly limited by) a clear understanding of the specific role of subnational government in China. As in other unitary countries, while local authorities are in principle agents of the central government, they still enjoy a high degree of autonomy. In many cases, the central government determines by law what types of activities subnational governments can engage in through a positive list of functions (an

ultra vires definition of subnational governments). But even if subnational government is granted a wide range of autonomy ("general competence"), the central government could consider specifying at least those functions that it must perform.

A second option would be for the central government to get involved in the subprovincial distribution of resources. For example, the center could, as a minimum, establish expenditure needs for each level of government and set limits on the disparities among subprovincial governments. Once the assignment of expenditure responsibility to subnational governments is decided, revenues would be assigned to ensure adequate resources to perform these tasks. In this process, the center could mandate some degree of uniformity in subprovincial revenue assignment and transfer. One very ambitious option would require the provinces to transfer revenues to the county level in the same way that transfers are allocated to the provinces. Alternatively, the center could require the provincial governments to achieve certain prescribed targets, such as a minimum level of education expenditure per student, and revenue capacity equalization at some level.

There also is further scope beyond the property taxes already noted for subnational governments to tap new sources of "own" revenue. The high disparity in development warrants some flexibility in revenue assignment. China could consider first granting new sources of own revenues to subnational governments in relatively developed cities. This step would free up fiscal resources for more transfers to poorer regions, and help bring a larger share of subnational financing on budget. It might also help reorient the enthusiasm of subnational governments from growth and investments to a more balanced growth strategy that reduces rural-urban disparities (discussed in more detail in the section on land policy). Finally, it could improve accountability, because citizens will hold officials more accountable if local public services are financed to a significant extent from locally imposed taxes.

A good local tax should meet several criteria. The subnational government should be able to set the rates itself, at least within limits. The tax should be visible to local taxpayers, large enough to finance a chunk of local services, and not easily exported outside the jurisdiction. In addition to the property taxes and motor vehicle and congestion charges noted earlier, own revenues could also include a local personal income tax, possibly as an add-on to the central government personal income tax rate. However, because the top national tax rate of 45 percent leaves little space for such an addition, reform to cut the top marginal rate may be crucial for meaningful progress on granting subnational governments more flexibility to raise own revenues.

Institutional reform to enhance accountability and transparency at all levels. Improved information and greater fiscal transparency at all levels of government would bring many benefits. These include greater efficiency, reduced corruption, and improved creditworthiness. Past reforms of government accounting classifications, and the construction of capital operating budgets and social fund budgets, have laid a good foundation for improving government self-regulation. A natural near-term step would be to further the reforms to make information accessible to taxpayers, research institutes, and universities. More information in the public domain would allow better policy analysis and evaluation and expand citizens' scope for active participation in policy debate. That, in turn, would ultimately lead to wider acceptance of policy choices and enhanced government credibility. Possible medium- and long-term measures include better aligning of budget formulation and execution, moving the budget calendar to better reflect the schedule of the National People's Congress, changing from cash to accrual accounting, producing an inventory of government financial and physical assets, and eventually constructing the government's balance sheet. The upcoming revision of the budget law is an opportunity to anchor more transparency in fiscal and intergovernmental fiscal matters in law.

Despite past improvements, China still faces considerable challenges in enforcing accountability. The lack of accountability reduces what the intergovernmental fiscal system can achieve in terms of efficiency and redistribution. Given the high degree of decentralization in China, a key issue is accountability of local authorities to the central government. Specifically, with limited accountability for results, more equalization of spending to poorer provinces could well lead to waste of resources rather than better service delivery for the poorer part of the population. To enhance accountability of subnational governments, the central government could consider the following four measures:

1. *Periodic evaluation of the fiscal implications of expenditure assignments.* Disparities among regions, the quality of basic infrastructure, priority areas for investment, and the technical capacities of subnational governments can all change over time. The central government must have flexibility to adjust to such changes. Such evaluation will need to bring out the fiscal implications (and necessary remedial policies) for the next 5 to 10 years if any restructuring takes place. This is a bigger issue than just expenditure assignment. The financing of this shift in responsibility would likely include a reassignment of some revenue sources and reallocation of transfers as well.

2. *Development of a medium-term fiscal framework and system for monitoring the fiscal development of subnational governments.* Local officials in China have inherent biases favoring the allocation of resources to physical investments and "leaping forward." These can lead to excessive (hidden) expansion of government debt, and fiscal stress in the medium and long run. One way to mitigate such risks is to require subnational government to develop a medium-term fiscal plan and

undertake the assessment of debt dynamics. Through this process, the fiscal implications of any reform can be calibrated and public expenditure and revenue decisions integrally articulated.

3. *Comprehensive evaluation of the performance of local officials.* Until recently, evaluation criteria for local officials were heavily focused on GDP growth. That growth is not hard to measure, and the accountability system has worked reasonably well. But the shift in focus to a "harmonious society" requires a greater focus on outcomes such as the health status of the population, educational attainment, energy efficiency, and environmental quality. As these mandates are spread among line ministries, it will inevitably be harder for the central government to know if the local government is doing a good job meeting these multiple objectives and to use that information in staffing and financing decisions.

4. *Cross regional and sectoral coordination.* China has quite a few revenue transfers: some are allocated among regions, and others are earmarked for specific issues: for example, transfers for rural education. Each transfer program is administered separately and often allocated in an ad hoc manner. It is important to ensure that the different transfer programs combine to provide solid foundations for regional development, and to ensure equity across regions and consistency with the national development strategy.

One bold option for enhancing subnational government accountability in public services would be to establish a budget committee under the direct oversight of the State Council, and to centralize the performance evaluation and monitoring of local agencies (including the noted four functions) in a single ministry. Such a practice is adopted in many countries including Japan and Finland, either as a separate ministry or as part of an existing ministry, such as the Ministry of Finance.

Enterprise Sector Reforms

The Enterprise Sector and China's Vision for 2030

A vibrant and increasingly efficient enterprise sector is key for sustaining relatively rapid growth and enhancing the innovativeness and global competitiveness of China's firms over the next two decades. It would support growth by promoting further productivity gains and by keeping returns to capital at levels that sustain high investment demand. Combined with a more favorable environment for small and medium enterprises (SMEs), service sector firms, and labor intensive firms, it would also promote China's objectives of moving to a more innovative and harmonious society.

Successful reform and the resulting structural change would leave China with a very different enterprise sector by 2030. In nearly all industries, a range of firms with diverse size and ownership would compete vigorously on a level playing field, facing similar market-driven factor and input prices. Many sectors would have been greatly consolidated, primarily by market forces. Entry barriers could remain in a few "natural monopoly" sectors where dominant providers (whether state owned or private) are subject to effective regulation. Large firms, including a diminished number of SOEs, would feature modern corporate governance with professional boards deciding key strategic matters. Having been made more competitive by vigorous competition from home and abroad, Chinese firms would be increasingly successful in global markets. Within government, the functions of policy making, regulation, and supervision would be better separated, each led by a single agency with strong capacity, clear mandates, and accountability. Finally, "industrial policy" may still be implemented, but in a more focused, consistent, predictable, and market-friendly way than it is today.

Going forward, China will need to determine the relative role of the state in relation to the market and the private sector in economic activity. While a large state role may have had beneficial effects during the recent crisis, China's own experience over a longer period supports its further scaling back. As elaborated below, China's nonstate enterprise sector is much more productive, profitable, and innovative than its SOE sector. Much of China's impressive productivity growth over the past decade was driven by manufacturing, which had just been opened to greater competition. To sustain rapid GDP growth, China will need to extract more productivity from its currently protected services and utilities sectors. One way to achieve this is through the same model that worked so well for manufacturing: expose firms to competition through deregulation, international trade, and private participation. In addition, the relationships between government and enterprises need to be reformed to allow firms with different ownership and sizes to have equitable access to resources and business opportunities.

China's Enterprise Sector: Key Developments to 2010

Significant enterprise sector reforms have underpinned China's successful past growth performance. In particular, bold reforms under the 9th Five Year Plan 1995–2000 led to a greatly expanded role for the private and other nonstate sector. Indeed, the state sector's share in the total number of industrial enterprises (with annual sales over RMB 5 million) fell from 39.2 percent in 1998 to 4.5 percent in 2010. During this same period, the SOE share in total industrial assets fell from 68.8 percent to 42.4 percent, while the SOE share in employment was slashed from 60.5 percent to 19.4 percent (figure 1.4). The SOE share in China's exports fell from 57 percent in 1997 to 15 percent in 2010. As a result, the nonstate sector has become not only the main generator of output (an estimated 70 percent of GDP) and employment and the strongest engine of growth but also the most active sector for innovation. According to one source, 65 percent of China's patents and 75 percent

FIGURE 1.4   **SOEs have declined in relative importance**

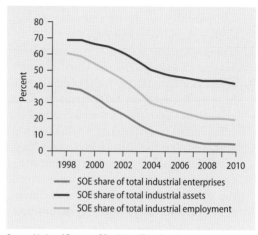

Source: National Bureau of Statistics (China), various years.

of technological innovations came from the nonstate sector.[22]

The 9th 5YP's guiding principle of "grasping the big, letting go of the small" left China with a distinctive industrial structure. Most small and medium-size firms became privately owned. Facing much domestic and external competition in an increasingly integrated domestic market, they became very dynamic and productive and now dominate many sectors.[23] In parallel, the "commanding heights" of the economy (most notably the 120 or so large central enterprises in sectors such as electricity, petroleum, aviation, and telecommunications) remained largely state owned. Even here, much progress was made. Many SOEs were corporatized, radically restructured (including the shedding of labor), and expected to operate at a profit. In some sectors, intra-SOE competition was promoted, and the scope for private participation was expanded. Later, the 2003 establishment of the State Owned Assets Supervision and Administration Commission (SASAC) to exercise authority over large centrally run firms laid a foundation for future improvements in governance and investment planning.

As a result, the profitability of China's SOEs increased. Their reported average return on equity (ROE) jumped from only

FIGURE 1.5   The rate of return for nonstate firms exceeds that of SOEs

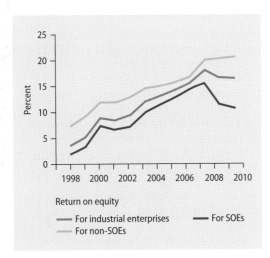

Return on equity

Source: National Bureau of Statistics (China), various years.

2.2 percent in 1996 to 15.7 percent in 2007, before sliding back somewhat to 10.9 percent in 2009 (figure 1.5).

However, the average profitability of SOEs remains well below that of nonstate (including private) firms. In 2009, the average ROE of nonstate firms had declined somewhat but still remained 9.9 percentage points above that of SOEs. In addition, a disproportionate share of SOE profits comes from a few monopolies that earn artificially high rates of return because of limits on competition, while SOEs as a class have enjoyed access to cheaper capital, land, and natural resources.[24] As a result, the profitability of SOEs in less-state-dominated sectors is generally poorer, suggesting an even greater underlying advantage for nonstate firms. The superior performance of private and other nonstate firms is also confirmed by a wide range of other research, although the financial performance of some SOEs has been weak in part because they have been responsible for delivering public services or have been constrained by regulated prices.

A significant expansion of competition contributed to productivity gains (World Bank 2009c). Privatization and market reform generated vibrant competition in most

manufacturing sectors. In some "strategic" or "pillar" sectors (airlines, telecoms, and the like), some inter-SOE competition was encouraged by the breaking up and corporatization of incumbent providers.[25] China's opening to the outside world, especially its accession to the World Trade Organization (WTO) in 2001, enhanced competition from abroad. Finally, the more recent phasing out of incentives that had favored foreign investors enhanced competition by leveling the playing field with domestically owned firms. For this reason, and also because of China's vast size, the overall industrial sector is not very concentrated (box 1.6), suggesting strong potential for competition between individual firms.

Competition remains curtailed in one key dimension, however—between state-owned and nonstate parts of certain sectors—especially in "strategic" industries and utilities. Large SOEs dominate certain activities not because they are competitive enough to keep the dominance but because the market competition is restricted and they are granted oligopolistic status by the authorities (Lin 2010). The weak and unfair competition resulting from such "administrative monopoly" (box 1.7) has been deemed "*the* current problem facing private enterprise in China" (Naughton 2011) and "the major source of monopolies in China's economy" (Owen and Zheng 2007). The strong direct ties between the government and incumbent SOEs, especially large SOEs, limit equitable market entry opportunities, hampering the efficient use and equal allocation of resources and restraining entrepreneurship and innovation.

The most problematic form of government intervention in competition and administrative monopoly in China is official lists that grant SOEs an exclusive or privileged role in certain sectors. Two lists stand out. First, in 2006, China identified seven "strategic" sectors in which the state would keep "absolute control"—defense, electricity generation and distribution, petroleum and petrochemicals, telecoms, coal, civil aviation, and waterway transport.[26] While a handful of state

BOX 1.6   China's industrial concentration remains low in most sectors

Sutherland and Ning (2008) compare the evolution of industrial concentration in China with that of earlier periods in Japan and the Republic of Korea. While such international comparisons are hampered by lack of strict comparability of data, they remain instructive. The authors use data from Amsden and Singh (1994), which shows that in Japan the average (unweighted) three-firm (C3) concentration ratio was 57.6 in 1937, 53.5 in 1950, and 44.1 in 1962. In Korea, the all-industry average C3 ratio was 62.9 in the 1980s. For China, the authors calculate a four-firm (C4) average of only 23. Thus, Chinese industry appears significantly less concentrated than Japan and Korea in earlier periods.

Looking at individual sectors, Sutherland and Ning find only three industries in which the C4 ratio exceeded 40 in 2006: extraction of petroleum and natural gas; processing of petroleum, coking, processing of nuclear fuel; and production and dis-

tribution of electric power and heat. These industries accounted for only 14.4 percent of total sales across the 37 surveyed industries. Only 5 of the 37 industries had eight-firm (C8) concentration ratios above 40 percent. By these definitions, only a small share of Chinese industry, found in traditional pillar industries, could be considered uncompetitive by these rather crude but often used metrics.

The Organisation for Economic Co-operation and Development (OECD 2010) also finds that standard measures of concentration are relatively low and declining in China. Using the Herfindahl-Hirschman index, and grouping results by U.S. Department of Justice merger thresholds, OECD finds that the number of industrial sectors at the four-digit level deemed to be highly or moderately concentrated has decreased from 27 percent in 1998 to only 14 percent in 2007. This is low compared with other countries, including the United States.

BOX 1.7   Administrative monopoly

"Administrative monopoly" refers to market power artificially created by government policies that restrict competition or compel anticompetitive conduct. It differs from a natural monopoly, where market power derives from structural factors such as economies of scale or scope. In China, the most important government policies contributing to administrative monopoly are explicit or implicit restrictions on (private and foreign) entry into (or expansion of capacity within) a still rather wide range of activities, particularly in services. They can also include government-mandated use of specific products or services, or discriminatory treatment of nonlocal firms or products by local governments ("regional blockades"). These policies can be exacerbated by government agencies requiring approvals for a range of activities, at times in the absence of statutory authority.

technology, construction, steel, base metals, and chemicals—the state has retained "somewhat strong influence" (Owen and Zheng 2007). In such sectors, private participants may face a range of entry barriers or other constraints.[27] Also, the clear signaling of the expected leading role of state enterprises may lead private firms to conclude that they would not be allowed to grow "too big" and thus may act as a powerful disincentive to expansion if not entry. As described in box 1.8, such barriers to entry and exit can reduce potential growth of both GDP and TFP.

These lists are long by high-income country standards and include many activities where vigorous competition is feasible. Most countries rightly limit entry into bona fide "natural monopoly" sectors. Until strong regulatory capacity has been established, there may also be a case for keeping such firms state owned. However, even in such sectors, technological advances have made large subsections potentially competitive, including much of the telecoms sector and a good part of electricity generation and distribution. Furthermore, in most high-income

firms might compete with one another in these sectors, they are protected from new entry (Naughton 2007). Second, in designated "basic or pillar" industries—including machinery, automobiles, information

---

BOX 1.8   Entry, exit, and "creative destruction"

Rates of entry and exit in China have been significant, but possibly different across market segments. Strong entry and exit is critical for competition. Brandt, Van Biesbroeck, and Zhang (2009) find that China has derived a large share of its total factor productivity growth from massive entry of new, productive firms and exit of inefficient incumbents. Over their sample period, net entry contributed more than two-thirds of total productivity growth, even more than its contribution in U.S. manufacturing. However, this average could hide variation across firms of different sizes, sectors, and ownership. Emerging evidence suggests that such creative destruction is indeed strong among smaller firms.

Low turnover among larger companies could work to limit gains in productivity going forward.

Several new studies suggest that dynamic economies with sustained high TFP growth tend to have relatively rapid turnover among large industrial enterprises. For example, Fogel, Morck, and Yeung (2007) study the impact of the stability of the top 10 firms in GDP and TFP growth in 44 countries. They find faster growth in countries where big business is less stable, that is, where "upstart firms undermin[e] stagnant behemoths." This relationship is particularly strong among higher-income countries. While rapid growth in low-income countries can arise from improved factor reallocation, higher-income countries also need "creative destruction" to push out the frontier and develop a more dynamic industrial sector.

---

countries, vibrant competition and extensive private participation now exist even in sectors that China has deemed "strategic," such as coal mining and air transportation. Most, if not all, of China's current "basic and pillar" industries are inherently competitive, and their counterparts in high-income countries are not (or are no longer) subject to high levels of government ownership. Thus, administrative barriers may be precluding significant efficiency-enhancing competition in China.

Policies that create an unlevel playing field or increase the uncertainty faced by businesses further limit efficiency gains. As a result, state and nonstate firms coexist while behaving differently in the face of very different incentives, leading to distortions in resource allocation. While nonstate firms have driven China's rapid economic growth, less efficient SOEs remain in business. In a detailed examination of the relative performance of these two groups of firms (using China's industrial census data), Li and Xia (2008) seek to explain how firms with different ownerships deploy resources and formulate strategies to achieve their goals. While nonstate firms outperform SOEs in labor productivity, cost control, and profitability, SOEs have had better and more stable access

to government-allocated resources such as bank credit (see discussion of financial sector below). This greater predictability and cost advantage has allowed SOEs to undertake longer-term investment and maintain greater slack in the form of inventories. In contrast, less effective property rights protection and less access to government-allocated resources has forced nonstate firms to take a shorter-term perspective and focus more on low-cost production and market-allocated resources.

Industrial Interventions

Finally, since the late 1980s, the Chinese authorities have implemented extensive interventions, including industrial administrations and industrial policies. Industrial administrations include administrative approval (*shen pi*) or reporting (*bei an*), administrative inspection, mandatory closure of business, and other controls on firms that are deemed to have inappropriate industrial activities. Industrial policies are more formal than industrial administrations but they are often connected. In broad terms, industrial interventions are designed to affect the allocation of resources among economic activities (across or within sectors) to achieve a different outcome from what otherwise would have occurred. Such policies are most critical in sectors with both state and private ownership, but with a dominant role envisaged for SOEs. They have involved a range of actors across all levels of government applying a variety of instruments to achieve multiple objectives across a large part of the enterprise sector.

Such interventions are implemented by three broad classes of actors (see annex 1B for details). The first are high-level national bodies. The second are central government departments, including the National Development and Reform Commission (NDRC), the Ministry of Industry and Information Technology (MIIT), and others. The third are subnational governments and their departments. While such governments are expected to help execute national policy, their extensive responsibilities also give them the means to influence industrial development, such as industrial planning, fiscal policy, access to land, and ownership of local SOEs.

The noted actors use at least five types of instruments to pursue industrial interventions. These are policy statements;[28] legislation; resolutions (of government departments or ministries, which require the subordinated system to follow); written and oral instructions; and "special inspection and reorganization."[29]

As elaborated in annex 1B, China's industrial policies have had seven defining characteristics. First, they have been scale oriented, that is, they have focused on the development of larger enterprises. As such, they have disfavored SMEs. Second, they have sought to control the expansion of sectors deemed to have excess capacity. Third, they have aimed to concentrate sectors deemed to be too fragmented. Fourth, policies to encourage technological advancement, such as requirements to use specific (local) technologies, have had industrial policy dimensions. Fifth, they have relied heavily on direct administrative intervention to introduce (withdraw) resources from preferential (prohibited) sectors. Sixth, they have often featured multidivision joint action. Finally, and importantly, such policies have been pursued at each level of government, often at cross

purposes. For example, while the central government may have aimed to consolidate a sector nationally, several provinces may have sought to make it a "pillar" for their own economy. With over 30 provincial and many more subprovincial authorities involved, the degree to which a particular sector is ultimately favored or discouraged becomes hard to discern. Enterprises facing such competing pressures face a treacherous business environment.

As in any country, views on the overall effectiveness of industrial policies vary widely. As might be expected, the more positive evaluations tend to come from government institutions,[30] while more critical perspectives tend to come from academic specialists.[31] There is more agreement on positive achievements in some more specific instances, for example regarding policies directed toward the textiles sector in the late 1990s.[32] Many also argue that excess capacity would have been even worse in the absence of efforts to restrain capacity expansion, for example in the steel industry over the past decade.

However, China's industrial policy has been unsuccessful in at least two dimensions. First, actual developments have often differed from those programmed by the authorities. In some cases, targeted sectors failed to emerge. For example, in 1982, the State Council set out to promote the Very Large Scale Integration (VLSI) industry. While these efforts were supported with significant funds from the 7th to 10th 5YP periods, the result was disappointing.[33] In other cases, the sectors did emerge but on a slower timetable. For example, the auto industry was identified as a "pillar industry" as early as the 7th 5YP period 1986–1990. Despite being nurtured, the industry made little progress during the 1990s, probably because China had not yet reached a level of income that would support rapid growth of auto ownership. The sector took off only in the past decade after incomes had risen and China had joined the WTO.[34] Finally, other industries flourished without being picked as winners, such as the construction machinery cluster in Changsha, Hunan Province.

Second, and most strikingly, despite concerted efforts to increase concentration, and despite much merger and acquisition activity, industries subjected to industrial policy have often fragmented further. Under the 10th 5YP, the authorities tried to increase the market share of the top 10 iron and steel producers from 50 percent in 2000 to 80 percent in 2005 (OECD 2006). In fact, this share dropped to 34.6 percent in 2004 before rising somewhat to 43 percent in 2009. Similarly, in 1994, the central government published "the development policy for China's auto industry," which aimed to nurture two or three large auto companies during the remainder of the 20th century. In fact, the concentration ratio of the auto industry remained very low and tended to decline over the 1990s (Hu 2008). While the central authorities can strongly influence the expansion of major producers, other firms are also expanding.

One key reason for the ineffectiveness of China's industrial policies is the country's five-layer government. In addition, the incentives faced by local officials exacerbate the fragmentation of strategically important sectors. Large industrial firms are important local employers and taxpayers. Because local authorities are entitled to 25 percent of the VAT levied on products produced in their jurisdiction, they may protect existing firms or compete vigorously to attract new ones. Local officials become especially anxious about cross-provincial mergers that could cut local jobs or transfer the tax base to another jurisdiction. In some cases, these may be the same firms that central authorities are seeking to close, for example because they use inefficient technology or produce high levels of pollution. Informational asymmetries and pressure from local interests can exacerbate such tensions.

Finally, industrial policies affect enterprise performance through three other channels:

1. *By discriminating between firms of different size and ownership, industrial policies distort resource allocation.* The "scale focus" of industrial policy works to favor larger firms, implying a bias toward SOEs that have the leading role at the "commanding heights" of industry. The resulting overabundant resource flows to (often less efficient) larger SOEs helped keep these firms alive while holding back SMEs. Furthermore, the scale orientation of policy can encourage Chinese firms to expand simply as a means of gaining policy support.

2. *The frequent use of direct administrative intervention raises the level of uncertainty faced by unfavored firms,* worsening their investment climate. Industries with long-term perspectives require a predictable environment for innovation, upgrading, and growth. Firms that fear the unexpected imposition of direct regulation, forced or "encouraged" merger, or even closure will be more reluctant to invest.

3. *The tensions created by competing policies of agencies across and within various levels of government further complicate doing business.* Each actor can have very different objectives, even within a given level of government. The roles and responsibilities of each player are not clearly delimited, with overlap leading to confusion. The result is policies that pull firms in many different directions, with unclear net impact.

Compared with industrial policies, China's "industrial administrations" are more heavily criticized. In particular, the use of discretionary powers and the regulatory approval system can lead to rent seeking and corruption and worsen the business environment. Industrial interventions provide a basis for the close direct links between government and business. They have also been broad (affecting an unusually large share of the economy); often direct and intrusive; and applied by many players using many instruments (Jiang and Li 2010; Shi and Wang 2011).

Enterprise Sector Reforms to Achieve China's 2030 Vision

To generate the productivity gains and enhanced innovation that can underpin further rapid growth, and thus get China on a critical path for achieving its vision by 2030, China needs to:

1. *Improve technical and allocative efficiency* by restructuring the state sector and further enhancing competition between state-owned and private firms, especially by scaling back the state sector and tackling "administrative monopolies."
2. *Improve allocative efficiency* by further leveling the playing field, especially between small and large firms, and implicitly between state and nonstate firms.
3. *Meet new challenges and improve the business environment* by moving to more limited, consistent, predictable, and market friendly industrial interventions.

All three spheres of policy relate primarily to larger enterprises. While the agenda for enterprise sector and business environment reforms in China is much broader, the commanding heights of the economy offer the greatest potential for further efficiency gains, reduced imbalances, and limits on direct links between government and business.

Restructuring the state sector and enhancing competition between SOEs and non-SOEs. To begin tackling "administrative monopolies," the authorities could review the lists that give SOEs a privileged role in strategic and basic and pillar industries. In China, these lists are very broad. They include sectors that are rather open in most high-income countries, and where the rationale for state ownership is not obvious, especially because the state could achieve its objectives through regulation and law enforcement. If this review does identify sectors or subsectors for removal from such lists, the authorities could next identify and cancel the explicit or implicit barriers that unreasonably limit competition in such sectors. A clear signal could be sent that the evolution of such sectors will now indeed be on a level playing field. Such steps can be taken unilaterally without changes in the Anti-Monopoly Law. Where the rationale for

state ownership is deemed strong, the focus could shift to strengthening the governance (boards and management) of such firms, and to regulating them effectively (see below).

Such a review would be facilitated by a clear state ownership policy that addresses both short- and long-term issues in the state sector. Given the explicit or implicit (from force of habit) role of ownership in China's current industrial policy, this policy could include an elaboration of the envisaged role for SOEs in the economy. Such a statement could serve as a benchmark against which more specific policies would be measured.[35] In 1999, a CPC plenum tried to define the function of state ownership, listing four areas to be controlled by state firms: state safety, natural monopolies, public goods sectors, and important enterprises in pillar and high-tech sectors. However, this declaration was not a clear state ownership policy, nor has it been well implemented. In 2006, SASAC declared that the state should have "absolute control" in seven sectors and "somewhat strong influence" in nine others. Going forward, the redefinition of China's state ownership policy should emphasize that state ownership should primarily focus on provision of public goods.

China could also make efforts to further downsize its state sector by a new round of SOE restructuring. In the late-1990s, some Chinese economists called for a "strategic restructuring of the state sector" (Wu, Zhang, and Liu 1998). The 15th Congress of the CPC decided to carry out this strategy. However, its implementation seems to have been frozen in recent years after notable progress during 1998–2003. According to recent research (Zhang 2010), state ownership is present in almost all competitive sectors. For example, 20,296 SOEs— 17.8 percent of all SOEs—are involved in wholesale trade, retailing, and restaurants. The downsizing of the state sector in the late 1990s and early 2000s was in reaction to serious financial distress. While ultimately successful, it came at a high cost of about RMB 2 trillion.[36] To limit such costs going forward, further front-loaded SOE restructuring would ideally be more proactive, rather than done in response to crisis, and be driven by the objectives of changing to the growth model needed to move to high-income status. Without further downsizing of the state sector, it will be hard to create a fair competition environment for private firms and to limit the direct ties between government and business.

Government ownership of enterprises is widespread and varied, covering most sectors and ranging from outright ownership to controlling interest to minority shareholder. The challenge for further SOE restructuring is thus twofold: how can public resources be best used; and how can China best transition from its current approach to managing its portfolio of state enterprises to one that is best suited for its long-term development objectives.

The response to the first challenge is straightforward. Public resources should be used solely for the provision of public goods and services—the production or consumption of which result in unremunerated positive externalities. These can range from defense at one end of a continuum to infrastructure, social protection, and basic R&D at the other—and the scope could evolve as conditions change. The recent emphasis on public housing for the poor is a good example of how government resources can be used to address a pressing social need. Indeed, the scope of public goods and services is quite broad and can even include reliable energy supplies and the widespread availability of communications and postal facilities. The share of public resources applied in a particular area will depend on the nature of the public good or service being supplied. In areas considered to be of high national priority, such as defense, government resources would be expected to provide the full or dominant share of finance. But in most areas, a smaller share is usually sufficient to achieve the government's objectives. Most important, in many cases, private sector firms are fully capable of delivering public goods and services, even though the government may provide the bulk of the finance. The

private delivery of public goods and services (with public financing) introduces the added dimension of competition and helps lower production and distribution costs.

The response to the second question is less straightforward. First, the government could securitize its implicit equity in state enterprises (in listed state enterprises, the value of the equity is already known) as soon as possible. Securitization would pave the way for state enterprise reform by separating ownership from management and introducing modern corporate governance practices—appointment of senior management, public disclosure of accounts in accordance with international practice, external auditing, and so on. Second, the government could consider establishing one or more state asset management companies (SAMCs) that would represent the government as shareholder and would professionally manage and trade these assets in financial markets where feasible. Each SAMC could specialize in certain sectors. They could then, on behalf of government, gradually diversify the portfolio and scale back state ownership over time. The dividends of state enterprises would need to be paid to the SAMCs who, in turn, would transfer them to the budget. Finally, a portion of state assets could be transferred to the national pension fund with the flow of returns being used to help meet future pension obligations.

While the operational details of the proposed SAMCs can be elaborated later, it is important that key principles are established early. It is critical, for example, that SASAC confine itself to policy making and oversight, leaving asset management to the SAMCs. The SAMCs should have clear mandates, be independently and professionally managed, and be subject to publicly announced performance benchmarks (depending on the nature of the enterprises in their portfolio). In addition, they will need to adhere to international standards for transparency, including on operations and results, value creation, profitability, and dividend payments.

In the medium term, the expanded scope for private participation could be complemented by the restructuring of remaining

SOEs. Building on China's own past experience with corporatizing and restructuring SOEs, more such large enterprises, especially those parent companies supervised by the central and provincial SASACs, could be restructured to mixed ownership enterprises and listed corporations. Furthermore, governments could reduce their ownership shares in those firms and build up modern governance featuring professional management. One additional benefit of narrowing the scope of the SOE sector would be to strengthen SASAC's capacity to supervise its remaining SOEs.

Also in the medium term, China could further spur competition by strengthening the Anti-Monopoly Law in two ways. First, it could further rein in administrative monopoly by making relevant clauses of the law clearer and more restrictive. China's new Anti-Monopoly Law, enacted in 2008, devotes one chapter to administrative monopolies and their impact on competition, broadly declaring them illegal. However, in its current version, the law lacks teeth. The clauses are very simple and focused on the cross-regional trade in goods. Moreover, the current law is not actionable, leaving enforcement as a voluntary matter for "higher authorities." The relevant provisions are explicitly subordinate to other laws and regulations, almost guaranteeing that they will be overridden. Within government, application and enforcement is spread out across several agencies. Such a cautious approach could well make sense at the beginning. Given the importance of administrative monopolies, a law that made no mention of them would be incomplete. On the other hand, an overly ambitious approach (beyond the initial capacity to enforce) could also erode authority of the law itself. For example, the Anti-Monopoly Enforcement Agency would have to bring cases against other parts of government at the same or higher rank. Clearly, enforcement of these provisions of the law will require both legal amendments and strong political will, including high-level support to the enforcement authorities.

Second, the scope for exemptions from the law could also be reviewed. All competition laws grant exemptions or exceptions to particular industries and certain types of economic activities and transactions (UNCTAD 2002). Exemptions may be sectoral in nature, such as a "natural monopoly," or functional, such as development of product standards or other practices where a single or few providers makes great sense. Some such exemptions might be necessary for furthering the objectives of competition policy. Other exemptions reflect pressures from special interest groups. In many cases, there is a clear need to revisit such exemptions. The UNCTAD report offers some general recommendations concerning procedures and principles for granting exemptions. After applying such principles, the number, nature, and scope of exemptions will tend to be more limited and procedures more accountable and transparent.

Further leveling the playing field. Greater competition needs to go hand in hand with fairer competition. This would enhance allocative efficiency by helping direct factors of production toward their most productive uses. To this end, firms of different size or ownership should compete on a more level playing field, not only in a strict legal sense, but also in the terms on which they gain access to inputs.

The most promising near-term reforms to address this issue are outside the scope of competition policy and would directly tackle key distortions. These include the preferential access to credit by larger firms or SOEs, including access resulting from moral hazard (see financial sector discussion below); the still low level of SOE dividend payments (which can leave savings within firms to be deployed less effectively than in other possible uses); and the implicit advantages that SOEs gain by their closeness to decision makers (including through the ministerial status of CEOs of large firms. A review of industrial policies (see below) to remove explicit or implicit biases in favor of firms of particular scale or ownership would also address such concerns.

In the medium term, fairer competition could be promoted by developing and enacting a set of laws that would limit potentially distortive discretionary actions, including in the realm of industrial policy. By defining clear "rules of the game," such laws would be in the same spirit as the limits that the WTO places on its members' trade policies, or that the U.S. Constitution places on restricting interstate commerce. Such rules could contain some of the most egregious attempts by central and subnational officials to pull in different directions using crude administrative means. One such law is the Anti-Monopoly Law, which has already been discussed. If a strengthened law still left important gaps, it could be complemented by additional legislation (possibly in the form of a special law) to restrict currently widespread industrial interventions by central or subnational governments. This law should be actionable, with any governmental departments liable to be charged if they impose interventions restricted by the law.

In the longer term, to safeguard fair competition in a single market, China could consider enshrining limits on the financial support that its governments can directly or indirectly provide to firms. One recent example is large capital injections into major state-owned airlines (Pan 2010). Such support, by allowing some firms to absorb losses that a purely commercial entity would not or could not absorb, results in unfair competition. To counter such tendencies, China should provide its governments with clear rules of the game in dealing with inevitable pressures for aid of one form or another (Leipziger and others 1997). This could build on experience of the European Union (EU) in implementing rules on "state aid." While the EU and China have many important differences, they face similar problem of regulating anticompetitive behavior either by member states (in the EU case) or by subnational authorities (in China's case). The EU experience emphasizes the necessity of a credible institutional framework to monitor industrial subsidy programs and enforce mutually agreed rules for industrial policy.[37]

Focusing and modernizing "industrial policies." China's industrial policy needs to adapt to changing circumstances. While such policy did not always work as expected during the past 30 years, it may have at times played a positive role in China's objective of "catching up." However, China's current system of industrial interventions could become an obstacle to achieving the innovation-driven growth to which the country now aspires. In distilling lessons of East Asian industrial policy, Weiss (2005) notes that for higher-income emerging economies, the agenda will be to upgrade export structure and move up the value chain. For these economies, old-style industrial policy of "second guessing" the market and creating winners will have less relevance. Instead, these economies will require a business climate that is more favorable to SMEs and new entrants, that encourages fair competition, that is more tolerant of low sectoral concentration and excess capacity, and that relies more on market mechanisms. The type of innovation that China seeks to unleash can initially result in rash new entry, ferocious competition, fragmentation, and excessive investment, developments that need not be unhealthy in industries that have yet to mature.

Reform of industrial policy should start from a clear elaboration of its role and purpose. Which market failures, externalities, or other circumstances need to exist for such policies to be applied? As Leipziger and others (1997) note, governments that follow a "hunch" to support a particularly prestigious industry without clear evidence of a market failure, or that identify favored sectors based on noneconomic criteria, will impose a high fiscal cost and generally fail. Such principles could be published to ensure transparency concerning policy objectives and the monitoring and evaluation of results.

Based on this clear elaboration, policies themselves would be more focused, implemented by fewer actors, simpler, and more market friendly. As noted, China's current industrial interventions can be extensive, inconsistent, unpredictable, and administrative. Greater focus means limiting their application to a few sectors where the case for such policies is strongest. That would avoid spreading scarce technical and entrepreneurial talent too thinly and crowding other established sectors with comparative advantage out of input and factor markets (Westphal 1990). The involvement of fewer actors (see below) would add coherence to policy. A more limited set of permissible interventions, including the provision of any support through fiscal rather than banking channels, would promote greater transparency and reduce collateral distortions in other markets (Leipziger and others 1997). For example, pursuit of more general objectives, such as consolidation of a sector, without prejudice toward specific (incumbent) firms, would avoid discrimination against potentially more innovative new firms. Support should be temporary and subject to strict "sunset clauses." The selection mechanism should lean toward innovation ability instead of scale and ownership. Finally, policies should try to work with the market, harnessing its power to achieve desired aims, rather than against it. For example, using market forces to spur mergers and acquisitions (by making more shares tradable for example) would promote concentration without prejudicing its outcome.

China's unique size, complexity, and high degree of decentralization should also affect the form of its industrial policies. Specific approaches that may have worked well in smaller and more centralized economies such as Japan, Korea, and Singapore could be problematic in China. With multiple layers of government possessing significant de facto autonomy, the central authorities could formulate policy but find it very hard to monitor or enforce. Within a given level of government, numerous agencies with overlapping mandates can pull in different directions. Local governments seeking to generate new jobs or tax revenues will have clear incentives to protect existing enterprises or attract new ones by providing resources such as land at a steep discount, by helping navigate the required permits and approvals, or by hindering or blocking cross-border mergers. Such forces can exacerbate industrial fragmentation, frustrating central government efforts to consolidate.

Changes in tax-sharing rules and in performance evaluation of local officials can help better align their incentives with national priorities. To the extent that local industrial policy is motivated by the desire for more revenues, different sharing rules for key taxes (especially the VAT) might reduce incentives for fragmentation. Similarly, performance evaluation that goes well beyond indicators of local GDP growth could limit excessive desire to attract or preserve industries in need of consolidation. All of this is a matter of degree, because competition among subnational units has also had positive features, and those features should be preserved. Any deeper realignment of incentives would require more fundamental changes to the relationship between levels of government in China, which we do not consider here.

Finally, as a general issue cutting across the themes discussed above, the assignment of functions related to ownership, policy, and regulation across government agencies needs to be rationalized. As a result of individually sound but piecemeal reforms, China now has a range of agencies with multiple and overlapping functions. For example, in addition to its core function of supervising state ownership in SOEs, SASAC also retains certain regulatory and policy-making roles. Similarly, responsibility for enforcing the Anti-Monopoly Law is split between three agencies with other broader responsibilities—the State Administration for Industry and Commerce (SAIC), the Ministry of Commerce (MOFCOM), and the NDRC. For example, MOFCOM is charged with encouraging foreign direct investment. Some SOEs, such as the tobacco enterprise, even retain responsibilities for sector policy while also seeking to earn a good return. This arrangement compounds already severe fragmentation across levels of government and tensions between various stakeholders. Such fragmentation can lead to a blunted focus, duplication of efforts, conflicts of interest, and weakened responsibility.

Going forward, China could review current functions and responsibilities, reallocating them so that one body would be the lead (if not sole) agency in a given area. For example, SASAC could focus entirely on the narrow mandate of maintaining and increasing the value of public assets. As in most high-income countries, a single government body would implement and enforce competition policy. A third agency (such as the NDRC) could take sole charge of industrial policy. Enterprises would be charged with doing business. Focused bodies will individually be more effective and work more coherently together. There has been some progress in establishing separate sectoral regulatory bodies—this needs to continue.

The performance of China's enterprise sector can also be improved by other reforms beyond the realm of industrial policy. These include issues on the general business climate, remaining barriers to a deeply integrated single national market, strengthening intellectual property rights, public procurement reform, contract enforcement, bankruptcy regimes, and trade policy, improving access to finance, and strengthening corporate governance.

Financial System Reforms

China's Financial System Developments to 2010

The Chinese financial system has served the purpose of savings mobilization and capital allocation to strategic sectors during the catch-up stage of economic development. It was successfully transformed from a socialist fund allocation system to a system that has proved effective for financing a rapid expansion of investment and thereby economic growth during the past three decades. The banking system has mobilized sufficient national savings to meet high investment demand by firms and local governments. Its extensive branch network, perceived stability by depositors in state-owned banks, reasonably stable inflation, and high household savings rate, among other things, have contributed to this successful role.

The past decade has also witnessed important progress in reforming and restructuring the financial system. There has been progress in interest rate liberalization. Reforms in the governance of state-owned commercial banks were introduced by selling a portion of shares to strategic investors and listing them on domestic and foreign exchanges. Entry restrictions on financial institutions and controls on capital flows were somewhat eased. Important regulatory reforms were undertaken by institutional restructuring and introduction of global standards. Various measures were introduced to boost the development of securities markets.

Despite the many reforms introduced so far, the Chinese financial system remains repressed, unbalanced, costly to maintain, and potentially unstable.

- *Repressed.* Pervasive controls remain in key areas.[38] The levels of state ownership in the banking sector (figure 1.6) and government intervention in the financial system are much higher than in other countries at a similar stage of economic development that later achieved high-income status. Despite changes in the ownership structure of commercial banks from the previous system of exclusive state ownership to the current system of joint-stock ownership, the government continues to dominate in the financial sector. Continued protection and intervention in the business decisions of financial institutions make them

FIGURE 1.6   Ownership structure of the banking sector, 2005

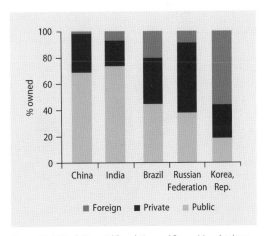

Source: World Bank Financial Regulation and Supervision database.
Note: The figure shows the share of banking sector assets held by majority-foreign, private domestic, and state-owned banks.

convenient policy instruments, the use of which prolongs the bureaucratic culture and distorted incentives that have prevented banks from full commercialization and from allocation of financial resources to the most productive uses.

- *Unbalanced*. Despite recent efforts to promote direct financing, bank credit still accounts for close to 90 percent of funds raised by the corporate sector. While it is not uncommon for financial systems to be weighted toward banks at China's stage of development, international comparisons show that China's is especially so (figure 1.7 and annex 1C). Recent research indicates that the optimal financial structure becomes more market oriented as economies develop (Demirgüç-Kunt, Feyen, and Levine 2011). This is consistent with theoretical arguments that economic development increases the demand for the services provided by nonbank financial institutions (NBFIs) and the securities markets relative to services provided by banks. The histories of developed countries such as Britain, Germany, Japan, and the United States also indicate major complementarities in the functioning and development of banking systems and securities markets (Allen and others 2010). So

far, China has not taken full advantage of these complementarities. If the histories of high-income countries are a reliable guide, China's future development likely hinges on achieving a more balanced financial system. Additional imbalance is found in the capital market in which the share of the fixed-income market is overwhelmed by the equities market, and the share of corporate bonds market remains small.

- *Costly to maintain*. The financial system is exposed to accumulated losses yet to be fully absorbed and new losses in the making. Banks have been used as instruments of the government's macroeconomic and sectoral policy goals and have not always been in a position to lend prudently. While this approach may have helped achieve policy goals, it has also exposed banks to a greater risk of deteriorating loan portfolios, increasing the ultimate costs of such public policies. Rounds of capital injections into state-owned commercial banks and disposal of nonperforming loans at the end of the 1990s and before public listing of their shares, not to mention the reported losses on lending to local governments incurred since 2008,[39] are indicative of the magnitude of real and potential costs to the government budget.

- *Potentially unstable*. The financial system is fragile and vulnerable to potential instability for several reasons. Systemic risks are embedded in the homogeneous behavior and operations of financial institutions, in part reflecting weak commercial orientation; in the widespread financial services integration and conglomeration that has been going on for years without a strong regulatory framework to monitor, measure, and mitigate risks across the financial services industries; in the rapid growth of shadow banking activities that, while providing useful channels to those underserved segments of the economy, are largely out of the official oversight; and in the large overhang of local government debts mentioned earlier. A major component of the financial safety net—the deposit insurance scheme—has yet to be

FIGURE 1.7   Financial system structure in comparison, 2009

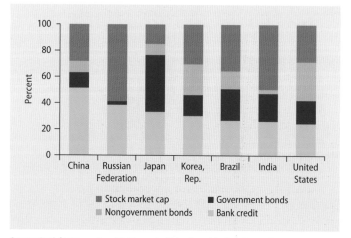

Sources: Bank for International Settlements, China Securities Regulatory Commission, IMF International Financial Statistics, World Development Indicators.

created more than 10 years since its initiation. The mechanism for resolution of troubled banks has not been institutionalized and crisis management mechanisms are not well established. Lack of information sharing and coordination among the fiscal, monetary, and financial regulatory authorities, and limited progress in building up a macroprudential framework against systemic risks, are also causes for concern.

Overall, financial sector reform and development have been out of step with the real economy. The current financial system, characterized by bank dominance and strong state intervention, served to mobilize savings and allocate capital to strategic sectors during the economic take-off, but such benefits are increasingly outweighed by the costs of the accompanying distortions and the resulting buildup of imbalances and risks. China could conceivably sustain high economic growth for a while longer even without fundamental reforms in the financial sector. However, in such a case, distortions in resource allocation would be intensified, income and wealth distribution worsened, and internal and external imbalance sustained. Eventually, these distortions and imbalances would undermine social stability, slow productivity growth, and erode competitiveness. The potential debilitating effect of a future forced financial liberalization, and lack of an integrated approach and concerted actions on the part of the government, can only serve to exacerbate the negative consequences. Now is the time for China to rethink its vision and strategy in the financial system, to avoid a situation where delays in financial system reform and development disrupt or impose a drag on the real economy.

China's 2030 Vision for the Financial Sector

China needs to build a more liberalized, balanced, efficient, safe, and sound financial system that meets the demands of corporate, household, and government sectors. China's future financial system should be free of repression and strike a balance between the banking and nonbanking financial institutions and markets, especially the capital market, with more diversified institutions and products reflecting the changing nature of China's economy. Financial institutions should be commercialized and rationalized, through installation of effective corporate governance, creation of a level playing field, establishment of effective oversight, and liability for bankruptcy regardless of ownership structures. The financial system should have better outreach to households, consumers, and micro, small, and medium enterprises (MSMEs), and be able to provide long-term and risk capital to support the upgrading and expansion of incumbent firms and the emergence and growth of new firms in high-tech and emerging industries.

A well-functioning financial system is essential in China's drive to become a harmonious and high-income society. First, as growth in the supply of labor and capital slows, China will have to rely more on productivity growth, which has to be supported by the financial system through improved allocation of capital. Second, the increasing importance of TFP in supporting economic growth requires innovation that cannot be realized without support from the financial system, especially a well-developed capital market. Third, a well-functioning financial market could provide reliable monitoring and corporate governance, and facilitate timely industrial restructuring by permitting the entry and exit of firms through various paths including mergers and acquisitions. Fourth, the need to rebalance the Chinese economy will require an inclusive financial system that provides widespread access to diverse financial services and products by households and by micro and small enterprises. Fifth, finance also contributes to preparing for old-age security and reducing poverty and inequality by improving opportunities for households to borrow and invest in assets whose value can grow in parallel with the economic advancement of China. Finally, finance that is not managed well can be disruptive to economic development, as shown in the recent financial crisis and China's own experience.

Key Reforms to Strengthen China's Financial System

Building a more efficient and robust financial system that can well serve China's transition toward a modern, harmonious, creative, and high-income society will require a systematic approach to reform. For the system to embark on a virtuous cycle, it will be critical for the government to gradually reduce its influence in the internal affairs of the financial institutions to focus on roles that belong to the government, including regulation, supervision, and infrastructure building, as well as creating and enforcing the right incentives and mechanisms.

Full commercialization and rationalization of the financial system. Macroeconomic and financial policies and instruments need to be better aligned to create incentives for a lasting transformation to a more commercially oriented and effective financial system. Mechanisms, structures, and institutions must be created that provide financial intermediation without distorting incentives, exacerbating moral hazard, and creating contingent liabilities for the government. To facilitate this process, the government should continue to reorient its roles and responsibilities, moving from direct controls to indirect measures. As an example, the central bank does not have the necessary independence to carry out its functions in monetary policy decisions. Monetary policy has been conducted through frequent changes in reserve requirement ratios, window guidance, and even credit ceilings. To enable banks to better manage their assets and liabilities, the central bank could conduct monetary policy in more market-friendly ways, that is, through open market operations.

It is important to move away from direct or indirect control of financial institutions and to develop alternatives to bank-based funding of government policy goals. The government at all levels has been closely involved in the commercial operations of financial institutions, either through direct holding of shares or through indirect influences, mainly because it is heavily dependent on the use of commercial bank credit for policy goals. Full commercialization of financial institutions will not be possible unless this practice is replaced by other mechanisms, including greater use of direct fiscal expenditures, government credit programs that work through the banking system, rationalization of the policy banks, and reforms to intergovernmental fiscal relations. The goal should be to first free the commercial banks from policy-oriented functions to enable them to compete with their peers from home and abroad, by subjecting them to market discipline and effective regulation and supervision. Policy loans and government-directed loans could be gradually phased out or transferred to those few policy-based banks with clear mission and mandates that operate under strictly enforced performance monitoring and evaluation.

A commercially oriented governance system should be introduced. While privatization would be the best way to make state financial institutions (SFIs) more commercially oriented, privatization of the big SFIs would not be easy.[40] Since the government is likely to remain majority owner of the commercial banks, state-ownership functions need to be strengthened. To be effective, state-ownership agencies need to act in ways similar to private owners. Otherwise, given the multiple objectives of the government, SFIs will not become truly commercialized. China may introduce a governance structure for banks after taking thorough stock of the existing state-ownership functions, agencies, and practices, and drawing lessons from international best practice and failures (box 1.9).

Further liberalizing interest rates. China has reached the stage where it needs to phase out remaining interest rate controls. Much progress has been made in liberalizing interest rates, but the remaining controls have been blamed for many distortions in the financial sector.[41] Such controls have played a key

BOX 1.9   Improving the effectiveness of the state-ownership functions in the financial sector

China has yet to establish consolidated and effective state-ownership functions in the financial sector. While the government has stated its intention to remain a dominant owner of key state financial institutions (SFIs) in the long run, there has never been a clear elaboration of why direct ownership is necessary for achieving its objectives. Many organizations are involved, each with responsibility for only a small aspect of ownership. None has either the perspective or the authority to take a broad view of the financial sector. Fragmentation leads to both ambiguities over decision-making authority as well as mismatches between rights and responsibilities. Moreover, there is insufficient public information on how the state ownership in the financial sector is organized, let alone about the objectives, mandates, division of rights and responsibilities, and performance indicators. In this setting, a meaningful monitoring and evaluation framework is not possible.

Several reforms are needed to further improve the effectiveness of state-ownership functions. The government needs to spell out the long-term and overarching goals of the financial sector, explain why it needs to own financial institutions, decide which institutions should continue to be held and which should be let go, and determine what level of ownership should be maintained over what period of time and how it should be done. The rights and responsibilities of state-ownership agencies need to be clarified in the law. An ownership policy should be developed and published to inform the general public as to why the government intends to own specific institutions and how its rights will be exercised and ownership responsibilities distributed and carried out. Transparency and accountability can be enhanced by implementing a performance-monitoring system and developing aggregate reporting on the performance of portfolio SFIs. In the medium to long run, a rational organizational format of functions should be considered. However, mere organizational changes can fail to achieve the intended results if they are not accompanied by fundamental changes in incentives and institutions.

role in the overall strategy of catching up through strategic capital allocation to priority sectors and in protection of the banking system. However, as the economy matures, the remaining controls become a drag on growth as artificially cheap capital contributes to overinvestment and delays restructuring. The development of capital markets also has been hindered by distorted risk pricing. The guaranteed interest spread has prevented the formation of a true risk culture, which is key to commercial banking, capital market development, and access to finance. In addition, market-determined interest rates will be crucial for an effective movement of monetary policy from direct quantitative control to indirect control.

While the floor for lending rates is easier to remove because it is no longer binding, liberalization of deposit rates is a complex matter, requiring several key prerequisites that cannot be ignored. Too rapid disintermediation or too rapid inflow to short-term financial products could raise the risk of financial crisis. There will also be a need to avoid a significant asymmetry in the pace of liberalization between banks and NBFIs, and between the direct market and indirect market. The moral hazard of financial institutions needs to be properly checked to prevent destabilizing interest rate competition. Effective regulation to prevent excessive competition for deposits by bidding up interest rates and by making loans to risky borrowers at unduly high rates should be secured before liberalization of the relevant bank interest rates.

Deepening the capital market. Deepening the capital market is conducive to a rebalancing of the financial structure and to the catch-up strategy of innovation in science and technology in which innovative, vibrant private firms could emerge and thrive. A country's financial structure influences the types of industries that get financed, with equity finance supporting more innovative industries and debt finance through bond issuance and bank lending better suited to existing industries. A key advantage of capital markets relative to banks stems from the evaluation of business opportunities by multiple potential investors, whose diligence can help assess the viability of new technologies. Venture capital and private equity industries will have to play a bigger role in financing technologically advanced industries. Institutional investors will also play an increasingly important role in the development of China's capital market. Deepening capital markets will also help to increase the access to bank loans by households and MSMEs as large and established firms rely increasingly on direct financing.

A market-based financial system is more dependent on the rule of law and market infrastructure than a bank-based system. An equitable, transparent, and efficient capital market is not achievable without a fundamental reorientation of the role of government. The authorities should gradually reduce administrative controls where market mechanisms could do better. As an example, China should move to a disclosure-based system from the current merit-based approval system for initial public offerings. The government should focus on improving the legal framework, enforcement of laws and regulations, upgrading financial infrastructure, and imposing stringent rules on information disclosure. Artificial segregation of the market should be avoided. The current segmentation of regulation in the fixed-income market among the People's Bank of China (PBC), China Securities Regulatory Commission (CSRC), and NDRC raises concerns about regulatory inconsistency. Their respective roles should be clarified to ensure regulatory consistency among different market segments.

Growth of the asset management business is essential to facilitate the deepening of the securities market. China's financial system needs to provide a reasonable variety of financial products with different risk and return profiles to meet different risk preferences of investors. Risk-averse individuals can choose bank deposits, while investors more willing to take risk may purchase corporate bonds, mutual funds, and stocks. That would facilitate the flow of funds to risky entrepreneurial ventures with potentially high return and long-term corporate investment with a long gestation period. The growth of asset management businesses could also assist in providing greater financial security for the elderly (through improved vehicles for accumulating retirement savings) and, more broadly, for securing social cohesion and stability. Asset management requires less strong regulation than banks, but it does require transparency, strong investor protections, market-determined interest rates, and mark-to-market of assets. The government has to provide a solid legal basis to nurture this business. According to other countries' experiences, once the market infrastructure and environment is provided, this business can grow quickly, taking a large part of household and corporate savings.

Upgrading financial infrastructure and the legal framework. China's financial infrastructure needs to be further upgraded to facilitate the financial market in general and the capital market in particular. Financial infrastructure includes many elements, such as credit information systems, rating services, accounting and auditing, payment and securities settlement systems, exchanges, and over-the-counter markets. While many key elements are formally already in place, more needs to be done to ensure their effective functioning. As an example, great strides have been made in the past few years in China's security interest filing system, as demonstrated in the registry system for accounts receivable and lease interest registry. What remains to be done is in the registration of inventory and equipment, which should be centralized and Internet-based. In addition to the enhanced payments and securities settlement system, efforts may include continuing to improve the coverage and quality of consumer credit information reporting as well as improving the independence and professional ethics and standards of credit rating agencies.

Adequate and accurate disclosure and transparency supported by credible accounting and auditing practices can go a long way in supporting financial development by minimizing informational frictions. China's legislative and regulatory framework on accounting and auditing has converged to international standards.[42] However, reviews and anecdotal evidence point to noncompliance in the financial statements of some listed companies and variations in the level of compliance with applicable auditing standards. More seriously, fraudulent activities can cause reputational damages and loss of investor confidence that is hard to restore. More efforts are needed to further strengthen the capacity of the regulators, as well as to improve the development of accounting and auditing professions. Strong and strict penalties should be imposed on improper accounting and auditing practices.

Strengthening the regulation and supervision framework. The independence and effectiveness of regulatory and supervisory bodies can be enhanced. Achieving this is a challenging task, especially because the government role as both an owner and regulator of major financial institutions creates potential conflicts of interest. Almost without exception, the experiences of other countries in a similar situation bear out the failure of regulatory oversight. The risk of failure becomes greater as financial liberalization progresses and competition in the financial market deepens. China's integration in the international financial system and the internationalization of the renminbi will put pressure on China to improve its regulation and supervision. The government needs to seek institutional reforms to secure the political independence of regulatory bodies to enable them to conduct arm's-length regulation and supervision, regardless whether it would remain the owner of financial institutions.

Institutional arrangements are needed to better align regulatory resources and structure to deal with increasing integration of the financial services industry. Despite laws that insist upon segregation among banking, securities, and insurance in the financial sector, the degree of financial conglomeration is stunning. The existing regulatory and supervisory structure does not provide the necessary monitoring and surveillance to deal with the spillover of risks among financial institutions and industries—the coordination mechanism is perfunctory, and information sharing is sporadic. The authorities may be forced to decide whether to unify all financial regulators under one roof or to maintain the current regulatory architecture but strengthen their ability to deal with cross-industry financial risks, probably through improved functional supervision.

A well-defined and functioning macroprudential framework is critically important for China to prevent or mitigate disruptive idiosyncratic risks, including those that may well emerge from the rapid growth of shadow banking activities. Currently, there is some interagency coordination on broad financial sector issues, but a comprehensive macroprudential framework needs to be developed, with a clear institutional setup (including mandate, powers, distribution of responsibilities, information-sharing arrangements, and the like). The PBC is deeply involved in microprudential regulation and supervision, as evidenced by the differentiated approach to required reserve ratios and capital requirements[43] and tight control of the interbank market participation and operations. But the financial regulatory authorities are reluctant to retreat from areas pertaining to macroprudence while not focusing fully on microprudential regulatory and supervisory work. While the concept of macroprudential regulation is yet to be fully defined in China, its importance for securing financial stability is being emphasized globally.

China could establish a high-level financial committee on the basis of the existing framework, with the main objective of reducing systemic risk and maintaining financial stability. Such a committee, if endowed with strategic significance and charged with forming an overall assessment of the financial system, would not only free the State Council from its current heavy burdens, but also enable sector supervisory authorities to concentrate on improving the effectiveness of financial regulation and supervision. It would also remove obstacles between the central bank and various supervisory bodies in coordination and information and analyze and supervise all institutions, products, instruments, markets, and transactions that might bring about systemic risks. The role of this financial committee could also include development and establishment of instruments, standards, and indexes for systemic risk monitoring and identification, and development of *macro*prudential instruments (possibly using microprudential means as transmission channel).

Building a financial safety net and developing crisis management and insolvency schemes. Financial liberalization will lead to a more efficient financial system but also will increase the risk of financial instability. Most countries have faced big or small crises in the process of opening their financial systems, often as a result of macroeconomic distortion and volatile changes in relative prices and asset values. While China's huge foreign reserves give it a strong buffer against a possible currency crisis, it cannot neglect the possibility of a domestic financial crisis.

An early warning system would be helpful for effective oversight, early intervention, and prevention of financial crisis. To identify threats, the authorities need to continue to deepen their financial stability analysis and develop a full range of early warning indicators. This warning system can be composed of two parts. The first would be a set of macroeconomic and sectoral models, possibly encompassing the housing market, foreign exchange market, banking sector, stock market, and labor market, among other things. It could specify the range of daily, weekly, and monthly changes in indicators that would dictate the severity of supervisory reaction. The second part would be to define the institutions responsible for monitoring and reporting market developments and for making decisions to address specific developments.

China should create an insolvency regime for the financial sector that would allow for an orderly exit of weak or failing financial institutions. In China, the sense of being "too big to fail" or "too connected to fail" is deeply rooted in the state ownership and control of financial institutions. Even small financial institutions that fail to pay off their debt rarely go bankrupt.[44] This situation creates the potential for rampant moral hazard. Signaling in an early stage of liberalization that poorly managed banks and firms could go under would be necessary even if it entails substantial short-run cost. Such a regime would include the designation of a resolution authority; the legal power to intervene promptly in a nonviable financial institution; resources to close, recapitalize, or sell such an institution; the capacity to manage the intervened institution, including its assets; and an effective safety net. A well-functioning insolvency regime would help contain moral hazard and also protect fiscal soundness. The authorities should establish an effective exit mechanism in the legal framework and streamline the court system to deal with troubled banks and firms in a timely fashion. It should allow for an orderly exit of weak or failing financial institutions and a clear definition of the role of the government in providing fiscal support. The roles of the PBC and regulatory agencies need to be reviewed. For example, it is important to limit central bank emergency liquidity support to solvent banks facing short-term liquidity problems, and to establish an out-of-court settlement system while streamlining the court system to resolve quickly failed financial institutions.

A formal deposit insurance scheme is needed to deal with potential bank runs on privately owned depository institutions and to protect the savings of small depositors (box 1.10). The preference to establish a deposit insurance fund instead of a multifunction deposit insurance system requires careful consideration. If such an institution becomes a fund only to pay for bank failures, it will bear the loss from risks incurred by banks with no ability to curtail those risks ex

A set of principles has emerged from cross-country evidence on the creation of an effective multifunction deposit insurance system. First, and most important, coverage should be limited so that large depositors, subordinated debt holders, and correspondent banks are convinced that their funds are truly at risk. This creates strong incentives for a relatively sophisticated set of depositors to monitor the activities of banks, while at the same time providing assurances of safety for depositors of smaller amounts of savings who generally lack the ability to effectively monitor banks. Second, membership in the deposit insurance scheme should be compulsory, so that stronger institutions cannot select out of the pool when new funds are needed to cover losses by other banks. Third, joint public-private management of deposit insurance schemes has proved more effective than either solely private or public management.[45] In Asia,

however, deposit insurance schemes have tended to be publicly managed and to have noncompulsory membership. Fourth, it must be made clear that funds to cover bank losses will come principally from the pool of surviving banks and that taxpayers will be tapped only in truly catastrophic circumstances. Fifth, deposit insurance premiums should be actuarially fair for the risks taken by banks, although in practice they tend to be lower in many countries. Sixth and finally, deposit insurers must play an active role in decisions about when and how to resolve a troubled bank, to minimize the cost of resolution and protect the remainder of the deposit insurance fund. Evidence shows that banks are less likely to become insolvent when the deposit insurer is responsible for intervening in failed banks and has the power to revoke a bank's membership in the deposit insurance scheme (Beck and Laeven 2008).

ante. Experiences from other countries show that deposit insurance institutions need to have some means to curtail the moral hazard associated with bank risk taking, sometimes involving a supervisory role, to better align their compensation rights (that is, the premium paid by banks) and obligations (payments to insured depositors) in the event of bank bankruptcy. Otherwise, the advantages of deposit insurance, such as deterrence of reckless risk taking by banks and improvements in the stability of the banking system by decreasing the probability of bank runs, are lost. Second, it is important to provide a legal basis for deposit insurance institutions to carry out their duties. The proposed "Regulations on Deposit Insurance" try to solve problems through administrative regulations rather than legislation.

An effective crisis management framework should be put in place. China has come out of the financial crises of Asia in 1997 and the recent financial crisis of 2008 largely unscathed. But that should provide no reason for complacency, because the Chinese financial institutions have been untested and are

not immune to external and internal shocks. A framework for crisis preparedness should be put in place that consolidates the various existing stand-alone arrangements and blocks, includes financial projection modeling and contingency planning, and involves all relevant agencies. Strategic design and capacity building are both key to the successful function of such a framework.

Recasting the rights and responsibilities of government. Most existing problems and potential risks in China's financial system can be traced back to the functions of government. An important distinguishing feature of China's financial system is the extensive involvement of the government in financial market activities. As mentioned, the government acts as owner and regulator of financial institutions and influences resource allocation through direct and indirect controls. The government is also widely perceived as an implicit guarantor of financial institutions. Despite the perceived advantages of government involvement and domination in the financial system, the negative impact on the financial sector has become increasingly felt: the conflicting roles of government in ownership and regulatory functions have made it impossible for regulation and supervision to be truly effective; continued patronage of financial institutions, including through appointment of senior executives, has prolonged the bureaucratic culture among banks; and the perception that the government will guarantee losses of failed financial institutions has exacerbated moral hazard, just to mention a few examples. To establish an effective financial system and ensure financial stability, China needs to reorient the rights and responsibilities of government in the financial sector.

First, the government should put more emphasis on creating an environment conducive to finance. The government could invest in financial infrastructure, allow the SFIs to price their services and products without interference, promote entry, and impose discipline on failures. A combination of conducive financial policies, enabling financial infrastructure, a reasonable degree of competition, and the threat of bankruptcy will go a long way toward bringing down transactions costs and providing the right incentives for SFIs to step up efforts to provide convenient, rapid, and reliable financial services.

Second, the conflict of interest caused by the multiple roles of government as owner, supervisor, and promoter should be resolved. Such conflicts of interest make it difficult for the supervisory authorities to carry out their roles in a neutral and just manner and thus to take decisive actions in case of serious offense. Besides, the regulatory authorities in China are deeply involved in the governance and operations of financial institutions through the power to appoint and remove top-level managers.

Third, the rights and responsibilities of local governments need to be aligned. Although local governments bear the responsibility for the failure of local financial institutions, they do not have relevant supervisory mandates and capabilities. Consistent with the overall trend toward decentralization, the central government has increasingly granted authority to local governments, especially since the late 1990s. There are more than a dozen types of (quasi) financial institutions under the administration of local governments. However, supervisory functions for these institutions are scattered across different departments. Lacking the means and capacity to ensure the safety and soundness of local financial institutions, provincial governments can resort to heavy intervention in their governance and operations, either through the provincial Rural Credit Cooperatives Union (RCCU) or through the Financial Affairs Office, or *Jinrongban*. In actuality, the provincial governments have assumed an ownership role in local financial institutions, at the expense of pursuing their regulatory functions.

In this regard, there is a need to establish an effective provincial-level financial supervisory framework. Local governments should focus on exercising their supervisory responsibilities, maintaining effective coordination with central government supervisory authorities, and gradually establishing regional supervisory capabilities, including establishing a supervisory framework, training a professional supervision team, and strengthening the effectiveness of on-site examination and off-site surveillance. Better provincial-level financial supervision will not only alleviate the supervision burden of the central regulator but also fill the vacuum and ultimately reduce regional financial risks. To establish such an effective regional financial supervisory framework, local governments should gradually separate the responsibilities of ownership and supervision.

Fourth, the government needs to define and effectively provide noncommercial financial services. A clear line between policy and commercial activities would determine what services and products should be provided by the government or by financial institutions owned by the government. In cases where policy-related finance is justified, principles and policies should be clearly set and supported by performance monitoring and evaluation. An exit strategy is also needed to avoid prolonged use of public resources and potential distortion of credit markets. All this will allow commercial financial institutions to focus on their commercial business, improving the effectiveness of capital usage and avoiding both financial and fiscal loss. A good understanding of the commercially sustainable frontier is essential for further reform in the policy banks and the promotion of inclusive finance to rural households and micro and small enterprises.

Obstacles to Reform

The main obstacles to reform and the difficulties faced in the process of financial liberalization are those commonly found in a financial system that has been dominated by state-owned banks or where the government has strongly intervened for a sustained period. The concerns over these obstacles tend to delay the reforms even as reforms are needed to meet the changing internal and external economic environment.

- *Moral hazard of state-owned banks and enterprises.* In a situation where major banks and firms are owned by the state, moral hazard can be pervasive. Without hard budget constraints, firms may continue to engage in reckless investment and borrowing that would lead to continued high demand for credit despite increased interest rates. Banks that put higher priority on gaining market share than on profit and prudential management would drive interest rate competition. Weak banks would have especially big incentives to offer higher deposit rates to mobilize funds and lend or invest them in high-risk borrowers or projects. That can lead to widespread distress borrowing and financial instability. If the strong incentives for moral hazard are not properly checked, interest liberalization, and financial liberalization more generally, may invite a high risk of financial instability.

- *Financial weakness of some SOEs.* Currently, SOEs pay much lower average interest rates for their debt than other borrowers such as private firms and cooperatives. The weighted average return on assets of SOEs is also significantly lower than that of other firms (see the previous section on enterprise and sector reform). On the other hand, the average debt to equity ratio of SOEs is substantially higher, exceeding 230 percent (Liu and Zhao 2009). If the financial system is liberalized, many highly leveraged SOEs would face difficulties in financing their investment or debt at low cost, resulting in deteriorating their financial situation and possibly leading to insolvency.

- *Political and bureaucratic resistance.* Financial repression has created economic rent that has been distributed to favored borrowers and nurtured vested interests. Banks have enjoyed a comfortable business environment provided by high entry barriers, interest rate control, and excess demand for credit, which allows credit rationing. Officials' power to control banks and their credit allocation is one source of their power over the economy and society. All these would work to mobilize resistance to financial reform and build a tendency of system inertia or regressing back to the old system.

Triggers for Change

Internal and external forces that build up as their economies grow and expand eventually lead to financial liberalization and opening. This is illustrated by evidence from other countries such as Korea and Japan (annex 1D). Such pressures from both domestic and external sources will also mount for the Chinese authorities in the course of transition from middle-income to high-income status. The following forces could intensify pressures for change in domestic financial system and drive the initiation of financial sector reform irrespective of the government's intentions over the next one or two decades:

- *Integration in the global market.* The Chinese financial system will have to become more integrated with the international financial system. China's rapid past economic growth results from, among other things, the opening and integration of the Chinese economy into the global economy. This integration has so far been led by the trade and real sectors, and to a limited extent by the financial sector. In transition to a high-income society, greater integration of the Chinese financial sector into global capital markets will be inevitable, as the business of Chinese firms becomes increasingly globalized and a growing number of foreign financial institutions penetrates the Chinese financial system.

- *Possible increase of nonperforming loans (NPLs) and deterioration of banks' balance sheets.* Without reforms in current lending practices and governance structures of state-owned commercial banks, the banks are likely to again accumulate large NPLs if the economic growth rate slows and the performance of SOEs deteriorates. The periodic increase in NPLs and repeated requirement to clean up bank balance sheets using taxpayer money could increase public discontent with the government's heavy regulation and control over the banking system.

- *Demand by the general public.* As income levels rise, and as households accumulate greater financial savings, Chinese citizens will demand a wider variety of financial savings options and asset investments. The demand for more equal and open access to economic opportunities will also increase. Likewise, as China's industrial structure and firms become more sophisticated and diverse, there will be a growing need for decentralized monitoring and governance of firms by market players. International experience indicates that as economies mature, financial services provided through securities markets become increasingly important for firms, particularly those in high-technology industries.

- *Pressure from the real economy.* As noted, to keep GDP growth at relatively high levels, China will have to rely more on total factor productivity growth through support for innovations and efficiency improvements. More efficient capital allocation through the financial system will

become increasingly crucial in sustaining growth.

- *External pressure from the global economy.* Relative to the global economy, China's ascendance toward an advanced high-income economy will be different from that of the ascendance of any other country in the past. Asian countries that took off earlier, including even Japan, could take the global economy and international economic system as an exogenous variable in the course of pursuing their development strategy. In contrast, the global economy and global economic system will no longer be endogenous to the development of the Chinese economy. In other words, the interplay between China and the world will be a key factor affecting the nature and pace of China's ascendance to high-income status. In the process, there could be tremendous potential for conflict and tension between China and the world economy. China is likely to play a major role in writing the rules of international trade and finance. It would be hard to imagine that such a country would maintain strong foreign exchange and capital controls with frequent interventions in the exchange market.

Sequencing of Reforms

Keeping adequate pace and sequencing will be very important for the successful progress of financial liberalization and opening. China's financial sector has served the rapid economic growth reasonably well over the past three decades, and in the process, it has been reformed and restructured. However, in view of the current and expected future economic circumstances, it should be further reformed and restructured. China may not need to pursue the same structure (including the ownership structure) and practices of financial market as are seen in most advanced economies these days. But it is also true that the liberalization and opening process will not be easy and could face many challenges including instability or temporary deterioration of economic performance, especially if it is not managed carefully. While managing financial reforms is as much art as science, and country-specific circumstances figure heavily, certain broad principles for managing reform can be put forth, drawing on the experience of other countries.

Reckless deregulation driven by the interests of the regulated should be avoided, as attested to by financial crises of many other countries, including the United States and Europe. Liberalization should be complemented by strengthened regulation and supervision. On the other hand, too much regulation will choke innovations and improvement in efficiency. Striking the right balance is not easy but is an essential consideration.

- *Financial reform is the result of a political economic process that can limit what is feasible in the near term and slow progress.* Certain market-based reforms cannot be deepened without accompanying measures. Premature reforms may also be a source of financial instability. The histories of both Japan and Korea indicate that partial deregulation of the financial system led to regulatory arbitrage that ultimately proved destabilizing. Deregulation thus must be introduced across various sectors in the financial system in ways that do not lead to major regulatory arbitrage. Banks and NBFIs should be liberalized along parallel tracks, so that a severe disintermediation or rapid expansion in some sectors does not take place and become a cause for financial crisis later.
- *The pace of domestic liberalization must be expedited when external opening of the financial system is envisaged.* While mounting external pressures eventually forced financial market opening in Japan and Korea, it also led to a significant shift of domestic financing toward offshore transactions or to severe financial instabilities because of a lack of concomitant progress in domestic financial liberalization. In this regard, further interest rate liberalization should be expedited according to the principles suggested above. While China

may be more able to resist external pressure, it would still need to accommodate demands by the rest of the world to grow and prosper together. By liberalizing the domestic system earlier rather than later, and in a systematic rather than piecemeal fashion, China could achieve the benefits of financial development without suffering undue instability.

- *Financial market infrastructure should be strengthened before liberalization.* For the system to embark on a virtuous cycle, the government will need to strengthen such infrastructure as quickly as possible and gradually reduce its influence in the internal affairs of the financial institutions, placing its focus on the roles that belong to the government, including regulation and supervision, securing credible accounting and audit practices and transparency in transactions, and creating and enforcing the right incentives and mechanisms.
- *Financial reform can progress successfully only when accompanied by institutional and organizational reforms.* Liberalizing market rules without changing old institutions can deepen distortions. Unless the government's organization changes, its modus operandi of intervention and involvement in the financial system may not significantly change. This gives the system strong inertia against real liberalization. Again, the Japanese and Korean experiences are cases in point. In this respect, in China, the reform of governance and incentive structures for management and staff of state ownership functions and institutional reforms of the relevant government bodies are two high-priority agenda items.

Land Policies

A Key Factor: Land

Land constitutes a key factor in China's quest for more efficiency-driven economic growth and more balanced and equitable development. Over the past three decades, land, together with investment, has fueled China's extraordinary levels of infrastructure development, urban expansion, and industrial growth and has contributed to maintaining social stability. Through its important links to the fiscal and monetary spheres, land use has critically affected macroeconomic stability. The state, especially local governments, has been skillful in using land, a key economic resource, to carry out its industrialization and urbanization strategies. Following the commercialization of finance, land has also become an important means to strengthen the links between government and business. Although China seemingly has some of the most rigid regulations for land use, land is often used by local governments to motivate investments, but often in a discretionary and distortionate fashion and to the detriment of rural land rights holders.

In the future, a sound land policy, legal framework, and enforcement mechanisms will be prerequisites for continued development and structural changes. More efficient land use will promote TFP and GDP growth, help maintain employment, and ensure China's domestic food production capacity. Well-functioning land markets will allow farms to grow into units that can raise rural incomes and promote efficient and livable cities. China's land policy will remain critical for maintaining social stability. In the context of rapid urbanization and migration, rural land will continue to serve as a social safety net in hard times. And land, in one form or another, will remain an important source of public revenue at local levels.

Over the past three decades, China has made impressive progress in reforming and developing its land-related policy and legal framework. From the introduction of the Household Responsibility System (HRS) in 1978 to the Property Law of 2007 and the 2008 CPC "Decision on Important Issues Concerning Rural Reform and Development," a range of policy decisions and legal reforms has addressed the questions of security of tenure and access to land, particularly agricultural land, and property. (See box 1.11 for a summary of key milestones in rural land reform.) In urban areas, a well-functioning

market for urban land use rights has been established and advanced since the mid-1980s, and robust regulations on land takings and compensation are in place.

However, previous reforms have left in place a number of problematic policies, institutional arrangements, and implementation practices. Additional significant challenges related to land policy have emerged in the course of rural-to-urban migration and urban expansion.

To transit successfully to high-income status and to realize a harmonious society, China will need to make some fundamental choices in land policy to overcome the constraints embedded in the current land tenure systems and to address the challenges that have emerged. Further reforms will have to reduce the complexity and contradictions inherent in the current system of collective and state ownership and emerging private property rights to land and ultimately treat the different types of land ownership and the associated private property rights equally within a clear legal, institutional, and policy framework. Such reforms will also have to set China on a path toward a more market-based allocation of land resources across rural and urban spaces, ultimately in the form of a unified land market. In parallel, the institutions to support such a market will have to be developed. Over this period, China will need to reconsider the state's unique monopoly power in the primary land market, which gives it the sole right to convert land for urban use. China will need to allow the state to be transformed into a market regulator, administrator, service provider, and enforcer of rules. It will also need to ensure the equitable participation and sharing of benefits from land management and transactions among its citizens.

In the most general terms, in realizing its vision for 2030, China will have incorporated and adapted the critical benchmarks from experiences in high-income countries to its specific economic, institutional, and societal context. It will have in place a policy and legal framework that provides clarity on land ownership and property rights. It will have open

BOX 1.11   Historical perspective: China's land-related policy reforms and emergence of the legal framework

China's land policy and legal framework is evolving continuously in response to economic and social changes. Policy directions provide clear evidence of a consistent appreciation of tenure security. There is also a clear trend of embodying policies into laws that is moving the country toward a comprehensive legal framework for land. The main reform milestones over the past three decades included the following:

China's Constitution provides that land in rural and suburban areas, except for that stipulated as state owned, is owned by rural collectives. The Household Responsibility System (HRS) of 1978 introduced the contracting of collective farmland to individual households for private farming, initially for a 5-year lease period that was later extended to 15 years (1984) and then to 30 years (1993). By 1983, virtually all arable land had been allocated to rural households. The HRS laid the foundation for strong agricultural and rural growth and for China's extraordinary performance in rural poverty reduction in the following decade (Lin 1992; Ravallion and Chen 2004).

The Party's No. 1 Document of 1984 laid down the foundation of China's current rural land rights system. It clarified the separation of collective ownership from individual land use rights and stipulated that collective land be contracted to households for a term of 15 years. It allowed for the voluntary transfer of individual land rights between farmers but did not provide guidance on land readjustments within the collective. The No. 11 Document of 1993 reinforced the HRS. It required that farmers' farmland rights be extended for a term of 30 years upon the expiration of the initial 15-year lease period. It endorsed transfers of farmland rights for value with prior consent from the collective and clarified the Central Government's view that administrative readjustments in response to population changes would violate famers' rights. The No. 16 Document of 1996 explicitly prohibited large readjustments and restricted small readjustments through the requirement of approval by two-thirds of the villager assembly or villager representatives and by township and county government. The document prohibited all forms of compulsory farming implemented through administrative order.

In 1988, the Land Administration Law, modeled on the Hong Kong Leasehold System, legalized the granting of use rights to state-owned land to private users and the transfer of such rights among them. In 1998, the law was revised to mandate that farmland be contracted to households for a term of 30 years. In the case of urban land, the revised law provided for marketable use rights of up to 70 years and created the legal foundation for an active urban land rights market. The law set out detailed procedures governing the taking of farmland by the state but did not provide for the meaningful participation by farmers, through such means as prior notification, participation in determining compensation, and appeal during the expropriation process.

The No. 18 Document of 2001 provided further policy direction by prohibiting the collectives from taking back land rights and recontracting those rights to nonvillagers for value. In 2002, these policies were embodied in the Rural Land Contracting Law. It clarifies the relationship between collective land ownership and farmers' land use rights, defines the contents of land use rights, and governs the transfer of individual farmland rights. It provides that rural land contracting and operation rights held by farmer households may be transferred (to other village households), leased (to nonvillage households), exchanged, assigned, or transacted by other means in accordance with law. It also provides legal remedies for any violations. The Property Law of 2007, the first comprehensive civil property code in modern Chinese history, articulates that all types of property in China—state, collective, and private—are entitled to the same level of legal protection. Furthermore, it characterizes farmers' rural land use rights as property rights rather than as the contractual rights defined by previous laws, and it provides greater protection for small farmers' land rights. It also reaffirms the provisions of the Rural Land Contracting Law. Regardless of the type of land transaction, transfers of use rights must adhere to the principles of voluntariness and free negotiation between transferor and transferee, compensa-

(Box continues next page)

BOX 1.11   (continued)

tion, freedom from compulsion, content and formal procedure, specification of contract terms, and a requirement that the transferee possesses the capacity to farm the land. In 2008, the CPC's "Decision on Important Issues Concerning Rural Reform and Development" introduced a landmark change to rural tenure by extending the 30-year term of famers' use rights for an indefinite period.

Land policy reform has been significant, but ensuring secure, marketable, and long-term land rights for all farmers remains challenging. A revision of the Land Administration Law was under way (as of 2011) and was expected to further strengthen tenure security, clarify the scope of state expropriations for public interest, determine compensation approaches for land takings, and extend the protection of farmers' rights to all types of land, including residential and collective construction land.

and integrated land markets that facilitate the accessibility and efficient allocation of land to various economic activities. And it will operate institutions that are efficient, transparent, and accountable and support the functioning of land markets, and it will apply technologies and skills that support the efficient administration and governance of land resources.

This report outlines three land policy themes or issues that will be particularly critical for achieving high-income status and social stability, along with relevant reform needs and options. The three needed reforms involve tenure security in rural areas and governance of collectives; land policy and rural-urban integration; and land policy and municipal finance.

Tenure Security in Rural Areas and Collective Governance

On its path to high-income status, China needs to improve overall tenure security in rural areas to create the right incentives for long-term investments and continued growth in agriculture and for rural-to-urban migration through effective implementation of its policies of indefinite land use rights to farmland and strengthening of the rights to other types of rural land; expanded land registration and strengthened rural land markets; and reform and modernization of the governance structure of rural collectives. (See box 1.12 for an international perspective on land policy.)

Despite a relatively clear legal and policy framework on rural land tenure, rural households continue to have weak rights over land and often face expropriation risks. The resulting insecurity creates strong disincentives for longer-term investments in agriculture and reduces land consolidation and rental activities. For example, one survey found that farmers who have at least one land document are 76 percent more likely to have made mid- to long-term investments than those who had not been issued a document (Landesa 2011). Farmers with documents that complied strictly with the law invested even more. Problematic aspects are found in persistent limitations in the tenure rights themselves, specifically with regard to the renewability and duration of existing farmland use rights and contracts that have not yet been embedded in the law. Equally important, the definition, protection, and the treatment of rights over rural residential and other collective land remain incomplete and problematic.

In addition, serious difficulties remain in the implementation of policies and laws, in improving governance and accountability at the local level, in the documentation of land rights, and in citizens' low awareness of existing rights. Taken together, these gaps create the potential for abuse of power and corruption. Disputes over rural land have become

BOX 1.12　Legal and policy framework: International perspective

High-income economies are typically characterized by widespread ownership of and access to land and property. Land is one of the most critical production inputs and accounts for a large share of national wealth in any given economy. Given the importance of land and property, high-income economies have generally moved toward ensuring clarity of definition of rights and security of tenure of land and property. Legal definitions and secure tenure have maximized land utility and its potential contribution to economic growth, while minimizing negative impacts of state interference and lengthy, unproductive disputes. Thus, for example, while the ultimate level of ownership might lie with the state, it has long been established that the state retains in effect only minimal rights.

Constitutional and legal frameworks define basic ownership and how this may be given effect with regard to alienation, inheritance, divorce, mortgaging, and the like. Registration and cadastral administrations record and thus further define these rights and parcels, covering an increasingly wide range of tenures and rights. Legal frameworks also define the bases for defining values (for example, in the con-

texts of compensation for compulsory acquisition or expropriation, taxation, and accounting) and for defining processes for change of use (through planning, zoning, and land use regulations). As a result, associated rights and responsibilities are generally considered secure and well defined, which facilitates economic activity. While uncertainties in tenure and transactions can never be entirely eliminated, they can be made somewhat predictable and be offset by risk management strategies, including insurances of various kinds.

High-income economies, reflecting in part the power of the vote and in part that of social groups and consumers, typically have well-developed legislated social policies and codes. Legislative provisions define basic landlord and tenant arrangements in both housing and commercial sectors. Similarly, legislated and regulated environmental policies defining restrictions and responsibilities significantly influence how land and property may be used and its value. Increasingly, social and environmental safeguards are conforming to international standards and codes of practice, facilitated by international forums, conventions, and agreements.

more frequent, for example, in cases where returning migrants want to resume farming and are claiming back their leased-out land. About one-quarter of villages across China is estimated to have been subjected to land consolidation and leasing arrangements to commercial enterprises, a recent and not yet well-understood phenomenon.

This complex set of problems needs to be addressed in a carefully sequenced and integrated set of reforms that strengthens tenure security in rural areas, likely involving the following elements:

Securing indefinite land use rights. Use rights to cultivated land need to be secured by expanding the renewability and duration of existing 30-year land use contracts and certificates. The CPC 2008 Policy Decision, with its stipulation of indefinite land use rights to agricultural land, was a landmark

document in this regard. Near-term reform is expected to anchor the provision of indefinite household rights to farmland, as articulated in the policy, in the relevant laws. The reform toward indefinite land use rights will need to clarify who will be eligible for such rights, for example through determining farmers' land-rights-related membership in a collective.

In the near to medium term, supplemental reforms will have to tackle the poor quality of current documentation on collective land ownership and individual use rights. These reforms could promote the introduction and implementation of a land certificate and contract system that not only specifies the property itself but includes core legal provisions and rights and responsibilities as well as sanctions in case of violations. Land contract and certificate documentation needs to be harmonized across the rural and urban spheres, for example, by following the standard format of China's existing urban land use rights certificate.

Improving land registration. China and most other developing countries lack a reliable complete national inventory of land parcels. While the full establishment of a national land inventory may not be feasible in the short or medium term, effective implementation of land rights will require some degree of clarity about the location and extent of the land to which the rights apply. More reliable, precise, and accessible records concerning the location of individual land parcels and who has what rights to a given parcel will help strengthen the trust and sense of security of contract owners, help reduce land disputes, and facilitate the more efficient implementation of land-related laws.

The government has recognized the role of land registration in promoting tenure security, rural growth, and rural-urban migration and has already piloted various land information management systems and methodologies. In the near term, the registration of farmland needs to be scaled up to realize its broader benefits. Significant start-up investments will be required to pursue the systematic and free initial registration of farmland. Ultimately, as international experiences show, land registration can be self-financing through fees for secondary transactions. Lessons from other countries indicate that administration of the land registry under a single agency could be one favorable option, because it avoids overlapping jurisdictions and parallel systems and approaches. Over time, land registration and the issuance of standardized rights certificates will gradually have to be extended to all types of rural land.

Developing rural land markets. The transition to transparent and efficient markets for farmland use rights will be important to promote productivity and GDP growth and to address China's rural-urban income gap. (For an international perspective on land markets, see box 1.13.) Gains in productivity of land use through land rental in a growing economy, such as China, can amount to 60 percent (Jin and Deininger 2009).

The functioning of markets for farmland serves as an important benchmark of tenure security. During the 1980s and mid-1990s, less than 5 percent of cultivated farmland in China was being planted under rental tenancy (Li 1999; Brandt and others 2002). Since the mid-1990s, rental markets for cultivated land have developed in a more vibrant way. Although little systematic official information is available, recent surveys provide some evidence of the expansion of the rural land rental market. The share of cultivated land being rented was only 7 percent in 2000 but increased to 19 percent in 2008, according to a survey conducted by the Center of Chinese Agricultural Policy in 2008. More land is being rented out in coastal and southern China than in inland areas or northern China. A DRC survey in 2007 covering almost 3,000 villages found that 21 percent of cultivated farmland had entered the rental market. In Anhui and Shandong, land turnover ratios were 12.4 percent and 6.1 percent, respectively (World Bank 2010b). Most of the current transfer activities are informal transactions and, in the absence of enforceable contracts, have led to inefficient and narrow market segmentations where sanctions can be enforced informally.

The transition to efficient markets for farmland rights over the coming decade will be complex and difficult. The development of appropriate market institutions will need to proceed in parallel with complementary reforms, including household registration reform, promotion of labor mobility and expansion and access to social security systems. In due course, tenure security to other types of collective land and their marketability will have to be strengthened in similar ways. (For an international perspective on land institutions, see box 1.14.) In the longer term, rural land use rights holders need to be given access to the urban land market and become full participants in the sharing of benefits whenever rural land is being converted to nonagricultural purposes.

Reforming the institution of the collective. The relatively low security of land tenure is part of a larger grassroots governance

---

BOX 1.13   Land markets: International perspective

One key pillar of economic development in high-income countries is the existence of efficiently functioning land markets. All economic activity requires access to land. Land markets facilitate accessibility, which allows land to be used in the most economic way, thus increasing economic activity and prosperity. Prerequisites for an efficient land market include clear land policies, an appropriate legal framework, secure land rights, capable institutional and professional services, transparency and availability of information, and easy access for all.

Land transactions are often complicated, because of the complexity of the property rights being transferred, the amount of money involved, and the regulatory framework within which the transactions take place. In the United States and the United Kingdom, sales by private contract (that is, for a price agreed directly between seller and buyer) are by far the most common form. There is no single land market. In addition to the different use sectors, separate markets reflect the diversity of tradable property rights, including freehold (or "full" ownership), strata title, fractional title, timeshare, leasehold, and other property-related rights such as quotas, carbon rights, and transferable development rights.

Efficient land markets depend upon buyers, sellers, professional advisers and other intermediaries having access to information. In developed countries, public sector land administration systems register transfers of ownership and transfer prices and make them available for public inspection. In addition, data on transactions is usually published through national statistics offices. With the recent growth in e-governance, the trend is toward improved web-based access and electronic public services in analyzing and disseminating data on property transactions.

---

deficit. The unresolved opportunities for abuse of power and rent seeking of village cadres at the expense of the members of the collective, for example in practices of land readjustment or commercial development, and the relative absence of transparent and accountable governance structures at the rural collective level, point to larger problems in the relationship between the collective entity and individual land use rights holders. Although recent surveys point to a reduction in the frequency of such reallocations, every village surveyed experienced at least one partial reallocation, on average, during the period 1998–2008 (Wang, Tao, and Man 2010).

A key policy challenge in rural areas of China in the coming two decades is how to modernize the institution of the rural collective to keep it relevant and consistent with the evolving shifts in law and policy, specifically the transition from the original land use rights contracted for a specified term under collective administration toward indefinite, inheritable, and transferable individual property rights to land. Reform will need to clearly define the nature of collective ownership and unambiguously identify the members of the collective; it will also have to clarify the relationship between collective ownership of land and individual rights to land in view of the government's push for a transition toward stronger and indefinite individual property rights. Such reform will not only require the strengthening of governance at the collective level but involve a fundamental redefinition of the remaining functions and roles of the collective entity as its responsibility for land management may no longer be relevant.

Land Policy and Rural-Urban Integration

On its path to high-income status, China needs to introduce fair and transparent rural land acquisition policies and practices, curtailing the role of the state in land requisition, and ensure more socially compatible rural-urban integration by allowing collectives and land use rights holders to share the benefits from urbanization.

The government promotes urbanization and rural-urban integration as part of China's overall development strategy. But

BOX 1.14   Land institutions: International perspective

To work efficiently, land markets must be supported by a wide range of institutions. In high-income economies, institutional development has progressed alongside economic development as a means of dealing with the complexities of land administration, management, and markets. The list of institutional stakeholders involved in well-developed land markets is long, ranging from policy makers to brokers, mortgage lenders to lawyers, and valuers to registrars.

Government institutions provide the policies, laws, and regulations governing all aspects of land use. Their interaction is often complex, with functions divided between ministerial departments and different levels of government. These functions include land-use planning and enforcement, the implementation of property taxation, management of state-owned land, and land registration. In recent years, there has been a trend toward commercialization, with government institutions operating as "agencies," outsourcing service provision to the private sector and entering public-private partnerships. These innovations have been driven by the demand to cut costs, improve accountability, increase accessibility, and enhance capacity. Examples in the United Kingdom include the Valuation Office Agency, which is responsible for valuing properties for taxa-

tion purposes and the extensive use of private sector firms by the Ordnance Survey, the national mapping agency.

Enforcement of laws and regulations is primarily a state function. Each country has its own unique and hierarchical court system. In many developed countries, these institutions are supplemented by special courts and tribunals that deal with specific areas such as land acquisition, taxation, and accounting. For example, in England and Wales, the Lands Tribunal determines disputes about compensation payable to owners and occupiers of land affected by expropriation, while independent Valuation Tribunals have jurisdiction over annual property tax appeals by taxpayers. In addition, many countries have developed dispute resolution systems that take place outside of court. These are usually administered by recognized independent professional bodies, such as the Royal Institution of Chartered Surveyors in the United Kingdom.

Competent, reliable, and accessible professional services provide an essential link between buyers, sellers, and government institutions active in land markets. In addition to bankers and financial service providers, these include lawyers and conveyancers, brokers or estate agents, valuers, land surveyors and structural surveyors, accountants, and others.

China's land tenure system remains biased toward urban development at a time when the rural-urban income gap has widened to levels rarely observed in other countries. The land tenure system also remains characterized by the strict separation and different treatment of rural and urban land. Within this separation, the state's exclusive power to acquire rural land and transfer it to urban users favors the currently uncontrolled and often inefficient pattern of urban development. The resulting land acquisition practices seriously disadvantage both the collective and the rural land use rights holder in sharing in the appreciating value of land entering the urban market.

These practices were historically determined and were justified in the early years of China's development when agricultural

surpluses supported the initial stages of industrialization. But these features, which are highly unusual in comparison with those in high-income economies, are now less advantageous to China's development and a major obstacle to a harmonious rural-urban integration. The widening rural-urban income gap, widespread land-related social conflicts caused by this separation, and other serious problems put this feature of the present land tenure framework and policy into question.

The persistent duality of rural and urban land systems needs to be managed and ultimately phased out. Various pilot efforts at the local level throughout China have experimented with rural-urban integration efforts with a view to developing a more comprehensive policy reform framework in the future.

BOX 1.15   Rural-urban integration and "linking mechanisms": Current and emerging issues

In contrast to farmland use rights, Chinese laws do not extend the same level of protection to farmers' residential land or other collective land, such as collective construction land. In 1962, when China's agriculture was still collectivized, residential land was allocated to farm households to use "for a long time without change," creating a de facto individual property right to residential land. The limited legal protection of rural residential land is a major disadvantage for farmers in the land conversion process. The legal vacuum has allowed many opportunities for experimentation and policy pilots that can infringe on farmers rights and contradict and circumvent Chinese laws.

Local governments throughout the country are pursuing a range of programs aimed at promoting urban-rural integration. These programs often target farmers' rights to farmland and residential land through an approach of "exchanging farmland rights for social security coverage and exchanging residential land rights and houses for urban apartments."

Initially put forward in 2004, these so-called linking mechanisms involve the reclamation of rural (collective) construction land, including farmers' residential land for conversion to farmland. Every unit of land, reclaimed corresponds to a reduction of one unit of rural construction land, and to an increase of one unit of farmland within a given jurisdiction

(discount factors apply to account for differentials in land quality). This unit of reclaimed farmland creates one unit of construction land quota that can be applied elsewhere in the jurisdiction. At this "somewhere else" place, usually the peri-urban areas where the urban land market price is high, the government can convert one unit of farmland to nonagricultural use and grant use rights to this new nonagricultural land to developers.

Through this mechanism, currently nontransferable rural residential land rights can be made marketable. However, because the rights pertaining to residential farmland and collective construction land are so weak, local governments have targeted these lands for expropriation and revenue generation, while developers have sought them for urban construction. While local governments often classify such "exchange" of farmland rights as voluntary land rights transfers, it can in fact constitute illegal appropriation of land rights.

More important, forcing farmers to give up their property rights to land in exchange for social security coverage also poses a moral dilemma because urban residents are not required to make a similar exchange. This practice also contradicts the intention of the Property Rights Law (2007), which requires that all type of property rights enjoy the same level of legal protection.

Many of the pilots have brought new challenges to the surface and often have created their own problems (box 1.15).

To promote a more harmonious integration of rural and urban areas and citizens, two fundamental reforms need to be pursued: the reform of China's current rural land requisition policies and practices is a pressing short- to medium-term issue; and integration of rural and urban land markets is required for more equitable benefit sharing in the longer term.

Reforming land requisition and compensation practices. Across the world, governments have the power to acquire land on a compulsory basis in certain circumstances and subject to certain conditions. In China,

the scope of this power is unusually wide by international standards, and its use has been very extensive. During 2003–08, a total of 1.4 million hectares of agricultural land, of which about 950,000 hectares were cultivated land, are estimated to have been requisitioned under current laws, while an additional 450,000 hectares are reported to have been requisitioned illegally during the same period. The impacts of compulsory land requisition have not been isolated and relatively localized as they might be in other countries. The process of land requisition needs serious reform in three dimensions.

First, Chinese law does not explicitly limit the purposes for which the state can use its power of compulsory acquisition. In contrast, no high-income country allows its government to use compulsory acquisition as the normal means of assembling land for purposes that are clearly commercial or industrial in nature. In the *near term,* to be more in line with international practices, tighter constraints on the use of state's power for land requisition will need to be clarified in the legal framework and implemented along the overarching principle that government's taking powers are extraordinary powers that should be limited to meet public needs that are not well addressed through the operation of the market. Such reform needs to go hand in hand with allowing the emergence of market mechanisms that span the urban-rural divide.

Second, current practices of compensation for requisitioned land need to be reviewed because they are a frequent cause of complaints about unfairness in the land requisition process. These are based on agricultural output value but do not consider the value of the land in its eventual urban use. The standard for compensation of cultivated land is a multiple (generally the duration of the land use contract, that is, 30 years) of the annual agricultural output averaged over three years. This practice is problematic in a context where the differential between urban and rural incomes and livelihoods is so large, and where this differential is reinforced by the separation of rural and urban land markets. A rethinking of the compensation practices, particularly where land is requisitioned for commercial purposes, is needed. It is recommended that the government consider international practices, where compensation is usually based on the market value for the best possible use.

Third, shortcomings in the land requisition process itself need to be addressed. While the laws set out the procedures for the taking of agricultural land by the state and require local government to make the resettlement plan public and to receive comments on it, these steps often take place only after the requisition has been approved. In addition, there is no explicit requirement that collectives or farmers be advised of the requisition ahead of time and be given an opportunity to react.

In the near term, reforms of the requisition process need to introduce key provisions such as advance notice, provide the opportunity for consultation and participation during the requisition process itself, and put in place workable channels for appeal and dispute resolution.

Integrating land markets for equitable benefit sharing. China's long-term land policy vision needs to consider more broadly how to rebalance the relationship between the state's monopoly in the primary land market and the collective and farmer participation in the conversion of agricultural land. Measures to decrease the urban-rural gap will have to consider fairer benefit-sharing approaches through, for example, gradually granting access for collectives or rural land-use-rights holders to participate in the transfer of rural land to the urban land market, while at the same time reducing and ultimately phasing out the state's monopolist power in the primary land market.

Experiences for successful rural-urban transitions and integration process exist, for example in Taiwan, China, and Korea. Both economies were able to make farmers' land rights secure and free from administrative intervention. That enabled farmers to invest in land, resulting in much increased land productivity, and to benefit from investments in urban development. In both economies, urbanization took place against a background of small farms with low per capita landholdings. Both economies adopted a farmer-friendly approach to the conversion of farmland for nonagricultural use and introduced comprehensive measures that let farmers capture a share of the increased land value as a result of conversion.[46] In both economies, farmers who sold their land rights and found employment in the city were automatically covered under urban social benefits. In China, land requisition and urban expansion have not only limited farmers' proceeds from their land assets but also led to an erosion of rural land rights by excluding collectives and farmers from the urban land market. A comprehensive reform program to better safeguard rural land ownership and, even more importantly, individual land use rights for farmland and residential land, in the process of urban-rural integration needs to be put forward.

Across China, several reform pilots are currently under way, most prominently in Chongqing and Chengdu. These pilots are experimenting with rural-urban integration approaches and promote the registration and definition of rural land ownership and property rights, the development of policies and mechanisms for the transfer and marketing of rural construction land for urban development, policies for the protection of farmland, and labor mobility and social protection reforms, as well as other elements. While the lessons and experiences of these pilots are to be collected and carefully evaluated over the coming years, the broader reform directions for making the rural-urban integration process more equitable could embody the following:

Curtailing the state's land requisition and opening the market for construction land. As noted, the state's power and scope for compulsory acquisition needs to be restricted to a more narrowly defined "public interest." This restriction will need to go hand in hand with the gradual introduction of a unified market for construction land. In such a market, collectives and individual land-rights holders would participate on an equal basis with the state in the conversion and trading of collective construction land in the primary land market without first converting the land to state ownership. Over the longer term and within a framework of approved and enforceable urban development and land use plans, collectives and individual holders of land use rights could also be empowered to participate in the conversion of collective farmland to nonagricultural purposes and be allowed to sell and buy land use rights across the rural-urban divide and benefit from it.

The capital gain accruing to collectives or individual holders of land use rights could be subjected to a tax to be set at a rate that accounts for the "public good" element of land converted to urban uses. Alternatively, the zone expropriation model practiced in Taiwan, China, or Korea's experiences with rural urban integration may offer valuable lessons on how to rationalize urban and industrial planning with fair participation and benefit sharing of the rural population in the development process (box 1.16).

Addressing the urban village problem. The move toward a unified market for construction land needs to be carefully sequenced. One option would be to begin in urban areas where collective land ownership is still widespread in the form of "urban villages"; collectively owned land is generally construction land that was not requisitioned by the state when it requisitioned land for city expansion. Because of the much higher compensation cost for collective construction land than for agricultural land, collective construction land remains scattered throughout many urban areas in China. The persistence of urban villages is one cause for inefficient city development and urban sprawl. Allowing collectives in urban areas to trade their collective construction land in the primary urban land would likely lead to more efficient development and to higher density land use in urban areas.

Strengthening checks and balances in urban development planning. The transition toward a unified urban land market will require a strict and enforceable implementation of urban and industrial land use planning. While a relatively rigorous urban planning process is in place, implementation and enforcement of long-term master plans is weak. In addition, there is no system for considering the long-term interests of urban residents or to hold decision makers responsible for the social and environmental consequences of urban development decisions. The weakness in checks and balances in the current urban planning system may be overcome by opening the planning process for public participation and scrutiny and transparency through mass media.

BOX 1.16   Land policies to promote rural-urban integration in Korea

Tenant farming predominated in the Republic of Korea before World War II. After the war, a massive land reform was conducted to distribute to former tenants the land purchased from Korean landlords or confiscated from the Japanese. As a result, more than 1.5 million farm households received land, and the farm ownership rate was raised from 13 percent to 71 percent.

To avoid social disruption in the course of urbanization, Korea took a series of legal and policy measures to prevent large-scale farming. During most of its period of urbanization, tenant farming was prohibited. This ban was eased in 1986 when the farming population dropped to less than 35 percent of the total population. The average farm size rose from 0.9 hectares in 1970 to just over 1.3 hectares in 1995. Korea also prohibited corporate ownership of farmland and corporate farming. This prohibition was lifted only in 1990, with two restrictions

remaining in place. First, half of the total investment by the corporation must come from farmers or farm families and more than half of the executive board must be farmers.

One of the important mechanisms adopted in Korea's urbanization process was its land readjustment program launched in 1966. Upon the designation of the project site agreed by 80 percent of owners of affected land, about 40 percent of the assembled land will be used by government to develop infrastructure and finance such development. The remaining 60 percent of the developed land is then distributed to participating landowners in proportion to their land contribution to the project. These landowners may choose to sell their value-added land or use it for other commercial uses. More than half of built-up areas in Seoul and over 40 percent in Pusan were developed through such land readjustment projects.

Land Policy and Municipal Finance Reform

On its path to high-income status, China needs to address the distortions in its municipal governance and finance system and reduce its excessive reliance on land-transfer-based revenue generation through the introduction of property taxes and reform of land requisition practices.

China's land policy and municipal governance and finance systems are closely interrelated, and both are shaping the country's urban land use and form for generations to come. Both the spectacular achievements as well as the enormous challenges in the area of urban planning and development grow out of the country's decentralized governance structure and fiscal systems.

In 1994, China adopted a tax-sharing system that provides separate tax collection powers for the central and subnational governments. This system has left many municipalities with a mismatch between local revenue and responsibilities for public service provision. In this setting, the combination of

the state's power to expropriate rural land and its monopoly in the urban land market, and the practice of evaluating local officials by their contributions to high GDP growth focus on generating high GDP growth, has encouraged local governments to generate additional income from land transfer fees.

Local governments have also become increasingly reliant on mortgage loans, using requisitioned land as collateral, through the vehicle of land banks. The practice of land banking by public entities created under local governments has grown phenomenally in recent years. Land banks can mortgage the land they hold to state banks and invest the loaned funds in urban development. The aggressive requisitioning of rural land to generate local revenue is risky and is contributing to unsound forms of urban growth, unsustainable local finance, and inefficient use of land resources.

Introducing market-value-based property taxes. Income from land transfer fees has become a significant source of local public revenue, and real property in China is subject to a range of minor fees, taxes, and charges, but there are virtually no annual taxes on property. Over time, property taxes could provide a sustainable substitute as receipts from land trading are reduced in parallel with a reform of land requisition practices. Property taxes are often one of the few major good sources of revenues for local governments and could in principle allow the cancellation of a range of difficult-to-collect "nuisance taxes" that can be harmful to the local business climate.

However, the property tax will take time to grow into a significant revenue source. Even in the long run, it is unlikely to fully replace income currently generated by sale of land use rights. Bahl (2009) notes that only a few countries like the United States and Canada raise on the order of 3–4 percent of GDP from such a tax, with the developed-country average being 2.1 percent of GDP. Among developing countries, the average collection is only 0.6 percent of GDP, with only a few countries (such as Uruguay) raising as much as 1.0 percent. Because the introduction of a property tax is institutionally complicated, and because difficulties in establishing initial valuation would also argue for setting initial

rates at relatively low levels, the initial take from a property tax would probably fall well below these averages. For this reason, local governments will also have to reduce their dependence on revenues from land use rights in a gradual fashion.

Implementation of a property tax is a complex task, and even in well-established systems, significant reforms are often required. International experience provides guidance on the necessary preconditions for effective implementation, such as the existence of adequate technical expertise for property assessments as well as the administration of appropriate land records (box 1.17). The development of such institutional capacity could begin in the near term. Political understanding and will are critical preconditions if the substantial challenges of implementing a highly visible and difficult-to-evade tax are to be overcome. The introduction of property taxes should be coupled with a simplification of the overly complex current system of property-based fees and taxes to ensure that these taxes fulfill their particular purpose and do not have an adverse effect on the real estate market.

BOX 1.17   Land valuation and taxation: International perspective

Most modern land administration systems include a significant valuation and taxation function. Public sector valuations are required for a variety of purposes, including property taxation; purchase, disposal, and rental of state land; and assessment of fair compensation where land is acquired through expropriation. An efficient land market, including easy access to reliable market data, provides the platform for transparent and accurate market-based valuations. High-income economies have well-developed public and private sector valuation professions using internationally recognized methodologies and standards. Valuers increasingly benefit from advances in information-technology-based automated valuation models, which particularly lend themselves to the mass appraisals required in countrywide land tax assessments.

Most developed countries impose property taxes—usually transfer taxes, estate duties, and annual property taxes—based on actual sale prices or assessed market values. Market value is generally considered to be a fair and equitable basis of taxation. In the United States and Europe, taxes on land and property provide a cornerstone of municipal finance. They have the advantage of being widely accepted by the taxpayer and are sustainable, predictable, and tend to provide a hedge against inflation over time, thus ensuring revenue maintenance in real terms. Over the past two decades, technology developments have made electronic billing and payment a central feature in both local and central government financial management.

Effectively regulating land banking. China needs to review the extent to which land banking has moved away from what was arguably its original purpose, namely, to serve as a planning tool devoted to the timed and targeted release of surplus government land in support of overall planning objectives. Today, land banking is too often an undesired conduit for requisitioned lands that are slated for disposal through auctions, which are devoted to profit maximization and securing land-backed loans. There is no national law or national regulation on land banking, although the practice is referred to permissively in some government documents. More effective regulation is urgently needed because land banking practices may be of a sufficient scale across the country to have serious implications for the economy generally, and for the financial sector in particular.

Annex 1A   Why Did China Grow So Fast?

A wide range of factors contributed to China's rapid growth. These can be viewed from three different perspectives: "growth accounting"; a review of exogenous factors that favored growth; and a discussion of the role of domestic policies and physical investments.[47]

First, China's growth performance reflected strong contributions from labor and capital accumulation as well as total factor productivity (TFP) growth. Favorable demographics, especially during the early reform period, generated a large "dividend" in the form of a labor force that grew faster than the overall population. Second, very high and rising investment rates, supported by even higher and more rapidly rising savings rates, allowed rapid capital accumulation. Over time, a gradual decline in the labor contribution was broadly compensated by the effect of a rising investment rate. Third, by World Bank staff estimates, TFP growth (including the contribution from improvements in human capital and factor reallocation) remained in the range of 3–4 percent a year, which is exceptionally high by world standards.[48]

Second, China's rapid growth was supported by three broad sets of exogenous factors. These were:

- The potential *"advantages of backwardness."* Under the "opening-up policy," China was able to borrow technology and models for social and economic institutions from the more advanced countries and thereby innovate and upgrade its industry at low cost and risk (Lin 2010). Lee and Hong (2010) find evidence that such forces were at work.

- *A high initial level of distortions.* The Chinese economy of 1978 was heavily distorted by previous policies that played to the country's comparative disadvantages. To achieve its aim of developing large, heavy, and advanced industries, the government was forced to protect such activities through various distortions, including suppressed interest rates, low input prices, and an overvalued exchange rate (Lin 2010). This left a sectoral and spatial misallocation of resources, as well as a closed economy with limited links to the rest of the world. While negative in their own right, such distortions also create greater scope for increases in TFP through policies aimed at their removal.

- *A supportive external setting.* The global environment for much of this period (Vincelette and others 2011) and the structural shift to more globalized forms of industrial production (Yusuf and Nabeshima 2010) both worked in China's favor as it pursued a strategy of opening to the rest of the world. This process included China's accession to the World Trade Organization (WTO) in 2001 and associated changes in tariffs and other policies, as well as a gradual opening to foreign investment.

Third, and most important, China was able to exploit these favorable conditions to generate rapid growth by implementing a stream of pragmatic, market-oriented reforms, and by deepening domestic market integration through improvements in infrastructure and logistics. Landmark reforms include the introduction of the household responsibility system in agriculture, the opening up of the tradables sector beginning with the establishment of special economic zones, extensive price liberalization, deep reform of the fiscal system, restructuring and privatization of state-owned enterprises, promotion of the private sector, and reforms associated with WTO accession. Other important contributors included improved macroeconomic management, factors supporting a high saving rate (the combined effect of rapid productivity gains, contained wage costs, and a managed exchange rate on enterprise profitability, with buoyant revenue growth and contained current spending on government savings), and strong subnational government-led interregional competition to attract investment. Improved policies and the sustained reallocation of factors to higher productivity uses helped keep the marginal product of capital high despite a high and rising investment rate (Bai, Hsieh, and Qian 2006; Song, Storesletten, and Zilibotti 2009).

Annex 1B   China's Industrial Policies: Key Actors and Defining Characteristics

China's industrial policy interventions are currently *implemented* by three broad classes of actors: high-level national bodies, central government departments, and subnational (provincial and local) governments and their departments. In turn, they are *influenced* by other stakeholders, such as industrial associations and firms themselves.[49]

The main high-level bodies include the State Council, the National People's Congress (NPC) and the Communist Party of China (CPC). The State Council can issue comprehensive multisector documents or policy guidance for a single sector, with the aim of promoting a particular structure across or within industries. Laws enacted by the NPC can include elements of industrial policy with significant impacts on certain industries. Finally, "work reports" to various national congresses of the CPC have included important strategic guidance (for example, on the selection of "pillar industries"), which has laid the ground for follow-up implementation measures.

Several central government departments release related policies in accordance with their responsibilities. These include the National Development and Reform Commission (NDRC), the Ministry of Industry and Information Technology (MIIT), and others. For example, the "Guiding Catalogue of Industrial Structure Adjustment" and "Catalogue of Industries for Guiding Foreign Investment" periodically issued by the NDRC are comprehensive policies, identifying industries to be "encouraged," "restricted," or "prohibited." The NDRC also issues industrial policy guidance for specific sectors. For its part, the MIIT has formulated "Opinions on Promoting the Merger and Reorganization of Enterprises," which was released by the State Council in 2010. The role of subnational authorities and their departments is discussed in the main report.

Currently, China's industrial policies have seven defining characteristics:

1. *They are scale-oriented, that is, they are focused on the development of larger enterprises.* For example, in 1993, the central government announced a strategic restructuring of state-owned enterprises, including through establishment of large-scale enterprise groups. In 1997, the 15th National Congress of the CPC issued the "Restructuring Major

Enterprises and Relaxing Control over Smaller Ones" strategy to develop large-scale enterprise groups. Since 2000, "fulfilling large enterprise group strategy in key industries" became a central element of China's industrial policy. Specific instruments include formulating a scale-oriented industrial development plan and establishing examination and approval conditions that limit entry while favoring large incumbents (Jiang and Li 2010).

2. *They have sought to control the expansion of sectors deemed to have excess capacity.* As early as the 1980s, when the basic thrust of policies was the promotion of industrial expansion, some sectors were already identified as having excess capacity; these sectors included textiles, automobiles, and home appliances. In the 21st century, curbing the development of industries with excess capacity has become a central pillar of China's industrial policy, especially in periods of macroeconomic adjustment. Since 2007, sectors targeted by the State Council as "controlled industries" included iron and steel, textiles, aluminum, coal chemicals, flat glass, caustic soda, cement, solar polysilicon, shipbuilding, chemicals, solar, and wind power. In such sectors, new entry can be restricted, capacity expansion projects might not be approved, companies can face prohibitions on financing through corporate debt and initial public offerings, and outdated production capacity can be targeted for elimination.

3. *They have aimed to concentrate sectors deemed to be too fragmented.* During the 11th five-year-plan period, the government vigorously encouraged stronger enterprises to acquire weaker firms and took other measures to encourage concentration. Subsequently, documents from the "restructuring and revitalization plans of ten industries" have all noted the need for "enhancing industrial concentration." Some provincial governments have in turn used such resolutions as a policy foundation to promote a similar concentration of their own sectors.

4. *Policies to encourage technological advancement have had industrial policy dimensions.* Such policies have included requirements to use specific local technologies; for example, one large mobile telecommunications operator was required to use the indigenous TD-SCDMA 3G technology. Some such technologies have scale economies that preclude their use by smaller producers, thus tilting the playing field toward larger firms.

5. *Industrial policies have relied heavily on direct administrative intervention to shift resources from prohibited to preferred sectors.* While market mechanisms also play a role, the authorities often use very direct means to "close down, suspend operation, merge and shift" resources. These have included market access controls, project examination and approval, land supply approval, loan approval, industrial guidance catalogue, and compulsory elimination of outdated production capacity.

6. *They have often featured joint action by many government divisions.* For example, the September 2009 "opinions on inhibiting excess capacity and redundant construction on some industries to guide the healthy development of industry" was jointly promulgated by 10 central ministries and commissions. It required joint action by departments for industrial management, quality management, investment management, environmental protection, land management, finance management, and local governments.

7. *These policies have been pursued at each level of government, often at cross purposes.* For example, while the central government may aim to consolidate a sector nationally, each province may seek to make this sector a "pillar industry" for its own economy. With over 30 provinces and many more subprovincial authorities involved, the degree to which a particular sector is ultimately favored or discouraged becomes hard to discern.

Annex 1C   Unbalanced and Incomplete Financial System

Although quantitative measures of financial depth seem to indicate that for the most part China's financial system is on par or even ahead of its economic development, the financial system is still unbalanced and incomplete (figure 1C.1). Although securities markets and insurance companies have grown, they are dwarfed by the banking system. The banking system itself is unbalanced, with the state-owned large commercial banks holding over half of banking sector assets (table 1C.1). While that share has been declining,

FIGURE 1C.1   **Select indicators of financial sector size/depth, 2009**

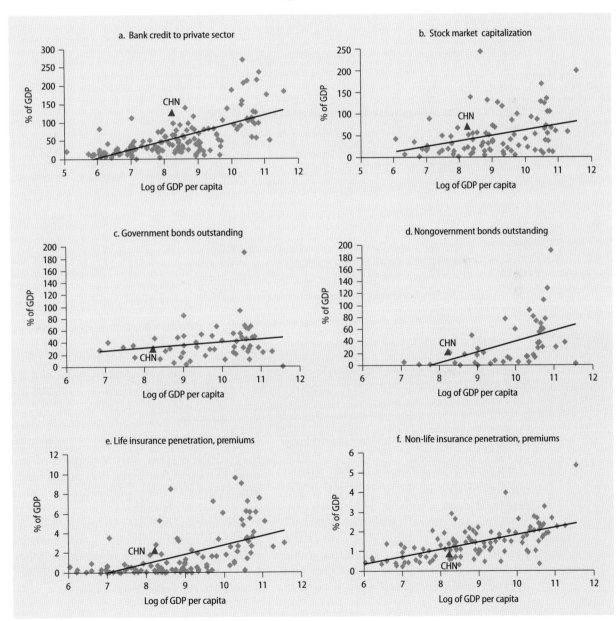

Sources: WDI, IFS, BIS, AXCO.

TABLE 1C.1   Share of banking sector assets by type of bank
Percent

Institution	2003	2004	2005	2006	2007	2008	2009	2010
Large state-owned banks	58.03	56.91	56.06	55.12	53.25	51.03	50.89	49.2
Policy banks	7.68	7.63	7.82	7.90	8.13	9.05	8.82	8.0
Joint-stock banks	10.70	11.54	11.92	12.38	13.78	14.12	14.96	15.6
City banks	5.29	5.40	5.44	5.90	6.35	6.62	7.21	8.2
Rural banks	0.14	0.18	0.81	1.15	1.16	1.49	2.37	2.9
Rural cooperatives			0.73	1.06	1.23	1.61	1.62	1.6
Urban credit cooperatives	0.53	0.57	0.54	0.42	0.25	0.13	0.03	0.0
Rural credit cooperatives	9.58	9.74	8.39	7.85	8.26	8.35	6.97	6.7
NBFIs	3.29	2.76	2.71	2.41	1.85	1.89	1.97	2.2
Postal savings banks	3.25	3.43	3.68	3.67	3.36	3.55	3.43	3.7
Foreign banks	1.50	1.84	1.91	2.11	2.38	2.16	1.71	1.8

Source: China Banking Regulatory Commission Annual Report 2009.

TABLE 1C.2   Size of financial sectors or markets as a share of GDP
Percent

	Assets of banking institutions	Assets of insurance companies	Assets of securities companies	Government bonds outstanding	Financial bonds outstanding	Corporate bonds outstanding	Stock market capitalization
1999	137.0	2.9	—	11.8	7.2	0.9	29.5
2000	138.5	3.4	—	13.1	7.4	0.9	48.5
2001	145.4	4.2	—	14.2	7.8	0.9	39.7
2002	169.8	5.3	—	14.8	8.2	0.5	31.9
2003	179.7	6.7	3.6	18.0	8.7	0.7	31.3
2004	175.0	7.5	2.1	22.4	9.1	0.8	23.2
2005	175.2	8.3	—	27.3	10.8	1.7	17.5
2006	204.0	9.1	—	28.9	12.1	2.6	41.3
2007	179.6	10.9	6.5	32.4	12.7	3.0	123.1
2008	204.3	10.6	3.8	31.3	13.4	4.1	38.6
2009	237.8	11.9	6.0	29.3	15.1	7.1	71.6
2010	241.6	12.7	4.9	28.1	15.0	8.6	66.7

Sources: China Bank Regulatory Commission, China Insurance Regulatory Commission, China Securities Regulatory Commission, Securities Association of China, Bank for International Settlements.
Note: Government bonds outstanding include both Ministry of Finance securities and Central Bank bills or notes.

China's Big Four remain among the 10 largest banks in the world.

There is also imbalance in the capital markets: stocks dominate while the corporate bond market remains underdeveloped. Stock market capitalization represents 67 percent of GDP, roughly seven times the size of corporate bonds outstanding (table 1C.2). Viewed through the lens of the share of funds raised, corporate bonds have been growing somewhat in recent years though they still represent only 9 percent of the total. In some recent years, the share of funds raised through bank loans has been as low as 50–60 percent, but those declines are mostly attributable to increasing shares of fundraising through government bonds and financial bonds (a large proportion of which are policy bank bonds), rather than increases in equities or corporate bonds (figure 1C.2).

FIGURE 1C.2   **Funds raised in the financial system (1993–2009)**

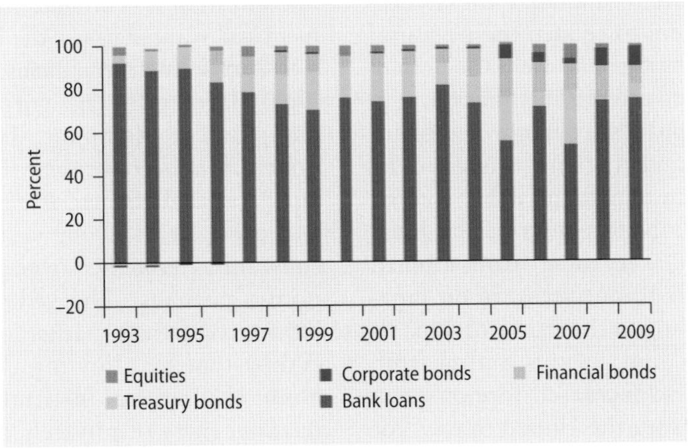

Source: China Securities and Futures Statistical Yearbook.

Annex 1D   Experiences of Japan and the Republic of Korea in Financial Liberalization

In both Japan and the Republic of Korea, financial liberalization was initiated by internal and external pressures. But the authorities were reactive, rather than proactive, to developments. Institutional and governance reforms in banks, firms, and regulatory bodies were very slow or even absent, leaving fertile soil for moral hazard while interest rate deregulation and capital market opening was in progress. In the process, regulatory arbitrage and risk were increasing. This ultimately led to financial crisis, which had to be dealt with at huge public cost.

In Japan, three main internal and external forces led to financial liberalization. First, as the period of high economic growth reached an end in 1974, the corporate sector's investment demand slowed, and firms started to accumulate surplus funds. The household sector had also accumulated substantial financial assets (deposits) by this time and started to seek assets with higher returns than bank deposits. At the same time, government budget deficits, which had expanded as economic growth slowed, had to be

financed by issuing larger volumes of government bonds. This led to the initiation of interest rate liberalization on government bonds and certificates of deposit as holders of those instruments required market-based interest, which also had to be applied to other interest rates to reduce the regulatory arbitrage.

Second, the internationalization of Japanese firms' operations required the domestic financial system to support the expansion of their international business, by among other things hedging risk exposure and meeting financing requirements in foreign currencies. This spurred the relaxation of the foreign exchange system and increased entry by Japanese financial institutions into international financial centers by establishing branches and subsidiaries. Once Japanese firms were able to issue debt abroad, and Japanese financial institutions could make investments in foreign assets more freely, Japanese households' savings started to find their way to the purchase of (Euroyen) bonds issued (at uncontrolled interest rates) by Japanese companies through Japanese banks and insurance companies located abroad. This process built up further pressure to liberalize the domestic financial system to reduce the potential for regulatory arbitrage and stem the flow of domestic finance to the offshore market.

Third, as the Japanese economy and financial market expanded, there was growing interest by foreign banks and other foreign financial institutions to penetrate the Japanese financial market; these firms lobbied their governments to put pressure on Japanese officials. The continuation of Japan's large current account surplus dating from the mid-1970s also increased foreign pressure, especially from the United States, for the opening of the Japanese service sectors and capital markets, a pressure that was eventually accommodated. That put further pressure on the government to liberalize the domestic financial system; without liberalization, the distortions and weaknesses in the domestic system would have intensified.

In Korea, the government's control over the financial system was more direct and pervasive than in Japan. As in China, all banks were owned by the state, and their lending activities were strongly controlled by the government through explicit policy lending programs and implicit window guidance. Interest rates were controlled and set substantially below the supposed market clearing rate. Government intervention grew stronger in the 1970s when the Korean government initiated a strong drive to develop its heavy and chemical industries (HCI). This led to substantial overcapacity in the HCI sector and a large amount of nonperforming loans in the banking sector, while light industries and small and medium firms were starved for credit. This in turn caused the deterioration of Korea's export competitiveness, slowed economic growth by the end of 1970s, and culminated in the assassination of President Park. Partly as a response to this negative experience with heavy financial repression, and as part of its overall economic liberalization efforts, the Korean government began gradual liberalization of the banking system by privatizing banks and relaxing entry barriers for other kinds of financial institutions.

However, true progress in banking sector liberalization was limited because the government still wanted to use the banking sector as a tool for industrial policies and also because highly leveraged large corporations needed cheap and stable finance from the banking system for their survival. By this time, the large corporate firms (*chaebols*) had emerged as a group with strong vested interests and substantial influence over government economic policies. The government instead introduced greater market forces in the financial system by allowing the expansion of nonbank financial institutions (NBFIs), by relaxing entry of privately owned (including foreign) institutions such as finance companies, merchant banking firms, and insurance companies, which were free from policy loan programs but could offer savings accounts similar to bank deposits. As in the Japanese case, this liberalization was also caused by increasing external pressure, especially from the United States, as Korean financial markets grew larger and as a substantial current account surplus emerged in the second half of the 1980s. These developments reduced banks' shares of total deposits and squeezed their profits by shifting deposits to NBFIs. This in turn pressured the government to allow banks to expand into products offered by NBFIs such as trust accounts.

The government started interest rate liberalization in the late 1980s but made little progress until the early 1990s when it liberalized interest rates on short-term money market instruments such as commercial paper and certificates of deposit (CDs), while maintaining control on bank interest rates. This accelerated the shift of funds to finance companies, other NBFIs, and the trust accounts of banks. The net effect was a reduction of average maturities in the liability side of corporate sector balance sheets, which increasingly had to rely on these short-term financing instruments. Foreign exchange controls were relaxed under pressures from both domestic firms, whose business had become more globalized, and foreign governments, which were pressured by their financial institutions to penetrate uncompetitive but expanding Korean financial markets. On the other hand, large chaebols and banks had built the perception that the government would not be able to let them fail for fear of the impact on overall economic performance. In fact, the Korean government had protected the chaebols and financial institutions (including small ones) from failures, and no significant chaebol or financial institution had gone bankrupt before 1997. The combination of these pressures led to two significant developments: increased reliance on short-term corporate finance; and increased foreign debt, especially short-term debt by financial institutions. In the first half of the 1990s, increased foreign capital inflows and domestic savings were channeled to large firms, which expanded their investment recklessly, due in part to pervasive moral hazard that came with the perception of "too big to fail." The first factor caused a domestic financial crisis when overly leveraged large corporate firms could not service their debt and were faced with an economic recession starting 1996. Together with the first, the second factor caused a currency crisis when foreign capital flowed out massively from Asian countries in 1997, which intensified the domestic financial and economic crisis.

Korea completed full liberalization and opening of the financial system under its post-crisis International Monetary Fund program, and undertook massive financial and corporate restructuring, with huge injections of public funds (equivalent to one-third of GDP) to clean up the balance sheets of financial institutions. In sum, government control over finance was an effective vehicle for rapid industrialization and economic growth in the early stage of Korea's economic advancement, but it led to pervasive moral hazard in both the banking and corporate sectors, which led to reckless investment by favored firms and poor risk management of banks. In the end, huge amounts of public funds were required to remedy the problems. Similarly, Japan experienced a domestic financial crisis as the asset bubble, which was built during the second half of the 1980s with the moral hazard of financial institutions and poorly managed financial regulation, started to deflate in 1991. Japan completed its financial liberalization and a restructuring of regulatory framework and government organization by 1998, and financial restructuring by 2004. In the course, it experienced a prolonged and deep financial crisis, which it has dealt with through injection of public funds at a huge public cost.

Notes

1. For a more extensive discussion of these imbalances, see the overview of this series.
2. Indeed, industrial employment grew by just 2.3 percent a year during 1993–2007, compared with annual value-added growth of 11.7 percent.
3. Investment rates would be supported by further reforms that work to sustain high rates of return to capital, by the large remaining scope for capital deepening, and by the new investment demand generated by emerging social and environmental challenges (Stern 2011).
4. http://english.peopledaily.com.cn/200412/06/eng20041206_166239.html.
5. Under the 12th 5YP, these gained added relevance through changes wrought by the global financial crisis. With subdued medium-term prospects for the global economy—and thus for exports—China will need to generate more growth from domestic demand if it is to sustain relatively high rates of overall GDP growth.
6. For example, see Kuijs and Wang (2006), Blanchard and Giavazzi (2006), Lardy (2007), and Aziz and Dunaway (2007).
7. The DRC–CGE model (2012 edition) includes 34 production sectors; 2 representative households distinguished by area; and 4 primary production factors: capital, agricultural labor, productive workers, and professionals. The 34 production sectors include 1 agricultural sector, 24 industrial sectors, and 9 services sectors. For a detailed description of the model, see Li and others (2010) and He and Kuijs (2007). This study has updated the previous simulations by incorporating new economic data and adjusting some parameters in light of new empirical research. The main drivers of growth are technological progress,

demographics, and capital accumulation. In this model, technological progress is exogenous and calibrated according to China's historical data and international experience. In addition, the growth rate of population and labor is exogenous. The growth rate of capital is determined endogenously by the savings-investment relationship. In this model, the basic factors driving structural change are the income demand elasticity of residents for different commodities (the Engel effect), the structural change of intermediate input demand resulting from technological change, and factor composition change resulting from different factor accumulation speeds.

8. These scenarios are not meant to be precise, detailed investigations of the future. Rather, they are somewhat stylistic, based on analysis of how key macroeconomic variables have related to each other in the past and assumptions on how these relationships may evolve in the coming 20 years. Many of those assumptions unavoidably have an arbitrary element.

9. Although this decline may seem fast, it is not out of line with experiences in other Southeast Asian countries. Korea witnessed a faster decline, from 50 percent in 1973 to 10 percent in 2001. Malaysia decreased its agricultural employment share from 37 percent in 1980 to 18.4 percent in 2001.

10. Such limits could include declining margins in the production of tradable goods, excess capacity, asset bubbles, insufficient employment generation, environmental degradation, and trade protectionism.

11. Chapter 2 looks at the other policies needed to advance the pace of innovation, a critical ingredient for rapid growth by improving China's technological capability and moving up the value chain.

12. This compares to headline budgetary government size of 19.9 percent of GDP in 2008 (22.5 percent in 2010). The IMF's Government Finance Statistics, a broader measure, includes government activities funded by some government funds and the social protection fund. As in other countries, these funds are separate from the core central budget. Nonetheless, they are subject to budget-type planning and management and are sometimes presented as part of a broader definition of consolidated spending. The budget preparation cycle for such funds is increasingly being aligned with that of the core budget.

13. This rose to more than 35 percent of GDP in 2010.

14. According to the Ministry of Finance (2011), the gross revenue from the sale of state-owned land use rights rose to 2.9 trillion yuan in 2010, equivalent to 7.3 percent of GDP. Because a substantial share of such revenues is paid out in the form of compensation to displaced residents, the net proceeds from such sales are lower but still significant.

15. In 2004, the Ministry of Finance released a list of government funds, stipulating that no government agency was allowed to charge fees beyond this list. In 2010, the State Council began compiling a national budget for social security funds on a trial basis. This budget initially included funds for five types of social security: basic old-age insurance, unemployment insurance for enterprise employees, basic medical insurance, workers' compensation, and maternity insurance for urban workers. The eventual aim would be to bring other social security funds within the control of the national budget. From 2011, the Provisional Rule on Government Funds Management includes a stipulation that all government funds revenues should be included in the fiscal budget and subject to the scrutiny of the National Peoples' Congress.

16. World Bank (2010a) provides a detailed discussion on SOE dividend policy and international practices.

17. Several such taxes address negative externalities. Unlike many other taxes, such taxes present few if any trade-offs when viewed in a more holistic way than through GDP alone, because they make prices better reflect the true marginal cost of a particular activity, including the damage to the environment.

18. Data are from Fiscal Reform and Economic Governance (2011), which takes into account only personal income taxes and contributions to pension funds. Including contributions to health insurance and housing fund, China's overall labor tax wedge is even higher.

19. Furthermore, the "revenue productivity" of personal income tax—measured as the revenue collected as a share of GDP divided by the weighted average personal income tax rate—is only 15 percent of global averages

and 11 percent of high-income-country averages.

20. This includes central government debt of RMB 6.75 trillion and subnational government debt of RMB 10.7 trillion. Of total subnational government debt, 62.6 percent is explicit debt, 21.8 percent is contingent debt (guarantees), and the subnational governments have only limited rescue responsibility for the remaining 15.6 percent.

21. The big three metropolises directly administered by the central government (Beijing, Shanghai, and Tianjin) have very small county-level governments.

22. Jia Qinglin, "Remarks in the 3rd Conference of Commending the Outstanding Builders of Chinese Characteristic Socialism in the Private Sector," *People's Daily*, November 7, 2009.

23. "Bamboo Capitalism." *The Economist*, March 11, 2011.

24. For example, Ferri and Liu (2009) find that the cost of debt is significantly lower for SOEs, even after controlling for individual firm features. They estimate that had SOEs paid the same loan rates as otherwise equivalent private firms, the additional interest payment would have wiped out their profit in 2004 and 2005, the two last years in their sample.

25. However, in some sectors such as telecoms, the splitting up was along geographic lines, still leaving a single dominant provider in any given area.

26. For example, in 2006, all of petroleum, natural gas, and ethylene production, SOEs controlled all basic telecoms services, about 55 percent of electricity generation, and 82 percent of airline and air cargo traffic (Owen and Zheng 2007).

27. Even if entry is allowed, and even beyond areas considered "strategic," private firms can face a range of other disadvantages. Ferri and Liu (2009) document significant advantages in borrowing terms for SOEs. In an overview of prospects for private airlines in China, Pan (2010) documents other regulatory and financial advantages of SOEs, including in securing bailouts through capital injections and in access to bank financing; and Tian (2007) documents entry barriers in the automobile industry.

28. Examples include sections of work reports to CPC congresses, policy guidance for 5YPs, and comprehensive or single-sector policy documents.

29. The latter policy is implemented by bodies such as the General Administration of Quality Supervision, Inspection, and Quarantine; the State Food and Drug Administration; and the State Administration of Work Safety. Such inspections and reorganizations can bring significant restructuring within sectors. For example, in April 2011, many of China's dairies were shut down after having their licenses revoked.

30. See, for example, State Information Center (2007), Ou and Liu (2007) on the NDRC, and Yuan (2010).

31. See, for example, Shi and Wang (2011), Jiang (2010), and Yang (2004).

32. At that time, the central government issued a policy aimed at eliminating outdated plants and reducing some capacity in that industry. Measures included mandatory closure of outdated plants, subsidies for restructuring and equipment replacement, and preferential placement for fired workers.

33. Similar cases can be found at the provincial and local level. For example, some local governments regarded the software industry as a local pillar industry and implemented preferential policies more than 10 years ago. However, the software industry remains weak in many of these localities.

34. Some automotive firms favored by industrial policy, such as Tianjin Xiali, Guangzhou Peugeot, and Beijing Jeep have in fact declined, while nationally less favored firms such as Geely, BYD, and Chery have grown.

35. The government can use state ownership as a policy tool to launch its industrial strategy, especially as SOEs can become excellent platforms for accumulating resources in times of economic prosperity. However, evidence suggests that a persistently large-size state sector can be harmful to efficiency and equitable competition in the long-term.

36. DRC staff calculation.

37. See Schneider (2010) for a detailed discussion of EU "state aid" rules in the Chinese context.

38. Controls take the form of directed credit and aggregate credit ceilings, floors for loan interest rates, and caps on deposit interest rates; business decisions of financial institutions are also controlled.

39. According to media reports, the potential losses of banks lending to local government platforms may be on the order of 2 trillion yuan.

40. Finding domestic strategic investors would be difficult. Selling banks to foreign strategic investors may not be politically acceptable, and it might be difficult to find willing and able buyers for a variety of reasons. Privatization by placement of government shares with small individual investors would not be a good option either, because the government would continue to be able to control the bank's management and operation.

41. Financial institutions continue to be subject to a floor on lending rates and a ceiling on deposit rates. The cap on deposit rates has been circumvented to a certain extent by the newly emerging credit-based wealth management products in the banking system, which further exacerbated the situation of shadow banking, with potential negative implications for financial stability.

42. The new Chinese Accounting Standards have achieved material convergence with the International Financial Reporting Standards. The Chinese Standards on Auditing are also largely comparable to the International Standards on Auditing.

43. The practice of differentiated reserve requirements and differentiated capital regulation would require bank-specific information that is available only to the banking supervisory authority gathered through its off-site surveillance and on-site examination. It would be logical for the PBC to focus on core central banking business and macroprudential functions instead and leave microlevel prudential matters to the banking supervisory authority.

44. In the past decade or so, only one bank, Hainan Development Bank, was closed. Several dozen minor financial institutions, mainly credit cooperatives, have been allowed to go under, but their resolution has been lengthy.

45. However, there are very few cases of solely private management, so the evidence here is based mostly on a comparison between joint public-private management and solely public management.

46. For example, Taiwan, China, adopted a law that introduced "zone expropriation" for the provision of land for urban development projects, especially those of a commercial nature. Under such processes, a farmer landowner may demand 40–50 percent of the expropriated land as compensation in lieu of cash and thus share partially but significantly in the gains from such development.

47. For more discussion of factors behind past performance, see Hofman and Wu (2009), Huang (2011), and Vincelette and others (2011).

48. Kuijs (2010) finds TFP growth of 3–3.5 percent a year from 1978 to 2009, of which about 0.5 percent comes from enhanced human capital. Bulman and Kraay (2011) find TFP growth of 3.0–4.1 percent a year from 1979 to 2008, over one-half of which they attribute to factor reallocation.

49. In the past, the NDRC (or its predecessor, the National Planning Commission) led the design and implementation of industrial policies, while specialized departments took charge of detailed work and local governments and other stakeholders participated in the process. With reform, most of the specialized economic departments have been abolished, while other stakeholders have become more powerful.

References

Allen, Franklin, Forrest Capie, Caroline Fohlin, Hideaki Miyajima, Richard Sylla, G. Wood, and Y. Yafeh. 2010. "How Important Historically Were Financial Systems for Growth in the U.K., U.S., Germany, and Japan?" Wharton Financial Institutions Center Working Paper 10–27, University of Pennsylvania, Philadelphia.

Amsden, Alice H., and Ajit Singh. 1994. "The Optimal Degree of Competition and Dynamic Efficiency in Japan and Korea." *European Economic Review* 38 (3–4): 941–51.

Aziz, Jahangir, and Steven Dunaway. 2007. "China's Rebalancing Act." *Finance and Development* 44 (September): Pages?.

Bahl, Roy. 2009. "Fixing the Property and Land Tax Regime in Developing Countries." February 25. Draft. [Sponsoring organization, location??]

Bai, Chong-En, Chang-Tai Hsieh, and Yingyi Qian. 2006. "The Return to Capital in China." Working Paper 12755, National Bureau of Economic Research, Cambridge, MA (December).

Beck, Thorsten, and Luc Laeven. 2008. "Determinants of Deposit-Insurance Adoption and

Design." *Journal of Financial Intermediation* 17 (3): 407–38.

Blanchard, Olivier J., and Francesco Giavazzi. 2006. "Rebalancing Growth in China: A Three-Handed Approach." Discussion Paper DP5403, Center for Economic Policy Research, London (January).

Brandt, Loren, Jikun Huang, Guo Li, and Scott Rozelle. 2002. "Land Rights in Rural China: Facts, Fictions and Issues." *China Journal* 47 (January): 67–97.

Brandt, Loren, Johan Van Biesbroeck, and Yifan Zhang. 2009. "Creative Accounting or Creative Destruction? Firm-Level Productivity Growth in Chinese Manufacturing." *Journal of Development Economics* 97(2): 39–51.

Brandt, Loren, and Xiaodong Zhu. 2010. "Accounting for China's Growth." Working Paper 4764, Institute for the Study of Labor, Bonn (February).

Bulman, David, and Aart Kraay. 2011. "Growth in China 1978–2008: Factor Accumulation, Factor Reallocation, and Improvements in Productivity." World Bank, Washington, DC (May).

Chen, Shiyi, Gary H. Jefferson, and Jun Zhang. 2011. "Structural Change, Productivity Growth and Industrial Transformation in China." *China Economic Review* 22: 133–50.

CBRC (China Banking Regulatory Commission). 2010. "China Banking Regulatory Commission Annual Report 2009." Unpublished.

CSRC (China Securities Regulatory Commission). Various years. *China Securities and Futures Statistical Yearbook*. Beijing: Academia Press China.

Demirgüç-Kunt, Asli, Erik Feyen, and Ross Levine. 2011. "Optimal Financial Structures and Development: The Evolving Importance of Banks and Markets." Policy Research Working Paper 5805, World Bank, Washington, DC.

Dollar, David, and Bert Hofman. 2006. "Intergovernmental Fiscal Reforms, Expenditure Assignment, and Governance." Paper presented at the Roundtable Conference on Public Finance for a Harmonious Society, Beijing, June 27–28.

The Economist. 2011. "Bamboo Capitalism." March 11.

Eichengreen, Barry, Donghyun Park, and Kwanho Shin. 2011. "When Fast Growing Economies Slow Down: International Evidence and Implications for China." Working Paper 16919, National Bureau of Economic Research, Cambridge, MA.

Ferri, Giovanni, and Li-Gang Liu. 2009. "Honor Thy Creditors before Thy Shareholders: Are the Profits of Chinese State-Owned Enterprises Real?" Working Paper 16/2009, Hong Kong Institute for Monetary Research, Hong Kong SAR, China.

Fiscal Reform and Economic Governance. 2011. Collecting Taxes Data System, 2009–10. http://www.fiscalreform.net/index.php?option=com_content&task=view&id=759&Itemid=134.

Fogel, Kathy, Randall Morck, and Bernard Yeung. 2007. "Big Business Stability and Economic Growth: Is What's Good for General Motors Good for America?" *Journal of Financial Economics* 89 (1): 83–108.

Gerschenkron, A. 1962. *Economic Backwardness in Historical Perspective*. Cambridge, MA: Harvard University Press.

Gill, Indermit, and Homi Kharas. 2007. *An East Asian Renaissance—Ideas for Economic Growth*. Washington, DC: World Bank.

He, Jianwu, and Louis Kuijs. 2007. "Rebalancing China's Economy—Modeling a Policy Package." China Research Paper 7, World Bank, Washington, DC.

Hofman, Bert, and Jinglian Wu. 2009. "Explaining China's Development and Reforms." Working Paper 50, Commission on Growth and Development, Washington, DC.

Hsieh, Chiang-Tai, and Peter Klenow. 2009. "Misallocation and Manufacturing TFP in China and India." *Quarterly Journal of Economics* 124 (4):1403–48.

Hu, Jiangyun. 2008. "Industrial Policies and the Development of China's Large Auto Groups." In *2007 Annual Report of the Development of China's Large Enterprise Groups*, ed. Wenkui Zhang. Beijing: China Development Publishing House (in Chinese).

Huang, Yiping. 2010. "Dissecting the China Puzzle: Asymmetric Liberalization and Cost Distortion." *Asian Economic Policy Review* 5: 281–95.

Huang, Yiping, and Kunyu Tao. 2010. "Causes and Remedies of China's External Imbalances." Working Paper 2010–02, China Center for Economic Research, Beijing.

Huang, Yiping, and Bijung Wang. 2010. "Cost Distortions and Structural Imbalances in China." *China & World Economy* 18 (4): 1–17.

Huang, Yukon. 2011. "China's Policy Reforms—Why They Worked." Processed, April 26. Background note for this report.

IMF (International Monetary Fund). Various years. Government Finance Statistics database. Washington, DC. http://elibrary-data.imf.org/FindDataReports.aspx?d=3306/6e=170809

Jiang, Feitao, and Xiaoping Li. 2010. "Market Intervention Directly and Competition Restriction: The Orientation and Fundamental Flaws of China's Industrial Policy." *China Industrial Economics* 2010 (9): (in Chinese).

Jiang, Xiaojuan. 2010. "Institution Reform and Industrial Development—Studies on Courses and Cases." Beijing Normal University Publishing (in Chinese).

Jin, Songqing, and Klaus Deininger. 2009. "Land Rental Markets in the Process of Rural Structural Transformation: Productivity and Equity Impacts from China." *Journal of Comparative Economics* 37: 629–46.

Kuijs, Louis. 2010. "China through 2020—A Macroeconomic Scenario." China Research Working Paper 9, World Bank, Washington, DC.

Kuijs, Louis, and Tao Wang. 2006. "China's Pattern of Growth, Moving to Sustainability and Reducing Inequality." *China and the World Economy* (January 2006): 1–14.

Landesa, Rural Development Institute. 2011. "Preliminary Survey Findings on Chinese Farmers' Land Rights and Future Reforms." Presentation Slides. Seattle, WA.

Lardy, Nicholas R. 2007. "China: Rebalancing Economic Growth." In *The China Balance Sheet in 2007 and Beyond*. Washington, DC: Center for Strategic and International Studies and Peterson Institute for International Economics.

Lee, Jong-Wha, and Kiseok Hong. 2010. "Economic Growth in Asia: Determinants and Prospects." Working Paper Series 220, Asian Development Bank, Manila (September).

Leipziger, Danny M., Claudio Frischtak, Homi J. Kharas, and John F. Normand. 1997. "Mercosur: Integration and Industrial Policy." *World Economy* 20 (5): 585–603.

Li, Guo. 1999. "The Economics of Land Tenure and Property Rights in China's Agricultural Sector." Unpublished Ph.D. dissertation, Stanford University.

Li, Shaomin, and Jun Xia. 2008. "The Roles and Performance of State Firms and Non-State Firms in China's Economic Transition." *World Development* 36 (1): 39–54.

Li, Shantong, and others. 2010. "Simulated Scenarios for China's Economic Growth: 2011–2030." *China Economist,* May–June.

Lin, Justin Yifu. 1992. "Rural Reforms and Agricultural Growth in China." *American Economic Review* 82 (1): 34–51.

———. 2010. "The China Miracle Demystified." Paper presented at the Econometric Society World Congress, Shanghai, August 19.

———. 2011. "China and the Global Economy." Remarks at the 20th Anniversary of the Hong Kong University of Science and Technology, March 23.

Liu, Lili. 2010. "Strengthening Subnational Debt Financing and Managing Risks." *Review of Economic Research* (Ministry of Finance, China) (August 16, 2010): 46 F-9.

Liu, Lili, and Juan Pradelli. 2011. "China Financing Infrastructure and Monitoring Fiscal Risks at Subnational Level: Strategic Considerations and Policy Options." Forthcoming Policy Note, World Bank, Beijing Office.

Liu, Xiaoxuan, and Xiaoyan Zhou. 2009. "How the Financial Resources Are Allocated to the Real Economy in China: Test for Relationships between the Financial and Industrial Sector." Working paper. http://www.wcu-snuecon.co.kr/upload/catalogue_file/b828a8d86c926d2d14372f04dc2742f7.pdf

Luo, Xubei. 2005. "Growth Spillover Effects and Regional Development Patterns: The Case of Chinese Provinces." Policy Research Working Paper 3652, World Bank, Washington, DC.

Ministry of Finance (China). 2010. "The Final Account of Chinese Central Government of 2010." Beijing.

———. 2011. "Report on the Implementation of the Central and Local Budgets for 2010 and on the Draft Central and Local Budgets for 2011." Presented to the Fourth Session of the Eleventh National People's Congress, March 5.

National Bureau of Statistics (China). Various years. "China Statistical Yearbook." Beijing: China Statistical Publishing House.

Naughton, Barry. 2007. "China's State Sector, Industrial Policies and the 11th Five Year Plan." Testimony before the US-China Economic and Security Review Commission Hearing, Washington, May 24. http://www.uscc.gov/hearings/2007hearings/written_testimonies/07_05_24_25wrts/07_05_24_25_naughton_statement.php.

———. 2011. "What Price Continuity?" *China Leadership Monitor* 34.{Page numbers?]

OECD (Organisation for Economic Co-operation and Development). 2006. "Current Situation of the Chinese Steel Industry." Report DSTI/SU/SC(2006)9, Paris.

————. 2010. *Economic Survey of China 2010*. Paris: OECD.

Ou, Xinqian, and Jiang Liu. 2007. *China's Industrial Development and Industrial Policy*. Beijing: Xinhua Press (in Chinese).

Owen, Bruce, and Wentong Zheng. 2007. "China's Competition Policy Reforms: The Antimonopoly Law and Beyond." Stanford Institute for Economic Policy Research (SIEPR) Discussion Paper No. 06-32 Stanford, CA.

Pan, Jane. 2010. "Focus: China's Private Airlines." (www.flightglobal.com/articles/2010/05/18/342125/focus-chinas-private-airlines.html.

Ravallion, Martin, and Shaohua Chen. 2004. "China's (Uneven) Progress against Poverty." Policy Research Working Paper 3408, World Bank, Washington, DC.

Rosenstein-Rodan, P. N. 1961. "Notes on the Theory of Big Push." In *Economic Development for Latin American*, ed. H. Ellis. New York: Macmillan and Co.

Schneider, Jacob. 2010. "Administrative Monopoly and China's New Anti-Monopoly Law: Lessons from Europe's State Aid Doctrine." *Washington University Law Review* 87: 869–95.

Shi, Yaodong, and Zhonghong Wang. 2011. "Evaluation on China's Industrial Policy—Based on Auto Industry." Internal report, Development Research Center, Beinjing (January) (in Chinese).

Song, Zheng Michael, Kjetil Storesletten, and Fabrizio Zilibotti. 2009. "Growing Like China." CEPR Discussion Paper 7149, Centre for Economic Research, London (January).

State Information Center (China). 2007. "Energy Saving and Emission Reduction: The New Start of China's Industrial Policy." Working paper, Beijing (in Chinese).

Stern, Nicholas. 2011. "Raising Consumption, Maintaining Growth and Reducing Emissions." Paper for China Development Forum, Beijing (March).

Sutherland, Dylan, and Lutao Ning. 2008. "Exploring and Explaining the Extent of Concentration and Diversification in Chinese Business Groups." Processed.

Tian, Lihui. 2007. "Does Government Intervention Help the Automobile Industry? A Comparison with the Chinese Computer Industry." *Economic Systems* 31: 364–74.

UNCTAD (United Nations Conference on Trade and Development). 2002. "Application of Competition Law: Exemptions and Exceptions." UNCTAD/DITC/cLP/ Misc.25, Geneva.

Vincelette, Gallina, Alvaro Manoel, Ardo Hansson, and Louis Kuijs. 2011. "China: Global Crisis Avoided, Robust Economic Growth Sustained." In *The Great Recession and Developing Countries: Economic Impact and Growth Prospects*, ed. Mustapha K. Nabli, 161–202. Washington, DC: World Bank.

Wang, Hui, Tan Tao, and Joyce Yanyun Man. 2010. "To Reallocate or Not? Reconsidering the Dilemma for China's Agricultural Land Tenure Policy." Lincoln Institute Working Paper Series 040, Peking University, Beijing (October).

Weiss, John. 2005. "Export Growth and Industrial Policy: Lessons from the East Asian Miracle Experience." Discussion Paper 26, Asia Development Bank Institute, Manila (February).

Westphal, Larry E. 1990. "Industrial Policy in an Export-Propelled Economy: Lessons from South Korea's Experience." *Journal of Economic Perspectives* 4 (3): 41–59.

World Bank. 2009a. *From Poor Areas to Poor People: China's Evolving Poverty Reduction Agenda; An Assessment of Poverty and Inequality in China*. Washington, DC: World Bank.

————. 2009b. "GET Note: Functional Reviews & Alternative Service Delivery." "Recently Asked Questions" Series 53458, World Bank, Washington, DC (August).

————. 2009c. *Mid-Term Evaluation of China's 11th 5 Year Plan*. Washington, DC: World Bank.

————. 2009d. *World Development Report 2009: Reshaping Economic Geography*. Washington, DC: World Bank.

————. 2010a. "Effective Discipline with Adequate Autonomy: The Direction for Further Reform of China's SOE Dividend Policy." Policy Note, World Bank, Washington, DC.

————. 2010b. "China Land Transfer and Registration Technical Assistance: Report on Survey of Rural Households and Other Stakeholders in Anhui and Shandong Provinces." World Bank, Washington, DC.

Wu, Jianglian, Junkuo Zhang, and Shijin Liu. 1998. "The Strategic Restructuring of the State Sector." China Development Press, Beijing (in Chinese).

Xu, Shanda. 2006. "On the Consistency of Tax Attribution and Tax Source." Paper presented at the High-level Roundtable Conference of Public Finance and Building a Harmonious Society, Beijing, June 27–28 (in Chinese).

Yang, Weimin. 2004. *Research on Integrated Policies for China's Sustainable Industrial*

Development. Beijing: China Market Press (in Chinese).

Yuan, Lei. 2010. "The Effectiveness Evaluation of 10 Industrial Adjustment and Promotion Plans." *China Economy and Trade Magazine* (zhongguo jingmao daokan) (October): (in Chinese).

Yusuf, Shahid, and Kaoru Nabeshima. 2010. *Changing the Industrial Geography in Asia.* Washington, DC: World Bank.

Zhang, Wenkui. 2010. "The Direction and Task for China's SOEs Reform in the 12th Five-Year Plan Period." Research Report 203, Development Research Center, Beijing (in Chinese).

Zhang, Xiaobo, and Kong-Yam Tan. 2007. "Incremental Reform and Distortions in China's Product and Factor Markets." *World Bank Economic Review* 21 (2): 279–99.

China's Growth through Technological Convergence and Innovation

Income gaps among countries are largely explained by differences in productivity. By raising the ratio of capital to labor and rapidly assimilating technologies across a wide range of activities, China has increased factor productivity manifold since 1980 and entered the ranks of middle-income countries. With the launch of the 12th Five Year Plan, China has reaffirmed its goal of becoming a moderately prosperous society by 2020. This chapter maintains that China can become a high-income country by 2030 through a strategy combining high levels of investment with rapid advances in technology, comparable to the strategy used by Japan from the 1960s through the 1970s and by the Republic of Korea from the 1980s through the end of the century. During the next decade, more of the gains in productivity are likely to derive from technology absorption and adaptation supplemented by incremental innovation, while high levels of investment will remain an important source of growth in China through capital deepening and embodied technological change. By 2030, China expects to have pulled abreast technologically of the most advanced countries and increasingly, its growth will be paced by innovation that pushes the technology frontier outward in areas of acquired comparative advantage.

Both technology catch-up through technological absorption and innovation at the technological frontiers will rest on several factors, including the success of policies focused on effective competition; the composition of the business sector and its strategic orientation; agile policy making and robust regulation that minimize the risk of crises (from asset bubbles, for example, that can depress innovative activity) and that position the economy to seize evolving opportunities; skill development; research and development (R&D); national and international networking to promote innovation; and the nurturing of innovation especially in the areas of green technologies, health and medical services, and urbanization modes, and in major urban centers.

A competitive market environment is the precondition for a steady improvement in productivity. Starting in the late 1980s, for example, market-enhancing reforms increased entry of foreign and private firms and stimulated competition in most of China's manufacturing subsectors. Even in some "strategic" or "pillar" industries (for example, airlines and telecommunications), the breaking up and corporatization or exit of incumbent, mainly state-owned enterprises (SOEs) in the 1990s strengthened competitive pressures. More recently, the phasing out of tax incentives that had favored foreign investors stimulated competition by leveling the playing field with domestically owned firms. China's accession to the World Trade Organization (WTO) in 2001 increased competition from imports, and the large volume of foreign direct investment (FDI) has led to a further intensification of competitive pressures. Sustaining this trend through institutional reforms and measures to enhance the supply of risk capital will be critical to the making of an innovative economy, because it will stimulate the deepening of the private sector, reduce barriers to firm entry and exit, promote the growth of dynamic small and medium enterprises (SMEs), prod the SOEs to raise their game (and pave the way for further reform), and result in national market integration as well as much needed regional or local specialization of industry.

The speed with which advanced technologies diffuse and the capacity to innovate will be keyed to the availability of a vast range of technical and soft skills such as management, research, design and production, the effective harnessing of information technology (IT) and of marketing and customer relationships. By 2030, China is expected to have up to 200 million college graduates, more than the entire workforce of the United States. Moreover, university-level education is improving—China now has 11 universities in the top-ranked 200 universities of the world.[1] Even so, the quality of tertiary education more broadly is a matter of concern, and some employers are experiencing a serious shortage of the skills required to upgrade processes and the product mix. For China to become an innovative knowledge economy, increased investment in human capital will be critical to build analytical and complex reasoning capabilities, enhance scientific literacy and the knowledge base of students, encourage creativity, and instill communication and teamwork skills. Raising the quantity and quality of skills demands innovation

in pedagogical techniques, with greater use of multimedia and flexible online training customized to the varying needs of students. That, in turn, will raise the productivity of the education sector overall and maximize the benefits from the limited pool of talented instructors and the available physical facilities. The effectiveness of traditional standardized approaches to training such as lectures to large classes may need to be reconsidered, with institutions being encouraged to experiment with supplementary modes of participatory learning and given the autonomy to do so.

China's spending on R&D is on a steep upward trend. This spending will increase the production of ideas and prepare the ground for innovation. But because most applied research and innovation are done within firms and because the majority of scientists will be employed by businesses, the commercialization of ideas will flourish and drive productivity only when firms make innovation a central plank of their business strategies. How quickly firms take advantage of the knowledge capital being created by R&D will be a function of market growth and competition, the quality of the workforce, and fiscal and other incentives that prioritize research-intensive activities. Agricultural research will also continue to contribute substantially to productivity gains, price stability, and food security.

An adequate volume of much-needed basic research, by virtue of its public good characteristics, will depend upon government initiatives and funding. Government agencies, key universities and research institutions, and some large corporations will need to take the lead, especially in high-risk, blue-skies research, through well-targeted incentives, by committing a sufficient (and sustained) volume of funding to high-caliber institutions, and by means of prizes and awards. In the United States, the National Institutes of Health have played a central role in boosting innovations in life sciences, as have agencies such as the Departments of Defense, Energy, and Agriculture and the Defense Advanced Research Projects Agency (DARPA).

Increased publishing of scientific papers and patenting is likely to have only a small impact on productivity growth—even if China is able to raise R&D spending to 2.2 percent of GDP by 2020—unless the quality of this research and its commercial relevance and uptake is substantially increased. Good research must be complemented by a stringent and disciplined process of evaluation and refereeing of research programs and findings, with the feedback incorporated in policies. The research community needs to take the initiative here to uphold ethics and set high standards, with public agencies providing the ground rules. Universities can reach out more actively than public research institutes to the business community to maximize the relevance of the research conducted and to serve the cause of learning by promoting public lectures and exhibitions, and contributing to the teaching of science in local schools. Beyond that, it is up to firms to transform research findings into profitable products and services.

The central government can help build countrywide research networks to mobilize national talent and create consortia composed of firms from inland and coastal areas to raise the technological levels of all participants through cross-fertilization. Governments in Japan, the United States, and Taiwan, China, have successfully sponsored similar consortia, and they can help China develop more firms that are "global challengers." The domestic research networks should be incorporated into global research networks so that Chinese companies can also participate in research conducted in other parts of the world. Such participation, and with it the creation of global research networks, will be promoted by measures that improve internal organizational and technological capacities and by policies that minimize protectionist tendencies in other countries.

Many high-tech multinational corporations have invested in R&D facilities in China (including in inland cities such as Xian and Chengdu). Such investment should be encouraged because of its potentially significant long-run spillover effects, the reputational gains for Chinese cities (a few of which are fast becoming science hubs), and the contribution such research can make to industrial upgrading. Closer collaboration and partnerships with multinational corporations on the basis of mutual trust and recognition will contribute to the making of a dynamic and open innovation system. In this context, an efficient and discriminating patenting system that learns from the experience of the U.S. and European systems (both of which are in the throes of reform) and effective protection of intellectual property, especially in technologically dynamic fields such as biotechnology, nanotechnology, software, and multimedia, will expedite the growth of China's innovation capabilities.

Smart cities will be the locus of technological innovation and of nascent green growth in China as in other advanced countries—and urban development strategy intersects with strategies for technology development and growth. Innovative cities take the lead in building large pools of human capital (especially in attracting many science and technology workers) and in embedding institutions that support the generating, debating, testing, and perfecting of new ideas. Innovative cities serve as the axes of regional and even international knowledge networks; they derive technological leverage from an industrial base that employs scientific and technological talent; they are home to a few leading, research-oriented firms and provide a business environment conducive to the multiplication of SMEs; and they invest in state-of-the-art digital networks and online services. Such cities thrive on the heterogeneity of knowledge workers drawn from all over the country—and the world. Moreover, such cities are closely integrated with other global centers of research and technology development. Finally, innovative cities are "sticky" because their knowledge environment, physical and cultural amenities, public services, and quality of governance attract and retain global talent.

International experience suggests that stickiness derives in large part from the presence of world-class research universities that China is committed to creating. China will need to endow its premier institutions with a measure of autonomy from government not only to succeed in stimulating urban innovation but also to ensure that they are disciplined by competition and indicators of performance and remain efficient providers of services. These universities must interact with employers to impart technical and soft skills as well as the latest industry know-how. China's front-ranked schools must mobilize the funding and staff faculty positions needed to sustain cross-disciplinary postgraduate and postdoctoral programs, introduce innovative approaches to imparting knowledge and analytical skills, and establish specialized, well-staffed research institutes, some of international standing. An important contribution universities can make to innovation is to groom the entrepreneurs of tomorrow who can transform ideas into commercial products and services.

With a yearly influx of more than 10 million people to its cities, China needs to optimize the planning of urban development, build energy-efficient mass public transportation systems, provide affordable housing, and inculcate sustainable urban life styles. Smart and green urbanization will stimulate both research on and the commercialization of green technologies. Energy pricing reform and enforcement of national environmental and energy efficiency standards will create pressures to upgrade technologies, and urban development will be the main venue for introducing new construction materials and technologies for transport, heating, cooling, and many others urban needs. Demand-side instruments such as government procurement and standard setting can also spur innovation. The key to success, however, will lie in genuine open competition supported by sound and responsive policy making.

China may need to develop a culture that encourages more people to boldly pursue new ideas and to push the frontiers of knowledge across a variety of fields.

Purpose of the Chapter

China is determined to become a global innovative powerhouse by 2020.[2] Policy analysis has shown that productivity gains from structural changes[3] and technological catch-up[4] will be largely exhausted within a decade and that thereafter, growth rates in the 6–7 percent range will be increasingly tied to productivity gains stemming from innovativeness in its several forms.[5] The purpose of this chapter is twofold: The first is to examine the scope for productivity gains even as the technological gap between China and the advanced countries narrows and to suggest how China could hasten the pace of technological catch-up by creating a more competitive economic environment and a world-class innovation system. The second is to sketch a menu of policies that could help to make innovation a major driver of growth in the new phase of development. The two are closely interrelated. Policies that promote technological catch-up over the medium run overlap with those that can enlarge innovation capacity over the longer term.

The chapter is divided into four parts. The first underlines the increasing significance of total factor productivity growth (TFP) as a source of growth,[6] describes China's performance since 1980, and examines sectoral trends. The second reviews China's progress in building technological capacity. The third assesses China's strengths and some of the constraints hindering the development of innovation capabilities. And the fourth is devoted to the discussion of national and subnational policies that would enable China to realize its ambition of eventually becoming an innovative nation on par with the United States,[7] Japan, Germany, and Korea, albeit one capable of sustaining a higher rate of growth than these mature economies.

Growth Drivers: Betting on TFP

Among the larger East Asian economies, only three were able to transition from the middle-income to the high-income category during the second half of the 20th century.[8] Japan did so in the 1960s,[9] and Korea and Taiwan, China, during the 1990s. Japan made the transition by means of a high-investment, manufacturing-sector-led growth strategy that combined technological catch-up with both incremental and disruptive innovations introduced by the private sector but enabled by the government's industrial and technology policies. The pocket transistor radio, the Walkman, compact automobiles, and lean manufacturing were some of the disruptive innovations introduced by Japanese firms that contributed to productivity gains and export successes.[10] Korea and Taiwan, China, also relied on technological catch-up facilitated by high levels of investment in manufacturing, and both benefited from incremental innovation as their industries matured. Research and development facilitated technology absorption although the contribution to productivity growth via breakthrough innovation was quite limited through the late 1990s except in Japan, whose technological capabilities in the 1950s and earlier put it in a different league from the other two. Governments actively engaged in deepening human capital, improving access to financing, and encouraging the borrowing and assimilation of technology and investment in productive assets. But it was leading manufacturers, assisted by clusters of smaller suppliers, that spearheaded technology absorption and innovation.[11] Korea and Taiwan, China, graduated from the middle- to the high-income group of economies largely on the basis of technological catch-up and the building of globally competitive electronics, transport, and chemical industries with strong export performance. The two economies began strengthening their innovation systems in the 1980s through public and private investment in research infrastructure, systematic borrowing from overseas through licensing and FDI (in the case of Taiwan, China), among other channels. The acceleration of technological progress during the 1990s and early 2000s enabled them to cross the threshold and join the club of high-income economies.[12] The importance of innovation has continued to increase and is now paramount for all three economies because their industries are at the cutting edge and growth must lean more heavily on productivity gains deriving in part from successful innovation.

This experience has a number of implications for China's growth strategy. First is the need to fully exploit the potential of technological catch-up in industry and services for at least the next decade. During this period, original innovation based on technological breakthroughs may not be as common as innovations combining different existing technologies or the introduction of innovative designs and special features customized for specific markets.[13] Second, innovation capability takes years to accumulate, and systematically defining and implementing an innovation strategy would begin yielding sizable dividends in the form of frontier expertise and groundbreaking discoveries most likely in the 2020s and beyond, when China would be more in need for a productivity boost from this source.[14] Third, the quality and efficiency of the innovation system deserves priority over indicators such as R&D spending, patents, and published papers—after all, innovation should create wealth. And, fourth, realizing productivity gains will be in the hands of the business sector, and it is the dynamism of firms that will be the ultimate arbiter of growth-enhancing innovativeness.

Accounting for China's Growth

A decomposition of China's growth rate is an appropriate starting point. A meta-analysis of 150 studies of total factor productivity growth in China (Tian and Yu 2012) concludes that since 1978, the annual contribution of TFP on average has been 2 percentage points, with the eastern region registering higher rates than the central and western regions (see below). Other research provides detail on subperiods and sectors. For example, a study conducted by Bosworth and Collins (2007) shows that physical capital and TFP contributed 3.2 percentage points and 3.8 percentage points, respectively, to China's GDP growth between 1978 and 2004.[15] From 1993 to 2004, their shares

TABLE 2.1   **Sources of growth, 1978–2004**
Annual percentage rate of change

Period	Output	Employment	Output per worker	Contribution of:			
				Physical capital	Land	Education	Factor productivity
Total							
1978–2004	9.3	2.0	7.3	3.2	0.0	0.2	3.8
1993–2004	9.7	1.2	8.5	4.2	0.0	0.2	4.0

Source: Bosworth and Collins 2007.

TABLE 2.2   **Sources of growth by industrial and services sectors, 1978–2004**
Annual percentage rate of change

Period	Output	Employment	Output per worker	Contribution of:		
				Physical capital	Education	Factor productivity
Industry						
1978–2004	10.0	3.1	7.0	2.2	0.2	4.4
1993–2004	11.0	1.2	9.8	3.2	0.2	6.2
Services						
1978–2004	10.7	5.8	4.9	2.7	0.2	1.9
1993–2004	9.8	4.7	5.1	3.9	0.2	0.9

Source: Bosworth and Collins 2007.

were 4.2 percentage points and 4.0 percentage points, respectively (table 2.1)[16] with industry overshadowing other sectors. Capital and TFP contributed 2.2 and 4.4 percentage points, respectively, of industrial growth during 1978–2004 and 3.2 and 6.2 percentage points from 1993 to 2004 (table 2.2). Agricultural output grew steadily at an average annual rate of 4.5 percent between 1978 and 2009, with TFP gains averaging 2 percent a year. The performance of agriculture was aided by market incentives, ownership reform, land-saving technologies, and the diversification of production from grains to higher-value items such as meat and vegetables. Chen, Jefferson, and Zhang (2011) show that TFP rose even more rapidly in most manufacturing activities during 1981–2008, with electrical and nonelectrical machinery, office equipment and telecommunications subsectors, which have benefited most from technological change, in the forefront (Jorgenson, Ho, and Stiroh 2007). However, metal and nonmetal industries, plastics, rubber, petrochemicals, and paper achieved comparable gains. Ito and others (2008) reaffirmed these findings. Growth of TFP was strongest for

machinery and motor vehicles during 1999–2004 (ranging from 2.71 to 2.83 percent a year). Glass and clay products and paper also registered large gains (see annex table 2A.1).

According to more recent estimates by Kuijs (2010), TFP growth slowed to 2.7 percent between 1995 and 2009, and the share of capital rose to 5.5 percent.[17] Growth of productivity in services also slowed from 1.9 percent (1978–2004) to just 0.9 percent a year between 1993 and 2004 (Bosworth and Collins 2007).

With capital spending subject to decreasing returns (as is evident from the upward trend in incremental capital-output ratios, or ICORs),[18] the scope for raising growth through larger injections of capital is being rapidly exhausted. Moreover, rebalancing of consumption spending will lead to a decline in the share of investment. At the same time, the structural transformation of the Chinese economy is entering a stage when productivity gains from the intersectoral transfer of resources will continue to taper off (Chen, Jefferson, and Zhang 2011). In most high-income countries, TFP growth averaged less than 2.0 percent a year between 1995 and

2009,[19] the exceptions being Korea and Ireland, which had rates of 2.7 percent and 3.1 percent respectively—although Ireland fell to 1.3 percent and Korea to 2.6 percent during 2005–09.[20]

International experience offers three pointers: First are the advantages of a continuing emphasis on those manufacturing industries that are likely to deliver the highest returns from catching up so long as Chinese firms are quick to pursue technological possibilities and strive to maximize efficiency gains. These include industries such as electrical machinery, office and computing equipment, pharmaceuticals, aircraft, motor vehicles, and nonelectrical machinery, which have demonstrated rapid improvements in technology because they are also the most R&D intensive (van Pottelsberghe de la Potterie 2008).

Second, catching up and innovation in services, promoted by information and communications technology (ICT), is likely to play a more prominent role over the longer run as the share of services in GDP begins to overshadow industry.[21] Services growth would involve encouraging innovation by firms engaged in banking, insurance, retailing, real estate, logistics, and data services as well as health care and education, two important and growing activities.

Third, lowering market barriers to the entry, growth, and exit of firms will contribute to economywide improvements in productivity growth by intensifying competition and with it the process of creative destruction (McKinsey and Company 2010).[22]

The trends in manufacturing are promising. Chinese manufacturers of transport and telecommunications equipment, consumer electronics, and textiles and garments are aggressively engaging in backward and forward integration, moving from the assembly and testing of standardized products to the design and manufacture of differentiated parts and components and of new products that generate higher profit margins.[23] These efforts, if they are aided by a consolidation of global production networks (resulting partly from the pull of agglomeration economies and partly from emerging supply chain vulnerabilities[24] and transaction costs), could increase the share of higher-tech items produced domestically and steadily reduce the imported content of China's manufactured exports, which has already declined from 52.4 percent in 1997 to 50.6 percent in 2006 (Koopman, Wang, and Wei 2009). This trend is likely to reverse past tendencies for imported inputs to increase initially as the skill intensity of production rises (Moran 2011b). Product space analysis pioneered by Cesar Hidalgo, Ricardo Hausmann, and others (Hausmann and Klinger 2006) suggests that the average sophistication of China's exports is comparable to that of Malaysia, Thailand, and the Philippines.

Since 1985, China has broadened its production base and, through massive investment, has enlarged production capacity and accelerated learning by doing.[25] As a consequence, China now produces a wide assortment of products that can be technologically upgraded and from which Chinese manufacturers can diversify into other related products. In product space terminology, more of the products lie in the densely networked core that multiplies options for industrial diversification and the scope for innovation.

A closer inspection of the products in China's export basket with the highest densities underscores China's rapid industrial progress. In 1987, the top 10 commodities were mainly low-tech items that offered minimal opportunities for diversification. By 2006, the product composition had altered radically, with many opening avenues for upgrading into more technologically advanced products with better market prospects. China's industrial capabilities are thus strengthening, as is its competiveness relative to higher-income countries. In recent years, the increase in product complexity and the share of products employing advanced technologies is linked to investment by multinationals in upscale manufacturing activities (Koopman, Wang, and Wei 2008, 2009). These findings are similar to those of Felipe, Abdon, and Kumar (2010).[26]

The trend in patenting during 2005–09 indicates that the changing composition of manufacturing is serving to upgrade domestic technology. The largest number of patents received by residents of China who registered with the United States Patent and Trademark Office (USPTO) was for electronic and electrical devices, followed by communications devices, software, pharmaceutical compounds, and optical devices (annex table 2A.2). Similarly, the overwhelming majority of patents granted to residents of China by the World Intellectual Property Organization (WIPO) was also for electronic, electrical, and telecommunication devices followed by chemical[27] and biological products[28] and products in the mechanical engineering category (annex table 2A.3).

Among manufactured products, electronic, telecommunication, and optical devices are likely to remain the technologically most dynamic products, the focus of innovation, and a continuing source of increases in productivity in the world and in China. Chinese companies such as Huawei and ZTE are emerging as world leaders in the telecommunications sector and role models for others seeking to establish a significant presence in the global market.[29]

Entry of Firms by Subsector

China's emerging comparative advantage in manufacturing subsectors is supported by data on the entry of new firms. The subsectors with high rates of new entry are metal manufacturing, machinery, and electrical, computing, and telecommunications equipment. Meanwhile, business, scientific, and technical services are growing robustly as China urbanizes and consumption shifts toward services. The statistics on firm entry for Guangdong reaffirm the importance of garments and leather products as well as the strength of industries producing metal products, machinery, and computing equipment. Business services are also a growth sector in Guangdong. Machinery and transport equipment and plastics are the favored subsectors in Zhejiang. And in both Zhejiang and Beijing, as well as in coastal provinces, the conspicuous growth drivers are business and scientific services (annex table 2A.4). Urban development and the continuing structural transformation of the economy are facilitating the entry of small firms, which in turn contributes to patenting and the introduction of new products. Small firms are, on average, more efficient in using R&D resources—financial and human—to generate patents (annex tables 2A.5, 2A.6, and 2A.7). Looking ahead, there is more room for growth of services activities and for competition that would raise efficiency.

The data on new domestic firms entering manufacturing subsectors is consistent with FDI data, which show that the two subsectors most favored by foreign investors are computers and other electronic equipment, followed by chemicals, universal machinery, and special purpose machinery. The share of computers and electronic equipment, while still high, has declined since 2004; the shares of the others have remained largely stable (annex table 2A.8).

International experience suggests that the contribution of small and medium companies to innovation is likely to increase. This desirable development can be facilitated by measures to reduce entry barriers, including transaction costs for SMEs, and to make it easier for them to access financing.

Building Technological Capacity

Before the Industrial Revolution in Europe, China led the world in technology.[30] After losing ground for more than 250 years, China now is sparing no effort to become a global force in technology, and possibly even again the leader, by 2030. China began piecing together a strategy starting in the 1980s with an emphasis on manufacturing capabilities and cost innovation in major product categories. The next step was to increase the acquisition of foreign intellectual property (IP) complemented by reverse engineering. Since the late 1990s, China has attempted to maximize technology transfer through foreign direct investment, in particular by encouraging multinational corporations to conduct more of their R&D in China.[31] The transfers and spillovers that resulted have fallen short of expectations. Research analyzing Chinese and international experience suggests—albeit with qualifications and exceptions—that multinationals thus far have generated few technological spillovers and those that have occurred are in high-tech sectors and have remained in the vertical plane, that is, from end users to suppliers, rather than also spreading horizontally to other sectors (Moran 2011a, 2011b). In low-tech sectors, the spillover effects might even be negative. Moreover, where multinationals fear that their intellectual property might be compromised, they are reluctant to introduce the latest technologies or to conduct frontier research aside from taking precautions to minimize technology leakage (Moran 2011a, 2011b; Fu and Gong 2011; Tang and Hussler 2011; Bai, Lu, and Tao 2010; Fu, Pietrobelli, and Soete 2011). In the light of this experience, China is redoubling its own efforts at technological upgrading, indigenous innovation,[32] and takeover of foreign firms and their brands by China's leading challengers, while supporting determined efforts by Chinese firms to innovate, build their own brand image, and expand their share of global markets.[33] This approach is exemplified by Lenovo (Tzeng 2011).

Planning Technology Development in China

The 11th Five Year Plan stated that China would build competitive advantage based on science, technology, and innovation, and this objective remains prominent in the 12th plan. In early 2006, the government announced its National Program Outline for Medium and Long Term Development of Science and Technology (2006–2020). Its key pillars include "indigenous innovation," "a leap-forward in key areas," "sustainable development,"[34] and "setting the stage for the future." The strategy seeks to encourage enterprise-led innovation; to strengthen intellectual property protection; to create a favorable environment for innovation in science and technology (S&T); to attract S&T talents; and to improve the management and coordination of S&T. More

important, the national program also has 16 specific subprograms—from core electronic components to moon exploration—aimed at achieving advances in core common-use technologies and enhancing the capabilities of Chinese enterprises. During the 11th 5YP period and through 2011, the central government's outlay on science and technology rose by 22 percent a year. By 2011, R&D accounted for 1.83 percent of GDP.

Innovation and technology development are assigned a central role in the 12th 5YP (2011–15), with the highest priority given to:

- Developing strategic industries such as energy-saving and environmental protection, next-generation information technology, biotechnology, high-end manufacturing, new energy, new materials, and clean energy vehicles. A number of megaprojects with a focus on basic research are earmarked for a large injection of resources starting in 2011. Two that have been singled out are in the life sciences—on drug discovery and on major infectious diseases—reflecting the view that research on biopharmaceuticals and stem cells might lead to profitable innovations.
- Promoting enterprise-led innovation.
- Strengthening supporting services.
- Raising expenditure on research and development to 2.2 percent of GDP.[35]
- Increasing the rate of patenting to 3.3 patents per 10,000 people.

An increase in R&D is being complemented by investments in the physical infrastructure supporting technological upgrading.[36] Strengthening and more fully exploiting the potential of multimodal transport is helping to raise logistics efficiency. And massive investments in renewable sources of power, a smart grid, and rail transport are expected to reduce energy consumption.[37] Mobile networks were serving 1.1 billion users by 2012, an increase of 650 million over 2006. In 2012, of the 564 million internet users, 530 million had access to broadband services, more than the total population of the United States[38] (figure 2.1).

FIGURE 2.1   China's communication infrastructure and mobile networks, 2002–12

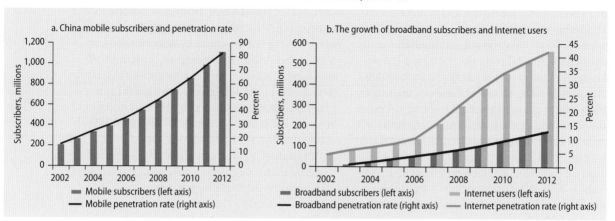

Sources: Data for mobile subscribers: Ministry of Industry and Information Technology, P.R. China (http://www.miit.gov.cn/n11293472/n11293832/n11294132/n12858447/index.html); data for broadband subscribers: Ministry of Industry and Information Technology, P.R. China (http://www.miit.gov.cn/n11293472/n11293832/n11294132/n12858447/index.html); data for Internet users: China Internet Network Information Center (http://www.cnnic.net.cn).

Furthermore, full-time equivalent R&D personnel tripled, from 750,000 to 2.3 million person-years, and the total number of personnel engaged in S&T activities reached 4.97 million in 2008. Some 6 percent of China's 1,700 institutions of higher education are elite Project 211 entities[39] responsible for training four-fifths of doctoral candidates, hosting 96 percent of key labs, and contributing 70 percent of the funding for university research. A total of 218 national priority labs now cover all the major scientific fields.[40]

Between 1996 and 2000, China's global science citation index ranking as measured by publications increased from 14th to 2nd place (Adams, King, and Ma 2009). The output of publications soared from 20,000 in 1998 to 112,000 in 2008, equal to 8.5 percent of global output of scientific publications. A study conducted by Britain's Royal Society found that between 2004 and 2008, China produced more than one-tenth of the published scientific articles while the United States, produced one-fifth, putting China in second place (ahead of the United Kingdom).[41] Chinese research publications lead the field in materials science, physics, chemistry, and mathematics. Moreover, Chinese research in nanoscience (which is likely to affect the development of advanced materials,

for example) is yielding promising results (Hassan 2005; Bai 2005; Preschitschek and Bresser 2010; Italian Trade Commission 2009; Leydesdorff 2008).

However, as yet, China has relatively few high-impact articles in any field (Simon and Cao 2009; Royal Society 2011), although according to the social science citation index, China's citation ranking rose from 19th place in 1992–2001 to 13th in 1996–2005 to 10th place in 1998–2008 (Hu 2011, 102).

Mirroring the trend in publications, the number of patents granted to Chinese enterprises dramatically increased from 5,386 in 1995 to 76,379 in 2006.[42] The number of patent applications to WIPO increased from about 23,000 in 1996 to 290,000 in 2008 (Hu 2011, 103).[43] A continuing sharp increase through 2009 propelled China to fifth place in WIPO's rankings, but again quantity has not yet been matched by the quality of the patents.[44] Incentives to patent (including incentives offered by provincial authorities) have produced a flood of minor design and utility patents that contribute little to advances in knowledge or commercial innovation.[45] Most of the high- and mid-value patents are being registered by multinational corporations (Boeing and Sandner 2011, table 9).[46] Triadic patent filings (with the patent offices of the United States, the European Union, and Japan), a better measure of the worth of a patent, are increasing but are still few in number. In 2009, China ranked 11th in the world, having filed 667 triadic patents compared with 1,959 by Korea, 12,715 by the United States, and 13,332 by Japan.[47] In 2010, the numbers of patent applications filed by Chinese residents to the United States Patent and Trademark Office, the European Patent Office, and the Japan Patent Office, stood at 6,978, 2,049, and 1,063, respectively, an increase over 2008 of 19.6 percent, 35.7 percent, and 37.7 percent.[48]

By official count, the number of science- and technology-based private firms in China increased from just 7,000 in 1986 to 150,000 in 2006,[49] and as of 2007, the assets of privately owned Chinese companies were approaching those of the SOEs, not including the 100 largest (OECD 2010). Now a small number of Chinese firms, such as Huawei[50] and ZTE in the ICT industry, Suntech Power in solar technologies, and Dalian Machine Tool Group in engineering, have reached or are approaching the international technological frontier and demonstrating a growing ability to create technology.[51] Chinese companies are also mastering the latest technologies in areas such as auto assembly and components, photovoltaic cells, biopharmaceuticals,[52] nanotechnology,[53] stem cell therapeutics (Gwynne 2010), high-density power batteries,[54] high-speed trains,[55] telecommunication equipment, wind turbines,[56] single-aisle passenger aircraft,[57] booster rockets, space satellites,[58] supercomputers, shipping containers, Internet services, electric power turbines, and many other products.[59] Many of the companies introducing innovative products are state owned.

These achievements notwithstanding, the reality is that much of China's export-oriented manufacturing industry is still engaged in processing and assembly operations, export competitiveness is predominantly based on low factor costs, and more than half of all exports are produced by foreign-owned firms or joint ventures. Foreign firms also account for more than 85 percent of high-tech exports since 1996 (Moran 2011b).[60] Having no big marquee brands or core technologies,[61] China reaps only a small portion of rents from high-tech exports, which accrue mainly to foreign designers and engineers. The most illustrative example is the case of Apple's iPad and iPhone. All iPads and iPhones on sale worldwide are assembled in China by the Taiwanese company Foxconn with homegrown Chinese companies supplying not a single component. In the case of iPhone, the only value captured in China is the wage earned by Chinese assembly workers, which accounted for 1.6 percent of the sales price; Apple's profits accounting for 58.8 percent (Kraemer, Linden, and Dedrick 2011).

China Versus Other Economies

How does China's performance to date compare with that of the leading economies? For one thing, China's growth has been higher over a longer period buoyed by above-average productivity gains. But the data on industrial value added and technological indicators suggest that plenty of rungs are left to climb on the technology ladder. By pouring resources into S&T development, China has moved faster than most of its neighbors in laying the foundations of a world-class innovation system. The efficiency of the emerging innovation system is questionable; however, the quality will need improving, and the urban dimension has been relatively neglected (see next section).

Starting in the 1980s, China began to reform its science and technology system and initiated four programs—Key Technologies R&D (1982), Spark (1986), High-Technology Research and Development ("863") (1986), and Torch (1988)—aimed at making science and technology serve economic growth and social development, and enhancing S&T capacity to complement China's investment in manufacturing capabilities.[62] These and other reforms and programs introduced since, with the focus shifting to innovation after 1990, are now producing results. A number of multidimensional indexes that measure capabilities across countries show that China is rapidly augmenting S&T skills, building research infrastructure, and assimilating information and communications technology.

According to a ranking of 40 countries produced by the Chinese Academy of Science and Technology for Development, China is in 21st place in its innovative capacity, with a point score of 58 compared with 100 for the United States. The index was constructed from five major subindexes based on 31 indicators. The various subcomponents indicate that China's performance has improved since 2000 in knowledge creation (it is now in 33rd place—a five-point improvement). Innovation performance has risen sharply to ninth place. But as the report observes, efficiency, intensity, and quality of research in China still lags behind the frontrunners—the United States, Switzerland, Japan, and Korea—it is seeking to match.

Another ranking of countries by innovativeness comes from the Information Technology and Innovation Foundation (ITIF).[63] This index covers 40 countries and is based on measures of human capital, investment in R&D, and numbers of scientific articles, entrepreneurship, IT, economic policy, and economic performance—in other words, this index casts its net broadly. Singapore leads the ITIF list with a score of 73, followed by Sweden, with the United States in 6th place and China ranked 33rd. The ITIF also prepares a separate ranking of the change in country scores to determine the scale of innovation effort and progress between 1999 and 2009. By this measure, China comes first, followed by Singapore and a number of northern European countries. Interestingly, the United States ranks dead last in this listing because it is the country at the technological frontier in most areas and because of its weak performance on a number of counts.

The European Business School is the source of a third measure, known as the Innovation Capacity Index, which rests on five pillars: the institutional environment; human capital; training and social inclusion; the regulatory and legal framework; and the adoption and use of ICT. [64] Sweden received the highest ranking in 2010–11 followed by Switzerland and Singapore, Finland, and the United States. This index puts China in 64th place even though the report recognizes its vast potential and huge investment in technology. The report observes, however, that China's R&D base is still somewhat weak as are the regulatory and legal frameworks.

The European Innovation Scoreboard compares China's performance on several benchmarks with the EU-27.[65] The most recent report concludes that the European Union (EU) countries are ahead of China on most of the indicators of education and innovation capability. However, China is increasing its lead in medium- and high-tech exports and drawing abreast of the EU in tertiary education, international publication, business R&D, and patenting, while the EU is extending its lead in public R&D expenditure and most-cited publications.

INSEAD's Global Innovation Index provides a fifth measure of China's capabilities. This index ranks 125 countries using measures of innovation input (such as institutions, human capital, infrastructure, and market and business sophistication) and output, both scientific and creative. China was ranked 29th in 2011, the three top-ranked countries being Switzerland, Sweden, and Singapore. Like the European Innovation Scorecard, this index points to China's improving performance—China's position actually declined from 37th place in 2009 to 43rd place in 2010 before reaching its current position.

A sixth index of "Science and Technology power," computed by Angang Hu, compares China with the four leading nations—Germany, Japan, the United Kingdom, and the United States—on five capacities: publications, patents, computer usage, Internet access, and R&D spending. Each of these is given equal weight, and Hu (2011, 110) finds that China's global share of S&T power rose from 0.82 percent in 1990 to nearly 4 percent in 2000 and to 9.7 percent in 2007, putting it in third place behind the United States and Japan.

These six by no means exhaust the indexes of innovation capabilities. Several others arrive at rankings for selected countries by fusing measures of competitiveness, scientific and technological knowledge, ICT, and human capital. Information on these rankings and a synthetic index constructed by Archibugi and Coco, are helpfully summarized by Archibugi, Denni, and Filippetti (2009). According to this consolidated set of rankings, the first place is assigned to Sweden, followed by the United States, Switzerland, Finland, Japan, and Denmark. China is ranked 42nd. Its ranking by the selected indexes range from 26th in the United Nations Industrial Development Organization index to 45th in the World Economic Forum index, with other rankings clustered around 44th place.

Technology development and innovation is a fairly recent focus of China's development strategy;[66] hence there are very few Chinese firms that can be counted among the technological leaders in their respective subsectors and that are significant producers of intellectual property. Although the research infrastructure and numbers of researchers have expanded many times over, quality, experience, and the institutions that undergird innovation, remain weak. Leapfrogging into the ranks of the top five contenders in most of the indexes will depend upon the efficiency of China's technology policies and the response these policies elicit from the business sector, academia, and the providers of supporting services. It will also crucially depend upon the creation of an innovation system that is alive to the global and open nature of innovative activities and their locus in a number of cosmopolitan urban hotspots.

The Urban Dimension of Technology Development

Science and technology activities and industrialization are primarily urban phenomena, and in East Asia, the most dynamic and fastest-growing industries have emerged in a relatively small number of cities. China's "reform and opening" since 1979 commenced with the establishment of four Special Economic Zones privileged with incentives for export-oriented industrialization, which were subsequently extended in 1984 to 14 coastal cities and to several new coastal economic zones. These urban centers and regions triggered and have crucially sustained China's remarkable economic performance. They have served as the locus for integrated industrial clusters that share a common labor pool, facilitate buyer-supplier relationships, allow collaboration between firms to refine and develop technologies, and encourage joint efforts to create marketing, information gathering, and training systems. Where cluster networking is taking root, it is internalizing technological spillovers and, in the most successful cases, providing a virtuous balance between competition and cooperation. To foster clustering, cities are relying upon science parks, incubators, and extension services; encouraging local universities to engage in research and to establish industrial linkages; inducing venture capitalists to invest in SMEs in the area; and trying to attract a major anchor firm, local or foreign, that could trigger the in-migration of suppliers and imitators. Higher-level governments have reinforced these initiatives with a variety of tax and financial incentives and investment in infrastructure and urban services (Yusuf, Nabeshima, and Yamashita 2008).

Some industrial clusters, as in Zhejiang[67] and Guangdong, materialized autonomously from long-established traditions of entrepreneurship and the strengths of local networks; others came together mostly as a result of initiatives taken by national and local governments (He and Fallah 2011; Fleisher and others 2010). In many instances, the attempts to create cluster dynamics failed even after a number of firms established production facilities at an urban location—these failures reflect the experience of cities world-wide. That notwithstanding, dense urban-industrial agglomerations, some with networked clusters of firms, have been vital for the growth of productivity, for stimulating technological change, and for promoting further industrialization by opening opportunities and crowding in capital and skills.

Three major urban-industrial agglomerations—the Pearl River Delta region centered on Shenzhen, Dongguan, and Foshan; the Yangtze River region around the Shanghai-Suzhou axis; and the Bohai region in the vicinity of Beijing and Tianjin—have spawned multiple clusters producing everything from toys, footwear, and garments to computers, electronic components, autos, and software (McGee and others (2011). Further industrial deepening in these three regions is continuing, and industrial agglomerations also are expanding in a number of the inland cities, such as Chengdu, Chongqing, Xi'an, Hefei, Wuhan, and Shenyang. Some clusters are evolving from industrial parks, such as the Zhongguancun IT cluster (Beijing), the Pudong pharmaceutical cluster (Shanghai), and the Wuhan opto-electronics cluster (Hubei Province), but most clusters are still operating at the lower end of the industrial value chain and lack horizontal integration (Zeng 2010).

Despite the rapid pace of industrial agglomeration nationwide, significant regional differentials remain between coastal and inland cities. Productivity (measured by the GDP output per labor force) of the East region is almost twice that in the Middle region and thrice that in the West region (annex table 2A.10). Scientific and technological advances measured by patenting also are much higher in the coastal regions (annex table 2A.11).

Technological capabilities and innovation would certainly benefit from a greater participation of major cities in the inland provinces, many of which have substantial manufacturing capabilities, growing stocks of human capital, and strong tertiary institutions. A two-pronged approach that stimulates innovation in coastal urban areas and cultivates more specialized expertise in the leading inland urban centers would increase the likelihood of achieving growth objectives and also serve to reduce income and productivity gaps

(Fan, Kanbur, and Zhang 2009). Inland cities are in a position to capitalize on favorable wage and rental gradients and, with suitable investment, some could offer more affordable housing, recreational amenities, and public services to attract knowledge workers and high-tech firms. According to a recent study by McKinsey Global Institute (2011), China's mid-sized cities with excellent growth prospects—such as Wuhan and Zhengzhou—would be contributing more to GDP growth than the leading coastal megacities.

The Road to Innovation

The imperative of building domestic innovative capacity is entwined with the dynamics of knowledge diffusion and the large rents that can accrue to lead innovators and first movers. Once a country is at the technological frontier and cost advantages have largely disappeared, producing and capitalizing on a steady stream of innovations provides a degree of insurance against economic stagnation. A compelling finding that has emerged from the analysis of patent data is that the intricacies of the research techniques underlying new findings are transferred, often through personal communication, among a small number of researchers, because they are tacit and not ready to be codified.[68] The circulation of new findings among firms in a cluster and between universities, research institutes, and firms proceeds slowly and can take three years or more, depending on the nature of the technology, the type of firm, and expenditures by firms on R&D.[69] A substantial body of research indicates that a few cities account for a high percentage of innovations and that these cities share certain attributes that make them "sticky" for knowledge networks and clusters.[70] The persistence of this tendency despite great advances in communications presents a strong case for investment in research to push the technological frontier and to grow innovations locally in sticky cities. The challenge for China is to arrive at a national innovation strategy that is cost efficient, optimally decentralized, rationally sequenced, and urban-centric.

Assets

In its pursuit of innovation as a driver of growth, China starts out with seven advantages:

First, the scale and wide-ranging capabilities of China's manufacturing sector are reaching the point where products can be reverse engineered and new product lines brought into large-scale production within months.[71] This is being aided by the co-location of R&D and manufacturing in China's leading industrial centers, which are providing the foundations of a robust innovation system. Advanced countries faced with a hollowing of their industrial sectors are rediscovering this complementarity: once manufacturing capacity is severely eroded, the skills and capabilities undergirding innovation are also imperiled.[72]

Second, having expanded its education system, China's efforts to innovate will be buoyed by the large supply of scientific and engineering skills, which is adequate to meet the demand for high-level skills. This demand is likely to remain strong, unlike the case in Japan, for example.[73] Moreover, the increasing attention to the quality of schooling at all levels, including the programs to develop world-class universities,[74] will reinforce the benefits from supply (Yusuf and Nabeshima 2010). Shanghai's top-ranked performance in the 2009 Programme for International Student Assessment (PISA) tests provided an inkling of what can be achieved through focused attention to raising quality of primary and secondary schools.[75] Similar progress in the quality of tertiary-level graduates nationwide would provide a quicker boost to innovativeness and productivity (Hanushek 2009; Pritchett and Viarengo 2010).

The third asset is the elastic supply of patient capital to support innovative firms, which are currently in need of risk capital, and new entrants attempting to commercialize promising ideas. Venture funds and China's private and state-owned banks are meeting some of the demand, especially in the coastal areas of the country, but a gap in funding remains. The creation of China's GEM (Growth Enterprises Market) in Shenzhen has provided innovative firms with an additional channel through which to access financing and to give investors an exit route.

A fourth advantage derives from China's successful penetration of the global market, increasingly complemented by the expanding market of domestic urban middle-class consumers (Cheng 2010; Kharas 2009). A large domestic market attracts multinational corporations and innovators, allows domestic producers to attain scale economies, and permits the formation of clusters and agglomerations that contribute to the competitiveness of firms. It tests and winnows products and services and rewards winners. China's middle class is expected to double in the coming decade and to double again in the next (Bhidé 2008; Zhou 2008).[76] Foreign firms first flocked to China because it was an attractive platform for low-cost manufacturing. During the past decade, however, the widening Chinese domestic market (and weakening demand in their home markets) has added to the appeal of investment in China for their existing product lines and for new offerings.

Fifth is the pro-business, entrepreneurial culture (staunchly backed by local authorities) in the Pearl River Delta, Zhejiang, Fujian, and elsewhere that is supportive of small firms and start-ups. Entrepreneurship is not synonymous with innovativeness (De Meyer and Garg 2005), but it can become a precursor as ideas and opportunities multiply. State sector reforms initiated in 1996–97 led to the exit, privatization, restructuring, and corporatization of thousands of state and collective enterprises and galvanized the private sector. Since then, there is ample evidence of entry and exit of private firms and of small and medium publicly owned firms under conditions of often intense competition, local and foreign.[77] This is conducive to innovation—initially, most firms are focused on cost innovation and customization for the domestic market, but that can change. Companies such as Huawei, ZTE, and Suntech can serve as role models for other domestic companies seeking to become more innovative.

The sixth advantage is the potential inherent in China's still underdeveloped and relatively unproductive services sector. The technology and productivity gaps in services are particularly large as are the opportunities for innovation. With the services sector expanding robustly and set to overtake industry during the next decade, the low-hanging fruit with regard to growth, productivity gains, and employment is increasingly tilting toward the services, tradable and nontradable. Thus far, services such as education and health care are largely nontradable, but IT-related and other technological and process-related advances could lead to breakthroughs. Indigenous innovations in marketing,[78] online sales, after-sale services, and IT services, to name just a few, are already on the rise, with many new firms entering the market. If the trend strengthens and leads to the emergence of a few national giants as is happening in the United States and Europe (with increasing activity among multinational corporations), and if innovation intensifies (assuming no easing of innovation pressures), productivity gains in services could begin to equal or overshadow those arising from manufacturing.[79]

Seventh, and finally, not only is China urbanizing but, relatively early in the game, some Chinese cities are realizing that the productivity and growth of urban economies will rest on the quality of life and the resilience of cities. These factors are a function of urban design, the adequacy and efficiency of hard and soft infrastructures, the testing and adoption of green technologies, environmental quality, affordable housing, and the effectiveness with which cities—or entire metropolitan regions—are managed and decisions coordinated. An urban development strategy, the objective of which is to build efficient, green, and innovative cities, will create enormous opportunities for innovation in urban planning, metro transportation systems, and green technologies. Successful innovation will be a function of both national strategy and its elaboration and regional implementation (Howells 2005).

Speed Bumps

These several advantages are counterbalanced by a number of challenges and constraints:

First, China's macroeconomic policies need to encourage the growth of the domestic market rather than continue to focus industrial attention mainly on exports.[80] An increase in domestic household consumption (currently accounting for a little over one-third of GDP) will have a positive impact on indigenous innovation meeting the needs and desires of Chinese buyers.

Second, China's SOEs control a huge amount of physical assets as well as human talent and have yet to realize their full potential for innovation.[81] Lack of competition or effective corporate governance means that some SOEs are indifferently managed and less receptive to strategies that give primacy to growth through innovation.[82] Even when SOEs invest in R&D—which many are doing under pressure from the state—the effort tends to be unproductive and poorly integrated with the rest of their operations. Compared with smaller enterprises, the SOEs are not as efficient at converting resources into patents and innovations (annex tables 2A.12 and 2A.13 for the industrial sector, annex tables 2A.14 and 2A.15 for high-tech industries only).[83] Annual growth of total factor productivity in the state sector averaged 1.52 percent compared with 4.56 percent in the nonstate sector.[84] Extracting high returns from R&D requires managerial ingenuity and experimentation with organizational structures; incentives; integration of research, production, and marketing activities; and a long time horizon. Many small and medium companies complain that some large companies, including large SOEs and multinational corporations, are abusing their market power by favoring their own connected companies and excluding other companies. Such favoritism inhibits innovation by other companies.

Third, China's universities, particularly the leading ones, are adding capacity and giving greater attention to research and its commercialization, but the procedures for recruiting faculty with superior qualifications from domestic and international sources could be improved, and many university faculty members need more experience.[85] Moreover, the quality of research is low, and there are worries that faculty members in the leading research universities are distracted from teaching by the financial rewards and recognition they gain from consulting, publishing, and patenting. Widespread concerns have been raised about research ethics and the rigor of peer review of publications and projects.[86] Heavy pressure on researchers to produce and to collectively raise China's standing in the world is leading to dysfunctional outcomes. The scarcity of talented young researchers is also an issue confronting universities as they attempt to recruit individuals with foreign PhDs or overseas experience. The tendency to tenure full professors from overseas institutions encourages others to spend their most productive years abroad.[87] Furthermore, although universities have embraced the "third mission" of commercializing technology, the effects of university-industry links on technological change have been minimal. Wu and Zhou (2011, 2) maintain that "the key role of universities so far centers not so much on cutting edge innovation but on adaptation and redevelopment of existing foreign technology and products. . . . The contribution of UILs [University Industry Linkages] as a part of university R&D income was largely stagnant in absolute amount and declined sharply as a proportion of the total R&D income during the 2000s. . . . The third mission of universities seems stalled." This conclusion is consistent with other observations, noted above, regarding the current state of innovation in China.

Fourth, China's venture capital industry is relatively inexperienced, as are other providers of services to start-ups and growing high-tech firms. Moreover, even with the emergence of local private firms and the entry of foreign firms, the venture capital industry remains dominated by government-funded or -controlled companies (Zhang, C. and others 2009). This situation is being corrected, and the amount of capital contributed by governments and solely state-owned investment institutions accounted for less than 40 percent of the total amount raised by China's venture capital industry in 2010 (Wang, Zhang, and Zhao 2011). However, more support to newly created companies is still required. In the meantime, entrepreneurs continue to lack the mentoring, professional assistance, networking links, and market insights that are invaluable for young firms. Moreover, some venture capitalists complain that exit is hindered because it takes too long for companies with venture-capital backing to be listed on the GEM.

Fifth, Chinese firms need to work closely with multinational corporations to build innovation capabilities, and it is in the interests of both parties to create a robust innovation infrastructure. But the multinationals may hesitate if they have to worry about intellectual property protection, exclusion from government contracts, newly introduced indigenous standards, rising domestic content requirements, and pressure to transfer technology to China in exchange for market access (Hout and Ghemawat 2010). Innovation policies need to establish greater trust between the government and foreign investors and stronger institutions that validate and operationalize the mutuality of interests. Western European experience starting in the 1960s suggests that, once such trust in institutions is established, technological transfer and spillovers begin to rise and multinationals begin to localize their latest production techniques. The European experience differs from that of developing economies. Given China's size and long-term importance for multinationals, however, China can learn from Europe and invest in the institutions, business practices, and cultural mores that undergird rapid technological diffusion. Chinese initiatives in these areas will be most fruitful if they are matched by a greater readiness to cooperate on the part of foreign companies in the pursuit of technology development.[88]

Sixth, although the benefits of smart (and green) urbanization are becoming apparent to many, much urbanization in China is proceeding inefficiently and untidily, characterized by low-density sprawl, ribbon development along new highways, real estate speculation, rising costs of housing (with low-income households increasingly disadvantaged), and neglect of long-term urban financing needs. These tend to hinder productivity, making it harder for cities to support an ecosystem of small businesses that are the lifeblood of urban economies and a major source of innovation (Glaeser 2011). Furthermore, the absence of longer-term fiscal planning jeopardizes urban sustainability.

Seventh, the signature characteristic of innovative economies is a learning and research environment that encourages new ideas and lateral thinking and that relies on market signals to guide the direction of innovation. In this model, the public sector plays a facilitating role, seeding experimental research with a long-term payoff, providing the legal and regulatory institutional scaffolding, and establishing enforceable standards. China is some distance from this model of an open, cosmopolitan, market-directed innovation system. It may well be that the *dirigiste* approach adopted by the Chinese state could deliver the goods with respect to innovation, as it appears to be doing with technological catch-up. China is putting fairly big bets on a number of technologies even as an innovation system is being pieced together, and without thoroughly evaluating the returns from R&D spending or the merits of recent policies to spur innovation.[89] The development of science and technology for the purposes of innovation remains a planned activity on an expanding scale spanning multiple sectors with a lot at stake and considerable uncertainty regarding the future productivity gains.

The experience of the former Soviet Union with its planned approach to technology development focused on the defense sector argues for caution. The Soviet Union achieved near parity with the United States in many areas of weaponry, but because the defense industry and its research were isolated from the rest of the economy, it soaked up talent and resources while generating few spillovers; in time, these shortcomings contributed to the collapse of the Soviet economy.

The time for a hard look at innovation strategy and policies is now.

Defining Policy Priorities

China is embarked on a longer-term strategy aimed at achieving technological parity with the advanced countries, and at deriving more of its growth impetus from higher productivity across the spectrum of activities and by capitalizing on the commercial benefits from pushing the technology frontier in selected areas.[90] Recent gains in technological capacity suggest that China is approaching the stage when it can transition to an innovation- and productivity-led growth path. How quickly it makes the transition will depend on strengthening the institutions that provide incentives to entrepreneurs, scientists, and engineers in companies, universities, and research institutions to be more innovative. Thus, priority should be placed on loosening institutional constraints.[91]

This transformation is likely to occur in two stages that will require shifting the policy focus between the first stage and the next (this division of stages is only for the purposes of illustration). In the first stage (2011–20), China will continue to benefit from imported technologies, supplemented by domestic incremental innovation, to increase productivity, and to deliver rapid economic growth. An emphasis on further reforming SOEs, improving the quality of the workforce, encouraging applied research in firms, strengthening the research infrastructure, and building market institutions to sustain the tempo of competition and facilitate the entry of SMEs may be appropriate. During this stage, China should achieve the transformation from the planned national innovation system to a system that is open, globalized, market oriented, and compatible with a market economy. The government needs to increase investment in basic research, push through university reform, raise the skill quality of its scientists and technologists, and launch large science and technology programs targeting some of the weak links in key industries.

In the second stage (2021–30), China will derive more of its growth impetus from home-grown innovations that rely not only on the generation of ideas through cutting-edge basic research—with risky blue-skies research supported by the state—but also on the harnessing of these ideas by dynamic Chinese multinational firms with global brand recognition, which are technology leaders in their own particular areas, committed to achieving competitiveness through innovation, and able to engage in technological exchanges and partnerships with foreign firms on equal terms.[92] In attaining such leadership, Chinese companies will necessarily be harnessing worldwide innovation resources much like their foreign counterparts.

As indicated earlier, policies for the first stage necessarily overlap with those for the second. The difference is in emphasis. Several of the policies listed and discussed below are frontloaded because the building of the innovation ecosystem is concentrated in the balance of the decade with the government playing a lead role. In the second stage, the burden of success will rest on the microstructure of the business sector, which is why a competitive environment and investment promoting macrostability are of paramount importance. National technology and innovation policies will need to be complemented by urban policies that recognize the vital role of cities in advancing ideas, extracting the maximum mileage from existing general purpose technologies, and helping germinate new green technologies. The roles of the various entities involved are further spelled out in annex table 2A.16.

1. Increasing market competition aided by greater national market integration, which promotes specialization of production and research activities
2. Making enterprises play a pivotal role in the national innovation system

3. Building national research consortia and networks
4. Improving the productivity and quality of tertiary education with the help of IT and other innovations
5. Strengthening technical and vocational skills to fully exploit technical advances
6. Tightening integration of a more productive national innovation system with the global innovation system
7. Sustaining an increase in R&D spending to raise the productivity of a national innovation system
8. Enabling policies and rigorous evaluation and refereeing of research programs to raise the quality of outcomes and to maximize productivity benefits
9. Increasing access to risk capital and mentoring of start-ups and SMEs by suppliers of venture financing
10. Using effective and disciplined government procurement to stimulate innovation

1. Deepen Reform to Develop a Competitive Market

A competitive market environment is a necessary condition for steady improvement in productivity. Creating this environment entails the opening of product markets, subjecting SOEs in the pillar industries to competition from private firms, enforcing, fairly and effectively, laws regulating competition, and protecting intellectual property as well as consumer rights (Owen, Zheng, and Sun 2007; Oster 1999). It also extends to competition and ease of mobility in factor markets. Starting in the late 1980s, for example, market-oriented reforms stimulated entry and competition in most manufacturing subsectors. Even in some strategic, or pillar, industries (for example, airlines and telecommunications), the breaking up and corporatization of incumbent providers in the 1990s released additional competitive pressures. More recently, the phasing out of tax incentives, which had favored foreign investors, stimulated competition by leveling the playing field with domestically owned firms. China's WTO accession in 2001 increased competition from imports, and the large volume of FDI has led to a further intensification of competitive pressures. Sustaining this trend through institutional reforms and measures to enhance the supply of risk capital as well as the mobility of the workforce will be critical to the making of an innovative economy. These steps will stimulate the deepening of the private sector, promote the growth of dynamic SMEs,[93] and induce the SOEs to raise their game (and pave the way for further reform). Greater national market integration would discourage local protectionism and lead to coordinated R&D activities at least by public entities—including universities—thus minimizing the duplication of suboptimally scaled research and the waste of resources it entails. It would mean intensifying the degree of competition and churning among firms,[94] encouraging firms to compete on the basis of technology, and promoting much needed regional or local industrial and research specialization.

Competition and market integration is inseparable from the efficient pricing of fossil fuels (with carbon taxes added to reflect externalities), electricity, and other nonrenewable resources as well as the setting of national standards (including environmental standards and standards encouraging energy efficiency) for products and the enforcement of these standards. This will also generate pressures to upgrade technologies, which some western countries have done to good effect.[95] Strengthening the industrial extension system and providing smaller firms with easier access to laboratory, metrology, testing, and certification facilities would facilitate meeting these standards by smaller firms. The German Fraunhofer Institutes provide a model for China to adapt. In Japan, the TAMA association makes laboratory facilities and testing equipment available to its member firms, most of which are small or medium in size. The association also offers assistance in obtaining product certification and in creating web pages for purposes of advertising, among other services.

2. Enterprises Have a Pivotal Role in the National Innovation System

Innovation is essentially about creating more wealth by discovering and using newer methods. In all innovative economies, be it the United States, the long-time innovation leader, or more recent entrants such as Japan and Korea, companies have successfully created national innovation systems. Most of the applied research and innovation of consequence for the economy is done by firms;[96] in the United States, for example, the vast majority of scientists are employed by businesses and governments and not by institutions of higher learning. Innovation will flourish if firms in particular provide researchers with the freedom to pursue interesting ideas in a stimulating work environment (Shapin 2010).[97] Mani (2010, 15–16) notes that, "due to various historical and structural reasons, the efficiency and innovation capacity of the business sector is still insufficient, despite a large and rapid increase in scale and scope." Mani uses a crude measure of firms' ability to develop local technological capabilities as the ratio of intramural R&D in business enterprises to the cost incurred in technology purchases from abroad. Over 1991–2002, China's average propensity to adapt grew from less than unity to only about 1.5 in 2002.

Government can support enterprises in developing technological capabilities and producing innovative products by establishing research and development platforms for the use of those companies. In China, there are a range R&D platforms and business service providers such as engineering research centers and productivity centers, but many of them lack the market orientation and the close involvement of potential employers in the design and teaching of curricula and suffer from shortages of funding and experienced trainers. It is important to make them more functional and more responsive to the needs of the economy through a public-private partnership approach. And there are some good examples of public platforms that could be more widely replicated.

FIGURE 2.2   Shanghai R&D Public Service Platform

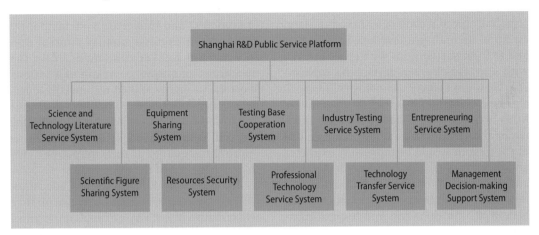

Source: Shanghai Municipality Science and Technology Commission 2006.

For example, Shanghai's R&D public service platform offers a wide range of business and extension services that cover the innovation development process from the sharing of scientific information to technology testing and transfer services to support for entrepreneurship and management (figure 2.2).

The influx of FDI and the recent brain gain is helping to enhance managerial experience as well as technical, research, and teaching skills, but a significant shortfall persists.[98] To move forward, both the private sector and the government need to invest more in improving human resources, especially the management of state-owned and private enterprises, in order to build and embed a culture supportive of innovation.[99] Too many Chinese senior managers from companies with global ambitions lack formal management training, and most are deficient in English language skills. They tend to rely more on informal networks to gather information and on intuition and instincts in making decisions. As a consequence, firm-level research and innovation strategies can be haphazard and do not systematically engage the relevant departments of a firm,[100] little effort is made to gather and analyze data to evaluate results and to guide decisions, and interactions with foreign firms—including foreign travel—are too often delegated to junior staff. Absent

improvements in management and the corporate culture, China may struggle to absorb technology at the desired pace and thus to make the leap from catch-up to a regime of steady innovation.[101]

3. Build Nationwide Research and Development Networks

The central government can take greater initiative in building countrywide research networks that mobilize national talent and reduce the relative isolation of inland cities by including firms from the inland cities in research consortia tasked with disseminating the latest technologies and advancing technology in areas where they have an existing or nascent comparative advantage.[102] Such consortia have been sponsored by governments in Japan and the United States, and they can help China develop more "global challengers" including from the inland metropolitan regions. Successful regional innovation systems are associated with universities that conduct some of the upstream research and generate ideas; a mix of smaller firms that often take the lead in introducing new technologies with mentoring from venture capitalists and angel investors; and larger firms with resources to perfect, scale up, and market the commercial outcomes of these technologies.[103] Recognizing the cost and complexity of research in frontier fields (especially green technologies), even the largest firms are finding it desirable to specialize and to form partnerships with other firms or with universities when developing sophisticated new products or technologies. Through a pairing of inland firms with more advanced firms from the coastal cities (including multinational corporations), the research potential of the interior would be more fully exploited and technological capabilities enhanced. In addition to consortia, the technological and innovative capabilities of inland cities would benefit if both domestic and foreign firms could be persuaded to locate some of their R&D centers in these cities, and not just production facilities. This process is already under way in Chengdu and Xian, for example,[104] but its success will depend on regional innovation policies actively pursued by local governments, which must provide the incentives and build the institutions tailored to local needs. Inland cities with a research orientation would benefit from a focus on a few specific industries, and, depending on what kind of activities achieve prominence, governments would have to act accordingly: developing a research-based biotechnology cluster would require very different policies from an engineering or a food-processing or a white goods cluster.

4. Improve the Quality of Chinese Universities

China's universities are graduating millions of students each year to meet the needs of the knowledge economy.[105] An estimated 6.6 million, including more than 50,000 with doctorates, entered the job market in 2011. But the quality of the training is weak, and many graduates are having difficulty finding employment, although this is likely to be temporary.[106] The low quality is explained by four factors: the massive expansion of enrollment, which has strained instructional capacity; the short duration of PhD training (three years); the inexperience and weak qualifications of instructors and pedagogical

techniques that favor lecturing over discussion and greater classroom involvement of students; and university systems poorly equipped to exercise quality control and to weed out weaker candidates.[107] In the meantime, employers complain of a serious shortage of highly skilled technicians, engineers, and executives. This low-skill glut and high-skill shortage poses a difficulty for the skill transfer needed for companies to improve the quality of their output or move to a higher rung of the value chain.

Because the demand for tertiary education is likely to keep rising and because quality will remain a major issue, China's universities will have to consider some disruptive innovations of their own in order to provide customized education for a vastly larger body of students at an acceptable cost (Christensen, Horn, and Johnson 2010; Zhong 2011). It must be recognized, however, that there is no simple technological fix.[108] Universities are more likely to embrace change if they enjoy a measure of autonomy for their own governance, modes of instruction, curriculum design, hiring, salaries, course offerings, and research orientation; are induced to compete and collaborate with universities throughout the country; and supplement traditional lecture-based training with new pedagogical practices and online and IT tools (especially now that great advances in video links have advanced to a point where a virtual seminar is becoming a reality).[109] Universities will need to recruit faculty from among some of China's brightest graduates, many of whom will be inclined to pursue careers other than teaching.[110] They will also need to tailor course offerings, instruction, and research to instill the desired mix of technical and soft skills (communication, team working, report and business plan writing) as well as the industry know-how in the greatest demand. Perhaps the greatest challenge is how to encourage creativity and initiative, attributes that are urgently needed as the country strives for technological maturity.

By harnessing IT and tapping the expertise and resources of leading firms, universities can improve teaching, motivate students to stick with demanding courses, limit the escalation of costs (which is crippling schools in many advanced countries), and help equip universities with the infrastructure they need to fulfill their missions. China's front-ranked schools must also be able to mobilize the funding and staff faculty positions to offer cross-disciplinary postgraduate and postdoctoral programs and set up specialized, well-staffed research institutes.[111] Universities can provide the precursors to innovation through basic research that leads to discoveries and novel findings. They can also incubate entrepreneurs[112] and skilled researchers, who are the vehicles for transforming ideas into commercial products and services. Together, the government and universities can enhance the dynamism and innovativeness of the private business sector.[113]

5. Strengthen Vocational Training

The development of high-tech industry envisaged by the 12th 5YP depends upon an increased supply and upgrading of technical skills through in-house training and vocational schools. Workers need to be trained in a vast range of technical skills to staff factories, engage in technically more demanding tasks as innovation ratchets up the level of industrial complexity, render IT support, maintain and repair complex equipment, and provide myriad other inputs and services. Smaller firms and start-ups frequently have difficulty finding such skills and can rarely afford to provide much training in-house. Hence, public-private initiatives are required to secure and replenish the base of technical skills essential for a smart city; aside from minimizing both frictional and structural unemployment, these initiatives can anticipate market failures and promote desirable forms of industrial activity. Labor market institutions can be strengthened and made nondiscriminatory by setting up multilevel professional advisory agencies and by increasing the provision of vocational training to meet the demand from expanding and new enterprises. In the most innovative and industrially dynamic European countries such as

Germany, Switzerland, and Finland, between one-fourth and one-half of all secondary school students take the vocational and technical route to a career in industry rather than opting for general education. Striking a better balance between the general and the technical would seem to be warranted.

6. Develop an Open Innovation System

Investment in R&D facilities by multinational corporations is on the rise and needs to be further encouraged and facilitated because of its potentially significant spillover effects that can enrich the knowledge and experience of the Chinese workforce, the potential gains in reputation for Chinese cities that will come to be seen as science hubs, and the contribution such research can make to industrial upgrading. Closer collaboration and partnerships with multinationals on the basis of mutual trust and recognition of the interests of both parties will contribute greatly to the creation of a dynamic and open innovation system.[114] The size and future growth of China's market means that many multinationals will be shifting the primary focus of their operations to China; as a consequence, technological spillovers are very likely to increase. In this context, an efficient patenting system that reflects the experience of the U.S. and European systems (both of which are in the throes of reform)[115] and effective protection of intellectual property will expedite the growth of China's innovation capabilities (Smeets and de Vaal 2011). Gwynne (2010, p. 27) writes that "even companies that possess legitimate Chinese patents have had problems defending their rights, because the scope for protection is much narrower. . . . And when it comes to enforcement, only [recently] have there been any large damage awards for infringement."[116] Legal developments in the form of specialized intellectual property courts is changing the picture.[117] It is also undeniable that China has made substantial progress in protecting intellectual property rights in furtherance of its ambition to become an innovative country. Not only did China launch reforms in 2008 to support the creation, utilization, management, and protection of intellectual property, but it may be the only country to have criminalized violations of intellectual property rights. As more and more Chinese firms file court cases charging violation of their rights by other Chinese firms, the awareness of intellectual property protection will be further raised and protection rendered more effective.[118] Furthermore, the Chinese government has recently relaxed some government procurement restrictions on multinationals, which should encourage these corporations to establish R&D centers in China. The government could also encourage home-grown multinationals to participate in international R&D and integrate into global innovative networks.[119]

7. Strengthen Basic Research to Sustain Continuous Support for Innovation

Central and provincial governments in China are seeking to enlarge the share of basic research in universities and research institutes as well as to raise the profile of R&D in firms, thereby building research capacity throughout the country.[120] They are more likely to succeed by committing a sufficient volume of funding and ensuring the continuity of funding, with the help of an enabling macro policy environment, and through a systematic evaluation of programs. The U.S. government proactively supported agricultural research starting in the mid-19th century and even through the 1930s, most public research funding served to promote agricultural productivity. More recently, the National Institutes of Health have played the central role in the boom in the life sciences in the United States because they were and are a source of large and stable funding, much of it for basic research done in the universities. This funding financed countless research programs, trained thousands of PhDs, supported postdoctoral students, and created the depth of expertise that has enabled the United States to become the leader in the field of biotech. TEKES and SITRA in Finland have also contributed along similar lines. One way to maximize the spillovers from

government-sponsored research and contests to develop particular types of technologies would be to make the findings of this research widely available. In the 1950s and 1960s, the research on electronics financed by the U.S. government was shared generously with private companies, which enabled many companies to come up to speed and become innovators themselves.

Although an increase of one percentage point of GDP in R&D will be one strand of China's growth strategy, the enabling characteristics of the domestic macroeconomic and business environments will be decisive if China is to maximize the longer term returns from R&D spending. Comin (2004) estimates that in the postwar period, R&D contributed between three-tenths and five-tenths of a percentage point to productivity growth in the United States. That higher R&D need have only a limited effect on growth is also apparent from the experience of Sweden, Finland, and Japan (Lane 2009; Ejermo, Kander, and Henning 2011).

8. Create a Stringent and Disciplined Process to Evaluate and Referee Research Programs and Findings

This is a difficult but unavoidable activity. As Lane (2009, 1274) observes, "The relation between science and innovation is nonlinear in nature, with complex outcomes that can vary substantially by discipline and are subject to considerable time lags. . . . Innovation is nonlinear because the demand side and the supply side of ideas are inextricably intertwined." It is an activity requiring initiative from the research community, particularly in strengthening research ethics,[121] instituting strict penalties against plagiarism, and strengthening the independence and quality of the refereeing process.[122] However, the government could provide some of the parameters and adopt a different approach to high-risk research (as is the case in the United States with the National Institutes of Health Pioneer and New Innovator Awards, and the Department of Energy ARPA-E program[123]), which promises to break new ground. Such projects should be evaluated by their potential for transforming a subfield. More broadly, the management and evaluation of R&D in China requires considerable enlightened strategizing and management by public agencies.

The development of innovation capacity in China since the mid-1990s has involved multiple agencies, and numerous policies have been introduced. Looking ahead, with the focus on innovation sure to sharpen, the tempo of policy making can only increase, and the economic outcomes will depend substantially on the quality and timeliness of the policy interventions. If past experience from other countries is a reliable guide, these policies will be multiagency and multidisciplinary, relying upon a mix of tax, fiscal, financial, and regulatory instruments. Good policies will depend upon:

- Strong leadership by the Communist Party Central Committee (CPCC)/State Council, by strengthening the leading group on Science, Technology, and Education, headed by the premier, which would have the requisite authority.
- Direct and consistent involvement of the National Development and Reform Commission, Ministry of Finance, and Ministry of Science and Technology, the key ministries involved with innovation policies, and effective coordination of their roles.
- Effective horizontal communication and coordination among other major ministries engaged in the making and implementation of S&T policies, such as the Ministry of Education, the Ministry of Commerce, the Ministry of Health, the Ministry of Industry and Information Technology, the Ministry of Agriculture, and others. The leadership role of a CPCC leading group would minimize past fragmentation of decision making among agencies, each of which pursues a narrow policy agenda within its own particular silo, as well the conflict among roles and mandates, thereby achieving greater policy coherence and effectiveness (Liu, Simon,

and others 2011). The weight of leadership and the engagement of the National Development and Reform Commission and the Ministry of Finance would also increase the commitment of subnational governments to the innovation agenda and lead to the strengthening of regional innovation systems.

- Leadership and coordination must go hand in hand with a concerted effort to raise the technical and implementation skills of the government bureaucracies tasked with driving the innovation strategy. It almost goes without saying that the growth of innovation capabilities will demand considerable farsightedness, agility, and innovativeness on the part of those responsible for guiding and managing a highly complex endeavor during a crucial stage of gestation. The quality of the bureaucracy matters everywhere; however, given the large role played by the state in China, the importance attached to building innovation capacity in the shortest possible time and the vast resources being invested, the caliber of the bureaucracy takes on an added significance.
- The experiences of the most innovative countries—such as Finland, Israel, the United States, and others—none of which can boast an unimpeachable innovation system[124]—underscore the contribution that a sound process of evaluating research-related spending can make to the design and conduct of innovation policies and to raising system productivity. Economists have generally tended to give high marks to R&D spending, claiming that it generates exceedingly high rates of social and even private returns, usually higher than spending on fixed assets.[125] But on closer scrutiny, it appears that many of these claims might be exaggerated. Ben Martin the editor of *Research Policy* observes that not infrequently, "there is some PR [public relations] rather than rigorous research involved."[126] Measuring the inputs and outputs of research is not a trivial exercise. The benefits from research are uncertain and variable and

they accrue over a long period of time. Moreover, the bulk of the returns take the form of spillovers for which there are no good metrics. The problem is especially severe with basic research. There are costs to research results and their assimilation, which can come to light much later and need to be factored in. For example, new medical technologies that extend the lives of elderly patients impose costs on society, nuclear power has imposed cleanup and disposal costs, and many defense technologies have not been unmitigated blessings. Collecting data on inputs and outputs from myriad and disparate sources and making the data consistent and readable is an additional and daunting task. Once the data are gathered, selecting an appropriate methodology for analyzing them presents a further challenge.[127] But all this is unavoidable in view of the sums involved and the need to obtain the greatest possible productivity mileage from public spending on the innovation system. The lesson from advanced countries is to start early by putting in place a system to rapidly evaluate research spending, to absorb the learning promptly into the policy-making process, and to be ready to make corrections or terminate programs that are not producing results. China is at the stage where it can begin building the elements of an evaluation process into its emerging innovation system, learning from others and fully utilizing the latest available data gathering, storage, and analytic technologies that promise to make a difficult task more manageable.[128]

9. Develop Multilayered Capital Markets to Support Innovation and Start-ups

Rising demand for risk capital calls for an increase in supply. The Chinese government is active in promoting both public and private venture capital, at least in the coastal cities. Although some public risk capital is available inland, private venture capital for smaller private firms, which are trying to scale up, is still scarce. Moreover, the level of professionalism and experience of venture capitalists and the degree of trust between providers of risk capital and borrowers is still fairly low; hence, further development of risk financing by venture capitalists and business angels will be needed. Banks can serve as a partial substitute, but such lending is rarely their forte. Nonetheless, such lending on a limited scale by local banks to local firms and the creation of bank-led relational networks is a mode of financing that seems to work in the United Kingdom and the United States and complements the resources of entrepreneurs, angel investors, and venture capitalists. Too little bank financing in China goes to private firms and especially the riskier high-tech ones (Hanley, Liu, and Vaona 2011). That said, the dot-com bubble and other bubbles have highlighted the waste arising from bouts of irrational exuberance fed by an excess of risk capital. The enormous investment in speculative real estate both in China (amounting to 12 percent of GDP in 2010) and in countries with sophisticated financial systems suggests that capital is not necessarily the constraint; more often it is investors who are rightly skeptical of technological offerings with uncertain prospects. Facilitating the exit for venture capitalists is as important as raising venture capital for start-ups and innovative firms (Guo, Zhang, and Li 2000; Guo 2009). So far, SMEs have only limited choices to raise capital by listing on stock exchanges, which normally takes a long time.

10. Make Better Use of Demand-Side Policies

Demand-side policy instruments such as government procurement and standard setting for equipment and services, combined with adequate efforts to guard against protectionist and rent-seeking activities that undermine market competition and discourage high-tech FDI, will stimulate the demand for innovation (Liu and Zhang 2008; Zhang 2007). Managing government procurement is a relatively new domain of policy in China. The first national guideline for government procurement was issued in 1999, and the National People's Congress adopted the law in 2002. Despite the relative newness of this approach, the government's determination to support innovation through procurement has been clear. However, procurement policy can be a double-edged sword. The key to success lies in open competition. In China, some potential risks in this area need to be fully recognized and reflected in government policies. These include the risk of turning the government procurement instrument into one that protects national and local products from international and national competition and the risk of the government becoming a passive taker of what domestic suppliers offer, rather than a demanding buyer of technologically sophisticated products (Zhang, C. and others 2009).

The demand for innovation could be increased through government standard setting. Standard setting allows governments and other entities to generate demand for advances in, for example, the performance, safety, energy efficiency, and environmental impact of products. Measures that could be taken to generate more demand for innovation include focusing exclusively on product improvement and resisting the tendency to use standard setting to protect or help domestic or local industry; taking EU or U.S. standards as a technical starting point while looking for ways to advance product performance; involving industry leaders more in standard setting (but that needs to be done in a productive way); and changing the role of government from sole standard setter to time-sensitive driver of industrial consensus (Zhang, C. and others 2009).

Emerging Priorities for Innovation

As per capita incomes rise, China's spending on health care will increase in parallel. The health care sector will become an important sector for China's economic growth and social development. In addition, as hundreds of millions of people emigrate from rural areas, developing green, smart, and innovative cities will be an important driver of China's growth through innovation.

Innovation in Health Care

The salience of health care in the Chinese economy is certain to increase, and innovation will be an important mechanism for controlling costs while raising quality and expanding access to health care. Health care in China confronts a "perfect storm," with steeply rising social and financial costs that could become a huge burden on the nation in a handful of decades. To quote from a *Lancet* editorial:

> The population demographics are uneven, exaggerated by rapid ageing, as a result of the single child policy, and by the large number of highly mobile workers within the country. The health infrastructure is variable, with world leading medical centers in the populous east of the country, whereas more rural areas lack basic sanitation. Despite better control, infectious diseases still account for considerable morbidity with an ever-present danger of new outbreaks. Alongside communicable diseases are the increasing burdens caused by the diseases of affluence and changing lifestyles. Meanwhile the ability to deliver care is compromised by an uneven distribution of human resources and the loss of doctors to other professions. In addition to the breadth of the challenges, the size of the task is enormous. A Chinese man smokes one in every three cigarettes. 177 million adults in China have hypertension but few receive effective treatment"[129]

The inexorable march of noncommunicable diseases is heightening concerns; these are now responsible for 80 percent of all deaths and 69 percent of the disease burden—higher than in the advanced countries—and they threaten to significantly erode China's economic gains (World Bank 2011). David Cutler (2003) has estimated that high-income countries can expect health care costs to rise by 5.7 percent of GDP just on the basis of demographic and technological changes. The increase could be greater in China given its stage of development, rising incomes, changing lifestyles, and epidemiological profile. Containing health care costs while providing modern health care to the entire population promises to remain a long-term policy objective. And the experience of advanced countries points to the urgency of policy intervention, before institutions have had time to solidify and strong vested interests have become almost politically invincible, as is the case in the United States, Europe, and Japan, and the system acquires an immense status quo bias (Starr 2011).

Clearly innovation is only a part of the answer, and in fact some of the cost escalation is directly attributable to advances in pharmaceuticals, diagnostic devices, medical implants, and others.[130] But technological improvements are also behind some of the advances in the quality of health care and increasing longevity (Lichtenberg 2008, 2010, 2011). Among the innovations that are likely to play a major role in the future, and that thus deserve the most prominence, are advances in preventive medicine, which reduce the risks from communicable diseases, ameliorate the effects of chronic ailments, bring about positive changes in lifestyles, and ensure that the majority of the population has access to clean water and good sanitation. Some of these advances will involve biopharmaceutical innovations, but many others also will play a role. Digital medicine is set to greatly expand its contribution by revolutionizing billing, ordering, record keeping and sharing, and medical administration. Digital medicine is also transforming access to medical information, communication between doctors and patients, and the monitoring of patients by providers. Advances in distance medicine have the potential to multiply medical assets and are only beginning to be tapped through new diagnostic and other devices as well as through the outsourcing of diagnosis. The potential of digital technology, how it can be assimilated (and the advantages of early action), and the many ethical, procedural, administrative, and financial hurdles

it raises are lucidly discussed by West and Miller (2009).[131]

ICT can also help to contain costs by enabling a much more exact measurement of total costs of care than is the case currently. Providers and insurers have had only a rough idea of the costs of caring for a patient but now are in a position to track the type and amount of resources used over the course of a medical treatment (Kaplan and Porter 2011).

Christensen, Grossman, and Hwang (2009) highlight another aspect of innovations in the biopharmaceutical and diagnostic fields with potentially disruptive and cost-reducing effects. This is the rise of so-called precision medicine tailored to the unique genetic profile of each patient, which would sharpen the accuracy of diagnosis and ensure that each ailment is treated with the medications calculated to have greatest effect and the fewest side effects.[132] The cost savings from this set of innovations could be large.

To strike the best balance between the quality of health care and costs, China will have to strive for medical innovation that is tempered by effective regulation (which minimizes red tape, optimizes incentives for providers, and fully harnesses ICT) and for competition among providers on results so that more patients migrate to better providers. Porter and Teisberg (2006) note that "good quality is less costly because of more accurate diagnoses, fewer treatment errors, lower complication rates, faster recovery, less invasive treatments, and the minimization of the need for treatment. Competition on results to improve patient value is an irresistible force for transforming the health care system without the need for top-down government intervention." Greater competition in health care would be very much in tune with the overall strategy to build a more competitive economic system.

Building Green, Smart, and Innovative Cities

Investment in technological capacity is more likely to result in a flourishing of innovation in a competitive environment and in "open" cities (Hu 2011). Learning from its experience with rapid industrialization in the 1980s, China initially sought to enlarge technological capacity in a small number of coastal cities (notably Shenzhen, Guangzhou, and other cities in the Pearl River Delta as well as Shanghai and Beijing) with the help of FDI, imported equipment embodying new techniques, licensing, and reverse engineering. The decentralized urban-centered approach, bolstered by suitable organizational and fiscal incentives and increased R&D, jump-started technology assimilation from abroad and created the framework for stimulating indigenous technology development. On the technological plane, these cities are performing the functions that the Special Economic Zones provided in the 1980s. The proposed intensification of R&D activities during 2011–20 and the increasing emphasis on achieving technological parity with the West and on greening growth to improve quality and minimize environmental costs offers an opportunity to develop the innovation capacity of coastal and some inland cities and, in the process, to increase the productivity of R&D expenditures.

Innovative cities rely upon the quality of human capital, on institutional mechanisms and basic research of a high order for generating ideas, and on ways of debating, testing, and perfecting these ideas and transforming them into marketable products. The innovative city achieves rapid and sustainable industrial growth by bringing together and fully harnessing four forms of intelligence: the human intelligence inherent in local knowledge networks, of which research universities are a vital part; the collective intelligence of institutions that support innovation through a variety of channels; the production intelligence of a diversified industrial base that is a source of urbanization economies; and the collective intelligence that can be derived from the effective use of digital networks, online services, and face-to-face contacts in a conducive urban environment (Komninos 2008).

The leading global innovative hotspots are open to ideas and thrive on the heterogeneity of knowledge workers drawn from all over the country—and the world (Page 2007). Moreover, such cities are closely integrated with other global centers of research and technology development, and their teaching and research institutions must compete with the best for talent and to validate their own ideas. For innovative cities, openness and connectivity are more important than scale. These contribute to the productivity of research and the generation, as well as the validation, of ideas. However, urbanization economies arising from size and industrial diversity can confer important benefits by offering a mix of technologies and production expertise out of which innovations can arise and that provide the soil for new entrants to take root.[133] Connectivity through state-of-the-art telecommunications and transport infrastructure—airports in particular (Kasarda and Lindsay 2011)—is a source of virtual agglomeration for an intelligent city, conferring the advantages of a large urban center without the attendant disadvantages of congestion and pollution. In this respect, the smaller innovative cities of Europe and the United States enjoy the advantages of livability without sacrificing the productivity gains accruing from agglomeration.[134]

To exploit the innovation potential inherent in virtual agglomeration, innovative cities need to actively network with other centers throughout the region and the world and build areas of expertise. This calls for embracing a culture of openness, and activism on the part of major local firms and universities to translate such a culture into commercial and scientific linkages that span the globe. For a city to be recognized as an innovation hotspot, however, one or a few local firms must join the ranks of the world's leading companies in a technologically dynamic field and account for a sizable share of the global market.

Last but not least, because innovative cities are at the leading edge of the knowledge economy, their design, physical assets, attributes, and governance need to reflect their edge over others. Industrial cities can become innovative cities, and a strong manufacturing base can be an asset, as it is for Tokyo, Stuttgart, Munich, Seoul, Seattle, and Toulouse. But industry is not a necessary condition: Cambridge (U.K.), Helsinki, San Francisco, and Kyoto are not industrial cities, yet they are innovative cities that have acquired significant production capabilities that are high-tech or "I-tech" (Markusen and others 2004).

Cities become innovative when existing industries or institutions act as a nucleus of new activities and start a chain reaction. The process can be initiated by any of a number of catalysts—decisive and visionary leadership by leading stakeholders, the upgrading and transformation of a local university, the creation of a new research institution, the arrival or growth of a major firm, a small cluster of dynamic start-ups, or some other catalytic event that energizes a combination of intellectual and productive activities. There are virtually no instances in the past two decades of innovative cities being successfully made to order anywhere in the world. The attempts to engineer science cities such as in Tsukuba in Japan and Daejeon in Korea as well as similar complexes in Europe have rarely lived up to expectations.

The science and technology capacity of China's coastal cites is well established and is being steadily augmented through rising investment in the research infrastructure; that of several inland cities is now being developed through increasing attention to regional innovation policies. Cities such as Xian, Chengdu, Zhengzhou, and Hefei are attempting to raise the profile of their leading universities, grooming local firms that could become industrial anchors for local clusters, much like ARM and Cambridge Consultants served as the anchors for the electronics cluster in Cambridge, U.K.[135] Several cities such as Chengdu, Shenyang, and Chongqing[136] have also been successful in persuading multinational corporations to set up production facilities, which augment manufacturing capabilities and create the preconditions for a concentration of the value chain.[137] Moreover, leading inland cities such as Changsha are investing in the transport infrastructure to improve connectivity, and all have established industrial parks to provide space and services for industry to grow. These plus a full suite of incentives satisfy most of the preconditions for the emergence of innovative industrial clusters. What might be missing is an industrial focus on specialization and on the quality of the environment.

Greening Urban Growth

Economic growth that is largely urban driven must be rendered climate friendly. Hence the "greening" of urban growth is becoming a priority worldwide, including in China. Although the precise meaning of green growth remains somewhat elusive, it points to the possibility of achieving sustainable urban development through a virtuous spiral of innovations. At the core of green growth is the assumption that the energy, capital, and emissions intensity of GDP can be contained or reduced as economies expand. The hope is that if greening can be mainstreamed, much more can be achieved: a green growth strategy should lead to development of and investments in low-carbon technologies and infrastructures that bring about a green industrial revolution, creating the jobs and raising incomes without the negative externalities associated with the fossil fuel–based growth of the past two centuries; greening can thus contain the trend change in the climate. An exploration of the possibilities is still at an early stage and hemmed in by the prevalence of entrenched technologies, but even now it is obvious that if the revolution is to succeed, much will depend upon the initiatives taken by cities and the effectiveness with which they are implemented.

To realize the potential of green urban growth, a conceptual framework can usefully provide the scaffolding for policies—national and local. In this context, an intersection of two concepts pertaining to general purpose technologies (GPTs) and to agglomeration economies can serve to identify and elaborate actions to promote green growth.

Long cycles of growth-augmenting technological change are associated with the emergence and diffusion of GPTs, which have protracted and economywide effects. A GPT has three characteristics (Bresnahan and Trajtenberg 1996):

1. *Pervasiveness:* It should spread to most sectors.
2. *Improvement:* It needs to evolve and improve over time with users benefiting from steadily falling costs.
3. *Innovation spawning:* The GPT should promote invention and provide the foundation for new products, processes, and related organizational and institutional changes.

Steam, electricity, the internal combustion engine, and now IT, are the emblematic GPTs (Jovanovic and Rousseau 2005). Each was and is responsible for urban industrialization extending over several decades, requiring a massive volume of investment. The effects were not limited to a single sector; instead, these GPTs unleashed innovations that diffused through and energized the entire economy. The innovations shifted the production frontier; triggered sustained investment in new products, business models, and modes of production; and served as the foundations of long-term economic growth. Starting in the 1970s, the benefits from IT began filtering through the global economy and very likely will continue to stimulate innovation and productivity for another decade or two. However, the looming threat of climate change from accumulating greenhouse gases largely released by urban centers (up to 80 percent of the total) and the increasing press of energy and resource scarcities has created a need for new energy and resource utilization systems that, in conjunction with IT, will gradually green the entire urban economy, with seismic network effects similar to those that arose from coal's displacement of wood as the primary source of energy.

A green growth strategy can potentially reinforce the productivity gains from urban agglomeration by introducing technological innovations and minimizing the productivity-eroding effects of urban sprawl, land use distortions, inattention to the design of cities, inefficient services, and infrastructures and transport systems that cater to ever-increasing automobility. Green urbanization suggests a number of policy directions:

- With respect to urban design, it would put a premium on the compactness of cities and mixed-use neighborhoods with due attention to and investment in public transport systems, green spaces, and recreational amenities to reduce energy intensity as well as environmental pollution.
- It would seek to more fully realize the returns from urban real estate and supporting infrastructures while remaining mindful of urban congestion and without compromising individual intraurban mobility and the quality of urban life.
- To deliver on its growth potential, green urban agglomeration would need to be hospitable to the continued vitality of existing industrial activities (while providing incentives for the greening of these activities) and to the emergence of new industrial clusters producing tradables so as to generate net employment and a flow of exports.
- It would support the growth of urban industries and services producing for the green economy: the adoption of energy and resource-conserving technologies (such as smart grids, energy-efficient housing and consumer products) backed by standards, regulations, and pricing and procurement policies plus consumer education campaigns that bring about a shift in preferences; of technologies controlling emissions and waste; and of techniques promoting recycling and disposal to minimize environmental impacts. To this end, green urbanization must strive after a mix of entrepreneurship and specialized skills to research, produce, transport, install, and service the technologies and products driving green cities. Thus the productivity of green urbanization would be closely related to technological change guided by market and nonmarket signals, as well as the quality and skills of the urban workforce.

- Fully exploiting the sources of green growth will be a function of creative urban and national bureaucracies committed to a green agenda and able to respond quickly to new information, formulate and implement policies, and achieve the necessary interdepartmental and interjurisdictional coordination, the lack of which all too often stifles change. More so than in the past, bureaucracies will need to be prodded by a vigilant, informed, and networked civil society to set targets, learn from best practice, and benchmark and produce results.

While the possibilities inherent in green technologies and green urbanization deserve serious attention, good policies are difficult to identify and will emerge only after a number of questions have been empirically addressed:

First, it is important to ascertain the practicality of the green growth concept for policy-making purposes and its compatibility with other views of economic growth. Moreover, given that the current share of green industries (producing "environmental goods") is small (accounting for about 1.5 percent of total employment in high-income countries), what would it take for the green economy to become a significant growth driver within the next two decades?

Second, it is desirable to canvas international experience with net job creation (are green jobs new jobs?), local industrialization, and productivity gains at the city level, of policies aimed at increasing energy efficiency and conservation (smart meters); substituting renewable energy for fossil-based energy, and developing advanced energy storage devices for use with intermittent power-generating sources; retrofitting existing residential and commercial structures and power, water supply, transport, and sanitation systems with new equipment based on green technology; and managing ownership and use of private cars (with the help of sensor technologies and ICT).

Third, China needs to learn from domestic and international sources about the more effective application of policy vehicles and instruments that support green urbanization and how might they be improved. These include:

- Public bureaucracies tasked with devising, implementing, and monitoring green strategies
- Local taxes, fees, and other charges to manage energy and resource consumption as well as to raise revenues, including some earmarked for green infrastructure and development.
- Use of local or national carbon markets to manage energy consumption
- Zoning, land use, floor area ratios, real estate and other property taxes (to limit urban sprawl), and urban design to arrest current trends; promote compact, green development; and begin transforming legacy urban infrastructure
- Subsidies, taxes, and other incentives in support of specialized training to enlarge the pool of relevant skills, provide incentives for research, and encourage start-up activity in green industries
- Standards and codes for structures and equipment; eco-labeling; incentives to use green energy; and education programs to stimulate use of green technologies
- Fiscal instruments and financing vehicles (public and private, foreign funded) to raise the capital for the substantial upfront spending needed to jump-start green development; implement green urban projects, many with long payback periods; and maintain the momentum of green development over the long haul
- Technology parks, seed capital, and tax exemptions to induce the formation of green industrial clusters.

Finally, it is important to take a measure of green technologies likely to mature over the next 15 years, most of which are already known, and judge whether a new green general purpose technology comparable to the Internet and the internal combustion engine is emerging, one that will transform many areas of activity and result in long-term productivity gains of the magnitude associated with the diffusion of ICT. Such a measure would help clarify whether reasonably tested and cost-effective low-carbon, green technologies (in the construction industry, for example, and related to the development of smart transport systems) are already accumulated and waiting to be exploited or whether the technologies expected to have the largest payoffs (such as lightweight electric cars connected by a mobility Internet) are still at an early stage of development or as yet undiscovered. In other words, tomorrow's green electrons should not just be expensive versions of today's brown electrons: greening should be part and parcel of a quantum leap in technology and productivity. The question to be asked is: How quickly could the most promising and relatively cost-effective technologies be scaled up given financing availability, technological expertise, industrial capacity, public readiness to adopt new technologies and lifestyles and constraints posed by legacy infrastructures, vested interests, and mainstream technologies?

Concluding Observations

Technological progress and the flourishing of innovation in China will be the function of a competitive, globally networked ecosystem constructed in two stages during 2011–30. Government policy will provide most of the impetus in the first stage, but success will hinge on the quality of the workforce, the initiative and strategy of firms, the emergence of supporting services, and the enabling environment provided by cities. Human talent is the source of innovation: its flowering depends on the research infrastructure in firms and cities and the degree of global networking. The innovativeness of the business sector is a function of many factors, some of which, such as management, competition, and strategy, are discussed here.

With respect to China's emerging innovative cities (coastal and inland), two points need to be emphasized. First, state-owned and state-controlled enterprises continue to account for a significant share of production in key industries. Second, although the innovation systems created by the cities are encouraging new entrants, it is not apparent from the low rate of entry and exit that truly innovative firms, especially privately owned SMEs, are being groomed or that struggling firms are allowed to fail in sufficient numbers. Making SOEs more innovative will contribute significantly to China's sustained growth. The best bet is an innovation system anchored to and drawing its energy from a competitive national economy.

Annex 2A   Annex Tables

TABLE 2A.1   Annual TFP growth rate: Major industries, 1999–2004
Percent

	China	Japan	Korea, Rep.
Construction	−1.74	0.18	−1.06
Food and kindred Products	−0.29	1.20	1.91
Textile mill products	0.16	1.56	1.65
Apparel	0.80	1.00	2.65
Paper and allied Products	1.47	0.57	1.57
Chemicals	0.60	1.94	−0.97
Stone, clay, and glass Products	3.70	2.09	3.48
Primary metals	−0.28	1.53	−2.85
Nonelectrical Machinery	2.71	1.78	1.65
Electrical machinery	2.83	5.18	11.05
Motor vehicles	2.78	1.13	1.39
Transportation	4.94	1.80	9.15

Source: Ito and others 2008.

TABLE 2A.2   Top USPTO patents by inventor resident in China, 2005–09
Percent

Class	Rank	Class title	Share of total patents
439	1	Electrical connectors	10.3
361	2	Electricity: electrical systems and devices	6.8
370	3	Multiplex communications	3.4
382	4	Image analysis	3.2
424	5	Drug, bio-affecting, and body treating compositions (includes class 514)	2.8
707	6	Dp: database and file management or data structures (data processing)	2.5
455	7	Telecommunications	2.1
438	8	Semiconductor device manufacturing: process	1.9
375	10	Pulse or digital communications	1.7
532	14	Organic compounds (includes classes 532-570)	1.4
435	17	Microbiology	1.1
385		Chemistry: molecular biology and optical waveguides	0.8
356		Optics: measuring and testing	0.6
280		Land vehicles	0.5
99		Foods and beverages: apparatus	0.2
123		Internal-combustion engines	0.2
180		Motor vehicles	0.1

Source: United States Patent and Trademark Office.

TABLE 2A.3   WIPO Patent Cooperation Treaty, share of international patents by sector, 2007–09

Percent

Sector of technology / field of technology	Worldwide Ratio	China Ratio	Share of patents held by China
Total	100.00	100.00	3.15
I Electrical engineering	29.48	53.14	5.67
1 Electrical machinery, apparatus, energy	5.20	5.38	3.25
2 Audio-visual technology	3.16	2.46	2.45
3 Telecommunications	4.61	11.33	7.73
4 Digital communication	4.69	25.76	17.28
5 Basic communication processes	0.87	0.78	2.84
6 Computer technology	6.37	5.11	2.53
7 IT methods for management	1.27	0.70	1.72
8 Semiconductors	3.31	1.62	1.54
II Instruments	16.23	7.86	1.52
9 Optics	2.96	1.59	1.69
13 Medical technology	5.90	2.72	1.45
III Chemistry	29.61	18.49	1.97
15 Biotechnology	3.61	1.98	1.73
16 Pharmaceuticals	37.67	4.55	2.34
18 Food chemistry	1.11	0.72	2.04
19 Basic materials chemistry	3.42	1.68	1.54
20 Materials, metallurgy	2.00	1.37	2.16
21 Surface technology, coating	2.04	1.08	1.67
22 Micro-structural and nano-technology	0.25	0.04	0.45
23 Chemical engineering	2.76	2.08	2.38
24 Environmental technology	1.51	1.20	2.49
IV Mechanical engineering	18.31	12.93	2.22
32 Transport	3.46	2.21	2.01

Source: China State Intellectual Property Office.
Note: Under the WIPO approach, one application may have several IPC classes and may belong to different technology fields. In this case, every technology field will be counted. As a result, the sum of the total number of all technology fields could be larger than the total number of applications in the year.

TABLE 2A.4   Sector composition of new entrants (legal unit) by established time, Guangdong, Beijing, and Zhejiang, 2008
Percent

	Guangdong		
	1996–2000	**2001–05**	**2006–08**
Manufacturing	*29.03*	*35.71*	*32.84*
Processing of food from agricultural products	0.84	0.58	0.32
Manufacture of foods	0.86	0.59	0.34
Manufacture of beverage	0.29	0.24	0.15
Manufacture of tobacco	0.01	0.00	0.00
Manufacture of textile	1.24	1.72	1.19
Manufacture of textile wearing apparel, footwear and caps	1.68	2.54	2.80
Manufacture of leather, fur, feather and its products	0.86	1.24	1.60
Processing of timbers, manufacture of wood, bamboo, rattan, palm, straw	0.46	0.54	0.61
Manufacture of furniture	0.97	1.02	1.16
Manufacture of paper and paper products	1.15	1.47	1.26
Printing, reproduction of recording media	1.52	1.67	1.00
Manufacture of articles for culture, education, and sport activity	0.62	0.67	0.55
Processing of petroleum, coking, processing of nucleus fuel	0.07	0.07	0.04
Manufacture of chemical raw material and chemical products	1.58	1.63	1.07
Manufacture of medicines	0.16	0.17	0.09
Manufacture of chemical fiber	0.04	0.06	0.02
Manufacture of rubber	0.33	0.45	0.43
Manufacture of plastic	2.56	3.21	2.89
Manufacture of nonmetallic mineral products	1.77	1.77	1.31
Manufacture and processing of ferrous metals	0.11	0.19	0.14
Manufacture and processing of nonferrous metals	0.26	0.40	0.33
Manufacture of metal products	3.22	3.87	3.75
Manufacture of general purpose machinery	1.15	1.57	1.51
Manufacture of special purpose machinery	1.09	1.64	1.87
Manufacture of transport equipment	0.70	0.80	0.56
Manufacture of electrical machinery and equipment	2.34	3.08	3.10
Manufacture of communication, computer, other electronic equipment	1.77	2.73	2.96
Manufacture of measuring instrument, machinery for cultural and office work	0.40	0.46	0.49
Manufacture of artwork, other manufacture	0.87	1.14	1.05
Information transfer, computer services, and software	*1.41*	*2.78*	*3.52*
Telecommunications and other information transmission services	0.25	0.43	0.55
Computer services	0.45	1.16	1.57
Software	0.70	1.18	1.40
Finance	*0.23*	*0.29*	*0.37*
Banking	0.08	0.01	0.05
Securities	0.04	0.02	0.01
Insurances	0.05	0.18	0.18
Other financial activities	0.06	0.08	0.13
Tenancy and business services	*9.04*	*9.01*	*9.93*
Leasing	0.10	0.17	0.20
Business services	8.95	8.84	9.73
Scientific research, technical service, and geologic perambulation	*1.98*	*2.87*	*3.16*
Scientific research and experiment development	0.30	0.63	0.92
Technical service	1.35	1.78	1.75
Scientific exchange and disseminate service	0.32	0.45	0.48
Geologic perambulation	0.01	0.01	0.01
Education	*3.97*	*2.42*	*1.56*

Source: Economic Census Yearbook, Beijing, Guangdong, and Zhejiang 2008.
Note: The table shows the share of newly entering firms in each category for the stated period. For example, 29.03 percent of the aggregate newly entering firms established in 1996–2000 in Guangdong province were manufacturing firms. New entrants are only those surviving in the survey year; firms that closed before the survey year were not counted. The data reflect the time a firm was established and do not reflect a possible move from one industrial sector to another. The new entry of S&T firms might thus be underestimated if a large proportion of them changed their industry affiliation from traditional sectors to high-tech sectors

	Beijing			Zhejiang		
1996–2000	2001–05	2006–08	1996–2000	2001–05	2006–08
14.65	*10.64*	*6.36*	*51.22*	*48.98*	*42.98*
0.49	0.26	0.14	1.25	0.75	0.55
0.53	0.29	0.19	0.50	0.33	0.27
0.20	0.11	0.05	0.65	0.46	0.31
0.00	0.00	0.00	0.00	0.00	0.00
0.33	0.21	0.11	5.30	5.78	4.86
0.95	0.76	0.69	2.22	2.34	2.30
0.09	0.06	0.06	1.78	1.40	1.32
0.20	0.22	0.24	0.75	0.78	0.82
0.46	0.44	0.42	0.55	0.58	0.63
0.38	0.28	0.21	1.77	1.45	1.20
0.62	0.41	0.21	1.85	1.56	0.89
0.17	0.11	0.05	1.01	1.04	0.88
0.14	0.06	0.02	0.05	0.04	0.04
1.07	0.66	0.24	1.86	1.53	1.05
0.30	0.18	0.06	0.29	0.21	0.13
0.02	0.01	0.01	0.21	0.23	0.14
0.10	0.06	0.03	0.69	0.58	0.44
0.75	0.48	0.25	3.72	3.74	3.26
1.02	0.84	0.43	1.82	1.73	1.41
0.05	0.06	0.02	0.40	0.41	0.35
0.11	0.09	0.03	0.52	0.50	0.40
1.40	1.13	0.63	3.59	3.39	3.09
1.28	0.90	0.56	6.46	6.64	6.00
1.05	0.80	0.43	2.30	2.41	2.18
0.51	0.43	0.20	2.87	2.65	2.73
0.87	0.64	0.41	4.43	4.07	3.79
0.70	0.52	0.25	1.18	1.22	1.11
0.58	0.43	0.21	1.23	0.87	0.66
0.28	0.20	0.20	1.84	2.09	2.01
4.86	*6.80*	*6.69*	*1.11*	*2.40*	*3.15*
0.74	1.05	0.92	0.18	0.20	0.21
1.78	2.23	2.23	0.56	1.60	1.98
2.34	3.52	3.55	0.37	0.61	0.96
0.24	*0.40*	*0.47*	*0.18*	*0.30*	*0.59*
0.05	0.01	0.04	0.05	0.03	0.03
0.05	0.04	0.05	0.01	0.00	0.02
0.06	0.21	0.18	0.04	0.09	0.14
0.09	0.14	0.20	0.08	0.17	0.40
12.77	*17.38*	*20.13*	*6.45*	*6.12*	*8.68*
0.71	0.68	0.72	0.16	0.20	0.38
12.05	16.71	19.41	6.30	5.91	8.30
6.68	*7.53*	*8.69*	*1.74*	*2.21*	*2.63*
0.63	0.79	0.75	0.17	0.18	0.22
2.67	2.93	2.74	1.05	1.30	1.23
3.32	3.72	5.12	0.50	0.72	1.17
0.05	0.08	0.06	0.01	0.01	0.01
1.89	*1.85*	*1.66*	*3.24*	*2.04*	*1.31*

TABLE 2A.5   Number of patents in force in the high-tech industry, by industrial sector and registration status, 2009

	Large enterprises	Share (%)	Medium enterprises	Share (%)	Small enterprises	Share (%)
Total	22,975	55.81	8,855	21.51	9,340	22.69
Manufacture of medicines	1,460	24.26	2,451	40.73	2,106	35.00
Manufacture of chemical medicine	795	32.41	967	39.42	691	28.17
Manufacture of finished traditional Chinese herbal medicine	646	29.16	1,031	46.55	538	24.29
Manufacture of biological and biochemical chemical products	10	1.32	284	37.47	464	61.21
Manufacture of aircrafts and spacecrafts	368	59.16	197	31.67	57	9.16
Manufacture and repairing of airplanes	367	69.11	113	21.28	51	9.60
Manufacture of spacecrafts	1	1.52	59	89.39	6	9.09
Manufacture of electronic equipment and communication equipment	17,120	69.70	4,178	17.01	3,264	13.29
Manufacture of communication equipment	14,000	89.68	770	4.93	841	5.39
Manufacture of radar and its fittings	12	24.49	31	63.27	6	12.24
Manufacture of broadcasting and TV equipment	83	27.04	66	21.50	158	51.47
Manufacture of electronic appliances	2,084	43.98	1,523	32.14	1,131	23.87
Manufacture of electronic components	328	18.50	848	47.83	597	33.67
Manufacture of domestic TV set and radio receiver	553	41.02	612	45.40	183	13.58
Manufacture of other electronic equipment	60	8.15	328	44.57	348	47.28
Manufacture of computers and office equipment	3,525	70.28	667	13.30	824	16.43
Manufacture of entire computer	2,630	94.47	108	3.88	46	1.65
Manufacture of computer peripheral equipment	437	27.96	444	28.41	682	43.63
Manufacture of office equipment	1	1.25	41	51.25	38	47.50
Manufacture of medical equipment and measuring instrument	502	10.14	1,362	27.50	3,089	62.37
Manufacture of medical equipment and appliances	112	7.85	322	22.58	992	69.57
Manufacture of measuring instrument	390	11.06	1,040	29.49	2,097	59.46

Source: China Statistics Yearbook on High Technology Industry 2010.

TABLE 2A.6   Innovation inputs and outputs of industrial enterprises in China, by enterprise size, 2009
Percent

Size of enterprise	Share with R&D activities	R&D spending as share of core business sales revenue	R&D personnel as share of total employment	Share of patents in force per RMB 100 million of R&D expenditure	Share of patents in force per 100 R&D personnel
Total	8.47	0.74	2.19	29.18	6.18
Large and medium	30.48	1.03	3.19	23.58	5.37
Small	6.16	0.28	0.99	61.90	9.27

Source: China Statistical Yearbook on Science and Technology 2010.

TABLE 2A.7   Innovation inputs and outputs of industrial enterprises in the high-tech industry in China, by enterprise size, 2009
Percent

Size of enterprise	Share of enterprises with R&D institutions	Share with R&D activities	R&D spending as share of core business sales revenue	R&D personnel as share of total employment	Share of patents in force per RMB 100 million of R&D expenditure	Share of patents in force per 100 R&D personnel
Total	17.52	25.53	1.63	4.96	42.51	8.67
Large-sized enterprises	53.61	61.68	1.71	6.06	43.67	10.81
Medium-sized enterprises	40.82	46.81	1.81	4.87	28.01	5.22
Small-sized enterprises	12.01	20.42	1.12	3.58	74.03	10.11

Source: China Statistical Yearbook on Science and Technology 2010.

TABLE 2A.8   Foreign direct investment: capital utilized by industry, 2004–09

Industry	2004	2007	2009
Total	100	100	100
Agricultural	1.84	1.11	1.52
Agricultural: farming	0.89	0.47	0.80
Mining	0.89	0.59	0.53
Manufacturing	70.95	48.93	49.72
Textile	3.88	2.21	1.48
Chemical material and product	4.38	3.46	4.24
Medical and pharmaceutical product	1.11	0.72	1.00
Universal machinery	3.58	2.58	3.17
Special purpose equipment	3.13	2.77	2.74
Communications, computer, and other electronic equipment	11.64	9.20	7.63
Electricity, gas, and water production and supply	1.87	1.28	2.25
Construction	1.27	0.52	0.74
Transport, storage and postal service	2.10	2.40	2.69
Information transmission, computer service and software	1.51	1.78	2.39
Wholesale and retail trade	1.22	3.20	5.73
Accommodation and catering trade	1.39	1.25	0.90
Banking and insurance	0.42	10.79	4.77
Real estate	9.81	20.46	17.86
Leasing and commercial service	4.66	4.81	6.46
Scientific research, polytechnic service, and geological	0.48	1.10	1.78
Water conservancy, environment, and public utility mgt	0.38	0.33	0.59
Residential and other service	0.26	0.87	1.69
Education	0.06	0.04	0.01
Health care, social security and welfare	0.14	0.01	0.05
Culture, sport, and recreation	0.74	0.54	0.34
Public management and social organization	0.00	0.00	0.00

Source: CEIC database.

TABLE 2A.9   Patent family applications by value and country absolute volume

Year	High value			Intermediate value			Low value		
	China	Germany	United States	China	Germany	United States	China	Germany	United States
1990	5	2,139	5,784	51	10,101	40,232	27,343	32,021	40,232
1991	5	1,781	4,747	37	10,445	39,887	33,158	35,216	39,887
1992	7	1,727	4,696	59	10,614	42,843	43,215	38,082	42,843
1993	4	1,868	4,314	47	11,014	48,298	44,879	40,573	48,298
1994	5	2,056	4,200	69	11,766	55,841	42,237	42,400	55,841
1995	3	2,107	3,888	64	12,073	62,261	41,296	43,300	62,261
1996	4	2,100	3,980	74	14,003	61,888	46,287	47,106	61,888
1997	8	1,851	3,977	97	15,218	68,525	48,099	49,319	68,525
1998	6	1,836	3,799	121	16,349	65,965	50,476	51,057	65,965
1999	5	1,543	3,743	160	17,167	66,363	59,659	52,417	66,363
2000	2	1,421	3,312	269	16,807	65,797	74,843	51,879	65,797
2001	10	980	2,564	333	16,143	62,624	87,826	49,961	62,624
2002	15	644	2,361	461	14,896	59,977	109,524	46,721	59,977
2003	13	556	2,027	759	15,603	50,830	133,444	47,140	50,830
2004	27	629	2,142	1,347	17,345	49,273	147,734	50,054	49,273
2005	25	606	1,722	2,528	18,321	50,098	187,067	47,245	50,098
Sum	141	23,843	57,254	6,476	227,867	890,706	1,177,087	724,491	890,706

Source: Boeing and Sandner 2011.

TABLE 2A.10   **Regional and provincial productivity in China**
RMB 10,000/person

	2004	2005	2007	2009
Eastern Region	***3.625***	***4.137***	***5.359***	***6.518***
Beijing	6.771	7.482	8.416	9.683
Fujian	3.171	3.516	4.627	5.642
Guangdong	4.371	4.757	5.873	6.996
Guangxi	1.296	1.508	2.158	6.996
Hainan	2.180	2.368	2.949	2.711
Hebei	2.481	2.912	3.843	3.834
Jiangsu	4.034	4.721	6.139	4.420
Liaoning	3.419	4.048	5.322	7.596
Shandong	3.041	3.623	4.934	6.946
Shanghai	9.938	10.696	13.905	6.220
Tianjin	7.373	8.662	11.671	16.192
Zhejiang	3.767	4.196	5.195	14.828
Central Region	***1.890***	***2.201***	***3.004***	***3.937***
Anhui	1.378	1.543	2.047	2.727
Heilongjiang	2.926	3.390	4.256	5.089
Henan	1.531	1.870	2.601	3.275
Hubei	2.176	2.436	3.341	4.285
Hunan	1.567	1.780	2.454	3.342
Inner Mongolia	2.984	3.742	5.632	8.526
Jiangxi	1.695	1.925	2.505	3.411
Jilin	2.799	3.293	4.821	6.144
Shanxi	2.422	2.831	3.699	4.600
Western Region	***1.436***	***1.625***	***2.199***	***2.939***
Chongqing	1.594	1.784	2.304	3.476
Gansu	1.277	1.435	1.966	2.408
Guizhou	0.774	0.893	1.201	1.671
Ningxia	1.802	2.023	2.873	4.120
Qinghai	1.772	2.030	2.836	3.787
Shaanxi	1.685	1.952	2.844	4.256
Sichuan	1.417	1.604	2.198	2.862
Tibet	1.634	1.789	2.227	2.610
Xinjiang	2.967	3.407	4.399	5.158
Yunnan	1.283	1.411	1.823	2.260

Source: China Statistical Yearbook 2005–2010.
Note: Productivity is calculated by dividing regional GDP by region's labor force.

TABLE 2A.11   **Domestic patents granted in different provinces in China, 2009**

Eastern Region		Central Region		Western Region	
Beijing	22,921	Anhui	8,594	Chongqing	7,501
Fujian	11,282	Heilongjiang	5,079	Gansu	1,274
Guangdong	83,621	Henan	11,425	Guizhou	2,084
Guangxi	2,702	Hubei	11,357	Ningxia	910
Hainan	630	Hunan	8,309	Qinghai	368
Hebei	6,839		1,494	Shaanxi	6,087
Jiangsu	87,286			Sichuan	20,132
Liaoning	12,198	Inner Mongolia	2,915	Tibet	292
Shandong	34,513	Jiangxi	3,275	Xinjiang	1,866
Shanghai	34,913	Jilin	3,227	Yunnan	2,923
Tianjin	7,404	Shanxi			
Zhejiang	79,945				

Source: China Statistical Yearbook on Science and Technology 2010.

TABLE 2A.12   Innovation inputs and outputs of industrial enterprises in China, 2009
Percentage

Enterprises	Share of enterprises with R&D institutions	Share with R&D activities	R&D spending as share of core business sales revenue	R&D personnel as share of total employment	Share of patents in force per RMB 100 million of R&D expenditure	Share of patents in force per 100 R&D personnel
Total	5.91	8.47	0.74	2.19	29.18	6.18
State-owned enterprises	10.61	14.12	0.69	2.63	17.92	3.71
Large SOEs	56.56	50.86	0.85	3.48	14.10	3.27
Private enterprises	6.38	4.07	0.39	1.22	43.42	7.44
Enterprises with funds from Hong Kong SAR, China; Macao SAR, China; and Taiwan, China	10.41	7.71	0.76	1.76	28.81	5.62
Foreign-funded enterprises	8.22	11.62	0.69	2.18	26.17	6.32

Source: China Statistical Yearbook on Science and Technology 2010.

TABLE 2A.13   Distribution of innovation inputs in China, by type of performer, 2009

	Number of enterprises (unit)	Share (%)	R&D personnel (thousands)	Share (%)	Expenditure on R&D (billions)	Share (%)	Number of patents in force (piece)	Share (%)
Total	429,378	100.0	1,914.27	100.0	405.20	100.0	11,8245	100.0
State-owned enterprises	8,860	2.06	174.77	9.13	36.16	8.92	6,478	5.48
Large-size SOEs	419	0.10	119.64	6.25	27.75	6.85	3,913	3.31
Private enterprises	253,366	59.01	356.35	18.62	61.09	15.08	26,528	22.43
Enterprises with funds from Hong Kong SAR, China; Macao SAR, China; and Taiwan, China	33,865	7.89	198.82	10.39	38.80	9.58	11,179	9.45
Foreign-funded enterprises	40,502	9.43	284.39	14.86	68.65	16.94	17,965	15.19

Source: China Statistical Yearbook on Science and Technology 2010.

TABLE 2A.14   Distribution of innovation inputs and outputs in high-tech industry in China, by type of performer, 2009

	Number of enterprises (unit)	Share (%)	R&D personnel (thousands)	Share (%)	Expenditure on R&D (billions)	Share (%)	Number of patents in force (piece)	Share (%)
Total	27,218	100.0	474.63	100.0	96.84	100.0	41,170	100.0
Domestic	17,922	65.85	297.83	62.75	60.69	62.67	29,254	71.06
State-owned enterprises	469	1.72	26.32	5.54	5.37	5.54	1,178	2.86
Enterprises with funds from Hong Kong SAR, China; Macao SAR, China; and Taiwan, China	3,809	13.99	70.39	14.83	13.37	13.81	4,713	11.45
Foreign-funded enterprises	5,487	20.16	106.41	22.42	22.79	23.53	7,203	17.50

Source: China Statistics Yearbook on High Technology Industry 2010.

TABLE 2A.15   Innovation inputs and outputs of industrial enterprises in high-tech industry in China, 2009
Percent

Enterprises	Share of enterprises with R&D institutions	Share with R&D activities	R&D spending as share of core business sales revenue	R&D personnel as share of total employment	Share of patents in force per RMB 100 million of R&D expenditure	Share of patents in force per 100 R&D personnel
Total	17.52	25.53	1.63	4.96	42.51	8.67
Domestic	18.32	27.11	2.97	7.32	48.21	9.82
State-owned enterprises	27.93	41.36	3.81	8.70	21.95	4.48
Enterprises with funds from Hong Kong SAR, China; Macao SAR, China; and Taiwan, China	16.30	22.92	1.13	3.29	35.25	6.70
Foreign-funded enterprises	15.73	22.18	0.83	3.16	31.61	6.77

Source: China Statistics Yearbook on High Technology Industry 2010.

TABLE 2A.16   **Roles of various entities involved in Nation Innovation System**

Entities in NIS	Primary objectives	Incentive mechanisms	The actions that the entities should and could take	Institutions and policies that could influence the behaviors of the entities
Domestic enterprises	Sustained profitability; Long-term competitiveness	Market competition as driving force for innovation (Schumpeter ian innovation)	Improve management; Purchase of technology; Long-term R&D investment; Research networking; Recruit talents	Promote effective competition; Protection of IPR; Enhance the supply of human resources; Encourage entrepreneurship Tax incentives for R&D investment; Demands-side incentives;
Foreign funded enterprises	Sustained profitability; Long-term competitiveness	Market competition as driving force for innovation (Schumpeter innovation)	Purchase technology from the parent company; Launch local R&D activities; Hire local talents	Promote a fully completive environment; Credible IPR protection; Enhance the supply of human resources; Incentives for establishing R&D facilities and investing in R&D
Universities	Cultivate talents; Frontier research	Teaching evaluation; Funds granted from the state; Peer pressure	Reform education philosophy; improve education methods; Recruit top-grade faculties; Encourage free thinking and independent research	Grant more autonomy to universities; Reform the evaluation and appraisal system of university; Reform the grant award and evaluation system of major R&D projects
R&D institutions	Applied and basic research; Cultivate talents	Funds granted from the state; Peer pressure	Design effective internal incentive mechanisms; Recruit first grade scientists and engineers	Reform grant award system for major R&D projects; Increase funds for hiring experts and postdoctoral fellows
Engineers and scientists	Wealth creation; Seeking after truth	Professional discipline; Peer pressure	Self-motivated lifelong learning; Perseverance	Reform grant award system for major R&D projects; Encourage freedom in research; Reform the appraisal and compensation system
Industry associations	Serve companies	Trust of the firms; Recognition by the society	Promote the cooperation between firms; Improve communications between governments and industry; Facilitate R&D alliances	Grant more autonomy to industry associations
Financial institutions	Profit maximization; Long-term competitiveness	High profits; market competition; Comply with the laws and regulations	Professional investment team; Good risk management mechanisms	Create good financial eco-system; Keep balance market competition and regulation; Provide tax deduction for the capital invested in the high-tech enterprises
Central government	Economic and social development; National security	Demand and needs of the people; Global competitive pressure	Improve the infrastructure, especially those related to ICT, to facilitate the transmission and flow of knowledge; Develop effective market; Strengthen the social security system; Increase investment in education and enhance the quality of education; Improve national innovation system; Sustained investment in basic research; Promote R&D by firms; Organize major R&D projects; Create initial demands through the first-buyer strategy of government procurement	Reform of the administrative management system; Create a rule-of-law government; Responsive to the people's demand
Local government	Sustainable regional economic and social development	Performance appraisal by superior; Competition between regions; Demand and needs of local citizens	Improve infrastructure and institutions to create an enabling environment for business start-ups and innovation; Promote R&D by firms; Promote the development of local industrial clusters	Reform appraisal system for local government officials; Promote regional competition in a unified national market; Responsive to the people's demand

Source: Authors.

Notes

1. As ranked by the Times Higher Education Supplement 2011. The list includes universities in Hong Kong SAR, China. http://www.topuniversities.com /world-university-rankings/qs-world -university-rankings-2011.

2. This projection is found in China's Science and Technology Medium-to-Long Term Plan. For more discussion and analysis, see Lu (2006); Xu (2006); Zhang, Liu, and Lu (2008); and Lu (2009). An earlier book by Sigurdson and others (2005) visualizes China as an emerging "technological superpower." See also Hu (2011, 95), who believes that by 2020, China will be an innovative country and the largest knowledge-based society in the world.

3. These are the findings of the Development Research Center's study on growth prospects. More than 320 million workers continue to derive their livelihoods from agriculture, and this number will shrink as agricultural productivity grows. Thus the transfer of workers from agriculture to more productive services will continue to yield a productivity bonus for some time. However, once this transfer is largely completed, the increasing absorption of workers in nontradable services that historically have registered very small or negative increases in productivity, could slow future gains in productivity. Two recent papers question whether China is close to this so-called "Lewis turning point." Knight, Deng, and Li (2011, 597) maintain that "there is a substantial supply of migrants still available in rural China. . . . Rural workers will have better opportunities to migrate for employment and older workers will have a stronger incentive to move with their families as central and local governments respond to the economic need for a more settled urban workforce." This view is echoed by Golley and Meng (2011, 571): "There is an abundance of rural workers who appeared to be under-employed with earnings well below their migrant counterparts."

4. Comin, Hobijn, and Rovito (2006) ascribe the bulk of productivity differentials among countries to lags in the assimilation of technologies.

5. In its original form as proposed by Joseph Schumpeter, innovation embraced new products, markets, sources of materials, new production processes, and new organizational forms. To these, one can add design and marketing and the list can go on. Dodgson and Gann (2010, 11), in their portrait of Josiah Wedgewood, the renowned serial innovator, maintain that the enduring truth about innovation is that it "involves new combinations of ideas, knowledge, skills and resources. [Wedgewood] was a master at combining the dramatic scientific, technological and artistic advances of his age with rapidly changing consumer demand. The way in which [Wedgewood] merged technological and market opportunities, art and manufacturing, creativity and commerce, is perhaps, his most profound lesson for us." According to a recent survey by Hall (2011), product innovation was unambiguously more productive than process innovation. In services, marketing, customer relations, and the clever use of IT can be decisive.

6. Jones and Romer (2009) explain the large differences in per capita GDP among countries with reference to both factor inputs and the residual. However, they note that "differences in income and TFP across countries are large and highly correlated: poor countries are poor not only because they have less physical and human capital per worker than rich countries, but also because they use their inputs much less efficiently."

7. Lester (2004, p. 5) observes that the real wellsprings of creativity in the U.S. economy are the "capacity to integrate across organizational, intellectual and cultural boundaries, the capacity to experiment, and the habits of thought that allow us to make sense of radically ambiguous situations and to move forward in the face of uncertainty."

8. This count excludes Singapore and Hong Kong SAR, China, which also achieved high-income status but, because of their small size, can shed very limited light on policies for China.

9. Japan differs from the other two because it was already an industrial power before World War II capable of fielding weaponry comparable to that of the Western nations. For comparative purposes, however, the Japanese experience remains relevant.

10. The Toyota Motor Company was among the pacesetters that borrowed techniques and ideas pioneered in the United States and adapted them to Japanese conditions. The

story of how entrepreneurs and inventors transformed the Japanese electronics industry is well told by Johnstone (1999). Japan's technology development and innovativeness is the subject of two excellent volumes written by Odagiri and Goto (1996, 1997).

11. The *keiretsu* in Japan, and the *chaebol* in Korea.

12. Among the innovations introduced by Korean companies was the 256 MB DRAM (by Samsung in 1998). The dedicated silicon merchant foundry pioneered by Morris Chang at TSMC in 1987 was a fundamental innovation, which built on the creation of standardized circuit design rules and electronic design automation to transform the chip manufacturing industry. This innovation greatly widened the options for chip designers, who had hitherto depended on excess capacity at vertically integrated chip manufacturers such as Texas Instruments to produce their chips (Perry 2011). See Mathews and Cho (2000); Breznitz (2007); Hsueh, Hsu, and Perkins (2001, specifically the annex by Ying-yi Tu); and Brown and Linden (2009) on the technological development of Korea and Taiwan, China. On fabless firms and production, see http://microlab.berkeley.edu/text/seminars/slides/RChen.pdf; http://cadlab.cs.ucla.edu/icsoc/protected-dir/IC-DFN_Agenda_Aug_2007/Jeremy%20Wang-FSA%20Industry%20Update.pdf.

13. Breznitz and Murphree (2011) argue that China does not need to master breakthroughs over the near term to achieve economic success. Instead, it can be a successful second-generation innovator since the spectrum of innovation possibilities is so wide. On innovation and China's sustainable development, see Fang (2007) and Gao and Liu (2007).

14. Translating promising discoveries into profitable innovations can take many years if not decades. The high-strength synthetic fiber Kevlar created by DuPont took 17 years to achieve commercial viability, and it is not an exception.

15. The estimates by Bosworth and Collins are among the higher ones. Total factor productivity is one of the most widely used indicators of growth, but its worth for policy-making purposes is uncertain. Felipe (2008), for instance, is outspokenly critical, claiming that "TFP a dubious, misleading

and useless concept for policy making." The sources of growth in China are estimated by, among others, Wang and Yao (2003); Badunenko, Henderson, and Zelenyuk (2008); and Urel and Zebregs (2009), all of whom find that capital played the leading role. Time series analysis arrives at similar results. Chen, Jefferson, and Zhang (2011) survey the sources of growth literature on China.

16. See also the estimates on sources of growth and China's share of the world economy in OECD (2010b).

17. Chen, Jefferson, and Zhang (2011) ascribe the slowdown in TFP growth since 2001 to industrial policies that have reduced allocative efficiency, factor market distortions that divert financial resources to less productive uses, and the diminishing productivity bonus from structural change.

18. Yu (2009). Perkins (2011) estimates that China's capital to output ratio rose from 3.79 in the 1990s to 4.25 in 2000–07 and to 4.89 in 2008–09. With a ratio of investment to GDP approaching 50 percent in 2011, China is now investing far more than Japan did at the height of its boom and deriving a roughly equivalent amount of growth.

19. Even at its peak, TFP growth was generally less than 3 percent for almost all countries. For example, even during its years of rapid growth, Finland averaged 2.8 percent a year.

20. The estimates differ. Those given here are from the OECD. See Groupe BPCE (2010); Fukao and others (2008); and OECD Statistics Portal, http://stats.oecd.org/Index.aspx?DatasetCode=MFP.

21. Eichengreen (2012) observes that the annual growth of productivity in China's services sector barely exceeds 1 percent, compared with 8 percent in industry, and that the sector conducts little R&D. He calls for a revolution in services for China to catch up with the United States.

22. Comin (2004).

23. As noted earlier, China's exports of manufactures overlap with those of the United States, but wide differences in quality and technological sophistication remain.

24. The Fukushima disaster has further sensitized companies to supply chain vulnerabilities.

25. An aspect of learning highlighted by Levitt, List, and Syverson (2011) and critical to the profitability of electronic component

manufacturing, for example, but also to that of autos, is a reduction in the number of defects, which is a function of worker skills and familiarity with the production process and of the plant's physical and organizational capital.

26. According to Felipe, Abdon, and Kumar (2010), as early as the 1960s, China was exporting 105 commodities (with comparative advantage) from the 779 commodities in their sample, many more than either Korea or Brazil. By 2006, the number had risen to 269, well ahead of Japan (192). Of these, 100 products were from the core of the product space. China continues to export, with comparative advantage, 69 labor-intensive products; its exports of machinery have risen from 1 in 1962 to 57; it has lost comparative advantage in less sophisticated metal products and gained it in products with higher PRODY, which is the average income of a country associated with that good. China has also forged ahead with telecommunication and electronic products and office equipment. As a consequence, the unweighted PRODY of China's core exports rose from $14,741 in 1962 to $16,307 in 1980 to $17,135 in 2006.

27. Data collected by Thomson Reuters shows that China's patent rankings by subsector are highest for chemical engineering, where it is second after the United States. The rankings are fourth or lower for other major subsectors (Zhou and Stembridge 2011).

28. The data generated by the Nature Publishing Group (2010) indicate that Chinese researchers are increasing their contribution to genetics, clinical medicine, and structural biology.

29. As of 2012, Huawei had emerged as the world's largest supplier of telecom equipment (in 2011, its revenues amounted to $32 billion), although Ericsson remains the leading producer of network infrastructure equipment; see "Huawei: The Company That Spooked the World," *Economist*, August 4, 2012, pp. 19–23. See also Nolan (2012), who compares the relative (global) standing of Chinese and other leading multinational corporations.

30. This leadership has been convincingly documented by the series of volumes on China's Science and Technology launched by Joseph Needham and published by Cambridge University Press (http://www.nri.org.uk /science.html). See also Subramanian (2011) on why China is well placed to regain its earlier preeminence. Subramanian computes a dominance index based on a country's GDP, trade, and status as a creditor. He is of the view, that as of 2010, China might already have pulled ahead of the United States and could be well in the forefront by 2030. And this dominance could very likely extend to the technological domain.

31. Walsh (2003). Zhang and Long (2011) provide detailed analysis on investment by multinational corporations in R&D activities in China.

32. See Gao, Zhang, and Liu (2007) on the efforts of Dawning and HiSense to cap manufacturing capability with own innovation.

33. The companies listed in the Forbes Global 2000 generate $30 trillion in annual revenue, equal to one-half the global GDP. China still has only limited representation in this group—with less than 5 percent of the revenue. The Chinese firms making headway in the sphere of manufacturing are Haier, Lenovo, BYD, Huawei, and ZTE. Lenovo's experience with the acquisition of IBM's personal computer business and that of TCL with the takeover of Thomson's TV arm suggest that the acquisition of large foreign firms with brand names can bolster the fortunes of ambitious Chinese companies if they can muster the managerial expertise to harness and grow the reputational capital of the acquired foreign assets and cope with the challenges posed by transnational operations. On Lenovo's circumstances, see "Short of Soft Skills: Lenovo's Bid to Become a Global Brand Is Coming Unstuck," *Business China*, June 8, 2009. The acquisition of Volvo, the Swedish carmaker, by Geely, the privately owned, Hangzhou-based Chinese manufacturer, will be another important test case of whether a Chinese firm can turn around an ailing foreign company and effectively sustain and capitalize on its reputation.

34. See Price and others (2011) on the success of China's efforts to reduce the energy intensity of the economy by 20 percent during the course of the 11th Five Year Plan.

35. Gao and Jefferson (2007) note that countries appear to experience an "S&T take-off" when their spending on R&D doubles as a

share of GDP and begins to approach 2 percent. China has doubled its spending since the mid-1990s and on current trends will exceed 2 percent by 2014. See "China Bets Big on Small Grants and Large Facilities," *Science*, March 2011, p. 1251. According to one estimate, a 10 percent increase per capita in spending on R&D raises TFP by 1.6 percent over the longer term (Bravo-Ortega and Marin 2011).

36. China has some of the best-equipped laboratories in the world with state-of-the-art measuring and testing devices. Computing power has also risen in leaps and bounds. As of November 2010, China, with 41 of the 500 fastest supercomputers in the world, was second only to the United States (IEEE 2011). For a period of less than a year (2010–11), China's Tianhe -1A was the world's fastest supercomputer, before being overtaken by the Fujitsu K computer. This might soon be eclipsed by IBM's Mira computer.

37. Installed electricity generating capacity rose from 350 gigawatts in 2000 to over 900 gigawatts in 2010 "China's power generation capacity leaps above 900 million kilowatts," *Xinhua News*, September 20, 2010. Temporary shortages of coal and rising prices constrained supply from coal-fired plants, while inadequate rainfall reduced the supply of power from hydro sources in 2011.

38. From the Ministry of Industry and Information Technology's "2010 Statistical Report on Telecommunications Industry."

39. China is attempting to groom up to 100 universities (including the 75 under the Ministry of Education) into top-flight, world-class universities—through the 211 and the 985 programs (buttressed by the 863 and 973 programs). Currently about 40 are being targeted by the 985 program.

40. Worldwide spending on R&D amounted to $1.1 trillion in 2007, with spending by Asian countries surpassing that of the European Union and approaching that of the United States (National Science Board 2010).

41. "China Shoots Up Rankings as Science Power, Study Finds," CNN, March 29, 2011. See also Gao and Guan (2009) on the increasing rate of China's S&T output relative to GDP growth.

42. Patenting is an unreliable indicator of innovation, and as patent offices have experienced an increase in applications, their ability to filter the good from the innocuous has declined—especially the filtering of business model, process, and software patents applications. Many if not most patents lie dormant, never leading to any commercial outcomes.

43. The National Patent Development Strategy (2011–20) envisages that patent applications of all kinds will increase from 1.2 million in 2010 to 2 million in 2015 and that overseas applications by Chinese residents will double.

44. See "China's Patents Push 2010," *Nature News*, February 15, 2010. However, foreign patent applications account for two-thirds of all effective invention patents (Hu 2011).

45. See "Patents, Yes; Ideas, Maybe. Innovation in China," *Economist*, October 14, 2010; and Li (2012), which refer to the generous incentives that are offered to researchers and companies and also to bureaucrats in patent offices to approve patents, many of which are of the utility model kind. So-called junk patents are not substantively examined or evaluated by China's State Intellectual Property Office (SIPO)—the patent being granted with the minimum of scrutiny. Breznitz and Murphree (2011) observe that most innovation in China thus far is of an incremental sort. Firms in the ICT sector account for the majority of the USPTO and many of the SIPO filings. These firms, according to Eberhardt, Helmers, and Yu (2011), tend to be young, large, R&D intensive, and outward oriented.

46. http://transatlantic.sais-jhu.edu/bin/k/u/cornerstone_project_lundvall.pdf; http://www2.druid.dk/conferences/viewpaper.php?id=502529&cf=47

47. *OECD Factbook 2011*, http://dx.doi.org/10.1787/888932505906. The small number of triadic filings also reflects the high costs. Some firms take the Patent Cooperation Treaty route, which establishes a filing date and needs to be followed up with national filings, but permits some delay. See http://en.wikipedia.org/wiki/Patent_Cooperation_Treaty.

48. Data supplied by SIPO.

49. Ministry of Science and Technology (2008).

50. In 2008, Huawei filed more international patents than any other company. It was also the leading filer of patents with SIPO during 1985–2006 with a 34 percent share. See

"Patents Yes, Ideas Maybe. Innovation in China," *Economist,* October 14, 2010; and Eberhardt, Helmers and Yu (2011). In general, firms in the electronics industries are the most prolific patenters, in part because a portfolio of patents serves as protection against patent infringement suits by others and as a basis for countersuits. Patents are also useful bargaining chips in highly contested industries and can be a source of revenue through licensing arrangements or outright sale.

51. Some of this technology is generated by the firms themselves, while some is acquired through the takeover of foreign firms. For example, Dalian Machine Tools purchased two businesses from Ingersoll International and bought a majority share in F. Zimmermann. Suntech Power acquired the Japanese MSK Corp and KSL-Kuttler Automation Systems in Germany (BCG, "The 2009 BCG 100 New Global Challengers," January 2009). See also Zhang, C., and others (2009).

52. Gwynne (2010) notes that Chinese contract research organizations (such as Shanghai Genomics/GNI) are now offering services ranging from the development and production of biological drugs using recombinant DNA technology, and research on edible vaccines is on the rise. Overall, however, Chinese companies hold only a limited portfolio of pharmaceutical patents and lag in this field.

53. Measured by purchasing power parity, China is likely to have spent more on nanotechnology research in 2011 than the United States—$2.25 billion vs. $2.18 billion—and several recently established nanotech centers in China are engaging in cutting-edge research (Oxford Analytica 2011). On some views regarding the future directions of nanotechnology, see Manoharan (2008).

54. See Adams, King, and Ma (2009) on China's R&D effort. Sinovel, Goldwind, and Dongfang Electric were the top Chinese producers of wind turbines in 2009, ranked third, fifth, and seventh in the world, respectively. China's BYD (Build Your Dreams) is a leader in high-density batteries. These and other firms (such as the Galanz Group, the HiSense Group, and SAIC) are among the New Challengers in BCG's list of 100 top firms in 2009.

55. About half of all worldwide investment in high-speed rail is occurring in China, and China's $300 billion investment in this industry to date has created state-of-the-art production facilities. See "China's Rail Exports Will Survive Wenzhou Crash," Oxford Analytica, August 24, 2011.

56. Goldwind has co-developed a direct-drive wind turbine, which dispenses with the cost and inefficiencies of a gearbox. See Zhao (2011) on the development of photovoltaic cells in China, starting in the mid-1980s with two silicon-cell assembly lines.

57. The first flight of the COMAC C919 is scheduled for 2014, with an in-service target of 2016. This might be optimistic in light of delays experienced by the ARJ 21 project initiated in 2002, which is running five years behind schedule. Whether the C919 can penetrate the single-aisle airliner international market in the face of competition from new entries from Boeing and Airbus and also Bombardier, Embraer, Sukhoi, and Irkut, will depend on the aircraft's performance, COMAC's marketing and support services, and its ability to win a few big orders from foreign carriers or leasing companies (Farnborough, "Is China Cracking?" *Flight International,* Special Report, July 3–9, 2012, pp. 86–88; and "A Dogfight for Duopoly," *Financial Times,* August 7, 2012, p. 7).

58. By 2011, China had launched more than 100 satellites for purposes of surveillance, remote sensing, weather forecasting, telecommunications, and, most recently, navigation and positioning via the Beidou Navigation Satellite System. China's Long March launchers are now among the world's most reliable. "Chinese Academy Takes Space under its Wing," *Science* 332, May 20, 2011, p. 904; "Beijing Adds Fuel to Global Space Race," *New York Times,* global ed., January 1, 2012, p. 3; Cliff, Ohlandt, and Young 2011). A space station is now in the works following the docking of two orbiters, Shenzhou-8 and Tiangong-1. "China Unveils Its Space Station," *Science* 473, May 5, 2011, p. 14; "China Forges Ahead in Space Race," *Nature* 479, November 17, 2011.

59. This list now includes stealthy jet fighter planes. See http://www.aviationweek.com /aw/generic/story.jsp?id=news/awst /2011/01/03/AW_01_03_2011_p18-279564 .xml&channel=defense.

60. See also http://www.sts.org.cn/sjkl/gjscy /data2010/2010-2.htm.

61. Lenovo and Haier now have the makings of global brands (Nolan 2012).

62. A full listing of national programs and policy initiatives from 1980 onward can be found in Lu (2008) and Liu, F. and others (2011). An overview of China's S&T system can be found in Swissnex (2011).

63. http://archive.itif.org/index.php?id=226.

64. http://www.innovationfordevelopment report.org/supplement/Supplement_ICI _profiles2010.pdf.

65. http://ec.europa.eu/research/innovation-union/pdf/iu-scoreboard-2010_en.pdf.

66. The Chinese government formally adapted the "Strategy for Raising the Nation by Relying on Science, Technology, and Education (Kejiao Xin Guo Zhanlue) in 1995" and established the State Leading Group on Science, Technology and Education in 1998, headed by then-premier Zhu Rongji.

67. See Huang, Zhang, and Zhu (2008) on the footwear cluster of Wenzhou. Other clusters producing cigarette lighters and eyeglass frames have also flourished, but as wages have risen, foreign demand weakened, and credit tightened in 2011, the Wenzhou-based clusters have come under considerable stress with weaker firms having to exit. Less well known is the industry in Hebei and Shandong. The so-called Gaoyang model—and its resilience through decades of turmoil—is described by Grove (2006).

68. Meisenzahl and Mokyr (2011) observe that the innovations responsible for the industrial revolution in Britain were the work of a small band of inventors and a limited contingent of skilled craftsmen who helped realize the industrial potential of the innovations. Lane (2009) observes that San Diego owes 40,000 jobs in the life sciences and 12,800 jobs in electronics to the research of just four scientists at the University of California, San Diego.

69. Adams, Clemmons, and Stephan (2006). Jaffe and Trajtenberg (1996) used patent citations to map the diffusion of knowledge. Others have observed that patents are only one of the avenues through which knowledge diffuses from universities. Certain informal means of communication are of greater importance (Agrawal and Henderson (2002). Keller (2001a, 2001b) substantiates earlier work by Jaffe and by others.

70. See Markusen (1996) on factors contributing to stickiness in slippery space. Gordon and Ikeda (2011) find that the most innovative cities combine scale with "Jacobs density," which maximizes informal contacts among city dwellers.

71. This development, noted by Stevenson-Yang and DeWoskin (2005), is unusual and affects the value of intellectual property, the return on manufacturing, and the speed with which manufactures are commodified.

72. This was the message of a major study conducted in the late 1980s by a group from MIT (Dertouzos, Lester, and Solow 1989). It is echoed in "When Factories Vanish, So Can Innovators," *New York Times*, February 12, 2011; emphasized by Andy Grove in "How America Can Create Jobs," *Bloomberg Business Week*, July 1, 2010"; and reflected in a recent report to President Obama by the President's Council of Advisors on Science and Technology on Ensuring American Leadership in Advanced Manufacturing.

73. "Education: The PhD Factory," *Nature* 472 (April 2011), 2776–79.

74. The reforms under way to make Shanghai's Jiao Tong University into a powerhouse comparable to MIT are described by Wang, Wang, and Liu (2011). The making of high-caliber universities is explained in detail by Salmi (2010) and Altbach and Salmi (2011). See also Kaiser (2010) on how MIT was transformed into a world-class university with strong links to business.

75. Students from Shanghai topped the list with a score of 575 in science and 600 in mathematics, and although the scores from a single city are not representative, the results demonstrate the potential China can exploit through improved schooling on a nationwide scale. Among the measures introduced by Shanghai to raise the quality of education are merit pay for teachers demonstrating results as measured by test scores, the designing of a new curriculum to prepare students for tertiary-level training, its mandating for all schools, and rigorous testing ("Chinese Lessons for the U.S," *Bloomberg Business Week*, April 14, 2011).

76. In purchasing parity power terms, private consumption per head in China was only a

tenth of the average for OECD countries; however, about 50 million households had incomes that exceeded 30 percent of U.S. households (OECD 2010a).

77. This has resulted in corner cutting and environmentally damaging practices (Midler 2011). The weakening of global demand and a tightening of monetary policy to contain inflationary pressures has increased the pressures on smaller firms.

78. This is where firms such as Lenovo have an advantage over foreign rivals such as Dell and HP and why foreign firms seeking to tap the Chinese market need to find reliable and savvy Chinese partners.

79. See Jorgenson, Ho, and Samuels (2010) on the contribution of IT to productivity in services. Brynjolfsson and Saunders (2009) provide additional evidence.

80. This is not to deny the innovation-stimulating effects of exports, which over the near term are likely to be greater than those of the domestic market. However, now that China is the world's largest exporter (and the leading manufacturer with 19.8 percent of global output in 2010 compared with 19.4 percent for the United States), a slowing of export growth and the concomitant restructuring of production and demand will increase the salience of domestic consumption on growth and on innovation—possibly of a different sort.

81. See Hsueh (2011) on physical assets. Half of the key national laboratories operating in companies certified during the 11th Five Year Plan period are located in enterprises owned by the central government.

82. The contribution of managerial competence and dynamism to productivity and profitability is analyzed by Bloom, Sadun, and Van Reenen (2009, 2010). Brandt and Zhu (2010) and Dollar and Wei (2007) discuss the inefficiency of SOEs relative to their counterparts in other sectors.

83. Although SOEs are less-efficient users of R&D resources, they have a higher ratio of invention patents to total patent applications.

84. SOEs also tend to use four times as much capital per worker on average as firms in the private sector, owing to their practice of reinvesting a portion of their profits to expand production capacity—profits not generally being paid out as dividends or transferred to the Treasury. Easier access to

credit from banks further encourages capital spending (OECD 2010b).

85. Recruitment of Chinese and foreign faculty members from overseas to introduce higher-quality talent and greater diversity is ongoing with the offer of generous incentives; however, these efforts are producing limited results and encountering resistance domestically. See the efforts by Shenzhen University, http://topics.scmp.com/news /china-news-watch/article/Shenzhen-University-in-global-search-for-top-talent.

86. Plagiarism is a serious issue and one commented on in leading foreign publications. http://factsanddetails.com/china.php?item id=1651&catid=13&subcatid=82; http:// www.npr.org/2011/08/03/138937778 /plagiarism-plague-hinders-chinas -scientific-ambition; http://www.nytimes. com/2010/10/07/world/asia/07fraud.html.

87. "High-Priced Recruiting of Talent Abroad Raises Hackles" *Science*, February 18, 2011, pp. 834–35.

88. Some Chinese companies have encountered barriers when trying to acquire certain kinds of foreign high-tech firms. The latest example is the opposition from the Committee on Foreign Investment in the United States to the acquisition by Huawei of a small U.S. tech company, 3Leaf (a server technology firm), on the grounds of national security. 3Leaf produces virtualization architecture that enables commodity servers to mimic the capabilities of mainframe computers. Huawei eventually dropped its takeover bid. See "Huawei Backs Away from 3Leaf Acquisitions," Reuters, February 19, 2011, http://www.reuters.com/article/2011/02/19 /us-huawei-3leaf-idUSTRE71I38920110219. See also "Huawei: The Company that Spooked the World," *The Economist*, August 4, 2012, pp. 19–23, on factors contributing to the resistance faced by Huawei.

89. See the suggestions in Lane and Bertuzzi (2011).

90. A comprehensive treatment of innovation policy can be found in World Bank (2010).

91. Wu (2002) and Chen (2011) elaborate on the primacy of good institutions for technological progress and innovation.

92. The off-shoring of R&D is set to continue (Dehoff and Sehgal 2009). See Carlsson (2006) on the internationalization of R&D and on the contribution of national institutions to the process of globalization.

93. Rising costs, tightening credit, and weakening export demand have dampened the performance and reduced the profitability of China's 2.5 million privately owned SMEs. The future contribution of this vital sector will depend on a moderation of these recent trends.

94. The gains from churning and creative destruction are analyzed by Fogel, Morck, and Yeung (2008); Liang, McLean, and Zhao (2011); and Bartelsman, Haltiwanger, and Scarpetta (2004).

95. Popp (2010) shows how environmental regulation and standards have contributed to green innovation.

96. The share of R&D expenditures by firms increased from 68 percent of the total in 2005 to 74 percent in 2009. This led to a decline in the share of expenditures by R&D institutions from 21 percent in 2005 to 16.5 percent in 2009. Hence, even though an increase in the proportion of R&D performed by business enterprises is interpreted as a desirable characteristic of a country that wants to become more innovative (Mani 2010), this trend in China is partly an outcome of its policy of converting R&D institutes into business enterprises.

97. Lane (2009, 1274–75) remarks that "science investment needs to generate an 'aha' moment or an idea that has value. Translating that 'aha' moment into an innovation also requires a well functioning team or organization, a well functioning patent system, a well developed firm ecosystem, or appropriate university links to industry." The experience of successful firms in China and elsewhere provides useful clues to how the innovative teams within firms interact with the policy and institutional framework in which they operate. A number of Chinese case studies are presented by Tan (2011). Case studies of foreign firms can be found in Herstatt and others (2006); and Boutellier and others (2000).

98. Active recruiting of overseas ethnic Chinese academics and researchers is leading to a brain gain for China and helping to improve the caliber of faculties and of research. However, less than 30 percent of those going abroad return, and very often the ones who do are not the leading lights. Nevertheless, the relative attractiveness and rewards to working in China have increased steadily, and the trend in brain gain seems to be positive (Oxford Analytica 2009).

99. Some recent research on enterprise restructuring in China can be found in Oi (2011).

100. This is a practice perfected by the leading Japanese firms, which, along with attention to customer feedback, accounts for their efficient commercialization of innovations.

101. Li (2011) finds that own R&D is critical for the absorbing of technology—a point underscored by Cohen and Levinthal (1990)—and that SOEs find it easier to absorb domestically generated technology than foreign technology, which might be related to the degree of sophistication, ease of communication, and proximity to the actual research source. This finding strengthens the case for indigenous innovation alongside international collaboration and borrowing from abroad. The importance of a corporate culture of innovation is empirically supported by Jaruzelski, Loehr, and Holman (2011).

102. See Mathews (2000) on the formation and working of consortia in Taiwan, China; and Branstetter and Sakakibara (1998) and Dodgson and Sakakibara (2003) on the utility of consortia in Japan and elsewhere in Asia. OECD (2007, p. 2) comments on the "islands" of science in China and urges the linking together of these islands; "the gates of thousands of science and technology parks [need to be] opened up through the promotion of networks for sharing human and capital resources. A greater national and regional concordance would avoid wasteful research duplication such as by issuing guidelines or creating an independent coordinating agency."

103. On China's regional innovation systems, see Research Group on Development and Strategy of Science and Technology (2011) and Liu, X. and others (2010).

104. Both house military research and production facilities. Chengdu is one of China's four space research centers and produces military jet planes.

105. Zhang and Zhuang (2011) find that tertiary education has a stronger impact on growth than primary or secondary education.

106. "China's Army of Graduates Struggles for Jobs," *New York Times*, December 11, 2010.

107. China's numerous business schools, which have made a great effort to imitate Western schools and attract academics from abroad, still lag behind on a number of counts, and

managerial talent remains in short supply. See "China's Schools Must Make the Leap Forward," *Financial Times*, Sept. 26 2011, and "Education: the PhD Factory," *Nature*, April 2011, p. 277.

108. For example, the initial enthusiasm with cheap laptops for children in developing countries is being tempered by the realization that it is likely to produce results only if it is combined with teacher training, a redesign of the curriculum, and an overhaul of weak school systems. The mixed results from the use of ICT in schools are also highlighted by Machin, McNally, and Silva (2007), who observe that the teaching of science and English benefited more than the teaching of mathematics.

109. Linking university funding on a sliding scale to the quality of outcomes is one way to spur innovation. The merits of online instruction should not be overstated. They can be meager unless complemented by personalized interaction with lecturers and with other students in a structured classroom setting.

110. Persuading a significant percentage of the best graduates and PhDs to take up teaching is key to achieving quality, but unless teaching is seen as rewarding monetarily and otherwise, only a small minority can be persuaded. (McKinsey and Company 2010).

111. Some Chinese universities are increasing their cross-disciplinary offerings by hiring foreign faculty members with the requisite experience; see Jane Qui, "Foreign Researchers Begin to Make Their Mark," *Science*, July 8, 2011, p. 144.

112. Experienced venture capitalists are more likely to "bet on the jockey and not on the horse" and to want to know how many PhDs a high tech start-up has on its payroll.

113. Wu and Zhou (2011) suggest that greater autonomy for universities, allocating more of the research funding to the leading research entities, and the leveraging of science parks adjacent to research universities might yield attractive dividends.

114. Highly successful and innovative companies such as Cisco eagerly pursue open innovation. In fact, according to Branscomb (2008, 916), "Cisco's most important innovation is its partnership with customers and competitors, making it a true networked enterprise. Li and Fung maximize the collective innovative capacity of dozens of partners needed for

a specific product by orchestrating them into a remarkably flexible, agile and skilled collaborative supply chain. They mix and match the special technical skills of the partners, creating a network enterprise." Collaboration needs to be encouraged at several levels. Peng (2011) writes of the increasing necessity of collaboration among scientists and observes that to catch up, China should be a more active participant on bodies such as the Intergovernmental Panel on Climate Change and FLUXNET (the global network of micrometeorological tower sites).

115. On the problems that the U.S. Patent Office is attempting to resolve, see "U.S. Sets 21st Century Goal: Building a Better Patent Office," *New York Times*, February 20, 2011; and on the European system see van Pottelsberghe de la Potterie (2010).

116. Suttmeier and Yao (2011, 19) observe, "Piracy and other forms of infringement remain extensive. Chinese culture still seems to have trouble valuing intangible assets. Elements of techno-nationalism in China's innovation policies . . . encourage suspicions that that the country's IP transition may not be one of harmonization. And it is difficult to see how an internationally harmonized IP system can exist where the concept of rights is so weakly established."

117. The number of courts equipped to handle commercial and financial litigation has also been increased to handle a sharp increase in the number of cases.

118. On rules, policy directives and statistics, see State Intellectual Property Office, http://www.sipo.gov.cn/.

119. Chinese officials and some company CEOs complain that certain international treaties that date back to the cold war era, such as the Wassenaar Arrangement on Export Controls for Conventional Arms and Dual-Use Good and Technologies, deny Chinese companies the right to purchase some technologies or high-end equipment. See Xue Yanping, "The Wassenaar Arrangement and EU's embargo on high-tech export to China," http://ies.cass.cn/Article/cbw/ozkj/201101/3394.asp.

120. The desirability of raising the share of basic research (only 5.2 percent of R&D spending in 2006 as against 10–20 percent in OECD countries) was noted by the OECD (2008). Since then, basic research has received

higher priority. See Zhu and Gong (2008) and Nature Publishing Index (2010, p. 5).

121. Greenberg (2007) points out that maintaining an ethical balance becomes even more important when universities draw closer to the business community and enter into multistrand research relationships. Troubling ethical issues have arisen in the United States, for example, as a result of corporate sponsorship of medical and pharmaceutical research.

122. Refereeing all too often relies on the "old-boy network," which predetermines the outcome. Many referees drawn from scientific fields also struggle to cope with socioeconomic effects of new technologies.

123. See Bonvillian and Van Atta (2011) on the application of the DARPA approach to innovation in the energy sector.

124. See http:/www.evaluation.fi for a measured assessment of the innovation system in Finland, widely viewed as having one of the best-performing innovation architectures.

125. See Wieser (2005) for a survey, and Lach, Parizat, and Wasserteil (2008) for an evaluation of returns from investment by the Israeli government in R&D.

126. "What Science Is Really Worth," *Nature*, June 2010, p. 683.

127. The difficulty faced by the United States in finding satisfactory answers for legislators as to the cost effectiveness of the Advanced Technology Program and the Small Business Innovation Research program highlights the difficulties governments face as they craft innovation policies that will deliver the sought-after growth and welfare dividends.

128. See the extensive and many faceted discussions of evaluation methods in Shapira and Kuhlman (2003). The STAR METRICS project is one example of a comprehensive approach to evaluating the full economic, scientific, and societal benefits of research. Massive data assembly and number crunching on a scale not imaginable a few years ago is now a reality and being widely harnessed by industry to study all kinds of behaviors and processes. These technologies, along with visualization techniques, could make it easier to chart innovation policy and to cope with its many uncertainties (Elmer 2004; Ayres 2007).

129. *Lancet*, October 25, 2008, p. 1437.

130. One explanation is that the incentives for innovation by providers are much too generous, particularly in the United States, and that the checks on cost escalation through the excessive use of new technologies, some of dubious efficacy, are too weak (Callahan 2009).

131. There is a vast literature on e-medicine and on distance medicine in the technical journals.

132. A profiling of patients would initially be based on the patient's genome, although later it could be done through the transcriptome. This approach would enable the medical establishment to anticipate and prevent diseases to which a patient might be susceptible in the future and to develop drugs for currently incurable diseases.

133. See, for instance, Henderson (2003, 2010); Carlino, Chatterjee, and Hunt (2007); and Carlino and Hunt (2009).

134. A city that is top ranked with respect to high-tech and I-tech scores is Seattle, the home of Boeing and also of Microsoft. The composition of employment in Seattle by subsector favors activities notable for their technology intensity such as aircraft and measuring instruments, and for IT intensity such as insurance, computer programming, and architectural services. Innovative cities are also likely to fulfill the criteria of livability such as good environmental quality, public services, recreational amenities, housing, and connectivity. Seattle, for example, is one of the better run and most livable cities in the United States with an attractive coastal location (Markusen and others 2004).

135. ARM (Advanced RISC Machines) was established in 1990 as a joint venture between Acorn Computers, Apple Inc, and VLSI Technologies. It is the leading producer of microprocessors for mobile telecommunications.

136. Chongqing, in particular, has demonstrated great initiative in persuading HP and Foxconn to relocate their laptop assembly operations and support operations—the lure being cheaper labor and land, lower taxes and strengthened logistics. See "HP, Foxconn to Build Laptop Manufacturing Hub in Chongqing," *China Daily*, August 5, 2009.

137. However, most of the more than 600 R&D centers established by multinationals are in the coastal cities, chiefly Shanghai and Beijing.

References

Adams, James D., J. Roger Clemmons, and Paula E. Stephan. 2006. "How Rapidly Does Science Leak Out?" Working Paper 11997, National Bureau of Economic Research, Cambridge, MA.

Adams, Jonathan, Christopher King, and Nan Ma. 2009. "China: Research and Collaboration in the New Geography of Science." Leeds, UK: Thomson Reuters.

Agrawal, A., and R. Henderson. 2002. "Putting Patents in Context: Exploring Knowledge Transfer from MIT." *Management Science* 48 (2002): 44–60.

Altbach, Philip, and Jamil Salmi, eds. 2011. *The Road to Academic Excellence: The Making of World Class Universities*. Washington, DC: World Bank.

Archibugi, Deniele, Mario Denni, and Andrea Filippetti. 2009. *"Technological Forecasting and Social Change."* 76: 917–31.

Ayres, Ian. 2007. *Super Crunchers*. New York: Bantam Books.

Badunenko, O., D. J. Henderson, and V. Zelenyuk. 2008. "Technological Change and Transition: Relative Contributions to Worldwide Growth during the 1990s." *Oxford Bulletin of Economics and Statistics* 70 (4): 461–92.

Bai, Chong-En, Jiangyong Lu, and Zhigang Tao. 2010. "Capital or Knowhow: The Role of Foreign Multinationals in Sino-Foreign Joint Ventures." *China Economic Review* 21 (2010): 629–38.

Bai, Chunli. 2005. "Ascent of Nanoscience in China." *Science* 309 (July 1): 61–63.

Bartelsman, Eric, John Haltiwanger, and Stefano Scarpetta. 2004. "Microeconomic Evidence of Creative Destruction in Industrial and Developing Countries." IZA Discussion Paper 1374, Institute for the Study of Labor, Bonn (October).

Bhidé, Amar. 2008. *The Venturesome Economy: How Innovation Sustains Prosperity in a More Connected World*. Princeton, NJ: Princeton University Press.

Bloom, Nick, Raffaella Sadun, and John Van Reenen. 2009. "Do Private Equity Owned Firms Have Better Management Practices?" London School of Economics and Political Science, London.

———. 2010. "Does Product Market Competition Lead Firms to Decentralize?" Working Paper 10-052, Harvard Business School, Boston, MA.

Boeing, Philipp, and Philipp Sandner. 2011. "The Innovative Performance of China's National Innovation System." Working Paper 158, Frankfurt School of Finance and Management, Frankfurt, Germany.

Bonvillian, William B., and Richard Van Atta. 2011. "ARPA-E and DARPA: Applying the DARPA Model to Energy Innovation." *Journal of Technology Transfer* 36(5): 469–513.

Bosworth, Barry, and Susan M. Collins. 2007. "Accounting for Growth: Comparing China and India." Working Paper 12943, National Bureau of Economics, Cambridge, MA.

Boutellier, Roman, and others. 2000. *Managing Global Innovation*. Berlin: Springer Verlag.

Brandt, Loren, and Xiaodong Zhu. 2010. "Accounting for China's Growth." IZA Discussion Paper 4764, Institute for the Study of Labor, Bonn.

Branscomb, Lewis. 2008. "Research Alone Is Not Enough." *Science* 321 (August 15): 915–16.

Branstetter, Lee, and Mariko Sakakibara. 1998. "Japanese Research Consortia: A Microeconometric Analysis of Industrial Policy." *Journal of Industrial Economics* 46 (2): 207–33.

Bravo-Ortega, Claudio, and Alvaro Garcia Marin. 2011. "R&D and Productivity: A Two Way Avenue?" *World Development* 39: 1090–107.

Bresnahan, Timothy, and M. Trajtenberg. 1996. "General Purpose Technologies: Engines of Economic Growth?" *Journal of Econometrics:* 65: 83–108.

Breznitz, Dan. 2007. *Innovation and the State*. New Haven, CT: Yale University Press.

Breznitz, Dan, and Michael Murphree. 2011. *Run of the Read Queen: Government, Innovation, Globalization, and Economic Growth in China*. New Haven, CT: Yale University Press.

Brown, Clair, and Greg Linden. 2009. *Chips and Change: How Crisis Reshapes the Semiconductor Industry*. Cambridge, MA: MIT Press.

Brynjolfsson, Erik, and Adam Saunders. 2009. *Wired for Innovation*. Cambridge, MA: MIT Press.

Callahan, Daniel. 2009. *Taming the Beloved Beast*. Princeton, NJ: Princeton University Press.

Carlino, Gerald A., Satyajit Chatterjee, and Robert M. Hunt. 2007. "Urban Density and the Rate of Invention." *Journal of Urban Economics* 61 (3): 389–419.

Carlino, Gerald A., and Robert M. Hunt. 2009. "What Explains the Quantity and Quality of Local Inventive Activity?" Working Papers 09-12, Federal Reserve Bank of Philadelphia, Philadelphia.

Carlsson, Bo. 2006. "Internationalization of Innovation Systems: A Survey of the Literature." *Research Policy* 35: 56–67.

Chen, Qing-tai. 2011. *Zi Zhu Chuang Xin He Chan Ye Sheng Ji* [Indigenous innovation and industrial upgrading]. Beijing: China Citic Press.

Chen, Shiyi, Gary H. Jefferson, and Jun Zhang. 2011. "Structural Change, Productivity Growth, and Industrial Transformation in China." *China Economic Review* 22 (1): 133–50.

Chen, Xiao-hong. 2009. "Zhong Guo Qi Ye 30 Nian Chuang Xin Ji Zhi, Neng Li He Zhan Lue" [Innovation in Chinese corporations in the last 30 years: Mechanism, capability and strategy"], *Chinese Journal of Management* 6 (11/12): 1421–29.

Cheng, Li. 2010. *China's Emerging Middle Class: Beyond Economic Transformation*. Washington, DC: Brookings Institution Press.

China Statistical Yearbook (volumes on each of Science, Technology, and Industry). 2010. Beijing: China Statistics Press.

Chinese Academy of Science and Technology for Development. 2011. "Guo Jia Chuang Xin Zhi Shu Bao Gao (2010)." [Report on the National Innovation Index 2010]. Beijing (March).

Christensen, Clayton M., Jerome H. Grossman, and Jason Hwang. 2009. *The Innovator's Prescription*. New York: McGraw Hill.

Christensen, Clayton M., Michael B. Horn, and Curtis W. Johnson. 2010. *Disrupting Class: How Disruptive Innovation Will Change the Way the World Learns*. New York: McGraw-Hill.

Cliff, Roger, Chad J. R. Ohlandt, and David Yang. 2011. *Ready for Take-Off: China's Advancing Aerospace Industry*. Santa Monica, CA: RAND Corporation.

Cohen, Wesley M., and Daniel A. Levinthal. 1990. "Absorptive Capacity: A New Perspective on Learning and Innovation." *Administrative Science Quarterly* 35 (1): 128–52.

Comin, Diego. 2004. "R&D: A Small Contribution to Productivity Growth." *Journal of Economic Growth* 9 (4): 391–421.

Comin, Diego, Bart Hobijn, and Emilie Rovito. 2006. "World Technology Usage Lags." Working Paper 12677, National Bureau of Economic Research, Cambridge, MA.

Cutler, David, M. 2003. "An International Look at the Medical Care Financing Problem." Harvard University, Department of Economics, Cambridge, MA.

Dehoff, Kevin, and Vikas Sehgal. 2009. "Innovators without Borders." *Strategy and Business* 44: 55–61.

De Meyer, Arnoud, and Sam Garg. 2005. *Inspire to Innovate*. Basingstoke, UK: Palgrave Macmillan.

Dertouzos, Michael L., R. K. Lester, and R. M. Solow. 1989. *Made in America: Regaining the Productive Edge*. Cambridge, MA: MIT Press.

Dodgson, Mark, and David Gann. 2010. *Innovation*. New York: Oxford University Press.

Dodgson, Mark, and Mariko Sakakibara. 2003. "Strategic Research Partnerships: Empirical Evidence from Asia." *Technology Analysis and Strategic Management* 15 (2): 228–45.

Dollar, David, and Shang-Jin Wei. 2007. "Das (Wasted) Capital." Working Paper 13103, National Bureau of Economic Research, Cambridge, MA.

Eberhardt, Markus, Christian Helmers, and Zhihong Yu. 2011. "Is the Dragon Learning to Fly? An Analysis of the Chinese Patent Explosion." CSAE Working Paper 2011-15, Centre for the Study of African Economies, Oxford University, Oxford, U.K.

Eichengreen, Barry. 2012. "China Needs a Service-Sector Revolution." http://www.project-syndicate.org/commentary/china-needs-a-service-sector-revolution.

Ejermo, Olof, Astrid Kander, and Martin Henning. 2011. "The R&D-Growth Paradox Arises in Fast-Growing Sectors." *Research Policy* 40 (2011): 664–72.

Elmer, Greg. 2004. *Profiling Machines*. Cambridge, MA: MIT Press.

Fan, S., R. Kanbur, and X. Zhang, eds. 2009. *Regional Inequality in China: Trends, Explanations and Policy Responses*. London: Routledge, Taylor and Francis Group.

Fang, Xin, ed. 2007. *Zhong Guo Ke Ji Chuang Xin Yu Ke Chi Xu Fa Zhan* [Scientific and technological innovation and sustainable development of China], Beijing: Science Press.

Felipe, Jesus. 2008. "What Policy Makers Should Know about Total Factor Productivity." *Malaysian Journal of Economic Studies* 45 (1): 1–19.

Felipe, Jesus, Arnelyn Abdon, and Utsav Kumar. 2010. "Development and Accumulation of New Capabilities: The Index of Opportunities." VOXEU (July 22, 2010. http://www.voxeu.org/article/new-measure-national-opportunities-development.

Fleisher, Belton, Dinghuan Hu, William Mcguire, and Xiaobo Zhang. 2010. "The Evolution of an Industrial Cluster in China." *China Economic Review* 21: 456–69.

Fogel, Kathy, Randall Morck, and Bernard Yeung. 2008. "Big Business Stability and Economic Growth: Is What's Good for General Motors Good for America?" *Journal of Financial Economics* 89 (1): 83–108.

Fukao, Kyoji, Tomohiko Inui, Shigesaburo Kabe, and Deqiang Liu. 2008. "An International Comparison of the TFP Levels of Japanese, Korean and Chinese Listed Firms." Japan Center for Economic Research, Tokyo.

Fu, Xiaolan, and Yundan Gong. 2011. "Indigenous and Foreign Innovation Efforts and Drivers of Technological Upgrading: Evidence from China." *World Development* 39 (7): 1213–25.

Fu, Xiaolan, Carlo Pietrobelli, and Luc Soete. 2011. "The Role of Foreign Technology and Indigenous Innovation in the Emerging Economies: Technological Change and Catching-Up." *World Development* 39 (7): 1204–12.

Gao, Jian, and Gary Jefferson. 2007. "Science and Technology Take-off in China: Sources of Rising R&D Intensity." *Asia Pacific Business Review* 13 (3): 357–71.

Gao, Shi-Ji, and Pei-lin Liu. 2007. "Ke Ji Fa Zhan Yu Zhong Guo Qi Ji" [Scientific and technological development and China's economic miracle]. In *Scientific and Technological Innovation and Sustainable Development of China*, ed. Xin Fang, 173–203, Beijing: Science Press.

Gao, Xia, and Jiancheng Guan. 2009. "The Chinese Innovation System during Economic Transition: A Scale Independent View." *Journal of Informetrics* 3 (4): 321–31.

Gao, Xudong, Ping Zhang, and Xielin Liu. 2007. "Competing with MNEs: Developing Manufacturing Capabilities or Innovation Capabilities." *Journal of Technology Transfer* 32: 87–107.

Glaeser, Edward L. 2011. *Triumph of the City.* New York: Penguin Press.

Golley, Jane, and Xin Meng. 2011. "Has China Run Out of Surplus Labor?" *China Economic Review* 22: 555–72.

Gordon, Peter, and Sanford Ikeda. 2011. "Does Density Matter?" In *Handbook of Creative Cities*, eds. David E. Andersson, A. E. Andersson, and Charlotta Mellander. Cheltenham, U.K.: Edward Elgar.

Greenberg, Daniel S. 2007. *Science for Sale: The Perils, Rewards, and Delusions of Campus Capitalism.* Chicago: University of Chicago Press.

Groupe BPCE. 2010. "Total Factor Productivity: A Reflection of Innovation Drive and Improvement in Human Capital (Education)." Special Report: Economic Research 41, Paris (February).

Grove, Linda. 2006. *A Chinese Economic Revolution: Rural Entrepreneurship in the Twentieth Century.* Lanham, MD: Rowman and Littlefield.

Guo, Li-hong. 2009. "Xu Yao Cong Su Jian Li KeJi Xing Zhong Xiao Qi Ye de Si Mu GuPiao Shi Chang" [China needs to establish private equity market for hi-tech SMEs quickly]. *Chan Quan Dao Kan* [*Property Rights Guide*] 7/12.

Guo, Li-hong, Cheng-hui Zhang, and Zhi-jun Li. 2000. *Gao Ji Shu Chan Ye: Fa Zhan Gui Lu Yu Feng Xian Tou Zi* [Hi-tech industry: Pattern of development and venture capital]. Beijing: China Development Press.

Gwynne, Peter. 2010. "The China Question: Can This Country Really Be the Next Life Science Superpower?" *Scientific American. Worldview 2010, Special Report:* 22.

Hall, Bronwyn. 2011. "Innovation and Productivity." Working Paper 17178, National Bureau of Economic Research, Cambridge, MA.

Hanley, A., W. Liu, and A. Vaona. 2011. "Financial Development and Innovation in China: Evidence from the Provincial Data." Working Paper 1673, Kiel Institute for the World Economy, Kiel.

Hanushek, Eric. 2009. "School Policy: Implications of Recent Research for Human Capital Investments in South Asia and Other Developing Countries." *Education Economics* 17 (3): 291–313.

Hassan, Mohamed H. A. 2005. "Small Things and Big Changes in the Developing World." *Science* 309 (July 1): 65–66.

Hausmann, Ricardo, and Bailey Klinger. 2006. "Structural Transformation and Patterns of Comparative Advantage in the Product Space." Center for International Development, Harvard University, Cambridge, MA.

He, Jiang, and M. Hosein Fallah. 2011. "The Typology of Technology Clusters and Its Evolution—Evidence from the Hi-Tech Industries." *Technological Forecasting & Social Change* 78: 945–52.

Henderson, J. Vernon. 2003. "The Urbanization Process and Economic Growth: The So-What Question." *Journal of Economic Growth* 8: 47–71.

———. 2010. "Cities and Development." *Journal of Regional Science* 50 (1): 515–40.

Herstatt, Cornelius, and others. 2006. *Management of Technology and Innovation in Japan.* Berlin: Springer Verlag.

Hout, Thomas M., and Pankaj Ghemawat. 2010. "China vs the World: Whose Technology Is It?" *Harvard Business Review* (December). http://hbr.org/2010/12/china-vs-the-world-whose-technology-is-it/ar/1.

Howells, Jeremy. 2005. "Innovation and Regional Economic Development: A Matter of Perspective?" *Research Policy* 34 (2005): 1220–34.

Hsueh, Li-Min, Chen-kuo Hsu, and Dwight H. Perkins. 2001. *Industrialization and the State: The Changing Role of the Taiwan Government in the Economy, 1945–1998.* Cambridge MA: Harvard University Press.

Hsueh, Rosalyn. 2011. *China's Regulatory State.* Ithaca, NY: Cornell University Press.

Hu, Angang. 2011. *China in 2020: A New Type of Superpower.* Washington, DC: Brookings Institution Press.

Huang, Zuhui, Xiaobo Zhang, and Yunwei Zhu. 2008. "The Role of Clustering in Rural Industrialization: A Case Study of the Footwear Industry in Wenzhou." *China Economic Review* 19 (2008): 409–20.

IEEE (Institute of Electrical and Electronics Engineers). 2011. "China's Supercomputing Prowess" (April). http://www.ieee.org/index.html.

Italian Trade Commission. 2009. "Market Report on China Biotechnology and Nanotechnology Industries." Shanghai.

Ito, Keiko, Moosup Jung, Young Gak Kim, and Tangjun Yuan. 2008. "A Comparative Analysis of Productivity Growth and Productivity Dispersion: Microeconomic Evidence Based on Listed Firms from Japan, Korea and China." Working Paper 259, Columbia University, Center on Japanese Economy and Business, New York (February).

Jaffe, Adam B., and Manuel Trajtenberg. 1996. "Flows of Knowledge from Universities and Federal Labs: Modeling the Flow of Patent Citations over Time and across Institutional and Geographic Boundaries." Working Paper 5712, National Bureau of Economic Research, Cambridge, MA.

Jaruzelski, Barry, John Loehr, and Richard Holman. 2011. "Why Culture Is Key." *Strategy and Business* 65 (Winter): 30–45.

Johnstone, Bob. 1999. *We Were Burning.* Boulder, CO: Westview Press.

Jones, Charles I., and Paul Romer. 2009. "The New Kaldor Facts: Ideas, Institutions, Population and Human Capital." Working Paper 15094, National Bureau of Economic Research, Cambridge, MA.

Jorgenson, Dale, Mun Ho, and Jon Samuels. 2010. "New Data on U.S. Productivity Growth by Industry." Harvard University, Department of Economics, Cambridge, MA.

Jorgenson, Dale W., Mun S. Ho and Kevin J. Stiroh. 2007. "The Sources of Growth of U.S. Industries." In *Productivity in Asia: Economic Growth and Competitiveness,* ed. Dale W. Jorgenson, Masahiro Kuroda, and Kazuyuki Motohashi. Northampton, MA: Edward Elgar Publishing.

Jovanovic, Boyan, and Peter L. Rousseau. 2005. "General Purpose Technologies." In *Handbook of Economic Growth 1B,* eds. Philippe Aghion and Steven N. Durlauf. Amsterdam: North Holland Press.

Kaiser, David. 2010. *Becoming MIT: Moments of Decision.* Cambridge MA: MIT Press.

Kaplan, Robert S., and Michael Porter. 2011. "How to Solve the Cost Crisis in Healthcare." *Harvard Business Review* 89 (9/10): 46–64.

Kasarda, John D., and Greg Lindsay. 2011. *Aerotropolis: The Way We'll Live Next.* New York: Farrar, Straus and Giroux.

Keller, Wolfgang. 2001a. "The Geography and Channels of Diffusion at the World's Technology Frontier." Working Paper 8150, National Bureau of Economic Research, Cambridge, MA.

———. 2001b. "International Technology Diffusion." Working Paper 8573, National Bureau of Economic Research, Cambridge, MA.

Kharas, Homi. 2009. "China's Transition to a High Income Economy: Escaping the Middle Income Trap." Brookings Institution, Washington, DC.

Knight, John, Qusheng Deng, and Shi Li. 2011. "The Puzzle of Migrant Labor Shortage and

Rural Labor Surplus in China." *China Economic Review* 22: 585–600.

Komninos, Nicos. 2008. *Intelligent Cities and Globalization of Innovation Networks.* New York: Routledge.

Koopman, Robert, Zhi Wang, and Shang-Jin Wei. 2008. "How Much of Chinese Export Is Really Made in China: Assessing Domestic Value-Add when Processing Trade Is Pervasive." Working Paper 14109, National Bureau of Economic Research, Cambridge, MA.

———. 2009. "A World Factory in Global Production Chains: Estimating Imported Value Added in Chinese Exports." Discussion Paper 7430, Center for Economic Policy and Research, Washington, DC.

Kraemer, Kenneth L., Greg Linden, and Jason Dedrick. 2011. "Capturing Value in Global Network: Apple iPad and iPhone." http://pcic.merage.uci.edu/papers/2011/Value_iPad_iPhone.pdf.

Kuijs, Louis. 2010. "China through 2020: A Macroeconomic Scenario." China Research Working Paper 9, World Bank, Beijing.

Lach, Saul, Shlomi Parizat, and Daniel Wasserteil. 2008. "The Impact of Government Support to Industrial R&D on the Israeli Economy." E.G.P. Applied Economic Ltd., Tel Aviv.

Lane, Julia. 2009. "Assessing the Impact of Science Funding." *Science* 324 (June 5): 1273–75.

Lane, J., and S. Bertuzzi. 2011. "Measuring the Results of Science Investments." *Science* 331: 678.

Lester, Richard K. 2004. *Innovation.* Cambridge, MA: Harvard University Press.

Levitt, Steven D., John A. List, and Chad Syverson. 2011. "How Does Learning Happen?" University of Chicago, Department of Economics, Chicago.

Leydesdorff, Loet. 2008. "The Delineation of Nanoscience and Nanotechnology in Terms of Journals and Patents: A Most Recent Update." *Scientometrics* 76 (1): 159–67.

Li, Xibao. 2011. "Sources of External Technology, Absorptive Capacity, and Innovation Capability in Chinese State-Owned High-Tech Enterprises." *World Development* 39 (7): 1240–48.

———. 2012. "Behind the Recent Surge of Chinese Patenting." *Research Policy* 41: 236–49.

Liang, Clair Y. C., R. David McLean, and Mengxin Zhao. 2011. "Creative Destruction and Finance: Evidence from the Last Half Century." Working Paper (April), International

Conference of the French Finance Association. http://papers.ssrn.com/sol3/papers.cfm?abstract_id=1720717.

Lichtenberg, Frank, R. 2008. "Have Newer Cardiovascular Drugs Reduced Hospitalization? Evidence From Longitudinal Country-Level Data on 20 OECD Countries, 1995–2003." Working Paper 14008, National Bureau of Economic Research, Cambridge, MA.

———. 2010. "Has Medical Innovation Reduced Cancer Mortality?" Working Paper 15880, National Bureau of Economic Research, Cambridge, MA.

———. 2011. "The Impact of Therapeutic Procedure Innovation on Hospital Patient Longevity: Evidence from Western Australia, 2000–2007." Working Paper 17414, National Bureau of Economic Research, Cambridge, MA.

Liu, Feng-chao, Denis Fred Simon, Yu-tao Sun, and Cong Cao. 2011. "China's Innovation Policies: Evolution, Institutional Structure and Trajectory." *Research Policy* 40: 917–31.

Liu, Shi-jin, and Wen-kui Zhang. 2008. "Yi Ji Li Ji Zhi Chuang Xin Cu Jin Zi Zhu Chuang Xin" [Promote indigenous innovation by new incentive mechanism], *Fa Ming Yu Chuang Xin, Zong He Ban* [Invention and innovation (Comprehensive Edition)] 4 (12).

Liu, Xie-lin, Ping Lu, Peng Cheng, and Ao Chen. 2010. *Gou Jia Jun Heng De Qu Yu Chuang Xin Ti Xi* [Construction of a balanced regional innovation system]. Beijing: Science Press.

Lu, Wei. 2008. Jian She Chuang Xin Xing Guo Jia: 30 Nian Chuang Xin Ti yan Jin [To Build an Innovative Nation: Evolution of Innovation System in the last 30 years]. Beijing: China Development Press.

———. 2009. *Zhong Guo Te Se Chuang Xin Zhi Lu: Zheng Ce Yu Ji Zhi Yan Jiu* [Innovation Path with Chinese characteristics: policy and mechanism research]. Beijing: People Press.

Lu, Yong-xiang. 2006. "Zou Zhong Guo Te Se Zi Zhu Chuang Xin Zhi Lu, Jian She Chuang Xin Xing Guo Jia" [Building an innovation-oriented country by boosting independent innovation featuring Chinese characteristics]. *Zhong Guo Ke Xue Yuan Yuan Kan* [Bulletin of Chinese Academy of Sciences] 5 (12).

Machin, Stephen, Sandra McNally, and Olmo Silva. 2007. "New Technology in Schools: Is There a Payoff." *Economic Journal* 117: 1145–67.

Mani, Sunil. 2010. "Have China and India Become More Innovative since the Onset of Reforms in the Two Countries?" Working Paper 430, Center for Development Studies, Trivandrum, Kerala, India (May).

Manoharan, Mano. 2008. "Research on the Frontiers of Nanoscience." *Technology in Society* 30 (3–4): 401–404.

Markusen, Ann. 1996. "Sticky Places in Slippery Space: A Typology of Industrial Districts." *Economic Geography* 72 (3): 293–313.

Markusen, Ann, Karen Chapple, Daisaku Yamamoto, Gregory Schorock, and Pingkang Yu. 2004. "Gauging Metropolitan 'High-Tech' And 'I-Tech' Activity." *Economic Development Quarterly* 18 (1): 10–24.

Mathews, John A. 2000. "Accelerated Technology Diffusion through Collaboration: The Case of Taiwan's R&D Consortia." European Institute of Japanese Studies, Stockholm.

Mathews, John, A., and Dong-Sung Cho. 2000. *Tiger Technology.* Cambridge, U.K.: Cambridge University Press.

McGee, T. G., G. C. S. Lin, A. M. Morton, M. L. Y. Wang, and J. Wu. 2011. *China's Urban Space: Development under Market Socialism.* London: Routledge.

McKinsey and Company. 2010. "Closing the Talent Gap: Attracting and Retaining the Top Third Graduates to Careers in Teaching." September.

McKinsey Global Institute. 2010. "How to Compete and Grow." Washington, DC (March).

———. 2011. "Cities of Tomorrow." Washington, DC.

Meisenzahl, Ralf R., and Joel Mokyr. 2011. "Is Education Policy Innovation Policy?" VOXEU, June 13th. http://www.voxeu.org/article/education-policy-innovation-policy.

Midler, Paul. 2011. *Poorly Made in China.* New York: John Wiley.

MOST (Ministry of Science and Technology). 2008. "China Science and Technology Development Report." Beijing: Science and Technology Literature Press.

Moran, Theodore H. 2011a. *Foreign Direct Investment and Development.* Washington, DC: Peterson Institute of International Development.

———. 2011b. "Foreign Manufacturing Multinationals and the Transformation of the Chinese Economy: New Measurements, New Perspectives." Working Paper 11-11, Peterson Institute

of International Economics, Washington, DC (April).

Nature Publishing Index, China. 2010. http://www.natureasia.com/en/publishing-index/china.

Nolan, Peter. 2012. *Is China Buying the World?* Cambridge, UK: Polity Press.

NSB (National Statistical Bureau of China). Various years. *China Statistical Yearbook.* Beijing: China Statistics Press.

Odagiri, Hiroyuki, and Akira Goto. 1996. *Technology and Industrial Development in Japan.* New York: Oxford University Press.

———. eds. 1997. *Innovation in Japan.* Oxford, UK: Clarendon Press.

OECD (Organisation for Economic Co-operation and Development). 2007. "Chinese Innovation: China Can Rekindle Its Great Innovative Past, Though Some Reforms May Be Needed First." *Observer* 263 (October).

———. 2008. *Reviews of Innovation Policy: China.* Paris: OECD.

———. 2010a. "China in the 2010s: Rebalancing Growth and Strengthening Social Safety Nets." OECD contribution to the China Development Forum, Beijing, March 20–22.

———. 2010b. *Economic Surveys: China 2010.* Paris: OECD.

Oi, Jean Chun. 2011. *Going Private in China: The Politics of Corporate Restructuring and System Reform.* Stanford, CA: Walter H. Shorenstein Asia-Pacific Research Center.

Oster, Sharon M. 1999. *Modern Competitive Analysis.* Oxford, UK: Oxford University Press.

Owen, Bruce Manning, Wentong Zheng, and Su Sun. 2007. "China's Competition Policy Reforms: The Anti-Monopoly Law and Beyond." Discussion Paper 06-032, Stanford Institute for Economic Policy Research, Stanford, CA.

Oxford Analytica. 2009. "China: Returnees Are Critical in Innovation Push." Daily Brief Services, Oxford, U.K. (July 2).

———. 2011. "China Leapfrogs to the Forefront of Nanotechnology." Daily Brief Services, Oxford, U.K. (September 26).

Page, Scott E. 2007. *The Difference: How the Power of Diversity Creates Better Groups, Firms, Schools, and Societies.* Princeton, NJ: Princeton University Press.

Peng, Changhui. 2011. "Focus on Quality, Not Just Quantity." *Nature* 475 (July 20): 267.

Perkins, Dwight H. 2011. "The Macro-Economics of Poverty Reduction in China." Presentation to the International Workshop on Challenges to Poverty Reduction in China's New Development Stage, Beijing, February 25.

Perry, Tekla S. 2011. "Morris Chang: Foundry Father." *IIEE Spectrum* (May).

Popp, David. 2010. "Innovation and Climate Policy." *Annual Review of Resource Economics* 2: 275–98.

Porter, Michael E., and E. O. Teisberg. 2006. *Redefining Healthcare*. Boston, MA: Harvard Business School Press.

Preschitschek, Nina, and Dominic Bresser. 2010. "Nanotechnology Patenting in China and Germany—A Comparison of Patent Landscapes by Bibliographic Analyses." *Journal of Business Chemistry* 7 (1): 3–13.

Price, L., M. D. Levine, N. Zhou, D. Fridley, N. Aden, H. Lu, M. McNeil, N. Zheng, Y. Qin, and P. Yowargana. 2011. "Assessment of China's Energy-Saving and Emission-Reduction Accomplishments and Opportunities during the 11th Five-Year Plan." *Energy Policy* 39 (4): 2165–78.

Pritchett, Lant, and Martina Viarengo. 2010. *Reconciling the Cross-Sectional and Time-Series Relationships between Income, Education and Health and Choice Based Framework for HDI*. New York: Palgrave Macmillan.

Research Group on Development and Strategy of Science and Technology. 2011. *Zhong GuoQu Yu Chuang Xin Neng Li Bao Gao 2010—Zhu San Jiao Qu Yu Chuang Xin Ti Xi Yan Jiu* [Annual report of science and technology development of China 2010—Research on regional innovation system of the Pearl River Delta Region]. Beijing: Science Press.

Royal Society. 2011. "Knowledge, Networks and Nations: Global Scientific Collaboration in the 21st Century." London.

Salmi, Jamil. 2010. "The Challenge of Establishing World-Class Universities." World Bank, Washington, DC.

Shanghai Municipality Science and Technology Commission. 2006. "The Innovation System of Shanghai." Presentation made to an OECD delegation in Shanghai, China, October 9.

Shapin, Steven. 2010. *Never Pure: Historical Studies of Science as if It Was Produced by People with Bodies, Situated in Time, Space, Culture, and Society, and Struggling for Credibility and Authority*. Baltimore, MD: Johns Hopkins University Press.

Shapira, Philip, and Stefan Kuhlman. 2003. *Learning from Science and Technology Policy Evaluation*. Cheltenham, U.K.: Edward Elgar.

Shi, Bingzhan. 2011. "Extensive Margin, Quantity, and Price in China's Export Growth." *China Economic Review* 22 (2011): 233–43.

Sigurdson, Jon, Jiang Jiang, Xinxin Kong, Yongzhong Wang, and Yuli Tang. 2005. *Technological Superpower China*. Cheltenham, UK: Edward Elgar.

Simon, Denis, F., and Cong Cao. 2009. *China's Emerging Technological Edge*. Cambridge, UK: Cambridge University Press.

Smeets, Roger, and Albert de Vaal. 2011. "Intellectual Property Rights Protection and FDI Knowledge Diffusion." VOXEU (March 15). http://www.voxeu.org/article/intellectual -property-rights-and-fdi-knowledge-diffusion.

Starr, Paul. 2011. *Remedy and Reaction*. New Haven, CT: Yale University Press.

Stevenson-Yang, Anne, and Ken DeWoskin. 2005. "China Destroys the IP Paradigm." *Far Eastern Economic Review* 168 (3): 9–18.

Subramanian, Arvind. 2011. *Eclipse: Living in the Shadow of China's Economic Dominance*. Washington, DC: Institute of International Economics.

Suttmeier, Richard P., and Xiangkui Yao. 2011. "China's IP in Transition." Special Report 29, National Bureau of Asian Research, Seattle.

Swissnex China. 2011. "A Quick Overview of the Chinese S&T System." http://www.swissnex china.org/background/a-quick-overview-of -chinese-st-system-2011.pdf/view.

Tan, Yinglan. 2011. *Chinnovation*. Singapore: John Wiley and Sons.

Tang, Mingfeng, and Caroline Hussler. 2011. "Betting on Indigenous Innovation or Relying on FDI: The Chinese Strategy for Catching-Up." *Technology in Society* 33: 23–35.

Taylor, Mark C. 2010. *Crisis on Campus: A Bold Plan for Reforming Our Colleges and Universities*. New York: Alfred A. Knopf.

Tian, Xu, and Xiaohua Yu. 2012. "The Enigmas of TFP in China: A Meta-Analysis." *China Economic Review* 23: 396–414.

Tzeng, Cheng-Hua. 2011. "An Evolutionary-Institutional Framework for the Growth of an Indigenous Technology Firm: The Case of Lenovo Computer." *Technology in Society* 33: 212–22.

Urel, B., and Harm Zebregs. 2009. "The Dynamics of Provincial Growth in China: A Nonparametric Approach." *IMF Staff Papers* 56 (2): 239–62.

van Pottelsberghe de la Potterie, Bruno. 2008. "Europe's R&D: Missing the Wrong Targets?" Bruegel Policy Brief 3, Breugel, Brussels (February).

———. 2010. "Patent Fixes for Europe" *Nature* 467 (September 22): 395. http://www.nature.com/nature/journal/v467/n7314/abs/467395a.html.

Walsh, K. 2003. "Foreign High-Tech R&D in China: Risks, Rewards and Implications for U.S.-China Relations." Henry Stimson Center, Washington, DC.

Wang, Qing Hui, Qi Wang, and Nian Cai Liu. 2011. "Building World Class Universities in China: Shanghai Jiao Tong University." In *The Road to Academic Excellence: The Making of World Class Universities,* eds. Philip Altbach and Jamil Salmi. Washington, DC: World Bank.

Wang, Y., and Y. Yao. 2003. "Sources of China's Economic Growth, 1952–99: Incorporating Human Capital Accumulation." *China Economic Review* 14: 32–52.

Wang, Yuan, Xiaoyuan Zhang, and Mingpeng Zhao, eds. *Zhong Guo Feng Xian Tou Zi Fa Zhan Bao Gao 2011* [Venture capital development in China 2011] Beijing: Beijing Economy and Management Publishinghouse.

West, Darrell M., and E. A. Miller. 2009. *Digital Medicine.* Washington, DC: Brookings Institution.

Wieser, Robert. 2005. "Research and Development Productivity and Spillovers: Empirical Evidence at the Firm Level." *Journal of Economic Surveys* 19 (4): 587–620.

World Bank. 2010. *Innovation Policy: A Guide for Developing Countries.* Washington, DC: World Bank.

———. 2011. "The Growing Danger of Non-Communicable Diseases." World Bank, Washington, DC (September).

Wu, Jing-lian. 2009. *Zhong Guo Zeng Zhang Mo Shi Jue Ze* [The choice of China growth mode]. Shanghai: Yuandong Press.

Wu, Jing-lian. 2002. *Zhi Du Zhong Yu Ji Shu—Fa Zhan Zhong Guo Gao Xin Ji Shu Chan Ye* [Development of China's hi-tech industry: institution priority to technology]. Beijing: China Development Press.

Wu, Weiping, and Yu Zhou. 2011. "The Third Mission Stalled? Universities in China's Technological Progress." *Journal of Technology Transfer* (September). http://sites.tufts.edu/wuweiping/files/2012/08/JTT-ThirdMission-PrePublished.pdf.

Xu, Guan-hua. 2006. "Guan Yu Zi Zhu Chuang Zhu Chuang Xin de Ji Ge Zhong Da Wen Ti" [Some key issues on indigenous innovation], *Zhong Guo Ruan Ke Xue, China Soft Science* 4 (12).

Yu, Yongding. 2009. "China's Policy Response to the Global Financial Crisis." Richard Snape Lecture, Productivity Commission, Melbourne.

Yusuf, Shahid, and Kaoru Nabeshima. 2010. "Two Dragon Heads: Contrasting Development Paths for Beijing and Shanghai." Washington, DC: World Bank.

Yusuf, Shahid, Kaoru Nabeshima, and Shoichi Yamashita, eds. 2008. *Growing Industrial Clusters in Asia: Serendipity and Science.* Washington, DC: World Bank.

Zeng, Douglas. 2010. "Building Engines of Growth and Competitiveness in China: Experience with Special Economic Zones and Industrial Clusters." Washington, DC: World Bank.

Zhang, Chuanguo, and Lihuan Zhuang. 2011. "The Composition of Human Capital and Economic Growth: Evidence from China Using Dyanmic Panel Data Analysis." *China Economic Review* 22: 165–71.

Zhang, Chunlin, Douglas Zhihua Zheng, William Peter Mako, and James Seward. 2009. *Promoting Enterprise-Led Innovation in China.* Washington, DC: World Bank.

Zhang, Wen-kui. 2007. "Chuang Xin Zheng Ce Ying Zhuan Xiang Zhong Shi Xu Qiu Gu Li" [Innovation policy needs to shift attention to demand encouragement]. *Zhong Guo Fa Zhan Guan Cha* [China Development Observation] 11 (12).

Zhang, Xiaoji, and Guoqiang Long, eds. 2011. *Wai Shang Tou Zi Yu Zi Zhu Chuang Xin: Zheng Ce Yu An Li* [Foreign investment and indigenous innovation: Policies and cases.] Beijing: University of International Business and Economic Press.

Zhang, Yu-tai, Shi-jin Liu, and Wei Lu. 2008. *Ji Li Chuang Xin: Zheng Ce Xuan Ze Yu An Li Yan Jiu* [Encourage innovation: Choice of policies and case study] Beijing: Intellectual Property Press.

Zhong, Hai. 2011. "Returns to Higher Education in China: What Is the Role of College Quality." *China Economic Review* 22: 260–75.

Zhou, Eve Y., and Bob Stembridge. 2011. "Patented in China: The Present and Future State of Innovation in China." Thomson Reuters, Philadelphia.

Zhou, Yu. 2008. *The Inside Story of China's High-Tech Industry: Making Silicon Valley in Beijing.* Lanham, MD: Rowman & Littlefield.

Zhu, Zuoyan, and Xu Gong. 2008. "Basic Research: Its Impact on China's Future." *Technology in Society* 30: 293–98.

Seizing the Opportunity of Green Development in China

Why Green Development?

The world's development process is at a crossroad. Given the unsustainability of current economic growth in both China and the world, a new approach to development is needed. The concept of green development is such an approach. Green development can become a potentially transformative process for the economy, for society, for the environment, and for the role of government. It is an opportunity, an open door.

Green development is a pattern of development that decouples growth from heavy dependence on resource use, carbon emissions, and environmental damage, and that promotes growth through the creation of new green product markets, technologies, investments, and changes in consumption and conservation behavior.[1] Green development is based on three key concepts: economic growth can be decoupled from rising greenhouse gas emissions and environmental degradation; the process of "going green" can itself be a source of growth; and "going green" is part of a virtuous circle that is mutually reinforcing with growth. Green growth is the means by which green development is achieved.

The Traditional Model of Development Is No Longer Feasible

Since 1978, China has been developing at an average growth rate of nearly 10 percent a year. Over just three decades, it has developed in one giant leap from a poor country into the world's second-largest economy after the United States. Great changes have taken place in the quality of people's lives. If this trend continues, then by 2030, China will have attained high-income status in an unprecedented short period of time. Some consider China's transformation as an economic miracle. But given the negative consequences of growth, it is, at best, an unfinished miracle. For various reasons, changes are needed in China's growth model.

First, China's development has resulted not only in past high emissions, resource consumption, and environmental destruction, but also in external, social, and regional imbalances. If these imbalances are not corrected soon, they have the potential to precipitate economic and social crises. Reforms are needed, and green development forms part of those necessary reforms. As income levels increase, the Chinese people are demanding improved welfare, a cleaner environment, and higher quality of life—without the recurring risks of environment-related disasters.

Second, whether China can attain high-income status by 2030 is still uncertain. According to projections by the State Council's Development Research Center (DRC) (Liu, S. and others 2011) and other research,[2] China's economic growth will slow down in the coming years, exposing yet more social and political challenges. Therefore, China needs to find new sources of growth, driven by innovation and supported by medium- and high-value-added production. Green development is part of the policy approach to overcoming future risks and finding new robust sources of growth.

Third, apart from domestic conditions, changes in the international arena have also made it important for China to change its model of development. Western countries are making the transition to a more competitive form of green development. As a result, a new race toward green development is now being played out in the global economy, with significant benefits accruing to early movers. In 2009, the Organisation for Economic Co-operation and Development (OECD) issued a Declaration on Green Growth in which its member countries set forth a comprehensive green growth strategy. Under the European Union's (EU) "Europe 2020" initiative, innovation and green growth form the core of a strategy to increase the competitiveness of European countries. At "Rio+20," the United Nations Conference on Sustainable Development held in Rio de Janeiro in June 2012, green growth was one of the main topics of discussion. In May 2011, Germany announced that it would strive to be the first industrial country to achieve a complete shift to clean energy. The United States has issued a 10-year clean energy strategy; the Republic of Korea has already made green economic development a part of its national strategy going forward; Brazil has aggressively merged its forward-looking policies for growth, climate change, and environmental management; and Japan is pushing for an additional 30 percent in energy efficiency

gains, starting from its position as one of the most energy-efficient countries in the world (box 3.1).

The current transition toward green development has deep historical roots. Developed countries, with 20 percent of global population, developed during a period of high fossil fuel and resource consumption. Now, the remaining 80 percent of the world's population also seeks to rise economically. However, if the 80 percent modernizes in the same way as the developed countries did—especially considering that by 2050 the global population will rise to over 9 billion people—the environmental costs will become insurmountable for all countries. Therefore, the traditional model of development is no longer feasible.

The global climate crisis is one of the most daunting of the crises precipitated by traditional economic growth. China will be one of the countries most affected by climate change. Therefore, addressing climate change is a pressing need for China, and a matter of self-interest. There is a scientific consensus that to limit the rise in global average surface temperatures to 2°C, global carbon emissions must peak in 2020 or so, then decline dramatically by 2 percent a year (UNEP 2011a). In short, there is simply not enough "carbon space" to satisfy the emission needs of all countries if they continue to grow in the traditional mode of development.

Because of rapid economic expansion, and despite strong measures taken since 2006, both China's total annual and per capita emissions are increasing at a high rate. Although its per capita emissions were historically low, they are now above those of France and Spain, and China's total emissions are the largest in the world (figure 3.1). During the period 2006–10, China reduced the energy intensity of its economy (a close measure to carbon intensity) by 20 percent, through strict energy conservation and emission reduction measures, even as it maintained overall growth of its gross domestic product (GDP) of more than 10 percent a year. China's current commitment is to decrease its carbon intensity (carbon dioxide, or CO_2, emissions

BOX 3.1   Examples of national green development strategies

Germany's new energy plan. In May 2011, Germany determined to close all of its nuclear plants by 2022 and to become the first industrial country to shift completely to clean energy by increasing investment and research and development for renewable energy and energy efficiency. Currently, nuclear power provides 22 percent of Germany's electricity. To fill the gap in its energy supply after it abandons nuclear, Germany has proposed vigorous development of wind, solar, and biomass and new standards for the thermal efficiency of buildings. It is also urging European and North African countries to create a continentwide super smart grid (which would allow the import of power from sun-rich North Africa and wind power from the North Sea).

Korea's green growth plan. In response to the global financial crisis of 2008, the Republic of Korea is a first mover in the implementation of green growth. Its move toward green growth combines three mutually reinforcing objectives: responding to the latest economic crisis through a green stimulus, reducing its energy dependency, and rebalancing its economy toward green sectors in the long term. The financial crisis exposed Korea's reliance on imported energy as a major weakness in its growth model. Korea imports 96 percent of its energy—accounting for two-thirds of all imports. To rebalance this situation by 2030, Korea aims to decrease its energy intensity by 46 percent and to increase the share of renewable energy in total primary energy from 2.4 percent in 2007 to 11 percent. Furthermore, the latest five-year plan allocates 2 percent of gross

domestic product to 10 green growth strategies, each containing quantitative objectives and well-defined projects. Korea also aims to increase its global market share of green technology exports from 2 percent in 2009 to 10 percent by 2020.

Japan's energy efficiency strategy. Japan's energy intensity decreased 26 percent between 1980 and 2009, and it is one of the most energy-efficient countries in the world. Nevertheless, in 2006, Japan pledged to improve its energy efficiency by another 30 percent by 2030 relative to 2006. The plan's implementation strategy fosters energy conservation technologies and develops a benchmarking approach to monitor energy conservation. In addition to promoting the most advanced technologies across the energy sector, the plan also introduces integrated energy consumption standards for all buildings and targets net-zero-energy houses by 2020 (which are to become the norm nationwide by 2030). Japan's Top Runner Program tests 21 types of appliances—ranging from vending machines and air conditioners to television sets—to determine the most efficient model and make that model's level of efficiency the new baseline. Then, manufacturers are required to achieve the new baseline within four to eight years. Japan's newest innovation is the concept of "smart community," a model city that maximizes the use of renewable energy and relies on smart grids to deal with its intermittent nature. Four large-scale pilot projects were started in 2010.

per unit of GDP) by 40–45 percent by 2020 from the level in 2005. Nonetheless, China's per capita GDP will have doubled by 2020, implying that both total and per capita emissions will continue to rise. It is clear that however global carbon budgets may be allocated through national actions and international negotiations over the next 20 years, there will never be enough carbon emission space for China to copy the past industrialization model of developed countries (DRC 2009; DRC Project Team 2011).

In sum, green development is being driven by harsh economic realities, changing global priorities, and growing technological possibilities (box 3.2). Many of the forces operating in the rest of the world are also present in China. Chinese leadership has already shown its commitment to green, low-carbon development, even though it is at the early stages of a long journey. This study focuses on how to achieve green development, not on whether it is an option.

FIGURE 3.1   **Emissions of CO$_2$ from energy, annually and cumulatively**

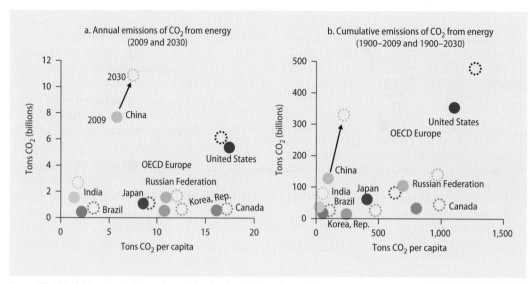

Sources: World Bank. Historic emissions and population data for 1950–2009 from Boden, Marland, and Andres 2010; World Bank World Development Indicators; and UN Population Division (2011). Projections of emissions for China from 2010 to 2030 are from World Bank and DRC. Projections for emissions from other countries are from U.S. EIA (2011) and WRI CAIT (2011); population projections from UN Population Division (2011).
Note: Solid dots = 2009; open dots = 2030.

BOX 3.2   Green development can help resolve the dilemma of global emission reductions

Traditional analysis shows that the benefits of climate change mitigation are global, while the costs are local. This asymmetry leads to difficulties in global coordination of emission reduction. However, this analysis fails to include the broader local benefits that accrue to mitigation investments, such as greater economic efficiency and competitiveness and local environmental co-benefits. As governments acknowledge these broader local benefits, the challenge of global emission reduction can begin to change from being a strictly zero-sum game to one with greater win-win potential.

Source: DRC Project Team on "Fighting Climate Change."

New Opportunities Arise

While the transition toward green development will not be easy, it will open the door to new opportunities. China's government has already clearly stated that "addressing climate change is an important opportunity to speed up economic restructuring as well as the transformation of China's mode of development and to hasten forth a new industrial revolution" (State Council 2011). The 12th Five Year Plan (5YP) contains many important prerequisites for China's efforts to "go green," including completing the transition to market through private sector development and factor market reforms, increasing the share of consumption, shifting toward less emissions-intensive service industries, increasing the pace of innovation, and developing human capital. It also supports increasing research and development (R&D) expenditure to 2.5 percent of GDP by 2015, among the highest levels of any country.

Transitioning to green development is critical to China's economic competitiveness in the future world economy. The core of global competition lies in technological innovation. The 12th 5YP has a strong focus on seven strategic industries—environmental protection and energy efficiency, new energy, next generation information technology, biotechnology, high-end manufacturing, clean-energy vehicles, and high-tech materials—which are all leading sectors for future growth. They are mostly all "green technologies" with high-value-added and export potential. Growth in these areas will make China's economic structure more competitive. Nevertheless, while technological breakthroughs are essential for green growth, the transition to green development is a much more profound process than technological change. The transition will span manufacturing and services, construction and transport, city development and management, and energy production and consumption. This is why green development would be a significant break from China's past pattern of development, cutting across all economic and social sectors.

Mounting global evidence shows that economic growth and carbon emissions and pollution have already begun to decouple. According to the United Nations Environment Programme (UNEP), the carbon intensity of the world economy has dropped 23 percent since 1992. Since 1990, economic growth has increased faster than carbon emissions for both the developed countries and developing countries, as represented by the five BRICS countries (Brazil, the Russian Federation, India, China, and South Africa),

although that decoupling is much more complete in OECD countries (figure 3.2). Overall, the data show that high growth is compatible with lower carbon emissions, and that China and the other BRICS have an opportunity to compete by going further down this path.

Even though the transition to green development is a long-term process, the next 20 years are a crucial strategic period for China to seize the opportunity, gain competitive advantages, and show global leadership. It could catch up with and even surpass the United States and Europe on green measures. If China does not seize this opportunity, however, then its economy will lock into a high-emissions structure, lose competitiveness, and face much higher low-carbon transition costs in the future.

As China positions itself to take advantage of green development opportunities, its vision can be defined by these major indicators:

- "Green" will become an important source of economic growth. The share of green products and green services in China's GDP will be among the highest in the world.
- China will become a world leader in key green technologies and business models and will be an important destination for

FIGURE 3.2   Decoupling economic growth from carbon emissions worldwide

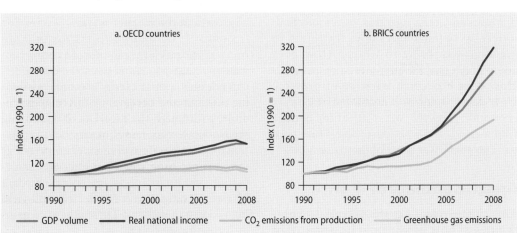

Source: OECD 2011.
Note: BRICS = Brazil, Russian Federation, India, China, and South Africa.

commercializing many globally important low-carbon technologies.

- China will have made real gains in low-carbon development. The correlation between growth and carbon emissions will be significantly weakened, and carbon emissions will have peaked.
- China will have adopted some of the world's most stringent and wide-reaching environmental standards, penetrating all sectors of the economy and society.
- Similarly, China will have established a resource-efficient society. Its resource efficiency through all phases of supply, consumption, and recycling will be among the highest in the world.
- China's cities will have low-carbon and smart transportation systems and buildings. They will be livable by international standards.
- The quality of air, water, and natural ecosystems will have improved dramatically. The recovery of the natural environment will significantly improve both public health and natural assets.
- Low-carbon living will become widespread and will involve all aspects of people's lives, from housing, to transportation, to food, to other consumer items.
- The risks posed by climate change will be addressed through proactive planning across all key sectors, including water, agriculture, urban, and health.

How can China turn this vision into reality? What opportunities does transition to green growth bring to China? How does going green make China more competitive? How does it become a *source* of growth? How does it improve the *quality* of China's economic growth? What advantages does China enjoy, and what obstacles? This chapter aims to answer some of these questions.

Green as a Source of Growth

This chapter identifies the potential opportunities of how green could be a source of growth. In the past, a clean environment has too often been considered an unaffordable

luxury—but green development goes far beyond the trade-off between growth and the environment. New evidence shows that the two goals—growth and a clean environment—not only may be realized simultaneously but may be mutually reinforcing. When it comes to climate mitigation, new literature developed by researchers in the United States (Acemoglu and others 2012), in Europe (Jaeger and others 2011), and in China (Zhang and Shi 2011) suggests it is possible to significantly reduce emissions without reducing long-term growth.[3]

How Green Contributes to Growth

Green development is primarily market driven. The prerequisite for green development is a sound market economy in which the governmental functions to correct environmental market failures through combined policies, regulations, and investments. One can say that past unsustainable growth represents the failure of government to fulfill this role. Once these government actions are introduced, the market will respond to reduce environmental and social costs. Furthermore, high-polluting, high-emitting, and resource-intensive products will become less competitive as their external costs are internalized. These changes in relative prices will help push resources into industries and services more consistent with green development objectives. To be specific, "green" is a source of growth in three major ways.

Source 1: Green transformation of traditional sectors. A large number of existing conventional techniques and management models can not only reduce energy use and emissions but also improve the level of corporate profitability. Although the greening of traditional sectors may seem less dramatic and revolutionary than the development of cutting-edge new technologies, it is clear that with information and financing, many energy-efficient investments are also cost-effective and yield high economic returns. These efficiency gains are growth enhancing.

Source 2: Expansion of emerging green industries. Emerging green industries include solar and wind energy, together with upstream and downstream industries such as relevant equipment manufacturing and electric vehicle industries. More broadly, however, new markets and incentives, supported by innovation and research, will likely stimulate new low-carbon, resource-light, and environmentally friendly technologies, goods, and exports. In addition, increased public awareness will help shift consumer demand toward green products.

Source 3: Expansion of the service sector. Services will also expand as a complement to new green product markets and changes in consumer preferences. Not only will the rising share of services in GDP help reduce the economy's carbon intensity, specialized services are likely to develop that specifically support green development. Examples of such services are ecosystem services, carbon asset management services, carbon trading, and contract energy management.

Of course, whether green becomes a dominant source of growth will depend to a great extent on future technological improvements, which are uncertain. Still, with stable green development policies, the pace of technological innovation and investment will no doubt quicken, thus increasing the possibility of technological breakthroughs. For example, between 1975 and 1997, growth in the number of patents for wind power, battery technologies, electric vehicles, marine power, solar power, and other green technologies was relatively slow. After 1997, with increased global awareness of climate change, more stringent environmental policies, and increased investment in renewable capacity coinciding with the signing of the Kyoto Protocol, the number of patents for green technologies increased dramatically (figure 3.3).

Although green development is still in an early stage and the speed of development in the future is highly uncertain, the opportunities it presents are increasingly recognized. For example, the OECD's latest Green Growth Strategy points out that "green growth has the potential to solve economic and environment problems and become a new

FIGURE 3.3   **Index of innovation in climate change mitigation technologies (1990 = 1)**

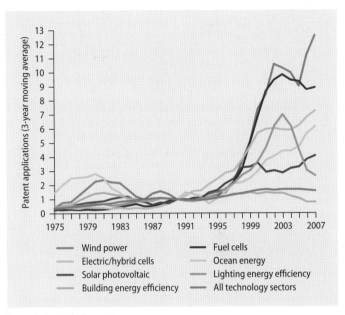

Source: Haščič and others 2010.
Notes: The figure shows total worldwide patent applications in EPO PASTAT database by priority date; it includes only claimed priorities (those patents for which an application is filed at an office other than the original "priority" office).

source of growth" (OECD 2011). According to Jaeger and others (2011), if Europe's emissions reduction target is raised from 20 percent to 30 percent by 2020, Europe's annual rate of economic growth may increase by up to 0.6 percent, generating 6 million new jobs and boosting investment as a share of GDP from 18 percent to 22 percent. Beyond these economywide benefits, additional sector-specific benefits may also accrue (box 3.3).

Source 1: Green Transformation of Traditional Sectors

Despite the unprecedented progress China has made in reducing the energy intensity of its economy over the past three decades, a large gap between China and the high-income countries remains (figure 3.4). The energy intensity of China's GDP, measured in terms of primary energy consumed per unit of output, was equal to 390 tons of coal equivalent (tce) per $1 million of output in

BOX 3.3   Further sectoral benefits of green development

In addition to the three broad reasons why green development contributes to growth, the implementation of green development policies brings several further sectoral benefits that are growth inducing:

- Rapid growth of energy consumption has strained China's domestic supplies of electricity, raised coal prices, and made it increasingly dependent on imported energy. With unchanged policies, China may have to import 75 percent of its oil (making it the world's largest oil importer) and 50 percent of its natural gas by 2030. Alternative energy sector policies will dramatically reduce this import dependence.
- The efficient use and better governance of land will help reduce urban congestion and sprawl.

- Agricultural output will be enhanced by reducing the degradation of land and water.
- Infrastructure constraints, particularly for handling coal, will be eased, and infrastructure investment requirements reduced.
- By anticipating climate impacts on agriculture, low-lying coastal areas, and areas vulnerable to extreme weather events, green development will reduce climate-related risks and improve investor and consumer confidence.

All of these measures will support growth through reduced costs, improved certainty, and the reduced need for risk management options.

Sources: World Bank analysis; IEA 2011b.

FIGURE 3.4   Energy intensity of GDP, 1990–2009

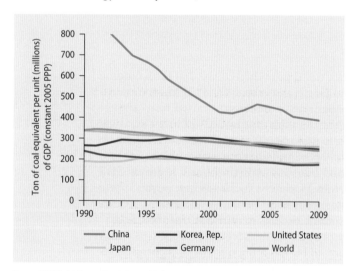

Source: IEA World Energy Statistics and Balances.
Note: Energy intensity is the energy used per unit of GDP; PPP = purchasing power parity.

2009. By comparison, the primary energy intensity of Germany's economy was 173 tce per $1 million.[4]

Whereas some new green technologies cost, many other technology and management changes that can help narrow the gap between China and the high-income countries already pay for themselves through lower energy and input costs. Policies and investments to improve efficiency, by increasing returns for investments in green technologies and products, will immediately add to growth. For example, according to estimates by McKinsey & Company, installing light-emitting diodes (LEDs) for lighting in buildings could generate RMB 184 billion ($25 billion) in annual financial savings a year by 2030 compared to business as usual (measured in 2009 dollars). Improving passive heating and cooling in buildings through design modifications could provide another RMB 44 billion ($6 billion). Industry was the largest sectoral user of energy, accounting for about 72 percent of primary energy demand in 2008 (NBS 2010b), and many efficiency gains can be found there. All together, the potential for direct savings through efficiency gains in China could be as high as RMB 480 billion ($65 billion) a year by 2030, if the full technical and economic potential of these so-called "no-regret" options can be realized.[5]

The direct benefits of these options are to reduce the amount of fossil fuels burned per unit of economic activity. However, they often have co-benefits that add further value

FIGURE 3.5   **No-regrets options for reducing CO$_2$ emissions in China, 2030**

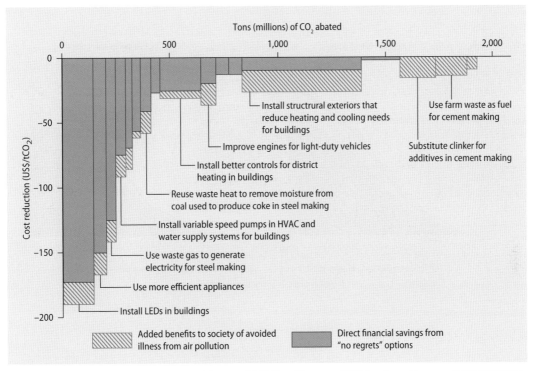

Sources: World Bank calculations, based on McKinsey & Company (2009); Ho and Jorgenson (2003); Cao, Ho, and Jorgenson (2009); NBS (2009b); Liu and Wang (2011), and Matus and others (2011).
Note: HVAC = heating, ventilation, and air conditioning; LED = Light-emitting diode; CO$_2$ = tons of carbon dioxide.

to the economy, such as improving local air quality and thus reducing the incidence of respiratory illness associated with air pollution; reducing infrastructure constraints in related sectors, such as transport and water; and reducing dependence on imports of fossil fuels. In other words, cost-effective energy efficiency and renewable energy investments offer triple-win ("win-win-win") outcomes by trimming production costs, mitigating emissions of greenhouse gases, and improving public health risks in various sectors. The potential for no-regrets measures to contribute to both the quantity and quality of growth is illustrated in figure 3.5. This figure shows the emissions reduction potential and leveled cost of certain energy efficiency technologies in 2030, as estimated for China by McKinsey, but adjusted to reflect the social value of these co-benefits. These health-related co-benefits are valued at RMB 148 billion ($20 billion, 2009 values) a year

in 2030, on top of the direct savings of RMB 480 ($65 billion) a year.

Feng and others (2011) estimate that several hundred mature energy-saving technologies are currently available to, but not fully deployed by, China's high-energy-consumption industries. The analysis shows that if energy-intensive industrial sectors widely applied 79 of these major technologies by 2020, the accumulated energy savings would be 456 million tce (with a corresponding reduction in emissions of 1.2 billion tons of carbon dioxide, or tCO$_2$) (figure 3.6). If all existing and emerging energy efficiency technologies available for energy-intensive industrial sectors were applied by 2020, the accumulated energy savings capacity would be 650 million–750 million tce (with corresponding reductions in CO$_2$ of 1.7 billion–1.9 billion tons). More detailed examples of the cement and iron and steel sectors are given in box 3.4.

FIGURE 3.6   Estimated energy savings and emissions reduction from installing 79 efficiency technologies in heavy industry, 2005–20

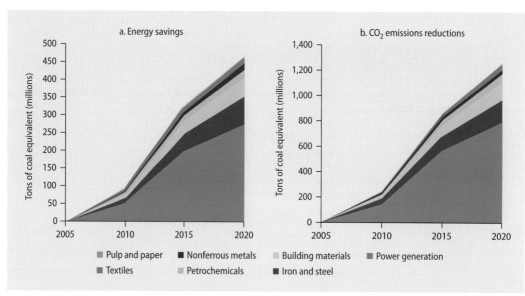

Source: Feng and others 2011.

Source 2: Expansion of Emerging Green Industries

Emerging industries are green if they emit low levels of pollution and greenhouse gases. The most concrete example of emerging green industries is clean energy, and some such as solar power, wind power, biomass, and hydropower have already been commercialized on a large scale. China's seven targeted strategic industries, mentioned earlier, are environmental protection and energy efficiency, new energy, next generation information technology, biotechnology, high-end manufacturing, clean-energy vehicles, and high-tech materials. Globally, business opportunities in many of these sectors, including clean-energy vehicles and clean energy, are shifting toward the developing countries.

China is now the world leader in renewable energy investment, surpassing all other countries (Pew 2010). The wind power industry alone could account for more than RMB 161 billion ($25 billion) a year in investment, assuming 20 gigawatts installed

a year. Furthermore, if the State Council targets are met, the contribution of emerging green industries to China's GDP will be 15 percent by 2020.

Cost reductions and technological progress in renewable energy technologies in China have exceeded expectations, mostly due to a massive scaling-up in the industry. In renewable energy, the cost of both wind energy and solar photovoltaic (PV) equipment has decreased dramatically during the past five years (Feng and Wang 2011). The wholesale prices of coal-fired and wind power are already very close (just under RMB 0.50 or $0.08 per kilowatt hour). The price of a solar PV module has decreased from RMB 149 ($23) in 1980 to less than RMB 20 ($3) in 2010 (U.S. DOE 2010). Following this long-term trend, the existing gap between coal-fired and solar PV power will likely close by 2020. Similarly, the costs of biomass, marine power, shale gas, coal gasification, and other clean energies will continue to decrease.

The rapid progress of clean energy technologies is illustrated by the dramatic rise in

BOX 3.4   Detailed analysis of two industries: Cement and iron and steel

Driven by an unprecedented construction boom over the past decade, China's iron and steel and cement sectors accounted for nearly one-fourth of the country's total energy consumption in 2009. As the construction boom is expected to last well into the 2020s, demand will continue to grow (Zhou and others 2011; Fridley and others 2011). By 2030, the amount of coal consumed to make steel and cement could reach 926 million tons a year, an increase of 276 million tons (42 percent) over 2008 (NBS 2010b; Zeng 2010; Zhou and others 2011).

Chinese cement makers have made impressive strides, reducing the energy intensity of production by 30 percent between 1998 and 2009. While now more efficient than the U.S. cement industry and on a par with Europe's, China's cement industry is still 30 percent above the energy efficiency level set by the world's best practice cement technologies.

China's iron and steel industry has farther to go to reach the efficiency levels of industry leaders (figure B3.4.1). By deploying the best available technologies, it could save more than 100 million tons of coal a year (IEA 2010a).

FIGURE B3.4.1   **Comparisons of iron and steel energy intensity**

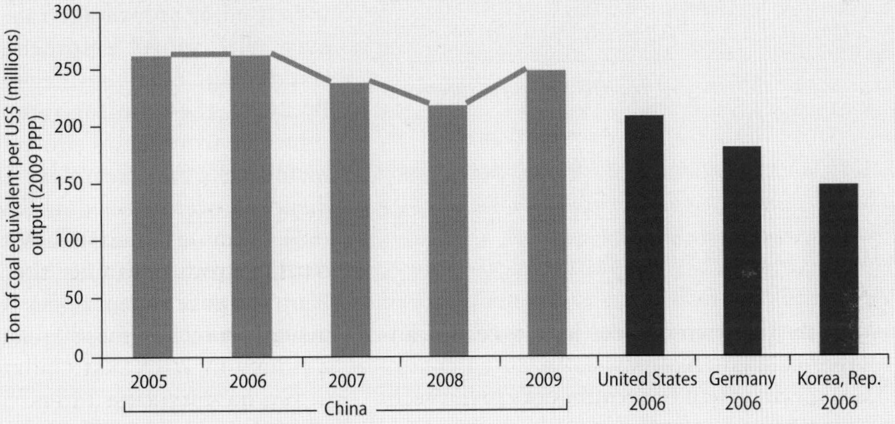

Sources: World Bank, based on IEA World Energy Statistics and Balances, NBS 2009b and 2010b, and UNIDO INDSTAT.
Note: The figure compares tons of coal equivalent per $1 million of output in constant 2009 US$.

Combined, the iron and steel and cement industries could achieve average net savings of RMB 73 billion ($9.9 billion) a year between 2008 and 2030 by using a basket of technologies that are already available on the market. This estimate includes net incremental capital, operating, and maintenance costs. Cost savings may be even greater depending on future energy prices. Energy-saving technologies also contribute to growth by reducing the burden of pollution-caused illness to society by an estimated RMB 8.9 billion ($1.2 billion) a year over the same period.

Sources: World Bank analysis; IEA 2011b.

the number of worldwide patent filings for wind power, solar PV, ocean energy, electric or hybrid vehicles, and lighting energy-efficiency technologies. China occupies a prominent place within this global trend of innovation. The number of wind power patents granted to Chinese inventors, for example, has surged within the past five to seven years, and transfers of wind power technologies to China from the developed countries

FIGURE 3.7   **Patent assignee origins for wind power technologies**

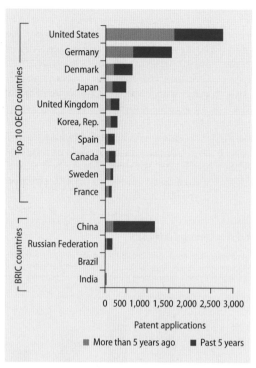

Source: Chatham House 2009, cited in Feng and others 2011.
Note: BRIC = Brazil, Russian Federation, India, and China.

over the past two decades have exceeded any other country (figure 3.7). As China continues to absorb and innovate new green technologies—supported in part by government investment and policies—these technologies will become increasingly competitive and contribute to the country's growth in the upcoming years.

The growth of China's nascent environmental protection industry, in particular, demonstrates the important role that the state will play in promoting the growth of green sectors. Take the flue gas desulfurization industry, for example. Under the 11th Five Year Plan, the central government mandated that sulfur dioxide (SO_2) emissions be reduced 10 percent nationwide from 2005 levels. This target was bolstered by additional standards set by the National Development and Reform Commission (NDRC) and the Ministry of Environmental Protection (MEP) for emissions from heavy industry. As a result, China's flue gas desulfurization industry has grown dramatically since 2006. Annual installations of sulfur dioxide scrubbers on coal-fired power plants have increased at an average rate of 34 percent, even with spotty enforcement of the new standards (China Greentech Initiative 2011). By 2009, the desulfurization industry and other environmental protection industries, including water treatment and solid waste disposal, were valued at RMB 480 billion ($74 billion) (Lan 2011). With stricter standards introduced under the 12th Five Year Plan, the government hopes that the environmental protection industry can grow to RMB 2 trillion by 2015 ($310 billion) (box 3.5).

Green emerging industries also create exports and jobs. By 2030, the projected exports of green technologies and services specifically related to renewable energy and clean energy (mainly electric) vehicles is projected to rise to RMB 1.691 trillion–2.916

BOX 3.5   **Robust growth projected for China's environmental protection industries**

In a speech in November, 2011, at the APEC (Asia Pacific Economic Cooperation) Summit, President Hu Jintao announced, "Continued rapid growth is projected for China's environmental protection industry during the 12th Five Year Plan (2011–15). By 2015, the total value of the industry may exceed RMB 2 trillion. Between 2011 and 2015, China's central government plans to invest RMB 3.1 trillion in protecting the environment, more than double

what was invested over the previous 5 years. China's energy conservation and environmental protection industries are seen as major sectors for foreign investment. A flourishing demand for 'green' products and services, combined with a favorable investment environment will provide a vast market and tremendous opportunity for enterprises from around the world. . . ."

trillion ($229 billion–$395 billion, measured in 2009 dollars) in export sales (figure 3.8) and lead to 4.4 million–7.8 million new jobs. These export sales are on the order of 6–10 percent of total projected exports, or 2–3 percent of projected GDP. Of course, this large scale-up is driven by global demand and depends on decisive action to address climate change by the world's governments.

As a driver of growth, green clearly creates jobs. But green also implies some higher costs, industrial restrictions, and layoffs as well as government actions that lead to changes in prices and production patterns. The positive impact on employment is greater the longer the time frame being considered and the wider the definition of green jobs being used. A recent study under the China Council of International Co-operation on Environment and Development (CCICED 2011) estimates that government spending of RMB 5.8 trillion ($910 billion) on measures to save energy, protect the environment, and replace polluting industries with high-tech firms would create 10.6 million jobs over the next 5 to 10 years. In contrast, eliminating the dirtier sectors of the economy would lead to the loss of 950,000 jobs. The previous paragraph noted that 4.4–7.8 million new jobs may be created by 2030 through

FIGURE 3.8   Projected annual Chinese exports of green products and services (2030)

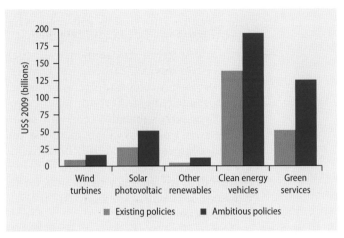

Source: World Bank calculations.
Note: The ranges given above compare two scenarios defined by the International Energy Agency (IEA). The "existing policies" scenario is one in which the G-20 countries follow through with their commitment to reduce fossil fuel subsidies, countries fulfill their Cancun Decision pledges to reduce greenhouse gas emissions, and other existing CO_2 mitigation policies are implemented (that is, the "New Policies" scenario in IEA 2010b). The higher estimates correspond to the scenario in which countries take ambitious action to prevent atmospheric concentrations of CO_2 from rising above 450 parts per million (that is, the "450" scenario in the IEA 2010b).

increased exports of certain green technologies. Although approximate, all of these estimates confirm the notion that the net trade-offs favor green as a source of job creation (box 3.6).

BOX 3.6   The relationship between green development and employment

Empirical research done in other countries has concluded that in the medium term, green growth will have a positive but small net effect on the number of jobs in the global economy (UNEP 2011b; Martinez-Fernandez and others, 2010; ILO 2009; Dupressoir and others 2007). Within this overall scenario, of course, some countries, such as China, will excel in creating green technology jobs. Furthermore, evidence from developed countries also suggests that those jobs that are created in the transition to green growth are often skilled and high paying. A recent nationwide study of green industries in the United States revealed that the median wage in these industries is 13 percent higher than the median wage in

the overall economy (Muro and others 2011). A study in Germany found that implementing measures to mitigate climate change led to more job opportunities for college graduates (cited in Dupressoir and others 2007). This finding is linked to the higher component of innovation found in newer technologies than in more traditional ones.[6] In contrast, extractive industries, utilities, marine fisheries, and some heavy manufacturing industries are likely to shed jobs over the upcoming decades, primarily as a result of gradually increasing energy prices, depleted natural capital (such as overexploited fisheries and forests), more efficient technologies, and the automation of production processes.

Source 3: Expansion of the Service Sector

The green transformation will impact the service sector in two ways. First, it will give birth to new green service industries, such as ecosystem services, carbon asset management services, carbon trading, and contract energy management. Second, it will support the country's intended economic rebalancing away from heavy manufacturing and toward a larger service sector. Both trends are important for reducing China's carbon footprint, as its efficiency in manufacturing may soon approach or even surpass the levels of high-income countries.

The emerging green service sector is already important. According to a trade association of energy conservation service providers in China, at the end of 2010, the total value of China's energy conservation service industry was RMB 80 billion ($12 billion). The industry reduced power consumption by 10.6 million tons of coal each year and reduced greenhouse gas emissions by 26.6 million tons of CO_2. Another important trend is that ecosystem management services are a growing industry in some poor areas of China, where farmers on marginal lands are paid to maintain the ecosystem rather than to sell wood or other crops.

China's traditional service sector is lagging and has significant room to develop. In 2010, the share of services in total value added was 43 percent, a figure that is much lower than the average for high-income countries (75 percent), and even lower than in most middle-income countries (52–54 percent in 2010) (World Bank, World Development Indicators) (figure 3.9).

Several reasons explain the low share of services in China's economy. First, the level of government public service is very low, particularly in the less developed regions. Historically, the role of government has focused on facilitating economic growth more than on providing social services. Second, government overregulation and in some cases monopoly has restricted development of the service industry and has inhibited the flow of private capital into these sectors. This is particularly true in finance, insurance, navigation, railway, telecommunications, petroleum, power, education, medical services, entertainment, sports, and the arts. Third, China's export-oriented development strategy has meant

FIGURE 3.9   Services, value added, as a share of GDP (2010)

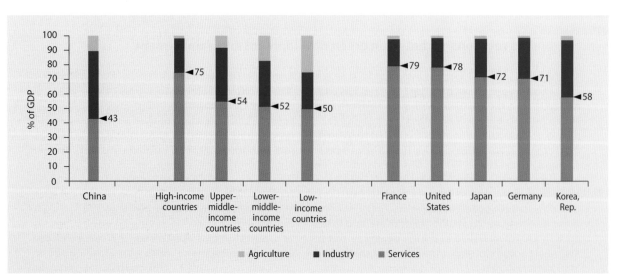

Source: World Bank World Development Indicators 2011.
Note: Agriculture corresponds with ISIC (International Standard Industrial Classification) Rev. 3.1 divisions 1–5, covering forestry, fishing, livestock production, and the cultivation of crops; industry includes divisions 10–45, covering mining, manufacturing, construction, and utilities; services are defined as divisions 50–99, which cover wholesale, retail trade, transport, government, financing, professional services, education, health care, and real estate. Data for France and Japan are from 2009.

that local government has been dependent on large-scale, capital-intensive industries for tax revenue, and there has been less support to the service industry. All of these forces are weakening, thus favoring the long-term development of China's service industry.

China's service sector growth over the long term will depend on the pace of reform of government restrictions, policies favoring the knowledge industries, and consumption patterns of the rising middle class. The rising share of services in GDP will help reduce the economy's carbon intensity. According to estimates by the DRC, the energy intensity of output (value added) by secondary industries in 2009 was eight times higher than agriculture and five times that of services. Every percentage point increase in the share of services in GDP is associated with a decline in energy consumption of 1.4 percentage points.[7]

Additional Opportunities for China's Underdeveloped Regions

The green development approach can help reduce China's interregional inequality by helping its relatively underdeveloped central and western regions catch up. Although historically the eastern provinces always led in economic development, since 2005, growth rates in the central and western regions have overtaken the east (Liu and He 2011). However, the interior provinces should not follow

the precedent of the eastern provinces by growing first and then cleaning up later. This is especially true for those central and western provinces with abundant mineral resources. Although extractive industries may have led to high GDP growth rates, the income levels of people living in these regions has not grown commensurately, and in some places, the natural environment has been severely degraded.

The interior provinces should avoid the conventional (and environmentally degrading) growth path of the east for several reasons. First, the ecological environment of the interior provinces is relatively fragile compared with the east, and the costs of "clean up later" would be prohibitive. Second, China's population is aging rapidly. As the surplus agricultural labor force that filled the factories of the east gradually shrinks, it will become impossible to sustain the kind of labor-intensive growth observed over past decades. Third, as China introduces more stringent policies to conserve energy and reduce greenhouse gas emissions, the potential for growth from high-emissions, resource-intensive industries will be limited. The interior provinces have a strong comparative advantage in clean energy resources (State Grid 2010). Fourth, with rapid expansion of cities onto increasingly scarce land, the national government has imposed stricter controls on the use of land for industry (box 3.7). Thus, China's underdeveloped regions

---

BOX 3.7   China's "Main Functional Area Development Plan"

To protect the environment and avoid "polluting first and cleaning up later," China's State Council launched the "Main Functional Area Development Plan" in 2010. This plan divides all of China's land area into four major types: relatively affluent, industrial, urbanized areas where development should be "optimized" to solve existing environmental problems; key areas for future development; areas where development should be limited; and areas where development is prohibited. These classifications are somewhat controversial: for example, restricting

the rights of different regions to development contains elements of a planned economy. Controversial aspects aside, the plan represents stringent environmental regulation and will prevent certain regions from following the more traditional path to development. Without the plan, local governments would likely be unable to implement such strict environmental policies. Thus, by limiting or prohibiting the development of certain regions, the Main Functional Area Development Plan will encourage these regions to take a new path to green development.

Source: DRC.

Source: DRC.

BOX 3.8   A "Big Push" model for green growth in poor areas: The case of Hunan

Huaihua in Hunan Province is endeavoring to take full advantage of improved transportation, telecommunications, and logistics networks to pursue a new strategy for economic growth. The previously undervalued intangible resources of the Wuling Mountain Area, such as its beautiful natural environment and rich cultural heritage, will provide a new source of income for local people and help promote local economic growth.

Through the coordinated efforts of government and private entrepreneurs, poor regions are making a "big push" to utilize new market mechanisms and build green economies that include conference centers, medical services, and eco- and cultural tourism. A more productive division of labor is evolving, with the local population benefiting as both farmers and service providers. The slogan of this experiment, "Villages Making Life Better," suggests that villages will no longer represent poverty in China but will be a symbol of a high-quality lifestyle. More important, the models are duplicable elsewhere.

have a direct interest in growing green while avoiding the cleanup costs being incurred by the eastern provinces.

Because their economies are currently less developed, many ecological, environmental, and cultural resources of these regions have been preserved. With high-speed rail, highways, improved logistics, the Internet, and other telecommunication technologies, the relationship between urban locations and economic development is changing. By capitalizing on better connectivity, the hitherto undervalued environmental resources of China's interior regions may provide economic benefits that enable them to grow in a way that does not require sacrificing their environment.

Many underdeveloped regions of China are now pushing to develop in new ways, in areas such as high-value-added agriculture, ecotourism, cultural tourism, training and conference centers, health care centers, and the arts. Some of these innovations require new business models, such as franchise businesses that draw on local labor. Important opportunities exist for payments for ecosystem services as well as for installations of renewable energy. For example, farmers in some poor parts of China have already transitioned from selling timber to marketing ecosystem services to earn a living. Another example is the more complicated "big push" that is being piloted to better connect a poor county of Hunan Province with the market economy (box 3.8). Elsewhere in China, other examples of green development are appearing every day. Searching out different forms of green development that are suited to local conditions has great importance not only for China but for other poor countries as well.

Green Improves the Quality of Growth

People's welfare includes such concepts as good health, quality of life, and a clean environment, in addition to income. While some of these welfare concepts are not quantified in traditional measures of GDP, they can, nevertheless, be measured. Improving the "quality of growth" implies improving some or all of these welfare measures. Even though China's current levels of environmental degradation and resource pollution, measured as a share of gross national income, are much higher than in high-income countries, China has already made great strides in improving these welfare measures. This section addresses the magnitude of the welfare gains that can be made through green development. It also indicates that some improvements in environmental quality are necessary investments that will benefit the quantity of growth in the medium and longer terms as well.

Improving the Quality of China's Growth by Reducing Environmental Degradation

Green development will reduce China's current high costs of environmental degradation and resource depletion, which is crucial for its continued growth and well-being.[8] Under no scenario can China achieve the quality of growth that is already articulated in its 12th Five Year Plan and longer-term social and economic targets without dramatic improvement in the use and sustainability of its natural resource base. The experience of Japan shows that stringent environmental policies do not interfere with economic growth. In fact, they may even catalyze growth. Intervention-style environmental policies play an important role in this (Kobayashi 2011). Economic growth and improving the quality of the environment thus may be mutually reinforcing.

The overall environmental benefits from green development can be substantial. At China's current level of development, the environmental degradation and resource depletion in the country is valued at approximately 9 percent of gross national income (GNI), more than 10 times higher than corresponding levels in Korea and Japan (figure 3.10).[9] A successful path of green development would cut this value, by 2030, to the much lower level of 2.7 percent of GNI a year (comparable to current levels in the United States)—at an estimated additional cost of 0.5–1.0 percent of GNI a year beyond current spending on environmental protection. While some of the benefits of this level of investment in the environment come in the form of financially viable "win-win" investments, others would take the form of economically viable investments in public welfare and ecological health.

China's specific environmental improvements would come from reducing reliance on fossil fuels, and achieving the lower levels of air pollution, water pollution, and resource depletion associated with high-income countries (table 3.1). The best way to achieve these improvements is to ensure that environmental

FIGURE 3.10 Environmental and natural resource degradation and depletion, 2008

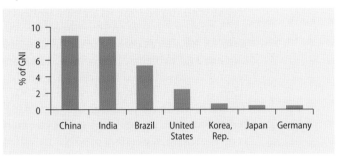

Sources: World Bank World Development Indicators 2011; World Bank 2007; Shi and Ma 2009.
Note: Here, environmental degradation includes damages from CO_2, small particulate matter (PM_{10}), and water pollution. Damages from CO_2 are estimated at $20 per ton of carbon (the unit damage in 1995 U.S. dollars) times the number of tons of carbon emitted. Damages from PM_{10} are calculated as the willingness to pay to reduce the risk of illness and death attributable to particulate emissions. Damages from water pollution for China are from 2003 and are based on estimates of health damages, calculated by monetizing premature mortality from diarrheal disease and cancer associated with water pollution and morbidity from diarrheal disease associated with water pollution (following World Bank 2007). Natural resource depletion is the sum of net forest depletion, energy depletion, mineral depletion, and soil nutrient depletion. Net forest depletion is unit resource rents times the excess of roundwood harvest over natural growth. Energy depletion is the ratio of the value of the stock of energy resources to the remaining reserve lifetime (capped at 25 years). It includes coal, crude oil, and natural gas. Mineral depletion is the ratio of the value of the stock of mineral resources to the remaining reserve lifetime (capped at 25 years). It covers tin, gold, lead, zinc, iron, copper, nickel, silver, bauxite, and phosphate. Soil nutrient depletion data come from Shi and Ma 2009.

TABLE 3.1 Getting to a greener China
Percent of GNI

Environment depletion and degradation	2009 value	"Greener" value, reachable by 2030	Net improvement
Energy depletion	2.9	1.9	1.0
Mineral depletion	0.2	0.2	0.0
PM_{10} health damage	2.8	0.1	2.7
Air pollution material damage	0.5	0.1	0.4
Water pollution health damage	0.5	0.1	0.4
Soil nutrient depletion	1.0	0.1	0.9
Carbon dioxide damage	1.1	0.2	0.9
Total depletion and degradation	**9.0**	**2.7**	**6.3**

Sources: http://data.worldbank.org; World Bank 2007; Shi and Ma 2009; World Bank analysis.
Note: PM_{10} = small particulate matter.

externalities are internalized as efficiently as possible in consumption, production, and investment decisions throughout the economy. Prices of natural resources and key factors of production will need to reflect scarcity value as well as environmental costs and benefits. Green development, such as reduced reliance on fossil fuels, will improve local environmental outcomes—such as reduced air pollution, land degradation, and water contamination.

The largest part of the projected improvement would be the economic benefits associated with improvements in human health and material damage from reduced air pollution. China faces one of the world's highest current and projected burdens of environmental disease linked to urban air quality (Cohen and others 2004; World Bank 2007). Trends in urban air pollution are improving, but the impact on health is still extremely large—nearly 3 percent of GNI in 2009. The government has responded strongly in recent years to address the problem of air pollution. But despite improvements in urban air quality, the urban population has grown so much that the total health costs associated with air pollution, and the exposure of the population most at risk, the elderly, continue to rise (figure 3.11).

A strong commitment to dealing with concentrations of particulate matter in cities will pay large dividends in improving health and social welfare. As China continues to grow, it will be possible to reduce air pollution levels dramatically—just as Japan did starting in the mid-1960s (figure 3.12). That is when

FIGURE 3.11   **Urban air pollution trends in China, 2003–09**

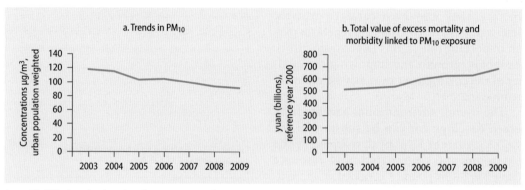

Source: World Bank analysis based on China Environmental Statistical Yearbook.

FIGURE 3.12   **Average annual SO₂ and NO₂ concentrations observed for the 10 largest cities in Japan and China, 1970–2009**

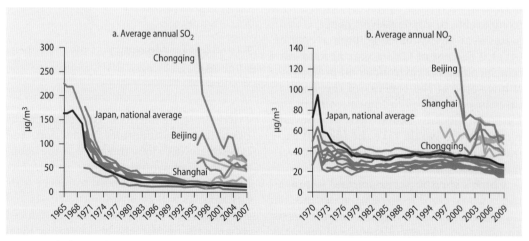

Sources: NIES database; Japan Ministry of Environment (1989); Kawasaki Air Pollution Monitoring Center; NBS, *China Environmental Statistical Yearbook,* various years; city statistical yearbooks for Beijing, Tianjin, Shenzhen, Chongqing, and Nanjing, various years.
Note: Includes 10 largest cities in Japan by population in 1970; 10 largest cities in mainland China by downtown population in 2009 (excluding Dongguan City, Guangdong). NO₂ = nitrous dioxide; SO₂ = Sulfur dioxide; μg/m³ = micrograms per cubic meter of air.

Japan's air quality and other environmental concerns reached crisis levels, and when it too was an upper-middle-income country. If air quality in China were brought to the level of Japan in 1980, these benefits would be valued at 3.1 percent of GNI. In addition, these air pollution improvements would bring large co-benefits associated with reduced use of fossil fuels, such as reduced depletion of fossil fuel resources, improved water quality, improved soil quality, and reduced CO_2 emissions.

Pollutants in water and soil also affect public health both directly and through the food chain. About 40 percent of the water sampled from the major rivers in the north and northeast is at Grade V or V+, making it unsuitable for most uses, whether recreational, agricultural, or industrial.[10] This exacerbates already

critical water shortages in the north and northeast, where freshwater resources are only 785 cubic meters per capita, about 200 cubic meters below the international standard for "severe water stress."[11] With the urban population growing by nearly 300 million over the next two decades, the stress on existing supplies will only increase. Cleaning up China's water supply is a clear priority (box 3.9).

Land degradation presents a similar problem of scarcity. Heavy use of agrochemicals, combined with pollution from cities and industry has degraded soil quality. According to the Ministry of Environmental Protection and the Chinese Academy of Engineering, heavy metal contamination of farmland is a serious issue raising concerns that these pollutants can make their way into the food

---

BOX 3.9   The challenge of China's water pollution

China's surface and groundwater supplies are low on a per capita basis, but useful supplies are much lower yet because of pollution. Although seen most vividly in pictures of an algae-choked Lake Tai, across water-stressed North China, 40 percent of the rivers fall into the two worst water quality categories (Grades V and V+), meaning direct use would endanger health. Water treatment is very expensive. The government has necessary, but ambitious, targets to control pollution:

Ministry of Environmental Protection Targets

- By 2020: 60 percent of China's surface waters meet the standards for Grades I–III (compared to 57 percent in 2009)
- By 2030: 70 percent of China's surface waters meet the standards for Grades I–III
- By 2050: 80 percent of China's surface waters meet the standards for Grades I–III.

Based on global experience, success in improving water quality will depend on a combination of aggressive regulatory monitoring and enforcement with a strong set of economic incentives. China's interventions to date have focused on industrial and municipal point-source pollution. While continuing

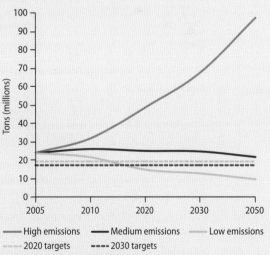

FIGURE B3.9.1   Wastewater emissions projections (COD), 2005–50

Source: MEP and CAE 2011.
Note: Chemical oxygen demand (COD) is an indirect measure of the severity of water pollution

to reduce those sources of pollution, the country will need to tackle the even more difficult problem of nonpoint sources.

chain (MEP and CAE 2011; Yang 2011). The presence of contaminated arable land may also restrict land availability for agriculture, which is already severely limited because of pressures from urban, industrial, and infrastructural development. Indeed, total agricultural land may drop below the amount mandated by the government as "the red line" below which self-sufficiency in grain production will be hard to maintain.

Environmental Co-Benefits of Green Development

As highlighted in the previous section, there are investments and management improvements that are cost effective (assuming efficient markets), emissions reducing, and pollution reducing. These "no-regrets" cases contribute, therefore, to economic growth,

climate mitigation, and local environmental benefits. McKinsey estimated the potential cost savings of these no-regrets low-carbon investments available in China to be on the order of $65 billion a year by 2030. However, the co-benefits of these investments associated with improved productivity of China's workforce, thanks to fewer cases of respiratory illnesses each year, puts additional economic gains at around RMB 148 billion ($20 billion) a year (measured in 2009 US$). The magnitude of various other potential "win-win" strategies to improving public health is highlighted in table 3.2. Of these examples, more efficient buildings that require less coal to be burned for electricity would generate the largest health-related co-benefits (as much as $9 billion), followed by the use of additives in place of clinker in cement production (as much as $2.7 billion).

TABLE 3.2   Direct savings and additional co-benefits of annual reductions in CO_2 emissions, 2030
($, millions per year)

Sector	Cost-saving abatement option	Direct savings from reduced costs	Additional benefits from avoided air pollution
Buildings	Replacing old bulbs with LEDs	24,992	2,364
	Appliances	9,007	978
	Efficient variable speed water pumps	3,453	750
	Water heating	2,085	489
	District heating controls	1,439	1,125
	Efficient buildings[a]	6,116	8,967
Transport	Light-duty vehicles, efficient combustion engines	5,018	950
Industry	Combined-cycle power plants (steel)	5,630	745
	Coal moisture control (steel)	2,085	827
	Utilizing or destroying coal bed methane (mining)	751	0
	Clinker substitution (cement)	229	2,669
Agriculture/forestry	Fertilizer management	2,280	162
	Cropland management and restoration	1,112	0
	Methane utilization	834	0
Total		**65,030**	**20,027**

Sources: World Bank analysis, based on McKinsey & Company 2009; NBS 2008a, 2009a, 2009b; Ho and Jorgenson 2003; Cao, Ho, and Jorgenson 2009; Liu and Wang 2011; Matus and others 2011.
Note: Figures are expressed in 2009 dollars. For this table, a sector-by-sector estimate was made of the local environmental co-benefits associated with energy efficiency investments. These co-benefits include the avoided costs of respiratory illnesses due to reduced air pollution, which is correlated with reduced burning of fossil fuels. For some industries, such as iron and steel and cement, most greenhouse gas emissions can be attributed to burning coal. For others, such as the transportation sector, the emissions come mainly from burning oil. Since certain fuels are "dirtier" than others, reductions in use have different impacts on local ground-level air pollution. A Chinese Academy of Sciences study calculated the fuel mix used by each industry type (Liu and Wang 2011) and estimated how many units of coal, oil, and natural gas were saved by reducing greenhouse gas emissions with the technology options in the McKinsey marginal abatement cost curve (McKinsey 2009). Damage estimates were taken from studies done by Harvard and Tsinghua University economists (Cao, Ho, and Jorgenson 2009; Ho and Jorgenson 2003) of the marginal cost of increasing people's exposure to higher concentrations of pollutants. The sum of the benefits from reduced coal, oil, and natural gas combustion for each abatement option gives the total estimated value of avoided illness.
a. Includes passive design, retrofit packages for commercial buildings, and other design improvements.

The Benefits of Investing in Environmental Protection

What are the costs China will face as it deals with the challenge of reducing the degradation of its natural assets (measured as a share of GNI) and makes targeted increases in spending on environmental protection? It is clear that cleaning up China's environment requires resources; otherwise, it would have been done already.

Current annual investment in the treatment of industrial pollution in China—about 0.15–0.20 percent of GDP—is roughly comparable with the amount spent in several European countries each year. Considering how fast China's economy has grown over the past decade, this spending reflects a great effort to reduce pollution, especially point-source pollution from industry.

Overall, however, cleaning up industrial pollution is a relatively small fraction of total environmental protection expenditures by government and business in high-income European countries. When the full range of environmental protection activities defined in the European System for the Collection of Economic Information on the Environment (EC 2002) are included, high-income European countries spent about 0.3 percent to 1.1 percent of GDP more than China on environmental protection overall, measured as a share of GDP in 2008 (table 3.3).[12]

Over the longer term, to improve its environmental quality, China's government expenditures related to the environment should be at least 0.5 percent of GDP above current levels. Any increased environmental expenditure in China would include increased spending both on pollution abatement and on efforts to protect and restore the health of its ecosystems. Although China is already spending RMB 83.7 billion ($13.0 billion) each year on tree planting programs to combat soil loss, flooding, and desertification, the cost-effectiveness of these programs can be improved by setting targets based on ecosystem health rather than on acres of forest planted. It can also direct more investment to relatively neglected areas, such as the conservation and restoration of wetlands and coastal ecosystems.

Evidence from the United States and elsewhere shows that such expenditures have extremely high rates of return when measured in economic terms (for example, the benefit-cost ratio of the U.S. Clean Air Act is projected to be 25:1 by 2015 and 31:1 by 2020) (U.S. EPA 2011). Increased environmental expenditure in China would have similar high rates of return by increasing natural and human capital in the economy. By this account, a relatively modest incremental increase in environment-related expenditures would go a long way toward securing the gain in social welfare of 6.3 percent of GNI shown in table 3.1.

TABLE 3.3   A comparison of total environmental protection expenditures, 2001–09
As a share of GDP

	2001	2002	2003	2004	2005	2006	2007	2008	2009
China	—	—	—	—	—	—	—	1.23	—
France	—	—	—	2.07	—	—	2.16	—	—
Germany	1.73	1.70	1.69	1.70	1.51	1.62	1.53	—	—
Hungary	1.68	1.76	1.85	2.00	2.14	1.95	1.59	1.52	—
Italy	—	—	—	—	—	—	—	—	—
Poland	—	1.75	1.78	1.74	1.79	2.04	2.06	2.38	2.42
Portugal	—	—	—	—	—	1.12	1.25	—	—
Spain	1.48	1.55	1.56	1.54	1.61	1.69	1.78	1.83	—
Sweden	1.19	1.19	1.18	1.16	1.26	1.20	—	—	—
EU-25	1.90	—	—	—	—	1.82	—	—	—

Sources: World Bank calculations based on Eurostat 2010, Eurostat database, OECD 2008, NBS 2010a, MEP and NBS 2010, MOF 2009, SFA 2009, Wang and others 2010, Chang and others 2010, and Wu and others 2007.
Note: — = no data.

Adapting to a Changing Climate by Increasing Resilience to Risk

A further benefit that green development would bring to the quality of China's growth is increased resiliency to climate risks.[13] China's climate is already changing, and changes are likely to accelerate in coming years. Even taking into account current scientific uncertainty about the extent and nature of future climate change impacts, preparedness for a more variable, unpredictable, and extreme future climate will be a prerequisite for sustained economic growth. Adopting planning and investment approaches to better address risks and uncertainties is a reason for China to fully incorporate climate change in its economic management.

Among the observed effects of climate change are average annual surface temperatures increased by 1.38°C between 1951 and 2009 for the country as a whole and much faster in the north and northeastern provinces (NARCC 2011). The number of rainy days has decreased for most regions, and more precipitation has come from shorter, more intense storms (Di and others 2007; Zhai and others 2005). The area of cropland exposed to drought has also increased for many regions. In the years to come, despite more rainfall projected for China as a whole, many regions may actually suffer from more droughts (Woetzel and others 2009). Agriculture will be particularly hard hit, because precipitation will come during the winters and less during the crucial spring and summer months. The area of cropland affected by flooding each year has increased significantly for parts of the Yangtze River basin. Although the projections are highly uncertain, flooding may continue to increase for this region in the coming decades (NARCC 2007; Ren and others 2008).

The agricultural sector is likely to have the greatest early climate change impacts. Annual crop losses due to drought in the Northern China plain and northeast provinces are projected to rise (Nelson, Ye, and d'Croz forthcoming). While warming will probably hurt rain-fed agriculture in parts of

the country where there is more indigent poverty, other areas may actually benefit from night-time warming, longer growing seasons, and increased water available to irrigation systems (Wang, J. X., and others 2008, 2010). Coping with the significant variability of future impacts will require geographic shifts in production and more flexible and robust water management.

Urban populations and industry will also be more exposed to extreme weather events. Much of the population lives in areas where sea-level rise, storm surges, flooding, and tropical cyclones are a concern (figure 3.13). Indeed, economic damages from typhoons, floods, and other severe weather events are already high: losses from typhoons alone in China averaged RMB 8.4 billion ($1.3 billion) each year from 1994 to 2005 (Guy Carpenter 2006). As the concentration and value of productive capital and valuable

FIGURE 3.13   Vulnerability to sea-level rise and storm surges by country, circa 2000

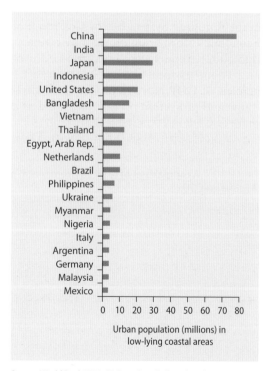

Urban population (millions) in low-lying coastal areas

Sources: World Bank 2008; McGranahan, Balk, and Anderson 2007.
Note: Low-lying coastal areas are defined as "the contiguous area along the coast that is less than 10 meters above sea level."

infrastructure increase in these areas, so will potential damages. This is particularly worrisome for long-term capital assets, such as power grids, water supply and wastewater treatment systems, and road and rail networks.

Institutions, planning processes, and policies that effectively manage future risk through green development will increase the resilience of China's economy. In turn, China will be able to mitigate, recover quickly from damage caused by adverse weather, and be ready to seize new opportunities for growth should these arise. For example, long-term glacier melt on the Himalayan plateau will generate both enormous challenges and opportunities for water conservation and storage technologies. Opportunities for both domestic and international gain abound in other sectors as well, such as agriculture, building design, and infrastructure design.

Factors Favoring and Impeding Green Development in China

In pursuing green development, China enjoys a number of unique advantages that other countries do not have. At the same time, it also faces unique challenges (table 3.4). The largest of these challenges is not a lack of financing but rather a lack of incentive structures to promote green development. If China can overcome these challenges in the next two decades, then it could position itself as a world leader in green development.

Factors Favoring Green Development in China

First, government has the ability to mobilize action on high-priority issues. China's top leaders have already reached a high level of consensus on the importance of green development. As President Hu Jintao remarked in a speech at the November 2011 Asian Pacific Economic Cooperation summit, China is committed to "vigorously developing the green economy." This commitment is also evident in the Work Program to Control Greenhouse Gas Emissions during the 12th

TABLE 3.4   China's unique advantages and challenges in green development

Advantages
1. Government ability to mobilize action on high-priority issues
2. The advantage of being a relative latecomer
3. Large domestic market in which to scale up green sectors
4. Abundant capital (including human capital) to invest in green sectors
5. Natural endowment of resources for clean energy
6. Potential to still avoid lock-in effects of higher levels of urbanization
7. A destination for global investments and R&D in green technologies

Challenges
1. Distorted prices of resource commodities
2. Overreliance on administrative measures for reducing carbon emissions
3. Weak incentives for environmental protection
4. Lack of a competitive market environment for green sectors
5. Sector coordination failures
6. Weak monitoring and enforcement of environmental standards, especially at the local level

Five Year Plan, in which the State Council (2011) makes clear that "addressing climate change will accelerate economic restructuring and the reform of economic development, driving forward the opportunities of the next industrial revolution."

Beyond expressions of commitment, the government has demonstrated numerous times that it can take decisive action on issues of high political and economic priority. Reforms undertaken over the past three decades have fundamentally redefined the functioning of the Chinese state in allowing the market to play a greater role. Green development is consistent with further market reforms that promote efficiency, while increasingly correcting for market externalities that can be addressed only with a proactive government.

Second, there is advantage in being a relative latecomer. Because developed countries industrialized following a high-carbon model, their economies have to a great extent been locked into a high-carbon path. On the other hand, China and other developing countries

TABLE 3.5 Comparisons of selected indicators for China and developed countries

Indicator	China	United States	Japan	OECD
Per capita GDP (US$, 2011)	5,445	48,442	45,903	37,029
Automobiles per 1,000 people (2009)	47	802	589	564
Per capita gasoline use for road transport (kg. oil, 2009)	45	1,134	332	470
Urbanization rate (%, 2011)	51	82	91	80

Source: World Bank, World Development Indicators 2011.

can meet additional demand by building new green productive capacity and infrastructure without having to eliminate equal amounts of existing physical capital. China's current level of economic development is only one-eighth to one-tenth the level of developed countries, measured in terms of per capita energy use, car ownership, and other indicators (table 3.5). Because China is still in a stage of rapid development, the incremental costs of green development will be relatively low. China can avoid the higher costs of transitioning to

FIGURE 3.14 Efficiency and CO$_2$ emissions of coal-fired plants in China and United States

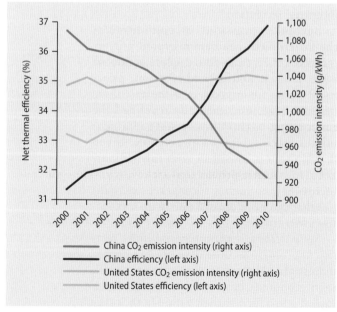

Source: Yuan and others 2011.

low-carbon technologies that face countries with less rapid growth and less rapid turnover of capital stock.

Nevertheless, capitalizing on this advantage and leap-frogging certain technological stages into the most efficient and greenest options will require early strengthening of incentives. This is clearly shown in how rapidly China has overtaken the United States in the efficiency of its coal-fired power plants (figure 3.14). In the past 10 years, due to large-scale installations of larger and more efficient supercritical and ultra-supercritical power plants have led to a qualitative leap forward in the overall efficiency of China's coal-fired plants; those plants overtook the U.S. coal-fired plants in efficiency in 2005.

Third, a large domestic market allows China to scale up green sectors. China has a vast domestic market that provides excellent conditions for the formation of industrial green sector supply chains, giving companies in China an advantage over competitors in other countries in seizing "first-mover advantages." The rapid expansion of both wind power and solar photovoltaics (box 3.10), for instance, has shown that China is capable of achieving economies of scale with the support of its large and growing domestic market. Large market size drives down production costs through learning by doing as well as by lowering unit costs. Scale combined with high investment levels and the ability to implement decisions quickly suggests that opportunities can be exploited ahead of competitors.

Fourth, abundant capital (including human capital) is available to invest in green sectors. China has traditionally enjoyed high rates of savings and investment (table 3.6); it attracts more direct foreign investment than any other country; it has built up an impressive research and development infrastructure; and it will have more than 200 million college graduates within the next 20 years. Clearly, China possesses an abundant amount of capital for green development that can be put to work, often with government support, to develop sunrise industries. The country is able to quickly acquire, adapt, and

---

BOX 3.10   China's solar photovoltaic (PV) industry

China is already the lowest-cost producer of solar panels in the world, thanks in no small part to the country's large domestic market, which has allowed the solar industry to rapidly specialize and establish an efficient division of labor. From equipment manufacturing to the production of accessories and auxiliary parts, the indigenization of the industry has been especially fast. As part of the supply chain for solar PV, by 2011, China already had 20–30 companies producing crystal silicon, more than 60 companies producing silicon panels, more than 60 companies making solar-powered batteries, and more than 330 companies producing components for solar technologies. Fourteen Chinese solar companies are already listed on foreign stock exchanges, and 15 are listed on domestic stock exchanges. The industry's annual production value now exceeds $45 billion, imports and exports have topped $22 billion, and the industry employs around 300,000 people.

Source: Li and others 2011.

TABLE 3.6   Comparative national investment, savings, and consumption rates
Percent of GDP

Country	Saving rate (%)		Investment rate (%)		Consumption rate (%)	
	1970	2008	1960	2008	1960	2008
Average of developed countries	27	20	26	22	75	79
Average of Russian Federation and Eastern European countries	26	25	31	27	70	69
Average of South American countries	22	24	23	24	76	74
Average of Asian and African countries	23	34	19	29	61	47
China	27	54	36	44	61	47

Source: World Bank World Development Indicators 2010.

---

master new technologies. Combined with the advantage of its large domestic market, China's ability to attract foreign companies and investors seeking to commercialize their own technologies brings additional know-how and spillover effects.

Fifth, China has an abundant natural endowment of resources for clean energy. China's natural endowments, such as wind, solar, biogas, and shale gas, favor new energy sources (table 3.7). The country's theoretic solar energy reserves are equivalent to 1,700 billion tons of standard coal a year, and two-thirds of the country receives more than 2,200 hours of annual sunshine. Compared with other countries at the same latitude, China's solar energy resource is at par with that of the United States and is much larger than that of Europe or Japan. China's wind resources are also very high—almost two times its power generation capacity 2005 (NDRC 2007). In addition, China's current dependence on and large endowment of coal also provides an opportunity—in the form of strong demand for cleaner coal, and the continuing dynamism of investment in the coal

TABLE 3.7   Total exploitable renewable energy resources in China
Gigawatts

	Potential capacity based on resources (GW)
Wind power (on shore)	2,560
Wind power (off shore)	190
Hydropower	542
Solar photovoltaic	2,200
Total	5,772

Source: Gao and Fan 2010.
Note: Small-scale hydropower includes retrofits.

sector—for lower emissions coal technologies given the right policy support (Shi 2008).

Sixth, China has the potential to avoid the lock-in effects of higher levels of urbanization. Although China's current level of urbanization is low (47.5 percent) compared with high-income countries, that will change. During the 12th Five Year Plan period (2011–15), the country is expected to invest $300 billion in basic infrastructure. According to UN estimates, by 2030, about 65 percent of China's people will live in cities (UN Population Division 2009).

The policy and investment choices made today and over the next two decades will have long-lasting implications for efficiency, lifestyle, the environment, and carbon emissions. For example, if cities lack adequate public transit facilities, commuters have no alternative but to resort to private vehicles. As vehicle density increases, so does congestion, which, in turn, sharply increases pollution, including emissions of CO_2. Similarly, commercial and residential building design will largely lock in energy needs for the life of the building, even if future price and other

policy incentives change dramatically. An electricity-generation plant has a lifetime of 30–40 years; its carbon footprint is fixed at the time it is built. *Only if China adopts green development policies sooner rather than later will it capture the lock-in benefits of efficient buildings, cities, transport systems, and industries* that use low-carbon, environmentally friendly technologies and standards (figure 3.15).

Conversely, high-carbon investments today will render it exceptionally difficult and expensive to achieve future emissions targets. If negative lock-in effects occur, China will have to either retire assets early, well before the end of their service lives, or purchase emissions reductions elsewhere in the market. The incremental cost of going low carbon now, by designing low-energy-intensive urban and transport structures, for example, is much less than the future cost to retrofit high-carbon cities to a lower carbon track. High-carbon power plants may not even be amenable to retrofitting. The prudent strategy is to introduce forward-looking low-carbon incentives now that lay the foundation

FIGURE 3.15a   What emissions growth path should China's cities take?

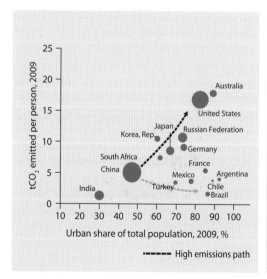

FIGURE 3.15b   Which way will China's transport sector efficiency evolve?

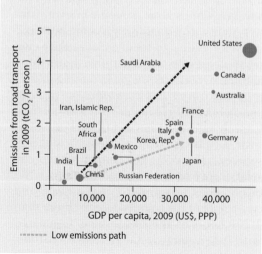

Source: World Bank analysis based on IEA (2011a) and UN Population Division (2009).
Note: Bubble size corresponds with total annual CO_2 emissions.

Source: World Bank analysis based on IEA World Energy Statistics and Balances, World Bank World Development Indicators.
Note: Bubble size corresponds with total annual CO_2 emissions.

for even stronger low-carbon policies in the future. The sheer speed and scale of China's urbanization and infrastructure construction lends urgency to this issue, as does the rapid expansion of the private automobile fleet.

Seventh, China is becoming a major destination for global investments and R&D. All of the above advantages, coupled with China's manufacturing capabilities, make it an excellent location for investments in many global green technologies. Regardless of whether future technologies are invented in China, they will likely be commercialized there. The cases of wind, solar, and cleaner coal technologies are illustrative: the transfer rate of clean energy technologies from developed countries to China is higher than to any other country or continent (OECD 2010). Since more than 70 percent of China's energy consumption comes from coal, there is a broad market space in China for technologies to clean up coal production and use. China can attract the world's best green technologies. This will not only promote China's own green transformation but will also accelerate the development of technical options available elsewhere.

Factors Impeding Green Development

China's advantages that favor seizing green growth opportunities notwithstanding, China also has to overcome a range of obstacles.

First, prices of resource commodities are distorted. Because of market distortions and rigidities, the major factor markets of land, labor, and capital have encouraged capital-, land-, energy-, and pollution-intensive development. As a consequence, damages to the environment and public health associated with the use of resource-intensive production technologies have not been included in production costs of companies; nor does the supply and demand of these resources on the market reflect their true scarcity. Inefficient pricing mechanisms, such as for water and land, is part of the cause, as are institutional weaknesses, such as the strong presence of monopolistic state-owned enterprises (SOEs). For example, water tariffs in China are

FIGURE 3.16   **Household water and wastewater tariffs in China's 10 largest cities compared with other major cities, 2008**

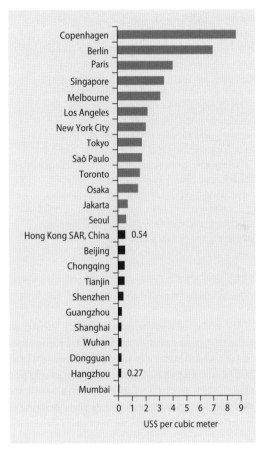

Source: Global Water Intelligence 2008.

extremely low by developed-country standards (figure 3.16). For China to focus investments and innovation in green industries and technologies, it must pursue deep-reaching policy and institutional reforms and establish markets in which prices reflect scarcity as well as social and environmental costs.

According to research by Huang (2010) and others, undervaluing China's labor, capital, land, energy, and environment is tantamount to offering subsidies to resource-intensive industries. For example, in 2009, subsidies embodied in artificially low energy prices were equal to about 0.7 percent of GDP. According to H. Li (2011), based on

BOX 3.11   International fossil fuel subsidies

The International Energy Agency (IEA) estimates that in 2010, fossil fuel consumption subsidies reached $409 billion. According to the IEA's analysis, if subsidies can be gradually phased out by 2020, then global primary energy demand would decrease 3.9 percent and CO_2 emissions from energy by 4.6 percent by that year, compared with a baseline in which subsidies are unchanged. At their 2009 summit in Pittsburgh, leaders of the Group of Twenty reached consensus on the need to gradually reduce subsidies, while providing support to low-income groups. "Inefficient fossil fuel subsidies encourage wasteful consumption, reducing our safety, obstructing investment in clean energies, and negatively influencing measures to mitigate the dangers of climate change," the leaders said in a statement.

Source: IEA (2011b).

2007 data, eliminating fossil fuel subsidies reduces China's emissions by 6.21 billion tons of CO_2. Similarly, Zheng and others (2011a, 2011b) predict that if electricity prices are not raised, then by 2020, China's urban residents will use 10 times the electricity they do today; and if water prices are not increased, then by 2020, the average urban household will use a multiple of current consumption. These research results suggest that raising electricity and water prices for urban residents may be an effective policy tool. In Beijing, for example, it is estimated that raising electricity prices by just RMB 0.02 ($0.003) a kilowatt hour will slow the average annual increase in household electricity consumption from 35.6 percent to 23.9 percent. Slightly raising the water tariff in Beijing from RMB 3.70 ($0.57) a cubic meter to RMB 4.00 ($0.62) is projected to reduce the average annual increase in water use from 14.7 percent to 5 percent. The use of tiered pricing could prevent undue burden on low-income households.

The distortion of factor prices in China is a serious problem, but not one that is unique to China. It is a global problem (box 3.11). Eliminating perverse subsidies for fossil fuels will dramatically improve the competitiveness of solar power, wind power, and other forms of clean energy. Going further and including the social costs of pollution and illness associated with the burning of fossil fuels would raise the price of fossil fuels even more.

Second, the country is overly reliant on command and control measures for reducing carbon emissions. Too much reliance on inflexible administrative measures has resulted in suboptimal allocation of resources for reducing carbon emissions and uneven compliance. The current provincial allocation of targets to reduce the energy intensity of economic output is an example. First, the targets are not allocated according to means or resources. During the 11th Five-Year Plan (2006–10), energy intensity targets for individual provinces were pegged to the national target of 20 percent. Although this method seems to make sense, it has placed an overly heavy burden on the less-developed provinces that are currently experiencing a period of heavy industrialization. Second, although targets for reducing energy or carbon intensity are the result of a negotiated political process, they are rigid (neither flexible nor tradable). This rigidity has increased the costs of compliance and made it more difficult for individual provinces to save energy and reduce emissions, leading to such phenomena as cutting off power (that is, resorting to "energy poverty") in order to meet targets that are even lower than what could otherwise be achieved.

Third, incentives for environmental protection are weak. Clear environmental regulations enforced by government are crucial for improving the quality of the environment. However, China's environmental regulations remain relatively weak, and enforcement has been inconsistent.

The problems associated with a lack of incentives for environmental protection are evident in both pollution monitoring and compliance and natural resource management. Of course, there are some successes as well, often market based. In agriculture, the lack of longer-term property rights in land and water has created a disincentive to farmers to invest in longer-term sustainability. Instead of increasing organic matter in their soil, for example, farmers find it more economical to increase output in the short run by using more fertilizers and pesticides. The same is true for China's grasslands, many of which have been overgrazed or encroached upon by expanding settlements and are in decline.[14] It was also true for China's forests, which, up until the late 1990s, experienced heavy cutting and were shrinking. This situation was changed, however, largely through the introduction of eco-compensation programs and reforms in forest ownership. Between 2000 and 2009, the central government invested RMB 365 billion ($56 billion) on afforestation programs, providing cash payments and other incentives for farmers who restored marginal lands in fragile watersheds, planted shelterbelts to protect against sandstorms, and protected natural forests. Reforms introduced in 2009 that extended the contract period for household forest rights to 70 years and allowed households to mortgage their rights strengthened the incentive for rural people to invest in sustaining forests.

Similar to land, China's water resources management system lacks incentives to promote efficiency at the scale required. As mentioned, the first obstacle to efficient water use is low tariffs. Other obstacles include the lagging water rights system reform and the inefficient use of market mechanisms. Some examples are the extravagant use of water for irrigation and the inefficient allocation of water between different crops and regions. As a result, water for agriculture accounts for 65 percent of total water use, but only 48 percent is actually used for crops (NBS 2010a; China Water Resources 2009). Only 40 percent of industrial water was recycled in China in 2003, compared with 75–85 percent in developed countries (although industrial water recycling has been improving in recent years).

China's existing fiscal policies have discouraged investment by local governments in environmental protection. Because many local governments lack fiscal resources, they have found it difficult to support long-term public investments in projects that promote environmental sustainability. In search of revenue, many have grown excessively reliant on rents from land in peri-urban areas that have been converted from farmland and leased for development. As localities have tried to attract outside investment and develop new industries to make up budgetary shortfalls, they have allowed projects that have damaged the environment and depleted natural resources.

Finally, the lack of incentives for environmental protection is tied to the inadequacy of the pollution control regulations that rely on command and control directives, and to the small scale of market-based pilot projects undertaken to date. For example, China has attempted to establish local SO_2 permit trading schemes, modeled after the system in the United States. But these programs have largely failed, because of overinvolvement by the government in trading that has weakened the role of the market, led to the unfair allocation of permits, introduced problems in the design of trading mechanisms, and interfered with monitoring of emissions.

Fourth, a competitive market environment for green industries is lacking. In reality, China's transition to green development has two levels: the first is "greening" its current economic base, and the second is a more fundamental shift toward emerging industries. Some Chinese green industries have experienced rapid growth in recent years, as exemplified by the rise of its clean energy industries. Yet, its emerging industries still lack a fair and open competitive market environment in which to grow.

The playing field for investment in emerging industries is still not level. In the case of the wind turbine and solar PV industries, for example, private companies are mainly concentrated in equipment manufacturing, while SOEs continue to monopolize the electricity generation market (SERC 2011). State-owned enterprises also dominate the development of shale gas, which will continue to be noncompetitive so long as the legal rights to shale gas resources are not clearly defined (box 3.12).

BOX 3.12   A lack of competition has held up China's shale gas exploration

China possesses abundant shale gas reserves with an estimated 25 trillion–35 trillion cubic meters of recoverable resources, comparable to the 38 trillion cubic meters of conventional natural gas on hand.[a] The country's richest shale gas reserves tend to overlap with areas in which state-owned oil companies have registered conventional oil and gas fields. Under current policies, these reserves can be explored only by existing state-owned oil companies. Yet, these companies are mainly interested in conventional oil and gas resources and have made very limited investments in exploring shale gas resources. Some resources are claimed by companies but not explored. In other cases, companies are interested in developing the resources but lack access rights. The result of this situation has been to hold up technological innovation in the sector.

Extracting shale gas involves surveying, drilling, fracking, microseismic monitoring, environmental monitoring, water treatment, and other advanced technologies. Exploiting shale gas resources requires sustained, successive investments over a span of many years. For that reason, it is particularly suited for exploration through coordinated investment by a diverse number of investors. For a single company to develop a site from start to finish often puts great strain on the investor and leads to low levels of efficiency and a lack of technological innovation.

Source: Zhang 2011.
a. China has yet to make a systematic exploration and assessment of its shale gas resources, and there are large discrepancies between various estimates. PetroChina, for example, has calculated that there are 21 trillion–45 trillion cubic meters of recoverable resources, while the U.S. Energy Information Administration puts this number at around 36 trillion cubic meters (Zhang 2011)

The Chinese government expects that SOEs will continue to play a leading role in strategic emerging industries, which may lead to disappointment given that SOEs have historically been unable to take on the role of green innovators. Not only do they lack the same incentives to innovate, they have also been placed in an awkward position by the government, which expects them to meet short-term GDP growth targets while also engaging in the innovation of high-risk, cutting-edge technologies. SOE managers are usually unwilling to take on the risk of failure; they are much more willing to purchase new technologies than invest in R&D on their own.

There is also a problem of regulation. Currently, wind power development projects smaller than 50 megawatts are approved by local governments, while projects larger than 50 megawatts are approved by the National Development and Reform Commission. With their powers of approval, local governments have spurred a "clean energy rush" that has quickly led to overcapacity by small projects. This campaign-style investment has long been a problem in China, and one that has been hard to correct.

Fifth, coordination between sectors is lacking. Coordination failures between government and the private sector, as well as between different levels of government, have stalled key green development projects. The complexity of coordinating different areas of public policy and investment is apparent with green industries, because they tend to span multiple sectors and because their infancy and focus on infrastructure often require some form of government support. Typically, since each agency working in a sector considers only what is in its own interest and within its own purview, different agencies may hold each other back. The same pattern holds for the central government and local government. For example, in the area of clean energy, investment in a single project may involve the National Development and Reform Commission, the National Energy Administration, the Ministry of Environmental Protection, and various local agencies. Generating electricity and connecting to the grid will involve the State Electricity

Regulatory Commission (SERC) and the state-owned power companies. Pricing subsidies are equally complicated and cumbersome to navigate. In the case of SOEs, top management will be evaluated by a number of different agencies.

For these reasons, the development of clean energy has been held back. For wind power, according to SERC, coordination problems exist in several areas. First is the difficulty in connecting wind power to the grid. In drawing up plans to develop wind power, local governments tend to consider only the availability of resources in one particular area in deciding the scale and timing of grid construction. Less thought is given to the long-term development of the wind power market. Second, the development of power generation capacity and the electrical grid is not well coordinated. For example, China had proposed to construct seven large wind-powered generating bases (with a capacity of 10 gigawatts) but did not lay down plans for how that electricity would be transmitted and distributed. Third, the development of wind power is not well integrated with the development of other types of power. The potential benefits of interprovincial trading and power switching are very high, although coordination has proven difficult.

Sixth, monitoring and enforcement of standards remain weak, especially at the local level. For example, green building design standards have been issued but are not strictly enforced, even though buildings account for about 30 percent of the country's energy demand. Standards for air conditioners and large-scale chillers are lax. In the case of wind farms, standards are lax or lacking for low-voltage ride-through, and for operating frequency (inactive versus active power). Since market externalities exist, by definition, in weak or distorted markets, the public market regulatory role based on standards is essential. Weak institutions will hinder progress in green growth unless adequate institutional strengthening is undertaken. There is no substitute for strong monitoring and enforcement, even when market-based instruments are used to reduce market externalities.

In summary, these six barriers will have to be overcome through appropriate policy and institutional reforms that together provide clear incentives for changes in technologies, investments, and behaviors. That the list of barriers is long should not be surprising; if it were otherwise, green development would already be a reality in China. In the absence of reforms, financing for green investments will not be forthcoming because the cost may continue to be seen as too high and the investments too risky.

Addressing Concerns on Green Development

While ample opportunities exist to increase the environment and natural resource efficiency of the Chinese economy, there will be trade-offs, winners, and losers. Policy makers need to recognize that relative price changes arising from changes in taxes, subsidies, regulations, and standards generate losers as well as winners. This section describes the impacts of these changes on the economy, industries, regions, and socioeconomic groups. The next section provides more details on the numerous policy options that government has available to dampen negative impacts on different groups.

First, economywide trade-offs can be balanced. Concerns are often raised that the economic, social, and even political costs of green development are unacceptably high. Those concerns are misplaced. Although pursuing green development will require greater public investment in certain areas, such as environmental protection and basic infrastructure, the core of green development is really to introduce market-based incentives that raise the efficiency and sustainability of China's economy while also improving social well-being. By no means does China need to undergo "shock therapy" to transition to green development.

Green development is unlikely to divert public expenditures from important public services. As China introduces new market incentives such as auctioning permits for carbon trading, strengthens a property tax, and raises prices of undervalued resources, green development may actually increase tax revenues and bolster the capacity of the government to provide funding for social services. Moreover, improving the quality of the environment will significantly reduce the need for spending on health care related to the burden of environment-related diseases.

FIGURE 3.17   Direct CO$_2$ emission intensities of various Chinese industries, 2007

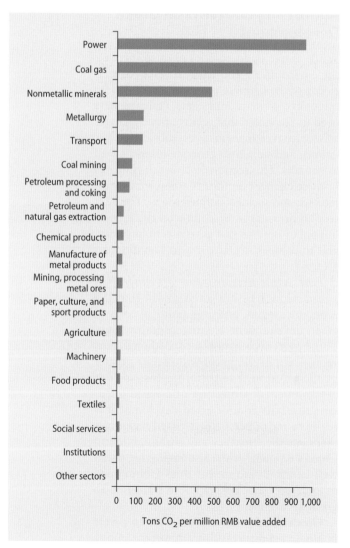

Source: DRC, based on the 2007 input-output table in NBS (2008a).

In terms of political costs, it is important to remember that the political economy of policy reform is complex and difficult in all countries, including China. Every subsidy creates its own lobby, whether the subsidy takes the form of preferential access to land and credit or access to cheap energy and resources. State-owned enterprises have political power and lobbying capacity, and energy-intensive export industries will also lobby for subsidies to maintain their competitiveness. Government will need to balance the broader social benefits of reforms with the losses of those adversely affected. Safety net policies for those likely to be negatively affected may include income support, access to alternative employment, retraining opportunities, and relocation assistance. Such policies will go a long way in mobilizing the political and workplace-based support for the changes that are needed (ILO 2011; UNEP 2008).

Second, different industries will face different impacts. High-emission industries include power generation, coal gas, metallurgy, nonmetallic mineral products, shipping, coal mining, and oil refining. Three industrial subsectors are the most energy-intensive ones and will be most directly affected by stringent carbon emissions policies (figure 3.17). More generally, raising the costs of energy, water, natural resources, and pollution will more directly impact those industries that incur relatively more of those costs. Some firms may even be eliminated, while others will survive and upgrade their production processes, supply chains, and management techniques by investing in greater efficiency.

Third, different regions will face different impacts. Because less-affluent provinces tend to invest more in heavy manufacturing and other lower value-added industries, they may be relatively more affected by green development policies. A number of China's poorer interior provinces are undergoing a period of heavy industrialization. If policies are administratively allocated and relatively rigid, as has been the case in China in recent years, they will place a heavy burden on these provinces. Conversely, relaxing price controls on energy so that the environmental costs of extracting fossil fuels may be passed onto the more affluent regions that consume more of these fuels, and introducing flexible trading mechanisms for emissions and energy intensity targets, may soften the negative impacts on the interior provinces.

As discussed, the less-developed regions of China will benefit in the long term by avoiding the costs of being locked into a high-carbon pathway. Once green development policies are put in place, they will also be able to better capitalize on previously undervalued resources, such as water, forests, grasslands, and renewable energy. Since these regions should no longer follow the precedent set by the more affluent provinces in growing first and cleaning up later, they will find new opportunities provided by green development.

Fourth, different socioeconomic groups will experience different effects. Since energy use is so pervasive in production and in the household, reforms in energy and carbon pricing will affect a broad range of consumer prices, and the net effect may be regressive for some households. In general, energy price increases will generally be progressive rather than regressive, since high-income households use proportionately more energy than poorer ones (Cao 2011). In contrast, some argue that poorer households are more emissions intensive because of their heavy dependence on coal (Golley, Meagher, and Ming 2008). In response, fiscal transfers to households, financed by revenues from eco-taxes, resource fees, or emissions reductions auctions, could be transferred to consumers to offset price increases without affecting incentives to use energy more efficiently. Even more important, carbon revenues might be best considered in a revenue-neutral fashion, in which the selection of revenue sources to be replaced would also have a distributional element. The specific distributional impact of a carbon emissions trading scheme can also be adjusted by freely allocating permits in the initial stage (Zhang and Wu 2011).

Other aspects of green growth reforms, such as strengthening rural property rights

and reducing air and water pollution levels, are typically progressive because the poor have traditionally suffered the most. Investments in improved ecosystem health, biodiversity, and watershed management will be sustainable with local people's engagement and employment through ecological protection, restoration, and related payments for ecological services.

The Road toward Green Development

Whether China can capture strategic green opportunities over the next two decades will depend on whether it can implement reforms sufficient to remove the obstacles in its way. Wide-ranging policies are needed to provide the necessary long-term incentives to the private sector and to strengthen the public sector's regulation of lingering environmental problems. Policies for green development should focus on six main goals, listed in table 3.8.

Goal 1: Provide Strong Market Stimuli for Transitioning to Green Development

The basic drivers of green development are market stimuli. The most pressing market reforms will kick-start the transformation of traditional sectors, start reducing environmental externalities, and mainstream long-term sustainability goals. The highest priority interventions are described here.

First, reform pricing mechanisms for coal, electricity, gas, water, and other resource commodities to provide the basic market conditions for green development. This is the

TABLE 3.8   Key policy packages to achieve green development

1. Provide strong market stimuli for transitioning to green development
2. Foster green sources of growth
3. Improve environmental quality
4. Minimize the negative impacts of green development
5. Manage risks associated with climate change impacts
6. Strengthen local institutions

most urgent reform so that prices reflect not only the market scarcity, but also as much as possible the external hazards imposed on the environment and health in the process of mining, producing, and using these resource commodities. At the same time, this reform requires removing and eliminating direct and indirect subsidies for the traditional energy and resource commodities and charging the SOEs full market price for their resource inputs (such as minerals, oil, natural gas, shale gas, and coalbed methane).

Second, continue to impose CO_2 emission reduction targets and accelerate the establishment of market-based mechanisms to reduce emissions. The Chinese government has announced ambitious plans to reduce emissions of carbon dioxide and expand environmental protection, and the emission reduction and environmental protection objectives set for local governments are binding. For example, in 2020, the CO_2 emissions per unit of GDP are targeted to be 40–45 percent lower than they were in 2005. However, these policy objectives rely too much on administrative measures, and emission reduction and environmental resources are not optimized. The measures do not promote technological innovation to the extent possible. According to the DRC Project Team (2011), the following short-term steps should be considered. First, the current target for reducing the carbon intensity per unit of GDP should be converted into a total emissions reduction target to create the conditions for introducing more flexible market mechanisms. Second, the emissions cap could then be distributed in accordance with advanced industrial emission standards, regional GDP per capita, and other criteria, and a carbon budget account could be established for each area. The carbon budgets set by the different provinces can be balanced to ensure the achievement of nationwide targets. Third, flexible and diverse mechanisms should be established to achieve emission reduction targets, including emissions trading, a carbon tax on fuels, emission technology standards, regional cooperation mechanisms for emission reduction, and administrative control measures. Among them, emissions trading

might initially cover about 1,000 high emitters, or about one-third of the country's total emissions.[15] The emissions of most other enterprises could be addressed through other emission reduction policy instruments. Fourth, new assessment methods should be established for emission reductions by province. Provinces should be able to reduce their actual carbon emissions, or achieve their reduction targets through cross-regional or national trading.

The approach described here puts a price on carbon using diversified instruments including a cap-and-trade market mechanism. Analysis shows that China will be able to limit its emissions significantly without reducing social welfare (see annex 3A for details). Any carbon revenue collections could be done in a revenue-neutral way. For example, recycling the revenue from emissions auctions by offsetting labor taxes normally paid by employers is one way to achieve job creation goals through green growth. In this way, governments tax "bads" such as CO_2 emissions rather than "goods" such as labor. Such a strategy has proven successful in Germany, where revenues from a tax on fossil fuels and electricity were channeled to workers' pension funds, thereby lowering the overall cost of labor and contributing to a net increase in employment (cited in ILO 2011).

Third, strengthen other environment-related markets and introduce market-based environmental incentives. Property rights for water, land, and forests should be strengthened, and market mechanisms for water, ecosystems, and land should be increasingly introduced. These resource issues are complex, politically as well as socially, but urgent. Poorer regions, for example, might bring new areas of land under cultivation and sell these quotas of farmland to the more developed regions to increase the efficiency of land use. For water-scarce regions, conservation and quality improvements can be driven by the market. For degraded ecosystems, expanded payments for ecological services in poor and ecologically important rural areas (for example, upriver watersheds or downriver flood plains) are needed (Bennett 2009). These programs have the potential to provide supplementary sources of financing for local governments and to create alternative job opportunities. For all of the above measures, reforms in property rights and land markets are fundamental to improving farmer and business incentives to protect the local environment.

Goal 2: Foster Green Sources of Growth

Beyond the provision of market stimuli for transitioning to green development is the need to more actively promote emerging green technologies and services. The national goal, as articulated in the current five year plan, is to turn China's green industries into a world-class example of innovation and competition. Further steps to be taken involve both focusing the role of the state and opening up competition to the private sector. Priority actions include:

Remove barriers to private capital to stimulate private investment. Great potential lies in investing in urban infrastructure and services (such as water treatment, waste disposal, and contaminated site cleanup), but various barriers exist for private capital entry, including information barriers. Once financial access restrictions are released, and new sources of capital are created, through such means as international climate policies, investment would grow.

Reform state enterprises to eliminate monopolies that limit new entrants to better promote innovation without excess state market presence. (For additional information on this subject, please see Supporting Report 2 "China's Growth through Technological Convergence and Innovation.")

Increase governmental investment in critical infrastructure for green development. Two examples are charging stations required by the emerging electric car market and improved electrical grids designed to absorb large amounts of fluctuating power generated by solar PV and wind generators. Related to expanding government investment is addressing institutional and governance issues (see goal 6, below).

Offer targeted support for R&D, especially in strategic industries, either through competitive grants to private research or through public research, development, and demonstration in sectors where public goods dominate. Complementary policies to "grow bigger fish by adding more water" may also be applied, such as through limited tax relief, enterprise bonds, and preferential financing to infant green industries. Subsidies should be phased out as each sector matures and the need for public support diminishes. To complement support for green sectors, the government should also draw up a schedule to cancel export tax rebates and perhaps set export quotas for the most polluting and most resource-intensive products.

Encourage green consumer habits and increasing demand for green products. For example, governments can advocate for green consumption; establish labels and standards for green products and services so that they are easily recognizable by consumers; and take steps to mobilize nongovernmental organizations, media, and other organizations to promote green consumption (box 3.13).

Goal 3: Improve Regulation of Environmental Quality and the Management of Natural Resources

Although market incentives are fundamental to achieving green development, regulations and other government actions are an important complement in several critical areas. The first need is to strengthen regulation generally by improving the monitoring and enforcement of existing regulations. In addition, other priority steps can to be taken to enhance the basic market incentives set out here.

Strengthened standards. Standards are a key regulatory area where improvements will shape behavior and create market incentives for green technologies. A key example is the automobile industry where standards can be set for fuel consumption. Another is the appliance and lighting industry where new standards for energy efficiency can have a direct and widespread impact. A third is the potential for national standards related to climate-robust green buildings, urban design, and transportation to prevent cities from

BOX 3.13   Energy efficiency and consumer behavior

Prices are typically very poor for signaling the carbon content of consumer products, even if a country has adopted carbon pricing, since it is likely a very small share of a product's price. As a result, guiding consumers to choose low-carbon goods and services through other means than pricing will be a key factor in determining the country's future emissions profile.

In the United States, households use one-third of total energy, and it is estimated that existing energy efficiency measures, if they were widely taken up, could save 30 percent of household energy use, reducing overall energy use by 10 percent (World Bank 2010). While these measures would be money saving as well as energy saving, many households never invest in profitable energy efficiency measures. Compact fluorescent lighting (CFL) provides one example: while the up-front cost of CFL bulbs is higher than it is for incandescent bulbs, the life-cycle cost is lower. In practice, the uptake of CFL bulbs by consumers continues to be low in many countries.

While this low uptake may be due to credit constraints, behavioral economics also offers a range of explanations for this household behavior, falling under the general heading of "cognitive biases" (Diamond and Vartiainen 2007):

- Status quo bias—the tendency to "continue doing what you are doing" instead of taking more profitable actions
- Anchoring—giving undue weight to one piece of information over other available information
- Heuristic decision making—for example, using "rules of thumb" to evaluate investments instead of accurately accounting for expected costs and benefits

Given these and similar divergences from what economists would consider rational behavior, traditional economic incentives such as taxes and subsidies may only weakly influence consumer behavior. A broader policy mix for energy efficiency could therefore include information programs (which can help to reduce anchoring effects and status quo bias) and quotas and technical standards (which can overcome the limitations of heuristic decision making). Similarly, promoting social norms in favor of saving energy and avoiding waste can help to change consumer behavior at relatively low cost.

Source: World Bank 2010.

"locking in" their carbon footprints, especially given the scale of urban construction. Compliance with standards can be increased through tougher inspections and buttressed by market-based incentives (such as insurance policies that require flood proofing or compliance with energy efficiency standards). And a fourth is to establish labels and standards for green products, services, and technologies so they are easily recognizable and understood by consumers.

Government procurement. Government can signal its seriousness about environmental goals by changing the way it conducts its own business. The most important and pervasive approach would be to introduce green standards for the roughly RMB 1 trillion ($155 billion) in government procurement each year, which can open up a huge market for green products and usher in a robust period of private sector growth.

Information disclosure. Health damages from air pollution in China's cities are increasing as the urban population grows faster than air quality improves. Investing in the monitoring of the most damaging pollutant, $PM_{2.5}$ (fine particles in the air 2.5 micrometers or less in size), and then regulating it, is the first step to curbing this trend. Better public disclosure of air quality data is critical for both awareness and effective action, and, indeed, China began to take steps in this direction when the State Council added $PM_{2.5}$ to national air quality standards in March 2012. In rural areas, an expanded network of water quality monitoring stations is needed to identify and reduce nonpoint sources of pollution from agriculture, the next major challenge to improving China's water quality.

Waste minimization and recycling in cities. Recycling guidelines and targets can reduce the need for new urban landfills or incinerators. By some estimates, China may need an additional 1,400 municipal landfills over the next 20 years, creating siting challenges and competition for scarce land resources. Waste separation and recycling could significantly reduce waste generation and landfill. Germany and the Netherlands, for example, send only 1 percent of their waste to landfills and recycle 60 percent. Reducing waste will be especially critical as the size and population of Chinese cities continue to grow and as land becomes scarcer.

Immediate measures to protect natural resources and biodiversity. The natural-resource-oriented market mechanisms mentioned above will take time to implement, and many of China's ecosystem problems are urgent and irreversible. Therefore, complementary measures are required to invest in ecosystem management programs, protected areas, and watershed conservation. (In some cases, maintaining healthy ecosystems, such as wetlands and coastal mangroves, can be the most cost-effective way to manage weather-related risks, such as storm surges and flooding.) In parallel, investments in water use efficiency and water quality monitoring stations would complement market-based initiatives concerning water rights, just as investments in agricultural R&D and extension services would complement reforms concerning agricultural land property rights.

Goal 4: Minimize the Negative Impacts on Vulnerable Groups

Overall, green development will bring enormous benefits for China; however, as with previous reforms such as those leading up to China's accession to the World Trade Organization, some sectors, regions, and groups will inevitably bear higher costs than others. The introduction of reforms, whether fiscal and financial incentives or nonmarket policy instruments (such as new standards and regulations), will inevitably alter relative prices and change the profitability of different sectors. Pollution-intensive sectors will see profitability reduced, while green sectors will see profitability enhanced. Resources will need to shift over time from one to the other, and

this shift may pose adjustment challenges. Similarly, jobs in pollution-intensive industries will decline, while those in clean industries will increase. Through a mix of properly designed policies, the adverse impacts of green development can be minimized.

First, for regions most affected by policies to reduce emissions, compensation for carbon pricing (whether through taxation or tradable permits) could be made through fiscal transfers. If done in a fiscally neutral manner, other taxes that may be more regressive could be replaced by carbon revenues. In addition, where price increases in water, electricity, oil, gas, and other markets specifically affect low-income groups, progressive "social" tariffs could be introduced.

Second, if carbon trading is introduced, the initial allocation of permits, both by sector and across regions, can be done in an equitable manner with the specific cost of the low-carbon transition in mind. Less-developed areas may have relatively fewer opportunities for emissions reductions and may therefore receive more favorable emissions allocations so that their economies are not negatively affected. High-emission enterprises that may be most affected (especially industries still subject to price controls or that cannot pass on the cost of carbon emissions to consumers) could receive free allocations at the beginning, moving to a partial and then full auction over time.

Third, for displaced workers, job retraining as well as labor market policies that permit workers to move to new jobs and locations at relatively low cost will be needed. Managing this transition, and ensuring that the pace of change is well within the capacity of the economy to absorb, will require careful policy planning and proactive implementation of social safeguards.

Goal 5: Reduce Risks Associated with Climate Impacts

In parallel to reducing the social and economic costs of green development, China's future strategy should also reduce environmental risks associated with the impacts of climate change. China's climate will not only become warmer, it will become more variable, with both greater extremes and increasing frequency of extreme weather events. Policies to better understand and manage risk—and recover from damages—are pro-growth by nature, because they reduce uncertainty and diversify risk. New planning tools can help ensure that long-lived infrastructure assets can withstand future climate change impacts, and new financial tools, such as insurance for disaster recovery, can help spread risks arising from adverse weather. The recommended steps include:

Improve information on weather-related risks. Already, China has invested considerably in its network of weather monitoring stations, and it has set up emergency alert systems in coastal areas. The country can continue to improve its understanding of past, present, and future impacts of climate change by increasing the quantity, quality, and accessibility of weather data. It should also continue to invest more in public institutions to research, analyze, and disseminate this information.

Update and develop new climate-robust technical standards for valuable infrastructure and physical assets. For example, China should ensure that transmission lines and distribution systems for power grids in coastal areas are designed to be resistant to increases in sustained peak wind speeds. Storm-water drainage systems in cities should be designed to handle changes in peak daily and weekly rainfall at least 30 to 40 years ahead. And ports should be assessed for exposure to at least 50–100 centimeters of sea-level rise.

Strengthen the enforcement of technical standards and building codes. Not only do building codes and other standards need to be climate robust, they should also be uniformly enforced. Compliance with standards can be increased through tougher inspections and the introduction of more market-based incentives (such as insurance policies that require flood proofing or compliance with energy efficiency standards).

Enhance disaster response systems. Emergency preparedness plans and coordinated procedures for government agencies to respond to disasters are critical, especially if the intensity and destructiveness of extreme weather events increases.

Offer insurance and other financial instruments to transfer risk and assist with recovery. Such instruments include disaster and calamity funds, contingent lines of credits, insurance, microinsurance, reinsurance, and risk pooling. Insurance schemes can be designed to encourage beneficiaries to avoid occupation of high-risk areas, comply with building standards, and implement flood- and storm-proofing measures.

Invest in agricultural R&D and extension services to help make the agricultural sector more resilient to the impacts of climate change. Well-funded research institutions can help develop new seeds and management techniques that require fewer agrochemical inputs and are better suited to changing climate patterns. More effective extension services can help to diffuse these technologies and practices. In this effort, cooperation between the public and private sector will be critical.

Mainstream risk management into development planning. China has issued laws for protecting cities against floods, the outbreak of disease, and other hazards; however, the current approach to risk management is highly fragmented, especially at the local level. Planning for weather-related risks should be better integrated into infrastructure and land use plans. Risk management audits should be incorporated into performance evaluations for local officials.

Goal 6: Strengthen Local Institutions

Smart urban planning, water supply management, pollution control, and disaster risk reduction planning all require coordinated action at the lowest levels of government. To achieve this, measures are needed to strengthen local-level governance and institutions and to provide clear incentives in the direction of green growth. New, sustainable sources of fiscal revenue and standards for evaluating the performance of local government agents are needed to provide the right incentives for provinces, cities, counties, and townships to pursue green growth strategies.

First, encourage different regions to explore different models. In the past, some of China's most successful reforms, such as the household responsibility system, originated as local experiments that were later scaled up. The same could be said for green development. Because green development is still in its infancy, some places will play a pioneering role. For example, in Baoding and Rizhao, bold efforts are under way to deploy clean technologies, improve energy efficiency, and reduce greenhouse gas emissions. The success of a few regions will have good demonstration effects and can be imitated elsewhere. Yet, local institutional innovation is often suppressed because local officials are still under immense pressure to grow their economies and protect jobs, and officials from different localities or bureaucracies often lack the incentives to cooperate in solving transjurisdictional environmental problems. The current competition between municipalities across China is healthy, but could benefit from following some basic principles for low-carbon urban development (box 3.14).

Second, improve coordination vertically, between the central state and provinces,

---

BOX 3.14   Low-carbon urban development in China

Cities account for about 70 percent of energy-related carbon emissions worldwide. That share is expected to increase to 76 percent by 2030, with most of the increase coming from rapidly urbanizing countries such as China and India. Chinese cities already have relatively high levels of per capita greenhouse gas emissions. With hundreds of millions of people expected to migrate to the cities in China over the next 20 years, implementing policies to reign in carbon emissions in urban areas will be a central feature of China's emissions reduction strategy. Taking into consideration the characteristics of Chinese cities, the following elements are essential building blocks for successful low-carbon urban development:

- *Increasing energy efficiency and clean energy sources.* Cities should make a consistent and dedicated effort to reduce carbon emissions by sustaining demand-side energy efficiency measures—particularly in industry, power, heating, and buildings. In addition, clean sources of energy supply can be developed within cities, with rooftop solar PV and solar water heating installations.
- *Reducing transport sector emissions.* To minimize emissions from the transportation sector, reduced motorization will be required. Decisive action should be taken to both adopt new technologies and provide high-quality public and nonmotorized transport.

- *Managing cities' physical growth.* Cities need to intervene in the shape and direction of their physical growth. Cities with higher densities emit less greenhouse gases. Cities not only need to grow denser but also *smarter*, fostering compact communities, multiple use buildings, and public transport networks.
- *Support of low-carbon lifestyles.* With rising income and higher individual purchasing power and consumption demands, a low-carbon lifestyle will be a key determinant factor of future energy demand in Chinese cities. Some tools have been developed internationally to engage citizens in understanding their household carbon footprint and taking action to reduce it. Similar partnerships at the city and neighborhood level in China could contribute to less carbon-intensive households.
- *Replacing energy-intensive manufacturing with low energy-intensive economic activities.* Changes in the urban economic base, such as through expanded services, will reduce emissions. However, such strategies need to be considered carefully. For today's industrial centers, simply relocating higher-emission industries outside a city boundary to reduce the carbon footprint of that city would make little (if any) difference on the national scale. But rapidly growing small and medium cities may have the opportunity to leap-frog and bypass the polluting, high-carbon growth paths taken by the earlier generation of Chinese cities.

Source: World Bank 2012.

and horizontally, between different agencies and across jurisdictional boundaries. Urban, transport, and environmental problems are not confined to the jurisdictional boundaries of local governments. The design aspects, costs, and benefits of land use planning, transport networks, and water resources management are not confined to one jurisdiction. Also, competition between local governments to attract business investment and create jobs can discourage coordinated planning on issues such as protecting against floods or preventing urban sprawl. Incentives are needed to encourage smart urban planning and risk management by local and regional government agencies. Transjurisdictional bodies, such as river basin commissions and regional planning boards, should be given more authority. Membership should be expanded to include representatives from multiple line agencies, local governments, and major users of natural resources.

Third, provide greater environmental protection incentives for local governments.

Adjusting the tax structure by establishing stable local revenue sources (such as a property tax, not land sales) is fundamental to more efficient land use. A property tax would also encourage localities to improve the quality of the environment so as to raise property values and thereby increase local tax revenues. The introduction of explicit performance indicators for local governments that support green growth is also key. Higher-level governments could reform the performance and promotion system to reward lower-level officials who place new and specific emphasis on measuring the quality of growth and the sustainability in the use of natural assets. Indicators of "greenness" and quality of growth should carry the same weight as GDP in performance reviews. To make these indicators work, local targets for ecosystem health will be needed, and jurisdictional authority of various agencies responsible for meeting these targets need to be clearly defined by law in anticipation of possible bureaucratic gridlock.

Annex 3A   Sequencing Actions and Confirming Results

The policy areas described in this chapter will have a profound effect on China's pattern of development. The demands on government to correct years of market failures and price distortions are enormous. This annex makes some cross-sectoral observations about how to sequence these recommendations, measure results, and confirm that the long-term targets for green development are being achieved. It was prepared by and represents the views of the World Bank team.

Sequencing of Green Development Actions

The concrete actions needed to achieve greener growth in China fall under the broad headings: creating market incentives that alter current behavior and foster technological innovation; using regulation, backed by enforcement, to complement these market incentives; financing public investments in domains where public goods, such as better weather monitoring, will not be provided by the private sector; and reforming and strengthening the local institutions that play a key role in allocating resources and managing environmental quality. While steps in all four of these areas can be taken now, the gains from green growth will follow a natural sequence (figure 3A.1):

- Short-term gains will come from improved economywide efficiencies, to be achieved through efficient pricing (land, water, carbon, and pollution), regulatory reform, and public investment in critical green infrastructure. Early steps should also be taken to tighten standards in areas that will pave the way for technical developments and behavioral change, such as more efficient buildings, transport vehicles, and household appliances.
- Medium-term gains will accrue from innovation and changed behaviors, which will come in response to government reforms to SOEs; targeted R&D in support of

new technologies, goods, and services; infrastructure and information support to green domestic and export markets; and scaled-up public education for all ages to help induce consumer and household behavior changes. The growth impacts of new technologies—in output, employment, and exports—should be measurable and significant by 2020.

- By 2030, important targets in lower-emissions growth, clean energy, air pollution, waste management, and efficient land markets can be met. In addition, risks associated with resource scarcity, climate change, and irreversible biodiversity losses can be managed. However, sustained government intervention will be required in all of these areas, at both the national and local levels, for the simple reason that most environmental gains require government intervention to help internalize

FIGURE 3A.1   Indicative sequencing of green development reforms

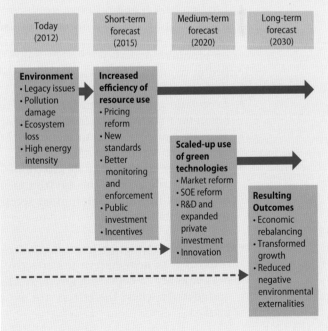

Source: World Bank analysis.

environmental externalities and government monitoring of compliance with standards.

Finally, while the 20-year time frame up to 2030 is sufficient time for some early and important successes—such as in renewable energy, air pollution, and waste management—other challenges will certainly remain, such as ecosystem conservation, water pollution, carbon emissions reduction, and adapting to climate change.

Measuring Progress Toward Green Development

Part of defining, pursuing, and achieving green growth is measuring progress. This point has been recognized both in OECD work on green growth (OECD 2011) and the World Bank's new program to develop a green growth "knowledge platform" to guide its activities in developing countries. For example, the OECD has identified four clusters of appropriate indicators for monitoring progress toward green growth:

- *Environmental and resource productivity,* to capture the need for efficient use of natural capital and to capture aspects of production that are rarely quantified in economic models and accounting frameworks.
- *Economic and environmental assets,* to reflect the risks to growth from a declining asset base and the need to maintain the asset base to sustain growth.
- *Environmental quality of life,* to capture the direct impacts of the environment on people's lives, through limited access to water, for example, or the damaging effects of air pollution.
- *Economic opportunities and policy responses,* to help discern the effectiveness of policy in delivering green growth and identify where the effects are most marked.

Not all of the desired OECD indicators are measurable today, and many countries and agencies are working to establish an optimal set of green development indicators. Although this topic remains a work in progress, the two most important areas for defining indicators are the *quantity* of growth and the *quality* of growth.

For the quantity of growth, in addition to measuring economic output (GDP or GNI), it is also important to measure changes in people's well-being.[16] Two indicators used by the World Bank are adjusted net national income (aNNI), a truer measure of income than GDP or GNI, and the adjusted net savings (ANS).[17]

For the quality of growth, indicators are needed at the sector or even subsector level. At this level, one challenge is to keep the list of indicators to a manageable size. A highly selective but informative set of indicators for the quality of growth includes:

- *Energy productivity:* increasing GDP per unit of energy used is greener because it is a sign of increasing energy efficiency
- *Share of fossil fuels:* decreasing the share of fossil fuel in total energy used increases greenness, as does increasing the share of alternative and nuclear energy
- CO_2 *emissions intensities of total energy and of GDP*
- CO_2 *emissions per capita*

One of the important functions provided by green growth indicator systems is the ability to benchmark performance against international good practice examples. These benchmarked indicators are shown in table 3A.1 and figure 3A.2, with these results:

- In terms of *quantity* of growth, the adjusted income and saving indicators show China's outstanding growth achievements. Over the period 2000–09, the average growth rate of real aNNI per capita in China was roughly ten times that in the OECD; and net wealth creation in 2009 as a share of GNI was seven times higher in China than in the OECD.
- The *quality* of growth indicators shows, however, where progress is needed. China's

TABLE 3A.1   Comparison of specific indicators, China vs. high-income OECD

Indicator	China	OECD	Year	Measure
aNNI % growth rate	5.5	0.6	2009	Growth of real per capita PPP $, 2000–09
ANS % of GNI	37.7	5.5	2009	Share of GNI
Energy productivity	3.77	6.73	2009	Constant 2005 PPP $ GDP per kg oil equiv.
Share of fossil fuels	92.6	82.9	2009	% of total primary energy use
Alternative and nuclear energy production	3.53	13.88	2009	% of total energy use
CO_2 intensity of energy	3.44	2.54	2009	tCO_2 per t oil equivalent
CO_2 intensity of GDP	0.91	0.38	2009	kg CO_2 per 2005 PPP $ GDP
CO_2 emissions per capita	5.67	10.36	2009	tCO_2 per capita

Sources: World Bank, based on World Bank World Development Indicators; BP (2011); and U.S. EIA database.
Note: aNNI = adjusted net national income; ANS = adjusted net savings; tCO_2 = tons of carbon dioxide.

FIGURE 3A.2 CO_2 emissions per capita and per unit of GDP, 1990–2009

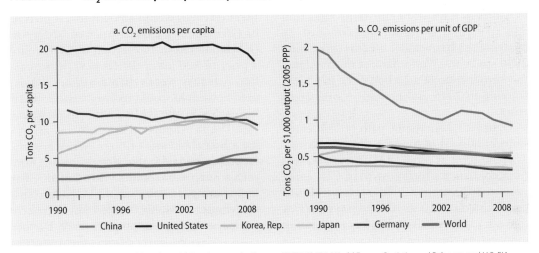

Sources: World Bank, based on World Bank World Development Indicators; BP (2011); IEA, World Energy Statistics and Balances; and U.S. EIA, International Energy Statistics.

energy productivity is half that of OECD countries; its fossil fuel share of energy is 10 percent higher than in OECD countries; its share of renewable and nuclear energy production is only one-quarter that of OECD countries, and its CO_2 intensity of GDP is more than twice that of OECD countries. (On a per capita basis, however, OECD countries emit 80 percent more CO_2 per capita as China.)

As China transforms its economy toward high-income status, both benchmarks and targets will be useful in measuring progress toward greening growth. For example, specific targets could be set, such as the share of

renewable energy, the declining share of coal in total energy use, the declining level of average urban air pollution; and the increasing value of water productivity. Chinese targets, based on international benchmarks, could include:

- An OECD benchmark of energy productivity that nearly doubles between 2010 and 2030
- The EU target of reaching a 20 percent share in renewable energy by 2020 and 30 percent by 2030;
- The Japanese air quality level of 25 micrograms per cubic meter ($\mu g/m^3$) in annual average PM_{10} concentrations

- A water productivity target of reaching best practice in OECD countries
- CO_2 emissions intensity falling by 60–65 percent between 2010 and 2030

As is the case in OECD countries, green growth indicators and future targets are a work in progress in China, but an important step to be taken in implementing a green growth strategy.

The Potential Impact of a Carbon Price

Carbon pricing, whether achieved through trading or taxation, would influence such variables as the cost of emissions reduction and structural shifts in the economy. By applying the base model used in this China 2030 study, the World Bank team simulated the introduction of a carbon price in China, starting in 2015 and phased in over eight years.

Figure A3.3 shows the path of CO_2 emissions in billions of tons for three scenarios. The "business as usual (BAU)" scenario features continued strong growth in CO_2 emissions to 2030, from 7.2 billion tons (5.4 tons per capita) in 2010 to 10.9 billion tons (7.6 tons per capita) in 2030. The key moderating influence on emissions in this scenario is the

decline in GDP growth rates in 2025–30. In contrast, the scenario in which a CO_2 price of $10 a ton is gradually phased in over eight years beginning in 2023 produces substantial reductions and flattens the upward growth in China's emissions, resulting in total CO_2 emissions of 9.2 billion tons (6.4 tons per capita) in 2030. And a CO_2 price of $20 a ton produces an even greater effect, with China's absolute emissions peaking by 2020 and then dropping down to 8.4 billion tons (5.8 tons per capita) in 2030—a total level about 17 percent higher than in 2010.

Carbon revenues in China could be significant in macroeconomic terms. By 2030, fiscal revenues would amount to 1.4 percent of GDP under a carbon price of $10 a ton (RMB 64) and to 2.7 percent of GDP under a price of $20 a ton (RMB 129). If the carbon revenues were rebated to households, each household would receive between RMB 2,126 ($329) and RMB 2,097 ($634) a year by 2030, depending on the price and assuming a household size of three. While government has considerable discretion on how such a lump sum could be distributed, a flat lump sum per capita would be progressive by definition, helping to offset any regressive tendencies of the carbon price itself. Further notes on lessons learned from other countries on selecting and implementing climate policy instruments are given in box 3A.1.

Although the simulated carbon price rates used in this analysis are too low to significantly affect the structure of the Chinese economy in 2030, they have a clear impact on the amount of coal the country would consume (figure 3A.4). In the $10 price scenario, China uses 492 million tons less coal compared with business as usual in 2030 (a difference of 15 percent). Under the $20 price scenario, coal use drops by 770 million tons compared with business as usual (a difference of 23 percent). *Both* scenarios result in a peak in China's coal use before 2020. This decline is driven largely by a shift in the relative prices of different fuels for electricity generation. The market share of coal-fired electricity in the power sector (in terms of the

FIGURE 3A.3   China's annual CO_2 emissions under three scenarios, 2010–30

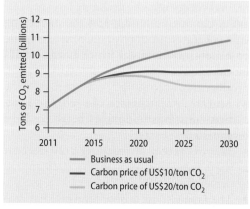

Source: World Bank analysis.

BOX 3A.1 Lessons from international experience on climate policy instruments

The *World Development Report 2010* on climate change outlines the issues concerning instrument choice for reducing carbon emissions. Permit systems give certainty on emission reductions but uncertainty about price. Taxes are the opposite—they give certainty on price, but uncertainty about emission reductions. Because price volatility is more of an issue with permits than taxes, investment in R&D for new technologies (especially without government support) may be depressed with permits. Revenue generation is possible under both regimes, although the administrative efficiency of the instruments differs considerably. Taxes can be integrated with fuel excise systems, requiring little additional monitoring effort. Permit systems require new regulatory institutions as well as monitoring and enforcement systems to ensure compliance.

The International Energy Agency recently reviewed existing and proposed carbon trading schemes in Alberta, Australia, the European Union, New Zealand, Switzerland, Tokyo, and the United States (both national and state-level schemes). Some of the key conclusions are:

- *Targets*. Ambitious long-run targets are needed if firms are to invest in lowering their carbon footprints.
- *Allocation*. Countries tend to allocate permits free of charge or to rebate costs to sectors heavily affected by taxes, since doing so eases the transi-

tion to a lower-carbon investment. It does, however, lead to some windfall profits and also delays adjustments by firms. The European emissions trading scheme is phasing out the free allocation of permits.
- *Start-up*. Trading schemes have tended to overallocate in the initial phase, leading to a price collapse. Allowing permits to be banked can overcome the price problem but also carries forward the surplus permits into the next phase. Other options include establishing a price floor with cancellation of any unsold permits or using a fixed price in the initial phase, which would aid in the collection of emissions and cost data to better guide subsequent phases.
- *Support to carbon-intensive sectors*. Concerns about potential competitive impacts on carbon-intensive sectors will lead to lobbying for financial support to these sectors. Any support should be time limited, and communicated as such, to reduce fiscal costs and provide incentives for firms to invest in less-polluting technologies.

In practice, many jurisdictions have opted for hybrid schemes, using tradable permits for the big emitting sectors and taxes for smaller sectors characterized by many actors, such as transport. Environmental taxes and levies are used in all OECD countries, raising revenues totaling 2.0–2.5 percent of GDP.

Sources: World Bank 2010; Hood 2010; OECD 2008.

portion of coal-fired power in total real output by the sector) drops 6 percent and 11 percent by 2030 in the $10 and $20 carbon price scenarios, respectively. This drop is made up for mainly by an increase in output volume for hydropower.

These results actually underestimate the benefits of the simulated carbon price, because they do not include the co-benefits for human health and crops that come from reducing fossil fuel use. One important study (Aunan and others 2007) shows that the cost to households of imposing a carbon tax of

RMB 290 a ton of CO_2 ($43 in 2007 dollars) generates the same amount of economic co-benefits associated with reduced air pollution, improved health, and increased crop production. According to this analysis, the co-benefits in China associated with reducing carbon emissions and recycling carbon tax revenues are substantial.

Sectoral Considerations

Fully pursued, green development will pervade all sectors of the economy, ranging from

FIGURE 3A.4   Coal consumption trends for China under three scenarios, 2011–30

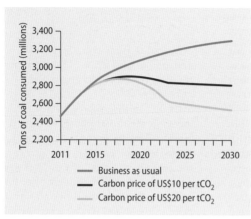

Source: World Bank analysis.

industry and energy to the management of cities, water resources, agriculture, forestry, and biodiversity resources. Background papers prepared for this report include sector-specific studies of the issues involved in achieving green development targets by 2030.[18]

Each sector-specific paper follows a similar structure; it first sets out a vision for China 2030 consistent with its status as a high-income country, and then analyzes the issues surrounding the implementation of that vision. While each sector is very different in its challenges and targets, the recommended actions fall into the various policy packages introduced in this chapter. Table 3A.2 summarizes the key findings of these seven sectoral background papers.

TABLE 3A.2   Sector-specific recommendations for achieving green growth in China

Today's challenges	Short-term targets and policies	Medium-term targets and policies	Long-term goals (by 2030)
Energy	Seek cost-effective, market-based solutions using existing technologies	Scale up and accelerate innovation	Develop a sustainable, efficient, and competitive energy sector
	Reduce energy sector subsidies and introduce market pricing	Scale up renewable energy in a competitive market	A greener energy mix in which renewable energy meets 30 percent of primary energy demand
	Invest in improving performance and reducing cost of existing renewable energy technologies	Cap fossil fuel consumption and deploy carbon capture and sequestration on a large scale	Carbon emissions peak and decline
	Amend energy legislation and create a more effective regulatory body	Implement carbon cap and trade	Chinese energy companies are world-class businesses, operating in an open, competitive market
	Continue to focus on reducing energy intensity and improving efficiency		A sound, fully functioning public regulator separate from the government focused on making policy
			China is the global leader in clean energy technologies and innovation
Water	Use directives and market-based approaches to control water use by main sectors	Deepen resource governance reforms; ensure clean water supplies and sanitation	Achieve efficient, balanced, and sustainable use of water resources
	Introduce consumption-based water allocation rights and fees for agriculture and industry	Expand water allocation right and fee programs to other major basins and industrial sectors	All major water users are covered by consumption-based allocation system
	Launch national rural sanitation program	Ensure safe drinking water from the tap for large cities and improved sanitation for all rural people	Safe drinking water for all urban residents
	Expand membership in a major river basin commission to include a wider range of water users	60 percent of China's surface waters meet standards for Grades I–III	70 percent of China's surface waters meet standards for Grades I–III

TABLE 3A.2 **Sector-specific recommendations for achieving green growth in China** *Continued*

Today's challenges	Short-term targets and policies	Medium-term targets and policies	Long-term goals (by 2030)
	Double efficiency of water use and achieve 50 percent reuse rate in industry by 2015	Expand river basin commission membership for all major rivers; new financial mechanisms such as flood insurance	Water use efficiency reaches current high-income country average
	Expand payment for ecosystem services	Water use efficiency doubles again	
Cities	**Pilot new regulations, policies, and financing mechanisms to alter current growth patterns**	**Scale up coordinated policies for land use planning, urban finance, and urban governance**	**Create efficient, livable, and sustainable cities**
	Pilot new performance indicators for local officials	Roll out green growth performance indicators for local officials across the country	Urban in-fill and higher density without spatial expansion
	Introduce new financing mechanisms to support green growth and steer cities away from land sales	Expand fiscal support tools	Livability achieved through connectivity, strategic development corridors, and efficient transport options
	Pilot a flexible land conversion quota and reallocation mechanism	Create functioning urban and peri-urban land markets in several municipalities	National integration of markets of goods, capital, and labor
	Change regulations and standards leading to inefficient land use	Coordinate all new development and mass transit plans with urban land use zoning regulations	Low-carbon status through overall resource use efficiency, bench-marked internationally
	Roll out market-based mechanisms to encourage efficient resource use		
Ecosystems	**Identify and implement immediate actions needed to restore ecosystem health**	**Bring all major ecosystems under sound management and significantly reduce the costs of ecosystem degradation**	**Halt biodiversity loss and the degradation of ecosystems**
	Introduce targets for all natural resource management (NRM) sectors based on measures of ecosystem health	Ecosystem health targets for NRM fully incorporated and given equal weight as production targets	Integrated ecosystem landscape-scale planning with full cost and valuation data
	New incentives introduced for restoration of degraded ecosystems and ecosystem services, providing rural employment	All KBAs are well-managed components of the national protected area (PA) system	Perverse environmental subsidies are eliminated
	Key biodiversity areas (KBAs) are designated and actions taken to begin management of these areas	Agrochemical and fertilizer use is halved	Biodiversity loss is halted
	Agricultural production targets reoriented and remediation measures taken to restore agricultural system health	Remediation actions started for farmland that is most contaminated with heavy metals	Land degradation is halted
	Inspection capacity is doubled and penalties are increased for illegal import or sale of native or imported wild products	Invasive species costs and illegal product trade are both halved	Health of major ecosystems is restored
	Urgent actions needed to protect forest health are identified and implemented in remaining natural forests		Efficient and effective national-level PA system is in place

(Table continued next page)

TABLE 3A.2   Sector-specific recommendations for achieving green growth in China   *Continued*

Today's challenges	Short-term targets and policies	Medium-term targets and policies	Long-term goals (by 2030)
Agriculture	**Remove market distortions**	**Create a competitive agricultural market focused on high-value products**	**Develop modern, commercial smallholder agriculture**
	Reforms in support of rural land rental markets	Land consolidation through improved rental markets and supporting institutions	Fully functioning land markets
	Limit growth of agricultural subsidies (even if WTO-compliant)	Expand extension services to better manage climate change risks	Measurable share of low-carbon agriculture
	Reform extension services	Scale up pilot schemes for input-saving technologies	Complete coverage of low-water technologies in water-scarce areas
	Reform producer cooperatives	Strengthen producer cooperatives in supply chain for high-value agricultural products	
Air pollution and waste	**Invest in systems to control the most damaging forms of pollution and waste**	**Bring pollution to within safe limits for people and ecosystems**	**Complete coverage and attainment of pollution targets**
	Agree on standards for $PM_{2.5}$	Achieve Class I targets for $PM_{2.5}$ in major cities	Achieve Class I targets for $PM_{2.5}$ for all cities
	Phase out inefficient waste disposal methods, pilot new methods	Pilot air quality management plans in major cities	Complete implementation of air quality management plans
	Pilot incentives for efficient waste utilization	All new landfills meet international standards; incineration of municipal waste reaches 10 percent	High-tech monitoring of waste stream and utilization
		Scale up waste utilization initiatives	
Adapting to climate change	**Improved information and understanding of climate risks**	**Mainstream climate risks into development policies**	**Develop an economy that is resilient to climate change impacts and uncertainties**
	Invest in weather information and warning systems	Update and enforce building codes	Fully functioning risk management and recovery mechanisms
	Make information on hazards accessible	Introduce financing frameworks for catastrophic risks	
	Identify cost-effective adaptation measures	Expand social services and support networks in vulnerable rural areas	

Notes

1. To date, no standard definition of green development has emerged from the public and policy debate (Huberty, Gao, and Mandell 2011).
2. See the other chapters and reports prepared as part of this China 2030 study, particularly the synthesis report.
3. Acemoglu and others (2012) found that government interventions to redirect investments toward green technologies would have a short-term cost but that long-term "green growth" rates would catch up to "non-green growth" rates. Growth would be unaffected overall. If immediate action is taken, then the catch-up period will be shorter. If action is delayed, the costs of intervention will be greater, and the catch-up period will be longer.
4. Differences in energy intensity are attributable to such things as output mix and relative prices as well as to energy efficiency. Nevertheless, the opportunity for further declines in China's energy efficiency is clear.

5. These estimates of cost savings are drawn from detailed work done by McKinsey & Company (2009) on technologies for CO_2 abatement in China. The McKinsey cost estimates are often considered an upper bound on the annual cost savings to be achieved, because, while they include potential technological gains, they do not include all transaction costs associated with implementing those technological gains.

6. At the same time, not all jobs produced by green investments are a priori "good jobs which offer adequate wages, safe working conditions, job security, reasonable career prospects, and worker rights" (UNEP and others 2008, p. 4). The creation of new employment opportunities through green investments may not improve the plight of informal workers in such industries as construction, waste removal, and recycling. The effect of green growth on work conditions across industries is also as yet unclear. Green growth is not a substitute for effective social protection and investments in human capital.

7. Of course, if reductions in China's manufacturing sector are offset by increased output in other countries, the rebalancing would have negligible effects on *global* emissions even as China's emissions intensity would decrease.

8. These costs are typically measured by valuing a country's environmental externalities, or the external costs associated with resource degradation (including pollution-related health damages, property damages, and global impacts) and resource depletion (soil erosion, deforestation, fisheries loss, biodiversity loss, water pollution, and watershed degradation).

9. It is recognized that figure 3.10 compares countries at different levels of development. That said, the figure is intended to illustrate the level of potential improvement that China may achieve as it rises to high-income status (for details, see table 3.1).

10. Grade V is defined as water suitable only for agricultural water supply and general landscaping use, and Grade V+ is water unsuitable for any use (NBS 2011a; MEP 2012; and MEP and AQSIS 2002).

11. The national average of 1,812 cubic meters of freshwater resources available for every person in China is only one-quarter of the world average.

12. This is a rough estimate; because of a lack of additonal publicly available information on China's national accounts, it may be an underestimate of China's expenditures.

13. Given the country's importance as a carbon emitter, green (low-carbon) development will reduce emissions, reduce the magnitude of climate change, and reduce the need for China to adapt.

14. China's Ministry of Agriculture (MOA 2007) estimates that 90 percent of the country's grasslands are degraded, about one-third of them seriously so.

15. These industries include power generation, iron and steel, nonferrous metals, chemicals, petroleum, and building materials.

16. The United Nation's work on a system of environmental and economic accounts (SEEA), building on the system of national accounts, is one such initiative to measure the change in social welfare as a measure of progress toward green growth. The World Bank's work on comprehensive wealth accounting (World Bank 2006, 2011) is a complementary initiative.

17. Adjusted net national income accounts for both the depreciation of produced capital and the depletion of natural resources such as forests, minerals, and fossil fuels. The growth rate of real aNNI is proportional to the change in social welfare, and so the sign of this growth rate indicates whether the economy is on a sustainable path. Higher levels of aNNI mean that a country is using its natural resources more efficiently. Adjusted net savings is a measure of net wealth creation that measures the depreciation of fixed capital, the depletion of natural capital, investments in human capital, and health damages from pollution. Positive savings represent an improvement in social welfare, while negative savings indicate a decline, implying that an economy is on an unsustainable path.

18. The seven sectoral background papers covered are Energy, Urbanization, Water Resources, Pollution and Waste, Agriculture, Natural Resource Management, and Adapting to a Changing Climate. They are available on-line.

References

Acemoglu, D., and others. 2012. "The Environment and Directed Technical Change." *American Economic Review* 102 (1): 131–66.

Aunan, K., and others. 2007. "Benefits and Costs to China of a Climate Policy." *Environment and Development Economics* 12: 471–97.

Bennett, M. 2009. "Markets for Ecosystem Services in China: An Exploration of China's 'Eco-Compensation' and Other Market-Based Environmental Policies." Forest Trends report. http://www.forest-trends.org/documents/files/doc_2317.pdf.

Boden, T. A., G. Marland, and R. J. Andres. 2010. "Global, Regional, and National Fossil-Fuel CO_2 Emissions." Carbon Dioxide Information Analysis Center, Oak Ridge National Laboratory, U.S. Department of Energy, Oak Ridge, Tenn. doi 10.3334/CDIAC/00001_V2010.

BP (British Petroleum). 2011. "BP Statistical Review of World Energy." http://www.bp.com/statisticalreview.

Cao, J. 2011. "Is Fuel Taxation Progressive or Regressive in China?" In *Fuel Taxes and the Poor: The Distributional Effects of Gasoline and Their Implications for Climate Policy*, ed. T. Sterner. Washington, DC: RFF Press.

Cao, J., M. S. Ho, and D. Jorgenson. 2009. "The Local and Global Benefits of Green Tax Policies in China." *Review of Environmental Economics and Policy* 3 (2): 189–208.

CCICED (China Council for International Cooperation on Environment and Development). 2011. "Development Mechanism and Policy Innovation of China's Green Economy." CCICED Task Force Report, CCICED Annual General Meeting, November 15–17.

Chang, D. H., and others. 2010. "Adjusting the Scope of China's Environmental Protection Investment Accounts" (我国环境保护投资统计口径调整方案研究). *Environmental Economy* (环境经济) 79: 34–39.

China Greentech Initiative. 2011. "The China Greentech Report: China's Emergence as a Global Market Leader." http://www.china-greentech.com/report.

China Water Resources. 2009. "Scientific Measurement of Irrigation Efficiency Rates Provides Policy Support for Developing Efficient Irrigation" (科学测算灌溉用水有效利用系数, 为发展节水灌溉提供决策依据). *China Water Resources* (中国水利) 3: 4–5.

Cohen, A. J., and others. 2004. "Urban Air Pollution." In *Comparative Quantification of Health Risks: Global and Regional Burden of Disease due to Selected Major Risk Factors*, eds. M. Ezzati and others, vol 2. Geneva: World Health Organization.

Di, P. M., and others. 2007. "A Survey of the Research on Changes in Extreme Precipitation Events" (极端降水事件变化的观测研究), *Advances in Climate Change Research* (气候变化研究进展) 3 (3): 144–48.

Diamond, P. A., and H. Vartiainen, eds. 2007. *Behavioral Economics and Its Applications*. Princeton: Princeton University Press.

DRC (Development Research Center of the State Council, China). 2009. "Greenhouse Gas Emissions Reduction: A Theoretical Framework and Global Solution." In *China's New Place in a World in Crisis: Economic, Geopolitical and Environmental Dimensions*, eds. Ross Garnaut, Ligang Song, and Wing Thye Woo, 389–408. Washington, DC: Australian National University E-Press, and Brookings Institution Press.

DRC Project Team. 2011. "CO_2 Emission Account: Governance Framework in Response to Climate Change and Green Growth" (二氧化碳国别排放账户：应对气候变化和实现绿色增长的治理框架). *Economic Research* (经济研究) 46 (12): 4–17, 31.

Dupressoir, S., and others. 2007. "Climate Change and Employment: Impact on Employment in the European Union-25 of Climate Change and CO_2 Emission Reduction Measures by 2030." European Trade Union Confederation, Brussels.

EC (European Commission). 2002. SERIEE: European System for the Collection of Economic Information on the Environment—1994 version (updated). KS-BE-02-002-EN-N.

Eurostat. Environment Statistics database. http://epp.eurostat.ec.europa.eu/portal/page/ portal/environment/ introduction.

———. 2010. Environmental Statistics and Accounts on Europe. http://epp.eurostat.ec.europa.eu/cache/ ITY_OFFPUB/KS-32-10-283/EN/KS-32-10-283-EN.PDF.

Feng, F., and J. Wang. 2011. "Focusing on New Developments in Wind and Solar Power" (注风电和太阳能发电领域的新变化). Survey Report 88, Development Research Center of the State Council, China (国务院发展研究中心调研报告《择要》第88号), Beijing.

Feng, F., and others. 2011. "China's Low Carbon Industrial Development Strategy." Report to the China Council for International Cooperation on Environment and Development (CCICED). CCICED 2011 Annual General Meeting, Beijing, November 15–17. http://www.cciced.net/encciced/policyresearch

/report/.(中国国际环境发展合作委员会委托课题报告).

Fridley, D., and others. 2011. "China Energy and Emissions Pathways to 2030." Paper LBNL-4866E, Lawrence Berkeley National Laboratory, Berkeley, CA.

Gao, H., and J. C. Fan. 2010. *Techno-Economic Evaluation of China's Renewable Energy Power Technologies and Development Targets* (中国可再生能源发电经济性和经济总量). Beijing: China Environment Press.

Global Water Intelligence. 2008. "Global Water Market 2008: Opportunities in Scarcity and Environmental Regulation." http://www.globalwaterintel.com.

Golley, J., D. Meagher, and X. Ming. 2008. "Chinese Urban Household Energy Requirements and CO_2 Emissions." In *China's Dilemma: Economic Growth, Development and Climate Change*, eds. L. Song and W. T. Woo. Washington, DC: Brookings Institution Press.

Guy Carpenter & Co., Ltd. 2006. "Typhoon Saomai: Impact and Historical Comparison." London.

Haščič, I., and others. 2010. "Climate Policy and Technological Innovation and Transfer: An Overview of Trends and Recent Empirical Results." OECD Environment Working Papers 30. OECD, Paris. doi: 10.1787/5km33bnggcd0-en.

Ho, M. S., and D. Jorgenson. 2003. "Air Pollution in China: Sector Allocation of Emissions and Health Damage." http://people.hmdc.harvard.edu/~mho/CCICED.report1.pdf.

Hood, C. 2010. "Reviewing Existing and Proposed Emissions Trading Schemes." IEA Information Paper, OECD/IEA, Paris.

Huang, Y. P. 2010. "Dissecting the China Puzzle: Asymmetric Liberalization and Cost Distortion." *Asian Economic Policy Review* 5: 281–95.

Huberty, M., H. Gao, and J. Mandell. 2011. "Shaping the Green Growth Economy: A Review of the Public Debate and the Prospects for Green Growth." Berkeley Roundtable on the International Economy, Berkeley, CA.

IEA (International Energy Agency). World Energy Statistics and Balances. Database. DOI 10.1787/data-00510-en.

———. 2010a. *Energy Technology Perspectives 2010: Strategies and Scenarios to 2050*. Paris: OECD.

———. 2010b. *World Energy Outlook 2010*. Paris: OECD.

———. 2011a. CO_2 *Emissions from Fuel Combustion*. Paris: OECD.

———. 2011b. *World Energy Outlook 2011*. Paris: OECD.

ILO (International Labour Organization). 2009. *World of Work Report 2009: The Global Jobs Crisis and Beyond*. Geneva: ILO.

———. 2011. "Promoting Decent Work in a Green Economy." ILO Background Note to "Towards a Green Economy: Pathways to Sustainable Development." http://www.ilo.org/wcmsp5/groups/public/@ed_emp/@emp_ent/documents/ publication/wcms_152065.pdf.

Jaeger, C. C., and others. 2011. "A New Growth Path for Europe. Generating Prosperity and Jobs in the Low-Carbon Economy." Synthesis Report for the German Federal Ministry for the Environment, Nature Conservation and Nuclear Safety, Potsdam, Germany. http://www.stakeholderforum.org/fileadmin/files/A_New_Growth_Path_for_Europe__Synthesis_Report%20%281%29.pdf.

Japan Ministry of Environment. 1989. "Quality of the Environment in Japan." http://www.env.go.jp/ en/wpaper/index.html.

Kawasaki Air Pollution Monitoring Center. "Air Pollution Monitoring Data." http://www.city.kawasaki.jp/30/ 30kansic/home/en/e_index.htm.

Kobayashi, Hikaru. 2011. "Basics of Eco-Business: Mutually Supportive Relationship between the Environment and the Economy." Paper presented at the Third International Forum for Sustainable Asia and the Pacific, Institute for Global Environmental Strategies, Yokohama, July 26–27.

Lan, X. Z. 2011. "China Drafts Plan for Development of Environmental Protection Industries over the Next Five Years" (中国制定未来五年节能环保产业发展规划). *Beijing Review* (北京周报), August 29. http://www.beijingreview.com.cn/2009news/guonei/huanbao/2011-08/29/content_386752.htm.

Li, H. 2011. *Equity, Efficiency, and Sustainable Development: China's Energy Subsidy Reform Theory and Policy Practice* (公平、效率与可持续发展：中国能源补贴改革理论与政策实践). Beijing: China Economics Press.

Li, J. F., and others. 2011. *Limitless Winds: China Wind Power Outlook 2011* (风光无限——中国风电发展报告2011). Beijing: China Environmental Sciences Press.

Liu, S. J., and others. 2011. *Trap or High Wall? Real Challenges the Chinese Economy Faces and Its Strategic Choice* (陷阱还是高墙？中国经济面临的真实挑战和战略选择). Beijing: China Citic Press.

Liu, X. L., and S. Y. Wang. 2011. "2011 Forecast of CO₂ Emissions from Primary Energy Consumption by Sector for China" (2011年我国分行业一次能源消费产生的二氧化碳排放量预测). *Science & Technology for Development* (科技促进发展) 1: 22–33.

Liu, Y. Z., and J. He. 2011. "Slowing Economic Growth in the East and Shrinking Regional Disparities: Short-Term Fluctuations or Long-Term Trends" (地区经济增长格局的变动与区域差距的缩小：短期波动抑或长期趋势). Working Paper, Development Research Center of the State Council, China, Beijing.

Martinez-Fernandez, C., and others. 2010. "Green Jobs and Skills: The Local Labor Market Implications of Addressing Climate Change." Working document, Center for Entrepreneurship and Local Economic and Employment Development Forum, OECD, Paris. http://www.oecd.org/dataoecd/54/43/44683169.pdf?contentId=44683170.

Matus, Kira, and others. 2011. "Health Damages from Air Pollution in China." Report 196, MIT Joint Program on the Science and Policy of Global Change, Cambridge, MA (March).

McGranahan, G., D. Balk, and B. Anderson. 2007. "The Rising Tide: Assessing the Risks of Climate Change and Human Settlements in Low Elevation Coastal Zones." *Environment & Urbanization* 19 (1): 17–37.

McKinsey & Company. 2009. "China's Green Revolution: Prioritizing Technologies to Achieve Energy and Environmental Sustainability." http://www.mckinsey.com/locations/greaterchina/mckonchina/reports/china_green_revolution.aspx.

MEP (Ministry of Environmental Protection, PRC). 2012. *2011 China State of the Environment Report* (2011年中国环境状况公报). Beijing. http://jcs.mep.gov.cn/hjzl/zkgb/.

MEP and AQSIS (General Administration of Quality Supervision, Inspection, and Quartine). "Environmental Quality Standards for Surface Water" (地表水环境质量标准). GB 3838-2002, issued April 28 2002, effective June 1, 2002. http://www.nthb.cn/standard/standard02/20030428174340.html.

MEP and CAE (Chinese Academy of Engineering). 2011. *Macro-Strategy for China's Environment: Strategy for Protection of China's Environmental Factors* (in Chinese), 2 vols. Beijing: China Environmental Sciences Press.

MEP and NBS (National Bureau of Statistics, China). 2010. *China Statistical Yearbook of the Environment.* Beijing: China Statistics Press.

MOA (Ministry of Agriculture, China). 2007. "National Grassland Monitoring Report" (in Chinese). Beijing. http://www.gov.cn/gzdt/2008-04/11/content_942549.htm.

MOF (Ministry of Finance, China). 2009. "2008 National Fiscal Revenues and Expenditures." Beijing. http://yss.mof.gov.cn/zhengwuxinxi/caizhengshuju/200907/t20090707_176723.html.

Muro, M., and others. 2011. "Seizing the Clean Economy: A National and Regional Green Jobs Assessment." Metropolitan Policy Program study, Brookings Institution, Washington, DC. http://www.brookings.edu/~/media/Files/Programs/Metro/clean_economy/0713_clean_economy.pdf.

NARCC (National Assessment Report on Climate Change Committee). 2007. *National Assessment Report on Climate Change* (气候变化国家评估报告). Beijing: Sciences Press.

———. 2011. *Second National Assessment Report on Climate Change* (第二次气候变化国家评估报告). Beijing: Sciences Press.

NBS (National Bureau of Statistics, China). 2000–2011a. *China Statistical Yearbook* (中国统计年鉴). Beijing: China Statistics Press.

———. 2009–2010b. *China Energy Statistical Yearbook* (中国能源统计年鉴). Beijing: China Statistics Press.

NDRC (National Development and Reform Commission) Bureau of Energy, NDRC Energy Research Institute, China Association of Resource Comprehensive Utilization Expert Committee, and China Renewable Energy Industry Work Committee. 2007. *China Renewable Energy Industry Development Report (2006)* (中国可再生能源产业发展报告[2006]). http://www.efchina.org/csepupfiles/report/200762245840354.3728109999679.pdf/China%20RE%20Industry%20Development%20Report_070330%20CN.pdf.

Nelson, G. C., L. M. Ye, and D. M. d'Croz. Forthcoming. "Chinese Food Security and Climate Change: Agriculture Futures." Discussion Paper, World Bank, Washington, DC.

NIES (National Institute for Environmental Studies, Japan). Monthly air quality database. http://www.nies.go.jp/igreen/td_down.html.

OECD (Organisation for Economic Co-operation and Development). 2008. OECD Environmental Data Compendium 2006/2007, Paris.

———. 2010. "Climate Policy and Technological Innovation and Transfer: An Overview of Trends and Recent Empirical Results." Working Party on Global and Structural Policies report ENV/EPOC/GSP(2010)10/FINAL, OECD Environment Directorate, Environment Policy Committee, Paris.

———. 2011. *Towards Green Growth*. OECD Green Growth Studies. Paris: OECD.

Pew (Pew Charitable Trusts). 2010. "Who's Winning the Clean Energy Race? Growth, Competition, and Opportunity in the World's Largest Economies." G-20 Clean Energy Factbook. http://www.pewtrusts.org/uploadedFiles/wwwpewtrustsorg/Reports/Global_warming/G-20%20Report.pdf.

Ren, G.Y., and others. 2008. "Overall Analysis of the Impacts of Climate Change on China's Water Resources" (气候变化对中国水资源情势影响综合分析). *Advances in Water Science* (水科学进展) 19 (6): 772–79.

SERC (State Electricity Regulatory Commission). 2011. "Monitoring Report on Wind and Solar Power" (风电、光伏发电情况监管报告). http://www.serc.gov.cn/zwgk/jggg/201102/W020110211528940195724.pdf.

SFA (State Forestry Administration, China). 2010. "2009 Report on the Development of Forestry in China." http://www.forestry.gov.cn/portal/main/s/62/content-437412.html.

Shi, M. J., and G. X. Ma. 2009. *The Real Price of China's Economic Growth—An Empirical Study of Genuine Savings* (中国经济增长的资源环境代价——关于绿色国民储蓄的实证分析). Beijing: China Sciences Press.

Shi, X. 2008. "Can China's Coal Industry Be Reconciled with the Environment?" In *China's Dilemma: Economic Growth, the Environment and Climate Change*, eds. L. Song and W. Woo. Washington, DC: Australian National University ePress and Brookings Institution Press.

State Council, PRC. 2011. "State Council Notice on the Work Program to Limit Greenhouse Gas Emissions during the 12th Five Year Plan" (国务院关于印发"十二五"控制温室气体排放工作方案的通知). State Council Directive 41 (December 1). http://www.gov.cn/zwgk/2012-01/13/content_2043645.htm.

State Grid (State Grid Corporation of China). 2010. "Green Development White Paper" (绿色发展白皮书). April 19, 2010. http://www.sgcc.com.cn/bps/_lsfzbps_/index.shtml.

UNEP (United Nations Environmental Programme). 2011a. "Bridging the Emissions Gap." Nairobi, Kenya: UNEP. http://www.unep.org/pdf/UNEP_bridging_gap.pdf.

———. 2011b. "Towards a Green Economy: Pathways to Sustainable Development and Poverty Reduction." http://www.unep.org/greeneconomy.

UNEP and others. 2008. "Green Jobs: Towards Decent Work in a Sustainable, Low-Carbon, World." Washington, DC: Worldwatch Institute. http://www.unep.org/labour_environment/features/greenjobs.asp.

UNIDO (United Nations Industrial Development Organization). INDSTAT. http://data.un.org.

UN Population Division. 2009. *World Urbanization Prospects: The 2009 Revision*. http://esa.un.org/unpd/wup/ index.htm.

——— 2011. *World Population Prospects: The 2010 Revision*. http://esa.un.org/unpd/wpp/index.htm.

U.S. DOE (Department of Energy, United States). 2010. "2008 Solar Technologies Report." Washington, DC. http://www1.eere.energy.gov/solar/pdfs/46025.pdf.

U.S. EIA (Energy Information Administration, United States). International Energy Statistics database. http://www.eia.gov/countries/data.cfm.

———. 2011. *International Energy Outlook 2011*. Washington, DC. http://205.254.135.7/forecasts/ieo/pdf/0484(2011).pdf.

U.S. EPA (Environmental Protection Agency, United States). 2011. "The Benefits and Costs of the Clean Air Act from 1990 to 2020." Washington, DC. http://www.epa.gov/air/sect812/prospective2.html.

Wang J. X., and others 2008. "Can China Continue Feeding Itself?" Policy Research Working Paper 4470, World Bank, Washington, DC. http://www-wds.worldbank.org/external/default/WDSContentServer/WDSP/IB/2008/03/03/000158349_20080303090028/Rendered/PDF/wps4470.pdf.

———. 2010. "Climate Change and China's Agricultural Sector: An Overview of Impacts, Adaptation and Mitigation." International Centre for Trade and Sustainable Development and International Food and Agricultural Trade Policy Council Issue Brief 5. Geneva and Washington, DC. http://www.agritrade.

org/events/documents/ClimateChangeChina _final_web.pdf.

Wang, X., and others. 2010. "How Have China's Environmental Protection Investment Statistics Become Inaccurate?" (环保投资统计为何失实?). *Environmental Protection* (环境保) 17: 35–37.

Woetzel, J., and others. 2009. "From Bread Basket to Dust Bowl? Assessing the Economic Impact of Tackling Drought in North and Northeast China." McKinsey & Company. http://www. mckinsey.com/locations/chinatraditional /From_Bread_Basket_Dust_Bowl_EN.pdf.

World Bank. World Development Indicators database. http://data.worldbank.org/data-catalog /world-development-indicators.

———. 2006. *Where Is the Wealth of Nations? Measuring Capital for the 21st Century.* Washington, DC: World Bank.

———. 2007. *Cost of Pollution in China: Economic Estimates of Physical Damages.* Washington, DC: World Bank.

———. 2008. *Climate Resilient Cities: A Primer.* Washington, DC: World Bank.

———. 2010. *World Development Report 2010: Development and Climate Change.* Washington, DC: World Bank.

———. 2011. *The Changing Wealth of Nations: Measuring Sustainable Development in the New Millennium.* Washington, DC: World Bank.

———. 2012. *Sustainable Low-Carbon City Development in China.* Washington, DC: World Bank.

WRI (World Resources Institute). Climate Analysis Indicators Tool (CAIT), version 8.0. http:// cait.wri.org/.

Wu, S. Z., and others. 2007. "Analysis of the Distortion of China's Environmental Protection Investments, and Some Recommendations" (中国环境保护投资失真问题分析与建议). *China Population, Resources, and Environment* (中国人口、资源与环境) 17 (3): 112–17.

Yang, C. M. 2011. "Solutions Urgently Needed for Health Risks from Heavy Metals in China" (中国重金属健康风险亟待寻找解决方案). In *Annual Report on Environment and Development in China* (中国环境发展报告), ed. D. P. Yang. Beijing: China Social Sciences Academic Press.

Yuan, X., and others. 2011. "CO_2 Emission Intensity of Coal Electricity in China and the United States." Manuscript. Development Research Centre, Beijing.

Zeng, X. M. 2010. "Cement Industry Launches Benchmarking for Energy Efficiency" (水泥行业全面启动能效对标). *China Cement* (中国水泥) 4: 25–27.

Zhai, P. M., and others. 2005. "Trends in Total Precipitation and Frequency of Daily Precipitation Extremes over China." *Journal of Climate* 18: 1096–108.

Zhang, Y. S., and H. Shi. 2011. "How Carbon Emission Mitigation Promotes Economic Development—A Theoretical Framework" (减排如何促进经济发展：一个理论框架). Project paper for "Fighting Climate Change," Development Research Center of the State Council, China, Beijing.

Zhang, Y. S., and J. Wu. 2011. "Auction or Free Allocation? Investigating the Effects of Different Allocation Approaches of Carbon Emissions Permits" (拍卖还是免费分配？不同碳排放权分配方案效果分析). Project paper for "Fighting Climate Change," Development Research Center of the State Council, China (国务院发展研究中心"应对气候变化"重大课题研究报告), Beijing.

Zhang, Y. W. 2011. "Recommendations to Accelerate the Development of China's Shale Gas Resources" (in Chinese). Investigatory Research Report 51, Development Research Center of the State Council, Beijing.

Zheng X. Y., F. H. Li, X. L. Li, and J. Guo, J. 2011a: "Determinants of Residential Water demand: Empirical Evidence from China." Energy Economics Research Paper, 2011-04, Renmin University of China, School of Economics, Beijing.

Zheng X. Y. P., Qin, Y. H. Yu, and F. H. Li. 2011b. "Estimating Demand Elasticity for Electricity in Urban China." Energy Economics Research Paper 2011-02, Renmin University of China, School of Economics, Beijing.

Zhou, N., and others. 2011. "China's Energy and Carbon Emissions Outlook to 2050." Paper LBNL-4472E, Lawrence Berkeley National Laboratory, Berkeley, CA.

Equality of Opportunity and Basic Security for All

China's social development over the past three decades has been impressive. The country has universalized compulsory education, expanded participation in higher levels of education, sharply reduced the burden from infectious diseases, and dramatically increased social security coverage. Labor has become more mobile, and the number of rural migrants moving to cities has grown. The "iron rice bowl" social protection system based on work units has been transformed into programs that are being expanded and consolidated.

At the same time, China's social development faces four broad challenges to which social and economic policies will need to respond.

Four Broad Challenges

The first challenge is high inequality, some dimensions of which may have worsened in recent years. Inequality remains high in incomes, consumption, and asset ownership, as well as in access to quality education, health care, jobs, and social protection programs across and within regions and social groups. Part of the higher inequality is the "Kuznets effect"—the result of structural change as labor moves from agriculture to manufacturing. But there are other drivers of inequality, including China's decentralized fiscal system and the mismatch at local levels between resource availability and social spending responsibilities, which have led to large spatial disparities in public expenditures per capita on social services; institutional arrangements and policies, such as the *hukou* system, and fragmented social security arrangements, which reinforce and even accentuate inequalities; high social insurance taxes and weak labor market institutions, neither of which favor labor; and significant segmentation in urban labor markets.

The second challenge is inefficiencies in social service delivery resulting from distorted incentives and market structures. Public organizations face little competitive pressure to improve efficiency or quality. And pressure from users of services is also limited because of lack of downward accountability. The incentive structure in health services, and to some extent education services, encourages public providers to act as profit-maximizing private sector entities. As a result, it is estimated that between one-third and one-half of hospital admissions in China are unnecessary, and the average length of stay in hospital is double the average in Organisation for Economic Co-operation and Development (OECD) member countries. School selection fees drive a further funding wedge between "key" schools and regular schools and exclude many.

The third challenge is rapid aging of the population. China is "growing old before growing rich." As the country ages, the labor force is expected to peak around 2015, with dependency ratios rising rapidly thereafter. These trends put a premium on deepening human capital to enhance labor productivity, place additional demands on education and training systems, and heighten the importance of allocating labor efficiently. Aging has also transformed the disease profile toward noncommunicable diseases, requiring a shift from curative to preventive care and better health education.

And the fourth challenge is managing growing economic, social, and cultural diversity. Significant changes in social structures and values have taken place since opening up, driven by changes in economic and industrial structure, employment and income distribution, and new social stratification patterns. The needs, expectations, and values of various groups are increasingly diverse, a situation that will present increased challenges in managing constructively the tensions of unity and diversity.

The Social Policy Response

In response to these challenges, this report argues that in the coming decades China needs to pursue social policies that promote *equality of opportunity with security*. Social policy will need to focus on human capital development, basic social welfare without welfare dependency, and growth and development. Simply stated, all citizens should have equality of opportunity in education, health, employment, and entrepreneurship; and security from deprivation through a moderate but sustainable social protection system, together with care services for the aging population.

Underpinning these reforms is the cross-cutting need to promote greater accountability for results in social services and social protection programs. Greater accountability would need to come through three channels: administrative systems that monitor performance and encourage quality and equity; market-based mechanisms that encourage private delivery and rely on competition with appropriate regulation; and direct accountability to citizens by increasing the role of civil society organizations.

To achieve these objectives, China needs to develop a vision, core values, and guiding principles for social policy development and social harmony. The report argues that China could benefit from its particular blend of social and economic characteristics. China could choose the "active welfare society" (also called "developmental welfare") model. Underpinning such a model would be the need to develop consensus on a common set of underlying values. These include social equity and justice for all; acceptance that society should help meet basic needs of all, especially the poor and vulnerable; respect and care for family members; maintenance of a strong work ethic and avoidance of welfare dependency; development of the professional ethics of service providers; and the sharing of responsibilities among the state, communities, families, social organizations, and the private sector.

In moving toward such a model, an overarching question will be what level of social services and protection the state should aim to finance. International experience suggests that social spending accounts for the bulk of incremental public expenditure as countries grow wealthier. At the same time, additional government-financed social services and social protection should be undertaken with considerable caution and with a strong focus on efficient public spending. In striking this balance, China will need to avoid the predicament that many advanced countries face from unsustainable entitlement programs.

The key elements of such a social policy model—some of which are already emerging—are:

Equitable and effective social services that build human capital for a healthy and productive population. By 2030, China would have an education system that provides quality general education for all children from preprimary to the end of senior secondary schooling. The latter would be fee-free, and the former available affordably to everyone, the most needy receiving subsidies. Underpinning this education system would be an early child nutrition program and expansion of childhood obesity interventions. Building the human capital base will also require a post-general-education system that provides a more flexible and demand-driven set of competencies. By 2030, the barriers between technical/vocational and academic educational streams would be reduced, with more core skills for technical students, more practical and applied higher education, and greater crossover between technical and academic streams. The health system would provide more uniform and deeper financial protection against health shocks for all. And the delivery system would be more accountable for the quality and cost-effectiveness of services through provider payment and other reforms. The restructured health system would be less hospital oriented and be built around a high-quality primary care network to meet more complex case management needs of noncommunicable diseases.

Flexible and secure labor and entitlement policies and institutions that not only promote an internationally competitive workforce but also ensure that workers share in growth and maintain basic protections. Achieving the balance between the interests of workers and employers requires "flexicurity" in the labor market not only to promote efficient allocation of workers to their most productive use, but also to provide the security to ensure decent pay and conditions that reflect their productivity. The first step would eliminate the remaining barriers to labor mobility, in particular barriers that are related to inherited characteristics. Most critically, the hukou system would be phased out no later than 2030 as an instrument of allocating social entitlements to the migrant population. Instead, entitlements would be linked to residential permits, stable employment, or

both, depending on the categories of rights. The higher levels of governments, in particular the central authorities, need to play a more proactive role to encourage local efforts that promote social inclusion of migrant populations, financially and politically, through a common policy framework. Labor mobility would be underpinned by a social security system where entitlements are fully portable across the country, and where pooling of risk at higher levels reduces the cross-regional disparities. And the burden of taxation on labor would be gradually reduced. In parallel, fair and representative collective bargaining would drive the wage determination system. Finally, by 2030, China would have extended the productive life of its urban workers through higher retirement ages, flexible work arrangements, and lifelong learning opportunities.

A basic but secure social protection system that provides for a moderate level of security for all while respecting fiscal constraints. By 2030, China would have full coverage of sustainable pension and health insurance systems, with more reliable security from all schemes and greater integration of all subsystems. In addition, China would have a well-developed system of aged and long-term care services that draws upon the human and financial resources of all stakeholders and provides a minimum level of service for the poor. Finally, the safety net for the poorest and most vulnerable would have greater coherence between different parts of the social protection system, providing acceptable coverage of benefits for poor households without at the same time creating "poverty traps" for the near poor.

While China's social policies have achieved some measure of success in the past 30 years, simply doing more of the same is unlikely to be sufficient as the country faces new challenges. The more complex challenges require greater collective action across regions and social groups in situations where interests diverge. They also require shifting emphasis from quantity to quality of services, from input to outcomes of programs, and from government dominance to cogovernance arrangements for social services that are complex to achieve and monitor. In this process, public resources need to be used more efficiently, along with structural shifts in policies and delivery systems; the country must recognize that the state cannot "do it all."

Implementing the necessary social policy reforms will need strong and sustained commitment to manage vested interests within the social sectors and beyond. Current patterns of service provision and outcomes result in divergent interests that are likely to generate resistance to reform among those who benefit from the status quo. As in other countries, careful management of reforms will be required, as will attention to creating the incentives to win the support of all stakeholders.

Challenges for China's Social Development

Since opening up, China has made great strides in social development. Educational enrollments have increased rapidly, with large increases in high school attainment and above. The real per capita stock of human capital has risen rapidly, especially since the 1990s (figure 4.1).[1] Since the collapse of the

rural health system in the 1980s, China has moved actively to rebuild the health delivery network. It dramatically reduced the burden of infectious disease and expanded coverage of basic health insurance to almost all rural and growing numbers of urban citizens. China is also transitioning from an enterprise-based "iron rice bowl" to consolidation of a market-compatible labor market and social protection system at a rapid pace. While hukou reform still remains an unfinished agenda, the strict constraints on population mobility have been gradually relaxed to release the largest flow of internal migration ever seen.

Despite these successes, China faces new social challenges and risks as it seeks to build a harmonious high-income society, perhaps the key one being the inequalities that have emerged during the reform period. The 11th and 12th Five Year Plans recognize the emerging limitations of the current growth model and place greater emphasis on addressing inequality and enhancing the basic security of the population. Part of the rising income and consumption inequality is the "Kuznets effect"—the result of structural change as labor moves from low-productivity and labor-intensive agriculture to higher-productivity and capital-intensive manufacturing. Some inequalities are unintended consequences of market reforms and past failures to deal appropriately with the public goods nature of investments in human development. Others, however, are direct products of policies that institutionalize inequality of opportunity (such as the hukou system) or that do not provide an effective framework for addressing inequalities (such as the intergovernmental fiscal system). Overlaying these challenges are ones of rapid demographic and epidemiological transitions, changing social structures, sustained urbanization, and the political economy of reform. Taken together, the challenges strongly suggest that "business as usual" in social policy will be insufficient to address China's needs in coming decades.

Just as important, there are significant challenges of quality and efficiency in education and health services, as well as in social

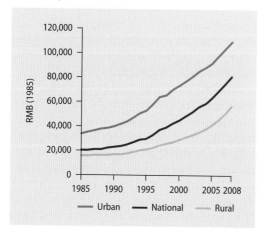

FIGURE 4.1 **Per capita human capital: national, urban, and rural, 1985–2008**

Source: China Center for Human Capital and Labor Market Research 2010.

security programs. Problems of quality risk compromising development of human capital and a healthy and productive population. The problems arise in part from *distorted incentives and market structures*. Public organizations and agencies exercise a monopoly or quasi-monopoly in delivering social services and face little competitive pressure to improve efficiency or quality. And pressure from users of services is also limited because of the lack of downward accountability. The revenue and incentive structure in health services, and to some extent education services, encourages public providers to maximize revenues and act as profit-maximizing entities. For example, it is estimated that between one-third and one-half of admissions to hospitals in China are unnecessary, and that the average number of days in hospital is double the OECD average (World Bank 2010a). School selection fees in urban areas drive a further funding wedge between "key" schools and regular schools.

Inequality of Outcomes and Opportunity

The sustained rise in income inequality during the reform period is a major source of concern. Income inequality was low in the mid-1980s but—as reflected by the Gini coefficient—rose rapidly to around 0.45 by the mid-2000s (figure 4.2). Subsequent analysis suggests that it may have climbed to 0.48–0.49 by 2007 (Li, Luo, and Sicular 2011).[2] The disparities across the whole population are mirrored by large divides between the richest and poorest citizens, with mean income in the richest decile more than 16 times that for the poorest decile by 2003, and more than 18 times greater by 2007 (World Bank 2009; Li 2012). Rising inequality reflects greater disparities between urban and rural areas and within rural and urban areas.

The sustained increase in income inequality places China at the high end of income inequality among Asian countries, and inequality is high by OECD country standards. While other countries have higher income inequality—notably in Latin America—few developing countries have seen the

FIGURE 4.2 The evolution of income inequality in China since the start of reforms, 1981–2005

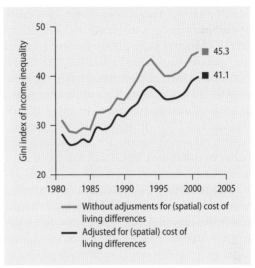

Source: World Bank 2009.

rapid sustained increase that China has witnessed since the mid-1980s, as can be seen in figure 4.3. Income inequality may have flattened in recent years—suggested, for example, by the rising relative wages of migrants and relative regional growth rates—but that remains to be confirmed.

Income inequalities are exacerbated by disparities in asset ownership, particularly

FIGURE 4.3 Global trends in per capita GDP growth and Gini coefficients, 1980s–early 2000s

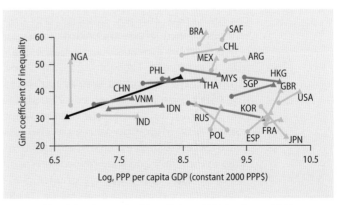

Source: World Bank (2009), except for China, which uses 2003 data. Start and finish years vary by country, but start years are in the early to mid-1980s and end years are in the late 1990s and early 2000s.
Note: PPP = purchasing power parity.

housing. Housing is estimated to account for around 60 percent of household wealth and for almost two-thirds of the inequality of wealth among households (Li and Zhao 2011; Zhao and Ding 2008). Nearly all rural and almost 90 percent of local hukou urban households owned their housing by the mid-2000s, but fewer than 10 percent of migrant households owned housing in their city of residence in 2007. In addition, while housing wealth increased rapidly for all homeowners between 2002 and 2007, the 15–20 percent annual rate of increase for urban households was significantly higher than the 7 percent annual increase of rural households. As a result, per capita urban housing wealth went from 4.5 times that of rural households in 2002 to 7.2 times only five years later, a gap significantly higher than the urban-rural income gap (Sato, Sicular, and Yue 2012).

Inequalities in incomes are mirrored and driven by major disparities in opportunities for quality social services and social protection. With China's success in expanding access to social services and coverage of social protection, new challenges of equalizing quality of services and depth of financial protection have emerged. Inequalities of opportunity start early in life and continue into working life. The opportunities for developing human capital, staying healthy, and having a reliable safety net vary greatly in China, depending on whether a person is rural or urban, lives in coastal or inland provinces, and is a migrant or a local resident in urban areas. In some cases (such as pre-schooling), inequalities are ones of access; in others (such as general education), the challenge is to promote "equality of quality" and affordability. The hukou system reinforces disparities by imposing high costs of education, health care, and housing on migrant households.[3] Migrant workers are also less able to access lucrative employment opportunities in the public and state-owned enterprise (SOE) sectors, and they face greater challenges than local workers in accessing decent work even outside these sectors. Inequalities in basic services have been compounded by lack of social security coverage and shallow

financial protection for migrant, rural, and urban informal sector workers (such as in the scale of protection under New Cooperative Medical Scheme, or NCMS). As a result, secondary distribution is in a number of cases regressive, despite the efforts of recent years to expand coverage. While the authorities recognize and are trying to address inequalities of opportunity, promoting greater equity in coverage and quality of social services and social security is hampered by the highly decentralized nature of financing.

Rapid Demographic Transition

China's demographic transition will be among the most rapid ever seen and is an emerging source of economic and social vulnerability. China has experienced the kind of fertility transition over the past 40 years that typically took more than 100 years in developed countries (Uhlenberg 2009). With rising life expectancy and the sharp drop in total fertility to only around 1.5, the country has "grown old before growing rich." Looking ahead, the share of people age 60 and over in the total population will accelerate in coming decades, from around 12 percent in 2010 to almost 25 percent by 2030 and to more than 33 percent by 2050 (figure 4.4). By 2030, China's population share over age 60 is expected to be just under the OECD average. As a result, the old-age-dependency ratio in China will increase at an almost unprecedented rate over the coming decades, with more than one in every three residents in rural areas and more than one of every five in urban areas being 60 or older by 2030. The emerging "4-2-1" extended family pattern of four grandparents, two parents, and one child will put deepening strains on family support networks.[4] Aging will also challenge social programs, in particular pensions and health care.

The end of the demographic dividend and exhaustion of the rural labor surplus will shift labor market dynamics. A source of growth in the reform era has been an expanding labor force, rising from under 600 million people of working age (15–64) in 1980 to around 990 million in 2012. This trend will reverse starting around 2015. The decline in the working-age population will not really take hold until around 2030, when it will drop sharply from just over 1 billion in 2026 to 850 million by 2050 (figure 4.5). The aggregate decline in the labor force is exacerbated by the rapid decline in rural surplus labor, which has until recently provided an unlimited source of cheap labor. Although the precise timing remains disputed, most researchers accept that China is at or nearing the Lewis turning point of exhaustion of the rural labor surplus, and the remaining rural working-age population may be too old, sick, or disinclined because of family obligations to migrate to urban areas.[5] The combined impact of a declining labor force, exhaustion of the rural labor surplus, and rapid aging means that productivity growth per worker will become critical as China seeks to move up the value chain. At the same time, in the short run, low-skilled workers could benefit from the shift in supply and demand in the labor market, which might provide negative incentives to investments in human capital beyond junior high level.

A further demographic challenge will be managing sustained urbanization. China's urban population grew from less than one-fifth of the total population in 1980 to almost half by 2010 and is expected to grow to around two-thirds by 2030. This growth has contributed to structural transformation and higher productivity and will continue to do so, facilitated by easing of population mobility restrictions in the hukou system. However, the failure to address entitlement reform for migrants through incomplete reforms of hukou and the ongoing challenges of managing farmers who have lost their land to urban expansion has resulted in a fundamental segmentation between the local and the nonlocal hukou populations. The social compact with migrants in urban areas remains for the most part different from that with local urban populations. Disparities in social entitlements that the original population of "floating" migrants was willing to accept will become harder to justify to second-generation,

FIGURE 4.4 **Number and share of population age 60 and over, 1950–2050**

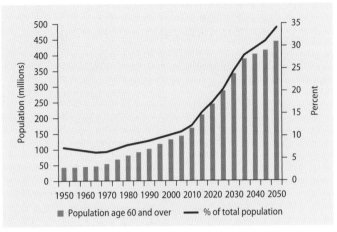

Source: For year through 2010, see China National Bureau of Statistics; for 2020 to 2050, see UN 2010.

FIGURE 4.5 **Total population and working age population, 1950–2050**

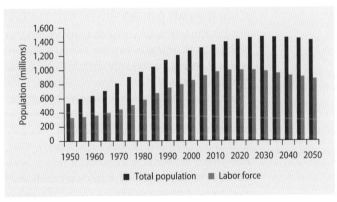

Source: UN 2010.

"permanent" migrants. Deepening reform of the hukou system to reduce social stratification and equalize entitlements for local urban and migrant populations presents major challenges, the resolution of which will have a major bearing on the social and fiscal sustainability of further urbanization.

A final demographic challenge will be sustaining a healthy and productive population in the face of epidemiological transition and the growing epidemic of noncommunicable diseases. Chronic illnesses such as heart

FIGURE 4.6   **Number of people with at least one noncommunicable disease, 2010–30**

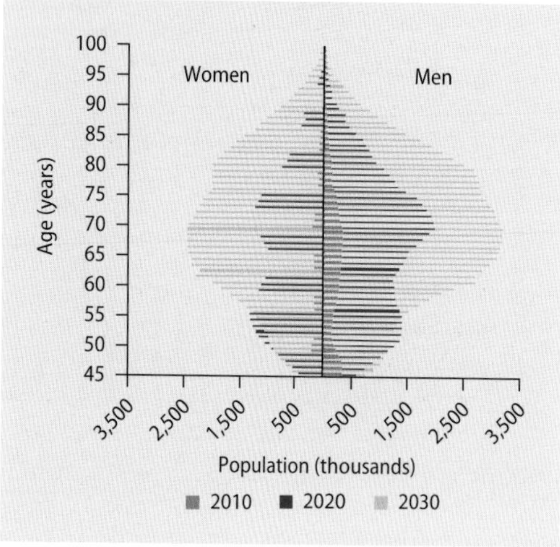

Source: World Bank 2011b.

disease, diabetes, and cancer are already the number one health threat. They account for more than 80 percent of the 10.3 million deaths annually and contribute to 82 percent of the total disease burden (WHO 2009). Around half of the noncommunicable disease burden is among those of working age, with significant costs to the economy. Urbanization and aging will accelerate a rapid increase in the prevalence of noncommunicable disease over the coming decades (figure 4.6), implying a major increase in demand for both curative and preventive health care. It will also require reorientation of the health delivery system in the face of more complex case management needs. If not addressed, health care costs could escalate rapidly, and labor productivity could be compromised. Rapid aging will make the need for health system reforms even more urgent.

Changing Social Structures and the Challenges of Response

Besides demographic transition and urbanization, significant changes in social structures have taken place since China's opening up, driven by changes in economic and industrial structure, ownership, employment and income distribution, and new social stratification patterns. As for economic structure, diverse ownership patterns and new sources of competition have emerged, although the state and collective sectors are still dominant. Social stratification has emerged as a major concern, with the expansion of new economic and social entities driven by private entrepreneurship. Employment opportunities have been created with the emergence of new social strata such as technical and managerial staff employed in private and joint enterprises, and self- and flexible employment. The traditional links between citizens through the work unit and even within families have weakened. The resulting diversification of interests and demands of stakeholders, together with changing social values reflecting the changes in social structures, requires greater efforts to manage conflicts of interests and rebuild consensus on core social values. In recent years, China has attempted to explore new institutional arrangements to build social consensus, but to date, these efforts have proven insufficient to cope with the challenges of profound social change.

China faces a range of new challenges as it seeks to achieve the social and economic policy goals that the country has set itself. Some of these challenges are discussed below.

The first challenge is navigating the divergent interests of different stakeholders in the current system. The current patterns of service provision and outcomes result in divergent interests that are likely to generate resistance to reform among those who benefit from the status quo. These divergent interests take many forms. They may be between service providers and users; between state and nonstate service providers; among different categories of users within localities and across space; between the elderly who expect good pensions and affordable health care and younger people whose wages are highly taxed; between richer regions that benefit from decentralized financing arrangements and those that would gain from greater equalization of public spending; or between employers, unions, and workers. Perhaps the most striking divergence is in the status of urban, migrant, and rural populations, where the social contract with the state is fundamentally different in a number of areas.[6]

In addition, sectoral reforms are likely to encounter the same resistance that they have faced in other countries. For example, increases in the pensionable age and the merger of different urban pension schemes will not be welcomed by those approaching retirement or working in public sector units (PSUs) and the civil service. At the same time, reorientation of the health delivery system toward greater reliance on primary care and reforms of provider payment systems are unlikely to be supported by specialist doctors and hospitals that have profited from current arrangements. More generally, efforts to strengthen the role of the nonstate sector and citizen voice in oversight of social services may run up against the desire for "business as usual." The fact that a number of social sector reforms and implementation of central directives have to date not made the desired progress (examples are higher-level pooling of social insurance funds; directives to provide free general education to migrant children; and reform of public hospitals) is indicative of the combination of technical and political economy challenges that will need to be navigated in coming years.

A second challenge is coordinating interests across agencies and regions to overcome fragmentation in policy design, financing, and delivery systems. Policies in China are fragmented between agencies at each level of government and across space between levels of government. As a result, policies are characterized by systems that are less than the sum of their parts and can lack systemic coherence. In some respects, the emphasis on local experimentation and innovation has served the country well in the reform period. The limits of this approach are now revealing themselves, however, and future progress will increasingly rely on cross-agency and cross-spatial coordination of policy and delivery to achieve more robust and coherent systems

and to promote more efficient use of public resources. This coordination can help to achieve as yet unrealized positive externalities in public policy.

A third challenge is the lack of consensus on core social values and social trust. Concerns are frequently expressed that China's cultural development has not fully matched its economic achievements, reflecting a degree of moral anomie, distorted values of some segments of society, and lack of trust in key social services.[7] Trust in health care providers is among the lowest of public services. More than two-fifths of people say they do not trust public hospitals, and almost two-thirds report they are suspicious of the medical industry, reflecting deep concerns about deterioration in professional ethics (Wang, J., and Yang 2011). Around one-third do not trust the educational system. The future of the pension system is also a major concern of urban residents (Ru, Lu, and Li 2011). Surveys of citizen satisfaction find an urban middle class in big cities that is least satisfied of all social groups, citing issues such as work stress, the costs of housing, and food safety.[8] Such "soft" indicators of insecurity are confirmed by the high levels of precautionary savings among citizens. China has recognized the urgency of rebuilding a moral foundation to guide individual behavior and collective action, but it is at the initial stage in seeking mechanisms to build a deeper consensus around core social values.

A fourth challenge is managing citizens' rising expectations as China becomes richer. The success of the Chinese economy and the pace of social sector reforms have created rising expectations that coverage and quality of services will continue to deepen at the same pace as recent years. For migrant populations, the shift in expectations is likely to be even sharper, because the children of first-generation migrants have higher expectations of urban hukou and associated entitlements.[9] However, with the likelihood of slowing growth in the medium term, China will inevitably face the dilemma seen in many OECD countries of setting a sustainable level of entitlements. The pace of wage growth, deepening financial protection from social insurance, and rapid expansion of the education system and other social reforms will inevitably slow also, and these adjustments will require careful expectations management by the authorities.

Finding the Way Forward

Despite the potential obstacles to social development, China has solid potential to address the above challenges. First, there is clear political commitment to address inequality of opportunity and to deepen security, and many policy initiatives to extend coverage and quality of services. Second, robust and sustained fiscal growth means that China is likely to have the resources to realize its policy goals, although improved efficiency in social spending will be required to translate increased resources into improved social outcomes. Finally, a strong tradition of local level experimentation provides ongoing lessons in how to turn policy commitments into better and more equal social outcomes.

The issues of inequality of opportunity and outcomes and lack of security are recognized by the Chinese authorities, but there are significant challenges and trade-offs in managing the demographic and social transitions. Synergy is needed among macroeconomic, fiscal, labor market, and social policies as China seeks to promote a more equal, high-income, and harmonious society. The rest of this chapter highlights the priority social sector reforms that will be needed. Many reforms are already starting to be addressed by Chinese policy makers, but others have not to date received the attention they may deserve. For both types of policies, the key issue is "how"—how to prioritize and sequence reforms, how to manage the inevitable resistance from certain players, and how to coordinate financing and actions across different parts of China and for different social groups to realize the public goods benefits of social sector investments.

The transition toward a high-income harmonious society will create a new set of social policy challenges that are in many ways more complex than those China has already faced. They require, for example, greater collective action across regions and across social groups in situations where interests diverge. They also require shifting emphasis—from quantity to quality of services, from input to outcome of programs, and from government-dominated to cogovernance of providers and users. These reforms are complex to achieve and monitor, and there are no easy answers from the experience of richer countries on a single "right" approach. The one certainty is that "doing business as usual" will be insufficient to achieve China's socioeconomic development goals.

Equality of Opportunity with Security: Goals and Principles

In response to the social and economic challenges facing China over coming decades, this report argues that China needs to pursue social policies that promote *equality of opportunity with security*. Simply stated, all citizens should have equal opportunities to access basic public services and contribute to the country's prosperity, regardless of place of birth, gender, or other factors; citizens should also have basic security from deprivation, for reasons of social equity (or harmony), to prevent any irreversible loss of human potential and to promote economic freedom of the population.[10] A combination of policies can promote both sustained productivity growth and a reduction in inequality to help ensure the social cohesion and stability necessary to underpin growth. Chinese policy makers will confront difficult trade-offs as they seek to realize their social policy goals, and their choices will require greater clarity on the underlying principles of reforms. This section first outlines the overarching goal and vision for social policy reform in China by 2030, before discussing the guiding principles in implementing those reforms. It then elaborates on three key cross-cutting issues that will be critical as social sector reforms evolve over the coming decades. Detailed discussion of the reforms and their prioritization and sequencing follows in the rest of this chapter.

The Goal and Vision for Social Development and Policies for China 2030

In light of China's social and economic challenges, the overarching goal of social development between now and 2030 would be progressive achievement of equality of opportunity with basic security for all. While notable progress has been made in China's social development in the past 30 years, simply doing more of the same is unlikely to be sufficient as the country faces new challenges. "Business as usual" will increasingly reveal its limitations, as the Chinese authorities have already recognized in the 12th Five Year Plan. The goal of equality of opportunity with basic security is not only fundamental to achieving greater equity in China, but would also contribute to sustaining growth by deepening the human capital base, ensuring a healthy and productive workforce, promoting a more efficient allocation of labor, and reducing overly high precautionary savings as people grow more confident in the public safety net.

Underpinning the social development vision is the need to develop consensus on a common set of underlying values. These values include social equity and justice for all, independent of place of birth or other characteristics; acceptance that society should help meet basic needs for all, especially the poor and vulnerable, in order to promote social cohesion; maintenance of a strong work ethic that avoids welfare dependency; respect and care for family members, in particular the elderly and disabled; development of the professional ethics of service providers, both public and private; and the sharing of responsibilities among the state, communities, families, social organizations, and the private sector.

Looking toward 2030, two fundamental issues for policy makers in formulating China's vision of social policy are the type of social contract they envision between the state and the population as China moves toward high-income status, and the respective roles of the state, communities, households, individuals, and the private sector in achieving that goal. There is no "right" social policy model that high-income countries choose.[11] In setting a model, China has the opportunity to benefit from its particular blend of social and economic characteristics. One characterization of such a model is the "active welfare society," or "developmental welfare model," which draws on the strengths of government, the nonstate sector (commercial and nonprofit), communities, and households. Such a model would promote human capital development, provide basic social welfare but avoid welfare dependency, and increase the synergy between economic growth and social development.

The goal of equality of opportunity with basic security provides a vision for social sector policies and outcomes in 2030 that would include:

- *Equitable and effective social services that build human capital for a healthy and productive population.* Based on the experience of OECD and successful middle-income countries, by 2030 China will have an education system that provides an expanded cycle of quality basic education that is accessible to all, starting in preschool and continuing to the end of senior secondary schooling. Senior secondary school would be fee-free, as it is in most high-income countries; preschooling would be available affordably to all, through subsidies for rural, migrant, and poor children as needed. An early child nutrition program would ensure that children have a sound cognitive base to maximize individual and societal returns to education; over time this program would also address the health risks of rising childhood obesity. Building the human capital base for the higher-value-added China will also require a system that goes beyond basic education to provide a more flexible and demand-driven set of competencies for young people. By 2030, the barriers between technical/vocational and academic educational streams would be reduced, by extending the period of development of core competencies for technical students,[12] building a more practical and applied higher education curriculum in universities, and allowing for crossover between technical and academic streams within an overall qualifications framework. To have a healthy workforce and promote healthy aging, the health system would provide more uniform and deeper financial protection against health shocks for its population, with general revenue financing likely to play a bigger role in total health funding. And the delivery system would have providers who are more accountable for the quality and cost-effectiveness of services through provider payment and other reforms. The reformed health system would be less hospital oriented than is the current case, and it will be built on a high-quality primary care network that is able to meet the more complex case management needs of noncommunicable diseases. Case management would also involve greater coordination of patient care across levels of the health system. Both health and education services would have institutionalized mechanisms for citizen voice to promote accountability and inclusiveness.

- *Flexible and secure labor and entitlement policies and institutions that promote an internationally competitive workforce where workers continue to share in growth and have labor protection.* Achieving the balance between the interests of workers and the need for competitiveness would require "flexicurity," that is, a labor market with the flexibility to promote efficient allocation of workers to their most productive use, but also the security needed to ensure decent pay and working conditions that reflect their contribution to productivity. The first step in this process would be the elimination of the remaining barriers to labor mobility with equity, in particular barriers that are related to inherited characteristics. Most critically, by 2030 at the

latest, the hukou system would be phased out as an instrument for allocating social entitlements to the migrant population. Instead, entitlements would be linked to residential permits, stable employment, or both, depending on the categories of rights. The higher levels of governments, in particular the central authorities, need to play a more proactive role to encourage efforts at the local level to promote social inclusion of migrant populations financially and politically, through a common policy framework. Labor mobility would be underpinned by a social security system where entitlements are fully portable across the country, and where risk pooling at higher levels has reduced the cross-regional disparities in social insurance protection. And over time, the burden of taxation on labor relative to other factors of production would be reduced. In parallel, core labor market institutions would mature. Key among these would be a wage determination system driven less by administrative direction and more by collective bargaining, where the interests of workers, employers, and the state are fully represented. Finally, China would need to make significant progress by 2030 in providing for a longer productive life from its urban workers. Retirement ages would be raised significantly, flexible work arrangements would make continued work more attractive, and life-long learning opportunities for workers would help to reduce the depletion of their human capital as they age.

- *A basic but secure social protection system that provides a moderate level of security for all while respecting fiscal constraints.* By 2030, China would have full coverage of pension and health insurance systems, with integration of currently separate subsystems for rural, urban, and migrant residents and for civil servants, PSU employees, workers, and residents. Differences in levels of benefits would remain, but the achievement of national pooling for pensions and provincial- or national-level pooling for health insurance would give policy makers more leeway to equalize basic benefit levels across the country. In addition, general revenue financing would play an ongoing important role in both pensions and health, through subsidies to rural and urban informal populations, and tax-based incentives to formal sector workers to participate in supplementary pension schemes. In addition to pensions, China would by 2030 have a well-developed system of aged and long-term care services that draws upon the human and financial resources of the government, the nonstate sector, communities, and households, and that prioritizes a minimum level of service for the poor. Finally, the safety net for the poorest and most vulnerable would have greater coherence between different parts of the social protection system so that it ensures adequate and affordable minimum coverage of benefits for poor households but without disadvantaging the near-poor and creating "poverty traps."

The Implementing Strategy for Social Policy Reforms

To achieve the goal of equality of opportunity with basic security and the vision of outcomes for 2030 outlined above, key principles underlying social policy reforms should include:

- *Promoting macroeconomic and structural reforms.* Social policy reforms should be consistent with, and ideally promote, macroeconomic and structural reform goals. China is pursuing several key macro and structural directions, including rebalancing of the economy toward higher domestic consumption, reducing distortions in factor markets, moving up the value chain in production, and integrating rural-urban activities. Different social policy choices may promote or hinder achievement of these goals, and assessing their contribution to macro and structural reform goals is vital.
- *Ensuring efficient and sustainable use of public resources.* Social sector reforms should be consistent with fiscal constraints and promote a more efficient use of public resources. The rapid growth in fiscal resources in recent years has diluted the emphasis on efficiency in use of public resources in the social sectors. With overall and revenue growth likely to slow in the medium term, there will be an increased premium on efficient use of public resources.
- *Promoting co-responsibility and citizen voice.* As in many areas of economic policy, social policy reforms should be guided by the principle that the state cannot "do it all." These reforms should seek to promote deeper participation of stakeholders such as communities, nongovernmental organizations, and the nonstate commercial sector. To achieve this goal, the state will need new and more differentiated roles not only as a provider and funder but also as a regulator and facilitator.
- *Supporting and cultivating prevailing cultural values, social institutions, and practices.* Effective and efficient social policies need to be designed with close attention to prevailing cultural values and practices. In China, the role of the family is of particular importance but has not always been taken into account in formulating public policies (examples are the absence of survivor pensions; individualized health insurance coverage; and hukou policy that splits families and leaves children of migrants behind). Ensuring a mutually reinforcing interaction between public policy and private behavior is thus vital to achieve both social harmony and economic efficiency.
- *Aligning policy reforms with implementation capacity.* The pace of social policy reform in China since the 1990s has been breathtaking. But delivery systems have often struggled to keep pace with policy reform, and the gap between policy and implementation has been highly variable across the country. The substance and sequencing of social policy reforms should be consistent with implementation capacity to avoid a mismatch between policy commitments and on-the-ground delivery.

This alignment will also promote policies that are simpler to understand and less prone to abuse.

- *Combining bottom-up with top-down reforms in a systematic way.* Chinese social policy has benefited from local piloting and innovation, both by government and the nonstate and community sectors. Local demonstrations have often been fertile testing grounds for subsequent national policies. At the same time, they have sometimes resulted in fragmented approaches and implementation mechanisms across regions that can make subsequent consolidation of policies and delivery systems challenging (for example, incompatible information systems and overly localized pooling of social insurance). A more systematic linkage of bottom-up local pilots and national policies can ensure that fragmentation is reduced and that national policies take local variation into account.

Key Cross-Cutting Issues in Social Policy Reform

As China's social reforms evolve, policy makers will seek to address a range of cross-cutting themes and trade-offs. Four in particular deserve elaboration in light of the above guiding principles of reform:

Financing and efficiency in social programs social sectors, where existing programs, planned reforms, and demographic transition will drive significantly higher social spending over coming decades. The transition from middle- to high-income status entails an almost universal increase in the size and share of public spending devoted to the social sectors, in particular social security programs and related services, especially for the elderly. For example, public spending on pensions alone accounted for over 10 percent of gross domestic product (GDP) on average in OECD countries in 2008. Similarly, public spending on health care is growing ever higher in OECD countries, averaging over 7 percent (and rising) in 2008 (OECD 2009, 2011b).[13]

China's recent health expenditure trajectory suggests that it will not be immune to such an effect. Even among middle-income countries, China's social spending is significantly lower than spending in other large countries such as Brazil, the Russian Federation, and Turkey. Moreover, China faces the double fiscal pressure of its demographics and policy commitments to rapidly expand pension and health insurance coverage and provide higher levels of education.

In assessing the appropriate level of future social sector spending, the impact of increased government social spending on consumption is an important additional effect to take into account. A contributory factor to China's high household saving rate is the need to "save for a rainy day" because of the historically high burden of private health and education spending and the underdeveloped social protection system. Research sponsored by the International Monetary Fund finds that every yuan of incremental public spending on health results in a 2 yuan increase in the consumption of urban households, and that an increase in social spending of 1 percent of GDP spread evenly across health, education, and pensions results in a 1.25 percent increase in household consumption as a share of GDP, with the consumption impact highest for incremental spending on pensions and health. These results are consistent with observed behavior among rural households, where saving rates are significantly lower among those with social insurance. [14]

While social spending will increase, international experience also suggests that the expansion of social sector spending requires a close eye on fiscal constraints to avoid unsustainable commitments. Projections done for this report suggest that by 2030, public spending on pensions as a share of GDP could double and public spending on health could increase by over 50 percent simply as a result of demographic trends (figure 4.7a).[15] If policy commitments to expansion of pension coverage to rural and urban informal workers, and to expansion of enrollments at higher levels of education are taken into account, the increases could be significantly

FIGURE 4.7   Projected social spending as a share of GDP

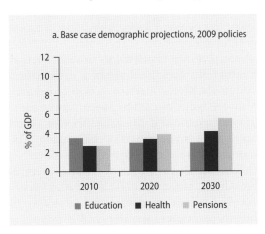
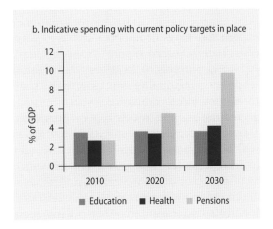

Source: Mason and Chen (2011), using National Transfer Accounts for China.
Note: Expenditures based on age-specific spending with 2009 policies, demographic and GDP projections. For GDP assumptions, see chapter 1 of this report. Education does not include preschool education spending.

higher (figure 4.7b). While these projections are at best indicative, even the "base case" growth due to pure demographics suggests a need for reductions in other elements of public spending and expansion of new revenues to accommodate social obligations as the population ages. They also confirm the critical role of ongoing reform of the urban pension system.

While social spending is certain to increase, ensuring that it achieves the desired social and economic outcomes will require a range of efficiency-enhancing reforms. Currently, inefficiencies in delivery models in the social sectors dilute the impact of incremental spending. The most notable inefficiencies are in the health sector, which relies too much on hospital-based care at the expense of primary and preventive care. Similarly in the area of pensions, negative real interest rates on individual accounts contribute to falling financial protection in old age, despite the continuation of high pension contribution rates. In these and other areas of social spending, simply putting more money into existing systems will have limited impact without continued structural reforms. Achieving such efficiencies will also require a further shift in administrative systems to promote accountability for results through better performance monitoring and a more rigorous system of impact evaluation for public programs.

Co-responsibility in service delivery and citizen voice. A second cross-cutting issue is how China can evolve toward a more diverse model of social service provision with new roles for the state and co-responsibility with the nonstate sector and households. To date, the public sector has been dominant as the main provider of social services, with a limited role for nonstate provision and a circumscribed role for citizen participation and voice. Looking ahead, the state cannot and probably should not do it all as it seeks to provide a wider and deeper range of social services and social protection programs. The experience of OECD countries suggests a range of innovations in unbundling financing, provision, and regulation of social services that China could explore and incorporate into national policies. Such approaches open up new roles for nonstate sector provision and public-private partnerships in social sectors: from hospitals and clinics to preschools and universities. In some fields, such diversification may also benefit from enhanced partnerships with international players, who can accelerate the adoption of good international practices. Plurality of service provision also offers a greater role for communities and the nongovernmental sector, two sectors that, according to pilot experience in China and international experience, have an important role to play, often with financial support from the state. Achieving plurality of social service provision while ensuring quality will require the state to assume more complex roles in licensing, accreditation, and regulation of providers. Developing regulatory capacity in particular will be challenging, as historical challenges in achieving effective regulation in areas such as pharmaceuticals, food safety, and pension and housing fund management demonstrate. It will also require in some areas a willingness to "step back" from micro-intervention in the operations of social services and to focus instead on setting rules-based policy, regulatory frameworks, and sets of incentives.

A related direction that will underpin social policy is the need to promote greater citizen participation and voice in social sector programs. A fundamental element of promoting accountability in social sectors is moving to a more rule-based system where access to quality public services is based on policy and progression in employment and education is based on merit or need rather than connections or wealth. There is an important and largely unexplored role for "bottom-up" accountability in promoting such a vision, through an increased role for people in monitoring and managing social services. Historically, citizen voice in the operation of social services has been limited, although localized innovations are spreading (Gong and Yu 2011). Increasing citizen participation in basic service delivery will require new ways of doing business for service providers and is also consistent with greater sharing of responsibilities in service provision.

Aligning the roles of levels of government to promote equalization. A third cross-cutting challenge in reorienting social policy is the need to reexamine the roles of the central and subnational authorities in promoting greater equalization of social services. Promoting greater equality of opportunity

is likely to involve a stronger role over time for central financing in the redistribution of spending across China. It will also require a stronger role for the center in setting national policy frameworks in areas such as hukou reform and management information systems where collective action is needed. However, current intergovernmental fiscal arrangements and the incentives for local authorities make progress challenging. The national authorities have already moved in this direction with central funding of rural education, pension subsidies for rural workers and urban residents, and subsidies to health insurance premiums. But financing remains highly decentralized by international standards, and disparities in quality of social services and the level of financial protection from social insurance remain high. Directions for reforms of the intergovernment fiscal system are discussed in chapter 1 on economic restructuring.

Strengthening institutional coordination. Stronger intra- and intersectoral coordination in policy development and delivery of social services will be vital to improve social outcomes. As economies grow richer and populations age, effective social services increasingly require better coordination within and across sectors. For example, within health services, coordination of care across levels of service is critical for managing noncommunicable diseases, and for education, the boundary between technical and vocational education and academic streams becomes more porous. Across sectors, new needs such as long-term care require inputs from social welfare, health, and other agencies, while labor policy for older workers requires coordination of social security and training initiatives. Developing an administrative system of cross-sectoral coordination requires the transformation of government functions and responsibilities.

There is increasing consensus on the goals and vision of social policy reform in China, but less clarity on how to reach them and how to navigate the obstacles that lie ahead. The following sections of this chapter discuss in detail the current situation and possible elements of reform around three proposed themes:

- *Expanding opportunities for all.* The report proposes action in four areas: expanding public investments in early childhood nutrition and education, especially for rural and poor children; promoting "equality of quality" in compulsory education among different areas and social groups and extending affordable access to postcompulsory education by universalizing free senior secondary education and reforming vocation and technical schooling and university education, including reducing the barriers between technical and academic streams; accelerating reforms of health financing and provider incentives and rebuilding China's primary care system as the basis of a system of coordinated care across levels of care to manage the epidemic of noncommunicable diseases and to avoid uncontrolled cost escalation of health services; and enhancing citizen voice and participation in the delivery and oversight of social services, and enhancing the role of the nonstate sector as service providers.
- *Developing a flexible but secure labor market.* To achieve this balance, the report proposes lowering barriers to mobility by ensuring the portability of pension and social security rights; phased reforms of the hukou system; ensuring that older urban workers do not exit the labor force prematurely, through pension system reforms, more flexible work arrangements, and expanded training opportunities; and building and reforming labor market institutions, in particular in the areas of labor taxation and wage determination policy and practice.
- *Enhancing security and helping people better manage risks.* Helping them manage these risks requires structural reforms of the pension system so that people have adequate support in old age from a sustainable system, as well as deepening financial protection from health insurance; expanded pension coverage, in particular for rural

citizens, migrants, and informal sector workers in urban areas; expanded aged and long-term care provision; and greater coherence across different elements of the social protection system to avoid poverty traps.

The scope and depth of social policy reforms points to the need for prioritization and close attention to sequencing of reforms within and across policy spheres. A process for agreeing on the top priorities is required, as are decisions on what is possible over the short, medium, and longer terms given fiscal constraints, implementation capacity, and political economy challenges. The following sections of this chapter suggest a possible sequencing of reforms that takes account of the constraints.

Expanding Opportunities and Deepening Human Capital

All people need equal access to quality, affordable education, and health services if China is to build the human capital base to reach high-income status by 2030 and share prosperity in a socially sustainable manner. This section outlines policies to achieve this vision, proposing action in six areas:

- Ensuring that all children get off to a good start in life by expanding public investments in early child nutrition and education, especially for rural and poor children.
- Narrowing the disparities in basic education quality across space and social groups and extending free access to senior secondary education in a phased manner that is consistent with fiscal possibilities.
- Deepening reforms of technical/vocational and higher education to promote a workforce with competencies that are relevant to the current labor market but also sufficiently flexible to adapt to the rapidly changing needs of the future labor market.
- Moving from an emphasis on treatment of disease to health promotion, which will require rebuilding China's primary care system to manage its new disease burden—particularly the epidemic of

noncommunicable diseases—and reorienting delivery systems away from overreliance on hospital care through incentives to promote use of primary care.

- Deepening reforms of financing and purchasing of health care services to promote more equitable health services for all citizens and ensure that the system provides quality services in a more cost-effective manner.
- Increasing the role of the population in oversight and some aspects of management of education and health services at the grassroots level to promote citizen voice and accountability.

An important cross-cutting theme in implementing the above policy and institutional reforms is diversification of the roles of state and nonstate players to promote greater plurality of social service provision. As noted, a key insight from international experience is the potential for unbundling the financing and provision nexus in social services, exploring diverse options including public financing with private provision and public financing through demand-side interventions. If China is to realize its ambitious social service expansion and quality enhancement goals within its fiscal constraints, an expanded role for the nonstate (for-profit and not-for-profit) and community sectors will be essential.

Running from the Same Starting Point: Early Childhood Development and Education

Evidence from developed and developing economies alike finds that investing in early childhood development and education (ECDE) yields high economic returns, is the most cost-effective strategy to break intergenerational transmission of poverty, and improves productivity and social cohesion.[16] An example can be seen in PISA (Programme for International Student Assessment) test scores for children attending at least one year of preschool, which are significantly higher across the developing and developed worlds compared with those of students without such schooling (figure 4.8).

FIGURE 4.8   PISA score differences between students with at least one year of preschool education and students without

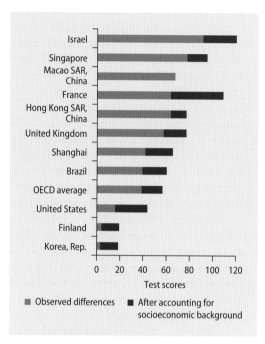

Source: OECD 2010b.
Note: Observed differences are differences in raw PISA test scores of students. Whole column = observed difference in raw scores.

Poor nutrition in childhood has immediate and serious impacts on children's health and educational performance, which can have lasting deleterious effects. Anemia results in cognitive impairment, altered brain function, and physical impairment. Apart from direct and immediate effects, poor child nutrition has been shown in developed and developing countries to have serious negative consequences for educational performance (Jukes, Drake, and Bundy 2008). Negative consequences of poor childhood nutrition can also be seen in adult health, human capital, and productivity during working life. In China, the Center for Disease Control and Prevention found that for every 1 percent of low height-for-age, physical productivity in adulthood is reduced by 1.4 percent (Chen and others 2010).

Current status and challenges in ECDE. The two major challenges for early childhood development and education are poor nutrition among plenty for China's rural children and low levels of preschool education that put children behind before they even start.

While China has made significant progress on child nutrition outcomes, it continues to face a major unfinished agenda in poorer provinces and poor rural counties nationally, especially for very young children.[17] Both national figures and studies within central and western provinces indicate that a substantial challenge remains in addressing early childhood nutrition. Data from the China Household Nutrition Survey over the past decade confirms overall progress but also large remaining disparities. Stunting affected more than 20 percent of children under age 5 in poor rural counties in 2010, more than twice the national average and almost six times the national urban rate.[18] Similarly, anemia rates among very young children in poor rural areas remained stubbornly high in 2005–10, especially for children 12 months or younger, with anemia rates above 40 percent in poor rural counties in 2009 (figure 4.9).[19]

Looking ahead, an emerging challenge in child nutrition is rising rates of obesity, a problem that Chinese evidence suggests will worsen with rising wealth. In the 1980s, overweight and obese children were not a big issue, with obesity only 0.2 percent

for boys and 0.1 percent for girls. But the prevalence rates of overweight and obesity have increased rapidly since the mid-1990s, especially in big cities. By 2005, the obesity prevalence rate among 7- to 18-year-olds in urban areas was 7.1 percent for males and 3.6 percent for females. For 7- to 9-year-olds, however, the rates were significantly higher: 10.6 for males and 5.3 percent for females. Average rates of overweight boys and girls were twice as high (table 4.1). Both levels and rates of increases in childhood obesity also show regional variation, with rates in coastal provinces increasing faster than rates in central and western provinces from 1985 to 2005.[20]

China's coverage rates for early childhood education are well below those of high-income countries and a number of major middle-income countries as well, and they and vary widely between urban and rural areas. In 2009, around 51 percent of Chinese children attended any school before beginning primary school, a share well below that in emerging economies such as Mexico and Brazil. The averages for early childhood education coverage in China disguise wide disparities between rural and urban areas: while coverage in urban areas averaged around 80 percent nationally in 2009, it was only

FIGURE 4.9   **Prevalence of anemia among children under age five**

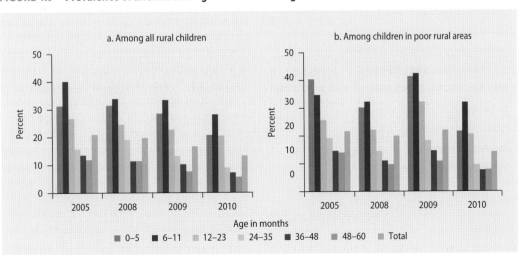

Source: China Health and Nutrition Survey, various years.

TABLE 4.1   Prevalence of overweight and obesity of students ages 7–18 in urban and rural China, 2005

percent

Age (years)	Urban areas				Rural areas			
	Male		Female		Male		Female	
	Overweight	Obesity	Overweight	Obesity	Overweight	Obesity	Overweight	Obesity
7–9	12.6	10.6	8.0	5.3	6.3	4.4	4.8	2.8
10–12	16.1	8.3	7.1	4.4	7.7	3.2	3.6	2.1
13–15	12.3	5.3	7.5	3.0	5.4	2.1	4.8	1.3
16–18	11.3	4.3	7.2	1.7	5.4	1.5	5.5	0.6
Average	13.1	7.1	7.4	3.6	6.2	2.8	4.7	1.7

Source: Ji 2007.

around 30 percent in rural areas. The rural average is well below the national average for India, which had coverage of 40 percent in the late 2000s (figure 4.10).

Just as important, among those enrolled in preprimary school, the *length* of attendance in rural areas is well below that in cities and towns. Urban children have a much earlier start in the education system, and children in counties and towns have an earlier start than their rural peers. In 2008, about 48 percent of preprimary enrollment in rural areas was in one-year-only classes, and the share goes as high as 87 and 83 percent in Guizhou and Ningxia, respectively (figure 4.11). In contrast, one-year preprimary enrollment accounted for only 13 percent of total preprimary in urban areas and 25 percent in county towns. In the general education system, rural and migrant children—particularly in poor areas and households—are thus behind before they start. International evidence shows that such early educational deficits are very difficult to overcome in terms of later school performance.

Major *quality* differentials in preprimary education between rural and urban areas are reflected in indicators of educational inputs, which in turn translate into large disparities in school preparedness. In 2008, the average rural pupil-to-teacher ratio was twice the national average of 17 to 1, while the urban average was under 10 to 1. The situation in some of the poorer provinces is even more striking, with ratios in Ningxia and Guizhou of 167 to 1 and 164 to 1, respectively, in 2008. The share of qualified preprimary teachers in rural areas was just over one-third of that in urban areas (Rozelle 2011). Two studies using the same measure of school readiness found that with a common score of 70 being needed to meet the basic school preparedness standard, urban children had a mean value of 100, with only around 3 percent of urban 4- and 5-year-olds being considered "unready" for school. In contrast,

FIGURE 4.10   International comparison of share of children attending nursery school or kindergarten

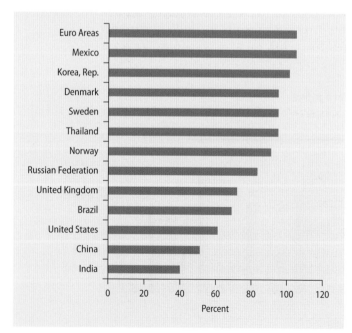

Source: World Bank 2011a.
Note: Date are for 2007, except for China, which are for 2009.

the same methods in a study in villages in Gansu, Shaanxi, and Henan provinces found that even the mean score for rural children (64) was below the minimal school readiness standard (figure 4.12).

A fundamental problem in improving equity of access and quality of preprimary schooling is the very low level of public financing. Financing of early childhood education remains overwhelmingly private even in most public facilities, with an estimated 70 percent paid out of pocket, compared with an OECD average of only 20 percent.[21]

Although China has targeted continued expansion of early childhood education in the 12th Five Year Plan, allocations within the public education budget have to date been very low relative to student shares and relative to OECD benchmarks. In 2008 in China, preschool programs accounted for 9.3 percent of total enrollment in education, but for only 1.3 percent of total public expenditure on education (0.01 percent of GDP)—far below the OECD average of 8 percent of total public education spending, or 0.5 percent of GDP (OECD 2007). In addition, large and growing gaps can be seen between richer and poorer provinces, with the share of extrabudgetary funds being significant and an incremental source of inequality (figure 4.13). Per-student government expenditures for early childhood education in the lowest-spending

FIGURE 4.11 **Comparative shares of children attending one-year-only early childhood education programs, 2008**

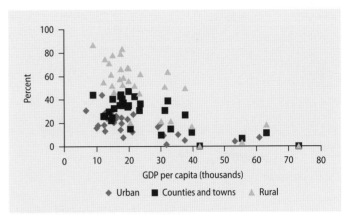

Source: World Bank 2011a.

provinces are less than one-tenth the level of spending in cities such as Beijing and Shanghai.

Lack of public financing means that rural and poor households struggle to afford preprimary education for their children. As an example, the study of preprimary education in Gansu, Henan, and Shaanxi found combined tuition and school lunch fees of RMB 800 a year in 2008, a considerable amount compared to average per capita income of just over RMB 1,000 for a rural family at the 2007 poverty line (Rozelle 2011). Although

FIGURE 4.12 **Distribution of educational readiness test scores for four- and five- year-olds in China**

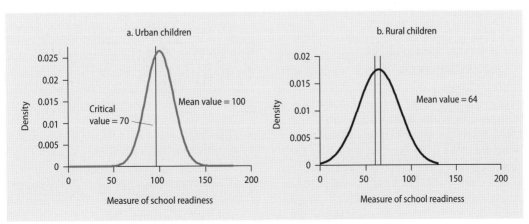

Sources: Data in panel a, Ou (2007). Data in panel b, Rozelle (2011) for Gansu, Henan, and Shaanxi provinces.

FIGURE 4.13   Budgetary and total spending per student on early childhood education, by province, 2009

Renminbi

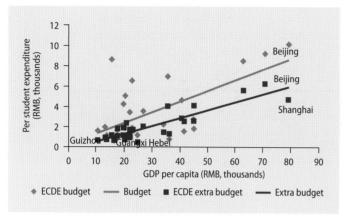

Source: Ministry of Education 2010.
Note: RMB = renminbi.

seemingly modest, such fees can therefore be a very high barrier to access for the poor.

Addressing the challenges of early child development. Early child development is a key investment in the productivity and good health of the workers of tomorrow and can also be a strong equalizer. Because children under age six today will be the labor force during the period of China's most rapid aging and accelerating labor force decline, it is essential to ensure that the human capital foundation is laid for all of them now. This section proposes measures to promote equality of opportunity in early child nutrition and to expand early child education, ensuring quality access for all.

Child nutrition in poor rural areas should be a high priority of government policy in the near term. Within these areas, targeting of specially vulnerable groups such as left-behind children will be crucial, as will be closer monitoring of the nutritional status of poor and migrant children in urban areas. China has huge potential to make a difference in a very affordable manner. Pilots by agencies such as China Development Research Foundation (CDRF), China's Center for Disease Control (CDC), and UNICEF demonstrate that major improvements in nutrition and cognitive functioning can be made at low

cost and at low risk. For example, a China CDC intervention of low-cost micronutrient supplementation in children under two years old in Gansu improved full IQ by up to 4.5 points, with effects persistent in follow-up studies to age six.[22]

Starting in the short term,[23] increased emphasis should be placed on coordinated action to combat childhood obesity. The levels and rates of increase in obesity in cities like Beijing, Tianjin, and Shanghai are precursors of those that all of China will experience over coming decades without action. But just as with undernutrition, there are cost-effective interventions that have been proven in China and globally to reduce obesity and improve child and subsequent adult health.[24]

To operationalize the enhanced policy commitment to address child nutrition—both undernutrition and problems of obese and overweight children—consideration should be given to rapid initiation of a national child and mother nutrition program. Designation of institutional leadership from the national to grassroots levels would be essential to promote coordination. Child nutrition is an area of interest for many public agencies in China, including the Women's Federation, Ministry of Health, CDC, State Council Working Committee on Women and Children (chaired by the vice premier), National Population and Family Planning Commission, Ministry of Education, Ministry of Civil Affairs, and the Leading Group on Poverty Reduction. However, significant hurdles remain in the areas of institutional coordination, standardization of approaches, and quality assurance. Coordination could be handled at the national level by the group led by the vice premier, but the agency that would take the lead at subnational level would need to be clarified. Key elements of such a program could include:

- *Universal implementation of nutritional supplementation for children under age three and pregnant or lactating women in all rural poor counties, and ideally in central and western provinces, and for migrant children in urban areas.*[25] The costs of such a program are not prohibitive: even at current low-volume production, the cost of a nine-nutrient supplement for one year is around RMB 260 per child—very cost-effective in light of high returns to health, cognitive development, and productivity.

- *Inclusion of a parenting education program.* Family feeding, hygiene, and other practices are major contributors to nutritional outcomes. International and Chinese evidence points to the benefits of parallel parenting education to ensure both that the supplementation itself is regularly administered and that practices negatively affecting nutrient intake and absorption are reduced. Such programs have proved effective in many developing countries, including Brazil, Mexico, and Vietnam (World Bank 2011a). In China, the Ministry of Civil Affairs' Social Welfare Department will be piloting community-based delivery of comprehensive child welfare service packages.

- *Identification of funding sources for pilot and rollout phases.* The key question will be what combination of incremental funding and reallocation of existing resources would be appropriate to support such efforts. A potential source for the pilot phase could be funds allocated by the State Council Leading Group Office of Poverty Alleviation and Development, which has indicated that reduction of child poverty would be a higher priority in the 12th Plan period.[26]

- *As part of the overall nutrition program, development of a national program against childhood obesity.* Pilot programs in China suggest that a combination of family-, school- and community-based interventions, including a focus on grandparents, can be very cost-effective. Direct interventions such as physical activity, health education, and dietary interventions could be combined with collaborations with local governments and industry to promote healthy school meals and control targeting of obesity-inducing foods at children.

- *Agreement on child nutrition outcome indicators that could be included in performance management indicators for officials.* Draft indicators that have been proposed by the China CDC could be reviewed as a basis for such indicators. It will be important to keep such indicators simple and to ensure that the monitoring system is capable of producing them with the required frequency.

For early child education, the major challenge lies in an effective expansion strategy for rural, migrant, and poor children. The National Plan for Medium- and Long-Term Education Reform and Development sets targets to 2020 for expansion of early childhood education, such as almost universal coverage of one-year kindergarten and enrolling three-quarters of children in three-year preprimary education programs. These are laudable goals, but do not answer questions of the appropriate (and fiscally feasible) role of public financing in the expansion, and the appropriate delivery models consistent with the financing strategy and the capacities of the state, communities, and the nonstate sector in early childhood education provision.

To achieve China's expansion targets, a significantly higher commitment of public resources to early childhood education is needed, in line with practices in most OECD countries (figure 4.14). While the OECD average of public spending of 0.5 percent of GDP on preschool programs may be ambitious in the short term, China does have significant scope for major expansion from its currently very low public spending base. If China achieved the share of total public education spending that OECD countries have (that is, 8 percent), that would suggest a sensible public spending target for early childhood education of just over 0.3 percent of GDP by 2020. The current levels of public spending on this education represent a missed opportunity for an investment that is highly productive and highly equitable. China's commitment to expand the overall educational budget, combined with the shrinking cohorts of young children, provide the possibility to change the situation.

In the short term, incremental public spending on early childhood education should

FIGURE 4.14   **Comparison of public expenditure on education by level, 2008**

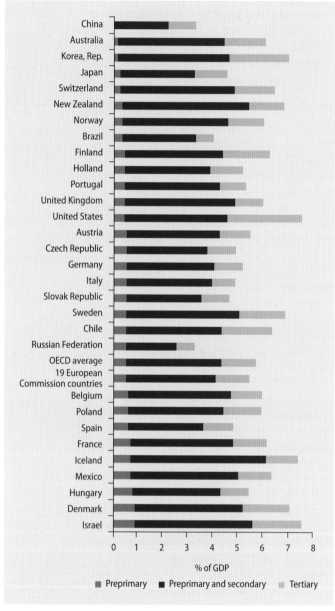

% of GDP

■ Preprimary   ■ Preprimary and secondary   ▪ Tertiary

Source: World Bank 2011a.

for the medium term. The recommendation of this report is that public subsidies in the coming 3–10 years focus initially on children in poor rural counties, gradually expanding to all rural areas in central and western provinces and to migrant children in urban areas. A significant fiscal injection from the national authorities would be required, which could in principle be done with supply-side subsidies to providers, demand-side subsidies or fee exemptions for targeted households, or a combination.

A financing option that could be piloted on a wider basis is conditional cash transfers (CCTs) targeted to poor children to encourage participation in preschool programs. This scheme has proven to be effective in other developing countries (Fiszbein and Schady 2009), and pilots in China indicate that it has significant potential. A pilot in Henan Province, for example, found that kindergarten attendance was 98 percent among poor rural children whose families received a RMB 200 stipend and had their fees covered, while only 19 percent of the children in a control group with no assistance attended.[27]

The second major direction of reform could be innovating with new models of preschool delivery that involve greater co-responsibility of state, communities, and households. This approach can be effective in terms of both impacts and costs, drawing on good international experience and emerging Chinese pilots.[28] Expansion of ECDE services could involve a range of models, guided by the notion of "welfare pluralism," in which public subsidies could go to support not only formal preschools but also community and parent provision (through carer allowances, for example). Given the high cost of center-based ECDE services, such as parent-child classes and formal kindergartens, local governments are unlikely to have sufficient revenue to fund center-based preschool services in rural areas for the three- to six-year age group. The financial constraints of local government limit supply, and parental inability to pay dampens demand.

Chinese pilots and international experience also offer many lessons for innovation in

prioritize rural, migrant, and poor children. Given China's starting point and simultaneous expansion in other parts of its education system, education for all three- to six-year-olds that is fully state funded seems unlikely models of formal center-based ECDE delivery. Even in formal settings, there is significant potential for greater efficiency and innovation. Reducing the length of shifts could accommodate more children in two shifts in the same facilities, perhaps even taught by the same teachers. A review of international literature found that most children had cognitive gains by participating in center-based preschool programs for 15–30 hours a week for at least 9 months of the year, and children from lower-income families benefit even more. Different models of formal provision are also possible and are already being tried in China; one example is the use of mobile kindergartens in remote rural areas. Piloting, evaluating, and gradually expanding different models of early childhood education suited to local fiscal and other conditions would be an agenda for the 12th Plan period.

Promoting Equality of Quality and Access across the Education Cycle

A key driver of China's sustained growth and economic transformation into a high-income country will be the development of a workforce with the competencies needed in a more complex and dynamic economy. A key distinction between countries that have successfully made the middle- to high-income transition and those that have stalled is the level, quality, and equity of investment in human capital. At the same point in their development paths, Japan and the Republic of Korea were sending almost all students to high school. In contrast, countries that have stalled at middle-income status—such as Argentina, Iraq, Mexico, and the Arab Republic of Egypt—are distinguished by low levels of human capital relative to their income levels.[29]

To promote and accelerate the human capital transition, reform efforts are needed in three directions in compulsory education and at the postcompulsory education level. The first is to reduce the remaining disparities in quality across space and across different groups of children in their access to quality compulsory education. The second

is to move toward free senior secondary education, with sufficient public resources to ensure access and quality for rural, poor, and migrant young people. The third direction would reform technical and vocational education and training (TVET) and higher education to promote a set of competencies that will continue to be in demand from employers as the economy evolves. Many elements of the vision for China's education system in 2030 are already visible in the National Plan for Medium- and Long-Term Education and Development, including promoting equality of access at all levels of the system, enhancing educational quality, and promoting innovation and greater diversity in the education system.

Promoting equality of quality in compulsory education. Promoting greater equality in compulsory education is a major priority from both social and economic perspectives and for maximizing China's human capital base. China has made great progress toward its goal of universal completion of primary and junior secondary schooling. Nonetheless, challenges remain in completion of the full junior secondary cycle in poorer areas and for certain groups such as migrant children, with around 9 percent of students nationally still not completing the full compulsory cycle in 2009 and higher shares in poorer provinces.[30]

The key challenge in basic education is "equality of quality" for children in different areas, social categories, and income groups. Disparities in quality of basic education remain substantial, and in some dimensions may have increased in recent years. Differences in per capita allocations of public spending across provinces (and often within provinces and prefectures) increased between 2000 and 2009, despite rising spending across the board as well as significant central subsidies to rural education as a result of the fee-free rural education reform (figure 4.15).

The equality of quality agenda is relevant to both rural and urban areas but in distinct ways. In rural areas, significant challenges include the recruitment, compensation, and retention of quality teachers and gaps in the

FIGURE 4.15   Spending per capita on education by province, 2000 and 2008

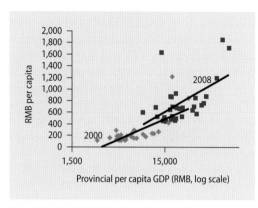

Source: China Statistical Yearbooks, in Brixi and others (2011).

The increased importance of family connections and "selection fees" to get children into elite urban public schools reinforces existing social disparities. Better-quality urban schools benefit from increased revenues from the school-selection fee, further setting them apart from ordinary schools. Despite national policies, significant challenges also remain in ensuring free access to schooling for migrant children in urban areas. In Guangdong Province, for example, 55 percent of migrant children from within the province and 79 percent of migrant children from outside the province enrolled in private schools (compared with only 13 percent of local urban residents) in 2009 (World Bank 2010a).

Although the authorities have been trying to address quality differentials in compulsory education, fiscal and other constraints make the task challenging. The removal of fees in junior secondary school has been an important reform in recent years and has had clear benefits in funding levels and the retention rates of poor students (Wang and Yang 2008). The authorities have initiated free tertiary education to encourage teachers to move to western areas and are promoting rotation of urban teachers, but the scale and consistency of approach varies.

Addressing "equality of quality" in compulsory education will require deepening reforms on several fronts, including:

quality of educational infrastructure and learning inputs.[31] Poor households also continue to experience difficulties in shouldering the non-fee costs of education (such as travel and learning materials), especially in the face of rising opportunity costs as real wages have risen. In urban areas, disparities are evident in the differential enrollment rates in higher quality "key" schools and regular schools among local, migrant, and poorer children and in indicators such as average class size and transition rates (figure 4.16).

- *Further financing inputs from governments above the county and district levels will be needed* to avoid further widening of disparities in educational quality across provinces and within them. This is particularly the case for rural schools, where aggregate funding shortfalls and disparities remain an issue in achieving quality. This equalization is part of a wider intergovernmental system reform agenda discussed in chapter 1 on structural reforms. The experience of cities such as Dalian and Chengdu in equalizing financial and other resources across districts and integrating poor and migrant children provides models, but such equalization efforts will eventually need to go beyond the

FIGURE 4.16   Type of urban schools attended by various subgroups in five Chinese cities, 2005

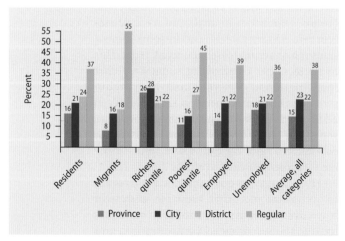

Source: Wang and Wu 2008.

prefecture. The experiences of countries such as Korea and Japan also offer insights into the potential for more proactive policies to promote equalization of access to good quality schooling.

- *A key focus will continue to be teachers*—teacher recruitment and career progression, allocation, compensation, and incentive policies. A combination of measures is required, including institutionalizing a rotation mechanism to ensure that quality teachers spend time in disadvantaged schools;[32] twinning arrangements between stronger and weaker schools; strengthened in-service training; incentives for hardship postings; and more fundamental examination of teacher compensation. China is experimenting with a number of such measures, including introducing a degree of performance pay for teachers.

- In urban areas, a key question is how to *reinvigorate the concept of a neighborhood school,* a concept that has been substantially undermined by the practice of selection fees and the growing importance of personal contacts in accessing the best schools. The issue of how to integrate migrant children into a stronger neighborhood school system is one that will require policy reform as well as close focus on their educational needs. The experiences of Japan and Korea suggest, however, that a strong neighborhood school system has a significant equalizing impact does not appear to compromise overall quality, given these countries' consistently strong results in international tests.

Achieving full senior secondary enrollment. While China has made great progress in expanding access to postbasic education, getting rural children into senior secondary academic high schools remains a major challenge. As shown in figure 4.17, the rate of graduation into the senior secondary academic stream among rural children remained almost stagnant from 1990 to 2006, increasing from 7 percent to only 9 percent. Getting the full picture for rural children is difficult,

FIGURE 4.17 **Official promotion rates from junior high school to academic high school, urban and rural, 1990–2006**

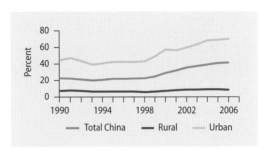

Source: Rozelle 2011.
Note: Rural promotion rate includes promotions only in rural areas.

however, because many go to high school in urban areas. Taking this into account gives an estimated junior-to-senior secondary academic promotion rate of 20–30 percent for rural children (Rozelle 2011). In contrast, urban rates rose rapidly during this period, from around 40 percent to around 70 percent. While a significant share of rural children go on to senior secondary vocational institutions, because of concerns about poor basic school training in TVET education, this section focuses on barriers to accessing senior secondary academic schools (Wan 2007; Xinhuanet 2009).

Several factors drive low rural progression to senior secondary academic schools: the entrance test, the high costs of secondary education, the perceived low quality relative to cost, and the rising opportunity costs. Many rural students simply fail the entrance exam to senior secondary academic school (*zhongkao*), with evidence even from rich provinces like Guangdong suggesting that fewer than half of rural junior high graduates pass the exam (Chen and Liang 2008). In addition, there is evidence that students pass the exam but choose not to enroll in senior academic school for quality or opportunity cost reasons (He 2009; Li 2007).

However, high cost and rising opportunity costs appear to be the main drivers of low rural graduation into senior academic high schools. Figure 4.18 compares average tuition fees for senior secondary school (or

FIGURE 4.18   International comparison of annual tuition per student in public high schools, late 2000s

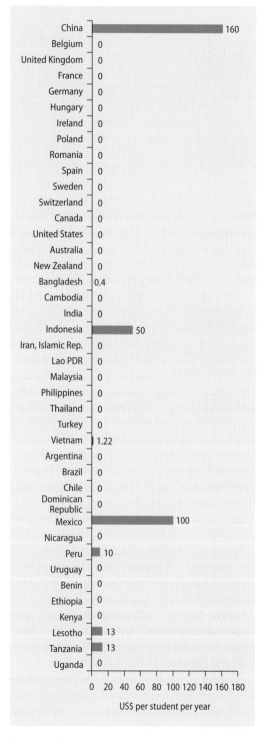

US$ per student per year

Source: Rozelle 2011.

general high school where relevant) in a range of countries relative to rural China (the latter based on evidence from rural Shaanxi as a representative poorer province). Even relative to countries at much lower levels of income, China is a major outlier. The situation is more pronounced when comparing the fees as a share of household income: in Mexico, three years' worth of school fees amount to only around 4 percent of per capita income, while in the China example, fees for the three-year cycle would cost 82 percent of net per capita income of a rural household at the time (Rozelle 2011). The costs of room and board in senior high school may more than double the tuition level. All of these are direct costs and do not take into account the rising opportunity costs of being out of the labor force because of substantial increases in the real wages of unskilled workers in recent years.

The government is aiming to provide financial aid to 20 percent of students in poor rural areas, but the level of aid relative to full direct costs remains low (leaving aside opportunity costs). The government's efforts are clearly a step in the right direction. However, survey-based estimates from Shaanxi Province in 2008 found that financial aid covered only around 6 percent of the total direct costs (tuition plus board) of senior secondary school (Rozelle 2011). The major policy questions for the authorities are:

- Should compulsory education cycle be extended to the end of senior secondary level?
- If so, should senior secondary education be free for all students, or should a targeted approach to financial aid be taken, and what should be the coverage in terms of groups/shares of total students and the degree of financial support provided?

Given the needs of the Chinese economy and the experience of countries that have moved from middle- to higher-income status, extending free education to include the senior secondary level seems inevitable in the coming decade. For China to continue deepening its human capital base, getting all students to finish senior secondary school is a necessity in the coming decades. China has already set a 90 percent senior secondary enrollment target (with half in the academic stream and half in the vocational stream) by 2020 in its National Plan Outline for Medium- and Long-Term Education Reform and Development. The 2020 quantitative target is comparable to Korea's senior high enrollment rate in 2000. However, the strategy on financing of senior secondary school remains to be developed, beyond the (appropriate) priority given to central and western provinces.[33]

Given the rising opportunity costs of senior high school, the government may need to consider a bolder financial commitment to achieving its 2020 target and the adoption of an even higher coverage target for 2030. Following the example of the rural fee abolition in the past decade, a similar policy would be advisable for senior secondary schools in rural areas; the government might also consider a parallel initiative for poor and migrant children in urban areas. A substantial injection of public funds would be required, with the bulk needing to be financed by the central and provincial levels. This could be financed in part by the incremental public funding China has already committed to in its Education Law, with a target of increasing the amount spent on education to 4 percent of GDP from around 3.5 percent. However, if such an initiative is to be combined with increased funding for preschool education for rural, migrant, and poor children, and if the planned continued expansion of higher education is to be achieved, public spending will most likely have to be increased beyond the 4 percent target. Fiscal constraints are likely to force prioritization of educational reforms by the authorities, with a sequenced approach.

Developing competencies for the 21st century. China has made great progress in expanding access to postbasic education in recent years. The share of postsecondary students enrolled in higher education, including higher vocational education, rose from only around 3 percent in the early 1980s to more than 24 percent by 2009. Similarly, technical and vocational training has expanded significantly at the senior secondary level, supported in part by major investments in student stipend schemes.

In both the technical and academic streams, however, quality and labor market relevance need to be strengthened to enable China to achieve sustained productivity growth. The greater openness and rapid technological adoption of the Chinese economy has created a demand for higher-skilled workers with more diverse competencies, posing an ongoing challenge to China's education and training systems. Employer surveys identify significant skills gaps in both higher education and TVET graduates. For example, a 2005 McKinsey report concluded that only 10 percent of the engineering graduates had the appropriate attributes for working in multinational corporations (Farrell and Grant 2005). The key shortcomings were in the "soft skills" such as practical and language (English) communication skills, innovative capacity, professional qualifications, and entrepreneurial capacity. Similarly, skills shortages were identified as a serious obstacle by more than 30 percent of Chinese firms by Investment Climate Surveys, with a further 30 percent identifying them as significant (Almeida 2009).

The TVET system faces several challenges in enhancing quality and the labor market prospects of students and their contribution to productivity growth:

- The TVET system is fragmented, with uncoordinated provision across a range of public sector agencies and a growing private sector. The bulk of colleges are operated by the Ministry of Education (MOE) or the Ministry of Human Resources and Social Security (MOHRSS) and their local branches, but many other line agencies are also operating significant subsystems. Governance is also decentralized within each of the subsystems.
- Consistent with the diverse governance arrangements, the system of qualifications and competency certification is also

fragmented, making it difficult to provide consistent standards on which employers throughout the country can rely for a consistent picture of the skills and competencies of TVET graduates.

- Financing of TVET faces several challenges, including the degree of decentralization and issues of vertical and horizontal equity, an uneven playing field in the allocation of public funding between public and private training providers, and a strong emphasis on inputs and the supply side of the system.
- The system lacks a framework for licensing and accreditation of private training providers, which both limits the growth of the private sector and results in lack of quality assurance and consumer protection for those undertaking private training.
- Systematic mechanisms for involving employers in the development of training curricula are lacking. While there is often a healthy transactional interaction between training schools and employers (for example, through "preordering" graduates by employers), the channels for involving employers in shaping course content remain largely ad hoc.

Apart from these institutional and policy issues, the role and nature of TVET in China needs to be considered. Overall, the shares of students in TVET versus academic streams varies considerably, from around one-quarter in Japan in TVET to 80 percent in parts of central Europe, with an average of 50 percent across OECD countries (about the same as China's current share at the senior secondary level). The bigger issue concerns the types of competencies being acquired in TVET programs and the extent to which they provide options for students for further study as well as labor market entry. The answers to these questions are crucial in assessing whether China's TVET system is well prepared for the faster pace of economic and labor market change and the types of skills needed by workers over coming decades.

Currently, TVET in China tends to be a dead end, with no pathway to further academic education for the large majority of students. In contrast, the expanding practice in many high- and middle-income countries is to allow for TVET students to stream into further academic education. This can be seen in reforms in Latin America and the Caribbean, the community college system in the United States, Nordic and apprenticeship countries such as Germany, and reforms over the past decade in Korea that allow technical students to cross over into academic streams. Some countries such as Norway and Austria have double qualifying pathways (Adams 2007). Given that the large majority of students in TVET are from rural, migrant, or otherwise disadvantaged or "blue collar" backgrounds, the structural segmentation of the TVET and academic streams also contributes to social segmentation.

Similarly, the Chinese TVET curriculum does not place a strong emphasis on continued acquisition of general "core" and academic skills. While that may be an appealing short-term strategy in preparing workers for immediate placement (as evidenced by the preordering system between enterprises and TVET colleges), it raises questions of how well prepared the TVET students will be for the medium- to long-term labor market, since specific skill demands will continue to shift. TVET reforms in OECD countries since the 1990s increasingly recognize this risk by blending vocational and academic curricula, with technical students receiving more academic content while academic stream students are taught greater practical application of their knowledge. Korea is a good example, with as much as 75 percent of curriculum being common between TVET and academic streams in senior secondary schooling (Adams 2007). This approach is consistent with a wider trend of deferring the introduction of vocational subjects in OECD education systems. These countries are also placing increased emphasis on general core skills such as communication, problem solving, and teamwork.

To help China ensure a sustained stream of appropriately skilled workers as it moves up the value chain, curriculum reform in TVET education should balance the continued acquisition of general core skills with technical skills. This will require a significant shift in the approach to TVET education as well as greater emphasis on the practical application of knowledge in tertiary academic education. Countries such as Finland and Korea provide a rich body of experience from which to draw as China develops such incremental reforms, including reforms such as dual academic/technical qualifications and for the possibility of transfer from the TVET system into academic streams with credit for prior learning.

The fundamental trade-off in TVET reform is between immediate employability and adaptability of skills across the life cycle to accommodate a rapidly changing economy. Global evidence indicates that, indeed, youth employment rates for those with TVET education are higher than those with academic education at the initial point of transition from education to work. That advantage decreases with age, however, as the narrow technical skills that initially helped in obtaining work become outdated and the absence of more general competencies for adapting and life-long learning become a constraint (Hanushek, Woessmann, and Zhang 2011). And the deterioration in TVET labor market benefits was found to be faster in countries experiencing more rapid technological change. The trade-off between short-term employability from TVET and China's long-run desire for a labor force with high but flexible skill sets as it strives for high-income status will become increasingly important in coming years.

In addition to reorienting the content of TVET education, structural reforms are needed to make TVET more responsive to employer demand and more accountable for quality. These include governance reforms to streamline and consolidate overall sectoral policy setting and oversight. One option for addressing the current fragmented

governance of the TVET sector is the establishment of a national (or provincial) training authority. Examples of national training authorities can be found in Australia, Brazil, New Zealand, the Philippines, South Africa, and the United Kingdom. The models vary, but governments hold primary responsibility for policy development and take the lead in promoting the orderly operation of training markets through regulation and institutional development and in ensuring equitable access to these markets. Rather than relying solely on public provision, new models of competition have emerged. Employers, worker organizations, and civil society are participating in policy development as stakeholders and assuming larger roles in provision and financing of training. Establishing an effective national training authority is not straightforward, but experimentation in advanced provinces in the medium term could build experience for wider institutional reform in the long term.

The TVET system can benefit enormously from an expanded role for nonstate sector provision to help meet demand, service niche skill sectors, and provide a healthy dose of competition. To help encourage greater plurality in TVET delivery, nonstate provision of training should be publicly financed within a solid regulatory framework to ensure that private trainers meet quality standards. This could in principle be done both on the supply side (by allowing for public financing of accredited nonstate training institutions) and on the demand side (by using public funds to provide vouchers to students who would freely choose among public and nonstate institutions). Local-level experiments with training vouchers in China (such as Meizhou in Guangdong; Jiangsu Province) can provide lessons for potential demand-side interventions. Licensing and accreditation for nonstate providers is a seriously underdeveloped area in China and would benefit from lessons of experience in countries with well-developed training markets. In Chile, for example, the Servicio Nacional de Capacitacion y Empleo (SENCE), a specialized agency of the Ministry of Labor, maintains no in-house capacity for provision of training and procures training services from public and private providers (Johanson and Adams 2004; Cinterfor/ILO 2001).

In the long run, adoption of a common standard for assessing the competencies of all students would promote greater integration across the education system. A national qualifications framework (NQF) could play an important role in this regard. Country-level frameworks linking existing qualifications of different levels and types of education in a coherent and consistent way based on a common set of criteria have proven to be valuable in a number of countries, including Australia, Ireland, the Netherlands, Russia, and the United Kingdom. The European Union (EU) has also established a voluntary European Qualifications Framework to promote mutual recognition of educational and skills qualifications.[34] The potential benefits of such a system in China, with its diversity of institutional subsystems of education and training (both geographically and across line agencies within the training system) are substantial. Given the challenges of coordination and agreement on common standards and implementation arrangements, implementing an NQF would be a long-term process. Nonetheless, it is a goal worth pursuing, because it can contribute to needed improvements in educational quality and labor market relevance.

Achieving and Sustaining a Healthy and Productive Population

Deepening health reform will be one of China's biggest social challenges in the coming years. At the same time, Chinese and international experience demonstrates that health sector reform is one of the most complex and politically challenging reforms that governments confront. This challenge is exacerbated in China by the explosion of noncommunicable diseases, and requires a fundamental realignment of the health delivery system away from the current hospital-centered model toward one that manages care across levels of the system with primary care providers playing the key role in care coordination.

Transforming the health system will be challenging, but if greater equalization and a more responsive and accountable system can be achieved, international evidence points to significant health, equity, and productivity dividends (Spence and Lewis 2009). China's Health System Reform initiated in 2009 recognizes many of these challenges. This section discusses three key elements of health reforms: reorienting the delivery system to put a greater emphasis on primary and preventive care; reforming health financing and incentive systems; and deepening reforms of the hospital system.

Current status and challenges in China's health system. In the past decade, China has sharply increased public expenditure on health care and undertaken a range of reforms in financing and delivery of health services. China has achieved expansion of its health insurance system at a speed that has few precedents globally. Health insurance coverage of the rural population rose from only around 20 percent in 2003 to around 95 percent by the end of the decade, and urban residents outside formal sector insurance schemes were also brought within the umbrella of insurance. Coverage of services and reimbursement rates have also been expanded gradually, and major investments have been made in health infrastructure. The expansion of health insurance has been complemented by ongoing structural reforms, most recently through the 2009 Health Systems Reform.

Despite increased spending, however, the health sector remains inefficient and fragmented, is misaligned with the burden of disease, and provides inadequate and unequal financial protection for the population. A key aspect of the changing context is the dominance of noncommunicable disease, which requires a different policy and delivery system mix. Following are the key issues and challenges for China's health sector:

- *Financial protection for households remains inadequate.* Although the share of out-of-pocket spending in total health expenditure has fallen in recent years to just under half (figure 4.19), health costs as a share of household income remain high. Despite the massive expansion of the New Cooperative Medical Scheme and urban residents' schemes in the 2000s, household health spending fell only marginally from 8.7 to 8.2 percent of average household income between 2003 and 2008 and actually rose slightly in urban areas (figure 4.20). Partial financial protection is driven by a combination of actual reimbursement rates (40–50 percent in nearly all provinces in the NCMS); annual caps on coverage that expose households to major financial risk from serious illnesses; and variable inclusion of services within insurance packages. Just as important, there is growing evidence of provider overservicing and health price inflation.

- *Financing is highly fragmented and unequal*, with risk pools fragmented across insurance schemes and across space. In most provinces, insurance plans are struggling to raise the pooling level beyond the prefecture level. As a result, coverage of services and the extent of patient reimbursement remain variable across space and across social groups, depending on which insurance scheme they are in. Funding sources are even more varied for primary care and include earmarked vertical program budgets, health insurance, central and local budgets, and user fees.

- *Financing and payment arrangements give weak incentives to health care providers to strive for efficiency and to deliver core primary care services*. For all levels of care, the dominance of fee-for-service provider payment systems and emphasis on self-financing of facilities has encouraged overservicing and lack of emphasis on efficiency. As a result, unnecessary hospital admissions account for 30–50 percent of the total, and average hospital lengths of stay are double the OECD average. In addition, the insurance-based financing model has for most people been

FIGURE 4.19   Out-of-pocket and government health spending as share of total health spending, 1997–2010

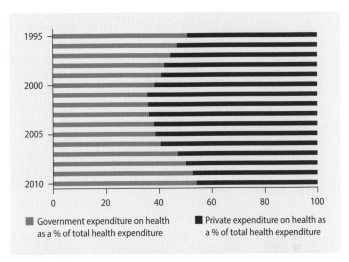

Source: China Health Economics Institute, *China Health Total Expenditures Statistics 2011.*

FIGURE 4.20   Household health spending as a share of total household income, 2003 and 2008

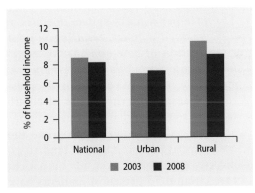

Source: Ministry of Health, third and fourth National Health Surveys.

biased toward inpatient care, until recently excluding outpatient care. The National Health Services Survey shows that in 2008, 33 percent of patients received reimbursement for outpatient care, compared with 85 percent who received reimbursement for inpatient care. Outpatient coverage within health insurance schemes has expanded significantly since then, but the process remains incomplete. Insurance plans often do not cover preventive services, which are particularly vital in early management of noncommunicable disease and illness. There is also a strong hospital bias in Chinese health spending relative to OECD countries (hospitals accounted for around 53 percent of total public health spending in 2010, compared with only 6.3 percent spent on township health clinics).[35] Second, the distorted price schedule and fee-for-service provider payment mechanisms have given health care providers strong incentives to generate demand for profitable high-technology services and drugs, rather than for basic services, particularly for the poor. Third, the capital funding model for public hospitals—with strong reliance on bank lending and "project cooperation," whereby third-party capital investors take an effective role in hospital management and even ownership—has reinforced incentives for profit maximization in public hospitals, led to unclear ownership and control of public facilities at times, and contributed to irregular practices (Liang 2007).

- *The three-tier delivery system operates in a fragmented manner, resulting in poor coordination of care and case management across the public delivery network.* Currently, there is very limited cross-referral across the three tiers of health facilities to ensure that health conditions are managed at the most appropriate and cost-effective level. Patients tend to go directly to hospitals even for outpatient care (around 53 percent of patients have their first contact with the system at a hospital), and there is no gatekeeping by lower levels. This "disintegrated" behavior is driven by provider incentives that promote profit maximization rather than appropriateness of care. This breakdown in the coordination of the three-tier system means that China is not well prepared for the more complex case management needs that noncommunicable diseases demand. Pilots to build relations and harmonize incentives between hospitals and lower-level providers are under way (in Shenzhen and Wuhan, for example), but these remain in their infancy.

- *Health insurance agencies and the budgetary authorities have a limited role in promoting cost effectiveness and quality of services.* To date, despite major increases in insurance financing of health services, insurance agencies remain largely passive financiers of services. As such, they do not effectively hold providers accountable for quality and cost-effectiveness. Similarly, budget subsidies are, to date, not used to contract for outputs and reward performance.

- *There are major challenges in building the human resources for the emerging system.* A particular challenge is building a primary care provider cohort of reasonable size and decent quality. In 2010, China had only 60,000 general practitioners, or around 3.5 percent of all licensed physicians in the country—a very low ratio compared with OECD countries. Notably, the OECD country with the highest ratio of health costs to GDP (the United States) also has the lowest general practitioner ratios (figure 4.21). The situation in China is exacerbated by assignment of responsibility to local-level CDCs for essential public health services and in-service training at the township and village level without allocation of adequate resources to provide such training or monitoring of provider practices. At the higher levels of the system, there is also a significant shortage of qualified hospital managers.

- *Trust in the health system and providers is low, and social accountability remains limited.* Currently, the hospital sector is considered to be one of the least-trusted public services by Chinese citizens (Wang and Yang 2011). Part of the concern is the perception of the need to make informal payments to providers to receive faster service and better-quality doctors.[36] More generally, there are concerns of an "erosion of medical ethics" (Yip and others 2010). While social accountability pilots in health are growing, there is limited accountability of providers and health facilities to the population.

FIGURE 4.21 Comparison indicators on density of general practitioners

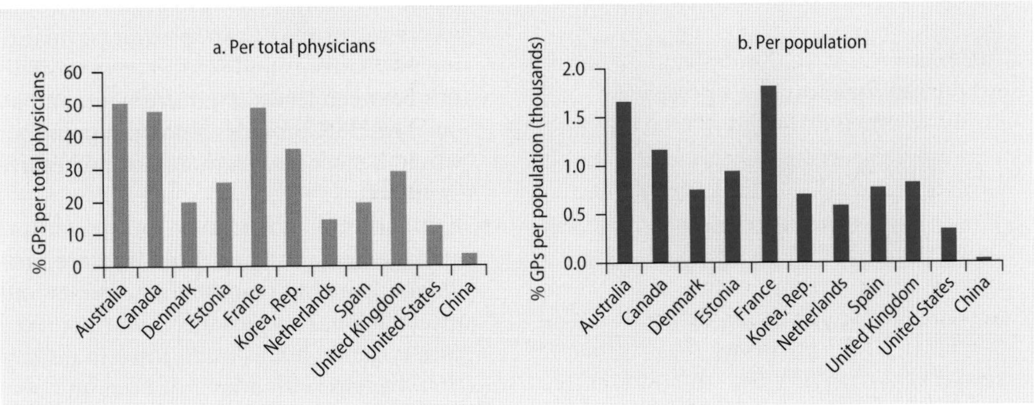

Source: OECD 2010a; World Bank 2011b.
Note: Data for OECD countries are for 2007; data for China are for 2010.

- *The nonstate sector has the potential to contribute more to realizing the government's objectives in the health sector.* Although around 20 percent of hospitals are private, they accounted for only about 5 percent of total inpatient and outpatient services in 2008. The situation is reinforced by public insurance systems that have so far provided an unlevel playing field between public and private health providers.

Reforms to promote a healthy and productive population. Many of the challenges of health reform are outlined in the 2009 Health Systems Reform (HSR), but questions remain on how much progress can be made in the absence of more fundamental realignment of the incentives in the health system.[37] The five areas of the HSR recognize the need to reorient care to greater reliance on primary and preventive services, contain costs, and reform financing and hospitals, but an overarching concern is whether the reforms will be sufficient to achieve the fundamental shift away from an inefficient and hospital-centered model of care to one that is more suited to the demands of a disease profile dominated by noncommunicable disease and is built around a primary care system that helps coordinate care across levels of the delivery system. This section discusses the reforms that

might be considered to achieve this, some of them extensions of existing reform initiatives. These include primary care reforms, deepening hospital reforms already under way, and addressing challenges in health financing and payment systems.

The Chinese authorities have emphasized *primary health care reform* in the ongoing health systems reform, but such reform is a generational change that is likely to encounter significant obstacles.[38] A modernized primary care system requires a set of comprehensive measures phased in over 10–20 years, including new delivery models, a new generation of primary care health professionals, financial and nonfinancial incentives, and a realistic transition plan (figure 4.22). The different elements of primary care reform are linked, and it is critical to move on all the major elements in tandem. In addition, primary care reform cannot succeed in isolation from reforms of other levels of the health system. An effective primary care system must be part of a broader model of "coordinated care" that ensures that patients are treated and that their condition is managed at the right level of the system to contain costs and improve quality.

International evidence shows that a disease profile dominated by noncommunicable illness requires more complex case management and coordination of care, and primary

FIGURE 4.22   **Pyramid of care model**

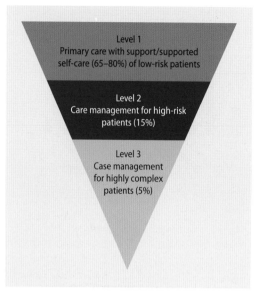

Level 1
Primary care with support/supported self-care (65–80%) of low-risk patients

Level 2
Care management for high-risk patients (15%)

Level 3
Case management for highly complex patients (5%)

Source: Palu 2011.

care level plays a critical role in the process. As shown in figure 4.22, a majority (65–80 percent) of such patients need low-level care because their conditions are reasonably controlled with self-management. This care can and should be provided by a strong primary care system. About 5 percent of patients with noncommunicable disease require complex case management delivered by specialized or hospital-based care. Between these groups are higher-risk patients who need less complex care management from specialists. Primary care plays the key role in managing care across these three groups. In addition, evidence from developing countries shows that expenditure on primary care is more pro-poor than expenditure on hospitals.

The key steps of primary health care reform are based on Chinese and global experience and are summarized in figure 4.23. In the short term, two broad steps should be taken:

• As a starting point, reach for consensus about the policy direction and key components of reform. This consensus would outline the key dimensions of

reform and include decisions about professional competencies, organizational forms for primary care providers, financing mechanisms and sources, responsibilities between levels of government, and so on. The HSR provides a starting point but would benefit from a more comprehensive approach.

• Experiment with new institutional arrangements for new primary care providers, learning from Chinese pilots and international experience. The primary care system remains fragmented in institutional terms with a host of often uncoordinated actors, including family planning agencies, maternal child health programs, township health centers (THC) for primary and secondary care, village doctors, public health agencies, and others. In rural settings, township health centers with links to village clinics are the natural unit to be strengthened or restructured to provide integrated primary care. A key question is to what extent THCs should retain an ambition to provide inpatient care. One possibility could be to convert THCs into ambulatory care centers, with family practitioners providing technical oversight of village doctors. The urban solution would be built around urban community care centers. Emerging experiences in Shanghai and Beijing indicate that they are able to fulfill primary care provision tasks when equipped with a new set of competencies and provided with professional support. Shanghai and Ningbo have also provided promising examples of a functional family doctor model for the past several years. Integrated care centers that include primary care providers along with other professionals (ambulatory specialists, social workers, geriatricians) should also be piloted.

In the medium to long term:

• *Equip a new generation of providers with new skills*, a process that will take a generation to complete. To achieve this goal by 2030, significant changes to medical

FIGURE 4.23 **Roadmap for PHC modernization**

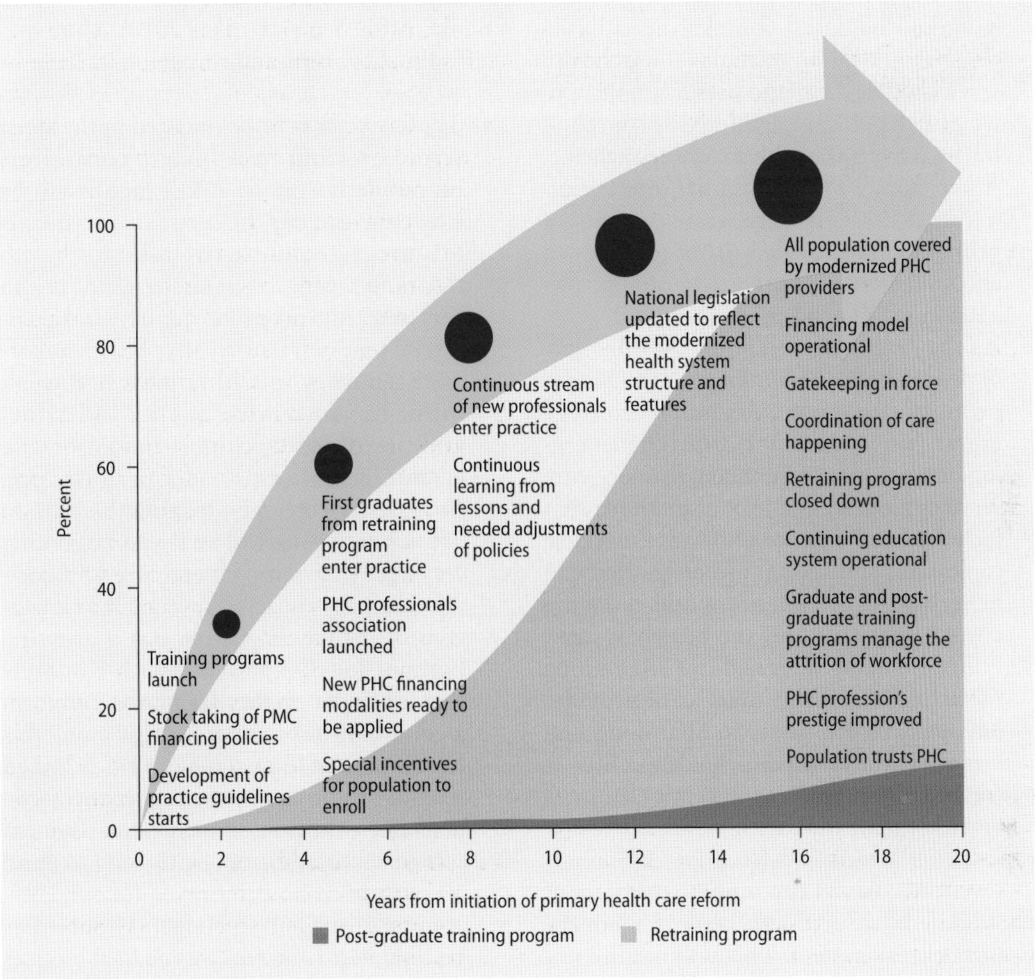

Source: Palu 2011.

education are needed.[39] OECD standards imply that China will need about 600,000 general practitioners and perhaps twice as many mid-level health professionals, but only a small number of universities in China currently provide training comparable to the eight-year Western medical training. Transitional arrangements will need to be put in place, balancing retraining the existing stock of providers (temporary programs) and establishment of new streams of training (permanent). The experience of former socialist countries in Europe and Central Asia provides lessons

in this regard (World Bank 2005). An important element of the in-service training strategy would be reform of the funding mechanism and incentives for local CDCs to provide essential public health services training at the grassroots level.

- *Further reform the resource allocation model supporting primary care development.* International experience suggests that resources could be allocated per capita, risk adjusted for gender, age, and mortality, possibly also including socioeconomic parameters (poverty, remoteness). High- and middle-income countries provide examples of models of varying complexity: for example, the United Kingdom has used complex need-based resource allocation formulas for its health service, while Thailand uses a simple non-weighted per capita allocation method for its universal health insurance scheme. A key step, which China has been piloting since 2005, is to separate incomes of primary care providers from revenues to encourage cost-effective and quality primary care (Yip and others 2010).

- *Adopt financing methods that provide appropriate performance incentives for primary care providers and encourage greater use of primary care.* The emerging best practice of financing primary care services globally is a mix of methods that includes fixed practice allowance, variable capitation, and special incentives that can help maximize benefits while reducing costs to patients and the health system. Pilots are being designed in China along these lines. In the primary care provider payment reform pilots in Shandong and Ningxia, the township health center is treated financially as a vertically integrated organization with village clinics.

Over time, China can move to a system of coordinated care across the three tiers of the health delivery system. This will require not only better-quality primary care providers but also strengthened coordination of care between primary and higher levels of the system and alignment of the financial incentives of providers and patients toward primary care. This process can benefit from global lessons (box 4.1) and from China's pilots on care coordination.[40] Such reforms can be a driver for wider reform of the health delivery system if well structured.

Hospital reforms will need to be deepened. Achieving the necessary reorientation to primary and preventive care and to promote a model of coordinated care in China will be difficult without further progress on hospital reform. Fundamentally, it will be necessary to change the current incentives for public hospitals and doctors to behave like private profit-maximizing providers (World Bank 2010b; Yip and others 2010). More specifically, short-term reforms could include:

- The key reform to be initiated in the short term is setting firm budget constraints on public hospitals. A key factor will be exerting greater influence over hospitals through more active roles for health insurance agencies as purchasers of health services that promote quality and cost-effectiveness. Historically, health insurance agencies in China have had weak influence on service quality indicators and use of information to monitor and encourage better provider performance. Moving from simply "paying the bill" to active purchasing will be key to promoting a system that puts patient care and cost-effectiveness ahead of revenue maximization of providers. China has a growing body of local experience with contracts that set wider quality standards and form a good basis for further strengthening this function over time. This reform is linked to wider reforms in provider payment systems (see below on financing and payment reforms). In addition, with only around 10 percent of hospital revenues currently coming from public budgetary subsidies (and the rest from fees for medical services and drugs), the influence of budgetary agencies on hospital and provider behavior is weak.

- A second set of measures would evaluate the experience in improving hospital governance and management. Given the diversity in hospital organizational reforms across China, it is necessary in the short run to have more rigorous evaluation of different models and the lessons from them. The national pilots in 16 urban areas from 2009 are a useful laboratory in this regard. In addition, there are improvements in adoption of new developments in information, communications, and record-keeping technology used in hospital and insurance management that can significantly improve efficiency of

BOX 4.1   Health care coordination in OECD countries

Health care systems in OECD countries have evolved significantly in recent decades and offer lessons in what to anticipate given an aging population, economic and medical progress, emergence of chronic diseases, and public dissatisfaction with access to and responsiveness of health care providers. The growing prevalence of chronic disease has been a major driver of calls for coordinated care.

It is well established that people with chronic conditions are high users of health services and absorb a higher share of costs (Machenbach 2005; Thorpe and Howard 2006). Care models are emerging to address the needs of these people to reduce costs for both patients and institutional payers, improve outcomes, and raise the quality of and satisfaction with care. Although models vary considerably, countries are consciously reducing their hospital capacity and moving toward a care model that places greater emphasis on primary care and coordination across care settings (OECD 2009; Hofmarcher, Oxley and Rusticelli 2007). Care coordination consists of a mix of measures that link professionals and organizations at all levels of the health system, emphasize patient-centered care integration, manage patient referral through the delivery system, and promote follow-up care as well as the continuity of long-term-service provision. The concept is often based on the strong role of primary care as the driver of coordination functions, including through gatekeeping (Saltman, Rico, and Boerma 2006).

Most coordination models target specific patient groups such as seniors or people with one or more chronic conditions. One approach is known as disease management. Disease management programs can consist of a number of components, including multidisciplinary teams, provider education, provider feedback, information technologies such as electronic medical records (to share patient infor-

mation), organized provider networks, patient reminder systems, use of evidence-based guidelines, financial incentives to providers, and the use of family physicians that coordinate treatment (Ofman, and others 2004). A similar approach, sometimes referred to as case management, consists of assessing, planning, managing, and monitoring of an individual's social service, prevention, and treatment needs. This is performed by a "case manager," who in principle works with providers across all levels to ensure cost-effective treatment. Other less common models involve the delivery of a comprehensive package of services to a defined population through integration of financing, professionals, and facilities under a single organizational and managerial structure. Kaiser Permanente and the Mayo Clinic in the United States are examples of an integrated delivery system.

The impact of coordinated care models suggests potential for improving system performance, although evidence on some indicators is mixed. In a review of the literature, Hofmarcher, Oxley, and Rusticelli (2007) found disease management programs appear to improve quality and outcomes. These programs may reduce hospitalizations, but their impact on cost containment appears inconclusive. Evidence from large integrated delivery systems suggests that these organizations are able to follow care management processes (such as clinical pathways), reduce unnecessary hospitalizations and lengths of stay, and provide higher-quality care at lower costs than other types of delivery arrangements (Weeks and others 2010; Tollen 2008). Finally, effective primary care systems have reduced unnecessary and costly hospitalizations in both high- and middle-income countries (OECD 2010a; Macinko and others 2010; Bynum and other 2011; Bitran, Escobar, and Gassibe 2010).

operations under any model of hospital organization. Moving from paper-based to electronic systems can facilitate adoption of tools such as cost-accounting software and electronic medical records. The key in expanding management information systems, however, will be the need for

consistent data standards and protocols across health facilities, to reduce the current fragmentation of systems and promote coordinated care across levels. And the effectiveness of any organizational change will depend on a new generation of hospital managers. Finally, following the co-responsibility direction of reforms, efforts to involve greater third-party and community involvement in the management and oversight of hospitals could be accelerated in line with the growing numbers of pilots throughout China.

- A further reform, to be initiated in the medium term, will be the introduction of greater competition for public hospitals from the nonstate sector. Government is looking to encourage greater entry of private providers, including international health care investors who can bring global best practice in facility management and quality assurance. Private providers could open their own facilities or enter under contract arrangements with public hospitals. There is significant potential to contract out management of public hospitals to nonprofit organizations, as several high- and medium-income countries, including Brazil, have done. To realize this goal, health financing and purchasing arrangements will benefit from proactive inclusion of nonstate providers. That in turn will require development of a licensing and accreditation regime to ensure minimum quality standards.

- A second area for attention in the medium to long term is the capital investment strategy for hospitals and the appropriate future mix of health facilities to manage the epidemic of chronic illness. While China has been trying to build up its hospital infrastructure in recent year, it is also important to learn the lessons of OECD and transition countries that overbuilt their hospital networks and struggled subsequently to adjust the system as use patterns shifted. In the European Union, for example, as chronic illnesses came to dominate the disease profile, hospital beds fell from around 850 per 100,000 population in 1985 to around 530 in 2009, and average length of stay declined from 10.5 days to just over 6.5 in the same period.[41] As a result, the delivery model has shifted from hospital-based care to community-based ambulatory centers and "teleportal" clinics. This has been facilitated by rapid advances in information and communications technology. In addition, hospital design is increasingly flexible to allow hospitals to expand or contract in response to shifting demand and to new technologies and care practices. Such trends suggest the need for a shift in the investment planning model for China's health system in the medium term to "right-size" the hospital network.

Health financing and payment reforms. *Health financing reforms* would benefit from a dual-track approach that focuses on reducing disparities between schemes and between localities, while in the longer run further examining the role of social contributions and general revenues in health system financing. Aiming for complete equality of coverage (services and financial protection) across all schemes and all areas is probably not realistic. However, it would be desirable to explore how increased funding at higher levels could help equalize a basic package of services that localities could top up with local resources and that could be further supplemented by expansion of private insurance arrangements.

In parallel, it is necessary to *accelerate provider payment reform* to increase the incentives for all health providers to improve efficiency and quality. A number of efforts have been made to control costs in the health system, including drug lists and zero mark-up policies, controls on use of technology, and the like. But without a more fundamental shift away from the current provider payment systems, the basic incentive structure for providers will continue to drive inefficiencies and inappropriate care. Payment reform needs to be complemented with a stronger emphasis on professional ethics among providers as well as tools for greater accountability of providers to patients.

The first step in the short term is to integrate management of health insurance schemes within pooling areas. This agenda is already being pursued in many areas and with central policy guidance toward integration of social insurance schemes. An increasing number of coastal areas (such as Dongguan) are already merging the management of the NCMS and urban residents' insurance schemes and have even achieved integration of the NCMS with insurance schemes for urban residents and urban workers. However, the effort is constrained in some provinces by the split management of different schemes across the health and human resources and social security departments.

Another short-term measure that should be considered is to move from the current model of individualized coverage in insurance schemes to household-based coverage. This approach makes sense from an insurance viewpoint, because it spreads risks across the household members of different ages with different intensity-of-care needs. But it also makes sense for supporting the core values of social policy, which include building on family institutions.

In parallel, it is necessary to accelerate pilots on provider payment reform and evaluate their impacts on efficiency, quality, and health outcomes. For all levels of care, the priority is to move away from the current fee-for-service model to alternatives. For higher-level care and hospitals, case-based payment is currently the main direction of pilots. This approach helps to contain costs and is relatively simply to manage, but it may raise issues in quality of care. Case-based payment can also have unintended consequences on spending on uncovered services. Other alternatives such as diagnostic-related groups avoid some of these problems but are also much more demanding of information, management, and monitoring systems.

For the medium term, integration of the three health insurance schemes seems a sensible and achievable goal, initially within prefectures and provinces. It would require gradual equalization of benefit packages and provider payment mechanisms across insurance schemes, as well as a financing mechanism to promote the equalization. A key question is to what extent the coverage package of the NCMS and urban residents is "scaled up" toward that of urban workers and, if so, over what time frame consistent with fiscal constraints. This issue could

be addressed in part by offering voluntary supplemental health insurance to those in the urban worker scheme.

To support such integration, the pooling level for health insurance should be raised to at least the provincial level and a common model of pooling defined to achieve more equalized health care coverage. Provincial-level pooling has been the direction of China's health policy for some time, but progress remains limited. The first question is what model of pooling will be pursued. International experience suggests that there is no single best model suited to all country contexts (World Bank 2010d). Japan has had a single "virtual" pooling fund since the early 1980s. Other countries such as the Netherlands use a risk equalization fund that adjusts premium and payment rates. Others pool at the national level (Sweden and the United Kingdom) or regional levels (Canada and Kazakhstan). In a number of countries, the process of moving to higher-level pooling took a decade or more, and a period of this length could be anticipated in China. Emerging experience in China suggests that some form of risk adjustment could be an intermediate approach, which could also help manage possible resistance from richer areas within each province.

Based on the evaluation of pilots, another key medium-term reform will be to roll out nationwide provider payment reforms that fundamentally realign the incentives of providers and patients. Both China's pilot experience and the growing body of global practice—including that of middle-income countries—on provider payment reform can inform rollout of provider payment mechanisms, which are case-based or move toward diagnostic-related groups (World Bank 2010c). This is an essential achievement if any of the other reforms and reorientation of the health delivery system are to be achieved, if uncontrollable cost escalation is to be avoided, and if public trust in the health system is to be restored.

In addition to payment reform for hospitals, continuing reforms of doctor salary and compensation systems will be needed.

Measures already being initiated to delink the incomes of doctors from prescription volumes are a welcome initial step in realigning doctor incentives with efficiency and appropriateness of care. But a more fundamental reconsideration of the incentives embedded in physicians' current salary structures will be needed over time, even with case-based or other payment system reforms. Building consensus in this area will be unusually challenging. The diverse experiences of OECD countries in striking the balance between fixed and performance-based pay, along with the different incentives and outcomes that result, provide useful lessons for China in this regard.[42]

In the longer run, a key question in health financing is the appropriate balance between insurance contributions, general revenues, and out-of-pocket spending. In the past decade, the balance of insurance contributions and general revenues has already shifted in favor of the latter with the reliance on budget subsidies to promote expansion of the NCMS and urban residents' schemes. Out-of-pocket spending has come down somewhat but is still well above the government's longer-term target of roughly 30 percent of total health spending. The increase in general revenues financing is a realistic acknowledgment of the challenges of covering rural and urban resident populations in a standard contributory insurance model and of the labor market risks of burdening workers with overly high social contributions. If merger of the three schemes can be achieved, combining the current demand-side budgetary subsidies in insurance schemes and supply-side subsidies to facilities into a basic scheme financed largely from general revenues becomes a real possibility in the longer term. Careful consideration of the alternative budgetary revenue sources to compensate for the removal or reduction of health contributions from workers would be required.

Rapid progress in this direction has been achieved recently within Asia (including in India, the Philippines, Thailand, and Vietnam), with general revenues being the source of substantial coverage expansion. Similarly, within OECD, a number of countries, such as Denmark, Italy, and Spain, moved from contribution-based to tax-financed health systems in the 1970s and 1980s, while those that have retained a contributions-based approach have in a number of cases reduced the rates of contributions and increased the share of general revenue financing (Austria and the Netherlands are examples) (World Bank 2010d). These experiences and China's own with the NCMS and urban residents' schemes suggest that the appropriate balance of social contributions and general revenues (and the role of higher-level and local authorities) in the longer-run financing of the health system is worth reconsidering.

The Role of Citizen Participation in Social Services

In recent years, initial efforts have been made to promote roles for citizens in service delivery. Historically, citizen participation in the management and oversight of social services has been weak in China. Lack of citizen inclusion is reflected in attitudes surveys indicating significant frustration with providers of public services. As the challenges in social services move from expanding coverage and quantity of services to ensuring that services are of adequate quality, initiatives to increase the role of citizens in promoting effective local services have expanded. However, efforts remain highly localized and for the most part in their infancy.

Current status and challenges. Increased citizen participation has several potential functions (Gong and Yu 2011). It can be a channel for citizens to better understand the challenges and trade-offs that service providers face in ensuring quality within budget constraints. It is one pillar of broader "social management" reforms in China that allow for some delegation of functions by the higher levels to the grassroots level. It can also help develop the capacity of citizen groups to express their grievances and provide an institutional basis for doing so. It can also build the capacity of communities for a future role as service providers in areas where community-based provision of social services has potential (such as care of the aged and early child development services); this in turn can help promote pluralism in service delivery in the longer run.

The roles of citizens in service delivery can take three forms progressively: consultation, presence and representation, and influence (Goetz and Gaventa 2001). Consultation involves opening channels for dialogue and information sharing. Presence and representation involves institutionalizing access for certain social groups in specific elements of decision making. Influence is the final stage in which the representation of citizens translates into influence on policies and the way services are run and organized. In general, China is at an early stage of developing these processes.

Emerging experience with different forms of citizen participation in social service delivery in China points to significant potential for increasing citizen voice. Recent experiences in Kunming, Chengdu, and Nanjing in the education and health sectors are summarized in box 4.2. The positive features include the following:

- Citizen satisfaction with services can be improved, through feeling that their views are being taken into account and through the increased accountability of service providers to citizens.
- The initiatives act as a localized and selective experiment in representative expressions of citizen voice.
- Citizens learn about the operating environment of local social services and are able to have a more informed dialogue with service providers on ways to improve quality.
- In the case of medical mediation, the initiative has the potential to resolve grievances in a more rapid and cost-effective manner than formal dispute resolution channels.

At the same time, the experiences reveal the challenges for effective citizen participation and the inherent trade-offs involved:

- While simple consultation may have value, for citizen participation to have a real impact, a clear policy and institutional framework is needed so their participation is not ad hoc but is truly linked to formal decision-making structures and the incentives of providers. Such a framework needs to spell out clearly the responsibilities and accountabilities of the citizens' group, service providers, and local officials. It should also provide a clear financing base for the sustained operation of such initiatives.
- The specific interests of citizen groups (such as parents of children in a school) may at times run counter to some wider social policy objectives. For example, parental pushes to tighten student entrance criteria to promote elite student selection may run counter to wider efforts to reduce disparities between schools—and may be a particular problem with respect to future inclusion of migrant children.
- Citizens may not at times have the information necessary to make informed decisions on matters involving questions of technical judgment, and this lack can weaken their influence and bargaining power. This challenge is likely to be particularly pronounced in the health sector, where asymmetry of information between providers and patients is significant. Information asymmetries can be addressed through appropriate involvement either of citizens who have such knowledge or experts who are able to provide such inputs to the decision-making process.
- There is not as yet good evaluation of the impacts on both processes and relevant outcomes (both qualitative such as client satisfaction and "harder" indicators such as student performance, health facility quality indicators, or patient outcomes).

Addressing the challenge of enhancing citizen participation in social services. National policies already set a clear direction for increased participation of citizens in social service delivery, but the key question is how to make their participation more effective in improving the quality of services and

---

BOX 4.2   Initiatives for public participation in social services

Field work for this report reviewed the experience of several local initiatives on promoting citizen participation in social service delivery. The cases reviewed include:

Kunming, the capital of Yunnan Province, following a pilot, in 2008 introduced *public election of primary and secondary school principals*. More than 2,000 schools now have elected principals for terms of three years. The elections involve voting by students and parents, teachers, and experts. In addition, a process has been set up for regular public supervision of performance and for dismissal and by-elections. The candidates are subject to an interview process by experts, faculty, and student and parent representatives. The second round of elections has recently been taking place. Candidates can come from anywhere in China, introducing wider competition to the local education market. The former practice of lifetime tenure for the principal has been removed as a result. Anecdotal assessment of the experience is positive among parents, students, teachers, and local officials. As one principal expressed it, his attitude changed from "I was told to do" to "I wanted to do." Teachers report more proactive school management and an increase in teaching quality. At the same time, there are concerns that candidates can easily "buy" the small number of experts and influence votes with promises of benefits to other groups. In addition, the interview panels and voters do not include migrants for the most part, so that the potential inclusiveness of schools in the future may be undermined.

In Nanjing, the capital of Jiangsu Province, *school councils,* consisting of two-thirds parents or community representatives and one-third school representatives, have been established in primary and secondary schools. Some schools allow parent representatives to

vote. The councils have internal powers to vote and recommend action to the school principal, although final decision-making authority rests with the principal. At the same time, important decisions of the principal can be put to opinion polls and further examination. While the anecdotal assessment of the experience generally points to improved transparency, concerns have been raised about unclear accountability for the final decisions of the principal and the legal basis of the school council's authority to recommend and review such decisions. Several other provinces have similar institutions from kindergarten to secondary levels. Some of them, including Shandong Province from 2009, and Chengdu city in the near future, have regulations that seek to clarify the scope of authority and underlying processes of the councils to give them a firmer jurisdiction. The 2010 National Educational Development Plan for 2010–20 has also suggested establishment of such parent councils on a nationwide basis.

In Nanjing, a *People's Mediation Council on Medical Disputes* was established in 2008. The council has at least two full-time mediators in each district with designated budgetary allocations. They come mostly from retired health bureau or legal systems. In 2008–10, 1,700 disputes were handled, with more than 90 percent successfully resolved. The number of disputes mediated doubled in 2010, including group medical disputes as well as individual claims. While the experience is judged generally positively, the legal basis for the council is not robust, and the difference in bargaining power and information between large hospitals on the one hand and claimants on the other can be high. The lack of clear legal basis for follow-up and enforcement is likely to result in patients settling claims on terms that may not be to their best advantage.

Source: Gong and Yu 2011.

---

user satisfaction and ensuring consistency with equity objectives. Chinese and international experiences point to several key challenges in promoting citizen participation that moves from consultation to structures and processes that give real authority and influence to citizens. The experiences reviewed

above point to the importance of having a clear policy and legal framework for citizen participation, and a robust institutional and financing framework for ensuring that citizen participation is truly representative and does not place the costs of participation unduly on citizens themselves. To date, most citizen participation in China can be considered "state-mediated," and there may be room in the future for initiatives that are more directly driven by citizens, as seen in many other parts of the world. There is also a major agenda for strengthening the capacity of citizens' organizations to play a more informed and effective role. International experience also suggests that unexplored possibilities for extending the areas of citizen participation upstream beyond service provision to involvement in development of emerging policies for social services. Finally, it is important to define the limits of citizen participation more clearly to avoid raising expectations that cannot be met.

Looking ahead, some measures that can support this agenda in the short term include:

- *Rigorous evaluation of experience in citizen participation in social services at the provincial and subprovincial levels.* This evaluation would include qualitative assessments of the policy, institutional, and financing frameworks for participation; surveys of providers, service users, officials, and other stakeholders; and development of indicators on the extent of citizen participation and its impacts on service quality, education and health outcomes, client satisfaction, provider behavior and attitudes, and so on.
- *Development of national policy guidelines that draw on the lessons of the evaluations.* The broad encouragement given by policies such as the National Education Development Plan will need to be made more concrete. In the health sector, the ongoing reforms would benefit from more explicit incorporation of citizen participation, which could include expansion of subnational pilots in tools for citizen feedback on service quality such as citizen scorecards and web-based feedback and complaints services (Brixi 2009).
- *In provinces where there is already experience, institutionalization of citizen participation processes and institutions,* for example, through the adoption of provincial policies (such as in Shandong with parent councils) and assured budgetary

allocations to fund the effective operation of relevant mechanisms.
- *Information and education campaigns* among citizens, officials, and providers on the benefits, challenges, and limitations of citizen participation along with practical guidance on how to initiate and institutionalize mechanisms. These campaigns should include expansion of information-technology-based tools for informing citizens and seeking their inputs.
- *Investment of public resources in capacity building of citizen groups and organizations* to increase their effectiveness in social service oversight and management.

Measures to be adopted over the medium to long term include:

- *Use of provincial policies and guidelines on citizen participation in social service delivery and oversight as a condition of receiving central transfers in the education and health sectors,* with a similar requirement for subprovincial levels as a condition for qualifying for provincial financing of social services.
- *Inclusion of indicators on citizen participation* in the monitoring and results systems of the education and health sectors and in the system for assessing the performance of local official.

Developing a Flexible and Secure Labor Market

An innovative and internationally competitive China will need a workforce that can adjust quickly to changing market conditions and whose workers continue to share in growth and have secure labor protection. To promote this notion of "flexicurity," the report proposes:

- Lowering barriers to labor mobility by ensuring the portability of pension and social security rights and phasing reforms of the hukou system so that all residents have equal access to a common set of social entitlements by 2030.

- Increasing the labor supply from the existing workforce. This will involve adopting a mix of measures to ensure that older urban workers—particularly women—do not exit the labor force prematurely; these measures including raising the retirement age. Higher rates of off-farm rural employment for those unlikely to migrate to urban areas should also be promoted.
- Building labor market institutions that allow for a sustainable balancing of the interests of workers with the need to maintain competitiveness. In particular, China should explore options to reduce labor taxation and to develop a more mature wage determination system.

A growing labor force has played an important role in China's economic performance, but supply and wage dynamics are shifting. From just under 600 million in 1980, the labor force is expected to peak at 1 billion around 2015. The dramatic increase in labor mobility has reinforced the contribution of labor to overall growth. The movement of rural labor has enhanced productivity and fed the low-wage model of Chinese growth. But the situation is changing. In the 1980s and 1990s, real wage growth for migrant workers was fairly flat, while labor market returns to higher levels of education were high and sustained (Cai, Wang, and Qu 2009). Since the mid-2000s, however, a notable degree of wage convergence has taken place across skills levels and across space within the country. While urban wage growth across all skill levels has been high in recent years, that of low-skilled workers has been particularly so, roughly doubling in real terms from 2001 to 2010 (Giles and others forthcoming; Cai, Du, and Wang 2011a).[43] Despite that, productivity growth has to date outstripped wage growth, avoiding inflationary pressures from the labor market (although there are signs of slower labor productivity growth in the second half of the 2000s) (Cai, Wang, and Qu 2009).

At the same time, the share of labor income in GDP fell during the 2000s, raising concerns about capital bias that may have contributed to rising inequality. The labor share was consistently around 60 percent of GDP from 1990 to 2004 before falling sharply to under 40 percent by 2008.[44] Although it has rebounded somewhat since then, questions remain concerning whether labor has been getting its "fair share" of the fruits of growth since the mid-2000s or whether the falling labor share was a short-run phenomenon produced by the transfer of labor to the more capital-intensive urban economy.

Looking ahead, China faces new labor market challenges as it seeks to move from middle- to high-income status. These include:

- *The aggregate labor force will start to shrink after about 2015*, initially slowly but then faster beginning in the late 2020s, and is projected to be more than 15 percent smaller than its peak by 2050.[45] The smaller labor force will support a growing elderly population.
- *China will no longer have the limitless rural labor surplus that has shaped the country's comparative advantage for the past 30 years.* Indeed, a number of researchers claim that the Lewis turning point was reached as early as 2003. The combination of shrinking or exhausted unskilled surplus labor and the concomitant massive increase in workers with senior secondary and higher education will fundamentally shift the dynamics of labor supply. This shift represents a huge opportunity for demand to adjust and move China up the value chain, but it also carries risks.
- *The rapid wage growth in recent years among migrants and low-skilled workers is accompanied both by rising expectations and by evidence of compression in the productivity growth premium.* While this wage growth has been a positive phenomenon, it raises the question of how to balance the continued need for upward real wage adjustments with sustained competitiveness as productivity growth eases

over the coming decades in the face of diminishing returns to capital investment.

- *As migrant workers shift from "floating" to become a more permanent urban population, they will increasingly expect better nonwage benefits,* including social security coverage and other urban social entitlements such as free education and social housing that historically have been available only to local hukou workers.

Unleashing the Potential of Labor

With China's labor supply beginning to decline beginning about 2015, ensuring that labor force participation among the current stock of working-age adults is adequate and that they are employed in the most productive ways will be essential. The discussion in the last section on human capital emphasized that the quality of *future* workers will need to improve for China to sustain robust productivity growth in the face of a declining labor force. However, there is also significant potential to increase labor supply among the *current* stock of working-age adults (primarily older urban workers). There is also scope to enhance the productivity of other groups: first, those who remain in rural areas, by increasing their participation in off-farm employment; and second, urban informal sector workers, many of them migrants. This section discusses these challenges and potential measures to address them.

Considerable debate swirls in China on the need to relax the one-child policy to offset the impacts of rapid aging. The policy has contributed to a fertility rate (1.54 according to the 2010 census) that is below what would be expected at China's income level. However, the experience of middle-income and East Asian countries and of parts of China raises questions as to whether eliminating the policy would have a significant impact on the fertility rate. The total fertility rates of countries such as Japan and Korea (both around 1.3) and Vietnam (1.8) suggest that the long-run fertility increase may not be major even if the policy were eliminated. Other social

FIGURE 4.24 **Urban labor force market participation rate among local workers, 1995–2009**

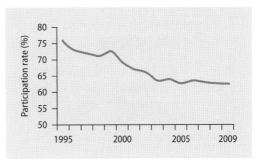

Source: Cai, Du, and Wang 2011a.

reasons might lead to relaxation of the policy, but from a labor supply standpoint, this report argues that China will still face significant challenges in coming decades.

The supply and structure of the labor force. While urban labor markets have seen a vast influx of migrant labor, they have also witnessed substantial declines in labor participation rates among local urban workers. Figure 4.24 shows a steady fall in urban labor force participation rates (LFPR) among local workers from mid-1990s to 2009.[46] While this decline appears to have stabilized at 62–64 percent, it is useful to understand the drivers.

The overall decline in LFPR among local urban workers masks different patterns among younger and older workers. The mid- to end-2000s saw slight increases in participation among younger urban workers but a notable decline among those in their 50s. A long-term phenomenon, the decline among older workers has continued since the main wave of SOE restructuring and more than offset the small increases in participation among younger workers. Even more striking is how early urban women withdraw from the labor force, with only around 20 percent participation by the official retirement age of 55.[47] It is difficult to say to what extent the decline in participation among older workers is a supply-side phenomenon or is driven by the combination of demand for younger and

FIGURE 4.25   **Employment rates of older workers by age, gender, and residence, selected years**

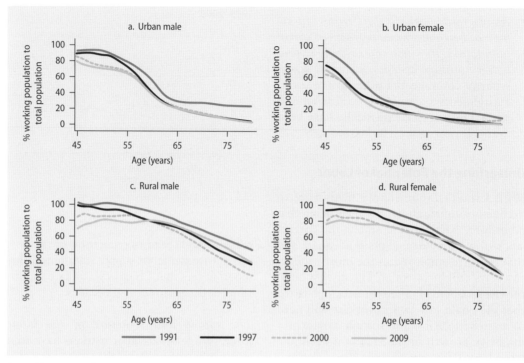

Source: Giles, Wang, and Cai 2012.

better-educated workers and the big influx of cheap migrant workers in the same period; regardless, it is clearly a long-term feature of urban labor markets. While LFPRs have also fallen for older rural workers, they remain much higher until much later ages than for their urban peers (figure 4.25).

International comparisons reveal that China's local urban population has a significantly shorter working life than their peers in other countries. Figure 4.26 shows LFPRs for older workers in Korea, Indonesia, the United Kingdom, and the United States. Women withdraw from the labor force earlier than men in all cases, but both urban men and women in the other four countries withdraw noticeably later than do those in China. The findings are strongly suggestive of challenges in the Chinese labor market and policy environment, which are likely to become more acute as the population ages. The issues include early and mandatory retirement for men and women, hiring policies of employers

who appear unwilling to hire older workers, and lack of opportunities for skill upgrading and "lifelong learning" among older workers.

Gender analysis of urban wages suggests that one reason for early labor market withdrawal by urban women may be the gender wage gap. Hourly wage differentials between urban men and women were consistently at 22–25 percent between 2001 and 2010.[48] Decomposing the differential to take account of both individual and job characteristics (sector and ownership type), the overwhelming bulk of the wage gap cannot be explained by observable characteristics, with the unexplained share of the difference ranging from 76 to 90 percent over the period (Cai, Wang, and Du 2011b). Recent analysis also confirms that returns to work experience in the labor market for women are notably lower than for men (China Center for Human Capital and Labor Market Research 2011).

A second issue in urban labor markets is the share of informal work and the potential

FIGURE 4.26 **International comparison of employment rates by age and gender**

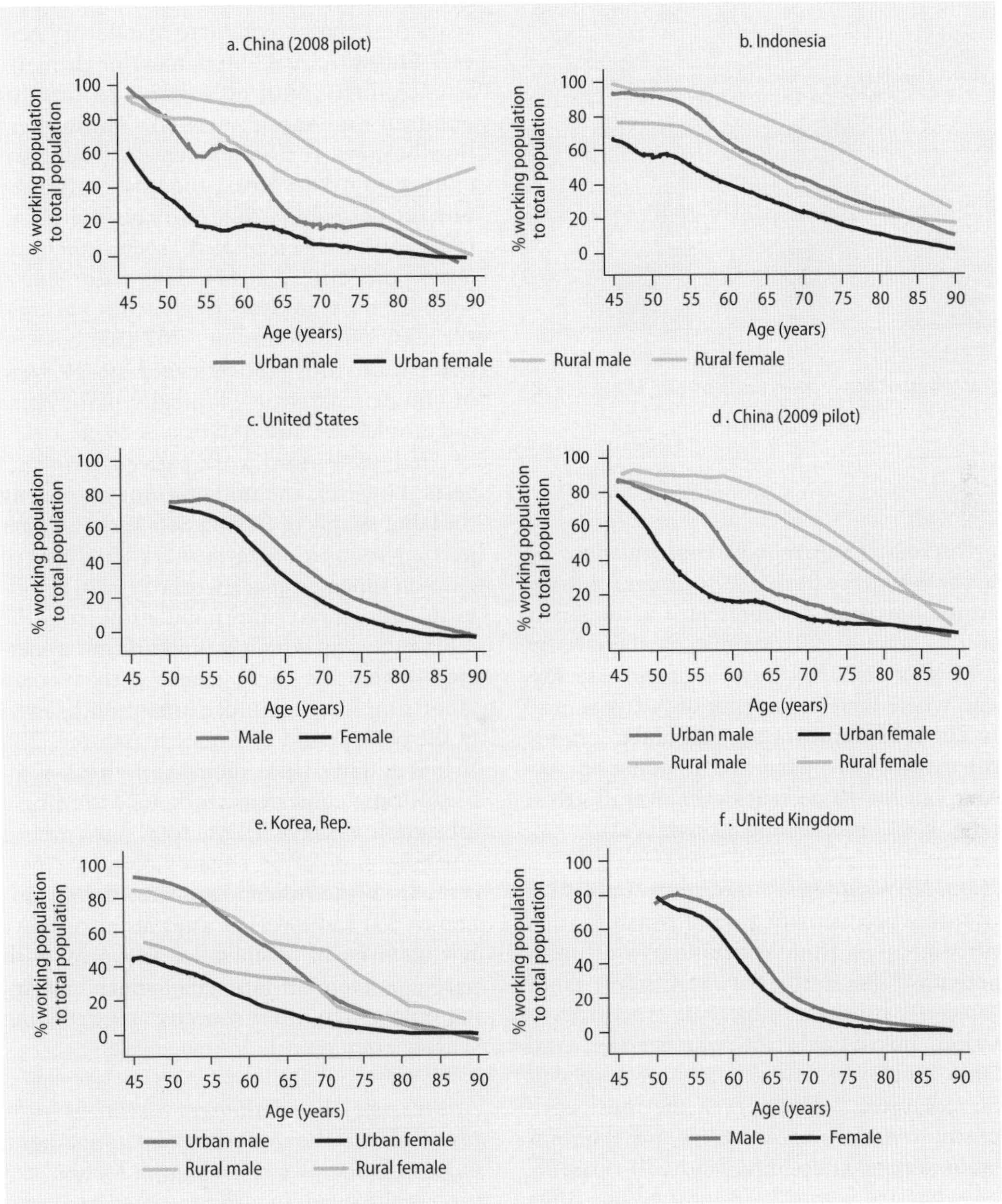

a. China (2008 pilot)

b. Indonesia

c. United States

d . China (2009 pilot)

e. Korea, Rep.

f . United Kingdom

Source: Giles, Wang, and Cai 2012.

to enhance productivity and worker protection through reforms that facilitate greater participation in the formal sector. Labor informality in urban China has undergone major transitions in the past two decades. Although the overall share of the informal sector in urban employment has decreased, it still accounts for a large proportion of the urban labor market (figure 4.27). Notably, more than 60 percent of migrant workers in 2010 were in the informal sector, indicating a remaining agenda for their incorporation into

FIGURE 4.27   **Size and composition of informal employment in the urban labor market, various years**

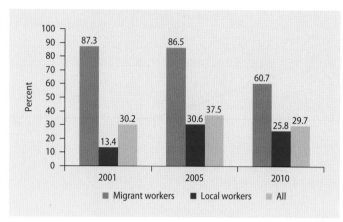

Source: Cai, Du, and Wang 2011b.

urban social security and labor regulation systems. Within the formal sector, migrant workers are heavily underrepresented in monopoly sectors (usually SOE dominated) where wages are higher than they are in competitive sectors and where there is evidence of "wage rents." In 2005, migrant workers accounted for only 3.1 percent of employment in monopoly sectors, but for 40 percent in the overall urban labor force (Yue, Li, and Sicular 2011).

Rural labor supply. Another potential source of future productivity growth is reallocation of rural labor from agriculture to off-farm activities. The decline of the Chinese labor force has been the subject of much speculation, in particular on whether the rural labor surplus has already been or soon will be exhausted.[49] Under even the most optimistic scenarios, it seems clear that the rural labor surplus is declining and will certainly be exhausted before 2030. At the same time, the profile of the remaining rural labor force suggests significant scope to increase productivity within rural areas through movement to off-farm activities in their localities.

Moreover, the profile of the remaining rural labor force indicates limited potential for substantial urban migration. Those still working in agriculture would not normally be in high demand in urban areas—they

are almost 47 years old on average, have average educational attainment of only 7.3 years (less than a complete mandatory general education), and 60 percent of them are women (often with obligations to care for children and aging parents). While there may be some further movement from agriculture to urban areas, the observation by one set of authors that "all the low hanging fruit has been picked" seems accurate (Park and others 2011). The argument is supported by analysis from other national surveys, which found in 2007 that over 80 percent of rural laborers ages 16–30 were in nonfarm activities, typically working as migrant labor (Park and others 2011).

Analysis of rural work patterns also suggests, however, the potential for increasing the labor supply of existing workers and their participation in off-farm work. Analysis of data on time and place worked (farm or off-farm) among the rural population from the 2005 minicensus indicates significant underemployment in rural areas, with average labor supply being under nine months even in the peak period of work life (figure 4.28). If one equates total months of rural work to full-time equivalent workers (assuming a 10-month work year), the total agricultural working population shrinks about 22 percent, from the official estimate of 297 million to 231 million. The analysis also shows low intensity of off-farm labor supply, with participation in off-farm employment averaging only around four months and dropping sharply after age 40.

Addressing the challenges in labor supply. Raising labor force participation among older urban workers, increasing formal sector employment in urban areas, and promoting further participation in off-farm rural work can help dilute the impacts of a shrinking labor force. One important point for policy makers is to avoid the "lump of labor" fallacy, which suggests that keeping older workers in jobs reduces employment opportunities for younger workers. International evidence consistently shows that is not the case. Some reforms and initiatives that

FIGURE 4.28   Labor supply by age for rural labor force and rural off-farm work, 2010

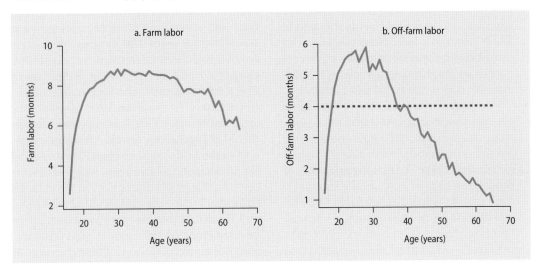

Source: Cai, Du, and Wang 2011a.

could help to address labor supply challenges include:[50]

- *Gradually raising retirement ages in the urban pension systems, removing the mandatory retirement age, and ending disincentives for later retirement.* These reforms are politically challenging but seem unavoidable as society ages. Initiating the reforms sooner can allow for a more gradual increase in retirement ages, to at least 65 for both men and women. Many OECD and transition countries have undertaken this reform in recent years, with the annual increase in the retirement age ranging from a more gradual pace of one to three months a year in OECD countries to six months a year in many transition countries. If reform can be started in the 12th Plan period, by 2030, the retirement age for men could reach 65 with a fairly gradual increase of three months a year; for women, full equalization of retirement age with men would take longer or require larger annual increments in the retirement age.
- *Facilitating access to part-time jobs and flexible work arrangements for older workers.* A key area of employment

experimentation in OECD countries is flexible work arrangements for older workers. These arrangements include "jobsharing," which splits a full-time position across more than one worker (as is common in Germany, for example) and more opportunities for part-time work. Such arrangements can facilitate greater labor force participation by women, which seems to be a particular challenge in China. Some countries have used wage subsidies for older workers to support such measures, although this needs to be done carefully to avoid distortions in the labor market. China would benefit from a close assessment of international lessons and an expansion of pilots domestically.

- *Enhancing mid-career skills training and upgrading.* By the time workers reach their 50s, employers may feel that investing in skills upgrading has low returns. OECD experience suggests that skills upgrading at mid-career is attractive both to employers in terms of returns on investment and to workers while they still have capacity and incentives to learn.
- *Strengthening the focus of employment services on placement of older workers.* A number of OECD countries have

introduced specific employment service programs for older workers, piloting new approaches to promote effective job search. These programs have been supported in some cases by special incentive payments for private employment agencies for placement of older workers (OECD 2006).

- *These measures would also be beneficial for rural workers, but additional policies could help facilitate their more active participation in off-farm labor.* To the extent that there is greater relocation of production away from coastal areas, more opportunities should be available for rural workers closer to their homes. That may increase their willingness to move into off-farm work, but in many cases, rural and migrant workers will need significant investments in training and skills upgrading to be able to take advantage of such opportunities. Substantial investments have been made in recent years.

Building Modern Labor Market Institutions

International evidence suggests that labor market institutions can have important impacts on the distribution of income. The effects of labor market institutions on macroeconomic performance, income distribution, employment, and other variables remain disputed.[51] Reviews of international evidence agree on one consistent finding, however: the strength of labor market institutions in determining wages has a significant impact on the distribution of income both within countries and across them (Freeman 2008). Given China's desire to reverse the rise in inequality, the potential role of labor market institutions is therefore of importance. This section focuses on two key labor market institutions: wage setting and labor taxation, including broader wage determination and minimum wages in the urban labor market.

Wage determination. Wage setting above the minimum is a highly decentralized process in China that is evolving toward a mature and uniform "system" of wage bargaining. The first provisions on collective contracts were in the 1994 Labor Law, and a series of guidelines and regulations have been issued periodically since then. The number of workers covered by collective contracts increased from around 50 million in 1998 to 94 million in 2009. Most recently, the Employment Contracts Law, effective from 2008, provides the legal framework. That was supplemented by the 2010 regulations for the "Rainbow Project" of the Ministry of Human Resources and Social Security, which urges complete coverage of collective contracting in firms with trade unions by the end of 2012 (Cai, Du, and Wang 2011b). Firm-level contracts are to be supplemented by regional- and industry-level collective contracts. The expansion of collective contracts has been mirrored by the increase in members of local branches of the state trade union, rising from around 100 million in 2000 to 226 million in 2009.[52]

Wage negotiations are guided in principle by wage guidelines issued by the local labor authorities.[53] The local guidelines are based on annual surveys of local firms for different occupations in various industries and work within national criteria. Each profession has a top, middle, and bottom wage level, and the national method is in principle meant to provide comparability across regions. The system is intended to provide an external reference point for employers in wage setting, and the number of occupations and sectors covered has gradually expanded since introduction.

In practice, collective bargaining is at an early stage of development and faces a number of challenges in becoming a truly bargained process. While the mechanism of collective contracting is spreading in urban firms, the practice can be considered more one of "wage consultation" rather than bargaining in the standard international sense (Shen and Benson 2008). Evidence shows that such consultation has reduced labor confrontations in multinational corporations that have such mechanisms, but it is also clear from the rising incidence of labor disputes in China that much remains to be done. A key challenge in the process of developing truly tripartite wage bargaining is the role of

TABLE 4.2 **Hourly wages of migrant and local workers, and share of difference explained by observable characteristics, 2001–10**

Indicator	2001	2005	2010
Migrant hourly wage as percent of local workers	35.0	46.7	78.0
Percent of difference explained by individual characteristics	74.7	62.3	63.7
Percent explained by individual and job characteristic	81.7	72.5	98.0

Source: Cai, Du, and Wang 2011b.

the All-China Federation of Trade Unions, which is still evolving toward a role as the representative of workers in wage discussions (Bai 2011). A second issue is the role of wage guidelines, which are based on surveys that often do not fully represent the local labor market, and in any event, play an unclear role in the discussions over wages at the firm level.

Public sector wages are determined separately, and the mechanism for wage setting is not systematic. On one hand, analysis suggests that more than half of the wage gap between monopoly (largely state-owned) industries and competitive industries cannot be accounted for by observable characteristics of workers (Yue, Li, and Sicular 2011). In contrast, in social services, the education sector introduced in 2009 an element of so-called performance-related pay (PRP), but these rules sought to address a complex set of issues related to the relative pay of rural teachers, the pay of teachers generally relative to civil servants, and a desire to reduce incentives for informal payments (Wang and Gong 2011). In the health sector, the fee-for-service system that has historically dominated naturally produces an indirect form of pay based on performance (or at least on volume of service), some of the negative effects of which were discussed earlier.

Wage outcomes in the urban labor market indicate that varied mechanisms are driving wage setting. In recent years, average wages of migrant and local workers appear to be converging rapidly, indicating that the labor market fundamentals of demand and supply are overcoming rigidities in wage-setting mechanisms. The convergence can be seen in the falling differential in average hourly wages over the 2000s and in the degree of difference that can be explained by

observable individual and job characteristics. Table 4.2 shows that the hourly wages of migrants relative to local hukou workers rose from only 35 percent in 2001 to 78 percent in 2010.[54] In addition, the proportion of the difference explained by observable characteristics rose from 82 percent in 2001 to 98 percent in 2010. In contrast, evidence on wages in monopoly sectors—mainly dominated by SOEs—indicates that in 2005, a high wage gap remained between SOE workers and those in competitive sectors. Around half of that difference could not be explained by the characteristics of the workers in monopoly and competitive sectors, such as gender, education, age, and so on (Yue, Li, and Sicular 2011).

Minimum wages. Minimum wages in China are a fairly recent phenomenon, and the system is still evolving, with as yet unclear significance in wage determination and market wages. The first minimum wage regulation was adopted only in 1993, with articles also in the 1994 Labor Law. However, more detailed guidelines on minimum wage setting did not emerge until 2004 and 2007.[55] Minimum wages are set at a decentralized level, most often at the municipal level, and should be adjusted at least every two years (although with no clear indexation mechanism). As shown in figure 4.29, real minimum wages across China have increased by almost two and a half times since the mid-1990s, with a rising share of cities making annual adjustments (except in 2009, with the global financial crisis).

Standards for minimum wage setting focus on the relationship to cost of living and relative wages rather than productivity. According to the 2004 and 2007 regulations, factors

FIGURE 4.29   Urban minimum wage adjustments, 1995–2009

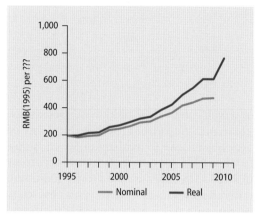

Source: Cai, Du, and Wang 2011b.

to be taken into account in setting minimum wages include the local minimum living cost, urban consumer price index (CPI), social insurance contributions and other mandatory personal contributions, average wages, and the economic and employment situation in the locality. Factors not mentioned include productivity, producer prices, and share of informal economy. City-level data on minimum wage elasticities show that minimum wages are most strongly associated with the

level of average wages, followed by local average consumption, while the urban CPI has a significant but much smaller effect (Cai, Du, and Wang 2011b).

While minimum wages have adjusted sharply upward in recent years, the vast majority of formal and informal workers in urban areas have labor incomes above the official minimum. Table 4.3 shows that almost all workers—whether migrant or local, men or women—receive labor income above the city-level minimum wage. Overall, the minimum wage is increasingly not a wage that workers generally are paid (or earn) in urban areas, but it serves as a reference point significant in its relativities to overall wage levels and to social benefits and thresholds. It therefore performs a benchmarking and administrative function, as well as an important political signaling function of the concerns of the authorities for low-wage workers. The question for coming years is whether the minimum wage will evolve toward playing a more direct role in the labor market, as discussed in the policy recommendations section below.

Improving approaches to wage determination: Looking ahead. Wage determination will play an increasingly important role in coming years in balancing the interests of workers and sustained competitiveness. The key will be to strengthen the linkage between wage setting and productivity growth. Real wages in urban China have enjoyed a period in which they have risen rapidly but are still below productivity growth. As the rural labor surplus is exhausted, productivity growth from labor transfer will decline over time. However, worker expectations of sustained rapid wage growth will be entrenched, increasing the challenges of sustaining wage growth of recent years.

Aside from minimum wage reforms, other reforms will need to be deepened to achieve a more uniform and market-based approach to wage setting in the formal sector. While the overall direction of such reforms is common across the public service, SOE, and private formal sectors, the starting points differ. The

TABLE 4.3   Share of migrant and local workers with income above minimum wage by gender, 2001–10

Percent

Indicator	Share of migrants above minimum wage	Share of locals above minimum wage
CULS2001		
Male	92.3	95.5
Female	86.3	88.9
Total	90.0	92.6
CULS2005		
Male	88.3	91.2
Female	76.4	83.5
Total	83.2	87.9
CULS2010		
Male	98.2	97.2
Female	97.1	97.3
Total	97.7	97.3

Source: Cai, Du, and Wang 2011b, using data from China Urban Labor Surveys (CULS).

pace of reform and factors to be considered thus also differ. Several directions should be considered:

SOE sector reforms. For SOEs, the initial priority is to establish a robust system of benchmarking wages so that they are increasingly determined by reference to relevant comparators in the wider labor market rather than simply by the amount of profits available for distribution to workers. The current wage premiums of SOEs are a reflection of underlying distortions in the operating environment of the enterprises and are difficult to justify on either efficiency or equity grounds. Although strengthening and enforcing a rigorous benchmarking system will be challenging for SOEs in sectors where only the state sector is active or in cases where a single employer is a monopoly, the more generic types of functions (accountants, secretaries, drivers) could be benchmarked against the outside market. It would also be useful to benchmark wages of local monopolies across regions to get a broad sense of within-industry comparability and identify outliers.

Enforcing wage discipline in the SOE sector will be challenging, but it could yield significant benefits for the Chinese economy and also result in a more equitable distribution of wages across society. The specific nature of the benchmarking process would be a matter for the Chinese authorities to consider further, but the evidence strongly suggests that a transparent system of some form is needed. Over the longer run, the direction of reform would be to have SOEs conduct collective consultation and bargaining in the same way as other firms under current labor legislation.

PSU reforms. The issues in wage setting for public service units are somewhat distinct, given the additional challenge of promoting accountability of public sector workers while ensuring that they are compensated adequately. Because of the unsystematic nature of PSU wage setting, it would be desirable in the short to medium term to develop a national strategy on reforming the process, including for social services. That could be linked to broader systems of human resource management, professional development, and promotions.

A big question for China is the extent to which it wishes to have performance-based pay as an element—and if so, to what degree—in setting wages for workers in the education and health sectors. Overall, there is a desire to explore the possibilities of PRP in the social sectors, but clarity on the objectives and potential modalities is lacking. The international experience in recent years suggests that PRP is not suitable for all types of public sector workers. In considering the appropriateness of PRP, several questions must be addressed: How closely is performance actually linked to pay, and what other factors are driving provider performance? How much are policy makers willing to shift the risk of low performance from the state to providers themselves? Are there indicators of performance that are consistent with the overall policy objectives of the sector and that have credibility among workers in the sector? If so, can those indicators be measured in a reliable, consistent, and transparent manner? What unintended consequences may result from an over-reliance on certain performance indicators?[56] Finally, are there alternative approaches to providing incentives for better performance by providers that may be more acceptable to the professions and less likely to induce unwanted behavior by providers. An example might be structuring the promotions system within the education and health sectors to place a higher emphasis on performance and results rather than on seniority or other factors. More broadly, if PRP is implemented primarily to address shortcomings in the wider system of governance and accountability in the education and health sectors, there may be other instruments for achieving the goals more effectively.

In considering whether PRP is appropriate, it is clear that pay based *purely* on performance is not suitable for teachers and health providers because of the perverse incentives that may result. If it is to be applied, a base compensation with some degree of bonus would be more appropriate. In addition, a stronger system for determining promotions and peer appraisal of performance is needed.

International experience also suggests that a "one-size-fits-all" approach to PRP should be avoided. The specific characteristics of the population being serviced should be taken into account in assessing provider performance—for example, through adjustments to account for remoteness or specific challenges of servicing particular population groups such as migrants or minorities. Box 4.3 summarizes some lessons of experience of PRP in OECD countries in the health and education sectors.

Formal private sector. For the formal private sector, the challenge will be to develop a mature system of collective bargaining. To make progress in this direction, the role of the union as an effective voice of workers in wage negotiations will be expected to strengthen. Gradual reforms in collective bargaining can be supported by efforts to make the labor market more competitive so that the relative bargaining strength of employers and workers reflects underlying supply and demand in

---

BOX 4.3   Lessons from performance-related pay experience for public servants in OECD countries

Despite a growing history of experiences with performance-related pay for health and education workers in OECD countries, the desirability and outcomes of PRP remain contested, and the gap between rhetoric and reality is often large. As of the mid-2000s, two-thirds of OECD countries had PRP for public sector workers or were introducing it (OECD 2005). The objectives underlying the introduction of PRP vary and are often related to the desire to promote wider organizational or management change, in addition to objectives related to the motivation or performance of individual workers. The scope of PRP initiatives has also varied, with schemes often more focused on managerial public sector workers and specific sectors. In addition, the actual assessment of performance varies, with some systems having no or low individual assessment.

While the share of PRP in total pay is not as great as may sometimes be claimed, salaries of civil servants in most OECD countries consist of three components: base pay, pay based on the specific duties of the position, and a performance-related element. The share of PRP has generally been fairly modest, with PRP bonuses rarely more than 10 percent of the base pay of civil servants, although closer to 20 percent for management-level staff. Some overall trends or features emerge from the review of OECD experience, including:

- There has been some expansion in the use of team or group performance as the benchmark for assessment of PRP.

- The countries with the strongest PRP emphasis are also those with the highest delegation of human resource and budgetary management responsibilities.
- In a number of cases, PRP systems have tended to become more decentralized over time.
- The criteria for assessing performance have become more diverse, with greater attention to outputs as well as competencies and social skills. At the same time, PRP systems have become less formalized and detailed, relying less on quantifiable indicators of performance.
- Many countries have experienced implementation problems, for example, before introduction of PRP in negotiations with unions and workers, during the deployment phase with management who may not well understand the system and objectives, and in terms of the costs in money and time for introducing PRP and the monitoring systems that it requires.
- International experience suggests that PRP itself may be only one factor in motivating workers, who emphasize other factors such as job content and satisfaction, flexibility of working arrangements, and promotion and other forms of recognition.
- PRP should not be used in isolation but as a tool to promote wider organizational reform, and the objectives and performance criteria should be set with this in mind.

Sources: OECD 2005; Wang and Gong 2011.

TABLE 4.4   **Minimum wage approach and criteria, various economies, end-2000s**

Economy	Approach	Key criteria for setting wage
Australia	Wage floor	Productivity, business competitiveness, relative standards of living, workforce participation rate
Korea, Rep. of	Wage floor	Cost of living, economic growth rate, average wage level, labor productivity, unemployment rate, consumer price index, and income distribution; there is no fixed weight for these factors, and the relevance of each is determined within the wage council debate and varies in time
Taiwan, China	Wage floor	Conditions of national economic development, price index, national income and average individual income, labor productivity of different industries and employment situation; workers' wages in different industries; survey and statistical figures on household income and expenditures
United States	Wage floor	Manufacturing productivity, affordability to employers, cost of living, wage levels
United Kingdom	Wage floor	Pay differentials, inflation, business costs, competitiveness, employment, economic conditions
France	Living wage	Overall wages and income, CPI, economic conditions, needs of workers and families
Hong Kong SAR, China	Wage floor	General economic conditions: latest economic performance and forecasts; labor market conditions: labor demand and supply, wage level and distribution, wage differentials and employment characteristics; competitiveness: productivity growth, labor costs, operating characteristics of enterprises, entrepreneurship, business sentiment and solvency, and relative economic freedom and competitiveness; standards of living: changes in employment earnings and inflation

Source: Hong Kong SAR, China, Provisional Minimum Wage Commission, 2010 (http://www.mwc.org.hk).

the labor market. This is starting to happen to some extent as the earlier labor surplus declines and workers now have a credible position of exit to other firms if wage settlements are inadequate. The bargaining process in the private sector can also benefit from better information on productivity growth through an improved system of labor statistics.

As a starting point, the basic function of the minimum wage in the private sector will need to be reoriented. That function is to ensure that workers are not exploited because of their limited bargaining power and that they receive a wage that fairly reflects their contribution to productivity growth. The minimum wage is not intended on its own to pull families out of poverty; keeping families out of poverty is the job of other policies, particularly social protection programs. Setting minimum wages too much according to their

poverty function could actually harm low-income workers by increasing unemployment or pushing them into the informal sector.

China's challenge over the coming decade will be to shift from its current "living wage" approach with respect to the minimum wage to a "wage floor" approach, which is more common in OECD countries. Like the current approach, the wage-floor approach takes into account several factors in determining the minimum wage. Table 4.4 provides examples of factors that are included in determining the minimum wage in some OECD countries as well as in Hong Kong SAR, China, and Taiwan, China. The major distinction is that some measures of productivity growth and competitiveness are the primary factors in setting the minimum wage. While price inflation and other factors remain important, the key is adjusting minimum wages to reflect

TABLE 4.5   Urban social insurance contribution rates in urban China

Type	Employer	Employee
Pension insurance	20 percent of payroll	8 percent of monthly wage
Unemployment insurance	2 percent of payroll	1 percent of monthly wage
Medical insurance	At least 6 percent of payroll	2 percent of monthly wage
Work injury insurance	0.5–2 percent of payroll	No contribution
Maternity insurance	0.5–1 percent of payroll	No contribution
Total	**29–31 percent of payroll**	**11 percent of monthly wage**

Source: Authors' compilation based on policy directives and documents of the Ministry of Human Resources and Social Services and the provincial departments.

productivity growth. China has elements of this approach in its current policy, but the relative balance between a needs-based approach and a productivity-based approach is toward the former.

Shifting toward a wage floor approach will require an improved system of labor market statistics to provide timely and reliable measures of productivity to the authorities setting minimum wages. Currently, the Chinese statistical system does not produce such measures on a timely basis. Reforms of labor market statistics will need to be deepened, with regular surveys of representative samples of firms and workers. Greater efforts will be needed to include small and medium-size firms in the samples. Historically, firm surveys have been based on information from large and state-owned firms, probably resulting in an upward bias in wage data.

Labor taxation. China is a high labor taxation country if all social insurance (SI) contributions are paid (table 4.5). The rates of social contributions are high by any standard and also exhibit considerable variation across and within provinces (for example, within Guangdong alone, the employer contribution rate for pensions in 2010 ranged from 9 percent in Dongguan to 22 percent in Zhanjiang). Pension dominates, in part driven by the high costs of funding legacy pension costs (see the next section).

By international standards, the "tax wedge" on workers in China is higher than in most OECD countries and well above East Asian regional comparators. Figure 4.30 shows the tax wedge on labor for a single worker on average wage in urban China (including the housing contribution) compared with other countries.[57] China's tax wedge of 45 percent is very high, especially considering that it is composed solely of social contributions (unlike most of the comparator countries the average worker in China does not pay personal income tax).

High average labor taxation leads low-income workers to avoid formal employment or to "selective formalization" of employment relations within the formal sector. The

FIGURE 4.30   Tax wedge on average formal sector worker, various countries, 2010

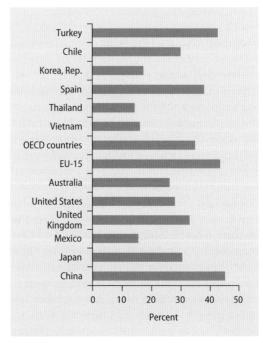

Source: OECD 2011c.

tax wedge on labor dampens incentives for formal sector participation for all workers, but an even more extreme impact can be seen when considering the marginal SI contribution rate of low-paid workers. This effect is produced by the policy of setting the minimum SI contribution wage at 60 percent of the average wage in each locality. Table 4.6 shows the distribution of urban workers in a selection of large cities whose wage falls below the 60 percent threshold. Around 33 percent of all workers fall below the minimum contribution base threshold. For those at 50 percent of the average wage (13–29 percent of all urban workers in these cities in 2010), the effective SI tax wedge if they are in the formal sector would be around 67 percent. This is clearly an exorbitant burden of labor taxation and could be expected to be a strong disincentive to formal sector participation at the lower end of the wage income distribution.

Selective formalization can be seen in the varying levels of participation in different types of "mandatory" SI in urban areas. In 2010, the latest available year, the total number of contributing urban workers ranges from 194 million for pensions, 178 million for health insurance, only 134 million for unemployment insurance, and under 80 million for housing funds.[58] Whether driven by employer or employee preferences, there is clearly large-scale and tactical "opting out" of social insurance schemes in response to high tax rates. At the same time, most urban SI funds continue to generate significant surpluses.

As part of its overall adjustment of the tax structure, it would be desirable for China to lower the tax burden on labor over time. The reform of labor taxation is only part of the broader tax restructuring discussed in chapter 1 on economic restructuring. If new revenues such as property taxes can be introduced, the potential to reduce taxes on labor may increase. Any reduction would need to be gradual and carefully sequenced to avoid overvolatility in public revenues.

Even within the current system, labor taxation could be reduced in some areas

TABLE 4.6 **Share of workers with income below minimum SI contribution base (40–60 percent of average wage), 2001–10**

		2001	2005	2010
Below 60%	Shanghai	32.35	29.05	31.37
	Wuhan	36.95	37.44	37.96
	Shenyang	28.10	33.84	31.41
	Fuzhou	32.88	30.69	31.30
	Xi'an	40.44	31.16	35.99
Below 50%	Shanghai	28.56	22.89	25.12
	Wuhan	11.53	28.89	29.07
	Shenyang	9.98	15.90	13.68
	Fuzhou	19.85	20.74	21.53
	Xi'an	20.72	17.64	18.05
Below 40%	Shanghai	13.91	12.58	13.09
	Wuhan	3.45	14.13	11.19
	Shenyang	4.87	9.80	7.52
	Fuzhou	11.66	13.12	12.51
	Xi'an	7.04	6.64	9.16

Source: Cai, Du, and Wang 2011b.

without unduly harming the benefits that workers derive from their contributions. These areas include pensions, unemployment, and housing. An additional issue that could be addressed in such reforms is the high marginal contribution rate for low-paid workers, which would be important to consider as part of a wider strategy to incentivize formal sector participation. More specifically:

• *The pension contribution* has potential for reduction, although it is a more complex matter if worker benefits are to be protected. However, a win-win solution appears possible for workers and employers that could reduce contribution rates significantly while protecting the replacement rates of pensions. This approach would involve financing the "legacy costs" of the current pension system from an alternative source that could spread the financing burden over a very long period, and considering switching the urban workers scheme to a Notional Defined Contribution approach. The details are discussed in the next section.

• A more marginal option for reducing social contributions is the *unemployment contribution*, which at 3 percent might be reduced given the surpluses in Employment Funds and the sustained low unemployment rate in China. The use of such funds for training and other purposes could be replaced by general revenues financing, which would most likely induce efficiencies that are not promoted currently through the guaranteed revenue of the unemployment insurance contribution.

- *The compulsory savings contribution to the Housing Provident Fund*—when paid in full—is very high and has questionable benefits for many workers. The high share of workers and employers already opting out of the housing scheme points to low demand for the program, in large part because of negative real returns and the inadequacy of benefits. While housing policy for workers needs to be looked at, housing funds have proven to be an ineffective way of achieving the desired protection and may have helped inflate property markets by acting as a cheap source of liquidity for local authorities. The primary source of resistance to such a reform would thus likely be local authorities rather than workers or employers.

Promoting Hukou Reform and Improving Labor Mobility

Hukou reform—current status and challenges. The hukou system is one of the key sources of inequality of opportunity in China, and the most distinctive feature of China's social policy.[59] The mobility restriction function of hukou has largely been eliminated in practice by reforms since the late 1980s.[60] However, the lack of parallel entitlement reform has meant that hukou continues to have significant negative impacts on welfare and equality of opportunity. Some comparative studies point out that the hukou system results in much more limited access to social entitlements than those for internal migrants within EU countries, and than immigration policies in Germany, Japan, and Mexico (Solinger 1999; Roberts 1997). The hukou system regulates many social entitlements of

citizens, including education, housing, utilities subsidies, and social protection, and also affects the ease of accessing formal sector jobs. It is widely acknowledged that deepening hukou reform in China has the potential to provide substantial equity and efficiency benefits. At the same time, it is also agreed that hukou reform is a gradual and challenging process.

Hukou reform can support China's transition to a high-income country in several ways. First, it can contribute to economic growth. Deepening reform of the hukou system could increase the allocative efficiency of the labor market and promote productivity-enhancing structural transformation and urban agglomeration effects. World Bank estimates indicate that moving 10 percent of the labor force out of the agriculture sector could lead to a 6.4 percent increase in GDP growth, with higher gains in western and central regions (World Bank 2005). Reform of social entitlements that are linked to hukou is key in deepening the human capital base and promoting a healthier workforce. Second, hukou reform can play a role in narrowing rural-urban and regional income gaps. Simulations show that completing hukou reform can have a dramatic equalization effect between rural and urban income.[61] Third, well-designed hukou reform can promote inclusive and manageable urbanization, which can help reduce the inequalities in income and access to services that create social tensions.

Hukou reform has been an important part of wider economic reforms in China (Wang, O'Keefe, and Song 2012). The early stages of hukou reform first encouraged the shift of agricultural labor off farm into township and village enterprises, then increasingly into small and medium cities; eventually restrictions were eased on movement into large cities, feeding the massive expansion of migrant labor from the second half of the 1990s. The 2000s saw increased policy emphasis on promoting rural welfare and deepening rural-urban integration, but hukou reforms in major urban centers have for the most part remained localized. At the national level, further measures are being used to ease hukou eligibility for small and medium cities. At the subnational level, different types of reforms have been initiated:

- *Unified hukou registration.* Between 2001 and 2009, 15 provinces had unified the registration function of hukou. The absence of supporting entitlement reforms, however, meant that in most places, people have continued to enjoy different rights depending on the place of their original hukou, so the reform has been largely symbolic to date. In practice, most medium and large cities have gradually lowered the criteria for migrants to change hukou identities and be granted accompanying entitlements. As illustrated in figure 4.31, the threshold for "full" hukou conversion to a status with the full entitlements of local residents has been higher in richer and larger cities. Box 4.4 describes some of the local innovations as well as the tendency in some provinces to treat migrants from within the province or prefecture differently from migrants from further afield.
- *Establishment of a parallel residence permit system,* which is intended to delink access to basic services for migrants from

hukou status itself. A number of large cities and provinces such as Shanghai, Shenzhen, Zhejiang, Guangdong, Jiangsu, Chongqing, and Chengdu have adopted the residence permit system. The approach differs across cities, with some offering easier access to permits but with more limited rights; others (Shanghai, for example) offering a better package of entitlements but with stricter criteria to obtain the residence permit; and still others (such as Zhejiang) mixing the two approaches for those with temporary residence permits and those with permanent and fuller entitlements.

Local pilots in hukou reform point to a number of challenges in achieving fuller rural-urban integration if pursued only at the subnational level. These challenges include:

- *Local reforms have been least complete in the large cities where rural migrants are most concentrated, at least for migrants from outside the municipal or provincial jurisdiction.* At the same time, urban hukou in small and medium cities entitles the migrant to less generous social services and social protection, contributing to the

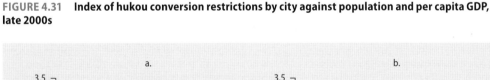

FIGURE 4.31   **Index of hukou conversion restrictions by city against population and per capita GDP, late 2000s**

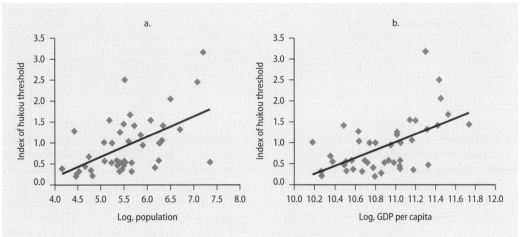

Source: Wu, Li, and Xiao (2010) for hukou index; China Statistical Yearbooks for population and GDP.

BOX 4.4   Recent innovations in hukou reform

Local hukou reforms are diverse and offer lessons for national efforts to deepen reform. They include:

- *A score system for hukou conversion.* In 2009, Guangdong introduced a cumulative points system to manage hukou conversion. This system is focused primarily on intra-Guangdong migrants, while the residence permit system regulates the entitlements of other migrants. Points are calculated based on education, vocational certificates and professions, years of social insurance contribution, charitable activities such as blood donation and volunteer work, and government awards. In parallel, all migrants are encouraged to apply for residence permits to receive additional public services and welfare. The impact to date has, however, been lower than expected. With a three-year target of 1.8 million conversions, only 100,000 hukou conversions were done in the first year.
- *Strict and fixed conversion criteria with rationing.* Shanghai was the first city to introduce the residence permit system open to all, but the qualifying conditions are among the strictest. The Shanghai system prioritizes three categories: those with college degrees or special talents and those who work, do business, or invest in Shanghai (and their families); those who have stable employment and housing; and those reunited with family members with Shanghai hukou. Residence permit holders enjoy equal public services including children's education, health and family planning services, training, social insurance, and driver's licenses. They must make seven years of social insurance contributions before applying for hukou. In addition, Shanghai has a tight overall quota on hukou conversions, and the number of conversions has to date been very low.

- *Localized hukou conversion through exchange of rural and urban entitlements.* Chongqing has encouraged family migration with hukou conversion but only for those who are rural residents of Chongqing. Hukou transfer to urban districts requires that migrants work or do business in the area for more than five years, purchase commercial property, or make significant investments or tax payments. Requirements are much lower for hukou transfer in small cities and towns. The key feature is the so-called "exchanging three rural clothes for five urban clothes" policy: the "rural clothes" being homestead land, farmland, and contracted forest land, while the "urban clothes" are pension, medical insurance, housing, employment, and education. Those converting from rural to urban hukou can keep their farm, homestead, and forest for three years but must give it up thereafter if they wish to retain their urban hukou. Chongqing has, however, been easing the exchange requirements in recent years.
- *Hukou conversion of local residents without exchange of rural rights.* Chengdu introduced a residence permit system with two types of permits: temporary and permanent. The residence permit and hukou conversion is only open to those who are already residents of rural areas of Chengdu prefecture. Local migrants apply for temporary permits if they stay between one month and one year and for a permanent permit if staying over a year. Local migrants will be issued residence permits if they have contracted jobs, register a business, purchase housing, or are dependents of residence permit holders. Residence permit holders enjoy more public services and welfare than temporary residence holders and are eligible for hukou conversion.

Source: Wang, O'Keefe, and Song 2012.

---

limited success of the policy aimed at attracting migrants to smaller cities.
- *Reforms in larger cities have generally been oriented to better-skilled and richer migrants, significantly limiting the labor market impacts of the reforms and reducing their equity benefits.* Migrants are excluded in a variety of ways, for example,

through entry barriers on skills, investments, or income or through rationing by strict income, work, and residence requirements.
- *Uncertainties and potentially high opportunity costs with respect to rural land holdings constrain demand by migrant workers for urban hukou.* In developed

areas, rural land values are high, and rural hukou holders could lose the windfall from land conversion if they change from agricultural to nonagricultural hukou.

- *Lack of social entitlement reform in hukou policies is likely to result in intergenerational losses and missed opportunities for higher human capital acquisition by migrant children.* For example, while national policy calls for free education for migrant children in urban areas, in practice, the localities that fund the education have failed to achieve the policy objective.

- *Local urban residents have concerns about the potential effects on service quality in cities if their localities have to absorb the costs of service provision for migrant populations.* Sociological research finds that urban residents are concerned about migrant workers compromising the quality of services in cities and driving down wages (Solinger 1999). Managing such perceptions may be as significant an element in hukou reform as the technical and policy issues.

- *Perhaps the key constraint to deeper hukou reform is financing public services and social welfare for migrants.* Under a decentralized finance system, local governments primarily finance core social services and social protection. They do not have incentives to provide free or subsidized services for migrant families given the limited public input and resources.

These challenges point to the key economic problem of hukou reform: the benefits of reform are national in scope, but the costs are overwhelmingly local because of the intergovernmental financing arrangements for basic services. This is a classic externalities issue, making collective action a major challenge. Cities capture only some of the benefits of financing entitlement reform, and the localized returns on investments remain unclear with a mobile migrant population. While their localized choices not to fund or to underfund basic services for migrants may therefore be rational, the resulting situation is suboptimal from a national perspective.

Reforming the hukou system. Hukou reform needs a phased strategy implemented over an extended period, with the end goal being a simple population registration system, delinked from social entitlements. It needs national-level planning in close coordination with provincial authorities. The key issue is not hukou reform per se, but rather the necessary preconditions of entitlement and welfare reform that will reduce the importance of hukou, turning it ultimately into a more typical population registration system such as exists in many other countries. These preconditions will require different types of collective action—across agencies and across levels of government—to ensure that reforms that are socially and economically optimal at the aggregate level do not continue to be delayed. They will also require consultation with the public to explain the rationale and strategy for reform.

The first step of the reform strategy could be to set a national framework for extension of the residence permit system, which would begin the process of delinking social entitlements of nonlocal residents from their hukou status. While common levels of eligibility criteria (such as the number of prior years of residence or of social insurance contributions) could not be expected in the short to medium term, having common indicators that urban jurisdictions could adapt to local conditions (such as the period of prior local residence) would be important. The criteria could be informed by the many local pilot programs and might avoid overly rigid rules by taking an approach like Guangdong's scoring system. A second practical implementation challenge would be establishing national standards for information systems and data exchange of information on mobile populations. While a fully centralized national database seems overly ambitious for the present, a common platform would be essential to underpin an effective reform.

A second dimension of the reform is the spatial expansion of more liberal residence permit and hukou conversion eligibility standards. A gradual expansion of the spatial scope of registration permit eligibility is also likely in such a framework—beginning with all rural residents of the prefecture, then extending to all people with hukou of that province, and ultimately opening up residence permits to those from beyond the province. This pattern, already visible in local reforms in places such as Chengdu, Chongqing, and Guangdong, provides a sequence for phased equalization of entitlements.

A third issue concerns the extent of rights to be conferred once a migrant obtains a registration permit, as well as the possible sequencing of such rights. Again, current pilots may be informative on this issue. In the initial phases, full social entitlements of local residents are unlikely to accrue immediately upon obtaining a residence permit. However, creating a pathway within the local permit system for gradual acquisition of the same social entitlements as local residents, and prioritizing rights such as children's education, would be important. The pace and scope of rights given to residence permit holders may also become a source of competition among cities in trying to attract nonlocal workers as the aggregate labor force shrinks and rural labor surplus is

exhausted. An illustrative graduation strategy is shown in figure 4.32.

Under such a common national framework, the residence permit could be rolled out nationally sometime between 2015 and 2020. Once universally established, the qualifying criteria and the pathway toward the same rights as the local hukou population could be accelerated over time. In this way, a residence permit could by 2030 have the same social entitlements as those of local hukou populations and could be obtained after a reasonably short period of residence in a city with modest qualifying criteria.

A key challenge in making such a transition effective would be agreement on the financing responsibilities for social services of those obtaining residence permits. This would be a complex negotiation between national and subnational authorities but should be guided by a clearer understanding of migrant flows across space and of the externalities of labor mobility. Fiscal burden sharing could be more weighted toward national financing in cases where migrants come from beyond the jurisdiction of the province, and it could involve a role for the province in the case of intraprovincial migrants. Certain entitlements would have a significant degree of self-financing by the migrant household that would be built into the qualifying criteria, for example, with social insurance contributions in the urban workers' system.

Figure 4.33 summarizes a possible sequence of hukou reform that gradually expands the residence permit system to diminish the relevance of hukou, ultimately leading to a simple population registry system. It shows the progressive expansion (in terms of both coverage of population and extent of entitlements) of the registration permit system among nonlocal populations over time and the parallel reduction in full hukou conversion thresholds. It also notes key steps to reach the end goal of all local and nonlocal citizens merged into a single population registry system with common entitlements based on city of residence rather than original hukou status. More detailed measures at each stage of this process are discussed in annex table 4A.

FIGURE 4.32   Progressive acquisition of social entitlements for nonlocal workers: An illustrative case

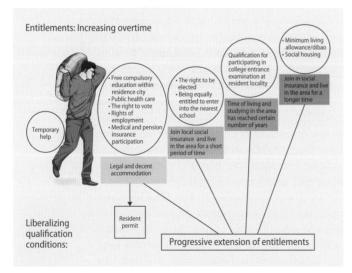

Source: Wang and Gong 2011.

Portability of pension rights. Lack of portability of pension rights has acted as an additional barrier to the mobility of workers, both across space and across sectors within urban areas. Until very recently, no national guidelines existed for portability of accumulated pension rights when moving to a different city or when moving employment from one subsystem of the urban pension system to another.[62] The level of pooling of contributions has been highly localized, with only recent efforts to pool partially to the provincial level. As a result, workers face uncertainty when moving across space, occupational sectors, or both. This uncertainty is likely to act as a barrier to greater labor mobility and efficient job matching, undermining productivity growth.

Recent guidelines recognize the need for portability reform and provide principles for its realization within the urban workers pension system.[63] Effective from 2010, there are principles for workers in the urban workers pension system to transfer both their individual account accumulations and their accumulated social pooling rights to other jurisdictions when they move jobs. This is a major step in reducing the welfare costs of labor mobility. However, principles for portability of pension rights across urban pension subsystems or between rural and urban systems have not yet been adopted.

While the new guidelines are a welcome step, their effectiveness will require progress on implementation systems. Even within provinces, significant practical barriers to reliable and timely transfer of pension rights remain. Most prefecture information systems are not compatible, so transfer of pension records from one to another is a cumbersome process of physical movement of paper records across cities. Moving to a system that can provide an effective clearing mechanism across cities and provinces is therefore an important but challenging agenda.

Portability of pension rights is a short- to medium-term priority that will in time be made less pressing as greater merging of rural and urban schemes and higher-level pooling of contributions and pension records take place. The guidelines on portability of

FIGURE 4.33   An indicative trajectory for residence permit expansion and hukou unification

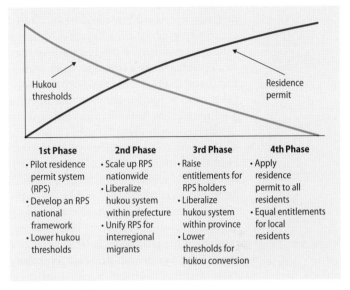

1st Phase	2nd Phase	3rd Phase	4th Phase
• Pilot residence permit system (RPS) • Develop an RPS national framework • Lower hukou thresholds	• Scale up RPS nationwide • Liberalize hukou system within prefecture • Unify RPS for interregional migrants	• Raise entitlements for RPS holders • Liberalize hukou system within province • Lower thresholds for hukou conversion	• Apply residence permit to all residents • Equal entitlements for local residents

Source: Author compilation.

rights within the urban workers' pension scheme provide a good foundation for phased expansion of portability across space, across schemes, and thus across different classes of workers. In principle, as fuller integration of pension schemes is achieved, the need for portability should be lessened. Similarly, to the extent that national pooling of the social pool portion of contributions can be achieved this decade, full portability within the urban workers' scheme would be facilitated. Pooling across schemes is a longer-term prospect. Key steps to increasing portability of pensions and thus reducing the welfare and transactions costs of labor mobility for workers and administrators would include:

• *Following the lead of the urban scheme, similar guidelines could be put in place during the 12th Plan period for portability of entitlements across all pension schemes to facilitate spatial and sectoral labor mobility.* For the individual account portion of any schemes, the principles are straightforward. The process of valuing and moving the implicit entitlements in the rural pension and urban residents schemes is more complex but can be achieved.

Principles for portability of entitlements across civil servant, public service unit, and urban worker schemes would also not be straightforward but could be facilitated greatly by gradual consolidation of urban schemes, starting with PSU and urban worker schemes (see social security section for discussion). Once developed, implementation of the guidelines could be initiated during the 13th Plan period and the system gradually consolidated.

- *To support the portability of both individual accounts and social pooling entitlements, a clearing mechanism would be needed for transfer of individual pension records and any necessary cross-jurisdiction or cross-scheme financial settlement.* This is a huge challenge and one that so far has proven difficult to achieve even within provinces because of fragmentation of information systems, lack of commonly agreed data standards, and lack of vision on the preferred models of data sharing. The first step would be agreeing on common standards for exchange of pension records and financial settlements. The *jin bao* program of MOHRSS would be the logical vehicle for developing consensus between the national and provincial authorities. However, design and deployment of a nationally integrated clearing mechanism likely will not be achieved until around 2020, and bilateral exchanges between sending and destination areas of mobile workers would continue to be the norm this decade.
- *The more fundamental reform that would facilitate portability of pension rights is the achievement of national pooling of social insurance contributions.* This is a long-held goal of national policy, not only for pensions but also for health insurance. Progress has been slower than hoped, however, with partial provincial pooling only recently achieved. Pooling of health insurance contributions has tended to occur only lower down the system, at the prefecture or county level. Higher-level pooling of pension and eventually health insurance contributions would be the single most effective measure to

facilitate portability. Realistically, it might be achieved in a phased manner with a gradually larger portion of provincial contributions pooled to the national levels over time as the information and administrative systems to manage information and funds flow are consolidated.

Enhancing Security and Improving the Social Security System

China has made remarkable progress in putting in place the core elements of a market-compatible social protection system since the transition from the "iron rice bowl" of work-unit-based social protection. Since the 1990s, it has introduced an array of social protection programs at a speed that is unprecedented internationally. Among other reforms, these include pension and health insurance programs for urban and rural populations; unemployment, sickness, workplace injury, and maternity insurance for urban formal sector workers; and a national social assistance scheme that now covers around 70 million people. This is a feat that took decades in OECD countries, and one that most middle-income countries have to date failed to achieve.

The vision of social protection development for 2030 has the following components:

- All households participate in the pension and health insurance systems, and the systems are integrated among different segments of population (rural, urban, migrants) and across different segments (civil servants, public service unit employees, and workers on the one hand, and residents and rural workers on the other). With rapid population aging, the pension system would also benefit from both parametric and structural reforms to ensure system sustainability and security at a basic level.
- China has a well-developed and decent quality system of aged and long-term care services that draws upon the human and financial resources of the government, the nonstate sector, communities, and

households and that provides a minimum level of service even for the poor.

- Greater coherence between different parts of the social protection system provides adequate and affordable minimum coverage of benefits for poor households but also ensures that the near-poor are not disadvantaged and that "poverty traps" are not created.

Building an Inclusive and Sustainable Pension System

With China's demographics, developing a sustainable pension system with wide coverage will be one of the country's most pressing social challenges over coming decades. The unfinished agenda is large, in part a product of the rapid pace of reform to date, but one that the authorities have begun clearly to address. The first element of the agenda is addressing historically low pension coverage among rural, migrant, and urban informal sector workers. The second is reducing fragmentation across different subsystems of the pension and health insurance systems, both to promote more seamless protection and to facilitate labor mobility. The third relates to financial protection and ensuring sustainability of financial protection for those in existing pension systems. Finally, in the longer term, structural reforms of the pension system may be desirable to achieve the reform goals of the authorities.

Expanding pension coverage. Until recently, China's pension coverage was well below the typical level for a country of its income level (figure 4.34). Low coverage has been driven by a few factors—the absence of a national rural pension program; the low participation rates of migrant workers in urban schemes; and the absence until mid-2011 of a pension scheme for urban residents, who make up 30–40 percent of the urban labor force.

Looking at the urban system, participation rates in pension schemes of different types of workers remain very different between local and migrant workers despite recent progress. Reliable nationwide survey figures are not available, but the China

FIGURE 4.34 **Pension coverage rate of active labor force, various countries, mid-2000s**

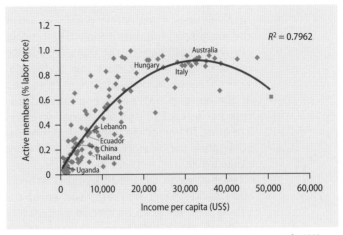

Source: Paralles-Miralles, Romero, and Whitehouse 2012. China coverage rate is for 2008.

Urban Labor Surveys (CULS) in 2005 and 2010 gives a reasonable picture from a selection of large cities. As seen in figure 4.35, participation in the pension system among migrant workers roughly doubled between 2005 and 2010 but still covered only around 25 percent of migrants, far lower than the 80 percent participation among local workers.

FIGURE 4.35 **Participation rates for pension programs among working-age adults in urban areas, by gender and residence status**

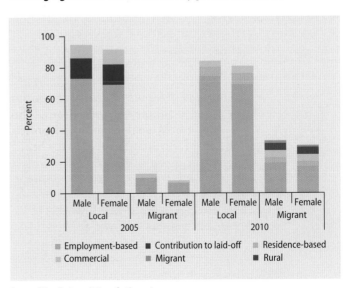

Source: Giles, Park, and Wang forthcoming.

Part of the expansion among migrants is in schemes other than the core urban workers' pension scheme, including participation in rural schemes. Factors that positively affect the marginal probability that urban workers will participate in the pension scheme include level of education (an additional year of school increases the chances around 4 percent and any postsecondary education by 7 percent) and age (older workers are more likely to participate). In contrast, controlling for other factors, migrants from other urban areas are 43 percent less likely to participate in the urban workers' scheme than local hukou workers, and rural-to-urban migrants are a further 26 percent less likely to participate than urban-to-urban migrants. While women are 5 percent less likely to participate, this effect disappears after controlling for the sector of employment, suggesting that it is occupational choice rather than gender per se that drives the gender gap in participation.[64]

Pension coverage in rural areas has historically been very low (10–12 percent) but has increased dramatically since the 2009 national rural pension pilot reform (figure 4.36). Although China has experimented with rural pension reform since the 1980s, it had failed, until the late 2000s, to make

significant inroads in expanding coverage, mainly because of the highly localized nature of schemes, fiscal constraints in many areas, lack of participation incentives for rural people, and weak implementation (Wu 2009; Lv 2005). The introduction of the national pilot in 2009 brought an impressive increase in participation.

In response to historical undercoverage, China has moved rapidly since 2009 to include groups formerly outside the formal pension system. Historically, the major groups with low coverage have been farmers, migrant workers, and the urban residents outside the formal sector schemes. In late 2009, China started rolling out a nationwide voluntary rural pension scheme that combines a matched contribution to an individual account with a basic flat pension benefit after retirement. The schemes are innovative efforts to encourage participation through public subsidies. The central government plays an important role in financing the full basic benefit for central and western provinces and half the benefit for coastal provinces. The broad design was replicated in mid-2011 for urban residents, with both rural and urban resident schemes aiming for full geographic coverage by end-2013. Both have a high public subsidy element, both during the accumulation phase through contribution matching and even more so through the payment of a basic benefit after retirement. Already the rural scheme has seen an increase of around 100 million contributors. The Social Insurance Law of 2011 and labor legislation in 2008 also place stronger obligations on urban employers to include migrants in urban workers' schemes, and there are indications of progress.

Financial protection and systemic risks to the urban system. Besides coverage, another key dimension of social security is the financial protection offered by schemes, an area of concern for pensions. While benefit levels in nominal terms have increased steadily in the urban schemes, wage replacement rates have fallen sharply in recent years (figure 4.37), although from a high base by international

FIGURE 4.36   Rural pension participation: total contributors and as share of rural employed

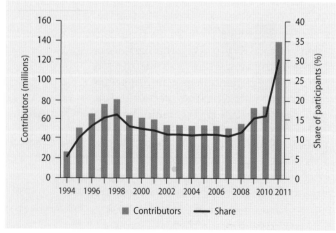

Source: Ministry of Human Resources and Social Security.

standards. The replacement rate in PSU and civil servants schemes remains relatively high at more than 60 percent, but the rate for regular workers has fallen toward the 40 percent threshold recommended by the International Labour Organization as an adequate minimum, raising questions about the longer-run financial protection from the scheme. These concerns are in part attributable to various design and implementation features, in particular the negative real rates of return on individual account accumulations (most of which are invested in bank deposits) and the prevalence of so-called "empty accounts" in many jurisdictions, where individual account deposits have been used in earlier periods to fund liabilities to current pensioners. The system also faces the challenge of managing the substantial "legacy costs" of promises to previous generations of pensioners.[65]

A number of structural challenges in design and implementation of urban pension systems risk undermining the system and impose significant inequities and labor market distortions. They include:

- *Legacy costs of the earlier, more generous urban workers' system,* which are financed largely through current pension contributions, sustaining high contribution rates and creating incentives for nonparticipation and inequities across generations of workers. Rough estimates of gross legacy costs range from 82 to 130 percent of 2008 GDP, depending on assumptions.[66]
- *Design weaknesses that affect incentives and undermine fiscal sustainability,* such as the low retirement age. Earlier studies of the urban enterprise pension system substantiate the threats to sustainability. Long-term actuarial projections suggested a baseline financing gap (present value of projected yearly financial shortfalls) from 2002 to 2075 of 95 percent of China's GDP for 2001. The same projections suggested that there would be marginal systemwide cash surpluses between 2009 and 2018, then deficits thereafter, despite the maturation of "young men" with lower replacement rates.[67]

FIGURE 4.37 **Pension benefits and replacement rates in urban China**

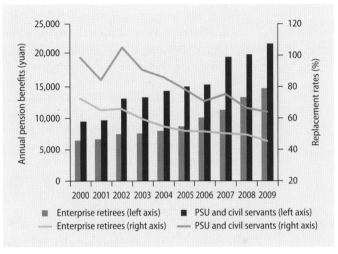

Sources: National Bureau of Statistics 2010.

- *Low returns on individual accounts,* which have meant that pension replacement rates have been significantly less than anticipated when the system was developed—a structural feature that cannot be removed so long as the bank deposit rate is mandated for individual account accumulations. In effect, the already high pension contribution rate for urban workers is thus made even higher by a negative real rate of return on these accumulations.
- *The multiplicity of urban pension schemes* for workers, PSU employees, civil servants, and in some areas, residents and migrants. This creates "entitlement segmentation" in the labor market and barriers to cross-sectoral worker mobility, and it also results in nontransparent disparities in worker compensation across public and nonstate sectors. The multiplicity of schemes is inconsistent with international trends toward consolidation of the pension policy framework across different categories of workers.
- *Major spatial fragmentation of urban systems and lack of portability of rights,* as discussed in the previous section. Lack of risk pooling and interurban resource

transfers limit the insurance function of the urban pension system and increase spatial disparities in financial protection. While the recent portability regulation for the urban system is a step in the right direction, considerable deepening of the management information and payment systems for transfer of information and funds will be needed to operationalize the policy. More broadly, similar guidelines do not yet exist for portability across rural, urban workers, PSU, and urban residents' schemes. In addition, the stated goal of provincial pooling remains incomplete, with very partial pooling beyond the prefecture level in most provinces.

Addressing the challenges in pension reform. The Chinese authorities have set sensible guiding principles for pension reform, but the parametric and structural reforms that will be needed will be challenging. In recent years, the government has articulated principles for a reformed pension system. The principles call for an urban system that "has broad coverage, protects at the basic level, is multilayered, and sustainable," while the principles for the rural system are "broad coverage, protects at the basic level, is flexible, and sustainable." Achieving expansion and integration of the pension system while trying to ensure adequate and sustainable benefits for all workers presents complex challenges that are likely to require structural and parametric reforms. The key challenge is how to manage the trade-offs and strike balances between the different objectives when they compete. Deepening pension reform is a long-term agenda, with several stages.

The key challenge in the short term is ensuring suitable incentives for coverage expansion of pensions to farmers, urban residents, and migrants. The use of public subsidies in the new rural and urban resident schemes provides a significant incentive to participate. At the same time, the fact that the subsidy is largely "back-loaded" to the retirement phase through the basic benefit—and that the vesting period is only 15 years—raises questions about whether those

under age 45 will participate in the new schemes to a significant extent. Initial evidence from surveys in Chengdu and Guangdong suggests that participation rates in the new rural scheme among younger farmers are indeed considerably lower than those closer to retirement (Wang, Chen, and Gao 2011; Wang, O'Keefe, and Thompson forthcoming). "Family binding"—whereby the parents of current workers can be covered in the rural and urban residents' systems if their working children contribute—is one important incentive, but this is a transitional provision. In the medium term, the authorities may need to consider stronger incentives for those under 45 to contribute, such as higher ex ante matching on individual account contributions or some increase in the basic benefit for those who contribute for more than the minimum period.

For migrant workers, the incentive challenge in expanding pension participation is somewhat different. While recent data indicate notable improvement in the participation of migrants in the urban workers' pension scheme, there is a three-way challenge of coverage expansion. First, the majority of migrant workers still remain in the informal sector and ineligible for the urban residents' scheme. Second, even those in the formal sector may be reluctant to participate because receipt of the pension benefit is so distant and because of uncertainty about their future location and ease of portability. Third, employers of migrant workers may be reluctant to make pension contributions for migrant workers because of the added labor costs. For migrants who wish to return home, participation in their local rural scheme would make sense, pending fuller integration of rural and urban residents' schemes. For migrants who intend to stay, a potential mechanism to address the first two issues in part would be linking social insurance contributions for migrants to registration permit and hukou reform by requiring a minimum period of contributions for conversion.

In addition to coverage expansion, there is also a need to initiate reforms of the urban formal sector schemes in the short run. These include:

- *Initiating an increase in the normal retirement age.* Given the need to do this gradually, initiating the increase in pensionable age sooner rather than later seems advisable. A caveat raised by some Chinese scholars is that the current cohort of older workers has lower skills and may struggle to remain productive and employable. This is a reasonable concern, but a gradual increase in normal retirement age, combined with availability of unemployment insurance and greater investments in mid-career training and lifelong learning, should mitigate the potential negative impacts on both older workers and overall productivity.
- *Defining a strategy to deal with legacy costs.* A sensible sequence of steps could be, first, separating legacy costs from other pension costs; second, estimating the financial requirements necessary to deliver on legacy costs (as part of wider actuarial modeling of the pension system financial position); and, third, agreeing on a financing strategy to meet legacy costs over the long term, using channels outside current pension revenues, such as government bonds and possibly resources from the National Social Security Fund (NSSF).
- *Taking preparatory design steps to integrate the PSU, civil servant, and urban workers' pension frameworks.* While five provinces have been designated as PSU pension reform locations, progress has been limited to date. Ultimately, the PSU and civil servant subsystems should aim to be fully integrated with the urban workers' scheme, and the first step in the short term is introducing contribution payments.[68] For some PSUs, this is already happening and needs to be widened. For civil servants, this step is more challenging, but countries such as India where new civil servants have been required to make contributions provide useful examples of how to manage such a transition to an integrated pension system. In both cases,

the key design question would be how to integrate within the urban workers' scheme while avoiding a dramatic downward adjustment in replacement rates. This would in turn require integrated policy development of PSU and civil service pension reform with broader compensation reforms.
- *Completing provincial-level pooling of pension funds.* Pooling contributions at the provincial level will allow for greater equalization of pensions within provinces and also strengthen the insurance function. To date, pooling remains only partial in most provinces, despite policy commitments to achieving full pooling.
- *Putting in place the information systems to facilitate portability of pension rights and pooling.* Currently, the information systems for pensions are highly fragmented, typically at the prefecture level, although efforts are under way to move toward common data standards within provinces and within the new rural and urban resident schemes. In the short run, it would be essential to set common data standards and data-sharing protocols under the lead of MOHRSS and develop a data management system strategy for phased convergence. Social insurance information systems would also need to be integrated within provinces to prepare the way for eventual sharing of beneficiary data and financial information across provinces.

The key medium-term challenge will be promoting greater harmonization across schemes and making progress on integration of schemes for different groups. As coverage is expanded, reducing fragmentation of schemes across groups and across space will come to the fore. Integration will be an important reform for creating a pension system that more fully reflects and facilitates the increased mobility of workers. It would involve several elements:

- *Completing integration of PSU, civil servant, and urban workers' schemes frameworks and management.* To move to a unified scheme for all formal workers, it will be necessary over time to integrate the policy frameworks and managements of the schemes for the three sets of workers. Integrating the PSU and urban workers' schemes is a sensible first step; integration of civil servants' schemes may require a longer phase-in period. To avoid a sharp decline in income replacement rates for both PSU and civil servants' supplementary occupational pension schemes may be needed that could top up pension benefit levels in the integrated urban formal sector schemes.

- *Integrating the rural and urban residents' schemes and their management.* Given the close policy harmonization between the schemes, integration of schemes for rural and urban residents should be somewhat more straightforward. In fact, a number of cities, including Beijing, Shanghai, Zhongshan, and Chengdu, have already achieved integration. The main practical challenge is ensuring that information and financial transactions systems are sufficiently integrated across provinces and prefectures to allow for scheme integration to be effective across wide areas as well as within jurisdictions.

The other main reforms in the medium term would build on preparatory steps taken earlier. These include:

- *Separating legacy-cost financing using a clearly defined financing strategy outside the pension system.* Separating the financing of legacy costs from the current and future pension system would allow the authorities to reduce the contribution burden of the pension system on current and future workers. This could also help reduce possible resistance to a raising of the retirement age. The legacy costs could be financed by the government at different levels and could also be shared with workers and retirees. The central government could establish a framework by which it finances a minimum level of acquired

rights, and the remainder could be financed by provinces and municipalities.

- *Raising the pooling level for the urban schemes to the national level.* This reform is a stated goal of national policy and would be desirable on several fronts. The two biggest challenges in achieving integration of schemes and higher-level pooling will be agreeing on the rules for distribution of pooled contributions across space and putting in place the platform for exchange of beneficiary data and financial information to support the portability of entitlements. One goal of pooled revenues should be to reduce gradually the spatial disparities in pension benefits as well as disparities across population groups. Progress on data sharing would require accelerated progress on the current efforts of MOHRSS to develop common standards for data sharing nationally. Both are challenging from a technical standpoint and in the coordination of many players with different interests.

- *Taking steps to ensure sustainable financial protection of pensions.* This reform would require measures both for ensuring adequate rates of return during the accumulation phase and for appropriate indexation of pension benefits after retirement. For pensions after retirement, introducing more systematic indexation would be desirable. Price indexation protects the retiree against inflation but would most likely result in a decrease in pension benefits after retirement relative to wages. An alternative could be to mix prices with the increase in covered wages in the pension system (Piggott and Sane 2009). During the accumulation phase, ensuring a better rate of return than produced by bank deposits would be vital. A more balanced investment approach for pension fund balances could be adopted, or a notional defined contribution (NDC) approach might be considered in the long term, with returns linked to GDP growth rates.

For the long term, it would be desirable to move to a system that distinguishes those with a formal employment relationship from those without one such as self-employed and informal workers. This reform would require unified pension systems for these two types of workers across rural and urban areas, breaking down the historical locational divide. Such a system would be consistent with deepening rural-urban integration and hukou reform and would help address issues of portability. It could also benefit from the lessons of OECD economies that have distinct schemes for the self-employed.

In terms of implementation, an integrated national data management system would be needed to underpin the nationally pooled and integrated system. This is a daunting task, but ultimately necessary. The real question is what model of integrated data management is feasible, both technically and politically. It need not be a fully centralized database but could instead have distributed provincial systems with a data clearinghouse function at the national level, or a cloud-based system.

In addition to integration of pension schemes, consideration should be given to the structure and mix of pension benefits. To balance financial protection, coverage expansion, and sustainability objectives, China should probably in the longer term consider moving the integrated schemes toward a three-pillar design consisting of a basic benefit pillar, a contributory pillar, and a supplementary pillar (figure 4.38):

- *The basic benefit pillar* would provide minimum elderly poverty protection through an integrated, noncontributory "social pension." This pillar would build on the basic benefit approach already being taken in the rural and urban residents' pension schemes but would go a step further in removing the link to even the low level of contributions required in those schemes. The social pension—set at a modest level to ensure fiscal sustainability—could be financed from general revenues with a strong role for the central government but some cost sharing with subnational levels. Depending on the extent of fiscal commitment and the

FIGURE 4.38 Potential design of long-term pension system

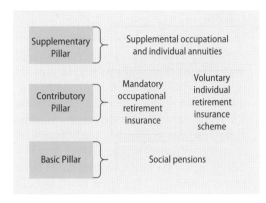

Source: Authors.

desired level of social pension, it could also be subject to a pension test that would take account of pension income from other sources or some other form of means testing (although a pensions test has the attraction of administrative simplicity). A key principle could be that the benefit would be set in a common way and would provide minimum income support higher than the *dibao* threshold. Social pensions of different forms are widespread in OECD countries as a method both for ensuring universal coverage of elderly benefits and avoiding old-age poverty (Palacios and Sluchynskyy 2006; Holzmann, Robalino, and Takayama 2009).

- *The contributory pillar* would have a mandatory defined-contribution scheme for workers with wage incomes and a voluntary defined-contribution pension savings scheme for the urban and rural population with nonwage incomes (temporary workers, the self-employed, and farmers). For workers with wage incomes, a notional approach to the contributory pillar could be considered. Such an approach offers a number of attractive features related to labor market incentives and facilitation of labor mobility, potential for reduction in contribution rates, and a lesser requirement for retained savings in the pension system to support benefit payments. Importantly, it would also allow for providing a positive real rate of return to contributors without imposing undue risks on investments or as many regulatory demands on government. For those with nonwage incomes, continuing (and possibly increasing) government matching of contributions would provide strong incentives to participate in the voluntary contributory scheme. The scheme for those on nonwage incomes could be fully funded, preferably with a rate of return guaranteed by the central authorities to reduce the risk to contributors from empty accounts. A question to address in such a dual scheme is the risk of encouraging informality through the subsidy to nonwage income earners. One solution to this concern could be to provide incentives for low-income formal sector workers as well, as has been introduced, for example, in Mexico and Colombia.

- *The supplementary pillar* for urban and rural residents would allow voluntary occupational and personal pensions that could supplement other pension benefits. For most people and employers, the supplemental pension could be an entirely voluntary arrangement used as part of the nonwage compensation package. It would also be a vital part of a strategy to integrate civil servants and PSU workers into the urban workers' scheme without a sharp fall in replacement rates.

Aged Care Services: Aging with Dignity

Current status and challenges. Although pensions are a crucial element of old-age support, the rapidly aging population will also need a range of aged care and long-term care services, which are currently underdeveloped in China. Historically, aged care in China has been primarily the responsibility of the family, and that is still the dominant approach culturally. At the same time, the state has provided for the poorest elderly people without other forms of support, who are known in rural areas as *wubao* people and in urban areas as the "three no's."[69] The wubao program covered just over 5.5 million people in

2011, and others often received benefits from the *dibao* program. However, with urbanization, the strains on children of the 4-2-1 family model, and rapid aging, demand is rapidly growing for a range of aged care services that traditional arrangements and the very targeted public programs are not well equipped to handle.

The policy framework for aged and long-term care services has been developed but does not yet fully reflect the demographic, policy, economic, and social changes of recent years.[70] China passed the Rights Protection Law for the Elderly in 1996 to guide and regulate rights on social security, aged welfare and services, health, and education for the elderly. In 2006, 10 line ministries, including the National Aging Commission, National Development and Reform Commission (NDRC), and the Ministry of Civil Affairs (MOCA), jointly issued a policy document that defined the aged care service sector.[71] Family-based and community-based elderly care services were piloted in Beijing, Tianjing, Qingdao, Daliang, Xiamen, Shanghai, and Changsha and were rolled out in more than 300 urban centers in 2009.[72] The 12th Plan also gives much more explicit attention to the issue of aged care services.

The multisectoral nature of aged and long-term care has posed institutional challenges to developing a coherent approach in China. Numerous ministries, levels of government, and nonstate actors are involved in aged and long-term care, contributing to fragmentation in the overall approach. At the central government level, responsibility for policy cuts across the NDRC, MOCA, MOHRSS, Ministry of Health (MOH), and China National Commission on Aging. At the subnational level, provinces, municipalities, counties, and townships have responsibilities for designing, coordinating, and implementing aged and long-term care services, sometimes in collaboration with voluntary organizations.

The lack of well-developed coordination mechanisms limits the overall effectiveness of aged and long-term care initiatives, and the effects are already visible. The lack of coordination has hampered the ability to adequately assess unit costs of different types of aged care services; assess the most appropriate options for funding services; determine clear and transparent eligibility criteria for services; identify appropriate splits between purchasing and commissioning functions and the delivery of services; and establish systems for quality assurance of aged care services (Joshua 2011).

China also has a large deficit of appropriately trained personnel in aged and long-term care services. In particular, social work education and practice are still in an embryonic state across China. Currently, around 250 institutions provide social work training with only 10,000 graduates a year, 60 percent of whom work in other professions upon graduation because of low pay and lack of career opportunities.[73] The scarcity of work settings and places in which to train staff in the application of social work skills makes it difficult to build a strong workforce for social work, which could have implications for the quantity and quality of aged care provision. Beyond social work, there are large shortfalls in most other areas related to aged-care services, including professional carers and gerontologists.

Community-based long-term care services have emerged in the context of the commercialization of state-owned enterprises but are generally fragmented and weak. In 2007, 31.4 million enterprise retirees were under the system of "social management services." These services aim to serve various social and health needs of the elderly but are often fragmented. In urban areas, community-based care services have begun to emerge. For example, the Beijing local government created a model, called "four nearby solutions," that offers elderly people resources for studying, social activities, and caregiving support, and opportunities to participate in community affairs. However, evaluations suggest that caregiving support functions in the community and at home are often ill-defined, suffer from weak coordination across different agencies and service providers, and have proven expensive to sustain (Cheng and Rosenberg 2009). In addition, the private sector has shown increasingly strong interest in the high-end aged care industry in China.[74]

The challenges in design and implementation of aged and long-term care services are not unique to China. Many advanced and emerging economies are further along the aging curve and have already undertaken reforms to address the needs that China is now confronting. They offer many relevant lessons and also point to quite diverse models of financing, provision, and regulation, which suggests that developing a model that is appropriate to China's context and affordable will be challenging (Joshua 2011, vol. 2).

Addressing the challenges of aged care. Given the early stage of development of aged care services in China, the fundamental question for policy makers is what vision they have for the system. The experiences of OECD and transition countries show significant variation in the ways aged care services are provided, financed, and regulated, reflecting to a large extent differences in the underlying social and cultural norms of different countries. Major variations can be seen both in the levels of spending on long-term care and in the structure of public and private spending (figure 4.39). China will need to decide on an appropriate model of aged care services that reflects its broader social service vision, cultural preferences, and fiscal possibilities. This section therefore points to the priority issues and options that Chinese policy makers will need to consider over different time frames rather than offering firm recommendations.

In the short term, the first need is to develop the broad policy framework for aged care services. In doing so, a central issue is the mixture of public and private financing and provision. Given the pace of aging in China and the scale of unmet need, aged care services will clearly be an area where the state cannot "do it all," and co-responsibility and plurality of provision—including the state, the nonstate commercial and nongovernmental sectors, communities, and households—will be essential. A mix of cost sharing and service provision is also likely to be consistent with Chinese cultural and family

FIGURE 4.39 **Long-term care expenditures in OECD, 2008**

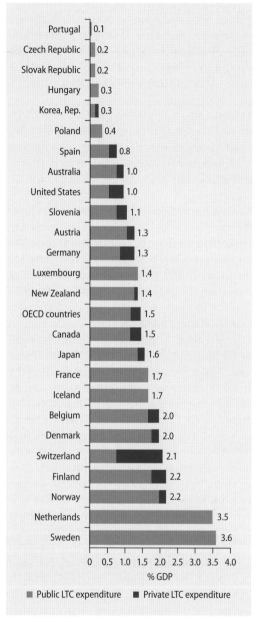

Source: OECD 2011a.

and neither finances nor provides services in yet other cases. More specifically:

- *Piloting different models of aged care services to gain deeper understanding of cost and quality issues and to test different mixes of public, nonstate, community-based, and household provision and financing.* Interesting experiments are already taking place (in Hangzhou and Shanghai, for example) and these can be expanded and carefully assessed to inform national policy development. National policy can also draw lessons from relevant international experience (OECD 2011a; World Bank 2010e).
- *Placing particular focus on the financing model for aged care services.* With respect to financing, public resources are likely to remain constrained for aged care in the short term. OECD approaches on public financing of aged care vary considerably, from models financed largely through general revenues (Scandinavia) to insurance-based approaches. For China, public financing is likely to continue to come from general revenues, but at much more modest levels than the countries with more generous general-revenues-financed systems. In providing public funding, policy makers may experiment in the short term with a mixture of supply-side subsidies to providers and demand-side funding directly to households. An increasing number of OECD countries are providing demand-side subsidies to households and giving households more choice in whether they provide care themselves or seek it from community-based or professional providers (OECD 2011a). The role of family and informal care arrangements—including community-based care—is critical in this regard, and it is vital that public investments do not crowd out informal and community-based care arrangements. At a minimum, public financing should not aim to disadvantage those who choose to care for their elderly family members in home or community-based settings.

values. It will require thinking about combinations whereby the state both finances and provides services in some cases, finances but outsources service provision in other cases,

- *In addition, public resources are likely to continue to be focused on the poor elderly in the short run.* Again, practice in the OECD varies between universal access systems financed either from general revenues or insurance contributions (in much of Europe, Japan, and Korea), and means-tested systems (in the United States, United Kingdom, and Australia). China may need to consider a phased approach that focuses on the poorest initially, with better-off households self-financing higher-quality care. The challenge for the medium term will be deciding on the appropriate role of public financing for the middle groups of the population who are neither very poor nor have adequate resources to fully self-finance care.
- *Another key issue will be the institutional and coordination arrangements for the aged care services sector, given the number of public and private actors involved.* MOCA has developed approaches in the 12th Plan, but elaboration of policy will benefit from a high-level coordination mechanism involving other players such as NDRC, MOH, MOHRSS, the National Commission on Aging, and others. Similarly, coordination mechanisms will increasingly be needed at the subnational level to oversee, regulate, and administer the aged care services system and subsystems.
- *Accelerated efforts to develop human resource capacity for the aged care sector are needed urgently.* This has been recognized and efforts are expanding to train social workers and other professionals, including gerontologists, aged care nurses, and other needed personnel. In 2011, MOCA set a target of having 2 million qualified social workers by the end of 2015 as part of coordinated efforts from 18 central agencies.[75] However, a complementary need will be addressing very low social worker pay and lack of career development prospects, factors that lead many who train as social workers to leave the field. This is also an area where having a clear strategy on the interaction between

formally trained personnel and the family and voluntary sector will be crucial.

In the medium to long term, the reforms initiated in the 12th Plan period will need to be deepened and new approaches are also likely to be needed as aging accelerates. Some of the key incremental reforms include:

- *Developing a regulatory framework for aged care services that encourages the entry of nonstate providers (community-based, commercial, and not-for-profit) but also ensures that basic standards of care are met.* The first step will involve better assessment of demand for different services and what households are willing to provide themselves. Another important element will be establishing a suitable licensing and accreditation framework to ensure that providers meet basic standards of care.
- *Experimenting with and potentially expanding long-term care insurance to help finance the growing need for services.* A number of OECD countries, including Germany, Korea, and Japan have introduced long-term care insurance as part of their national social insurance programs in recent years, and these models may provide lessons for China. Given the existing high burden of social insurance contributions in China, the space for a dedicated long-term care payroll contribution is likely to be available only as other contribution rates in areas such as pensions and housing are reduced over time. Such pilots should be complemented by a system of carers' allowances for poor and possibly middle-income households who choose to care for dependent elderly members in the home or with the support of community-based organizations.
- Moving to integrated aged care and assisted living models that have a more differentiated range of services across the spectrum of needs and that draw on the skills of service providers from a wider range of agencies.

Promoting a More Integrated Social Security System

The impressive pace of expansion and reforms of China's social protection programs over the past two decades has created the second-generation challenge of promoting greater coherence in the system. Both within individual programs such as pensions and social assistance as well as across programs, new issues of compatibility have arisen as the social protection system has expanded. These issues need to be addressed to develop a system that is a coherent whole, not simply an accumulation of programs (World Bank 2012). Greater coherence will need to be informed by a clear vision of the goals of the social protection system and the underlying social values those goals reflect.

Greater system coherence will require balancing the desire for deepening security and protection of the poor with appropriate incentives for people to work and increase participation in formal sector employment. This is an agenda both within different parts of the social protection system and across them. Some issues that the current system will need to navigate in the coming years to strike the appropriate balance between protection and incentives include:

Deepening reforms of the social assistance system can help better achieve its poverty alleviation and promotional objectives. The expansion of *dibao* in urban and rural areas to cover around 70 million beneficiaries has been impressive over the past decade. Consolidation of the program provides the opportunity to improve the program design and linkages further:

- *One area for development is the relative impact of the program on the poor and the "near poor."* While the *dibao* program has performed well in excluding the nonpoor, its design raises risks of "poverty traps" for households just above the *dibao* eligibility threshold. Eligible households have their incomes topped up to the *dibao* threshold and also receive noncash benefits including exemptions or reductions on education fees, subsidized health insurance, public housing, and subsidized utilities. As a result, they may be better off than households just above the *dibao* threshold that are not entitled to such noncash benefits but have only slightly higher incomes. This raises the risk that *dibao* households face high effective marginal tax rates upon graduation from the program (and thus incentives to remain dependent on welfare) and that the near-poor will feel unfairly treated. Cities such as Beijing are trying to address this issue by allowing some subsidies on selected basic services for the near-poor, but such programs are not affordable for all localities. In OECD countries, the problem is often addressed by tax credits or other preferred treatment of nonpoor households with low incomes, but such options will not be possible for China while the large majority of households remain outside the personal income tax net in the foreseeable future.

- *A second challenge will be developing a more systematic approach to determination of dibao eligibility thresholds and benefit levels.* Currently, both the methods of determining *dibao* thresholds and the benefit levels themselves vary enormously, reflecting the highly decentralized nature of implementation. While some diversity in threshold levels is appropriate, a more consistent method for setting them would be desirable. MOCA has made progress in this direction, and assessment of emerging experience can inform future policy development.

- *A third direction is promoting greater synergies between social assistance programs and the antipoverty interventions in poor counties.* Traditionally, areas-based antipoverty programs have operated in parallel to household-based social welfare support. The government's new rural poverty strategy points the way to greater convergence of social assistance, social services, and antipoverty programs over time (such as prioritizing *dibao* and near-poor households in training under antipoverty programs).[76]

• *Over time, and in parallel with hukou reform and further labor market integration, greater convergence of rural and urban dibao programs would be expected,* with the gap between rural and urban thresholds within prefectures and provinces likely to narrow.

Another challenge for social assistance programs is the interaction between *dibao* and the host of national and local welfare schemes for the poor, including *wubao*, temporary assistance, and residual programs for *tekun* households. The draft Social Assistance Law is a positive step in this direction in its effort to make *dibao* the "backbone" social assistance program. It will be important to avoid the mistakes of many OECD countries that have seen a gradual proliferation of social assistance and welfare programs that are often inconsistent in their objectives and create inefficiencies in program administration.

In both the pension and health insurance systems, the use of public subsidies to encourage coverage expansion creates a future risk of disincentives for rural and urban informal sector workers to move into the formal sector, where they face high social contribution rates. This may in the long run harm both the economy (because of the lower productivity of informal sector employment) and workers themselves, who will continue to have worse working conditions. For the present, this risk seems worth taking in the interests of expanding coverage and promoting greater security for all workers, formal and informal. In the medium term, however, it may be necessary to look for ways to reduce the high marginal tax rates that informal sector workers face when moving into formal employment, caused by the combined effect of loss of subsidy on their social insurance coverage and high social contribution rates. The experience of middle-income countries such as Mexico and Colombia, which offer continued subsidies for low-income workers within formal social insurance systems, may provide lessons for managing such challenges. More fundamentally, the balance between general revenues and social contributions may need to be reconsidered in financing the social insurance benefits of all workers, both formal and informal.

Issues of coherence across social assistance and social insurance schemes will require closer attention in the medium term. One example is the consistency of coverage and treatment of elderly people across programs: with the expansion of basic pension benefits to rural and urban informal retirees in coming years, the interaction with measurement of household income for *dibao* needs to be examined closely. Currently, basic pension income is ignored in the *dibao* eligibility determination, but as the pension system expands, it may be necessary to look more closely at the rationale for such an approach.

Finally, given the dramatically increased imputed value of housing for urban households in recent years, the interaction of government policy on affordable housing and social assistance programs will need to be considered. The government has placed increased emphasis on affordable housing for lower-income households, in addition to public housing for the poor. While this is a welcome policy direction, it will also require more rigorous evaluation of the implicit value of social assistance packages that include free or subsidized public housing, and comparison of the value of the full *dibao* package with subsidies on offer to non-*dibao* households.

These issues are natural challenges to be expected in a social protection system that has expanded so rapidly and that has such diversity across space. Advanced economies continue to struggle with such issues in their more mature social protection systems. Considering such issues in future policy development will be vital to ensuring that the dual goals of protecting the poor and ensuring fairness for all are appropriately balanced. The lessons—including the numerous failures—of OECD and middle-income countries in balancing such considerations can be valuable, but the appropriate approach for China is also very dependent on its specific social, cultural, economic, and political values.

Annex Table 4A   Illustrative Sequencing of Hukou and Supporting Reforms

Phases	Hukou reform policies	Supporting reform policies
First phase	• Deepen and rigorously evaluate the local/provincial hukou reforms to inform national policy • Develop a national framework and national standards for residence permit system and indicators • Issue national guidelines and encourage prefecture cities to promote local hukou reform based on the national framework and guidelines • Pilot the national framework of residency permit system and prepare for scaling up • Start to establish a shared information system and platform from population registration and management	• Roll out rural-urban integration programs based on experiences learned from the national pilots in Chengdu and Chongqing • Implement specific plan for the equalization of basic public services and social welfare • Continue to increase the standards in rural areas to lower the gap to urban areas and harmonize key policies • Increase real pooling level of social security system (pension at the provincial level, unemployment insurance and health insurance at prefecture level) and issue social security card nationwide
Second phase	• Adopt the residence permit system nationwide and national guidelines for hukou conversion indicators, standards • Universalize open hukou access for rural residents in all prefectures, and liberalize/standardize access standards for all intra-provincial migrants • Undertake costing and sensitivity analysis of net costs of basic local-level service provision for migrants by type of city and volumes of migrants • Deploy and roll out population information system	• Continue to implement the equalization programs and pay more attention to lagging areas • Complete rural-urban integration of key social policies and programs (pension, health and health insurance, *dibao* programs) • Establish full coverage of social security system to provide basic social security, upgrade pooling level of social security (pension and unemployment insurance at national level, health insurance at provincial level), and establish national standards for *dibao* and social welfare programs
Third phase	• Based on costing, agree fiscal sharing arrangements for provision of basic public services to migrants and implement national net-settlement system to incentivize open hukou access by all cities through an incentive-based approach rather than an "ordering" approach • Further lower thresholds and requirements for hukou conversion based on cost-sharing and financing by central and local governments	• Incorporate hukou reform financing into budgetary management system and social economic plan • Make budgets for public services and social welfare based on the information of permanent residence population (>6 month) • Arrange special budget and establish an adjustment fund to compensate the net cost in receiving areas
Fourth phase	• Apply residence permit to all residents to restrict the function of the hukou system to population registration • Open accesses to all migrants	• Establish a standardized budgetary approach based on the information of permanent residence population

Notes

1. The measure of human capital used is the Jorgenson-Fraumeni lifetime income-based approach.
2. The 0.48 estimate uses data from China's National Bureau of Statistics and the 0.49 estimate uses China Household Income Project survey data.
3. See World Bank (2010a) for a detailed example of differential access to urban public education for migrant children.
4. See Cai and others (2012) for evidence on emerging strains on family support in rural areas. Commentators have also pointed to the longer-term prospect of an 8-4-2-1 family structure.
5. A useful symposium on the issue can be found in *China Economic Review* (2011).
6. The term *social contract* is not commonly used in China but is used in this report in the sense of the relationship between the government and its population as originated by Jean-Jacques Rousseau.
7. Yongkang Zhao, "Strengthening and Improving Social Management and Promoting Social Stability and Harmony," *People's Daily*, October 25, 2006. See also resolutions of the 6th Plenary session of the 17th CPC Party Congress.
8. See report in *China Daily*, March 18, 2010, on results of happiness survey of 70,000 Chinese residents.
9. See CASS (2011), which reports on surveys of nine large cities in 2009 and villages in 20 provinces in 2010.
10. See World Bank (2006) for an elaboration of the general framework for equity and development.
11. At one end of the spectrum, the governments of the social democratic welfare states of Scandinavia have a dominant role in providing highly equal access to high-quality social services and social protection. In contrast, the "liberal" welfare state model exemplified by the United States relies more on market-based approaches and may have higher tolerance for differential access to and quality of social services and social protection. In between lie the "conservative" welfare state models of other European countries, the "productivist" welfare states of richer East Asian countries, and hybrid models in countries such as New Zealand and Australia. Each model exhibits considerable diversity; see Esping-Andersen (1990) and Arts and Gelissen (2010). See Holliday (2000) regarding East Asian models.
12. Core competencies include communication skills, team work, and problem solving.
13. See also chapter 1 for benchmarking of social spending among OECD countries.
14. Barnett and Brooks 2010; Baldacci and others 2010. See Cai and others (2012) regarding rural savings.
15. The projections use national transfer accounts (NTA) modeling assuming constant real age-specific unit costs for social services and pensions by age cohort over time and overlaying China's demographic trajectory for the base case. The "explicit targets" scenario overlays the base case with policy commitments already made by the authorities to expand coverage of social programs (such as rural and urban resident pensions; expanded senior secondary and higher education) (Mason and Chen 2011).
16. Early child development and education covers children from conception to age six, and their parents, with a range of interventions including nutritional and health care interventions for young children and mothers to ensure optimal physical and cognitive development; early education programs—institution, community, and home-based—that aim to improve school readiness skills, including language, numeracy, and psychosocial skills; and parenting and caregiver education and counseling. High rates of return to investments in ECDE can be seen in studies from the United States as well as developing countries, including Colombia (ECDE attendees 100 percent more likely to be enrolled in later grades), Turkey (20 percentage points higher school enrollment in teens), and Bangladesh (58 percent better performance on standardized tests).
17. There were, as of late 2011, 592 poor counties in China, where around 20 percent of the country's population lives, although this number increased with the raising of the rural poverty line in December 2011.
18. According to the World Health Organization (WHO), stunting rates over 20 percent are considered medium level globally, and 40 percent anemia prevalence is "severe."
19. See WHO Global Database on Anemia, various years. Notably, the data show volatility in the anemia rate in the short period 2008–10

in poor rural counties (particularly among children 0–2 years of age) where anemia rates rose 31–45 percent in a single year from 2008 to 2009, then dropped below 2008 levels by 2010. This spike was presumably a consequence of the global financial crisis. Given the long-term effects of nutritional deprivation, both the average levels and their fluctuation are real causes for concern. While the comparison of the very youngest in poorest counties in a crisis year with the cohort 6–60 months in other countries can be misleading, it is nonetheless instructive to note that the poor county anemia rates for the very young in 2009 were equal to or above the most recently available rates for 6–60-month-old children in Afghanistan (37.9 percent prevalence in 2004), Arab Republic of Egypt (29.9 percent in 2000), Guatemala (38.1 percent in 2002), Namibia (40.5 percent), Tajikistan (37.7 percent in 2003), and Vietnam (34.1 percent in 2000–01).

20. Ji, Sun, and Chen 2004; Ji 2007; Ma and Wu 2009. While obesity levels as measured by the China Health and Nutrition Survey are notably lower, rates still more than quadrupled in the 1980s and 1990s (Li, Y., and others 2008). For comparison, in the mid-2000s, the national rate of childhood obesity in the United States was around 11 percent (Dehghan, Akhtar-Danesh, and Merchant 2005).

21. World Bank 2011a. The out-of-pocket spending estimate for China needs to be explored further. It is based on estimates from information on fees in public and private preprimary schools and on education statistics on government spending.

22. Chen and others 2010. Results on development quotient (DQ) and IQ were all statistically significant.

23. For the purposes of this chapter, the short term is the next two to three years, the medium term from then until 2020, and the long term from 2020 to 2030.

24. See Gao, Griffiths, and Chan (2008) for a review of 20 studies on obesity interventions in China that combine dietary intervention, physical activity, and health education; 17 of the studies found significant improvements.

25. It could be the "yin yang bao" packages already piloted in poor areas of China (Chen and others 2010).

26. Speech of Deputy Chief of the Office of Poverty Alleviation and Development at China Child Poverty Forum, reported in *China Daily*, May 27, 2011.

27. Rozelle 2011. See also CDRF pilots on ECDE in Qinghai (http://www.cdrf.org.cn/en).

28. See, for example, World Bank (2011b), which summarizes a range of preschool innovations in Latin America. For details, see Vegas and Santibañez (2010).

29. OECD (2007); Zhang and Zhang (2008) regarding Asian countries; Miguez (2006) regarding Argentina; and Hanson (2010) regarding Mexico.

30. National Plan for Medium- and Long-Term Education Reform and Development (2010–2020). http://www.moe.edu.cn /publicfiles/business/htmlfiles/moe/moe _177/201008/93785.html.

31. See Wu, Boscardin, and Goldschmidt (2011), background paper for this report. See also National Inspectorate sample survey of teachers 2007, which found major challenges in retention of rural teachers—particularly key teachers—and high incidence of substitute teachers in western and central provinces (http://www.moe.edu.cn/publicfiles/business /htmlfiles/moe/moe_914/201001/81660.html).

32. Some researchers have suggested that shifting the employment status of teachers to that of civil servants would be one way to facilitate a teacher allocation and transfer system that promotes greater equalization of quality (Wang and Gong 2011).

33. The plan says, "More assistance shall be granted to senior middle school education in impoverished areas in central and western regions."

34. European Training Foundation, various publications. See http://www. etf.europa.eu.

35. China National Health Development Research Centre 2011.

36. Evidence from 2001 in China found that 74 percent of patients reported making informal payments (Bloom, Han, and Li 2001).

37. Opinions of the CPC Central Committee and the State Council on Deepening the Health Care System Reform, 2009 (http://www.china. org.cn/government/scio-press-conferences/ 2009-04/09/content_17575378.htm).

38. The background paper for this section is Palu (2011).

39. The Global Independent Commission for Education of Health Professionals provides best-practice guidance on training of primary care professionals.

40. See Hofmarcher, Oxley, and Rusticelli (2007) for a summary of OECD experience on coordinated care reforms, and Ma and Lu (2011) on Chinese pilots in cities such as Shenzhen and Wuhan.

41. WHO Europe, European HFA Database, 2011 (http://www.euro.who.int/hfadb).

42. See, for example, Ould-Kaci (2011) on the French medical salary system, which relies on a higher fixed salary component in total doctor compensation, an approach similar to that of Japan.

43. Some commentators point to higher food and rental shares of migrants and low-income workers in consumption relative to the consumer price index (CPI), both items that have risen faster than the overall CPI.

44. Adjustments in statistical measures around the time of the initial decline raise questions of how much it was a statistical artifact, but there appears to be a consensus that a significant fall in labor income share occurred.

45. These trends appear to be accelerated in the light of the 2010 census results.

46. LFPRs are not reported in official statistics in China and have to be constructed (Cai, Du, and Wang 2011a).

47. Analysis also finds that work intensity among older urban workers has not increased to offset the falling supply and, if anything, has slightly declined over the same period (Cai and others 2012).

48. This is comparable to the gender wage gap in OECD-26 countries of 16 percent in 2008. However, both Korea (at 38 percent) and Japan (at 30 percent) were outliers, against countries such as Italy, which had a less than 2 percent gap (http://www.oecd.org).

49. There are many contributions to the Lewis turning point debate in China. See the symposium on the subject in *China Economic Review* (2011).

50. OECD 2006. Murrugarra (2011) discusses policy responses in Latin America to similar challenges.

51. The effects of labor market institutions on indicators such as employment and unemployment rates are the subject of debate. See Freeman (2008) for a review of the literature.

52. http://www.mohrss.gov.cn.

53. A Notice on Establishing the Wage Guideline System of Labor Market, Ministry of Labor and Social Security, 1999 (http://w1.mohrss.gov.cn /gb/ywzn/2006-02/15/content_106794.htm).

54. The *total* average monthly wages of migrant workers are in fact higher than those of local workers as migrant workers work more hours.

55. Regulations on Minimum Wages in Enterprises (1993); Provisions on Minimum Wages (2004); and MOLSS Notice on Further Developing the Minimum Wage System (2007).

56. The standard example in education is teachers "teaching to the test" when examination results are a key indicator, perhaps neglecting the development of other skills in students. Another example is overservicing by health providers when "performance" is determined according to the volume of services provided.

57. The tax wedge is calculated as (total labor cost − net take home pay)/total labor cost. So for China, assume payroll = 100 RMB, then total labor cost (100 + 42) = 142; net take home pay (100 − 22) = 78, and tax wedge = (142 − 78)/142 = 45.1 percent. For many countries, one would also calculate the personal income tax levied after deduction of social insurance contributions; OECD also allows for transfers from the state (for example, income tax credits). In China, neither of these is included in the calculation for the average urban worker who falls below the personal income tax threshold.

58. MOHRSS data from end-2010.

59. Hukou divides the population into rural (agricultural) and urban (nonagricultural) residents, as well as local and migrant residents, largely according to the place of birth. The hukou status of parents is generally transferred to children. The match is not exact, but the majority of rural people have agricultural hukou.

60. However, this process remains incomplete in very large cities, such as Beijing, where applicants for government jobs and in many enterprises require a Beijing hukou to be considered.

61. See Hertel, Zhai, and Wang (2002) and Whalley and Zhang (2004), both of which used CGE models to explore the impacts of removing all migration restrictions. See Zhu and Luo (2010) for a detailed study of Hubei province on the positive distributional effects of labor mobility.

62. The urban pension system has separate systems for civil servants, public service unit workers, and regular urban employees, each with different rules, replacement rates, and the like (World Bank forthcoming).

63. State Council Interim Provisions on Portability of Pension Benefits of the Urban Enterprise Pension System, December 2009.
64. See Giles, Park, and Wang (forthcoming) on determinants of participation across different urban SI schemes, using CULSS 2005 and 2010 data. The paper also notes significant discrepancies in estimated participation of migrants in the urban pension scheme and other social insurance schemes (medical, unemployment, and work injury insurance) between official sources and between official and survey-based sources.
65. In China, several reforms of the pension system since opening up have resulted in different cohort benefit frameworks: the different groups are described as "old man," "middle man," and "new man," depending on their period of entry into the system (World Bank forthcoming).
66. The net costs could be lower, as financing for civil servant and PSU pensions already involves significant public subsidies (World Bank forthcoming).
67. Sin (2005). These estimates were based on a sample of seven municipalities and need more representative and updated modeling, which includes the 2005 change in annuity factor for individual accounts.
68. The global trend is toward greater integration of civil servant and general worker pension schemes, either through full integration or integration with supplementary "top-up" schemes for public sector workers (Palacios and Whitehouse 2006).
69. *Wubao* refers to the five guarantees that such elderly people are meant to be provided: food, oil, and domestic fuel; livelihood necessities such as clothing and bedding, as well as spare money; basic housing; medical care; and funeral and burial services. Three no's means no family support, no sources of income, and no work capacity.
70. Long-term care is not the same as aged care services, which generally include a wider range of services, but long-term care tends to be the major funding need within aged care services.
71. Suggestions on Accelerating the Development of Aged Care Service Industry, February 2006 (http://www.gov.cn/zwgk/2006-02/17/content_202553.htm).
72. http://zyac.mca.gov.cn/article/ldjh/201203/20120300290474.shtml; http://chinau3a.com/lndx/html/?2952.html.
73. *China Daily,* November 11, 2011 (http://www.chinadaily.com.cn/bizchina/2011-11-09/content_14065471.htm).
74. See, for example, the Retirement Communities World Asia Conferences (http://www.terrapin.com/conference/retirement-communities-world-asia).
75. *China Daily,* November 11, 2011 (http://www.chinadaily.com.cn/bizchina/2011-11-09/content_14065471.htm).
76. Outline for Poverty Reduction and Development of China's Rural Areas (2011–2020) (http://www.gov.cn/jrzg/2011-12/01/content_2008462.htm).

References

Adams, Arvil V. 2007. "The Role of Youth Skills Development in the Transition to Work: A Global Review." World Bank, Washington, DC.

Almeida, Rita. 2009. "Does the Workforce in East Asia Have the Right Skills: Evidence from Firm-Level Surveys." World Bank, Washington, DC.

Arts, Wil, and John Gelissen. 2010. "39 Models of the Welfare State." In *Oxford Handbook of the Welfare State,* ed. Christopher Pierson, Herbert Obinger, Jane Lewis, Stephan Leibfried, and Francis Castle. Oxford, UK: Oxford University Press.

Bai, Ruixue. 2011. "The Role of the All China Federation of Trade Unions: Implications for Chinese Workers Today." *Journal of Labor and Society* 14 (1): 19–39.

Baldacci, Emanuele, Giovanni Callegari, David Coady, Ding Ding, Manmohan Kumar, Pietro Tommasino, and Jaejook Woo. 2010. "Public Expenditures on Social Programs and Household Consumption in China." IMF Working Paper 10/69, International Monetary Fund, Washington, DC.

Barnett, Steven, and Ray Brooks. 2010. "China: Does Government Health and Education Spending Boost Consumption?" IMF Working Paper 10/16, International Monetary Fund, Washington, DC.

Bitran, Ricardo, Liliana Escobar, and Patricia Gassibe. 2010. "After Chile's Health Reform: Increase In Coverage and Access, Decline in Hospitalization and Death Rates." *Health Affairs* 29 (12): 2161–70.

Bloom, Gerald, Leiya Han, and Xiang Li. 2001. "How Health Workers Earn a Living in

China." *Human Resources for Health Development Journal* 5 (1–3).

Brixi, Hana. 2009. "China: Urban Services and Governance." Policy Research Working Paper 5030, World Bank, Washington, DC.

Brixi, Hana, Yan Mu Beatrice Targa, and David Hipgrove. 2011. "Equity and Public Governance in Health System Reform: Challenges and Opportunities for China." Policy Research Working Paper 5530, World Bank, Washington, DC.

Bynum, P.W. Julie, Alice Andrews, Sandra Sharp, Dennis McCollough, and John E. Wennberg. 2011. "The Care Span: Fewer Hospitalizations Result When Primary Care Is Highly Integrated into a Continuing Care Retirement Community." *Health Affairs* 30 (5): 975–84.

Cai, Fang, Yang Du, and Meiyan Wang. 2011a. "Labor Market Institutions and Social Protection Mechanism." Background paper for China 2030, Institute of Population and Labor Economics, China Academy of Social Sciences, Beijing.

———. (2011b). "Overview of China's Labor Market." Background paper for China 2030, Institute of Population and Labor Economics, China Academy of Social Sciences, Beijing.

Cai, Fang, John Giles, Philip O'Keefe, and Dewen Wang. 2012. *The Elderly and Old Age Support in Rural China: Challenges and Prospects*. Washington, DC: World Bank.

Cai, Fang, Dewen Wang, and Yue Qu. 2009. "Flying Geese within Borders: How Does China Sustain Its Labour-Intensive Industries?" In *China's New Place in a World in Crisis*, eds. Ross Garnaut, L. Song, and W. T. Woo. Canberra: Asia Pacific Press.

CASS (Chinese Academy of Social Science). 2011. "Report on China's Migrant Population Development." Beijing.

Chen, Chunming, Wu He, Yuying Wang, Lina Deng, and Fengmei Jia. 2010. "Nutritional Status of Children during and post Global Economic Crisis in China." *Biomedical and Environmental Science* 24 (4): 321–28.

Chen, Y., and Z. Liang. 2008. "Educational Attainment in Migrant Children: The Forgotten Story of Urbanization in China." In *Education and Reform in China*, ed. Emily Hannum and Albert Park, 117–32. New York: Routledge.

Cheng, Y., and M. W. Rosenberg. 2009. "Financial Security of Elders in China." Social and Economic Dimensions of Population Aging Research Paper 241, McMaster University, Hamilton, Ontario.

China Center for Disease Control and Prevention (CDC) and Carolina Population Center. Various years. *China Health and Nutrition Survey*. University of North Carolina at Chapel Hill. http://www.cpc.unc.edu/projects/china.

China Center for Human Capital and Labor Market Research. 2011. *China Human Capital Report*. Central University of Finance and Economics, Beijing.

China Economic Review 2011. The Lewis Model Applied to China—Symposium." 22, Pt. 4: 535–625.

China National Health Development Research Centre. 2011. China National Health Accounts Report 2011. Beijing: China National Health Development Research Centre.

CINTERFOR/ILO. 2001. *Modernization in Vocational Education and Training in Latin America and the Caribbean*. Montevideo (http://www.cinterfor.org.uy/public/english/region/ampro/cinterfor/publ/sala/moder_in/moder_in.pdf).

Dehghan, Mahshid, Noori Akhtar-Danesh, and Anwar Merchant. 2005. "Childhood Obesity, Prevalence and Prevention." *Nutrition Journal* 4: 24–32.

Esping-Andersen, Gosta. 1990. *The Three Worlds of Welfare Capitalism*. Cambridge, U.K.: Polity Press.

Farrell, Diana, and Andrew Grant. 2005. "China's Looming Talent Shortage." *McKinsey Quarterly* (4): 70–79.

Fiszbein, Ariel, and Norbert Schady. 2009. *Conditional Cash Transfers: Reducing Present and Future Poverty*. Washington, DC: World Bank.

Freeman, Richard. 2008. "Labor Market Institutions around the World." Centre for Economic Performance Discussion Paper 844, London School of Economics and Political Science, London.

Gao, Yang, Sian Griffiths, and Emily Chan. 2008. "Community-Based Interventions to Reduce Overweight and Obesity in China: A Systematic Review of the Chinese and English Literature." *Journal of Public Health* 30: 436–48.

Giles, John, Albert Park, Fang Cai, and Yang Du. Forthcoming. "Weathering a Storm: Survey-Based Perspectives on Employment in China in the Aftermath of the Global Financial Crisis." In *Labor Markets in Developing Countries during the Great Recession: Impacts and Policy Responses*, eds. Arup Banerji, David

Newhouse, David Robalino, and Pierella Paci. Washington, DC: World Bank.

Giles, John, Albert Park, and Dewen Wang. Forthcoming. "Expanding Social Insurance Coverage in Urban China." World Bank Policy Note, World Bank, Washington, DC.

Giles, John, Dewen Wang, and Wei Cai. 2012. "The Labor Supply and Retirement Behavior of China's Older Workers and Elderly in Comparative Perspective." In *Aging in Asia: Findings from New and Emerging Data Initiatives*, eds. J. P. Smith and M. Majmundar. Washington, DC: National Academies Press.

Goetz, Anne-Marie, and John Gaventa. 2001. "Bringing Citizen Voice and Client Focus into Service Delivery." Working Paper 138, Institute for Development Studies, University of Sussex, Brighton, U.K.

Gong, Sen, and Dong Yu. 2011. "Cases of Public Participation for People's Well-being" (in Chinese). Development Research Center, Beijing.

Hanson, G. H. 2010. "Why Isn't Mexico Rich?" *Journal of Economic Literature* 48 (4): 987–1004.

Hanushek, Eric, Ludger Woessmann, and Lei Zhang. 2011. "General Education, Vocational Education, and Labor Market Outcomes over the Life Cycle." Working Paper 17504, National Bureau of Economic Research, Cambridge, MA.

He, Y. 2009. *Weishenme Shangdaxue de Nongcun Haizi Shaole* [Why so few rural students go to college?]. http://focus.cnhubei.com/original/200903/t604450.shtml.

Hertel, T., F. Zhai, and Z. Wang. 2002, "Implications of WTO Accession for Poverty in China." Paper for the Development Research Center of the State Council/World Bank Conference on China's WTO Accession and Poverty Alleviation, June 28–29, Beijing.

Hofmarcher, Maria, Howard Oxley, and Elena Rusticelli. 2007. *Improved Health System Performance through Better Care Coordination*. Paris: OECD.

Holliday, Ian. 2000. "Productivist Welfare Capitalism: Social Policy in East Asia." *Political Studies* 48 (4): 706–23.

Holzmann, Robert, David Robalino, and Noriyuki Takayama, eds. 2009. *Closing the Coverage Gap: The Role of Social Pensions and Other Retirement Income*.

Ji, Chengye. 2007. "Report on Childhood Obesity in China: Prevalence and Trends of Overweight and Obesity in Chinese Urban School-Age Children and Adolescents, 1985–2000."

Biomedical and Environmental Sciences (20): 1–10.

Ji, Chengye, Junling Sun, and Tianjiao Chen. 2004. "Dynamic Analysis on the Prevalence of Obesity and Overweight School-Age Children and Adolescents in Recent 15 Years in China." *Chinese Journal of Epidemiology* [Zhonghua Liuxingbingxue Zazhi] 25 (2): 103–08.

Johanson, Richard, and Arvil V. Adams. 2004. *Skills Development in Sub-Saharan Africa*. Washington, DC: World Bank.

Joshua, Laurie. 2011. *International Experience with Long Term Care: Lessons for China's Evolving Policy Framework for an Aging Population*. 2 vols. Beijing: World Bank.

Jukes, Matthew, Lesley Drake, and Donald Bundy. 2008. *School Health, Nutrition and Education for All: Levelling the Playing Field*. Oxford, U.K.: CABI Publishing.

Li, Q. 2007. "Shi Lun Woguo Zhiye Jiaoyu Fazhan de Pingjing he Duice" [Technical and vocational education and training in China: Bottlenecks and Countermeasures], *Fujian Taoyan* 3: 19–23.

Li, Shi. 2012. "The Current Situation and Trend of Income Inequality in China and Factors behind Changes." In *Income Distribution during the Transition Period*. Beijing: China Development Research Foundation.

Li, Shi, Chuliang Luo, and Terry Sicular. 2011. "Overview: Income Inequality and Poverty in China, 2002–2007." CIBC Centre for Human Capital and Productivity Working Papers 2011/10, University of Western Ontario, London, Ontario.

Li, Shi, and Renwei Zhao. 2011. "Market Reform and the Widening of the Income Gap." *Social Sciences in China* 32 (2): 140–58.

Li, Yanping, Evert Schouten, Evert, Xiaoqi Hu, Zhaohui Cui, Dechun Luan, and Guansheng Ma. 2008. "Obesity Prevalence and Time Trend among Youngsters in China, 1982–2002." *Asia Pacific Journal of Clinical Nutrition* 17 (1): 131–37.

Liang, Zhaoguo. 2007. "Yiyuan rongzizulin gudingzichan de kongzhiguanli yu caiwuhesuan. zhongguobaojian-yixueyanjiuban" [Management and financial accounting of finance leasing of hospital's fixed assets]. *China Health,* (Medical Research Edition). 25 (22): 35–38.

Lv, Jiming. 2005. "Current Situation of Rural Social Security and Analysis of Its Development Path" (in Chinese). *Journal of Ningxia Communist School* 6.

Ma, Jin, and Lin Lu. 2011. "Responsibility Division and Work Condition between Public Hospitals and Primary Health Care Institutions." World Bank East Asia Health Unit, Beijing.

Ma, Jun, and Shuansheng Wu. 2009. "Trend Analysis of the Prevalence of Obesity and Overweight among School-Age Children and Adolescents in China" (in Chinese) *China School Health* 30 (3): 195–97, 200.

Machenbach, Johan. 2005. "Health and Health Care." In *Health, Aging and Retirement in Europe—First Results from the Survey of Health, Ageing and Retirement in Europe*, eds. A. Borsch-Supan, A. Burgiavini, H. Jurges, J. Machenbach and G. Weber. Mannheim: MEA.

Macinko, James, Ines Dourado, Rosana Aquino, Palmira de Fatima Bonolo, Maria Fernanda Lima-Costa, Maria Guadalupe Medina, Eduardo Mota, Veneza Berenice de Oliveira, and Maria Aparecida Turci. 2010. "Major Expansion of Primary Care in Brazil Linked to Decline in Unnecessary Hospitalization." *Health Affairs* 29 (12): 2149–60.

Mason, Carl, and Qiulin Chen. 2011. "Projecting China's Expenditures on Health Care, Education and Pensions with Data from the National Transfer Accounts: Results and Documentation." Background paper for China 2030 report, Berkeley, CA.

Miguez, Eduardo. 2006. "The Argentinean Failure: An Interpretation of Economic Evolution in the "Short 20th Century." Desarrollo economico 1 (Special Edition).

Ministry of Education of the People's Republic of China. 2010. *Educational Statistics Yearbook of China 2009*. Department of Development and Planning, Ministry of Education. Beijing: People's Education Press.

Murrugarra, Edmundo. 2011. "Employability and Productivity among Older Workers: A Policy Framework and Evidence from Latin America." World Bank Social Protection Working Paper Series 1113, World Bank, Washington, DC.

National Bureau of Statistics. 2010. *China Labor Statistical Yearbook*. Beijing: China Statistics Press.

———. 2010. *China Statistical Yearbook*. Beijing: China Statistics Press.

OECD (Organization for Economic Cooperation and Development). 2005. *Performance Related Pay for Government Employees*. Paris: OECD.

———. 2006. *Live Longer, Work Longer*. Paris: OECD.

———. 2007. *Education at a Glance: OECD Indicators 2007*. Paris: OECD.

———. 2009. *How Expensive Is the Welfare State?* Paris: OECD.

OECD. 2010. *OECD Health Policy Studies: Improving Value in Health Care Measuring Quality*. Paris: OECD.

———. 2010b. *PISA 2009 Results: Executive Summary*. Paris: OECD http://pisa2009.acer.edu.au/.

———. 2011a. *Help Wanted? Providing and Paying for Long-Term Care*. Paris: OECD.

———. 2011b. *Society at a Glance*. Paris: OECD.

———. 2011c. *Taxing Wages 2011*. Paris: OECD.

Ofman, J., and others. 2004. "Does Disease Management Improve Clinical and Economic Outcomes in Patients with Chronic Disease? A Systematic Review." *American Journal of Medicine* 117 (3): 182–92.

Ou, M. 2007. *The Intelligence Development of Children in China: The Ability Training and Test for Children Aged 3–7* (in Chinese). Beijing: China Women's Publishing House.

Ould-Kaci, Karim. 2011. "Introduction to Human Resources in French Hospitals." Paper prepared for DRC/WHO Joint Project on Medical Services Regulation, Beijing.

Palacios, Robert, and Oleksiy Sluchynskyy. 2006. *The Role of Social Pensions*. World Bank: Washington, DC.

Palacios, Robert, and Edward Whitehouse. 2006. "Civil-Service Pension Schemes around the World." Social Protection Discussion Paper 0602, World Bank, Washington, DC.

Palu, Toomas. 2011. "Modernizing Primary Care in China." Background report for the China 2030 report, Beijing.

Paralles-Miralles, Montserrat, Carolina Romero, and Edward Whitehouse. 2012,, "International Patterns of Pension Provision II: A Worldwide Overview of Facts and Figures." Social Protection Discussion Paper 1211, World Bank, Washington, DC.

Park, Albert, John Giles, Fang Cai, and Yang Du. 2011. "Labor Scarcity, Labor Regulation, and Prospects for China's Labor Markets." Paper based on paper titled "The Chinese Labor Market: Prospects and Challenges," prepared by Albert Park for the Conference on the State of the Chinese Economy: Implications for China and the World, US-China Institute, University of Southern California, February 25–26.

Piggott, John, and Renuka Sane. 2009. "Indexing Pensions." Social Protection Discussion Paper 0925, World Bank, Washington, DC.

Roberts, Kenneth. 1997. "China's 'Tidal Wave' of Migrant Labor: What Can We Learn from Mexican Undocumented Migration to the United States?" *International Migration Review* 31 (2): 249–93.

Rozelle, Scott. 2011. "China's Human Capital Challenge and Investments in Education, Nutrition and Health." Background paper for China 2030 report, Beijing.

Ru, Xin, Xueyi Lu, and Peilin Li, eds. 2011. *Society of China Analysis and Forecast*. Beijing: Social Sciences Academic Press.

Saltman, Richard, Ana Rico, and Wienke Boerma, eds. 2006. "Primary Care in the Driver's Seat? Organizational Reform in European Primary Care." European Observatory on Health Systems and Policies Series, World Health Organization, Copenhagen.

Sato, Hiroshi, Terry Sicular, and Ximing Yue. 2012. "Housing Ownership, Incomes, and Inequality in China, 2002–2007, Rising Inequality." In *China: Challenge to a Harmonious Society*, eds. Shi Li, Hiroshi Sato, and Terry Sicular. Cambridge, U.K.: Cambridge University Press.

Shen, J., and J. Benson. 2008. "Tripartite Consultation in China: A First Step towards Collective Bargaining?" *International Labour Review* 147 (2–3): 231–48.

Sin, Yvonne. 2005. "Pension Liabilities and Reform Options for Old Age Insurance." East Asia and Pacific Human Development Unit Working Paper 2005-1, World Bank, Washington, DC.

Solinger, Dorothy J. 1999. *Contesting Citizenship in Urban China: Peasant Migrants, the State, and the Logic of the Market*. Berkeley, CA: University of California Press.

Spence, Michael, and Maureen Lewis, eds. 2009. "Health and Growth." Commission on Growth and Development, Washington, DC.

Thorpe, K. E., and D. H. Howard. 2006. "The Rise in Spending among Medicare Beneficiaries: The Role of Chronic Disease Prevalence and Changes in Treatment Intensity." *Health Affairs* 22 (August).

Tollen, L. 2008. "Physician Organization in Relation to Quality and Efficiency of Care: A Synthesis of Recent Literature." Kaiser Permanente Institute for Health Policy and Commonwealth Fund (http://www.commonwealthfund .org/usr_doc/Tollen_physician_org_quality_ efficiency_1121.pdf).

Uhlenberg, Peter, ed. 2009. *International Handbook of Population Aging*. New York: Springer Science and Business Media Press.

United Nations. 2010. World Population Prospects, 2010 Revision. http://esa.un.org/wpp /unpp/panel_population.htm.

Vegas, Emiliana, and Lucrecia Santibanez. 2010. *The Promise of Early Childhood Development in Latin America and the Caribbean*. Washington, DC.: World Bank.

Wan, P. 2007. "Gaozhi Zhiyegangwei Xing Shixun Jidi Jianshe de Gouxiang" (A concept to build up training centers for vocational education"), *Zhiye Jiaoyu Yanjiu* (Vocational Education Research) 7: 18–19.

Wang, Dewen, Jiaze Chen, and Wenshu Gao. 2011. "Social Security Integration: The Case of Rural and Urban Resident Pension Pilot in Chengdu" (in Chinese), World Bank, Beijing.

Wang, Dewen, Philip O'Keefe, and Jin Song. 2012. "Hukou Reform in China: A Roadmap to 2030." Background paper for China 2030 report, Beijing.

Wang, Dewen, Philip O'Keefe, and Larry Thompson. Forthcoming. "China's Pension System Integration: The Case of Guangdong." World Bank, Beijing.

Wang, Junxiu, and Yiyin Yang, eds. 2011. *Annual Report on Social Mentality in China* (in Chinese). Beijing: Social Sciences Academic Press.

Wang, Liejun. 2010. "Experiences of Hukou Reform and Overall Strategy for Next Step Reform" (in Chinese). *Social Sciences of Jiangsu* 2: 59–65.

Wang, Liejun, and Sen Gong. 2011. "Gonggong bumen xinchou jili de guoji bijiao ji qishi,Guowuyuan fazhan yanjiu zhongxin Diaocha Yanjiu Baogao" (International comparison of salary and incentive in public sector and its implications for China). DRC Research Report 179, Development Research Center of the State Council, Beijing.

Wang, Rong, and Kin Bing Wu. 2008. "Urban Service Delivery and Governance in Education in Five Chinese Cities." East Asia and Pacific Department, World Bank, Washington, DC.

Wang, Rong, and Jianfang Yang. 2008. "Empirical Study on Educational Expenditures of Local Government in China." China Institute for Educational Finance Research, Beijing.

Weeks, W.B., D.J. Gottlieb, D.E. Nyweide, J.M. Sutherland, J. Bynum, L.P. Casalino, R.R. Gillies, S.M. Shortell, and E.S .Fisher. 2010.

"Higher Health Care Quality and Bigger Savings Found at Large Multispecialty Medical Groups." *Health Affairs* 29 (5): 991–97.

Whalley, John, and S. M. Zhang. 2004. "Inequality Change in China and Hukou Labor Mobility Restrictions." NBER Working Paper 10683, National Bureau of Economic Research, Cambridge, MA.

WHO (World Health Organization). 2009. "Global Health Risks." Comparative Risk Assessment Project, WHO, Geneva.

World Bank. 2005. "Review of Experience of Family Medicine in Europe and Central Asia." Human Development Sector Unit, Europe and Central Asia Region, Washington, DC.: World Bank.

———. 2006. *World Development Report 2006: Equity and Development*. World Bank, Washington, DC.

———. 2009. "From Poor Areas to Poor People: China's Evolving Poverty Reduction Agenda. An Assessment of Poverty and Inequality in China." East Asia and Pacific Region, World Bank. Washington, DC.

———. 2010a. "China: Compulsory Education for Migrant Children in Guangdong Province." Human Development Unit, East Asia and Pacific, World Bank, Washington, DC.

———. 2010b. "Fixing the Public Hospital System in China." China Health Policy Notes, Human Development Sector Unit, East Asia and Pacific, Beijing.

———. 2010c. "Health Provider Payment Reforms in China: What International Experience Tells Us." China Health Policy Notes, Human Development Sector Unit, East Asia and Pacific, Beijing.

———. 2010d. "The Path to Integrated Insurance Systems in China." China Health Policy Notes, Human Development Sector Unit, East Asia and Pacific, Beijing.

———. 2010e. "Long-Term Care Policies for Older Populations in new EU Member States and Croatia: Challenges and Opportunities." Europe and Central Asia Human Development Sector Unit, World Bank, Washington, DC.

———. 2011a. "Early Childhood Development and Education in China: Breaking the Cycle of Poverty and Improving Future Competitiveness." Report 53746-CN, Human Development Sector Unit, East Asia and Pacific Region, World Bank, Washington, DC.

———. 2011b. "Towards a Healthy and Harmonious Life in China: Stemming the Rising Tide of Non-Communicable Diseases." Human Development Unit, East Asia and Pacific Region, Washington, DC.

———. 2012. "Resilience, Equity and Opportunity." World Bank Social Protection and Labor Strategy Paper, 2012-2022, Social Protection and Labor Anchor Unit, World Bank, Washington, DC.

———. Forthcoming. "A Vision for Pension Policy Reform." Human Development Sector Unit, East Asia and Pacific Region, World Bank, Washington, DC.

Wu, Kin Bing, Christy Kim Boscardin, and Peter Goldschmidt. 2011. "A Retrospective on Educational Outcomes in China: From Shanghai's 2009 PISA Results to Factors that Affected Student Performance in Gansu in 2007." Background paper for the 2030 report.

Wu, Kaiya, Li Zhang, and Xiao Cheng. 2010. "The Barrier of Hukou System Reform: An Analysis of the Qualifications for Urban Hukou." *Chinese Journal of Population Science*, No. 1, pp. 66-74.

Wu, Yuning. 2009. "Literature Review of China Rural Pension System." Paper prepared for World Bank East Asia Social Protection Unit, Beijing.

Xinhuanet. 2009. "Zhu Yong Daibiao: Zhiye Jiaoyu Buneng "Heibanshang Kai Jiqi." (http://job.workercn.cn/content-file/2009/03/09/172319604621006.html).

Yip, Winnie Chi-Man, William Hsiao, Qingyue Meng, Wen Chen, and Xiaoming Sun. 2010. "Realignment of Incentives for Health-Care Providers in China." *Lancet* 375 (9720): 1120–30.

Yue, Ximing, Shi Li, and Terry Sicular. 2011. "High Incomes in Monopoly Industries: A Discussion." *Social Sciences in China*, Special Issue on Income Inequality in China 32 (2): 178–96.

Zhang, Ruoxue, and Tao Zhang. 2008. "Jingji Zengzhang he Shouru Chaju Suoxiao Heyi Jiande." *Jingji Xuejia* 5: 96–101.

Zhao, Renwei, and Sai Ding. 2008. "China Household Wealth Distribution Research." In *China Household Income Distribution Research*, eds. Shi Li, Terry Sicular, and Bjorn Gustafsson. Beijing: Beijing Normal University Press.

Zhu, Nong, and Xubei Luo. 2010. "The Impact of Migration on Rural Poverty and Inequality: A Case Study in China." *Agricultural Economics* 41 (2): 191–204.

5

Reaching "Win-Win" Solutions with the Rest of the World

After an absence of two centuries, China has returned to center stage of the global economy. Domestic reforms and integration into global markets have resulted in 30 years of unprecedented growth, making China the world's second-largest economy and premier creditor. The integration of China into the world economy has yielded huge benefits, both for China and the rest of the world. In China, poverty has been reduced dramatically and new employment opportunities have been created for hundreds of millions of people. Substantial flows of foreign direct investment (FDI) into China have helped drive productivity in domestic firms with new technologies, training on the job, and intensified competition. China has imported foreign practices in a host of areas ranging from banking regulation to product standards. For the rest of the world, manufactured products have become more affordable, while the FDI flows into China represented new investment opportunities for foreign firms, and the efficiency of global production networks has sharply risen.

This remarkable story is set to continue. China has the potential to reach high-income status and to become the world's largest economy within the next two decades. However, wide-ranging transformations in the relation between China and the rest of the world are required if China is to avoid the "middle-income trap." The next 20 years will radically differ from the previous 20 years as China moves toward a successful transition to high-income status.

- In recent decades, China's growth has been exceptionally high and driven by manufacturing sectors. In the coming decades, however, growth will likely be lower and will depend more on the services sectors. In the past, the main concern was about the impact of sustained high growth. The focus was on bottlenecks in the fast-growing export-oriented manufacturing sectors: limited availability of necessary natural resources, adverse environmental impacts, and slow-growing foreign markets. Those problems will not disappear, but in the future, an equally important concern could become the impact of decelerating growth. What tensions and imbalances, especially in China's financial sector, will be revealed if growth slows?
- In recent decades, FDI inflows were instrumental in China gaining access to global markets and global technologies. In coming decades, further access to markets and technologies will instead come more and

more through globalization of Chinese firms (and thus FDI outflows). Through investments abroad, globalizing Chinese companies can not only enter new markets and acquire new technologies, but they can take advantage of economies of scale and move production up the value chain. Large global companies are a prerequisite for the transition into a high-income economy.

- In recent decades, China's presence in global financial markets has been limited. In coming decades, China will have to become a more dominant player. In the past, China protected itself from volatility in international financial markets by restricting capital account transactions, by pegging the renminbi to the dollar, and by accumulating large foreign exchange reserves. In the future, that strategy will become less effective, and stability should come from a more international and independent role for China's currency.

- In recent decades, China has often approached international policy debates from a purely domestic perspective. In future decades, it is in the interest of both China and the rest of the world that China adopt a more proactive approach and take responsibility for proposing solutions to global governance problems and for the provision of global public goods.

Such a successful transformation can create more win-win opportunities for China and the world, but the next 20 years will pose new challenges and come with new uncertainties. In thinking about the challenges that China (and the world) will face over the next two decades, it is useful to consider three questions. The answers are not obvious, and the policy choices involved are difficult and in some cases risky.

First, to what extent should China prepare for significantly lower growth? Growth prospects are obviously highly uncertain, not only because of the short-run uncertainty linked to the global financial crisis but also because structural growth trends are contingent on innovations that are virtually impossible to

predict. Nevertheless, strong signs suggest that population aging and the shift to services will slow growth in China and many other parts of the world. Even if new sources of productivity growth in services could be unleashed, it would be prudent to anticipate decelerating growth and to stress-test the sustainability of institutions in case of low growth.

Second, should China slow the pace of global integration or rather step up its globalization in new areas? Some argue that the penetration of China in global manufacturing has reached its limits. Further expansion of market shares is becoming increasingly difficult, while the slow recovery in high-income countries may magnify calls for protectionist measures against Chinese exports. Consequently, future growth has to come more from domestic demand. Moreover, with globalization, China has become more exposed to volatile global financial markets. China cannot achieve its goal of becoming a high-income country by retreating from the world economy, however. Indeed, China will have to integrate more into financial markets and markets for services to facilitate the globalization of its firms, to strengthen the international use of its currency, and to increase efficiency in its delivery of services. As a result, China will likely become the main champion of globalization. Nevertheless, in some areas (the financial sector, in particular), a lengthy transition period is required to reduce the risk of instability.

Third, to what extent should China take responsibility for the provision of global public goods? Even if China reaches high-income status, its per capita income will still be far behind those in more advanced economies, and its domestic problems will remain daunting. Still, it would be a mistake for China to leave the initiative to more advanced economies. Global governance structures and procedures to provide global public goods should be brought much more into line with the need of fast-growing developing economies. Not only is China's participation critical in providing global solutions for environmental problems and financial stress, but its active role in negotiations can ensure that the solutions adequately reflect the interests of China and other developing countries.

These questions and the policy issues they raise are explored through three main sections that consider scenarios for the future of the global economy, China's integration into global markets, and China's participation in addressing global public goods. Together, they outline a strategy for deepening China's integration into the global economy over the next two decades to upgrade production to more sophisticated manufactures, establish a world-class services sector, and contribute to the preservation of global public goods.

Scenarios of China's Evolving Economy

Following this introduction, the chapter presents scenarios for the evolution of the global economy and China's role through 2030. To capture some of the many uncertainties, both a low-growth and a high-growth scenario have been developed. Both scenarios include anticipated structural changes, because China's future role in the global economy cannot be explored by simple extrapolations of gross domestic product (GDP). The next two decades are unlikely to bring a mere continuation of current growth patterns. Indeed, comparative advantages will change, economies will move up the value chain, production and trade patterns will shift, and relative prices will adjust. Therefore, detailed, model-based scenarios were developed for this study to capture the main changes that are expected. The scenarios incorporate key drivers of change during the next two decades, including technological catch-up, demographic transformations, and further capital accumulation.

Several striking features emerge in the scenarios. First of all, a further rise of other emerging economies as drivers of global growth should be expected, rather than mainly a further rise of China, which has already established a dominant position. More rapid growth than in advanced countries, combined with exchange rate appreciation, will make the emerging markets the main destinations for world trade. In both scenarios, domestic demand in other developing countries will contribute more than 40 percent to global growth in 2030. That is more than the contribution of all high-income countries together, where roughly one-third of global growth will originate. China alone would contribute 20 percent (in the low-growth scenario) to 28 percent (in the high-growth scenario).

Second, aging populations, declining investment rates, and a shift to services, with relatively low-productivity growth all point to a slowing of GDP growth in many countries, including China. In the low-growth scenario, growth in all developing countries combined is expected to slow from 6.5 percent currently to 4.5 percent in 2030. The slowdown in China will be even sharper, from 9 percent currently to just below 4 percent in 2030, although on average China will remain one of the fastest-growing countries during the next 20 years. High-income countries would see their annual growth rates more than halved, from 2.5 percent now to just above 1 percent in 2030. In the high-growth scenario, with more innovations in the services sectors worldwide, the slowdown is minimal. For example, China's growth remains for many years at current levels, dropping to 7 percent only after 2025.

Third, despite the slowing of overall growth, environmental pressures will increase. That is clearly illustrated by the anticipated increase in greenhouse gas emissions. Without additional policies, even in the low-growth scenario, emissions of the four main gases that the model tracks are expected to more than double in China and India between now and 2030, while only minimal increases are anticipated in high-income countries. This means that China and other emerging countries will increasingly hold the key to the solution for global environmental problems.

Fourth, middle-income countries will continue to dominate international trade in manufactured products but will experience a significant shift toward services domestically. Globally, the share of services in value added would increase from 56 percent now to 65 percent in 2030, while the share of manufacturing would decline from 19.5 percent now to 11 percent in 2030. As middle-income countries shift to services and move up the value chain in manufacturing, new opportunities will be created for low-income countries to expand their low-skill labor-intensive production.

Fifth, even in the high-growth scenario, with large investment needs and a decline in the savings rate in China from 45 to 35 percent, capital will remain abundant in China. Not only does that create opportunities for substantial investments in new markets, it will also open up the opportunity for more productive investments abroad, a trend that might well become one of the most distinctive developments during the coming decades.

A final character of the scenarios is that, despite China's dominant position in the global economy and the sharp rise in average incomes, making China formally a high-income country, a large part of the population will still be relatively poor. It will likely take significantly more than 20 years for the whole population to reach high-income status.

Many of the opportunities and solutions to the challenges that emerge in this scenario can be found in global markets. Countries, developing and high-income alike, that maintain an outward orientation will be among the successful ones during the coming decades, while an inward-looking policy will increasingly prove self-defeating. Three outward-looking policy areas are of special interest for China: trade policies, policies that govern cross-border investments, and policies that will facilitate the internationalization of the renminbi.

China's Interaction with the Global Economy

The chapter then reviews how policies in the areas of trade, FDI, exchange rates, and capital controls will need to be modified in the light of China's interactions with the global economy. Increasing economic openness has been a critical driver of China's remarkable success over the past three decades. Reductions in import barriers have boosted the efficiency of domestic firms by strengthening competition and increasing access to imported inputs. These reductions have also promoted China's participation in components trade and facilitated rapid expansion into foreign markets through reciprocal reductions in foreign import restrictions and eventual entry into the World Trade Organization (WTO). Dismantling most barriers to FDI inflows has increased access to foreign technology and business practices. The integration of foreign standards into regulation and business practices has improved the quality of domestic production. Greater exposure to foreign ideas through the education abroad of Chinese students and increasing communications through the Internet have enriched China's, and the world's, economy and society.

Despite the obvious benefits of economic openness to China, pressures for slowing China's economic integration with the rest of the world are still evident. These pressures stem from concerns over China's vulnerability to foreign protectionism, China's increasing financial dependence on low-yield U.S. government liabilities, and the disruption to Chinese economic activity from the recent global financial crisis and its aftermath, as the full implications of the expansionary activities required to support demand are still not clear.

Despite these real concerns, China cannot achieve its full potential and become a high-income country by turning its back on the global economy. We argue that China needs to continue its outward orientation but that the focus of that orientation should change during the coming decades. China (and the world) will continue to benefit from maintaining an open trading system and from welcoming investment in its economy to improve competitiveness, but it will need an open financial sector and policies that enable an acceleration of investments in foreign markets. It is in the interest of other countries, both high- and low-income, to welcome these investments. Only through openness will China be able to obtain the oil and metals required to support domestic industry and absorb the technology necessary to upgrade production to supply consumers with rising incomes and penetrate new foreign markets.

That does not mean that the government should move rapidly to dismantle all its controls on transactions with the global economy, which would be excessively risky. The pace of change in each sector should take into account the risks involved. China already receives large FDI inflows and is generating increasing FDI outflows; most remaining limits on investment and approval requirements (except those to ensure compliance with national laws and maintain national security) could be eliminated easily. China should continue to pursue opportunities to increase its market access and maintain its relatively open trading system. By contrast, the transition to an open financial system and a flexible exchange rate will require time to ensure that China's institutions are adequate to maintain stability in the face of shocks from the international financial system.

China's huge size, its presence in most markets, the threat of rising protectionism, and limited regional agreements argue for continued support for a global trading system based on multilateral negotiations. While China will continue to have a comparative advantage in manufactures, it should focus on services in future trade negotiations. Opening the services sector to foreign participants, if done in the context of a strong regulatory framework to ensure competition, can improve the efficiency of the services sector and thus improve efficiency in goods production as well. In addition, despite the rapid reduction in barriers to entry in services (from a high level of restrictions) undertaken for WTO accession, China still has a relatively high level of protection in services. Thus it has more concessions to offer in future negotiations on trade in services than in most traded goods, where its tariffs are relatively low.

The division of the world into regional trading blocs is a challenge to the multilateral

trading system and to China's market access. China should emphasize both multilateral and regional arrangements. It will benefit from abiding by and protecting existing multilateral agreements as well as pushing for further opening of global markets using multilateral channels. China should also proactively push ahead with the negotiations for accession to the WTO government procurement agreement as part of its effort to improve procurement procedures, enhance transparency, reduce costs, and enhance quality in government purchases. At the same time, China needs to participate proactively in regional trade agreements that lower trade barriers at and behind borders and that introduce trade facilitation arrangements. Where possible, China should advocate "open regionalism," which would require that tariff levels agreed among regional partners be offered to other countries on a most-favored-nation (MFN) basis.

In an integrated world, it is especially important that countries press for disciplines that limit the use of export restrictions at times of food scarcity. Although governments understandably take steps to avoid sharp increases in food prices, export restrictions should be discussed with consuming nations and the extent of the threat documented. Without some provision for review, the exceptions to WTO strictures against export restraints are open to abuse, resulting in an exacerbation of food shortages and sharper fluctuations in international prices. Trade restrictions make it difficult for importers to rely on the international trading system in times of scarcity and thus reduce food security.

Outward flows of FDI from China have increased markedly over the past decade, despite attempts to restrict Chinese investment in some markets. The government has supported outward investment through bilateral investment treaties that provide for national treatment of Chinese investors already established in the host country. Future efforts to protect overseas investment could shift toward gaining pre-entry national treatment, essentially ensuring that

Chinese investors are allowed access to host-country markets on the same basis as nationals. Even this more liberal approach to investment guarantees will not overcome obstacles to investment based on national security concerns, which has been an argument used to block some highly publicized deals. Such agreements, however, could support less controversial investments in developing countries where the legal system may not be reliable in protecting investors' rights. And achieving pre-entry national treatment may be necessary to maintain the competitiveness of Chinese investors if such agreements proliferate in coming years. China should also consider supporting a multilateral agreement on investment, provided the terms of such an agreement can be shaped to be appropriate for developing country circumstances.

Sustaining access for overseas investment would require reciprocal concessions, including the dismantling of many of the sectoral controls on inflows of FDI. Such controls will in any event become less necessary, and less effective, as rapid growth continues to increase the complexity of the economy and as the financial system becomes more open to external capital flows.

China's tightly managed exchange rate and closed capital account have supported rapid growth and helped limit financial instability. Linking the renminbi to the dollar has avoided sharp changes in the renminbi value of foreign assets and trade flows that are largely denominated in dollars. And restricting capital movements has protected China's relatively undeveloped financial markets from the volatility experienced by many of its East Asian neighbors. However, these policies have also led to sharp swings in China's competitiveness with third countries, necessitated inefficient administrative controls to control inflation, resulted in a large buildup of low-return and risky reserves, and constrained financial sector development.

Going forward, as other parts of the world become more important and economic relations diversify, greater use of the renminbi as an international currency would provide more economic stability than a managed exchange rate. If a substantial portion of China's assets and trade were denominated in renminbi, then fluctuations in the exchange rate would not have major implications for domestic stability. Moreover, an open capital account is needed to facilitate the internationalization of Chinese companies. Further integration with global financial markets would also support the creation of a robust and efficient domestic financial sector. With unrestricted capital movements, a floating exchange rate will be necessary to enable the government to use monetary policy to control inflation. This strategy entails risk, however: opening the capital account before China has in place the regulatory framework required to effectively supervise financial institutions as well as the credibility and experience with indirect monetary controls required to limit inflation could be destabilizing. Thus, a relatively conservative approach, stretching over many years, is recommended in transitioning to a more open and efficient financial and exchange rate system.

Shaping Policy for Public Goods

Over the next few decades, China will have a major impact on, and will be greatly affected by, the supply of global public goods. The final section of the chapter reviews China's role in global governance surrounding select public goods, such as climate change, financial stability, and official finance. In the medium term, the government will face important choices in its policies toward global public goods. It can essentially leave the determination of these global policies to a multilateral consensus, with specific interventions to protect China's interests, or it can actively help to shape global agreements. Active involvement in international negotiations would likely imply shouldering some of the costs of preserving global public goods by, for example, diverting resources toward limiting environmental damages. Nevertheless, China has much to gain from helping to shape international agreements on public goods. The country's huge size means that effective agreements are unlikely in its absence, and in many areas China has a critical interest in ensuring the preservation of global public goods. In addition, having a say in the design of agreements can minimize the costs for China and in some cases open up opportunities for gain.

Climate change is one of the most critical policies and the best example of why China should not only participate in global negotiations but proactively help shape new global solutions. Absent changes in policy to reduce energy intensity, global carbon emissions could rise by about 50 percent over the next 20 years, with a quarter of this increase coming from China alone. The resulting increase in average temperatures could have disastrous implications for China and the global economy. Effective global policies to combat climate change are not feasible without China's participation, both because limiting China's emissions is critical and because other countries are unlikely to participate in the absence of the largest source of carbon emissions. If China fails to take steps to reduce carbon emissions while other countries do, China would get an artificial comparative advantage in energy-intensive production, making the country even more dependent on uncertain future energy supply and worsening its already considerable environmental challenges. As chapter 3 shows, limits on carbon emissions would not necessarily reduce China's GDP because "green" technologies may become a new source of growth. Finally, it is important that China continue to push actively for a global climate change treaty to ensure that emissions targets reflect developing countries' low levels of per capita emissions and leave room for future growth.

The integration of international prudential norms into China's banking regulations has helped the government improve the soundness of the banking system. Likewise, following the guidelines of Basel III should serve to improve regulatory standards and provide an anchor for continued reform. Heretofore, China has played little role in defining international standards, but that may need to change. For example, advanced countries may be concerned that controls on derivative

transactions not overly impair the efficiency benefits (and the profits of their financial institutions) from sophisticated derivatives. In contrast, Chinese banks lack the technology and banking relationships required to play a major role in these markets, while China's economy suffered from the extreme volatility generated by the failure to properly regulate them. Thus, it may be in China's interest to promote a stricter regulation of derivatives than is currently envisioned.

China has recently transitioned from a receiver to a provider of foreign aid. China's official finance has boosted the social and economic development of recipient countries and strengthened bilateral political and economic ties. China's current practice of tied aid, minimal project conditionality, and competitive terms for export credits resemble those of advanced countries a few decades ago. The South-South type official finance provided by China is used to achieve multiple objectives, not only aiding the social and economic development of recipient countries but also promoting its exports, securing future flows of natural resources, and improving diplomatic relations. During the coming decades, as the development objective becomes a more independent one, aid effectiveness should receive more emphasis. That will require transparency in reporting data on aid flows and greater attention to environmental and governance standards. China could also improve global aid effectiveness by urging traditional donors to adopt China's more efficient approaches to infrastructure projects.

The World in 2030

Despite intermittent crises, developing economies have been strikingly successful during the past two decades. Their GDP volume increased, on average, by 4.6 percent a year. That was more than twice as fast as the 2.1 percent annual growth in high-income countries. Prices in developing countries also rose twice as fast as those in the high-income countries, raising their share in the global GDP value from 16.7 percent in 1990 to 31.3

percent in 2010. This strong performance was achieved after broad-based domestic reforms in many countries and rapid integration into global markets, which pushed up potential growth from 3 percent during the early 1990s to 6.5 percent currently. Developing countries' share in world trade roughly doubled, from 14.6 percent in 1990 to 30.3 percent in 2010. Export volumes increased 8.8 percent a year during the past two decades, compared with merely 2 percent annually during the previous 20 years. That acceleration in exports coincided with a similar acceleration in import volumes, from 3.5 percent annual growth during the 1970s and 1980s, to 9.5 percent annual growth during the past two decades.

China's success has been an important part of the strong performance of developing countries, with its share in global GDP increasing from 1.5 percent in 1990 to 9.5 percent in 2010. But growth outside China was strong. The share of other developing countries in global GDP increased from 15 to 22 percent over the same period. The penetration of developing countries in global markets has reduced the market shares of high-income countries but has not come at the cost of export growth in those countries, which averaged 5.2 percent a year between 1990 and 2010, exactly the same as during the previous 20 years. While competition increased for high-income exporters, accelerating imports in developing countries also created new opportunities. High-income countries also benefited from the increased supply of affordable imports and from new investment opportunities in the emerging economies. Although the integration and catching up of emerging economies has also caused new tensions, on balance the last two decades have shown many winners and few losers.

The question now arises whether the pace of recent rapid growth can be sustained over the next two decades and whether the world economy can continue to produce win-win solutions. The uncertainty is obviously large, especially in the short run, as turmoil in financial markets has the potential to seriously disrupt global activity. Long-run trends

are easier to predict than short-term fluctuations, but these trends are ambiguous too. High-income countries are currently facing structural problems that restrain competitiveness; even in the case of adequate policy responses, it is uncertain when growth will strengthen and unemployment will return to normal levels. Fundamentals in most developing countries remain strong, but there are limits to the current pattern of growth, if only because the share of services will increase over time.

To illustrate the long-term uncertainty, we explore two scenarios. In the first scenario, technological progress within sectors will continue at the same pace, even though one could argue that technological progress in manufacturing could slow as several emerging economies approach the slowly advancing global technological frontier. Despite the assumption of constant intrasectoral technological progress, overall growth will slow for two main reasons. First, aging populations (particularly in the Russian Federation, China, and high-income countries) will limit labor force growth and push down savings rates and, thus, investment. Second, since productivity growth is much higher in manufacturing than in services, the shift to services will reduce overall growth. In emerging economies, the share of services will rise because richer consumers will demand more services and because the price of basic services will increase relative to manufactures. In the advanced countries, the aging population will demand more health and personal services, and the relative price of those services will also increase. Furthermore, many new products in the global economy (coming from innovations in information and communications technology and biotechnology) have a large service component and require higher levels of education, in turn increasing demand for (education) services.

In the second scenario, we assume further domestic reforms and more rapid innovations in the services sector that lead to higher productivity growth than in the past. The higher productivity is supported by globalization of both production and consumption

TABLE 5.1   Past and future growth trends
Percent

Time period	Low- and middle-income countries	China	High-income countries	United States
1990–2000	3.3	10.4	2.7	3.4
2000–10	5.9	10.5	1.6	1.7
2010–20[a]	5.6–7.4	7.4–10.1	2.0–3.1	2.3–3.5
2020–30[a]	4.2–6.6	4.2–7.8	1.3–2.7	1.5–3.0
Average annual per capita GDP growth				
1990–2000	1.6	9.3	2.0	2.3
2000–10	4.6	9.8	1.0	0.7
2010–20[a]	4.4–6.1	6.8–9.5	1.6–2.6	1.5–2.7
2020–30[a]	3.4–5.8	3.9–7.6	1.1–2.4	0.9–2.4

Source: World Bank calculations using Envisage Model.
a. The lower and upper bounds reflect average growth rates in the low-growth and high-growth scenarios.

of services, which boosts innovation, competition, and economies of scale. As a result, volume growth is higher than in the first scenario in both high-income and developing economies, but the relative price increase of services is significantly smaller.

Average annual GDP growth during the next 20 years in developing countries ranges from 4.9 percent in the low-growth scenario to 7 percent in the high-growth scenario (table 5.1). The actual growth during the past 10 years was 5.9 percent, exactly in the middle of the two scenarios. So the two scenarios seem to describe a range around a continuation of the recent trend. However, that perception is not correct. The past decade includes the global financial crisis, which pushed average growth down, and trend growth had been accelerating in the developing world. In the two years before the crisis, growth in the developing world exceeded 8 percent; in 2010, growth was 7.3 percent, higher than the average growth in the high-growth scenario. That means that in both forward-looking scenarios, growth will come down over time from its recent very strong pace; in the low-growth scenario, it falls to 3.5 percent in 2030 and in the high-growth scenario to 6 percent in 2030.

The decline in growth is somewhat steeper in China than the average growth decline in the rest of the world, because China's exceptionally high growth of the last decade will

be difficult to maintain (figure 5.1). Especially after 2025, forces that curb growth will become strong. Nevertheless, China is expected to remain one of the fastest-growing economies in the world. Average annual growth is 5.7 percent in the low-growth scenario and 9 percent in the high-growth scenario, respectively 1 and 3 percentage points higher than average growth in the other developing countries. Growth in high-income countries will likely continue to be substantially lower than in developing countries. In both scenarios, developing countries are growing more than twice as fast. Average growth in the high-income countries ranges from 1.6 percent in the low-growth scenario to 2.9 percent in the high-growth scenario. And again, growth is likely to decelerate over time, to 1.1 percent or 2.5 percent in 2030 in the respective scenarios.

In both scenarios, developing countries will have established themselves in 2030 as the dominant force in the global economy. They will be responsible for two-thirds of global growth, with only one-third originating in the current high-income countries (figure 5.2). A quarter of global growth will come from China—slightly more in the high-growth scenario, slightly less in the low-growth scenario. That implies that developing countries other than China will have a larger impact on global growth (contributing over 40 percent to global growth) than

FIGURE 5.1   Growth trends

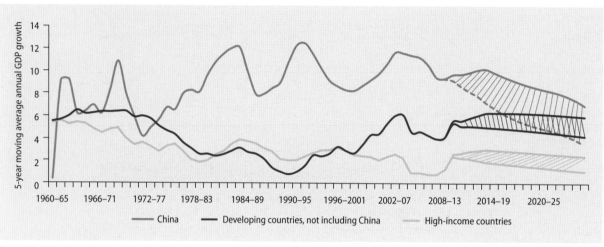

Source: World Bank calculations.

all high-income countries together. That has important consequences for China. Not only will competitors to Chinese firms be predominantly in other developing countries, but increasingly, markets for Chinese products will be there too.

Driving Forces of Future Long-Term Growth of the Global Economy

The expected deceleration of growth over time and the associated structural changes are suggested by mechanisms incorporated in an elaborate general equilibrium model. The model contains 14 countries or country groupings and describes shifts over 21 sectors as a result of differentiated technological progress and different income elasticities. The model also distinguishes between skilled and unskilled labor and a segmented labor market, differentiating between rural and urban employment and describing endogenous migration to cities. The allocation of land between rural and urban areas can have significant impacts on relative prices, as does the availability of natural resources. Savings depend on youth and elderly dependency ratios and are positively correlated with growth. Together with capital flows, they determine capital accumulation. In each sector, international trade is based on

the Armington assumption of differentiated products. To analyze global environmental policies, a climate change module is incorporated in the model.

The main drivers of growth are technological progress, demographics, capital accumulation (including education, so-called human capital accumulation), changes in the use of land, and domestic migration from low- to high-productivity sectors. All these drivers imply higher growth in developing countries than in high-income countries during the next 20 years, but they also suggest that growth will slow over time. As a result, overall growth tends to drop as economies mature. The drivers can be summarized as follows:

• Technological progress is relatively high in developing countries as these countries catch up to efficiency and skill levels already achieved in high-income countries, but the more they close the gap with the global technological frontier, the more difficult it will be to maintain the same pace of technological progress. Moreover, technological progress is still high at a macroeconomic level in developing countries because the share of services is smaller than in high-income countries. However, as a consequence, the future shift toward

FIGURE 5.2   Growing share of developing countries in global growth (five-year moving average)

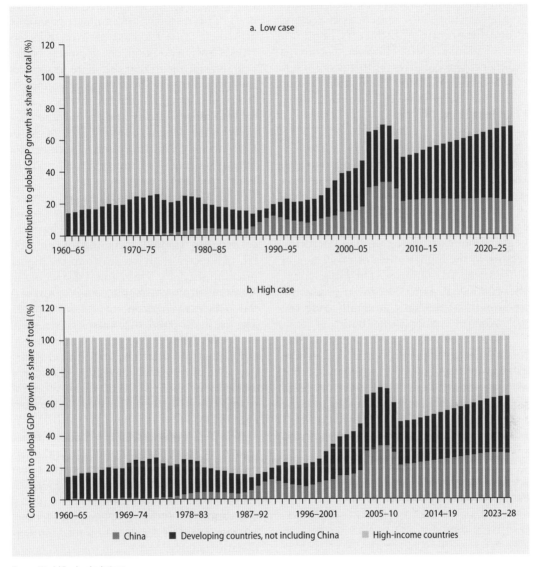

Source: World Bank calculations.

services will tend to lower technological progress.

- Growth of population and of labor supply is higher in developing countries than in high-income countries, but over time, those growth rates will decline.

- In many developing countries, savings rates are large enough to allow for rapid growth in the stock of capital, making it possible not only to keep the capital stock in line with the rapidly growing output

but also to increase the capital-output ratio more than in high-income countries. However, as the capital intensity rises, further increases will be more and more difficult to achieve.

- Urbanization is an important part of the growth advantage in developing countries. The capacity of urban areas to transition labor and land from low-productivity sectors to high-productivity sectors is a significant part of productivity increase at a macroeconomic level. Segmented labor and land markets keep the factor prices relatively low in low-productivity sectors, and the transition of factors implies a jump in value added. However, as with the other drivers of growth, this process has inherent limitations. The potential gains decline as the share of low-productivity sectors drops.

In the low-growth scenario, historical trends in technological progress are extrapolated, which means that productivity growth remains higher in manufacturing sectors than in services and agricultural sectors. That is especially true in developing countries, which benefit from catching up in manufacturing sectors to the higher levels of efficiency in more advanced countries. The latter countries continue to experience lower productivity growth as they only gradually push the technological frontier further out.

The fast growth in manufacturing sectors makes developing countries as a whole grow faster than developed economies, but it also carries the seeds for a future deceleration of macroeconomic growth because the relative prices of services will rise as a result of differentiated productivity growth across

sectors. That in turn will increase the size of the services sectors in the developing economies. The result is lower macroeconomic growth, because productivity growth in services is low. In addition, developments on the demand side mean that the share of services is expected to rise. In developing countries, that will happen mainly because per capita incomes grow quickly and the income elasticity of the demand for services is high. In high-income countries, it will happen mainly because aging will increase demand for health care and personal services.

The increasing importance of services will have far-reaching consequences beyond the lowering of macroeconomic technological progress. Capital, including foreign capital, will increasingly be drawn to the higher prices in services. This capital deepening in sectors with slow technological progress further reduces macroeconomic volume growth. The rise in the prices of domestic services will also reduce the relative price of internationally traded raw materials, including the relative price of energy. That reduces the energy efficiency of services and makes the need for stringent environmental policies even more urgent.

The high-growth scenario assumes faster growth of technological progress in the services sectors, that is, additional progress over and above the historical trend. All countries benefit from the accelerating pace of global innovations in services and from the fact that a larger share of services becomes internationally tradable. As a result, macroeconomic growth is faster and slows less over time than in the low-growth scenario. The mitigated deceleration results from the smaller share of services in nominal GDP because the prices of services do not rise as quickly as in the low-growth scenario. Nevertheless, in the high-growth scenario, the share of services will still increase in China and other developing countries, very much in line with experience in other countries that have already achieved higher per capita income levels (figure 5.3). The additional technological progress in the services sector is the only difference in assumptions between the two

FIGURE 5.3 China's future share in services and historical experiences of other countries (high-growth scenario)

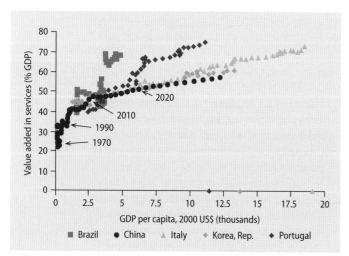

Source: World Bank calculations.

FIGURE 5.4   **Labor supply growth will vary greatly among countries**

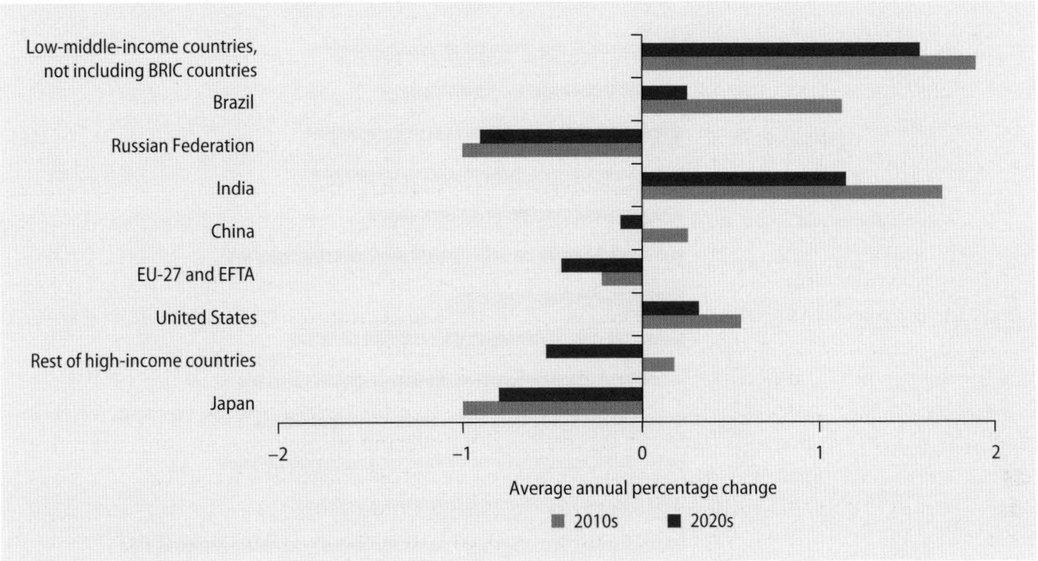

Source: World Bank calculations.
Note: BRIC = Brazil, Russian Federation, India, China; EFTA = European Free Trade Association.

scenarios. However, this difference endogenously has consequences for other drivers of growth. The higher macroeconomic growth results in more capital accumulation and also slightly more internal migration from low- to high-productivity sectors.

Growth in labor supply is another key driver of economic growth and does not differ between the two scenarios. As in the case of technological progress, the expected demographics during the coming decades point to faster growth in the developing world than in the high-income countries, while over time growth should slow.

In 2030, world population is expected to have grown to 8.3 billion people, an increase of 1.3 billion over the current 7 billion. All the additional population will be added in the developing world, which will grow from 5.9 billion currently to 7.2 billion in 2030. This is one of the driving forces behind the growing importance of the developing world. At the same time, demographic changes will lead to slower growth worldwide, including in many developing countries. Despite the 20 percent increase in the world population during the next 20 years (0.9 percent a year),

the pace of increase will be slower than in the previous 20 years, when the average annual rate of growth in world population was 1.3 percent. In parts of the world, the change in the labor force is even more dramatic as a result of aging. Toward 2030, the labor force in China, Russia, Japan, and Europe will be declining at an annual pace of 0.4 percent or more. On the other hand, India and many African countries will still experience high, albeit declining, growth rates of labor supply (figure 5.4). These developments will obviously change the comparative advantages among developing countries, with labor-intensive (especially low-skilled intensive) production shifting to Africa and South Asia.

The trends triggered by technological progress and demographics will be reinforced by capital accumulation. In the long run, capital tends to grow at the same rate as overall output. Capital-to-output ratios change only gradually, if at all, over time. If output increases, more savings are generated that allow a corresponding increase in the capital stock. This phenomenon explains the rapid capital accumulation in developing countries. The result of this process is that

FIGURE 5.5   **Capital output ratios will further rise, especially in emerging economies**

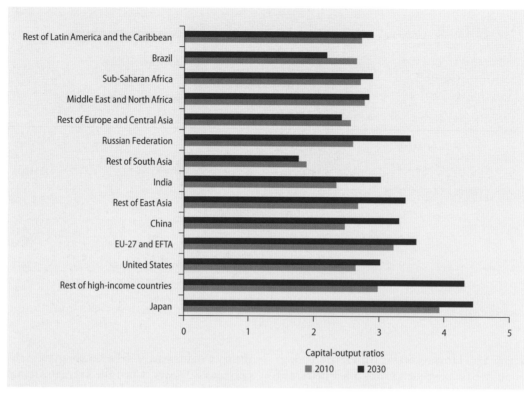

Source: World Bank calculations, derived from low-growth scenario; EFTA = European Free Trade Association.

capital-to-output ratios are surprisingly similar across countries, even where capital-to-labor ratios vastly differ.

On top of this mechanism, several emerging economies, with China as a prime example, are experiencing capital deepening (rising capital-output ratios) (figure 5.5). That allows labor productivity to rise even faster. That capital deepening is expected to continue, albeit at a slower pace, in China and India, where ample savings will allow more capital accumulation than is needed to keep pace with output growth. By contrast, capital-output ratios in the relatively young emerging markets in Latin America and Sub-Saharan Africa will fall, while advanced countries will experience only small changes in capital-output ratios.

Another driver of growth is the availability of land, which can become a constraint for agriculture and urban development. The rapid transformation of rural to urban land

in developing countries contributes to the higher growth rates than in high-income countries, but over time the scarcity of land makes this transformation more difficult and curbs macroeconomic growth. Densely populated countries with high economic growth should experience the highest increases in land and real estate prices. And indeed, the scenarios generate the sharpest increases in land prices in India and China, with relatively modest increases in Latin America, Africa, and emerging Europe (figure 5.6).

Finally, internal migration from rural to urban areas is an important driver of growth in developing countries because it allows workers to move to more productive jobs where wages are higher. Like many other drivers of growth, this one explains not only why developing countries outperform high-income countries but also why growth is expected to slow over time. The existence of segmented labor markets with low-wage jobs

FIGURE 5.6   Land prices in China and India will rise sharply

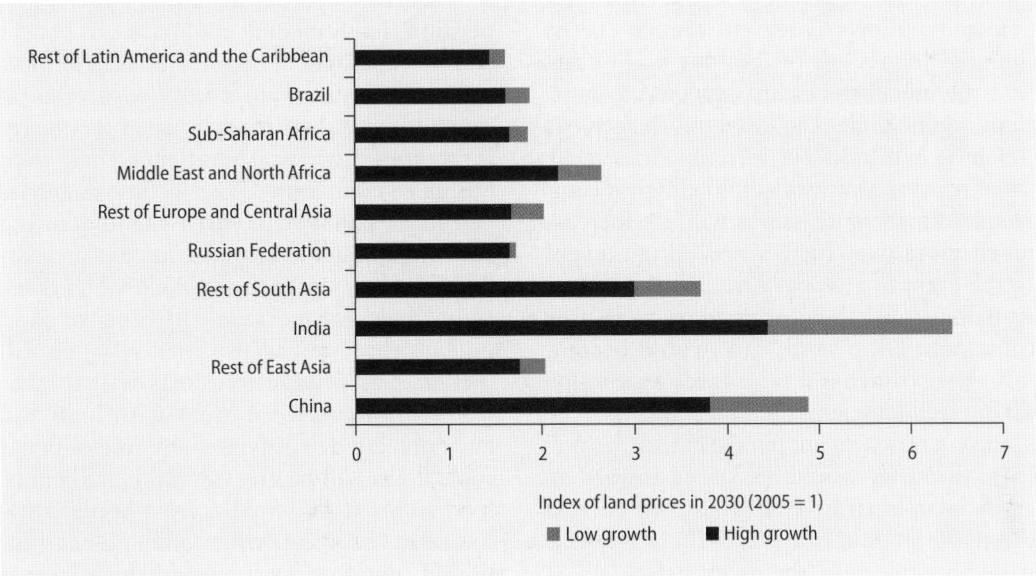

Index of land prices in 2030 (2005 = 1)

■ Low growth   ■ High growth

Source: World Bank calculations.

in rural areas provides developing countries a large growth potential. However, that potential will diminish over time as the rural population shrinks. In the low-growth scenario, China's internal migration in 2030 will be 9 percent lower than it was in 2010. Other developing countries also are expected to experience substantial declines. Only in Sub-Saharan Africa does the migration potential remain large, and internal migration is actually expected to increase by 50 percent over the next 20 years. Developments in the high-growth scenario are even more pronounced. Because of the higher productivity growth in cities, migration flows are larger than in the low-growth scenario during the early years. As a result, however, the deceleration also will be faster as the remaining pool of rural workers declines faster. The migration flows in that scenario are expected to decline by 12 percent in China, while in Africa the increase, from the higher levels achieved early on, is only 5 percent.

Changing Trade Patterns

Emerging markets will likely become the main destinations for world trade, and the sectoral pattern of trade within the developing world is expected to shift radically. Rapidly growing middle-income countries, including China, will experience a declining comparative advantage in low-skilled labor-intensive products relative to other developing countries. As these countries move up the value chain, new opportunities arise for lower-income countries, which will become increasingly competitive in labor-intensive production.

Middle-income countries will continue to dominate trade in manufactured products, even if the share of services in total value added in their domestic economies is increasing sharply. Exports of high-income countries would, in both scenarios, shift more to services. As middle-income countries move up the value chain in manufacturing, and as low-income countries export more (low-skilled) labor-intensive manufactured products, the comparative advantage of high-income countries will shift even more to internationally tradable, cutting-edge services.

Trade patterns will also change once additional environmental policies are put in place, an assumption not reflected in the baseline scenarios. The mounting environmental pressures are clearly illustrated by the anticipated increase in greenhouse gas emissions. Without policy changes to reduce energy intensity, emissions of the four main gases that the model tracks are expected to more than double under the low-growth scenario in China and India between now and 2030. This increase contrasts with the high-income countries, where emissions will not increase much more over their already high levels. In the event of a global agreement to reduce emissions (see below for more discussion on these policies), overall trade would become less energy intensive, and trade in energy-saving technologies would increase. If developing countries do not pursue mitigating policies, then they would be pushed toward an artificial comparative advantage of energy-intensive production, and their exports would become more energy intensive.

Despite the increased competition from low-income countries, and the slowing global economy, plenty of opportunities will still emerge for China to penetrate further in existing markets and to explore new markets. With the high growth in other emerging economies, new fast-growing markets will open up. With higher schooling levels and further accumulation of capital, Chinese firms can move to higher value-added segments of global markets. Globalization of Chinese firms will also create new opportunities, as these firms expand their investments abroad, and acquire new technologies. And even environmental policies might create new growth opportunities in global markets. Bold, new environmental policies (that will price externalities in a consistent and predictable way) are likely to create win-win solutions as they address domestic bottlenecks, make developing countries competitive in new global growth markets, and contribute to the solution of global environmental problems such as climate change.

With all the changes in the global economy that are anticipated, it is clear that many of the opportunities and the solutions for many of the challenges will be found in global markets. Middle-income countries can move up the value chain and create enough

productivity growth only if their service sectors can benefit from increased global competition. High-income countries can benefit from the new global opportunities in services only if they maintain an outward orientation and keep their markets open for emerging competitors that challenge their own advanced companies. Low-income countries can step into labor-intensive manufacturing sectors that middle-income countries are exiting only if they participate in global markets. In agricultural markets, the costs of food policies that are based on self-reliance will increase, as production costs will further differentiate between areas with high and low population density. Reliable international trade flows will be an essential ingredient of food security. And finally, cross-border environmental problems will require global solutions. Countries, developing and high-income alike, that maintain an outward orientation will be among the successful ones during the coming decades, while inward-looking policies will increasingly prove self-defeating. In short, many win-win solutions are possible, but only if protectionist attitudes that aim to defend old positions and vested interests are avoided.

The Transformation of China

China has become a dominant global economy. In 2010, China outstripped Japan to become the world's second-largest economy (while remaining less than 40 percent of the U.S. economy), as measured in nominal GDP. Still, even this remarkable achievement does not fully reveal how important China has become in terms of changes in the global economy. Between 2005 and 2010, China added $3.7 trillion to global nominal GDP; that amount represented almost a quarter of global growth and was almost twice as large as the $2 trillion added to global output by the United States. A similar picture emerges even if the role of real appreciation of the renminbi is excluded. This pattern continued in 2010, when China was by far the largest contributor to global GDP growth; its economy added $638 billion to growth in global nominal GDP, compared with $497 billion added by the U.S. economy.

China is yet more important if one looks at the parts of the economy that are internationally tradable. In 2010, the value of investment in China already exceeded the U.S. investment value by 50 percent, and between 2000 and 2010, China contributed half of the growth in global investments. China also holds a dominant position in other internationally tradable products. For example, in many metals markets, China is responsible for half of global demand.

The low-case scenario envisions a slowing of GDP growth in China and sharp changes in the composition of output over the next two decades. The labor force in the modern sector will fall as the population grows older and as migration from rural to urban areas declines. The net rural-urban migration during the 1990s was 125.5 million in China (Chan and Hu 2003), which would indicate an annual outflow of about 4 percent. However, that migration rate likely has slowed significantly in more recent years and is projected to be around 1 percent (of a slowly declining rural population) in the coming years.

The decline in the labor force means that China will continue to lose its comparative advantage in labor-intensive production. Only 10 years ago, roughly 2 of every 10 additional jobs in the world were created in China. Over the next 5 years, China's labor supply will be declining and, if participation rates do not change, employment will decline in 2030 at a rate of 3 million jobs a year. That decline will be much larger if the current moderation of the still very high participation rate continues.

Savings rates will fall 10 percentage points, with a larger drop in investment rates. The share of services will rise from 38 percent in 2010 to 67 percent by 2030, resulting in lower average productivity growth.[1] Despite the decline in investment rates, the high initial level of investment (45 percent of GDP) will mean that the capital stock will continue to grow, by more than 7 percent over 2010–30, or 1.5 percentage points more rapidly than output. Capital deepening

will place downward pressure on the return to capital, which will shift China toward a comparative advantage in capital-intensive sectors and create opportunities for substantial investments in new markets. It also will open up the opportunity for more productive investments abroad, a trend that might well become one of the most distinctive developments during the coming decades.

Finally, it is important to realize that China will continue to struggle with significant levels of poverty. Even measured in purchasing power parity (PPP) terms, China's per capita income is only one-tenth of that in the richest countries in the world. More than 80 countries have higher per capita incomes than China, while the income distribution in China is more unequal than in many of the rich countries. Despite the sharp rise in average incomes anticipated over the next 20 years, which will make China a high-income country, a large part of the country's population will still be relatively poor. It will likely take significantly more than 20 years for the whole population to reach high-income status. Unlike the current high-income countries, in which virtually all inhabitants are part of the highest deciles in the global income distribution, China will still have, in 2030, key characteristics of a developing country, with a population much closer to a cross-cut of the world population (figure 5.7).

In the next section, we consider policies that would facilitate the shift to services, more capital-intensive production, and continued rapid productivity growth, focusing on outward-looking policies in trade, cross-border investment, and the internationalization of the renminbi.

China's Integration in Global Markets

China's economic miracle is built on the adoption of market-oriented policies and openness to the world economy. The progressive reduction in trade barriers and the dismantling of many restrictions on FDI have generated great benefits in the form of access to foreign technology, increased competition

FIGURE 5.7   China's population will have more low-income people in 2030 than the United States does now

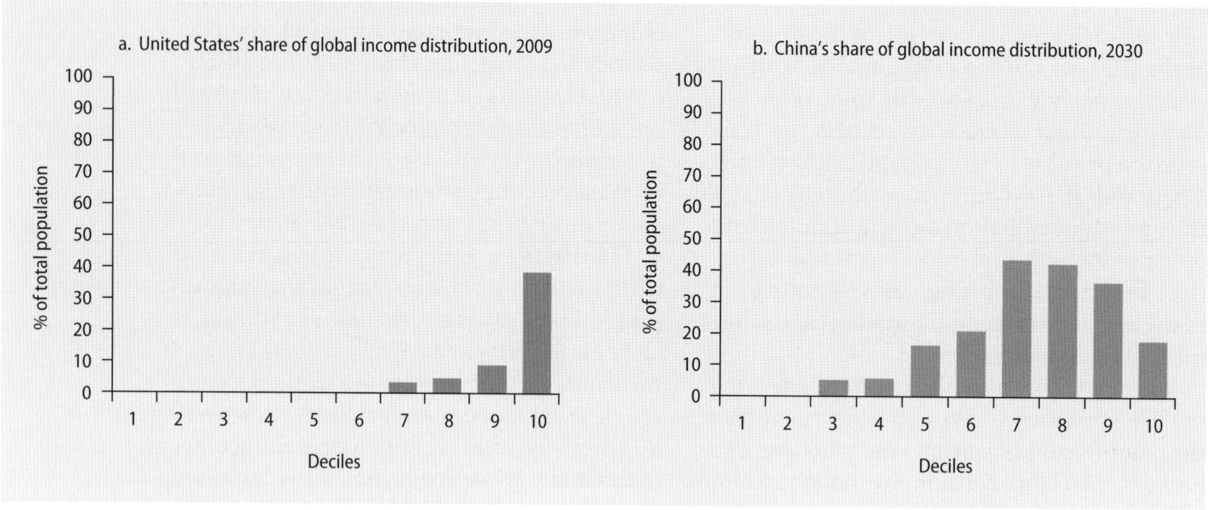

a. United States' share of global income distribution, 2009

b. China's share of global income distribution, 2030

Source: World Bank calculations, based on the low-growth scenario.

in the domestic economy, and the growth of a mammoth industrial sector built on exports. Despite this remarkable progress, pressures can be seen for a change in direction: either a slowing of efforts toward global integration or a measured withdrawal from international economic interactions. The arguments for a retreat from integration are not trivial. China's dependence on exports has increased its vulnerability to foreign protectionist measures, and the threat of such measures is apparent in the political climate, for example, in the United States. The huge export surplus is reflected in an apparently never-ending accumulation of low-interest and potentially risky foreign assets. The financial crisis generated in the United States posed a severe threat to stability. Although massive stimulus policies maintained growth, they also engendered a risky increase in bank lending and local government debt that may yet have to be addressed. Looking at the risks of international economic relations over the past few years, it is not difficult to understand calls for a retreat from global integration.

We argue, however, that this view is short-sighted. China has the opportunity by the end of the next two decades to join the ranks of high-income countries, to substantially eliminate absolute poverty, and to become the world's largest economic power. The country cannot achieve these goals by looking inward. Instead, China needs to embrace further steps toward global integration to improve the competitiveness of its economy and sustain increases in living standards. Using its capital surplus to invest in foreign markets, increasing exports of more sophisticated goods, encouraging domestic competition in services sectors, and deepening the financial sector through the participation of foreign financial institutions will enable China to avoid the "middle-income trap" and continue its development.

We emphasize that these reforms are essential to achieve broad-based development, regardless of the particular specialization of production that China may adopt over the next two decades. For example, an efficient financial system and world-class business services generate broad economic benefits, but they are also necessary to support the production and trade of sophisticated manufactured products. Thus, emphasizing services does not mean the neglect of manufactures production but rather a choice for technological progress and continued upgrading in all sectors through integration in the global economy.

This is a vision of how China should look in 2030. The transition to a more globally integrated economy and, in particular, the opening to capital flows transactions needs to be accomplished at a pace consistent with the strengthening of Chinese institutions required to ensure stability. We do not recommend that the government dismantle all of its controls on economic activity in the interest of promoting efficiency. Instead, we would set a goal over the next two decades of transitioning to an open financial system, a flexible exchange rate, limited controls over FDI transactions, and a services sector that can compete with the world's best. There are risks in this transition, but these policies promise to support a prosperous society for the next generation.

Trade

Those arguing for a retreat from global integration point to the threat of protectionism against China's exports.[2] And, as China's exports further penetrate foreign markets, increasing market shares in China's traditional products and competing in higher-value-added segments, protectionism against imports from China may well increase. Already China faces higher-than-average protectionist barriers. But the policy response that is consistent with

long-term development is to seek to strengthen the world's open trading system built on multilateralism. At the same time, China should advance its own agenda in future negotiations, which could include reducing barriers to trade in services, seeking regional partners to achieve deeper integration, strengthening WTO disciplines to require "open regionalism," and limiting the use of export restrictions at times of rising food prices.

Rapid export growth has dramatically increased China's share of global manufactures. China's exports have risen by 17 percent a year (in dollar terms) over the past two decades, transforming the country into the world's largest exporter of goods and dramatically increasing the country's presence in global markets, particularly of manufactures. China's share of world manufactures trade doubled during the past decade, and China now accounts for 35 percent of manufacturing imports in Japan, 30 percent in the European Union, and slightly over 25 percent in the United States (figure 5.8). China's exports are particularly significant in markets with the highest tariff levels (figure 5.9), indicating that China is exporting to markets that are politically sensitive and likely to be the source of trade frictions.

FIGURE 5.8   China's share in industrial imports of the world's 10 largest importers has increased

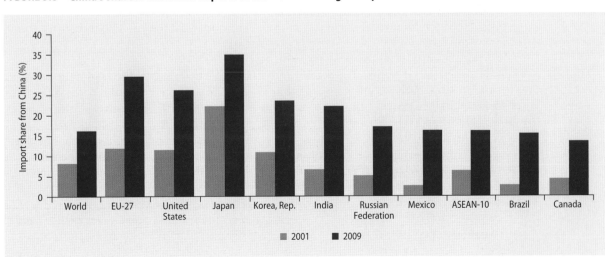

Source: UN COMTRADE database.

FIGURE 5.9   China's share in imports of 10 most-protected sectors in the 10 largest importers has increased

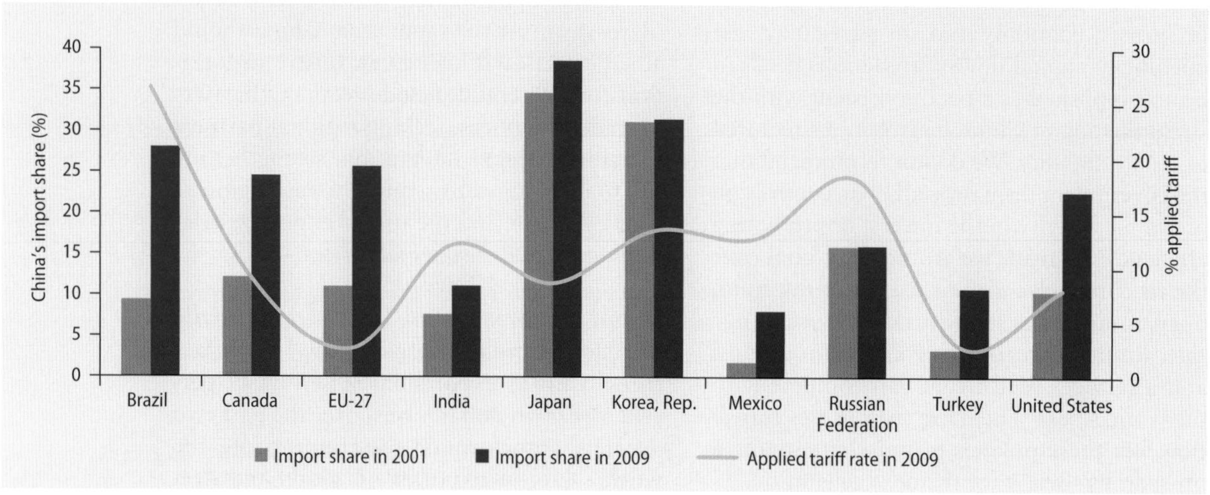

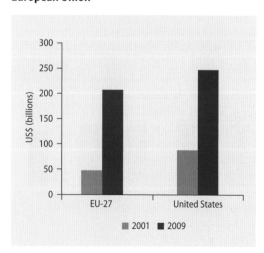

Source: UN COMTRADE database (trade data) and UNCTAD TRAINS database (tariff data).
Note: Sectors defined at the Harmonized Schedule (HS) 2-digit level of aggregation in 2009.

China has seen a substantial widening of its trade surplus in industrial goods with all of its major trading partners, with the exception of the Republic of Korea and Japan. For example, China's manufacturing trade surplus with both the United States and the European Union has increased more than three times to $200 billion and $250 billion, respectively (figure 5.10a). China's trade surplus on manufactures with other large emerging-market countries has also increased sharply (figure 5.10b).

These bilateral surpluses are sometimes seen as signs of imbalances and can trigger protectionist responses. However, bilateral trade balances with individual countries

FIGURE 5.10a   China has a large trade surplus in industrial goods with the United States and the European Union

FIGURE 5.10b   China has a large trade surplus in industrial goods with major trading partners

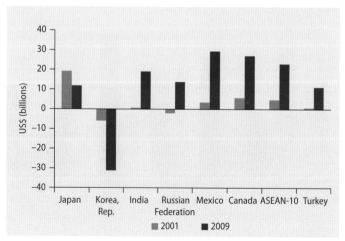

Source: UN COMTRADE database.

Source: UN COMTRADE database.

TABLE 5.2   China's trade with developing East Asia differs from that of Sub-Saharan Africa
Share of exports to China, %

	1990	2010
Developing East Asia		
Final manufactures	33	33
Parts and components	10	47
Raw materials	35	16
Sub-Saharan Africa		
Final manufactures	7	5
Parts and components	8	0
Raw materials	67	88

Source: UN COMTRADE database.
Note: Export categories exclude some products.

provide no information on overall balance of payments pressures and give at best an incomplete picture of bilateral trade patterns. China is a major exporter of manufactures and a major importer of natural resources, so surpluses in manufactures trade may be (partly) balanced by deficits in natural resources trade. The pattern of trade with China also differs in part based on geographical proximity and economic capabilities. Close by and relatively industrialized East Asia is becoming part of a manufacturing network with China, where these countries export manufactured products to China, some of them inputs to goods that are assembled in China and then shipped to advanced countries. While the share of manufactures in developing East Asia's exports to China has remained at about a third since 1990, the share of parts and components has risen from about 10 percent in 1990 to almost half in 2010 (table 5.2). Over the same period, the share of manufactures in the exports to China of distant and less-industrialized Sub-Saharan Africa fell slightly, while the share of raw materials rose from two-thirds to almost nine-tenths.

China's trade surplus in manufactures is likely to decline over time. Domestic production should shift toward services to meet the growing demand from consumers with rising incomes. This shift will require increased manufactured imports and will draw resources away from industrial production.

China's exports already have met increased protectionist barriers. China was the target of 15 percent of the antidumping actions initiated by the 10 economies that accounted for 79 percent of new antidumping investigations during 1995–2001, while it accounted for only 4 percent of these countries' imports (Bown 2007). Discriminatory practices increased after China's WTO accession, as the share of developing-country antidumping actions against China (as a share of their total actions) increased from 19 percent in 2002 to 34 percent in 2009. The corresponding figures for industrial countries were 11 and 27 percent, respectively.[3]

The current threat from protectionism should not be overstated, because the share of China's exports subject to quantitative restrictions or WTO processes does not appear to be large. In 2009, for example, 2.6 percent of China's exports to developing countries and 1.6 percent of its exports to developed countries were subject to antidumping (Bown 2010). Recourse to this instrument will become more difficult when China attains market economy status in 2016. Moreover, the product-specific transitional safeguards that were negotiated at the time of China's WTO accession are scheduled to expire in 2013. But tensions over trade and disputes concerning exchange rate parities indicate the potential for increased protectionism in the future.

Protectionism may rise as China's exports continue to expand and move into new markets. China's exports are expected to rise by 6 percent a year from 2010 to 2030, a more moderate rate than in the past two decades but still representing some increase in penetration in the country's traditional export markets. In addition, continued rapid growth in incomes will drive rising wage levels and exchange rate appreciation, somewhat reducing China's competitive advantage in labor-intensive goods compared with lower-wage economies. Thus, as outlined in the global scenarios described above, Chinese firms will need to move into the production and export of more capital- and knowledge-intensive

BOX 5.1   The Japanese experience with voluntary export restraints

Episodes of agreements between the United States and Japan to restrain the latter's exports occurred in textiles in the late 1930s and 1950s, in automobiles in the early 1980s, and in steel in the mid-1980s. While "voluntary" export restraints were far from trivial (according to one study, they covered 32 percent of Japanese exports to the United States in 1984[a]), their economic impact on Japanese firms (although perhaps not on Japanese employment) was limited. The automobile export restraint was on the number of cars, for example, not their value, so firms sold higher-value (and more profitable) cars to the United States than before the export restraints. Firms could also circumvent the export restraints by opening plants in the United States. Japanese foreign direct investment into the U.S. auto sector increased from $200 million in 1980 (before the export restraints) to $850.8 million in 1986, and by the early 1990s, Japanese brands accounted for some 30 percent of the U.S. auto market, up from 21 percent in 1981. Japanese firms also exported from third countries not covered by the export restraint. Similarly, when the United States and major steel exporters (Japan and Europe) agreed on voluntary export restraints, steel was exported from the restrained countries to the nonrestrained countries, and then underwent some further fabrication and was later exported to the United States.[a]

Source: Carbaugh and Wassink 1991.
a. This is the share of existing products covered by export restraints. The share of potential exports (if the restraints did not exist) would be higher.

goods and services. The need to absorb the technology, business management practices, and market knowledge required for this transition is an important reason why continued openness is essential to China's development.

China is so large, and the pace of its growth so rapid, that expanding into new markets is likely to elicit protectionist responses from both the high-income countries that traditionally have dominated these markets and from other rapidly growing emerging economies that wish to promote domestic production. All of these countries have a great deal invested in an open international trade regime. Nevertheless, China should be prepared for actions that are designed to limit competition, whether compliant with WTO rules or not. A useful historical parallel is the pressure that Japan faced during the 1980s to limit exports to the United States (box 5.1). This experience underlines the importance of supporting outward foreign investment as a means of exploiting market opportunities in the face of protectionism, apart from the obvious advantages for Chinese firms if they internationalize.

China should meet the protectionist threat by seeking deeper integration with regional

partners, supporting multilateral trade negotiations and open regionalism. China's response to the threat of rising protectionism should be anchored in support for an open trading system based on multilateral agreements. It is important to remember that China remains an extremely open economy, particularly given its large size (for example, in 2009, China's total trade in goods and services equaled 49 percent of GDP, compared with 25 percent in the United States). Thus, continuing to pursue international agreements to preserve and further open markets should be a cornerstone of China's trade policies going forward.

China faces relatively high tariff rates in many of its export markets. Therefore, in further multilateral negotiations, the government should push for proportionally larger reductions in relatively higher tariff levels, rather than across-the-board tariff reductions.

Preferential agreements may ultimately present a greater challenge to China's market access than MFN tariff levels. The number of preferential agreements has increased from about 70 in 1990 to almost 300 today. About half of the exports of the 30 largest exporting countries, including China, go to partners with whom the country has some sort of preferential agreement. This statistic overstates the impact of agreements on trade flows, however, because only 16 percent of trade actually takes place on preferential terms (WTO 2011).[4] Nevertheless, preferential agreements are of particular concern for China, for two reasons.

First, China gains only limited benefits in the form of increased access through preferential agreements. Only about 6 percent of its exports enjoy preferential access—significantly below the world average, and low compared with other large traders, such as the European Union (EU) (13 percent), United States (22 percent), India (26 percent), and Brazil (15 percent). Moreover, China's nonpreferential exports are somewhat disadvantaged compared with other major exporters. For most countries or trading blocs, including the European Union, United States, India, and Brazil, only about 4 percent of nonpreferential exports face MFN tariffs greater than 10 percent, but the proportion for China is twice as high.

Second, in the future, preferential agreements in services may have a more exclusionary impact. Today, preferential agreements in services tend to cover more sectors and include greater legal commitments to openness than under the General Agreement on Trade in Services (Marchetti and Roy 2009). However, these commitments tend to be weaker than existing policies and thus have had little role in opening markets.[5] Even in the rare cases where preferential agreements have induced liberalization—for example, in Costa Rica's elimination of its telecommunications monopoly—the new policies are at least in principle applied on a nondiscriminatory basis. Thus, the cost of exclusion today from a preferential agreement in services is not worse access but less secure access, because these agreements involve not more liberalization but wider and deeper bindings.

In the future, however, any deepening of preferential agreements in services could create significant discrimination against outsiders because MFN levels of protection are significant, and there is considerable scope for the preferential recognition of standards, licensing, and qualification requirements. Strong exclusionary effects could also arise from "deeper integration" along other dimensions: preferential agreements increasingly have provisions on investment protection, intellectual property rights, government procurement, competition policy, and technical barriers to trade. A discriminatory tariff may matter less than the selective recognition of product safety standards or selective access to government procurement markets.

The government should pursue a two-track strategy to confront the potentially adverse impact of regional trade agreements. On the one hand, on the basis of abiding by and protecting multilateral agreements, China should make efforts to push for the further opening of markets through multilateral organizations as a prime policy objective. It should also proactively push ahead with the negotiations on its accession to the WTO government procurement agreement as part of its effort to improve procurement procedures, enhance transparency, reduce costs, and enhance quality in government purchases. On the other hand, China should proactively participate in regional trade arrangements and, where possible, strongly advocate "open regionalism," which requires that tariff levels agreed among regional partners be offered to other nonmember countries on an MFN basis.

Further liberalizing services trade and joining the government procurement agreement could boost export opportunities. In the context of joining the WTO, China committed to one of the most rapid programs of services market opening ever seen. Over 2001–08, many restrictions on banking, telecommunications, transport, retail, and a range of business services were phased out. Nevertheless, China's services sector policies remain more restrictive than those in many developing countries and much more so than in the high-income countries, in all sectors except transport.[6] Easing remaining restrictions could provide the reciprocity required to open foreign markets as well as improve efficiency in the Chinese economy.

International commitments could encourage both increased market access and improved domestic efficiency in government procurement, which represents well over 20 percent of China's economy. The European Union Chamber of Commerce recently studied foreign-invested enterprises competing in China's public procurement markets and found that the regulatory framework governing this enormous and increasing amount of economic activity is fragmented, inconsistent, and unevenly implemented. The WTO's Trade Policy Review on China also found that "China continues to face challenges in implementing a consistent and transparent approach to procurement across all levels of government" (WTO 2010).

China has applied for accession to the WTO's government procurement agreement. Establishing the transparent and reliable procurement procedures necessary to gain access could enormously increase the efficiency of government operations.[7] Joining the agreement would also open potentially huge markets for Chinese firms. The total size of government procurement markets of the current and possible future accession candidates to the agreement is $2.3 trillion to $3.0 trillion annually, while the portion of these government procurement markets that is likely to be covered by the agreement is in the range of $380 billion to $970 billion annually (Anderson and others 2011).

Improving commodity security. Multilateral negotiations may also be a useful forum for improving China's assured access to food imports. China is increasingly dependent on imported food. Already, China accounts for 54 percent of world imports of soya beans, and 98 percent of its imports come from just three countries—the United States, Brazil, and Argentina. Considerable potential remains for increasing global food production (World Bank 2009), and prolonged food shortages are likely to be localized rather than affecting the global economy as a whole. However, short-term supply disruptions and demand-driven

price spikes are still possible, owing to rising demand from increased incomes in developing counties, volatile fuel prices, and climate-change induced pressure on agricultural supplies. Multilateral disciplines could be useful in limiting export restrictions that tend to exacerbate price hikes. During the global financial crisis and its continuing aftermath, 18 developing countries imposed some form of export restrictions (World Bank 2008). Each country is trying to keep domestic supplies high on the grounds of food security. But, as more countries implement export controls, global supplies contract, pushing prices up further and impairing global food security.

There are few restrictions on the use of export taxes in the WTO, and the disciplines on export restrictions are incomplete. Article XI of the General Agreement on Tariffs and Trade (GATT) does prohibit quantitative restrictions on exports, but its paragraph 2(a) permits temporary restrictions to prevent critical shortages of food or other goods.[8] To ensure continued access to critical foodstuffs, the government should consider pressing for a multilateral approach to dealing with temporary shortages. This approach could involve a requirement that countries justify how export restrictions would relieve critical domestic shortages and include a provision for consultations between importing and exporting countries at times of scarcity. While governments are unlikely to forgo trade restrictions in the face of sharp increases in prices that endanger the welfare of their populations, ensuring that such measures are undertaken only when essential would provide greater assurance to importers that they can rely on the world trading system, rather than bilateral deals, to ensure food supply at times of scarcity.

Similar considerations apply to China's participation in global trade in raw materials. Ensuring that the country has a reliable supply of raw materials will be an important element of China's trade strategy over the next two decades. China is a significant producer of several metals that are critical to production and has large reserves of oil. Nevertheless, the high commodity intensity of production and rapid growth of China's huge economy has made the country a significant presence in global trade in these commodities. China accounts for a quarter or more of world imports of most of the main metals and is a major energy consumer (Coxhead and Jayasuriya 2010). For example, in 2009, China produced half the world's supply of coking coal but still accounted for 17 percent of global imports. China also produced 15 percent of global iron ore but consumed more than half of global production and accounted for more than two-thirds of total imports (Christie and others 2011).

Current efforts to secure the supply of commodities include restrictions on export of selected minerals (such as coke, antimony, bauxite, magnesium carbonate, molybdenum, silicon carbide, tin, and tungsten), limits on foreign exploration and mining, investment in commodity-producing activities abroad, long-term contracts with suppliers, and loans to energy-producing nations where minerals are used as collateral for eventual repayment. The combination of the dramatic increase in China's demand for raw materials and efforts to secure foreign sources of supply has raised foreign alarms about the country's efforts to monopolize access to minerals (for example, see Brightbill and others 2008) and calls for restrictions on Chinese minerals investments in some producing nations.[9] These views are gaining some public hearing, even though Chinese firms' investments in raw material production differ little from efforts at vertical integration by Western multinationals and China's share of global mining mergers and acquisitions (M&A) remains small.[10]

Continued efforts by Chinese firms to gain reliable access to raw materials seem rational from China's perspective, and, to the extent that these efforts lead to increased global supply, they can also benefit other countries. However, a segmentation of the global market for commodities should be avoided. If major consuming nations have fixed, long-term contracts that tie up a large share of global production, shocks to the system (for example, increased demand caused by changes in technology or supply interruptions

resulting from political instability or natural disasters) could be accommodated only by changes in the share of global production that is not subject to such contracts. That would prevent the right price signals in the controlled parts of the markets and would introduce tremendous volatility in the free part of the market. The resulting substantial differences in prices with the more controlled parts of the market would ultimately be arbitraged and could trigger smuggling or the breaking of contracts, thus imposing increased volatility on the market in general. Such a system is not in China's long-term interest, and the government should help ensure that, globally, investment and consumption decisions remain responsive to the right pricing signals. Thus, while attempts to secure access make sense from an individual country perspective, the world as a whole (and given its huge presence in the market, China in particular) will benefit from maintaining an open trading system for raw materials.

Foreign Direct Investment

China has adopted FDI-friendly policies since 1980, beginning with permitting FDI in Special Economic Zones but steadily broadening it to the rest of the nation. As a result, China is now host to almost 700,000 partly foreign-owned companies with accumulated foreign investment of $1.05 trillion. These companies account for 22 percent of tax revenue, 28 percent of industrial value added, 55 percent of exports, 69 percent of the trade surplus, and 50 percent of technology imports. Foreign direct investment has enabled China to integrate gradually into global manufacture networks, as well as contribute to exports, employment, technology, and institutional reform.

As China grows richer, its attractiveness to foreign investors changes. Transnational corporations no longer invest in China merely because of low labor costs but increasingly because of its rapidly expanding domestic market, supporting industries, excellent infrastructure, and human resources (about 7 million university graduates every year).

According to a survey by China's Development Research Center, since the global financial crisis, China's attractiveness to transnationals has gone well beyond low costs. The top 5 (of 17) reasons for investing in China were given as the domestic market, infrastructure, labor cost, access of FDI, and industrial clusters, in which the large market was the most important.

Following this change in the strategy of transnationals, China needs to take several steps to capitalize on the potential advantages. First, the Industrial Guidelines for FDI should be adjusted to encourage investments in emerging industries and research and development (R&D). Second, policy should be shifted from giving preferential incentives to improving the investment climate: ensuring a level playing field between domestic and foreign investors, improving the quality and efficiency of public services, improving human resources, and strengthening the service sectors. Third, to make full use of FDI's spillover effects, FDI's R&D should be integrated into the domestic innovation system. The government should encourage greater cooperation and exchange between foreign companies and domestic institutes and companies related to the human resources, information, and R&D sectors. Finally, the government needs to enhance international competitiveness of its service sectors by further liberalizing FDI in services.

Even more important than these changes toward inward FDI, China can benefit from promoting outward FDI, because investments abroad will play an important role in the transition to a high-income economy. At first glance, it can be difficult to understand why a poor country like China should encourage its firms to invest overseas, and it is easy for those arguing for a more inward-looking development strategy to ignore the implications for outward FDI. Indeed, openness to FDI inflows and domestic policy reforms to ensure that technology spillovers from foreign firms can disseminate quickly to domestic firms remain an important element of China's development strategy. However, Chinese multinationals also can play an important role in the country's development, by transferring technology obtained in foreign markets and by integrating business practices and organizational approaches observed in foreign countries into domestic operations. The government should strive to strengthen legal protections for Chinese overseas investments, either through bilateral investment treaties or a multilateral agreement on investment. Achieving stronger protection for Chinese investors would require granting reciprocal concessions to foreign investors in China, implying a dismantling of most restrictions on FDI inflows and continued improvements in the autonomy of state enterprises. These policies also are in the long-term interest of China's development.

FDI outflows are increasing. FDI outflows have risen rapidly since inauguration of the "Going Global" policies in the late 1990s, from \$1 billion in 2000 to \$44 billion in 2009. China's total FDI outflows over the period were greater than for any other emerging markets except Russia and Hungary (table 5.3). Since 2003, almost 55 percent of China's greenfield FDI and 27 percent of M&A transactions have been in the mining sector, compared with 10 percent in M&A transactions from advanced countries (figure 5.11).[11] Investment projects in services and manufactures tend to be smaller than in mining, and these two sectors were more important over this period in terms of the number of deals.

TABLE 5.3   FDI outflows by emerging markets rose sharply in 2000–09

	FDI 2000	Total 2000–09
Russian Federation	3	215
Hungary	1	160
China	1	159
India	1	75
Korea, Rep.	5	84
Singapore	6	97
Brazil	2	60
Malaysia	2	51
Mexico	0	40

Source: IMF Balance of Payments database.

FIGURE 5.11 China's outward FDI is directed more toward mining, compared with advanced countries' FDI

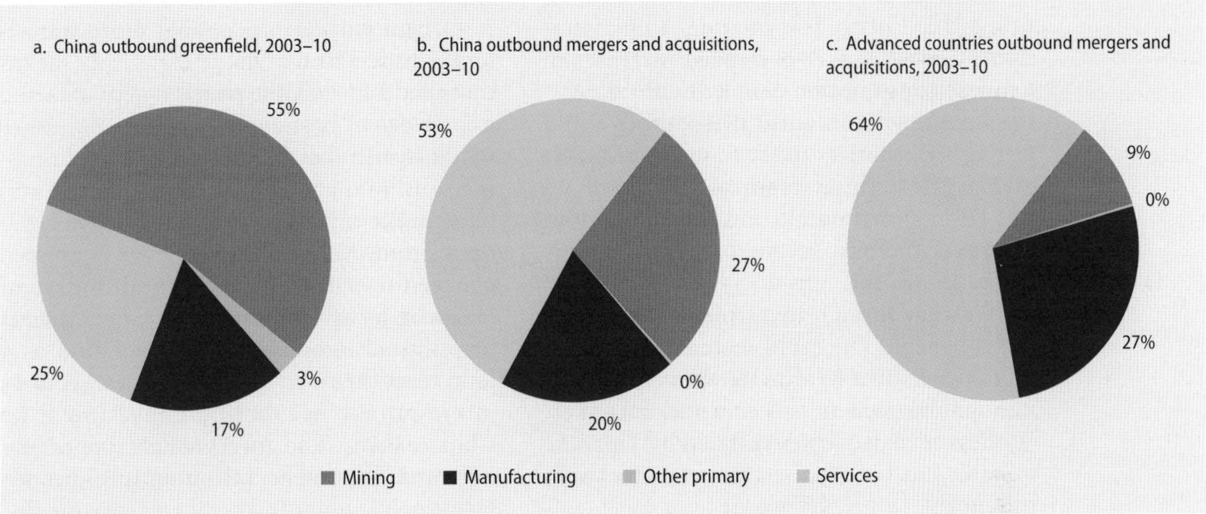

a. China outbound greenfield, 2003–10
55%
25%
17%
3%

b. China outbound mergers and acquisitions, 2003–10
53%
27%
20%
0%

c. Advanced countries outbound mergers and acquisitions, 2003–10
64%
9%
0%
27%

■ Mining   ■ Manufacturing   ■ Other primary   ■ Services

Sources: For mergers and acquisitions data, World Bank staff estimates based on Thomson-Reuters SDC Platinum. For greenfield data, World Bank staff estimates based on FDI markets.

China's FDI outflows have increased at about the same annual rate of growth as outflows from Japan and Korea, to take regional examples that have achieved rapid growth (beginning from the year that these countries' outflows exceeded $1 billion), but less than outflows from Malaysia. Given China's huge size, FDI outflows could quickly rise to high levels. For example, by 2030, China's per capita GDP will exceed $10,000. If China's FDI outflows relative to GDP equaled the level of Japan's at a similar level of income (about 0.5 percent), then China's outflows would almost double to $75 billion.

Outward FDI can generate important benefits for Chinese firms and the country's development. Outward FDI can play an important role in exploiting global business opportunities. China's rapid increase in incomes means that firms may need to relocate to lower-wage locations to employ their expertise and technology. Trade barriers may increase the profitability of locating production in host-country markets (see above). China's multinationals can become an important source of technology, brand names, distribution networks, market contacts, and skilled workers for domestic firms. China's large stock of

foreign exchange reserves is largely invested in low-return assets (such as U.S. Treasuries), and demand for foreign exchange by firms to invest abroad represents some diversification of foreign assets, from the perspective of the country as a whole.[12]

More controversially, FDI can be used to secure essential commodities for the domestic economy. The high energy and metals intensity of production mean that the economy is dependent on a stable, secure supply.[13] There are two reasons why China might be concerned about its future ability to secure commodities. First, while these commodities do trade in international markets, their supply is heavily influenced by government decisions: oil prices depend greatly on Organization of Petroleum Exporting Countries (OPEC) production, while several important metals are located in a few, relatively unstable countries, where the governments could potentially affect supply, at least in the short term. China's political influence and investments in oil and metals could encourage supportive government policies in supplying countries. Second, China accounts for a significant share of global consumption of some commodities (for example, in 2008, China's consumption of oil and net imports of oil equaled almost 9 percent and 4.5 percent, respectively, of global oil consumption, according to the U.S. Energy Information Administration). Concerns over continued increases in Chinese consumption coupled with increasing investments in natural resources could lead other countries to try to safeguard their own access to these resources. China's share of FDI in global natural resources has doubled over the past seven years but remains below 15 percent.

Not that foreign investment is an unalloyed benefit. The rapid increase in foreign investments by a relative newcomer to international investment can engender mistakes. Witness the huge losses suffered by Japanese investors in U.S. real estate and other sectors in the 1980s.[14] There is also some concern that government influence over the large state-owned enterprises (SOEs) may encourage unprofitable, but politically important, foreign takeovers and that limits on interest rates reduce resources allocated to project evaluation and increase incentives to lend to public sector firms, thus reducing the efficiency of FDI projects (Morck, Yeung, and Zhao 2008).

Chinese outward FDI has encountered obstacles. China's investment outflows have already stirred concern among some commentators in host countries, and efforts by Chinese firms to purchase foreign companies and to operate in foreign countries have in some cases met with political opposition. For example, the state-owned China National Offshore Oil Corporation withdrew its bid for Union Oil Company of California (Unocal) in the face of political opposition in the United States. And a 2008 deal to double Aluminium Corporation of China's (Chinalco) stake in Rio Tinto, an Anglo-Australian iron ore producer, was scrapped in the face of opposition from Australian lawmakers (Xu 2009). The reasons for opposition to Chinese investments are varied but do not (or, at least, should not) reflect fears of Chinese domination of the global economy. Despite its rapid growth, China's outward FDI remains a small share of total FDI flows and a minuscule amount

compared with total investment in most host countries.

Other issues are probably more important. Chinese firms' lack of experience means that they may lack the political networks and knowledge of host-country culture necessary to avoid mistakes in public relations, branding, and management. Chinese companies have made mistakes that have engendered opposition. Many observers have expressed concern over the environmental impact of investments by Chinese firms. Governments or political interests who view China as a long-term threat to other countries' security interests may not welcome investment by Chinese firms. The government's support for outward investment, including subsidies for investments in natural resources, tax breaks, and low-interest financing from state-owned banks (Luo, Xue, and Han 2010), has raised resentment over competitive practices that undermine domestic investors, although some of these practices are hardly unique to China.

Perhaps most important, the prominent role played by SOEs rather than private firms may engender suspicion in host countries about potential strategic behavior by Chinese investors. More than two-thirds of FDI outflows were from centrally controlled SOEs in 2009, and a portion of the remainder came from firms partially owned or controlled by the state or by provincial or municipal governments (Salidjanova 2011). The important role played by SOEs in China's foreign investment is not surprising—most of the large Chinese companies that have the resources and expertise to invest abroad are owned by the state. Only 2 of the 43 Chinese companies in the Fortune 500 list of the largest global firms are privately owned.[15] This legacy of central planning notwithstanding, the government should ensure that private firms are given the same opportunity to invest abroad and should avoid burdensome approval processes that might inhibit such investment. The main reason for encouraging outward investment is to enable Chinese multinationals to absorb foreign technology and use it to improve domestic production. Since private firms are typically more successful in adopting new technology than government-owned firms, it is important to ensure that private firms participate in foreign investment.

The government can help improve the legal framework for outward investment. Given the potential benefits of outward FDI and the political obstacles and tensions that some Chinese investments have engendered, the government has an interest in demonstrating support for Chinese investors, to ensure that they are treated equally with other investors and to provide adequate recourse in case of disputes. This issue is set to intensify in coming years, because Chinese outward investment will no doubt continue to expand as China becomes richer and its firms more exposed to international competition.

Chinese policy has focused on international treaties to protect foreign investors. Since the early 1980s, China has signed 127 bilateral investment treaties (through May 2010) and 112 double taxation treaties (through May 2009) (Davies 2010). Since 2000, China's bilateral investment treaties (BITs), mostly concluded with developing countries that are the main destinations for Chinese FDI, have expanded protections for investors. These include commitments by host countries to treat foreign investors, once established in the country, equally with domestic investors, and to provide investors with virtually unrestricted access to international tribunals (such as the World Bank's International Centre for the Settlement of Investment Disputes), when they believe that host-government policy violates these commitments (Berger 2008a). The latest Chinese BITs do allow for the continuation of existing provisions that discriminate against existing foreign investors, subject to a "best effort" commitment to roll back such measures over time.

Bilateral investment treaties can provide important support to overseas investors by cementing political relationships, offering some leverage to foreign investors where political concerns are not paramount, and demonstrating the government's commitment

to its foreign investors. Indeed, the failure to participate in today's proliferation of investment agreements could be taken as a symbol of government indifference.

Nevertheless, BITs cannot address many of the obstacles to China's outward investment. Even the U.S. BITs, which embody the most stringent investment protections, include an exception for national security concerns (Cai 2009), and such concerns were cited in the most prominent examples of barriers to Chinese FDI. Thus, while useful, BITs cannot in and of themselves resolve most of the barriers to investment described above.

Should China enter into more liberal investment treaties? The most liberal investment treaties, as exemplified in treaties promoted by the United States, include commitments to eliminate any existing discriminatory practices and to treat foreign investors equally with domestic investors in all respects, including giving foreigners the right to invest in the country if they meet the criteria (if any) that are imposed on domestic investors (referred to as pre-entry national treatment).[16]

Securing pre-entry national treatment for Chinese overseas investment could be beneficial. In the absence of such protection, Chinese firms could be at a competitive disadvantage in some markets. That is, Chinese firms could potentially be subject to time-consuming processes that firms from countries with treaties guaranteeing pre-entry national treatment could avoid. Firms that are seeking a foreign purchaser may choose investors who are not subject to such delays.[17] To the extent that BITs with strong investor protections proliferate over time, this constraint could become important.[18]

A distinction should be made between BITs with developing countries that are not major sources of FDI flows and treaties with the advanced countries. Explicit investment guarantees and access to international tribunals are not so critical in the advanced countries, where legal redress through relatively fair judicial procedures is available. By contrast, securing protection for Chinese investors in the more uncertain policy environments in developing countries may be more important in supporting outward FDI.[19]

Bilateral investment treaties or a multi-lateral agreement on investment? Assuming that the government decides to strengthen the legal protection for Chinese outward FDI, it then confronts the question of how to do so. One choice would be to enter into bilateral investment treaties that provide strong investor protections. Another would be to press for a multilateral agreement on investment that includes most countries.

A global agreement would have advantages. The existence of multiple BITs can increase transactions costs for firms, which face different investment rules depending on the host country (although the importance of these costs is disputed).[20] A multilateral investment agreement could provide more certainty to investor protections than a BIT, by increasing the costs to host countries of violating the agreement. Thus, a multilateral agreement could play a more important role in encouraging FDI than multiple BITs (studies provide mixed evidence about the extent to which stronger investment protection secured through BITs encourages greater foreign investment).[21] By joining hands with other developing countries, China may be able to achieve a more development-friendly multilateral framework for investment than it could through individual BIT negotiations.[22] A multilateral investment framework could also curb the power of multinational companies to implement restrictive business practices such as transfer pricing to evade taxation, restrictions on the ability of subsidiaries to trade with some domestic firms, and restrictions on the licensing of technology by subsidiaries (Xiao 2010; Crystal 2009).

On the other hand, pursuing multiple BITs would provide China more leverage over specific terms. Thus, for example, a BIT might specify the sectors in which national treatment would be provided, while such sectoral restrictions (apart from general provisions such as national security or health and safety exceptions) would be more complicated to negotiate through a multilateral framework.

Thus, if China decides to pursue a multilateral approach to investor protections, it is important that it play an active role in shaping the agreement. Allowing the advanced countries to negotiate such an agreement among themselves and then deciding whether to accept it, is unlikely to serve Chinese interests. Instead, the Chinese government needs to act to help define the specific terms of such an agreement, to ensure that the level of investment protection is suitable and that the particular circumstances of developing countries are recognized.

Guaranteeing national treatment to foreign investors has important implications for domestic policy. Securing pre-entry national treatment for Chinese investors would require providing the same protection for foreign investors in China. The large share of production accounted for by state enterprises and government subsidies for productive activities complicates efforts to credibly ensure a level playing field for domestic and foreign investors. Increasing state enterprises' autonomy and phasing out subsidies that explicitly favor domestic firms (as opposed to demand-side subsidies that do not discriminate between foreign and locally owned firms) could provide more credibility to policies guaranteeing national treatment and thus help secure such rights for Chinese investors in other markets.

Providing pre-entry national treatment would also imply reducing restrictions on FDI inflows. While China has progressively simplified approval procedures for foreign investment, local or central government review is still required for many investments.[23] Investment can be encouraged, restricted, or prohibited depending on the sector, the level of technology, and (formerly) the extent of exports. Elimination of at least some of these restrictions would significantly expand the sectors open to foreign investment.

It is difficult to argue that such dramatic changes in development policy should be undertaken simply to achieve reciprocity for Chinese investments overseas. As it happens, however, the domestic reforms that could help achieve stronger legal protection for

Chinese overseas investments are also likely to further Chinese development. Increasing the autonomy of state enterprises and reducing the role of subsidies would be consistent with efforts to improve the efficiency of SOEs.[24]

Rationalizing the system of approvals and restrictions for inward FDI could reduce the costs confronting foreign investors, by providing greater assurance that they would be able to invest without excessive delays and to operate without undue interference. In particular, reducing restrictions on service sector FDI would promote service sector efficiency,

the importance of which will rise as China strives to become a high-income economy. Encouraging FDI inflows can be particularly useful in improving the efficiency of service sectors that are less affected by competition through trade (box 5.2). Also, as China becomes a richer and more globally integrated economy, the usefulness of government review of foreign investment will decline. The economy will become much more complicated, making it more difficult to control investments and to understand all of the ramifications of guiding investment in the way practiced when the economy was

---

BOX 5.2   FDI and competition in services

FDI can have a positive impact on the services sector and thus more broadly on the overall economy (several studies show that FDI in services can improve productivity in manufacturing through vertical linkages—see, for example, Arnold and others 2007). Many developing countries have limited FDI in services, in part because they lack an adequate regulatory framework to oversee a more competitive sector. But inefficient services sectors can be a severe constraint on development, so opening services to FDI can be important to future growth as incomes rise and the resources available to regulate the sector increase.

Foreign direct investment that results in increased competition can encourage lower prices and improvements in quality, expand the set of available producer services, and improve the productivity of domestic firms through knowledge spillovers. For example, cutting-edge retail practices (central warehousing, appointment system, use of pallets) introduced in Mexico by Walmart were quickly adopted by other retail chains (Javorick, Keller, and Tybout 2006; McKinsey 2003). Similarly, with the opening of Korea's retail market, competition from Walmart and Carrefour encouraged domestic firms to lower prices and expand consumer choice, while enabling them to absorb advanced technology that increased the productivity of distribution networks. While smaller businesses were driven out of the market, the larger Korean retail stores flourished and bought out Walmart and Carrefour within 10 years.

Foreign direct investment can have a positive impact on infrastructure. A study covering 85 developing countries from 1985 to 1999 found that telecommunications services improved after foreign entry (Fink, Mattoo, and Rathindran 2002). In countries with strong regulatory systems, FDI has led to improved telecom services and contributed to higher economic growth (Norton 1992; Roller and Waverman 2001). FDI improved the reliability of electricity and telecommunications services provision in Latin America (World Bank 2004). The positive impact of FDI in infrastructure, however, requires a regulatory environment that encourages competition. In Argentina, Mexico, and República Bolivariana de Venezuela, telecom enterprises were transformed from loss-making, subsidized entities into tax-paying firms, but part of their profitability arose from monopoly positions and captive regulators. In Argentina, the privatization of Entel did not result in lower service prices (UNCTAD 2004), and in Brazil, greater efficiency was accompanied by higher prices (Anuatti-Neto and others 2003).

Both cross-country and case studies find that FDI can strengthen the banking sector.[25] Again, however, the regulatory environment is critical. Studies find that foreign bank participation improved efficiency and competition in Colombia (Barajas, Steiner, and Salazar 2000) and Argentina (Cull and others 1999). But studies of Mexico (Haber and Musacchio 2005; Schulz 2006) argue that high concentration in the sector before and after foreign entry meant there was no improvement in efficiency.

simpler. And, establishing an open capital account (see below) will complicate the issues involved in imposing restrictions on foreign investment (for example, by making it simpler to invest through local intermediaries).

Thus, with Chinese development, the usefulness of investment restrictions will decline, while the potential benefits of stronger investment protections in foreign markets will rise. In short, China does have an interest in continuing to ease restrictions on inward FDI and to undertake commitments to strong investor protection in international agreements. A transition period is likely necessary to ensure that government agencies have the ability to regulate foreign investment effectively without extensive approval procedures. Also, in some sectors, domestic investors may need time to be able to compete with foreign investors who enjoy national treatment. Limited exceptions to national treatment could be incorporated into investment agreements that generally provide for an open regime toward FDI. It is important, however, that such restrictions have sunset clauses to ensure that eventually the protected sectors can enjoy the benefits of increased investment. Overall, in a decade or so, developmental interests likely will be better served by the replacement of the current regime for regulating inward FDI with international agreements that will also achieve strong protection for Chinese firms investing abroad.

Deeper Integration into the Global Financial System

China's tightly managed exchange rate and extensive capital controls have been linchpins of China's economic policies. These policies have helped support spectacular export-led growth and supported financial stability. This policy mix has also played an important role in insulating the economy from global financial crises. Continued economic and financial stability requires the gradual adoption of an alternative policy mix, however, one involving greater exchange rate flexibility, modernization of the financial system, and liberalization of capital controls leading

eventually to full convertibility. These policies also would support the rebalancing of growth toward greater domestic demand and greater production of nontraded goods and services; this rebalancing is required for China to become a high-income economy. In the long run, when the economy becomes even more integrated in the global economy, the internationalization of the renminbi will provide more stability than the current system of a managed exchange rate. The transition to a more financially integrated economy involves risks, however. Careful attention must be paid to the timing and sequencing of policies and to the building of strong institutions to manage the financial system.

Exchange rate stability and capital controls have supported stability in China. China has achieved remarkable growth by opening to the world economy. But at the same time, its global relationships have on occasion created significant challenges for domestic economic stability. Most of China's foreign investments and a significant share of external trade transactions are perforce largely denominated in dollars, so that changes in the dollar/renminbi exchange rate have enormous implications for the profitability and balance sheets of domestic firms, and for the prices faced by consumers. A stable (albeit not fixed) exchange rate with the dollar has helped to limit domestic economic instability.

China's official exchange rate depreciated sharply in 1994 with the unification of the formerly dual exchange rate system.[26] Thereafter, the government essentially fixed the renminbi/dollar rate until July 2005 when the managed floating exchange rate regime was adopted, after which the renminbi gradually appreciated. By October 2011, the real effective exchange rate had appreciated 66 percent compared with that of January 1994, and 31 percent compared with that of January 2005.[27]

At the same time, the managed exchange rate policy has required maintaining a closed capital account, so that the domestic monetary policies could be more independent and effective; with limited exchange rate flexibility and an open capital account, the government would lose the ability to use monetary policy to influence domestic inflation and economic activity.[28] This strategy has enabled China to achieve rapid growth and maintain a highly competitive exchange rate to support exports.

Nevertheless, the tightly managed exchange rate is now posing more difficult challenges for macroeconomic policy. First, while tight management of the renminbi's exchange rate does help stabilize the nominal value of a large portion of China's overseas investments and trade, it occasionally has engendered sharp swings in China's competitive position with third countries.[29] The most dramatic example occurred when countries hit by the East Asian crisis in the late 1990s depreciated sharply against the dollar, while the renminbi/dollar exchange rate remained stable (table 5.4). The real exchange rate of Korea, Malaysia, the Philippines, and Thailand fell by an average of 24 percent, while China's real exchange rate appreciated slightly. The collapse of demand in the crisis-hit countries further reduced China's exports, with the U.S. dollar value of China's merchandise export growth falling from 20.9 percent in 1997 to 0.5 percent in 1998. The stability of the renminbi has been credited, however, as a significant factor in reestablishing regional growth and shortening the effects of the crisis, while doing little damage to China's medium-term growth.

Second, the managed exchange rate policy impairs the government's ability to control inflation. Inflationary pressures are strong to the extent that in China, as in other rapidly growing developing countries, the prices of nontraded goods have a natural tendency to rise relative to traded goods (that is, for the currency to appreciate in real terms).[30] If the prices of nontraded goods cannot rise through an appreciation of the nominal exchange rate, then they will tend to rise through inflation. It is difficult for the government to control inflation by increasing interest rates sufficiently in response to excessive demand growth, in part because rising interest rates will attract some capital inflows

TABLE 5.4   China's exchange rate was relatively stable during the East Asian crisis
Percentage change in exchange rate, 1997–98

	Real exchange rate	Normal exchange rate
China	−5.0	−0.1
Korea, Rep.	32.0	47.3
Malaysia	25.3	39.5
Philippines	19.4	38.8
Thailand	19.0	31.9

Source: World Bank.

(to the extent that capital controls are not 100 percent effective) that will further boost domestic liquidity. Thus, the government has had to rely on administrative controls (such as guidance to banks to reduce lending and direct controls of prices) to restrain inflation. For example, the government was initially reluctant to raise interest rates to cope with the overheating economy in 2004, leading to a plunge in the real rate of interest to corporate borrowers, which contributed to excess demand (Goldstein and Lardy 2006). Instead, the government imposed administrative controls (which are inconsistent with the long-term goal of increasing the autonomy of state enterprises) to reduce commitments to large-scale projects (Gallagher 2005). While these efforts were ultimately successful in bringing inflation down, they introduced distortions that have hampered efficiency and undermined the credibility of government policy.

Currently, very low interest rates in the United States and other advanced countries are contributing to another episode where inflation is rising above government targets. Thus, under the dollar-dominated international monetary system, the tightly managed exchange rate has, to a considerable degrees made China's monetary policy hostage to decisions by the U.S. Federal Reserve, the European Central Bank, and other central banks in advanced economies. While exchange rate volatility can also be undesirable, in current circumstances, less resistance to upward pressures on the exchange rate (if accompanied by appropriate monetary and fiscal policies) would help dampen

---

BOX 5.3   **Japan's transition to a floating exchange rate**

Japan's adoption of a floating exchange rate provides useful lessons for China's policies. Japan in the 1970s had several similarities with China today: a fixed exchange rate (360 yen to the dollar from shortly after World War II until 1971), capital controls, limits on interest rates that helped finance industrial investments, an underdeveloped financial system, a history of rapid growth propelled by rapidly increasing exports, a large trade surplus, and tensions with trading partners over rapid market penetration. Japan faced similar challenges in maintaining stability with a fixed exchange rate, relying on various administrative controls to contain inflationary pressures. Rising inflation (which peaked at 7.7 percent in 1970) and complaints from trade partners over the low valuation of the yen increased pressures for a change in parity. Events came to a head with the breakdown of the Bretton Woods system, and after some initial attempts to support the existing rate, the Japanese government allowed the yen to fluctuate (and appreciate) with only limited intervention.

The adoption of a floating exchange rate strengthened monetary autonomy and helped Japan cope with the significant economic turbulence of the 1970s. The floating exchange rate in the context of a steady decline in monetary growth led to a sharp fall in inflation (after the oil price shock), which averaged 4 percent in 1978–79 when inflation in the United States was about 10 percent. And the variability of both prices and output was considerably lower than under the fixed rate regime (Meltzer 1986). Lower inflation was accompanied by average GDP growth of 4 percent from 1974 to 1982, a comedown from pre-1970 growth rates but significantly higher than Japan's advanced-country trading partners (the period includes the severe global recession).

---

inflationary pressures, similar to the experience of Japan during the 1970s (box 5.3).

Third, maintaining the managed exchange rate policy in the face of the booming trade surplus has contributed to a huge buildup of foreign exchange reserves. Reserves rose to almost $2.9 trillion in 2010 and were projected to reach almost $3.5 trillion by the end of 2011, representing about 200 percent of annual imports. The buildup of foreign reserves, largely held in U.S. government and agency paper, has saddled China with assets that earn very low rates of return and, given the continued deterioration in the U.S. fiscal position and the Euro Area debt crisis, have also become increasingly risky. Reportedly, the authorities are making efforts to diversify reserve holdings away from dollar-denominated assets toward higher-yielding investments through various sovereign wealth funds, including the China Investment Corporation.[31] China is also taking a lead in moving forward international discussions to encourage alternatives to the dollar as a reserve currency. Such diversification is a slow process, however, particularly because any attempt to shift a large portion of reserves out of U.S. Treasuries could precipitate a sharp depreciation of the dollar, thus severely reducing the real value of the remaining stock of reserves, and could also be highly destabilizing to the global economy.

Fourth, while allowing greater flexibility of the exchange rate may not immediately reduce the trade surplus by a substantial amount, over time, movement to an equilibrium exchange rate will act to stimulate domestic absorption, reduce the current account surplus, and stimulate greater investment in nontraded goods and services. Such a readjustment would contribute to raising standards of living in China, increasing macroeconomic stability; it would also contribute to reducing global imbalances.

A different policy mix will be required to maintain stability as China's development continues. A tightly managed exchange rate regime with the rate deviating from equilibrium levels and a largely closed capital account are unlikely to continue to contribute to stability over the medium term. The dollar has been subject to considerable instability vis-à-vis other major currencies, which may become critical if it is no longer a reliable store of value owing to U.S. fiscal mismanagement. The renminbi's close relationship to the dollar, and the large amount of foreign reserves dominated by the dollar, would thus not be conducive to the future development of China's international economic activities. Also, over time, capital controls are likely to become increasingly less effective, as the sophistication of China's financial system develops, as Chinese firms increase their overseas operations, and as international financial players become more adept at circumventing controls. To the extent that capital controls become more porous, an inflexible exchange rate regime will make it increasingly difficult for the central bank to undertake an independent monetary policy, and the economy would become increasingly vulnerable to the global economic cycle.

Gradually liberalizing capital controls would enhance China's ability to achieve high-income status. Capital controls inhibit the development of the financial sector, thus reducing the scope of domestic investment by firms, limiting asset diversification opportunities for Chinese households, restricting the provision of sophisticated financial services required by complex modern economies, and impairing the ability of the financial system to allocate resources to the most productive activities. In the past, the government's domination of the financial system and the channeling of resources to large industrial projects and exports have supported development by overcoming impediments to the coordination of economic activities, reaping economies of scale, and increasing confidence. However, China's future development will require a more efficient services sector and more diversified manufactured production to serve domestic demand. A market-based financial sector is essential to support these new requirements as China's economy becomes more complex and incomes continue to increase. The gradual removal of capital controls will be required to support an efficient and well-regulated financial sector.

Increasing the use of the renminbi in international transactions could support economic stability. Thus, continued development will require greater monetary independence, exchange rate flexibility, and a modern, more open, financial system. Increased use of the renminbi in international transactions could make an important contribution if a significant share of foreign assets were denominated in renminbi, and if Chinese firms that operate abroad could borrow in renminbi, then exchange rate fluctuations would have less impact on economic and financial stability. From the perspective of individual firms, use of the renminbi in external activities (such as trade) would allow diversification in the sense of reducing exposure to risks specific to the Chinese economy without increasing foreign exchange risk. From the perspective of the country, the danger of capital outflows during crises is smaller if the renminbi is recognized as an international currency.

Achieving greater use of the renminbi in international transactions would have other, perhaps less important, benefits. To the extent that nonresidents are willing to hold the currency, the government would enjoy seigniorage revenues.[32] The government and firms could face lower interest rates on their debt if foreigners increased their demand for renminbi-denominated assets. Chinese traveling abroad would be able to use renminbi to purchase domestic currencies with relatively low transactions costs if currency traders had access to well-established markets for trading in the Chinese currency.

Having the rest of the world use one's currency does have some downsides. If some regional trading partners choose to peg their exchange rates to the renminbi, future Chinese authorities could face some economic and political challenges in pursuing purely national objectives when conducting monetary and exchange policy. The increased demand for renminbi assets associated with external use of the currency likely would result in a more appreciated exchange rate than otherwise, potentially reducing the attractiveness of China's exports. Chinese monetary policy would become a greater focus of attention if foreigners hold significant renminbi assets (witness the considerable reaction to the U.S. Federal Reserve's quantitative easing, as opposed to little interest in similar policies followed by the Bank of England), while foreigners' demand for renminbi could increase the instability of money demand, potentially complicating monetary policy. Counterfeiting of the renminbi could become an issue, as it has for the dollar. But these issues are manageable and would not greatly reduce the significant benefits involved from the renminbi becoming an international currency.

What is required for the renminbi to become a more widely used international currency? For a currency to be accepted in international transactions by other countries and held as assets by foreigners, the country's shares in international trade and financial transactions have to be significant. Inflation and inflation expectations need to be low, so that the currency is a reliable store of value. Nonresidents should have confidence in the independence and competence of monetary authorities. Domestic capital markets need to be deep and liquid (so that investors can buy and sell large volumes of securities without greatly affecting the market price) and include a broad range of financial instruments with different risk-return characteristics.

China currently meets only some of these necessary conditions. The country is now the second-largest trading economy. The scenarios presented earlier indicate that China's share of world trade is likely to increase by two-thirds over the coming 20 years, and its share of global output will nearly double, making China the world's largest economy. Officially recorded inflation is currently just above 5 percent, somewhat above the government's target, as a result of expansionary policies during the financial crisis. But inflation was relatively low (about 2 percent, albeit somewhat unstable) over the past decade.

In most respects, however, the renminbi is not yet a suitable international reserve currency. While the Chinese authorities' concern over inflationary pressures has contributed

to the credibility of stabilization policies, the inability to understand how monetary policy decisions are made makes it difficult for market participants to anticipate changes. An international ranking finds that the transparency of China's central bank improved substantially in the early part of the last decade but remained below that in most middle-income countries (Dincer and Eichengreen 2006). Thus, further moves to improve the independence of the central bank and to increase the transparency of monetary policy decision making would be essential to support greater international acceptance of the renminbi.

But perhaps the greatest challenge that China faces in expanding the cross-border use of the renminbi is its underdeveloped financial system. China lacks the diversified financial instruments and the secondary markets that would enable investors to quickly and cheaply convert their renminbi assets into cash, even if capital controls were removed. Low efficiency, high transaction costs, and weak supervision and regulation are major limitations on financial sector development (Wu, Pan, and Wang 2010). Administered interest rates and the lack of transparency in the regulation of banks and financial markets inhibit market competition and the development of advanced financial products (Dobson and Masson 2009). For example, interest rate controls allow the large SOEs to fund their activities with retained earnings and cheap credit, which has meant little issuance of corporate debt and asset-backed securities and a relatively illiquid market. Financial market infrastructure is improving but remains challenged: bankruptcy procedures are not widely understood, modern accounting standards are not applied uniformly, and issues often lack transparency (Zhou 2005). Restrictions on the kinds of foreign institutions allowed to acquire domestic securities, on the size of investments, and on the pace of repatriation (necessary to ensure that capital controls are not evaded) severely limit foreigners' ability to participate in the market.

Strengthening of financial regulation and supervision is essential to ensure stability in the context of a more liberalized financial environment. Considerable progress has been made in strengthening the capital adequacy of the banking system, although the implications of the recent sharp increase in lending are as yet not fully clear. Improved coordination among the various institutions involved in financial regulation will be important. Further progress also will be necessary to ensure that state-owned banks operate on market principles, rather than being responsive to political decisions. At the same time, the regulation and supervision of nonbank financial institutions involved in these markets will be essential, particularly because, in the absence of such improvements, restrictions on the banking sector will be reflected in the transfer of funds to nonbanks. The regulation of nonbank financial institutions is probably the most difficult challenge the government will face in establishing a market-based financial system. It will be necessary to encourage the growth of alternative instruments and sources of funds, while ensuring the soundness of all institutions that borrow short and lend long (and are thus potentially subject to sudden failure). Industrial countries spectacularly failed to achieve adequate regulation of nonbank financial institutions during the recent boom, with dismal results.

The government is taking steps to increase financial integration with the rest of the world. Government policies are increasing the use of renminbi in trade and financial transactions. On the trade side, settlement in renminbi is growing rapidly, accounting for around 7 percent of total trade in April 2011, up from almost nothing at the beginning of 2010 (IMF 2011). The pattern of settlement in renminbi, however, is very unbalanced, with almost 90 percent of the settlements on the import side.

The government is also undertaking cautious steps toward allowing foreigners to participate in capital account transactions denominated in renminbi. A few qualified investors, including international development institutions in China, have been allowed to issue bonds in China's domestic market (Makin 2010), and some foreign participation in the banking system is under way, although foreign banks' share of financial assets remains below 2 percent, and their activities are restricted.[33] The government is developing an offshore market in renminbi in Hong Kong SAR, China, including provision for renminbi balances to be held by foreigners, the development of instruments for hedging currency risk, and the issuance of renminbi-denominated government bonds (Huang 2010). The goal, according to Subacchi (2010), is to develop an offshore market while maintaining capital account restrictions, reminiscent of the development of the offshore Eurodollar market when the United States had controls on capital outflows during the 1960s and 1970s (He and McCauley 2010). Some Chinese companies have issued renminbi-denominated bonds in Hong Kong SAR, China, but the size of the available renminbi-denominated assets is still small, resulting in the bulk of the trade settlements held in deposits in the Hong Kong SAR, China, clearing bank. Since October 2010, China has allowed three types of foreign institutions, including foreign central banks or monetary authorities—renminbi clearing banks in Hong Kong SAR and Macao SAR, China, and foreign banks participating in cross-border renminbi trade settlements—to invest in domestic Chinese interbank bond markets using renminbi.

So far, these policies have played little role in encouraging a broader role for the currency. Overall, the renminbi remains little used internationally, accounting for one side of only 0.9 percent of foreign exchange trades (BIS 2010). An expanded offshore market and expanded trade invoicing will encourage some greater international use of the renminbi. However, even a flourishing offshore market is unlikely to encourage widespread adoption of renminbi-denominated assets when the domestic capital markets remain small and illiquid.

A program to deepen China's financial integration with the global financial system will require careful planning. Deepening China's financial integration with the global financial system will require more aggressive measures to modernize and regulate its financial system and to open it more to foreign competition, increased exchange rate flexibility, and gradual removal of capital controls. But these policy changes, particularly the transition to an open capital account and removal of domestic financial sector controls, entail significant risks. Many countries in Latin America, Eastern Europe, and East Asia that have eliminated capital controls have suffered dramatic financial crises accompanied by calamitous declines in output and large increases in poverty. These crises have typically been driven by large financial sector weaknesses and imbalances, coupled with failures to manage increases in aggregate demand from unrestrained capital inflows, real exchange rate appreciation (often reflected in real estate booms), and an eventual withdrawal of capital and a major collapse in asset prices. The European experience with financial sector and capital account liberalization was more positive, and holds some lessons for China (box 5.4).

To minimize stability risks, the reform agenda must be carefully timed and sequenced. China can limit the instability often experienced during financial sector liberalization and capital account opening through a gradual approach that involves careful attention to the appropriate sequencing of policy changes. A detailed blueprint for financial and capital account liberalization is impossible to lay out because some flexibility will be required to take into account economic developments and the degree of success of various reforms. It is nonetheless useful to provide an overview of the steps that will be required, along with some information on their order. In particular, there are several prerequisites for an opening of the capital account.

The most important first step is to reform the renminbi exchange rate mechanism in the direction of a more market-determined, flexible regime. That will indicate the extent to which the currency is misaligned. Indeed, an important goal of China's capital controls has been resisting pressures to appreciate the renminbi (Yu 2009). Dismantling capital

controls in the context of a widespread expectation of an appreciation of the exchange rate would encourage huge capital inflows. Establishing a market-based exchange rate, while not eliminating the potential for instability from capital inflows, would at least reduce one reason for it. Moreover, providing for exchange rate flexibility would improve the authorities' ability to control inflationary pressures through monetary policy and reduce the pace of the buildup of foreign reserves. At the same time, the government should proceed with steps to increase the independence of the central bank, improve the transparency of monetary policy, and strengthen financial sector regulation.

Even before the exchange rate reaches an equilibrium level, parallel efforts should be undertaken to improve the methods for conducting monetary policy as well as financial market regulation and supervision. As progress is made on these fronts, the government can proceed with financial liberalization. Deposit interest rates would be raised toward market levels, perhaps in stages to gauge the impact on bank balance sheets. Experience shows that the removal of deposit rates can lead to excessive credit expansion, so it will be necessary to ensure that monetary conditions are sufficiently tight to maintain stability (Feyzioğlu, Porter, and Takáts 2009). Controls on lending rates can also be gradually removed. Although the reforms required for successful financial liberalization take time, there is some urgency in implementing them. Financial innovation and stronger banking regulation are encouraging greater flows to nonbank institutions, potentially challenging the government's ability to control inflation through administrative means (IMF 2011). Improving the regulation of nonbank financial institutions while establishing market-based interest rates is necessary to enable the government to manage macroeconomic policy successfully and ensure financial stability.

To set the stage for further capital account liberalization, the government could increase current initiatives to encourage the use of the renminbi in settling current account

BOX 5.4   Lessons of the European experiences with capital account liberalization

Today's Europe of open financial markets and unrestricted capital flows took a long time to establish. Many western European countries imposed extensive restrictions on their financial sectors for three to four decades following World War II, and exchange controls were not fully abolished by the European Union until 1990 (Wyplosz 1999). Capital account restrictions were often used to dampen pressures for exchange rate changes, by restraining capital outflows that could force a depreciation and (at other times) limiting capital inflows that would otherwise tend toward appreciation and a decline in competitiveness. In addition, several European countries used capital account restrictions to sustain financial sector policies that maintained low interest rates (primarily to reduce the costs of financing government deficits) and directed credit toward favored borrowers. With interest rates artificially low, quantitative ceilings were used to control credit. Thus, controls on capital outflows were necessary to prevent asset holders from placing their wealth at the higher interest rates available abroad, and controls on inflows were sometimes required to avoid exchange rate appreciation as borrowers sought to circumvent credit constraints. In short, some European countries' financial sector controls, monetary policies, and capital account restrictions, along with the challenges faced in the potential disintermediation of the banking system and growing circumvention of controls, resemble China's current experience.

Financial repression and capital account controls gradually became less popular, for several reasons. The effectiveness of controls declined as financial markets became more sophisticated. The growth of derivative products significantly reduced the costs of, and increased the potential for, circumventing controls, while funds increasingly flowed out of the tightly regulated banks to other financial institutions. Controls also became increasingly costly in terms of administrative procedures, efforts at evasion that introduced competitive distortions among firms, and the diversion of commercial and financial activities to other countries. The process of European integration provided an impetus for more stable macroeconomic policies to maintain the fixed exchange rate with low-inflation Germany, and

improving macroeconomic stability reduced the need for controls to respond to foreign exchange crises.

The European countries' approach to financial sector liberalization and opening the capital account varied. Most countries employed a gradual approach to liberalization. For example, France began a process of liberalization in 1983 (after aborted attempts in the 1960s) that involved financial sector deregulation and a shift to indirect means of monetary control while capital account restrictions were still in place. Once the macroeconomic situation was favorable and the financial sector was viewed as able to withstand foreign competition, capital controls were gradually withdrawn. The sequence of measures to ease controls began with direct investment flows within the European Economic Community, then FDI from others countries along with travel allowances, then restrictions on foreign exchange operations, then restrictions on bank lending to nonresidents and administrative controls on import and export settlements (initially imposed to avoid the use of current account transactions to circumvent capital controls), then controls on foreign borrowing and holding of foreign currency accounts by domestic enterprises, and finally restrictions on bank lending in French francs to nonresidents. The full process of liberalization took six years.

Some countries adopted a much more rapid approach to capital account liberalization. The United Kingdom abolished all capital account restrictions in 1979 in conjunction with floating the exchange rate, the removal of credit controls, and a tightening of fiscal and monetary policies. These measures, undertaken when the country had a strong balance of payments position owing to the rise in the oil price, were largely successful in improving macroeconomic stability and establishing a more efficient financial sector, although there were some transitional costs from higher exchange rate volatility and an asset price bubble at the end of the 1980s.

Denmark, Finland, Norway, and Sweden also rapidly implemented capital account liberalization and a deregulation of financial markets during the 1980s, with asset price booms leading to banking crises in Norway, Finland, and Sweden (in the first two countries, also driven by lower oil prices and the

(Box continues next page)

BOX 5.4   (continued)

collapse in trade with the Soviet Union). In contrast, improvements in banking supervision allowed Denmark to escape significant financial sector difficulties despite loan losses.

The European experience has some useful lessons for China. First, in China's situation, reform must cover a broad agenda, including the removal of credit controls and restrictions on interest rates, the reliance of monetary policy on interest rates and open-market operations rather than quantitative controls, a move to a more market-determined exchange rate, and the gradual opening of the capital account. However, none of these reforms will function effectively without the others. Second, steps to ease financial sector restrictions and open the capital account should be undertaken when the country is in a strong balance of payments position. This perspective argues for China initiating this process soon, when the country's huge current account surplus could cushion downside risks involved in unanticipated capital outflows, which is likely a more serious problem than unanticipated inflows. Third, it is critical to achieve adequate supervision of the financial sector before opening the capital account. While defining "adequate" in this context is difficult, the potential for asset price booms followed by collapses is high when the banks are unaccustomed to dealing with the increased potential for both profits and risks in a newly liberalized financial sector. Fourth, financial sector reform and capital account liberalization must be supported by a stable macroeconomic environment. Thus, the recent rise in inflation needs to be addressed before, or in conjunction with, taking any steps toward liberalization. Finally, some European countries removed controls and then reinstituted them when their exchange rates came under pressure. The reversal in policies made it more difficult for market participants to anticipate government policy and reduced long-term investment.

Nevertheless, the applicability of the European experience for China is limited because of the substantial difference in levels of development and changes in the international financial system. Western European countries had a long history of established financial sector institutions and prudential frameworks, which China is now developing. European countries also had much more extensive stock and bond markets that could absorb large capital inflows without putting at risk depositors' money, and thus potentially inducing rescues of insolvent institutions and the attendant moral hazard that can spur excessive lending. A stronger and more diversified financial sector in Europe likely contributed to the relatively mild impact of financial sector liberalization in most countries, as compared, for example, with the severe crises experienced in East Asia and the Southern Cone of Latin America. Thus, the risks facing China in embarking on this process, and the need for caution and experimentation, are likely greater than in the Europe of the 1980s.

China also faces a much more complex and sophisticated global financial environment than Europe did. The availability of standardized derivative instruments and a multiplicity of offshore centers that lack controls on external transactions should make it easier to circumvent controls today than in the 1980s. While China's control regime remains effective, the more sophisticated international financial environment implies some greater difficulty in opening the capital account gradually, because initial steps to free some transactions (by removing all controls on FDI, for example) could be exploited to effect more extensive capital account transactions. This possibility implies the necessity to maintain some vigilance, perhaps in the form of requiring the reporting of transactions, during the process of capital account liberalization so that large anomalies can be checked.

Source: Bakker and Chapple 2002.

transactions; it could also expand bilateral currency swap arrangements to more trade partners. But as these initiatives progress, achieving a more balanced settlement pattern will be difficult while the exchange rate remains significantly undervalued (IMF 2011). A further early measure would be to abolish approval processes for inward and outward FDI flows, which tend to be more stable and long term than portfolio flows. Given China's large current account surplus and large and growing official reserves, it would make sense to consider lifting controls on outflows before lifting controls on inflows. Programs to allow residents greater access to external financial markets could reduce upward pressures on the exchange rate and lessen official reserve accumulation. The range of qualified investments by foreigners could then be increased and restrictions on foreign investment in the stock market gradually eliminated. Cross-country experience strongly suggests that restrictions on short-term capital inflows be removed last.

Establishing the renminbi as an international currency will take time. The reforms outlined above are necessary, but not sufficient, to ensure that the renminbi becomes a major international currency. More time, perhaps many years, will be required to develop sufficiently deep capital markets and to establish the reputation for stability that is required for foreigners to hold large amounts of a country's currency. The pace of international acceptance will be determined in part by international conditions. To the extent that alternative reserve currencies, notably the dollar and the euro, are subject to instability and mismanagement, reliance on the renminbi would increase more rapidly. One informed estimate places the earliest year that the renminbi would become a global currency beyond 2025 (Wu, Pan, and Wang 2010); another model-based simulation predicts the currency could account for up to 12 percent of international reserves by 2035 (Lee 2010); and one market analyst sees the renminbi likely to become one of the world's major reserve currencies sometime after 2030 (Jaeger 2010).

The policies required to establish the renminbi as an international currency will have important implications for China and the world. The implications for China's development model will be profound. State-owned banks would have to be allowed to act like private banks and not be subject to instructions from the government to increase lending for macroeconomic reasons (Eichengreen 2010). State-owned enterprises would have to face

hard budget constraints, that is, those that become insolvent would have to be allowed to go bankrupt, so that creditors would not be tempted to lend in the expectation that their loans enjoyed an implicit government guarantee. Similarly, some constraints will need to be placed on borrowing by local governments, either through greater administrative control from the center or statutory limits on local government deficits. Another problem worth noting is the double mismatch between currency and maturity of borrowing and lending—borrowing short in foreign currency while lending long in local currency. This double mismatch has been a major cause for heightened exchange rate risk and debt crises in many developing countries, most notably in the Asian financial crisis of 1997.

The implications of these policies go beyond ensuring financial stability in government and government-owned institutions. To the extent that prices are allowed to clear markets, reliance on influence and contacts should become less important than innovation and efficiency for economic success. That would be beneficial to the economy but may also imply that some formerly successful firms are no longer profitable, underlying the importance of social insurance for providing health care and pensions. A more market-based exchange rate would mean less reliance on exports and a rebalancing of the economy from manufacturing to services. All of these changes would be beneficial in their own right, in addition to being consistent with a greater international role for the renminbi. They do, however, imply dramatic changes in the way that business is transacted in China.

Finally, China should not ignore the international implications of increasing the use of the renminbi. As Barry Eichengreen (2010) has emphasized, the emergence of the renminbi as an international currency would provide a useful diversification away from the dollar, helping to limit financing of the sort of excessive current account deficits pursued by the United States before the 2008 financial crisis, and thus reducing the likelihood of a repetition. China's efforts to establish the renminbi as an international currency would support global economic stability, which, given China's size and openness, is an essential ingredient of stability in China.

Global Public Goods

China's future prosperity depends to a large extent on the preservation of global public goods—a wide variety of issues that are important for many countries where market forces cannot be relied upon to achieve efficient outcomes. In such cases, coordinated government policies are necessary to ensure the efficient provision of global public goods. For example, the market cannot be relied upon to limit environmental damage, either domestically or cross-border, so issues such as climate change and threats to the ozone layer can be resolved only through international coordination. Similarly, preservation of global resources such as ocean fisheries, seabed minerals, and the Antarctic requires coordinated interventions by governments. The benefits of communications networks increase with the number of users, so international agreements and domestic regulations that promote efficient Internet use, for example, are in everyone's interest. International trade and financial transactions require a framework of rules to promote cooperation; reductions in import barriers and steps to ensure global financial stability often require international discussion. Efforts to reduce global poverty, thus enhancing global stability, will be more effective if all countries with sufficient resources are encouraged to participate. Indeed, the term "global public goods" is, to an extent, misleading: much of the work involves establishing effective institutions that take into account the global impact of the provision of goods and services. While all of these issues touch on domestic policies, they all also involve international coordination; thus, this section also considers aspects of domestic regulations that have a significant international impact.

While China has certainly cooperated in efforts to sustain global public goods, the government faces an important policy question.

Should China rely on a multilateral consensus to determine global policies, with specific interventions to protect China's interests, or should China actively help shape global agreements? This question is particularly difficult for environmental agreements, where it might be argued that, because the advanced countries are principally responsible for damages to the environment, and are richer and thus better able to forgo income for future benefits, they should shoulder the costs involved.

While the moral argument concerning advanced countries' responsibility has resonance, it remains in China's interest to play an active role in shaping agreements on global public goods. China's huge size imposes on the country both a responsibility to contribute to safeguarding public goods (else others will refuse to cooperate as well) and the opportunity to shape global agreements so that they support China's development.

Here we consider a few examples of global issues that cannot be resolved efficiently by relying on the market, and where China should actively participate in international solutions, for its own and the world's benefit. Some of these issues will be critical to China's development in coming years, while others, though important, will have less impact. Our purpose is to provide examples of common problems where China plays an important role, not to enumerate all of the challenges in preserving global public goods over the next decades.

Climate Change

The global economy faces an enormous challenge in reducing carbon emissions to avoid the worst effects of climate change. Absent changes in policies to reduce emission intensity, the increase in average global temperatures over the next several decades could be calamitous, with a rise in the sea level that would inundate vast regions where millions of people live as well as the degradation of agricultural land that millions of poor depend on for their livelihood. China will be severely affected, both directly in some regions and indirectly as the global economy deteriorates.

FIGURE 5.12   Carbon emissions will rise in the baseline scenario

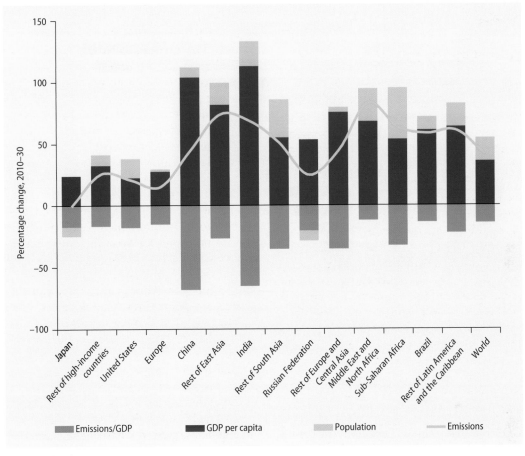

Source: World Bank.

Here we discuss how global emissions could evolve over the next 20 years, the role China might play in multilateral efforts to reduce emissions, and the implications of different agreements for China's economy.

Emissions are set to increase. Global annual emissions are expected to increase around 50 percent over the next 20 years, largely because of growth in GDP per capita and, to a lesser extent, population growth. Emissions per unit of GDP are expected to decline slightly (figure 5.12).

More than four-fifths of the rise in emissions over the next 20 years will come from developing countries. The large share of developing countries in the global increase reflects higher population growth and higher

per capita GDP growth compared with high-income countries, although the relationship between growth in developing countries and global emissions is complex.

While developing countries will be responsible for the bulk of new emissions, their emissions per capita are much lower than in high-income countries (figure 5.13). While developing countries' per capita emissions are expected to rise somewhat, they will not approach the levels in high-income countries. However, emissions per unit of GDP are relatively high in developing countries, and China is among the countries with the highest emission intensity in the world. A key reason for the high emission intensity in the developing world is the low valuation of nontradable products in those countries, which makes

FIGURE 5.13   **Emissions per capita in developing countries are much lower than in advanced countries**

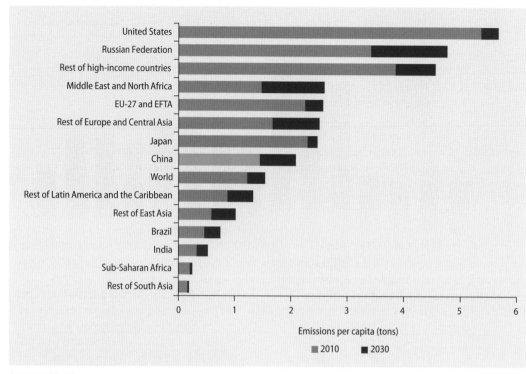

Source: World Bank.
Note: EFTA = European Free Trade Association.

GDP relatively small. Especially in China, another reason is the small share of services and the large share of manufacturing. As a consequence of the high emission intensity, GDP growth in the developing world leads to more than proportional growth in global emissions, even as the emission intensity is expected to decline sharply along with the shift to services and the rise in the relative price of nontradable products.

It is in China's interest to actively promote global efforts to reduce carbon emissions. China is the largest source of carbon emissions, accounting for 23 percent of global carbon dioxide (CO_2) emissions (although note that China's large export sector means that a significant portion of the goods produced in generating these emissions are actually consumed abroad). Moreover, during the next 20 years, China is expected to be responsible for one-quarter of the increase

in emissions, even in a baseline scenario that assumes a significant shift toward the service sectors in China. Effective global policies are not feasible without China's participation, both because limiting China's emissions is critical and because other countries are unlikely to participate in the absence of the largest source of carbon emissions.

It is in China's interest to reduce carbon emissions significantly; otherwise, China would create an artificial comparative advantage in energy-intensive production and be stuck with the current emission structure, making the country even more dependent on future energy supply. Over the long term, the supply of energy is one of the most binding constraints on growth potential, so having a comparative advantage in energy-intensive production is not desirable. In addition, greater reliance on energy-intensive production would worsen China's already considerable environmental challenges.

Limits on carbon emissions would reduce China's GDP in the short run. These limits would not necessarily reduce consumption, however, because a large share of relatively energy-intensive production is devoted to exports. Global limits on carbon emissions would increase the relative price of these exports, which would reduce the volume of exports but also generate tax revenues for the government. The impact on consumption would depend on the government's allocation of these tax revenues. More important, as chapter 3 argues, a green strategy may well become a new source of growth, increasing long-term growth potential.

A fair and effective global climate agreement is important to China. China should actively push for a fair, reasonable, and sustainable global climate regime based on common but differentiated principles. Failure on the part of major countries to reach agreement on climate change and contain the climate crisis will lead to serious consequences for the world economy, in particular, developing countries, including China, that are likely to be the most severely affected by climate change. A fair global climate regime can be consistent with China's implementation of its domestic commitment to reduce greenhouse gas emissions. China's 12th Five Year Plan already includes declining intensity of such emissions as a binding target. China's earnest efforts to reach this target and establish a market-based emissions reduction mechanism will not only spur other major economies to adopt forceful measures for greenhouse gas reduction but also facilitate transformation of the development model, advances in technology, and economic growth within China, thereby turning emission reduction from a burden into an opportunity.

Global limits on carbon emissions have to take into account the need for continued growth in developing countries. Developed countries, having reached an advanced phase of industrialization, have high existing emissions levels and low future economic growth potential. Developing countries, on the other hand, have relatively low existing emission levels and high future economic growth potential. That growth potential has to be realized to meet pressing development needs. Therefore, emission targets in a global climate change agreement should not be based on existing emission levels, but on future needs.

International Financial Regulations

The global financial crisis highlighted the importance of effective supervision of financial systems for global stability. International agreements can enable individual country authorities to impose regulatory rules without impairing the competitive position of their banks relative to banks in other jurisdictions. International norms can also provide an anchor for domestic reforms. China has consistently supported international prudential norms for banking regulation and has made considerable progress in integrating these norms into its domestic financial system. Going forward, the government may need to take a more proactive role in helping to shape these norms. This discussion does not cover all, or necessarily even the most important, areas where China relies on international coordination to preserve financial stability. For example, our focus on the long term means we do not consider the current financial controversies concerning China's criticism of U.S. monetary policies and debt burden an important, albeit short-term, area for stability in China.

China has benefited from adopting international regulatory norms for banks. China accelerated its program to implement Basel standards in the late 1990s, as a guide for the recapitalization of state-owned banks in response to the large amount of nonperforming loans (NPLs). Adopting international norms provided a useful benchmark and a means of enhancing the credibility of the government's program. Authorities combined elements of the implementation of Basel I (such as capital requirements) with elements from Basel II (supervisory review and disclosure procedures), in what officials of the China Bank Regulatory Commission (CBRC)

FIGURE 5.14   State-owned banks dominate China's banking sector
Share of types of banks in total assets, 2009

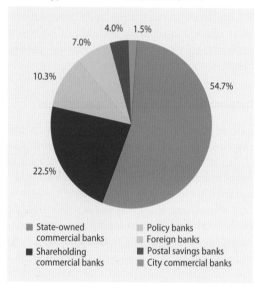

- State-owned commercial banks
- Shareholding commercial banks
- Policy banks
- Foreign banks
- Postal savings banks
- City commercial banks

Source: UBS.

Moreover, the stimulus program adopted in response to the global financial crisis involved a substantial expansion in credit extended by the state-owned banks. The size and necessary speed of this process is likely to result in some rise in NPLs going forward.[37] As happened with Basel I, the implementation of Basel III will provide an external standard for Chinese regulators in the necessary future cleanup and again will help to defuse potential domestic criticism of the process.[38] The Five Year Development Plan (covering 2011–15) envisions the continued implementation of Basel regulatory norms, and the CBRC announced in May 2011 the imposition of increased capital adequacy ratios, with higher levels for "systemically important banks."

China also should take advantage of informal bilateral relationships related to international banking supervision to share experiences and information. Membership in the Financial Stability Board puts Chinese authorities into direct and regular contacts with other regulatory organizations, which also have an interest in formal and informal exchanges of information with their Chinese counterparts.[39]

China's reliance on international prudential norms in its domestic financial reform process does not mean that the country should passively accept norms that are defined by the advanced countries. Although developing countries have recently become more involved in international financial discussions,[40] the agenda is still essentially set by high-income countries.[41] These international norms should be reviewed both for their relevance to China's financial system and for their implications for China's interactions with the global economy. The first issue does not present great difficulties, because the government has been successful in adapting norms to domestic circumstances.[42]

The second issue may require further study. International prudential norms have changed in response to the vulnerabilities exposed by the financial crisis. These changes reflect a difficult trade-off (from the perspective of the advanced countries) between the desire for increased stability and the wish to

sometimes called "Basel 1.5." As a result of this process and strong economic growth, the banks' NPLs dropped from a staggering 23 percent of GDP in 2000 (Allen and others 2008) to below 2 percent in January 2010 (according to the CBRC).[34]

Support for the use of international prudential norms also comes from the large, state-owned banks, which hold over 50 percent of total banking assets (figure 5.14). These banks have an interest in adhering to an internationally recognized regulatory framework to support their efforts at international expansion and to ensure that other domestic banks cannot compete by adopting more lax prudential norms.

The government remains committed to integrating the Basel prudential norms into its regulatory practices, despite the financial crisis resulting from poor regulation and supervision in the U.S. banking system (Walter 2010).[35] It is recognized that considerable work remains in establishing an efficient financial sector,[36] and the implementation of international norms is seen as a part of this still unfinished reform process.

avoid unduly reducing the efficiency benefits (and bank profits) generated from the use of sophisticated derivatives. China's view of this trade-off may differ from those of authorities in advanced countries. China's banks lack the technology and banking relationships required to sell these products, while China's economy suffered from the extreme volatility generated by the failure to properly regulate them. Thus, it may be in China's interest to promote a stricter regulation of derivatives than is currently envisioned.

For example, one difficult issue is the extent to which certain kinds of derivatives held by major financial institutions should be moved to central clearinghouses and subject to strict capital requirements. Establishing a single clearinghouse that spans a broad range of over-the-counter (OTC) derivatives would be desirable to ensure adequate regulatory control. However, recent proposals that would reduce the capital threshold for a clearinghouse and exempt some OTC derivatives from movement to clearinghouses would encourage a proliferation of clearinghouses and increase systemic risk (Singh 2011). China profits little from such sophisticated derivatives, and the most recent five-year plan envisions little progress in easing restrictions on such trades. It would, therefore, be logical for China to push for aggressive measures to limit the risks from OTC derivatives. This is simply one illustration of the many technical issues where a developing-country perspective would likely take a more conservative view of the trade-off between efficiency and risk in today's financial markets.

In short, as China becomes more integrated into the global financial system, the implications for China of external instability will rise. China should, thus, play an active role in promoting more stable financial sector regulation.

Official Finance

One global issue where China is playing an increasingly important role is official development assistance (ODA). While China has provided financial assistance to developing countries since the 1950s, the size of its program and its importance for development in the poorest countries is increasing rapidly. China's program of financial assistance has provided substantial benefits to developing countries, in some respects through mechanisms that are superior to the programs of Organisation for Economic Co-operation and Development (OECD) countries. In the future, China could improve the effectiveness of its overseas development finance (and avoid the same mistakes that the advanced countries made in their aid programs) by exchanging information about policies and procedures with the OECD. At the same time, the OECD countries should consider integrating some aspects of China's overseas financing policies, including flexible application of debt-sustainability guidelines and steps to improve the efficiency of infrastructure projects, into their own programs. The government also should consider potential competitive responses by the advanced countries to China's growing export credit program.

China's official aid statistics differ from OECD's in classification. The recent publication of an official paper on China's foreign aid is a welcome step toward greater transparency (State Council 2011). However, the statistics provided in the paper generally follow the Chinese practice of providing cumulative totals of annual figures over many years (China's aid totaled RMB 256 billion by end-2009). Data on the government's annual expenditures on external assistance (published in the *China Statistical Yearbook*) show a sharp rise in concessional assistance, from a total of about $700 million in 2001 to almost $5 billion in 2009 (figure 5.15). However, these figures cannot be directly compared with those reported as ODA by other major donors (see below), because of different classification of aid statistics between China and OECD countries. The difference is partly related to the differing features of aid policies and development experiences.

Both China and recipients have benefited from China's program of official finance. China's

FIGURE 5.15   China's official finance increased sharply in the past decade

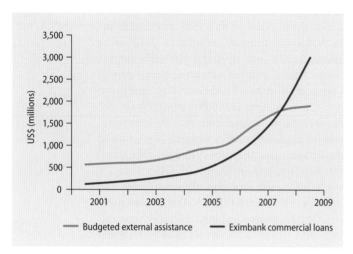

Source: Originally from Brautigam (2009), as reported with modifications by the author in Christensen (2010).

aid procedures are simple, allowing for quick implementation because no policy conditions are attached. Most of the funds go to projects that enhance infrastructure and living standards (roads, hospitals, clean water projects, personnel training programs, and the like), fostering economic and social development in the recipient country. The provision of finance has assisted China's efforts to improve strategic relationships with other developing countries, to foster trade and other business opportunities for Chinese firms, to improve access to key commodities, and to boost awareness and appreciation of China's political and economic system. China's aid institutions do require evaluation of social and environmental impacts and the efficacy of the aid programs. Perhaps not as specific and detailed as required by traditional donors, these evaluations can be strengthened to ensure the quality and effectiveness of China's program and maximize developmental benefits for recipient countries.

China does not impose formal conditions for receiving finance. Unlike traditional donors, China does not systematically impose formal conditions concerning governance or economic policy. Indeed, a central principle of

China's program is respect for the sovereignty of recipient governments and the refusal to become involved in their internal policies, although the government has on occasion vigorously expressed concerns about corruption and the possible diversion of its finance (Mold and others 2010). Embezzlement in China's official loans is limited by paying Chinese firms directly for building infrastructure.[43] China provides very little direct budget support. China also has provided several rounds of substantial debt relief since 2000, but without linking debt relief to policy reforms. And China's loans to a few heavily indebted poor countries have raised concerns of a renewal of debt problems.

China's policies are in some respects beneficial to recipients. China's provision of finance in different forms and with a different approach from the traditional donors can provide recipient countries with greater policy autonomy; they have an alternative source of funding if traditional donors' conditionality appears onerous or unproductive. China is willing to finance dams, power plants, stadiums, and other government buildings—projects that traditional donors have largely stopped financing. China finances projects in countries without regard to political or governance concerns. China's lack of conditionality reduces the burden on government officials, as well as the delays and costs inherent in demonstrating compliance with conditionality. All of this can increase the attractiveness of Chinese finance for recipient governments.

China needs to be vigilant about corruptive behavior in its aid programs. Preventing corruptive behavior in China's aid program and ensuring effectiveness of aid will become increasingly important to maintain the real diplomatic benefits that China has garnered from its financial program. As China's program increases, examples of mismanagement and corruption may also rise. For example, the China Eximbank's system of relying on Chinese companies to generate projects for financing by concessional loans can increase the risk of illicit payments or kickbacks.

Concerns have been raised about a lack of attention to operations and maintenance costs in projects (Hanson 2009). Of course, cases of corruption are sometimes found in traditional donors' programs. But China can impose more transparency as an important measure to tackle corruption in its aid programs. It is encouraging that China has signed and ratified the 2005 UN Convention Against Corruption, and recently followed through by making corrupt practices by Chinese companies overseas illegal under Chinese law. The challenge now will be effective enforcement (Brautigam 2011).

China can learn from the failures and successes of traditional donors' development assistance. In some respects, such as the heavy reliance on tied aid and lack of conditionality, China's policies can logically be seen as similar to the approaches by traditional donors. Official finance programs, including aid and export credits, were initially designed to expand diplomatic influence and commercial interests. Over time, however, some policies were modified to focus on development effectiveness and to adopt more cooperative approaches to the provision of official finance. This process, in part, responded to obvious aid failures and growing pressures from civil society. It also reflected the increasingly important institutional role played by the multilateral institutions, growing cooperation among bilateral aid agencies, the realization that competition among export credit agencies was counterproductive (from the standpoint of creditors), and more recently the need to achieve fair burden sharing in debt relief to heavily indebted poor countries. Overall, global goals rose in importance compared with national and commercial goals. These changes are only partial, and donors' financing programs still often serve narrow interests, either that of the nation or specific firms. But the goals of promoting development effectiveness and financial cooperation have taken on more and more importance over time. For example, most Development Assistance Committee (DAC) countries have considerably reduced tied aid requirements

to improve the effectiveness of competitive bidding in reducing costs. On average, only about 13 percent of ODA in DAC countries was tied to purchases in donor countries (Perroulaz, Fioroni, and Carbonnier 2010).[44] In contrast, projects financed by concessional loans from China Eximbank are required to give priority to Chinese suppliers for equipment, raw materials, technology, and services procurement.[45] Because of their competitiveness, Chinese companies would likely still win most, if not all, contracts even if they were not formally tied.

As China's financial programs increase in size, the government will confront pressures to take on a similar perspective. Greater openness in China will increase the importance of civil society and its ability to lobby for policies that promote aid effectiveness. Higher levels of official finance will increase the importance of coordinating with other countries. And China's increased impact on recipient countries will inevitably generate pressures to improve effectiveness.

The government should focus on improvements in transparency and standards over the medium to long term. China is still a developing country, and its aid policy should be seen more as South-South cooperation than as the unilateral aid provided by traditional donors. Therefore, China's classification and data gathering of its official aid is also quite different from those of the developed economies. Naturally, China's aid is now much more integrated into its trade policies and its own development strategy. However, as China transitions into a high-income economy, it is logical that its aid policy becomes more independent, with its own objectives and its own effectiveness measures.

Already China has adopted higher technical and environmental standards in its aid programs and is paying more attention to the people's livelihood and natural environment in recipient countries.[46] However, increasing transparency and learning from the well-established practice and experience of official aid programs of the developed economies (for example, hiring professional institutions for independent evaluation) will be conducive to enhancing the quality and reputation of China's aid programs.

The government could take several concrete steps as its aid program develops during the coming transition. First, transparency can be improved. One possible way to enforce an improvement in transparency would be to report the country's official finance according to DAC categories, as 20 non-DAC donors do already (World Bank 2011) or according to alternative categories that are consistent with independent aid flows.[47] Collecting this data in a systematic way could also improve the government's monitoring of its financing program. Second, the government could introduce independent evaluations of projects or country programs. Such evaluations would impose a useful discipline on officials responsible for projects, and the lessons learned would ultimately improve program effectiveness. At the same time, integrating research on the impact of projects into project design would force officials to be explicit about the goals of projects and provide invaluable information on project results.

The issue of conditionality in projects raises thornier issues. On the one hand, the lack of conditionality in Chinese projects means that they can be implemented more rapidly, more cheaply, and with less of a burden on government officials than projects undertaken by traditional donors. On the other hand, from the angle of traditional donors, the lack of conditions raises the risk of undesirable consequences. The challenge is to take side effects of aid projects into account, while avoiding excessive interference in recipient government policies. Finding the right strategy is not straightforward. Many traditional donors still provide aid to countries where governance has been sharply criticized (witness the rise in U.S. assistance to Iraq and Afghanistan over the past decade). Nevertheless, many studies have shown that aid is more effective in an overall environment of good governance.

Rising official finance may require greater global coordination. As China becomes a more significant source of concessional assistance, efforts to improve coordination with other donors will become more important. Coordination will require adjustments in the aid programs of both China and the traditional donors. Extension of current initiatives, such as the dialogue initiated with the British Department for International Development and the collaborative workshop with the Australian government on aid to the Pacific Islands, and new initiatives would be useful vehicles for learning and for considering proposals for improved coordination between China, traditional donors, and recipient countries.

As its size and influence expand, China's official finance should take more factors into consideration. The rapid growth of China's overseas finance implies that China will increasingly be responsible for financial flows that are large relative to the size of some recipients' economies. To ensure the continuing effectiveness of its economic cooperation, it will be necessary to take into account broader considerations than simply the quality of specific projects. The government will have to pay attention to whether project allocation across the economy is sensible, whether the government's resources devoted to operations and maintenance are adequate, and whether the recipient is adequately coping with potential macroeconomic implications of large inflows of finance (Christensen 2010).

Notes

1. The actual share of services was 43 percent in 2010. Because the model adopted 2004 as the baseline year and does not include some of the more recent data revisions, there are differences between simulation results of past data and actual data.
2. Most of this section on trade is based on Mattoo and Subramanian (forthcoming).
3. Antidumping is hardly the only mechanism used to discriminate against China's exports. Others include the Transitional Product-Specific Safeguard Mechanism (a unique feature of China's WTO accession that allowed importers to invoke safeguards against China

through 2014, with fewer evidentiary requirements than under the normal safeguards regime), the traditional safeguards regime, voluntary export restraints (particularly as a result of U.S. and EU investigations of China's textile and apparel exports, and despite the banning of voluntary export restraints under the WTO Agreement on Safeguards), and countervailing measures under antisubsidy policies (Bown 2007).

4. Over half of trade is already subject to zero MFN rates where there is no room for preferences; and many products with high tariffs (in agriculture, for example) are excluded from preferential agreements, so trade in those goods still occurs at MFN rates.

5. For example, India has committed to allowing maximum foreign ownership of 25 percent in basic telecommunications under the General Agreement on Trade in Services and 49 percent in some of its preferential agreements, but in practice it already allows 74 percent.

6. Restrictions of foreign firms in banking are meant to ensure that they are not used to evade capital controls, insurance remains closed in many respects, majority foreign ownership is prohibited in some sectors (such as telecommunications and air transport), and provision of domestic legal services is restricted.

7. To join the procurement agreement, countries must (for the transactions covered) eliminate discrimination against foreign suppliers, enhance ex ante transparency (advertising for bids for all procurements above a given threshold) and ex post transparency (explain why suppliers were chosen), and establish procedures to review complaints.

8. This exception appears to have been interpreted relatively broadly in justifying the application or threat of export barriers, in cases such as the U.S. proposal for an export ban on soybeans in 1973. Article 12 of the WTO Agreement on Agriculture requires that developed-country members and net-exporting developing-country members introducing export restrictions under this provision take into account the implications for importing members' food security, and notify the Committee on Agriculture, preferably in advance. However, notifications have rarely been issued; it appears that the most recent is from Hungary in 1997 (Gamberoni and Newfarmer 2008).

9. See, for example, http://schumersenate .gov/Newsroom/record.cfm?id=331896&& year=2011&.

10. In 2010, only 6 percent of buyers in global mining M&A deals were Chinese, and few Chinese buyers have secured controlling stakes in global mining corporations (Price WaterhouseCoopers 2011).

11. The data on M&A transactions may overstate the share of services and thus understate the share of mining and manufacturing. The M&A data are reported by the acquirer. Because many acquiring firms are banks acting as intermediaries, the M&A data may not accurately represent the business of the acquired firms. Fung, García-Herrero, and Siu (2009) find that proxies for natural resources do not have a significant relationship with the location of Chinese outward FDI flows. Cheung and Qian (2009) find that resource seeking is an important motive, although China does not appear to invest in African and oil-producing countries mainly to obtain natural resources.

12. The government also is beginning efforts at diversifying foreign exchange reserves through the China Investment Corporation.

13. China's per capita demand for steel rose from 0.06 ton in 1990 to 0.37 ton in 2008, about 2.5 percentage points more rapidly than the rise in per capita GDP (McKay, Sheng, and Song 2010). In 2010, China's consumption of refined metals exceeded the total of all OECD economies combined.

14. Japanese investment in U.S. real estate totaled nearly $300 billion in the 1980s, and the "value of many of these assets fell by as much as 50 percent in the early 1990s." See Terry Pristin, "Commercial Real Estate; Echoes of the 80s: Japanese Return to the U.S. Market." *New York Times*, January 26, 2005.

15. He and Lyles (2008) claim that fears of government domination of SOEs are outdated after three decades of reform have improved the SOEs' autonomy and responsiveness to market forces.

16. It is also necessary to define the assets to be covered by the agreement, for example, to decide whether short-term flows are also protected, although a substantial transitional period would be required until China can achieve an open capital account. Xiao (2010) argues that China should press for a hybrid approach. Access to investment should be

based on a narrow definition (such as kind of activity), while protection of existing investments should be determined by a broad asset definition.

17. For example, one complaint concerning the process for approval of Chinese investment in Australia's Rio Tinto was that the responsible agency took three months longer than expected before ultimately approving it.

18. The same issues are not as pressing for national treatment after entry, because MFN provisions of Chinese BITs imply that Chinese firms would enjoy the same protections as granted under other treaties.

19. Even there, however, the importance of access to tribunals is suspect. Investors are understandably reluctant to appeal to international tribunals against governments of host countries. For example, despite the inclusion of arbitration provisions, albeit with exceptions, in several Chinese BITs, no investor has brought a case against China to international arbitration (no doubt largely because of the fear that doing so would impair the investor's relationship with China) (Economist Intelligence Unit 2010).

20. Hoekman and Saggi (2000) find that a multilateral framework would result in little reduction in transactions costs for either governments or investors compared with reliance on BITs.

21. Some empirical studies find that BITs have little impact on FDI flows (Nunnenkamp and Pant 2003). On the other hand, Berger and others (2010) find that BITs with liberal investment provisions guaranteeing market access for FDI are significantly and positively related to cross-border investment flows.

22. For example, transparency provisions could reflect weak administration in developing countries, and technical assistance could be provided to help developing countries implement the agreement.

23. The State Council has assigned most of its authority for approving foreign investments to the Ministry of Commerce and local governments, although the council retains final authority for investments with significant macroeconomic or foreign policy implications (Berger 2008b).

24. The subject is beyond the scope of this paper, but such reforms of state enterprises will have to take into account a host of concerns, most notably the implications for employment, and will need to be phased in over time.

25. Claessens, Demirgüç-Kunt, and Huizinga (2000) use data from a sample of 80 countries to show that foreign entry reduces the profitability of domestic banks and enhances their efficiency. Claessens and Lee (2003) conclude that the increased presence of foreign banks in low-income countries reduced financial intermediation costs and made the banking system more efficient and robust.

26. From 1988 to 1993, the government maintained a dual exchange rate system where businesses involved in trade had access to the swap market with a market-determined exchange rate, while most others had to undertake transactions at the official, controlled rate. During the early 1990s, the rate in the swap market (which accounted for about 80 percent of foreign exchange transactions by 1994) depreciated sharply, and the official exchange rate became increasingly overvalued. Thus, the official rate records a large nominal depreciation with the unification of the exchange rate system (Huang and Wang 2004).

27. BIS (Bank of International Settlements) effective exchange rate.

28. China's capital controls also serve other purposes, including supporting interest rate controls and limiting the impact of capital movements on China's relatively undeveloped financial markets.

29. In 2005, the authorities announced that the renminbi would no longer be pegged to the U.S. dollar but to a basket of currencies, although the composition of that basket has not been announced. This shift may explain why the real effective exchange rate has been more stable than the exchange rate against the dollar (Frenkel 2009).

30. Increasing productivity in the production of traded goods will increase the demand for labor, thus increasing wages in both traded and nontraded sectors. But because productivity growth is slower in the production of nontraded goods, the rise in wages will require an increase in the relative price of nontraded goods.

31. The exact currency composition of China's reserves is not known because China does not participate in the International Monetary Fund's COFER database.

32. Because issuing additional cash is virtually costless, the government earns a real return on monetary expansion, part of which would come from foreigners if the renminbi were to circulate internationally as the dollar does now.
33. Reuters, "Factbox: China's Decade in the WTO," November 29, 2011, http://news.yahoo.com/factbox-chinas-decade-wto-055550276.html.
34. The process of reducing NPLs of the four major state-owned banks involved the transfer of the loans to asset management companies and subsequent sales to the public, in conjunction with capital injections into the banks.
35. By contrast, the Asian crisis and the prolonged Japanese stagnation eliminated the attractiveness of alternative regional models (for instance, during the 1990s, Korea's regulatory framework was considered as a possible reference; this ended after 1997).
36. The Chinese banking system remains underdeveloped in many areas. The scope of bank services is extremely limited in comparison with more developed systems (for example, consumer credit remains a small share of total credit), and the regulatory system is limited (for example, there is still no formal system-wide deposit insurance scheme in China, and the government maintains ceilings and floors on interest rates).
37. The existing figures for the current level of NPLs, at around 2 percent of GDP, are widely considered to significantly understate the dimension of the problem (OECD 2010). Nevertheless, the CBRC has already used its considerable "moral suasion" powers to force an increase in capital adequacy ratios, which reached an estimated average of 9 percent in the 14 domestic listed banks by 2010.
38. Basel III is the successor of the ill-fated Basel II, but now with risk-adjusted capital, leverage, and liquidity standards of an (arguably) simpler, more strict and transparent nature.
39. An example of those more informal exchange processes is provided by the regular dialogues held by Directorate General for Internal Market, the regulator of the financial markets in the European Union, with its Chinese counterparts (see http://ec.europa.eu/internal_market/ext-dimension/dialogues/index_en.htm). From a more formal point of view, the new sectoral agencies created in the postcrisis overhaul of the financial regulatory environment—the European Systemic Risk Board, the European Banking Authority, and the European Securities and Markets Authority—are institutionally mandated to engage in administrative agreements with third-country authorities in the pursuit of their respective mandates, and contacts with their Chinese counterparts to that effect have already started.
40. Developing countries are playing a more important role in discussions of international financial decisions through reliance on the Group of 20 as the main body for international economic coordination and through the expansion of the Financial Stability Board.
41. Among other things, this agenda includes strengthened international governance; training of supervisors for cross-border banks; the expansion of the Financial Stability Board; better regulation of credit rating agencies and private pools of capital (hedge funds); improvements in accounting standards; standardization and increased resilience of credit derivative markets; principles for employee compensation; improved corporate governance and prudential supervision (including macro supervision); reducing evasion of standards through off-shore financial centers; and addressing the procyclical nature of capital requirements.
42. As noted, authorities pursued a somewhat selective implementation of Basel prudential norms during the past decade. And with the onset of the financial crisis, CBRC statements signaled an implicit rejection of Basel II's market-based and self-regulatory approaches to capital adequacy standards.
43. See "The Chinese in Africa," *The Economist*, April 20, 2011.
44. Note, however, that these figures exclude aid related to technical cooperation and administrative assistance (which often are tied) and thus probably underestimate tied aid levels. Also, research shows that even when OECD aid is untied, donor country firms still win the vast majority of contracts (Nichol and Gordon 2011).
45. China Eximbank website.
46. It is important to distinguish between technical and environmental standards adopted in overseas business ventures by Chinese enterprises

and those adopted in official aid programs, which are normally higher than the former.

47. This would require presenting China's aid according to DAC definitions, which differ somewhat from China's. For example, China does not count scholarships as aid, while DAC does; China includes military assistance in its external assistance budget, but DAC excludes military assistance from ODA; China does not count debt relief as aid, while DAC does include debt relief on nonconcessional loans; and China includes only the interest subsidy in concessional loans as aid, while DAC includes the face value as ODA while deducting repayments in subsequent years (Brautigam 2010).

References

Allen, F., J. Qian, M. Qian, and M. Zhao 2008. "A Review of China's Financial System and Initiatives for the Future."

Anderson, Robert D., Philippe Pelletier, Kodjo Osei-Lah, and Anna Caroline Müller. 2011. "Assessing the Value of Future Accessions to the WTO Agreement on Government Procurement (GPA): Some New Data Sources, Provisional Estimates, and an Evaluative Framework for Individual WTO Members Considering Accession." World Trade Organization Secretariat. Geneva. http://www.unescap.org/tid/projects/procure2011-docII1.pdf

Anuatti-Neto, Francisco, Milton Barrosi-Filho, A. Gledson De Carvalho, and Roberto Bras Matos Macedo. 2003. "Costs and Benefits of Privatization: Evidence from Brazil." Working Paper 164, Inter-American Development Bank, Washington, DC.

Arnold, Jens Matthias, Beata Smarzynska Javorcik, and Aaditya Mattoo. 2007. "Does Services Liberalization Benefit Manufacturing Firms? Evidence from the Czech Republic." Policy Research Working Paper 4109, World Bank, Washington, DC. http://ssrn.com/abstract=956489.

Bakker, Age, and Bryan Chapple. 2002. "Advanced Country Experiences with Capital Account Liberalization." International Monetary Fund, Washington, DC.

Barajas, Adolfo, Roberto Steiner, and Natalia Salazar. 2000. "Foreign Investment in Colombia's Financial Sector." Working Paper 99/150, International Monetary Fund, Washington, DC http://ssrn.com/abstract=218069 or doi:10.2139/ssrn.218069.

Berger, Axel. 2008a. "China and the Global Governance of Foreign Direct Investment: The Emerging Liberal Bilateral Investment Treaty Approach." Discussion Paper 10/2008, German Development Institute, Bonn.

———. 2008b. "China's New Bilateral Investment Treaty Program: Substance, Rationale and Implications for International Investment Law Making." Paper prepared for the American Society of International Economic Law Interest Group 2008 conference in Washington, DC, November 14–15.

Berger, Axel, Matthias Busse, Peter Nunnenkamp, and Martin Roy. 2010. "Do Trade and Investment Agreements Lead to More FDI? Accounting for Key Provisions Inside the Black Box." Working Paper 1647, Kiel Institute for the World Economy, Kiel, Germany.

BIS (Bank for International Settlements). 2010. Triennial Central Bank Survey. Basel.

Bown, Chad. 2007. "China's WTO Entry: Antidumping, Safeguards, and Dispute Settlement." Working Paper 13349, National Bureau of Economic Research, Cambridge, MA.

———. 2010. "Taking Stock of Antidumping, Safeguards, and Countervailing Duties, 1990–2009." Policy Research Working Paper 5436, World Bank, Washington, DC.

Brautigam, Deborah. 2009. *The Dragon's Gift.* New York: Oxford University Press.

———. 2010. "China, Africa and the International Aid Architecture." Working Paper Series 107, African Development Bank Group, Tunis, Tunisia (April).

———. 2011. "Origin of China's New Anti-Corruption Law." March 22. http://www.chinaafricarealstory.com/2011/03/origins-of-chinas-new-anti-corruption.html.

Brightbill, Timothy C., Alan Price, Christopher Weld, Charles Capito, and Robert E. Morgan. 2008. "Raw Deal: How Governmental Trade Barriers and Subsidies are Distorting Global Trade in Raw Materials." Wiley Rein LLP. Washington, DC.

Cai, Congyan. 2009. "China-US BIT Negotiations and the Future of the Investment Treaty Regime: A Grand Bilateral Bargain with Multilateral Implications." *Journal of International Economic Law* 12 (2): 457–506.

Carbaugh, R., and D. Wassink. 1991. "Steel Voluntary Restraint Agreements and Steel-Using Industries." *Journal of World Trade* 25 (4): 73–86.

Chan, K. W., and Y. Hu. 2003. "Urbanization in China in the 1990s: New Definition, Different

Series, and Revised Trends." *China Review* 3 (2): 49–71.

Cheung, Yin-Wong, and Xing Wang Qian. 2009. "The Empirics of China's Outward Foreign Direct Investment." Working Paper 17/2009, Hong Kong Institute for Monetary Research, Hong Kong SAR, China.

Christensen, Benedicte Vibe. 2010. "China in Africa: A Macroeconomic Perspective." Working Paper 230, Center for Global Development, Washington, DC.

Christie, Virginia, Brad Mitchell, David Orsmond, and Marileze van Zyl. 2011. "The Iron Ore, Coal and Gas Sectors." *Reserve Bank of Australia Bulletin* (March): 1–8.

Claessens, Stijn, Asli Demirgüç-Kunt, and Harry Huizinga. 2000. "How Does Foreign Entry Affect Domestic Banking Markets?" World Bank, Washington, DC. http://siteresources.worldbank.org/DEC/Resources/84797-1114437274304/final.pdf.

Claessens, Stijn, and Jong-Kun Lee. 2003. "Foreign Banks in Low-Income Countries: Recent Developments and Impacts." In *Globalization and National Financial Systems*, eds. James Hanson, Patrick Honohan, and Giovanni Majnoni, pp. 109–44. Washington, DC: World Bank.

Coxhead, Ian, and Sisira Jayasuriya. 2010. "The Rise of China and India and the Commodity Boom: Economic and Environmental Implications for Low-Income Countries." *World Economy* 33 (4): 525–51.

Crystal, Jonathan. 2009. "Sovereignty, Bargaining, and the International Regulation of Foreign Direct Investment." *Global Society* 23 (3): 225–43.

Cull, Robert, Laura D'Amato, Andrea Molinari, and George Clarke. 1999. "The Effect of Foreign Entry on Argentina's Domestic Banking Sector." Policy Research Working Paper 2158, World Bank, Washington, DC.

Davies, Ken. 2010. "Outward FDI from China and Its Policy Context." Columbia FDI Profiles, Vale Columbia Center on Sustainable International Investment, New York.

Dincer, Nergiz N., and Barry Eichengreen. 2006. "Central Bank Transparency: Where, Why and with What Effects?" Working Paper 13003, National Bureau of Economic Research, Cambridge, MA.

Dobson, Wendy, and Paul R. Masson. 2009. "Will the RMB Become a World Currency?" *China Economic Review* 20: 124–35.

Economist Intelligence Unit. 2010. "Evaluating a Potential US-China Bilateral Investment Treaty: Background, Context and Implications." Report prepared for the U.S.-China Economic and Security Review Commission, London (March).

Eichengreen, Barry. 2010. "The Renminbi as an International Currency." University of California, Berkeley, http://www.econ.berkeley.edu/~eichengr/renminbi_international_1–2011.pdf.

Feyzioğlu, Tarhan, Nathan Porter, and Elöd Takáts. 2009. "Interest Rate Liberalization in China." Working Paper WP/09/171, International Monetary Fund, Washington, DC.

Fink, Carsten, Aaditya Mattoo, and Randeep Rathindran. 2002. "An Assessment of Telecommunications Reform in Developing Countries." Policy Research Working Paper 2909, World Bank, Washington, DC.

Frenkel, Jeffrey. 2009. "New Estimation of China's Exchange Rate Regime." *Pacific Economic Review* 14(6): 346–60.

Fung, K. C., Alicia García-Herrero, and Alan Siu. 2009. "A Comparative Empirical Examination of Outward Direct Investment from Four Asian Economies: China, Japan, Republic of Korea and Taiwan." Workshop on Outward FDI from Developing Asia, July 21. BBVA Working Paper 0924. http://ssrn.com/abstract=1471776

Gallagher, Mary E. 2005. "China in 2004: Stability above All." *Asian Survey* 45 (1): 21–32.

Gamberoni, E., and R. Newfarmer. 2008. "Export Prohibitions and Restrictions." World Bank, Washington, DC (May).

Goldstein, Morris, and Nicholas Lardy. 2006. "China's Exchange Rate Policy Dilemma." *American Economic Review* 96 (2): 422–26.

Haber, Stephen, and Aldo Musacchio. 2005. "Foreign Banks and the Mexican Banking System, 1997–2004." Harvard Business School, Boston.

Hanson, Fergus. 2009. "China: Stumbling through the Pacific." Lowy Institute for International Policy Brief. July. http://www.lowyinstitute.org/Publication.asp?pid=1084.

He, Doong, and Robert N. McCauley. 2010. "Offshore Markets for the Domestic Currency: Monetary and Financial Stability Issues." Working Paper 02/2010, Hong Kong Monetary Authority, Hong Kong SAR, China (March).

He, Wei, and Marjorie A. Lyles. 2008. "China's Outward Foreign Direct Investment." Indiana

University, Kelley School of Business, Bloomington, IN.

Hoekman, Bernard, and Kamal Saggi. 2000. "Assessing the Case for Extending WTO Disciplines on Investment-Related Policies." *Journal of Economic Integration* 15 (4): 629–53.

Huang, Haizhou, and Shulin Wang. 2004. "Exchange Rate Regime: China's Experience and Choices." *China Economic Review* 15 (3): 336–42.

Huang, Yiping. 2010. "RMB Policy and the Global Currency System." Working Paper 2010–03, Peking University, China Center for Economic Research, Beijing.

IMF (International Monetary Fund). 2011. "People's Republic of China Article IV Consultation." Country Report 11/192, International Monetary Fund, Washington, DC. http://www.imf.org/external/pubs/ft/scr/2011/cr11192.pdf.

Jaeger, Markus. 2010. "Yuan as a Reserve Currency: Likely Prospects and Possible Implications." Deutsche Bank Research. http://www.dbresearch.eu/PROD/DBR_INTERNET_EN-PROD/PROD0000000000260162.PDF.

Javorcik, Beata Smarzynska, Wolfgang Keller, and James R. Tybout. 2006. "Openness and Industrial Responses in a Wal-Mart World: A Case Study of Mexican Soaps, Detergents and Surfactant Producers." Working Paper 12457, National Bureau of Economic Research, Cambridge, MA.

Lee, Jong-Wha. 2010. "Will the Renminbi Emerge as an International Reserve Currency?" Asian Development Bank, Manila. http://aric.adb.org/grs/papers/Lee.pdf.

Luo, Yadong, Qiuzhi Xue, and Binjie Han. 2010. "How Emerging Market Governments Promote Outward FDI: Experience from China." *Journal of World Business* 45: 68–79.

Makin, John H. 2011. "Can China's Currency Go Global?" Economic Outlook, American Enterprise Institute for Public Policy Research, Washington, DC (January).

Marchetti, Juan A., and Martin Roy. 2009. *Opening Markets for Trade in Services.* Cambridge, U.K.: Cambridge University Press.

Mattoo, Aaditya, and Arvind Subramanian. Forthcoming. "China and the World Trading System." World Bank, Washington, DC.

McKay, Huw, Yu Sheng, and Ligang Song. 2010. "China's Metal Intensity in Comparative Perspective." In *China: The Next Twenty Years of Reform and Development,* ed. Ross Garnaut,

Jane Golley, and Ligang Song. Canberra: Australian National University E Press.

McKinsey. 2003. "Multinational Company Investment: Impact on Developing Economies." http://earth mind.net/fdi/misc/mckinsey-fdi-impact.pdf.

Meltzer, Alan H. 1986. "Monetary and Exchange Rate Regimes: A Comparison of Japan and the United States." *Cato Journal* 6 (2): 667–83.

Mold, Andrew, Annalisa Prizzon, Emmanuel Frot, and Javier Santiso. 2010. "Aid Flows in Times of Crisis." Paper presented at the Conference on Development Cooperation in Times of Crisis and on Achieving the MDGs, Madrid, June 9–10.

Morck, Randall, Bernard Yeung, and Minyuan Zhao. 2008. "Perspectives on China's Outward Foreign Direct Investment." *Journal of Inernational Business Studies* 39:337–50.

Nichol, William, and Ann Gordon. 2011. "Implementing the 2001 DAC Recommendation on Untying Aid: 2010–2011 Review," Development Co-Operation Directorate, DCD/DAC(2011)4/REV1, OECD, Paris (March 14). http://www.oecd.org/officialdocuments/ publicdisplaydocumentpdf/?cote=DCD/DAC%282011%294/REV1&docLanguage=En.

Norton, Seth W. 1992. "Transactions Costs, Telecommunications, and the Microeconomics of Macroeconomic Growth." *Economic Development and Cultural Change* 41 (1): 175–96.

Nunnenkamp, Peter, and Manoj Pant. 2003. "Why the Economic Case for a Multilateral Agreement on Investment is Weak." EU-India Network on Trade and Development, Jaipur, India.

OECD (Organisation for Economic Co-operation and Development). 2010. "Economic Surveys: China." 2010/6, OECD, Paris.

Perroulaz, Gérard, Claudie Fioroni and Gilles Carbonnier. 2010. "Trends and Issues in International Development Cooperation." International Development Policy Series, The Graduate Institute, Geneva. http://poldev.revues.org/142?lang=en.

Price Waterhouse Coopers. 2011. "You Can't Always Get What You Want: Global Mining Deals 2010." New York, March. http://www.pwc.com/en_GX/gx/mining/mergers-acquisitions/pdf/mining-deals-2010-annual-review.pdf.

Roller, Lars-Hendrik, and Leonard Waverman. 2001. "Telecommunications Infrastructure and Economic Development: A Simultaneous Approach." *American Economic Review* 91 (4): 909–23.

Salidjanova, Nargiza. 2011. "Going Out: An Overview of China's Outward Foreign Direct Investment." US-China Economic and Security Review Commission Staff Research Report, Washington, DC (March 30).

Schulz, Heiner. 2006. "Foreign Banks in Mexico: New Conquistadors or Agents of Change?" Working Paper 06-12, University of Pennsylvania, Wharton School, Philadelphia.

Singh, Manmohan. 2011. "Making OTC Derivatives Safe—A Fresh Look." Working Paper 11/66, International Monetary Fund, Washington, DC.

State Council. 2011. "China's Foreign Aid." Information Office of the State Council. April 2011. http://news.xinhuanet.com/english2010/china/2011-04/21/c_13839683.htm.

Subacchi, Paola. 2010. "'One Currency, Two Systems': China's RMB Strategy." International Economics Briefing Paper 2010/01, Chatham House, London.

UNCTAD (United Nations Conference on Trade and Development). 2004. *World Investment Report: The Shift Towards Services.* Geneva: UNCTAD.

Walter, Andrew. 2010. "Global Regulatory Norms after the Crisis: The Case of China and Basel Standards." Paper prepared for Dublin 2010-ECPR Conference "Regulation in the Age of Crisis," Dublin, June 17–19.

World Bank. 2004. *World Development Report: A Better Investment Climate for All.* Washington, DC: World Bank.

———. 2008. "Liberalization of Trade in Financial Services: Lessons from Latin America and the Caribbean." Trade Issues in East Asia, China Focus, World Bank, Washingotn, DC (January).

———. 2009. *Global Economic Prospects: Commodities at the Crossroads.* Washington, DC: World Bank.

———. 2011. *Global Monitoring Report: Improving the Odds of Achieving the MDGs.* Washington, DC: World Bank.

WTO (World Trade Organization). 2010. "WTO Trade Policy Review, China." WTO Document WT/TPR/S/230, Geneva (June 4), p. 41.

———. 2011. *World Trade Report 2011.* Geneva: WTO.

Wu, Friedrich, Rongfang Pan, and Di Wang. 2010. "Renminbi's Potential to Become a Global Currency." *China and World Economy* 18 (1): 63–81.

Wyplosz, Charles. 1999. "Financial Restraints and Liberalization in Postwar Europe." Discussion Paper 2253, Centre for Economic Policy Research, London.

Xiao, Jun. 2010. "The ASEAN-China Investment Agreement: A Regionalization of Chinese New BITs." Paper presented at Second Biennial Global Conference, University of Barcelona, July 8–10.

Xu, Jodi. 2009. "Rio Tinto-Chinalco: China Is Not Amused." *Wall Street Journal* Blogs. June 4.

Yu, Yongding. 2009. "The Management of Cross-Border Capital Controls and Macroeconomic Stability in China." Third World Network. Penang, Malaysia.

Zhou, Xiaochuan, 2005. "China's Corporate Bond Market Development: Lessons Learned." BIS Papers 26, Bank for International Settlements, Basel.

Index

Boxes, figures, notes, and tables are indicated by b, f, n, and t following the page number.

capital market deepening, 119–20
challenges for, 55–56, 125
change drivers for, 125–26
commercialization and rationalization of
system, 118
crisis management planning, 122–23
deposit insurance and, 123b
development strategy and, 19, 22
exchange rate stability and, 392–94, 393t
financial infrastructure and, 120–21
government financial management and, 59,
123–25, 397–98
history of, 115–17, 143–44, 143f, 144t, 145f
insolvency schemes and, 122–23
interest rate liberalization, 118–19
legal framework for, 120–21
local government resources and, 58–59, 58f
poverty reduction and, 47b
proposals for, 56–59
public expenditures and, 57, 397–98
regulatory framework for, 64, 121–22,
400b, 405–7, 406f
revenue mobilization, 57–58
securitized financing, 30
sequencing of, 88, 126–27, 398–401
state-owned enterprises and, 119b
transparency in, 66
financing health care, 52, 310–12
Finland
capital account liberalization in, 399b
innovation in, 166, 167, 178, 179
performance evaluation of local officials in,
103
TVET in, 300
vocational training in, 177
fiscal stimulus package (2009–10), 55
fiscal sustainability, 97–100
fiscal system reforms, 78, 89–103
accountability and, 102–3
challenges for, 92–103
efficiency and, 86–87
fiscal sustainability and, 97–100
functional reviews, 95b
government expenditure restructuring,
92–94, 93f
history of, 90–92, 91–92t
policy options for, 92–103
regulatory framework and, 99b
state role in, 89–90
subnational governments and, 99b,
100–102, 100t
taxes and revenue sources, 94–97, 95–96f
transparency and, 102–3
flexible work arrangements, 321
flexicurity, 49, 53–54, 54f, 273, 282, 315–36

flood control, 44, 238
floor area ratios (FARs), 186
flue gas desulfurization industry, 228
Fogel, Kathy, 107b
food security, 7, 30, 384–85, 411n8
Forbes Global 2000, 200n33
foreign aid. *See* official development assistance
(ODA)
foreign direct investment (FDI)
bilateral investment treaties and, 412n21
global trends in, 6
green development and, 240–41
inflows, 361–62, 365
innovative cities and, 38
interregional competition and, 5
Japan's investments in U.S. auto industry,
382b
legal framework for, 389
outflows. *See* outward FDI
restrictions on, 377–78
services sector and, 391b
technology transfer and, 175
trends in, 14
in university system, 37
foreign exchange reserves. *See also* exchange rate
capital markets and, 29
exchange rate management and, 394
FDI and, 60, 61–62, 387–88
risk management for, 69
Foshan, cluster networking in, 168
fossil fuels
in energy mix, 40
international subsidies for, 244b
pricing of, 174
Foxconn, 165, 207n136
France
capital account liberalization in, 399b
public expenditures on social protection in,
93, 93f
Fraunhofer Institutes (Germany), 174
free trade agreements, 7, 62
fuel efficiency standards, 43
Fujian Province
entrepreneurial culture in, 34, 169
green development performance indicators
in, 44
functional reviews, 95b
Fung, K. C., 411n11
F. Zimmermann GmbH, 202n51

Gann, David, 198n5
Gansu Province, preprimary education in, 291
Gao, Jian, 200n35
Gao, Xudong, 200n32
Gaoyang model, 203n67

García-Herrero, Alicia, 411*n*11
GATS (General Agreement on Trade in Services),
    383, 411*n*5
GATT (General Agreement on Tariffs and
    Trade), 384
Geertz, G., 69*n*6
GEM (Growth Enterprises Market), 169
gender wage gap, 353*n*48
General Administration of Quality Supervision,
    Inspection, and Quarantine, 149*n*29
General Agreement on Tariffs and Trade
    (GATT), 384
General Agreement on Trade in Services (GATS),
    383, 411*n*5
general budget, 56, 57
general purpose technologies (GPTs), 184–85
Germany
    aged and long-term care in, 347
    capital account liberalization in, 399*b*
    financial system in, 116
    green development strategy in, 218, 219*b*,
        229*b*
    industrial extension services in, 174
    labor migration in, 330
    recycling in, 253
    science and technology power in, 166
    TVET in, 300
    vocational training in, 177
Gerschenkron, A., 86
Giles, John, 354*n*64
global economic integration, 361–417
    economic growth scenarios and, 363–64
    financial system integration, 392–402
    growth drivers for, 370–75, 371–75*f*
    integration with, 6–8, 377–402
    projections for, 367–77, 369*t*, 370–75*f*
    public goods and. *See* global public goods
    trade patterns for, 375–76, 379–85,
        379–80*f*, 381*t*
global financial crisis, 6, 65, 123, 406
global governance, 63–64
Global Independent Commission for Education
    of Health Professionals, 352*n*39
Global Innovation Index, 166
global public goods
    climate change and, 402–5, 403–4*f*
    defined, 70*n*17
    development strategy and, 18
    economic integration and, 362–3, 402–10
    financial regulations, 405–7, 406*f*
    official development assistance, 64, 407–10,
        408*f*
    policies for, 366–67
    public financing of, 17
    structural reforms and, 26

Goldwind, 202*n*54, 202*n*56
Golley, Jane, 198*n*3
Gordon, Peter, 203*n*70
governance
    corporate, 103
    land policies and, 31, 32
    state-owned enterprises and, 27
    in tertiary education, 37
    urbanization and, 24*b*
government financial management, 59,
    397–98. *See also* fiscal system reforms; public
    expenditures
government-funded budget, 56
GPTs (general purpose technologies), 184–85
Great Recession, 60
Greece, transition to high-income country status
    by, 12*b*
Greenberg, Daniel S., 207*n*121
green development, 39–45, 217–70
    advantages for, 239–43, 239–41*t*, 240*f*,
        241*b*, 242*f*
    "big push" model for, 232*b*
    carbon markets and, 260–61, 260*f*
    challenges for, 41, 239*t*, 243–47, 243*f*
    climate change risks and, 238–39, 238*f*,
        253–54
    compensation for negatively impacted
        groups, 45, 253
    development strategy and, 21
    economic growth and, 232–39, 251
    emerging green industries, 226–29, 228*b*
    emission reductions and, 220*b*, 220*f*, 225,
        225–26*f*, 236, 236*t*
    employment and, 229*b*
    environmental degradation reduction and,
        233–36, 233*t*, 233–34*f*, 235*b*
    as growth driver, 40, 222–32, 223*f*
    innovation and, 42, 158, 184–87
    institutional framework and, 44–45,
        254–56
    market incentives and, 41–43, 249–51
    measuring progress in, 258–60, 259*f*, 259*t*
    need for, 39, 217–22
    opportunities for, 220–22
    public investment in, 43–44, 237, 237*t*
    recommendations, 41–45, 249–56, 249*t*
    regulatory framework and, 43, 251–53
    research on, 38
    sectoral considerations, 39, 40, 223–26,
        224*b*, 227*b*, 261–64, 262–64*t*, 262*f*
    sequencing of reforms for, 257–64, 257*f*
    in service sector, 40, 230–31, 230*f*
    in underdeveloped regions, 231–32
    urbanization and, 255*b*
green technologies, 367